Amnesty International is a worldwide movement of people who campaign for internationally recognized human rights to be respected and protected.

Amnesty International's vision is of a world in which every person enjoys all of the human rights enshrined in the Universal Declaration of Human Rights and other international human rights standards.

In pursuit of this vision, Amnesty International's mission is to undertake research and action focused on preventing and ending grave abuses of the rights to physical and mental integrity, freedom of conscience and expression, and freedom from discrimination, within the context of its work to promote all human rights.

Amnesty International is independent of any government, political ideology, economic interest or religion. It does not support or oppose any government or political system, nor does it support or oppose the views of the victims whose rights it seeks to protect. It is concerned solely with the impartial protection of human rights.

Amnesty International is a democratic, self-governing movement with more than 1.8 million members and supporters in over 150 countries and territories in every region of the world. It is funded largely by its worldwide membership and public donations.

The *Amnesty International Report 2005* documents human rights issues of concern to AI during 2004 and reflects AI's activities during the year.

The absence of an entry on a particular country or territory does not imply that no human rights abuses of concern to AI took place there during 2004. Nor is the length of individual entries any basis for a comparison of the extent and depth of AI's concerns.

Regional maps have been included in this report to indicate the location of countries and territories, and each individual country entry begins with some basic information about the country. Neither the maps nor the country information may be interpreted as AI's view on questions such as the status of disputed territory.

Amnesty International
Report 2005

the state of the world's human rights

This report covers the period January to December 2004.

It is dedicated to the memory of
Peter Benenson (1921-2005),
founder of Amnesty International.

First published in 2005 by
Amnesty International USA
5 Penn Plaza
New York, NY 10001
USA

www.amnestyusa.org

© Copyright
Amnesty International Publications 2005
ISBN# 1-887204-42-3
AI Index: POL 10/001/2005
Original language: English

Printed by:
The Alden Press
Osney Mead, Oxford
United Kingdom

Cover design by Synergy

Regional maps by András Bereznay,
www.historyonmaps.com

Images of earth from space © Corbis

Inside cover: Schoolgirls taking part in the
launch of AI Benin's Stop Violence against
Women campaign, Porto-Novo, Benin, 2004.
© AI (Women Teachers Group Porto-Novo)

**For more information on Amnesty
International's work in the United States of
America, or for a complete listing of AI
publications with dollar prices, write to:**

**Amnesty International
National Office
5 Penn Plaza
New York, NY 10001
USA**

CONTENTS

CONTENTS

ABBREVIATIONS

The following abbreviations for international human rights treaties and monitoring bodies are used in this report:

■ UN Convention against Torture refers to the Convention against Torture and Other Cruel, Inhuman or Degrading Treatment or Punishment.

■ UN Women's Convention refers to the Convention on the Elimination of All Forms of Discrimination against Women.

■ UN Children's Convention refers to the Convention on the Rights of the Child.

■ UN Convention against Racism refers to the International Convention on the Elimination of All Forms of Racial Discrimination.

■ UN Refugee Convention refers to the Convention relating to the Status of Refugees.

■ European Convention on Human Rights refers to the (European) Convention for the Protection of Human Rights and Fundamental Freedoms.

■ European Committee for the Prevention of Torture refers to the European Committee for the Prevention of Torture and Inhuman or Degrading Treatment or Punishment.

FOREWORD

By Irene Khan, Secretary General, Amnesty International

Last September in a makeshift camp outside El Jeniena in Darfur, Sudan, I listened to a woman describe the attack on her village by government-supported militia. So many men were killed that there were none left to bury the dead, and women had to carry out that sad task. I listened to young girls who had been raped by the militia and then abandoned by their own communities. I listened to men who had lost everything except their sense of dignity. These were ordinary, rural people. They may not have understood the niceties of "human rights", but they knew the meaning of "justice". They could not comprehend why the world was not moved to action by their plight.

It was yet another example of the lethal combination of indifference, erosion and impunity that marks the human rights landscape today. Human rights are not only a promise unfulfilled, they are a promise betrayed.

Take, for instance, the failure to move from rhetoric to reality on economic and social rights. Despite the promises in the Universal Declaration of Human Rights and international human rights treaties that every person shall have the right to an adequate standard of living and access to food, water, shelter, education, work and health care, more than a billion people lack clean water, 121 million children do not go to school, most of the 25 million people suffering from HIV/AIDS in Africa have no access to health care, and half a million women die every year during pregnancy or childbirth. The poor are also more likely to be victims of crime and police brutality.

In September 2000, world leaders adopted the Millennium Declaration, with human rights as a central thread, and a set of Millennium Development Goals, which established some concrete and achievable targets by 2015. They cover issues such as HIV/AIDS, illiteracy, poverty, child and maternal mortality, and development aid. But progress on the Goals has been agonizingly slow and woefully inadequate. They cannot be achieved without a firm commitment to equal respect for all human rights — economic, social and cultural as well as civil and political.

The indifference, apathy and impunity that allow violence against millions of women to persist is shocking. In countries around the world women suffer many forms of violence including genital mutilation, rape, beatings by partners, and killings in the name of honour. Thanks to the efforts of women's groups, there are now international treaties and mechanisms, laws and policies designed to protect women, but they fall still far short of what is required. In addition, there is a real danger of a backlash against women's human rights from conservative and fundamentalist elements.

Women's human rights are not the only casualty of the assault on fundamental values that is shaking the human rights world. Nowhere has this been more damaging than in the efforts by the US administration to weaken the absolute ban on torture.

In 1973 AI published its first report on torture. It found that: "torture thrives on secrecy and impunity. Torture rears its head when the legal barriers against it are barred. Torture feeds on discrimination and fear. Torture gains ground when official condemnation of it is less than absolute." The pictures of detainees in US custody in Abu Ghraib, Iraq, show that what was true 30 years ago remains true today.

Despite the near-universal outrage generated by the photographs coming out of Abu Ghraib, and the evidence suggesting that such practices are being applied to other prisoners held by the USA in Afghanistan, Guantánamo and elsewhere, neither the US administration nor the US Congress has called for a full and independent investigation.

Instead, the US government has gone to great lengths to restrict the application of the Geneva Conventions and to "re-define" torture. It has sought to justify the use of coercive interrogation techniques, the practice of holding "ghost detainees" (people in unacknowledged incommunicado detention) and the "rendering" or handing over of prisoners to third countries known to practise torture. The detention facility at Guantánamo Bay has become the gulag of our times, entrenching the practice of arbitrary and indefinite detention in violation of international law. Trials by military commissions have made a mockery of justice and due process.

The USA, as the unrivalled political, military and economic hyper-power, sets the tone for governmental behaviour worldwide. When the most powerful country in the world thumbs its nose at the rule of law and human rights, it grants a licence to others to commit abuse with impunity and audacity. From Israel to Uzbekistan, Egypt to Nepal, governments have openly defied human rights and international humanitarian law in the name of national security and "counter-terrorism".

Sixty years ago, out of the ashes of the Second World War, a new world order came into being, putting respect for human rights alongside peace, security and development as the primary objectives of the UN. Today, the UN appears unable and unwilling to hold its member states to account.

In the latest incident of paralysis, the UN Security Council has failed to muster the will to take effective action on Darfur. In this case it was held hostage to China's oil interests and Russia's trade in arms. The outcome is that poorly equipped African Union monitors stand by helplessly and bear witness to war crimes and crimes against humanity. It remains to be seen whether the UN Security Council will act on the recommendation of the International Commission of Inquiry to refer Darfur to the International Criminal Court.

The UN Commission on Human Rights has become a forum for horse-trading on human rights. Last year, the Commission dropped Iraq from scrutiny, could not agree on action on Chechnya, Nepal or Zimbabwe, and was silent on Guantánamo Bay.

At the national level, the ability of the state to protect human rights is in crisis. In some places, armed groups – warlords, criminal gangs or clan chiefs – hold sway over people's lives. In many countries, governance has been undermined by corruption, mismanagement, abuse of power and political violence. In a globalized economy, it is increasingly international trade agreements, international financial institutions and big business which are setting the terms. And yet there are few mechanisms for addressing their impact on human rights, and even fewer appropriate systems for accountability.

The time has come for a sober reappraisal of what needs to be done to revive the human rights system and our faith in its abiding values. That is the import of the judgments of the US Supreme Court on Guantánamo detainees and the UK Law Lords on indefinite detention without charge or trial of "terrorist suspects". That is the message of the spontaneous and massive turnout of millions of people in Spain protesting against the Madrid bombings, the popular uprisings in Georgia and Ukraine, and the growing debate on change in the Middle East.

Within the UN too, the appointment of a new High Commissioner for Human Rights in 2004, and the report commissioned by the UN Secretary-General from a High-level Panel on Threats, Challenges and Change, created an environment conducive to reform and renewal of the human rights system. This must be based on shared values and goals, on the rule of law rather than arbitrary power, on global cooperation rather than unilateral adventurism.

The credibility of the international human rights system rests on its ability to reassert the primacy of human rights, and their centrality in tackling the full range of threats to international peace and security. The leadership challenge for the UN and its member states is clear:

- Reaffirm and reassert human rights as embodying the common values and universal standards of human decency and dignity, equality and justice. Acknowledge them as the basis for our common security, not a barrier to it.
- Resist all efforts to water down the absolute ban on torture and cruel, inhuman or degrading treatment. Torture is unlawful, and morally reprehensible. It dehumanizes the victim and the perpetrator. It is the ultimate corruption of humanity. If the international community allows this fundamental pillar to be eroded, it cannot hope to salvage the rest.
- Condemn unequivocally human rights abuses by those who have taken humanity to new depths of bestiality and brutality by blowing up commuter trains in Madrid, taking school children hostage in Beslan, and beheading humanitarian workers in Iraq, but stand firm on the governments' responsibility to bring them to justice within the rule of law and the framework of human rights. Respect for human rights is the best antidote for "terrorism".
- Close the impunity and accountability deficit in human rights. At the national level, a full and independent investigation of the use of torture and other human rights abuses by US officials will go a long way to restoring confidence that true justice has no double standards. At the international level, the International Criminal Court must be supported to become an efficient deterrent for atrocious crimes and an effective lever to advance human rights.
- Listen to the voices of the victims, and respond to their cry for justice. UN Security Council members should commit themselves not to use the veto in dealing with genocide, crimes against humanity and war crimes or other large-scale human rights abuses. They should promote an international treaty and other means to control the trade in small arms which kill half a million people every year.
- Reform the UN's human rights machinery urgently and radically in order to improve its legitimacy, efficiency and effectiveness. In particular, strengthen the capacity of the UN and regional organizations to protect people at risk of human rights abuse.
- Link the achievement of the quantitatively formulated Millennium Development Goals to the qualitative achievement of human rights, particularly economic and social rights, and equality for women. Bring corporate and financial actors into the framework of accountability for human rights.
- Protect human rights activists who are increasingly threatened and labelled as subversives. The space for liberal thought is shrinking, and intolerance is on the rise. Be vigilant in protecting civil society, because the pursuit of freedom depends on it as much as on the rule of law, an independent judiciary, free media and elected governments.

Will governments and the UN take up this agenda? Now more than ever human rights activists must play their part, mobilizing public opinion to put pressure on governments and international organizations. In very different ways in the course of 2004, popular mobilization for the victims of the Madrid bombings and the Indian Ocean tsunami showed the power of ordinary people to promote hope over fear, action over inaction and solidarity over indifference. Amnesty International believes in the power of ordinary people to bring about extraordinary change, and with our members and supporters we will continue in 2005 to campaign for justice and freedom for all. We remain the eternal hope-mongers.

AI REPORT 2005

PART 1

INTRODUCTION

RESPONSIBILITIES HAVE NO BORDERS

"When the institutions of collective security respond in an ineffective and inequitable manner, they reveal a much deeper truth about which threats matter. Our institutions of collective security must not just assert that a threat to one is truly a threat to all, but perform accordingly."
Report of the UN High-level Panel on Threats, Challenges and Change, December 2004

One of the defining events of 2004 happened in its closing days. On 26 December, in the seas off Indonesia, a powerful earthquake sent a series of deadly waves across the Indian Ocean, striking the shores of Indonesia, Sri Lanka, India, Thailand, Malaysia, Myanmar and east Africa. The devastation that followed was almost beyond comprehension. Nearly 300,000 people were killed, around 100,000 were missing and presumed dead, and over five million others were left homeless, hungry and at risk of disease.

The tsunami and its aftermath brought home our global interconnectedness and shared vulnerability. In a year in which "terrorism" dominated the international agenda, the disaster highlighted how the most devastating threats to security arise from a much greater range of sources than the suicide bomber. Whether environmental, political or economic in nature, today's most pervasive threats to human rights

and human security are international in scope — they cannot be dealt with exclusively by individual countries, but require globally coordinated action.

The global response to the tsunami was just as striking in its scale and impact. Unprecedented levels of empathy and solidarity were shown by people around the world towards those with whom they seemingly shared nothing more than space on the planet. Everywhere, people were united in grieving and giving. Media outlets, weblogs and other new and informal media instantaneously linked people to the events and each other. The actions and generosity of citizens and non-governmental organizations embarrassed donor governments into substantially increasing their promised aid and assistance.

At least initially, the worldwide reaction to the disaster was cause for cautious optimism about an emerging sense of global citizenship. There were signs of an increased awareness that only multilateral action can contribute to global shared security. As 2004 drew to a close, the international community appeared to have recognized that in this age of globalization, the responsibility to protect human security transcends the borders of the nation state.

However, the reaction to the tsunami of the international community, including the response of ordinary people, was painfully at odds with the failure to deal effectively with other global crises which throughout 2004 left comparable numbers of victims in their wake. Economic interests, political hypocrisy and socially orchestrated discrimination continued to fan the flames of conflict around the world. The so-called "war on terror" appeared more effective in eroding the international framework of human rights principles than in countering the threat of international

© REUTERS/Yusuf Ahmad

A man walks through the aftermath of the tsunami in the town of Banda Aceh, Indonesia.

© AP Photo

A fundraising event in Fuzhou, Fujian province, China, for victims of the tsunami.

"terrorism". The security of women facing gender-based violence in the home, in the community or in situations of conflict barely received attention. The economic, social and cultural rights of marginalized communities continued to be largely ignored.

Armed conflict

"When we tried to escape they shot more children. They raped women; I saw many cases of Janjawid raping women and girls. They are happy when they rape. They sing when they rape and they tell us that we are just slaves and that they can do with us how they wish."
A., aged 37, from Mukjar in Darfur, Sudan

The failure of the community of nations to address human rights crises appropriately and effectively was seen most clearly in Sudan's Darfur region, where another humanitarian tragedy on a vast scale unfolded throughout 2004. Unlike the tsunami, this tragedy was not one of nature; it was man-made. And in this instance, the international community made relatively little effort to stop or alleviate the suffering.

Throughout the year, countless women and girls in Darfur were raped, abducted and forced into sexual slavery by the Janjawid, nomad militias armed, paid and supported by the Sudanese government. The mass rapes, including gang rapes of school children, were clearly war crimes and crimes against humanity.

The Janjawid, often dressed in Sudanese military uniform and accompanied by the Sudanese army, also burned villages, killed civilians and pillaged property and livestock. The Sudanese air force added to the suffering by bombing villages, while the security forces routinely tortured those in their custody, often by heavy beatings with hoses, whips or boots and sometimes by ripping out nails or burning with cigarettes. By the end of the year, the conflict had forced more than one and a half million people to flee their homes, their villages destroyed, their herds and possessions looted. Nearly every village in the region was devastated. During the final months of the year the scale of the crisis in Darfur escalated, with attacks on civilians mainly by government forces and government-supported militias, fighting between government and rebel forces, and attacks on humanitarian convoys.

The brutality in Darfur was a critical test of the ability of the UN to respond effectively to major human rights crises. And, again, the UN failed the test. "Safe areas" designated by the Sudanese government and the UN for the internally displaced of Darfur, for example, proved to be anything but safe. Monitored by the government's security and military intelligence, the displaced people remained vulnerable to arbitrary arrests, rape and killings by government security forces. When the El-Geer camp was bulldozed and residents were assaulted and tear-gassed, with UN and African Union (AU) representatives present, the protests of the international officials were simply ignored.

Meanwhile, three UN Security Council resolutions in less than six months showed the UN largely failing the people of Darfur. It appeared that human rights protection sat awkwardly with attempts to secure a peace deal for the North-South conflict. By adopting a resolution in November that failed to send a strong message that human rights violations would not be tolerated, it is likely that the Security Council created the impression that the Sudanese government could act with impunity. The deployment of the enhanced AU Mission in Darfur had not, by the close of 2004, resulted in improved security and protection for civilians. Nor had it acted as a deterrent to attacks.

Despite clear international awareness of the abuses being committed in Darfur, a long list of governments knowingly or unwittingly allowed arms to be sent to the country that were then used by the Sudanese government forces and allied militias to commit atrocities. Calls by human rights groups for an arms embargo to end military and related supplies reaching all parties went unheeded, and the establishment of an international investigation to examine evidence of war crimes and crimes against humanity was only agreed at the end of 2004. The international community had at its disposal tools that could have saved lives and prevented suffering; the simple truth was that it chose not to use them. Instead, the violence and abuse in Darfur illustrated, starkly and bleakly, the continued failure of the UN Security Council – under strong pressure from some of its members – to prevent and punish crimes against humanity and war crimes.

In 2004 Darfur was not the only place where human rights became a casualty of the narrow interests of powerful states. The US-led military intervention in Iraq, justified in the name of security, left millions of Iraqis feeling deeply insecure as they faced widespread violence and growing poverty. In Chechnya, the conflict continued into a sixth year. Reports emerged of torture, rape and other sexual abuse of Chechen women by Russian soldiers. To cite just one case, 23-year-old Madina (not her real name) was detained by Russian federal forces on suspicion of being a suicide bomber. A mother with one child, she was kept incommunicado and allegedly tortured for two weeks at the Russian military base in Khankala. Madina told AI: "They warned me on the first day that I would be begging to be dead. But at that time I really wanted to live because I have my baby... I could not imagine that I would ask them for death... But on that day... exhausted, tired, breathless, I started to ask them to shoot me."

In 2004 people who had given up hope of securing justice in Russia and sought redress through the European Court of Human Rights found themselves deliberately targeted by the authorities, as did human rights defenders and activists who attempted to speak out within the region against injustice.

Half a world away, in Haiti, armed government opponents, led by men convicted of committing serious violations under the de facto military dictatorship of the early 1990s, attacked state institutions in February. Following the departure of President Jean Bertrand Aristide, a Multinational

Interim Force arrived, mandated by the UN Security Council to help ensure law and order and protect human rights. Even though disarmament of armed groups and the re-establishment of the rule of law were clearly essential to ensure the safety of civilians, neither the Multinational Interim Force nor the interim government made any credible attempts to initiate comprehensive nationwide disarmament programmes.

Individuals responsible for serious human rights violations in Haiti steadily regained positions of authority. Devastating floods, and further outbreaks of violence in September and October, underlined the need for the international community to tackle the humanitarian and human rights crisis in the country.

The human rights situation deteriorated in the Occupied Palestinian Territories. There was an increase in killings and destructions of homes by the Israeli army in the West Bank and Gaza Strip. Attacks by Palestinian armed groups against Israeli civilians continued.

The civil war in Côte d'Ivoire, meanwhile, was a reminder of how easily a country can lurch back into war if the root causes of conflict are left unaddressed. In November the Ivorian armed forces bombed the rebel-held town of Bouaké in the north of the country, breaking an 18-month ceasefire. In the aftermath, in the capital Abidjan, there were indiscriminate attacks and violence against civilians, notably French and other foreign nationals who had lived in the country in some cases for decades. The violence was fuelled by xenophobia and allegedly led to rapes of some French and other foreign women by Ivorian civilians. In response to anti-French demonstrations, French troops, who were under a UN peacekeeping force mandate, used excessive force against civilians, most of them unarmed,

© Evelyn Hockstein/Polaris

A woman building a shelter in a camp for internally displaced persons in South Darfur, Sudan, September 2004.

A man searches for relatives among the bodies of dead hostages at a morgue in Vladikavkaz, southern Russia. Nearly 350 people are thought to have died in the hostage-taking tragedy at a school in Beslan in September, when explosives were detonated in the school and in the ensuing shoot-out between hostage-takers, armed local civilians and security forces. Shamil Basaev, leader of a Chechen armed opposition group, claimed responsibility for the hostage-taking.

© REUTERS/Sergei Karpukhin

and shot dead at least 15 of them. Other civilians were killed apparently while fleeing the shooting.

One of the major factors that fuels the continuation of wars is the proliferation of arms. Easy availability of weaponry and munitions tends to increase the incidence of armed violence, to prolong wars once they break out, and to enable grave and widespread abuses of human rights. The majority of current armed conflicts could not be sustained without the supply of small arms and light weapons and associated ammunition.

In Colombia's 40-year armed conflict, where rape and other sexual crimes have been committed by all parties to the conflict, military equipment, including large quantities of small arms, have been supplied in the past few years to the Colombian authorities by the USA, Israel, Brazil, France, Germany, Spain, South Africa, the Czech Republic and Italy. The failure to control the international arms trade has also enabled guerrilla groups to obtain large supplies of arms.

Most governments are still failing in their duty to take stringent measures to prevent the flow of arms to those who openly flaunt international human rights and humanitarian laws. A comprehensive international framework of controls is needed to close the loopholes that allow weapons and munitions to get into the wrong hands. That is why AI has joined forces with Oxfam and the International Action Network on Small Arms (IANSA) in the Control Arms campaign, to work towards tighter controls, including an international Arms Trade Treaty.

Another characteristic of contemporary conflict is the role of powerful economic interests in fanning the flames and reaping the profits of conflict and militarization. As more conflicts are fought over natural resources in the future, the role of corporate actors will be all the more significant and decisive.

The role of external players in prolonging conflict can be seen starkly in the Democratic Republic of the Congo (DRC), where more than three million civilians have been killed or have died from hunger and disease since August 1998. This conflict has been characterized by illegal killings, torture and rape by forces on all sides, and by the intervention of other states and international

© AP Photo/Dario Lopez Mills

Marchers flee gunfire in Port-au-Prince, Haiti, March 2004. Four demonstrators were killed after their calls for deposed President Jean Bertrand Aristide to face trial for corruption ended in violence.

Tens of thousands of people demonstrate in Brazil to demand an end to gun crime.

corporations in pursuit of their own interests, regardless of the human costs. Many countries have continued to supply arms to the DRC, often arranged and delivered by international arms brokering networks using circuitous routes to breach the UN arms embargo on the DRC.

In 2004, almost all of eastern DRC, where numerous armed groups are fighting for control of the land and its resources, remained under the de facto control of different armed groups or militia. Unlawful killings and torture persisted. Men, women and children were attacked with machetes, homemade weapons and small arms. Sexual violence was used as a weapon of war. There was extensive looting and destruction of homes, fields, schools, medical and nutritional centres, and religious institutions. All armed forces used children as soldiers.

2004 witnessed horrific levels of gender-based violence committed with impunity against women of all ages, including very young girls, in the DRC. A young woman who was twice raped during the DRC conflict told AI: "In the community they made such fun of me that I had to leave the village and live in the forest... I am hungry, I have no clothes and no soap. I don't have any money to pay for medical care. It would be better if I died with the baby in my womb."

The scale of rape has created a human rights and health crisis requiring both an immediate and a long-term response. Yet although tens of thousands of women, children and even babies, as well as men, were systematically raped and tortured in eastern DRC, the government and international community failed to develop an organized or comprehensive response to assist survivors.

Violence against women

The DRC and Darfur were not exceptional in terms of the widespread abuse of women and girls. In other armed conflicts around the world, women and girls were raped or otherwise sexually attacked, mutilated and humiliated.

Those who committed the abuses were many and varied: soldiers of the state's armed forces; pro-government paramilitary groups or militias; armed groups fighting the government or at war with other armed groups; the police, prison guards or private security and military personnel; military forces stationed abroad, including UN and other peacekeeping forces; staff of humanitarian agencies; neighbours and relatives.

When AI launched its campaign to Stop Violence Against Women in March 2004, one of its pivotal aims was to end impunity for crimes of violence against women in conflict, building on the progress made by international tribunals and the International Criminal Court in identifying such crimes.

The campaign also seeks to demonstrate that the violence women suffer in conflict is an extreme manifestation of the discrimination and abuse they face in peacetime, when such attitudes contribute to the widespread acceptance of domestic violence, rape and other forms of sexual abuse against women. When political tensions degenerate into outright conflict, all forms of violence increase, including rape and other forms of sexual violence against women.

Many of the conflicts of 2004 were based on perceived racial, ethnic, religious, cultural and political differences, and set community against community. In such contexts, sexual violence was often used as a weapon of war, with the torture of women being seen as a means to attack the community's "honour". Moreover, most of the conflicts were internal – between governments and armed groups, or between several competing armed groups, rather than between professional national armies. As a result, there was little chance that many of the atrocities suffered by women would be punished as it is notoriously difficult to hold armed groups to account for abuses.

During 2004, AI produced several reports to highlight different aspects of violence against women around the world. One focused on Turkey, where between a third and a half of all women are estimated to be victims of physical violence within their families. They are hit, raped and in some cases even killed or forced to

Rape survivors gather to meet Amnesty International delegates in Kindu, Maniema province, Democratic Republic of the Congo, March 2004.

commit suicide. Young girls are bartered and forced into early marriage. Husbands, brothers, fathers and sons are responsible for most of these abuses. This violence is widely tolerated and even endorsed by community leaders and at the highest levels of the government and judiciary. The authorities rarely carry out thorough investigations into women's complaints about violent attacks or murders or apparent suicides of women. Courts still reduce the sentences of rapists if they promise to marry their victim, despite recent moves by the government to end the practice.

Another report issued by AI in 2004 looked at the trafficking of girls and women into Kosovo for forced prostitution. It showed that many of the young women and girls come from the poorest countries of Europe and are vulnerable because of economic deprivation or because they have already been physically abused. They dream of a better life, which the traffickers use when offering them "work" in the West. But instead of getting a proper job, they find themselves trapped, enslaved, forced into prostitution. With clients including international police and troops, the women and girls are often too afraid to escape and the authorities fail to help them.

In countries around the world, poverty and marginalization continue to fuel violence against women. Women have a higher incidence of poverty than men; their poverty is more severe than that of men; and increasing numbers of women are poor. While globalization has opened up opportunities for women, it has also had negative effects. It has left more and more women trapped on the margins of society. Such women find it extremely difficult to escape abusive situations and to obtain protection and redress.

When AI launched its Stop Violence Against Women campaign, it deliberately set out to work with local women's groups in their own countries as well as with the international women's movements in order to build a new constituency for human rights. Women throughout the world have organized to expose and counter violence against women. They have achieved dramatic changes in laws, policies and practices. Above all, they have challenged the view of women as passive victims of violence.

One of the achievements of women's rights activists has been to demonstrate that violence against women is a human rights violation. This changes the perception of violence against women from a private matter to one of public concern and means that public authorities are required to take action. The parallel development of international and regional human rights standards reinforces this accountability. Women's rights activists were central to ensuring that the founding statute of the International Criminal Court explicitly recognizes rape and other forms of sexual violence as crimes against humanity and as war crimes. In December 2004 the International Criminal Court announced that its first investigation would examine allegations of mass murder, summary execution, rape, torture, forced displacement, and the use of children as soldiers in the DRC.

AI's campaign to Stop Violence Against Women aims to show that women's self-organization, bolstered by the solidarity and support of the human rights movement, is the most effective way to overcome violence against women. The campaign is designed to mobilize both men and women and to use the power and persuasion of the human rights framework to end violence against women.

'Terror', 'counter-terror' and the rule of law

"Then [the guard] brought a box of food and he made me stand on it, and he started punishing me. Then a tall black soldier came and put electrical wires on my fingers and toes and on my penis, and I had a bag over my head. Then he was saying 'which switch is on for electricity?'"

Iraqi detainee, Abu Ghraib prison, 16 January 2004 (statement given to US military investigators, obtained by *The Washington Post*)

US President George W. Bush has repeatedly asserted that the USA was founded upon and is dedicated to the cause of human dignity. It was a theme of his speech to the UN General Assembly in September 2004. Yet during his first term of office, the USA proved to be far from the global human rights champion it proclaimed itself to be.

These double standards were perhaps most vividly captured by the appalling photographs from Abu

Ghraib prison in Iraq – a detainee, hooded, balanced on a box, arms outstretched, wires dangling from his hands with electric torture threatened; a naked man cowering in terror against the bars of a cell as soldiers threaten him with snarling dogs; and soldiers smiling, apparently confident of their impunity, over detainees forced into sexually humiliating poses.

The Abu Ghraib photographs prompted official investigations and reviews by the US authorities, but none was comprehensive in scope or had the independence or reach needed to investigate the role of the Secretary of Defense or agencies, departments or individual office holders outside the Pentagon. Moreover, a series of government memorandums that emerged after the Abu Ghraib scandal broke – which suggested that the administration was discussing ways in which its agents could avoid the international ban on torture and cruel, inhuman or degrading treatment – indicated that the US administration's stated opposition to torture and other cruel, inhuman or degrading treatment was paper-thin.

Throughout 2004, violence was endemic in Iraq, whether in the form of unlawful killings, torture and other violations by US-led Coalition troops and Iraqi security forces, or attacks against civilians and others by armed groups. Delivery of aid and reconstruction assistance was debilitated by the violence. Millions suffered the consequences of destroyed infrastructure, mass unemployment and uncertainty about their future. Dozens of hostages were brutally killed, some beheaded on film that subsequently received worldwide media attention. Criminal gangs kidnapped scores of Iraqis, especially children, for ransom. And there was little or no progress in bringing to justice those responsible for past and present human rights abuses.

Meanwhile, the main human rights body of the UN ignored the crisis in Iraq. In April, the UN Commission on Human Rights decided to discontinue its review of the situation in Iraq at a time when monitoring, assistance and cooperation were of crucial importance to a successful transition from a brutal dictatorship to a government respectful of human rights. By doing so, the Commission showed yet again it had no stomach for confronting grave abuses of human rights in the face of intransigent governments.

In June, in a resolution unanimously adopted on the transfer of power in Iraq, the UN Security Council included a commitment by all forces in the country to act in accordance with international law, including their obligations under international humanitarian law. However, a crucial opportunity to make clear the specific obligations of the multinational force and the Iraqi authorities under international human rights and humanitarian law was missed. A proposal to state these obligations in unambiguous terms and include them in the binding part of the resolution was blocked by the drafters of the resolution – the USA and the UK – even though a majority of Security Council members supported the proposal.

Meanwhile, Afghanistan slipped into a downward spiral of lawlessness and instability. Anti-government forces, which were aligned to the Taleban, carried out violent attacks on election staff and aid workers. Throughout the country, levels of violence against women were extremely high, and there were ongoing allegations of human rights violations including torture and ill-treatment by the US military in US-managed detention facilities.

The human rights abuses in Iraq and Afghanistan were far from being the only negative repercussions of the response to the terrible events of 11 September 2001. Since that day, the framework of international human rights standards has been attacked and undermined by both governments and armed groups.

© Rei Shiva

A former football pitch in Falluja, Iraq, now used as a graveyard for people killed since the US-led invasion of Iraq in March 2003.

The USA continued to hold hundreds of foreign detainees without charge or trial in the US naval base in Guantánamo Bay in Cuba. The refusal of the US authorities to apply the Geneva Conventions to the detainees and to allow detainees access to legal counsel or the courts violated international law and standards and caused serious suffering to detainees and their families. The ruling by the US Supreme Court in June that the US courts have jurisdiction to consider challenges to the lawfulness of such detentions appeared to be a step towards restoring the rule of law for the detainees, but the US administration sought to empty the ruling of any real meaning in order to keep the detainees in legal limbo. The USA also failed to clarify the fate or whereabouts of detainees that it held in secret detention in other countries.

Death penalty statistics

In 2004 at least 3,797 people were executed in 25 countries. At least 7,395 people were sentenced to death in 64 countries. These figures include only cases known to AI; the true figures were certainly higher.

As in previous years, the vast majority of executions worldwide were carried out in a tiny handful of countries. In 2004, 97 per cent of all known executions took place in China, Iran, the USA and Viet Nam.

By the end of the year, 84 countries had abolished the death penalty for all crimes. A further 12 countries had abolished it for all but exceptional crimes, such as wartime crimes. At least 24 countries were abolitionist in practice: they had not carried out any executions for the previous 10 years or more and were believed to have a policy or an established practice of not carrying out executions. Seventy-six other countries and territories retained the death penalty, although not all of them passed death sentences or carried out executions in 2004.

Such serious abuses carried out by a country as powerful as the USA created a dangerous climate. The US administration's unilateralism and selectivity sent a permissive signal to abusive governments around the world. There is strong evidence that the global security agenda pursued since 11 September 2001, the US-led "war on terror", and the USA's selective disregard for international law encouraged and fuelled abuses by governments and others in all regions of the world.

In many countries, new doctrines of security continued to stretch the concept of "war" into areas formerly considered law enforcement, promoting the notion that human rights can be curtailed when it comes to the detention, interrogation and prosecution of "terrorist" suspects.

The "security excuse", whereby governments curtailed and abused human rights under the cloak of the "war on terror", was particularly apparent in a number of countries in Asia and Europe. For example, thousands of members of the ethnic Uighur community were arrested in China as "separatists, terrorists and religious extremists". In Gujarat, India, hundreds of members of the Muslim community continued to be held under the Prevention of Terrorism Act. In Uzbekistan, the authorities rounded up and detained hundreds of people said to be devout Muslims or their relatives, and sentenced many people accused of "terrorism-related" offences to long prison terms following unfair trials. In the USA, there have been reprehensible attempts by officials to argue that torture was not torture, or that the USA bore no responsibility for torture carried out in other countries, even if it had sent the victim there.

Despite widespread "counter-terrorist" measures aimed at securing nation states and their citizens, armed groups in many countries launched appalling acts of violence designed to increase levels of insecurity. The massacre of hundreds of people on their morning train journey to work in the Spanish capital Madrid in March, or the taking hostage of hundreds of families, including children, in the middle of a festive school event in Beslan, Russian Federation, in September, showed complete contempt for the most fundamental principles of humanity.

Governments have a duty to prevent and punish such atrocities, but they must do so while fully respecting human rights. Not only is it a moral and legal imperative to observe fundamental human rights all the more stringently in the face of such security threats, in practice it is far more likely to be effective in the long term. Respect for human rights and fundamental freedoms is not optional in efforts to defeat "terrorism". States' efforts to combat "terrorism" must be firmly and unconditionally grounded in the rule of law and respect for human rights.

The establishment of the International Criminal Court opens a number of new avenues for pursuing international criminal prosecutions, including against armed groups, although it will only be able to investigate and prosecute a limited number of cases itself. The continued opposition of the US administration to the International Criminal Court is therefore counter-productive to its own stated aim of countering "terrorism". The International Criminal Court needs strong political and practical support to be able to deliver justice for international crimes committed by armed groups or governments.

Economic and social insecurity

The persistence of poverty — more than a billion people live in extreme poverty — remained perhaps the gravest threat to human rights and collective security. The fact that so many people live in inhuman conditions, and that the gap between rich and poor is widening between and within countries, directly contradicts the notion that all human beings are born equal in dignity and rights.

The Universal Declaration of Human Rights and international human rights treaties hold out the promise of a life with dignity, where every person enjoys an adequate standard of living and access to those essentials that give practical meaning to such a

© REUTERS/Tim Wimborne

Demonstrators in central Sydney protest against the Australian government's policies restricting the rights of refugees and asylum-seekers, October 2004.

life – including food, water, shelter, education, work and health care.

These fundamental economic and social entitlements must be recognized as rights on an equal footing with the right not to be tortured or arbitrarily detained. Until the corresponding obligations are built into public policy at the national and international levels, efforts to tackle poverty will remain tokenistic and ineffectual.

In several countries, economic and social rights have been invoked successfully in efforts to remedy injustices. For example, the human rights framework has been used to confront the forced eviction of slum dwellers in the Angolan capital Luanda and the political manipulation of food shortages by the Zimbabwean government. In 2004 AI supported efforts in these countries to claim the right to housing and the right to food.

AI's work throughout the year also highlighted how poverty, marginalization and exclusion deprive people of the conditions for enjoying other rights, including freedom of expression and access to a fair trial. The relative powerlessness of the poor leaves them vulnerable to the arbitrary exercise of state power, from repressive policing in urban shanty towns to the denial of access to essential public services.

The UN Millennium Declaration set a range of targets, later complemented by the Millennium Development Goals, which include halving extreme poverty, promoting women's equality and reversing the spread of HIV/AIDS by 2015. The Millennium Development Goals should be seen not as a limited aspiration for selected countries, but as an opportunity to advance a broader range of economic and social rights obligations which apply to all states and to the international community as a whole. They should

provide the context for promoting transnational obligations for human rights which should inform international decision-making on policy and practice in the fields of trade, aid and debt.

In 2004 these obligations continued to be woefully neglected in the international forums and global governance institutions charged with these matters. An indication of the relative neglect of economic, social and cultural rights was the slow progress made within the UN human rights system in adopting a new mechanism to hear complaints of violations of the International Covenant on Economic, Social and Cultural Rights. Despite renewed momentum generated by non-governmental organizations and sympathetic governments, such a mechanism remains a distant prospect.

Another indication of the shortcomings of existing global governance structures is the lack of acceptance that corporate actors have human rights responsibilities. December marked the 20th anniversary of the gas leak in Bhopal, India, which left 20,000 people dead and 100,000 living with chronic illnesses. Twenty years on, the tragedy and contaminated environment continue to ruin the lives of the surrounding communities. The companies involved, Union Carbide Corporation (UCC) and Dow Chemicals, have still not cleaned up the site or stopped pollution that started when the plant opened in the 1970s. Survivors are still waiting for just compensation and adequate medical care. No one has been held to account for the toxic leak. Dow Chemicals and UCC both deny legal responsibility, with UCC refusing to appear before Indian courts to face trial.

Businesses provide employment for countless millions of people and constitute the driving force in most national economies today. Companies therefore exercise tremendous influence and power, and many businesses have a global reach. Corporate activities have significant effects on the human rights of those they influence. In many countries government regulation and enforcement are inadequate to protect individuals when corporate activities harm workforces or communities. National systems are often unable or unwilling to hold companies operating in their countries accountable. The complex structure of multinationals can create obstacles for local courts in exercising jurisdiction over abuses committed by a corporation with headquarters outside the country.

Most companies oppose any move towards binding international regulations, although many businesses operate across boundaries in a way that exceeds the regulatory power of any one state. Voluntary codes and initiatives such as the Global Compact, the international network in support of responsible corporate citizenship, can be useful in promoting good practice, but have failed to reduce the negative consequences of corporate behaviour on human rights.

In 2004 the process to codify the human rights responsibilities of transnational corporations and related business enterprises gained momentum in the UN.

UN reform

2004 revealed the inadequacy of the UN's response to global human rights challenges, and the need for more effective and impartial mechanisms for human rights protection.

The UN came under strong criticism during 2004, some of it justified, some of it aimed at weakening the UN itself. AI believes that the role of the UN remains central to the protection and promotion of human rights, but needs to be strengthened through constructive reform of its human rights machinery. In

order to recapture people's trust in the language of human rights, and to strengthen efforts to improve human security, the UN must reform. Governments must recognize that sidelining human rights creates greater insecurity, and greater scope for abuse.

The need for reform was recognized in the report of the UN High-level Panel on Threats, Challenges and Change – *A more secure world: Our shared responsibility* – published in December 2004. The report provides a critical opportunity to strengthen the UN and to re-establish the central importance of human rights and the rule of law in tackling complex global threats and challenges. The governments that make up the UN must use this chance to strengthen human rights protection and promotion in the UN system by giving human rights the authoritative position which the UN Charter requires and by providing the UN's human rights machinery with the necessary political and financial support.

AI believes that the following reforms, among many others, are needed. In developing a comprehensive, principled "counter-terrorism" strategy, the UN must integrate human rights as a central component. The Security Council must be encouraged to address the human rights deficit in the work of its Counter-Terrorism Committee so that the instruments and measures it promotes remain strictly within a legal framework that is respectful of human rights.

The Security Council should invite the High Commissioner for Human Rights to participate routinely in relevant thematic and country debates. The High Commissioner has an invaluable contribution to make to the Security Council's debates, including on the mandates of peace operations, on early warning, and on the effective implementation of human rights-related provisions in its resolutions.

© Maude Dorr

Residents of Bhopal, India, demonstrate for clean water, July 2004. Twenty years after a pesticide plant owned by Union Carbide leaked toxic gases, which killed thousands of people, a proper clean-up of the contaminated site has not been carried out.

© REUTERS/Gustau Nacarino

A crowd in Barcelona's Plaza de Catalunya joins millions of other people in city centres across Spain to protest against the Madrid train bombings, March 2004.

The Security Council's Permanent Members should commit themselves not to use the veto when dealing with genocide, crimes against humanity, war crimes or other large-scale human rights abuses.

The Commission on Human Rights – the legitimacy of which has been undermined by the political manoeuvrings of its members – should be reformed to ensure the most effective protection and promotion of human rights in all countries at all times. Any proposal to expand membership of the Commission to include all UN member states should be undertaken only as part of a comprehensive strategy to strengthen the UN human rights machinery. Any institutional changes must ensure that the role of non-governmental organizations is maintained.

Governments should substantially increase financial support for the Office of the High Commissioner for Human Rights. The lack of sustained and adequate financial support (it receives only two per cent of the UN budget) has hampered the human rights programme's ability to attract the stable, professional resources that are essential for effective work.

The High-level Panel's report on UN reform discusses the issue of shared responsibilities towards human rights, but the debate is framed largely in terms of a duty to intervene militarily in the case of mass human rights abuses. AI believes that this narrow focus is both limited and dangerous. The international responsibility to respect, protect and fulfil human rights goes well beyond the use of military force in so-called humanitarian interventions and covers a much broader range of obligations. These include: taking early measures to prevent conflict; not selling arms to states that violate human rights; providing asylum to refugees fleeing persecution; and helping other states combat problems such as endemic inequalities, poverty and HIV/AIDS.

A challenging year

Human rights activists had a difficult year in 2004. The disturbing pictures of torture in Abu Ghraib highlighted the need to defend principles once thought inviolable, like the prohibition of torture. The prevalence of horrific sexual violence against women in conflicts was a reminder of how rapidly men thrown into battle are dehumanized, and how consistently women and girls are targeted. The escalating levels of xenophobia in many countries showed the importance of confronting every manifestation of racism. These, and many other problems, revealed the scale of the challenges facing human rights defenders around the world.

However, there were grounds for optimism. Five countries – Bhutan, Greece, Samoa, Senegal and Turkey – joined the growing list of states that have abolished the death penalty for all crimes. Prisoners of conscience were released in several countries. The International Criminal Court continued to make progress, providing new hope of justice for victims of horrendous crimes.

Around the world, vast numbers of ordinary people demonstrated the power and influence of civil society. The World Social Forum in Mumbai, India, in January; the European Social Forum in London, UK, in November; the widening debate on human rights in the Middle East; and the protests on the streets of Ukraine in December, were all examples of solidarity in action. The millions who massed on the streets of Madrid to protest against the train bombings showed the power of ordinary people to mobilize, to claim their right to live free from fear, to repudiate the acts of the "terrorist", and to demand that their governments be truthful and answerable to the people.

Global activism is a dynamic and growing force. It is also the best hope of achieving freedom and justice for all humanity.

AI REPORT 2005
PART 2

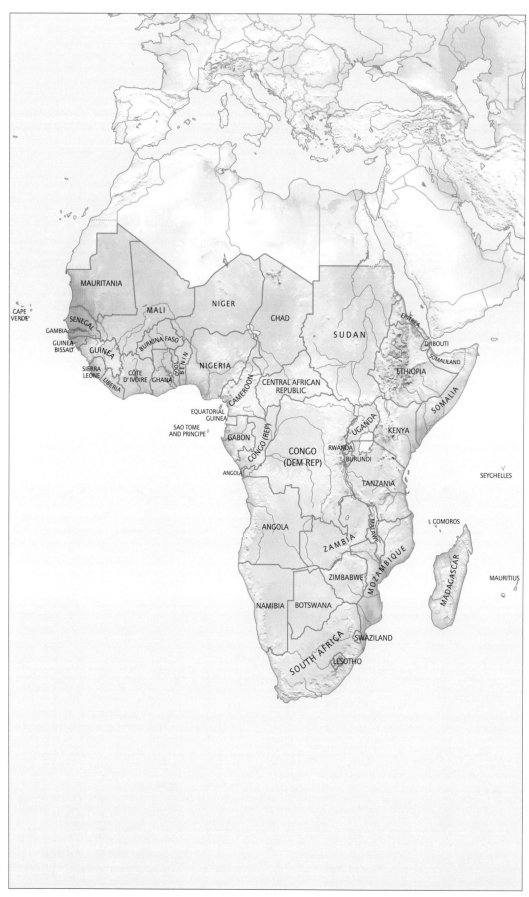

AFRICA REGIONAL OVERVIEW 2004

Armed conflicts continued to bring widespread destruction to several parts of Africa in 2004, many of them fuelled by human rights violations. Refugees and internally displaced people faced appalling conditions. There were international initiatives to hold perpetrators of abuses accountable. Across the region, there was discrimination against people living with HIV/AIDS, the vast majority of whom were denied the right to medical treatment. Political repression was widespread and human rights defenders came under attack. Pervasive violence against women was exacerbated by poverty and lack of access to health care and education.

Regional institutions, established to ensure respect for human rights, to carry out peacekeeping functions or to prevent and resolve conflicts, became operational. In addition, in January the Protocol to the African Charter on Human and Peoples' Rights on the Establishment of an African Court on Human and Peoples' Rights entered into force. However, the Court was not fully established because a decision of the African Union (AU) Assembly to integrate it with the African Court of Justice caused considerable delays.

Governments reaffirmed commitments to promote and protect human rights. Yet broken promises, weak or collapsed criminal justice systems, corruption and illegal exploitation of resources contributed to deny basic rights to many.

Armed conflict

Killings, abductions and rape by government forces and armed opposition groups remained widespread in armed conflicts in the Democratic Republic of the Congo (DRC), Somalia, Sudan and Uganda. The progress made on a number of peace agreements remained fragile in Burundi, Côte d'Ivoire and Somalia, where sporadic outbreaks of violence persisted in localized areas.

The parties to the north-south warfare in Sudan made commitments to reach an overall peace agreement by the end of 2004. Wealth and power sharing agreements had already been signed, and interim security arrangements made. In stark contrast to these peace negotiations, thousands of people were killed or raped in the escalating conflict in Darfur, western Sudan, and hundreds of thousands driven from their homes, many of them by government supported militias. Ceasefire agreements were regularly violated by the various fighting forces.

In Somalia, in the final stages of a reconciliation process to end over a decade of state collapse and factional violence, a newly appointed President formed a government and a transitional parliament was created. Most of the faction leaders were made members of the newly formed government.

Eastern DRC remained volatile. Armed political groups continued to carry out killings, rapes and other torture of civilians, and occasionally resumed fighting with rival forces. The direct support of armed groups by neighbouring countries contributed to the persistent instability.

The role of peacekeeping missions in Africa expanded throughout 2004. The UN mission in Côte d'Ivoire and the African Mission in Burundi were transformed into UN peacekeeping missions, and additional troops strengthened the UN peacekeeping mission in the DRC. The AU Peace and Security Council sent a force to Darfur with a mandate to protect civilians. In spite of the increased presence of UN and AU forces on the ground, the protection of civilians often remained inadequate in Bukavu, DRC, or in Darfur.

The proliferation of small arms in the region continued to be a major cause of human rights abuses, and the UN Security Council declared an arms embargo against all non-governmental forces in Darfur. However, no proper monitoring mechanisms were put in place and the embargo was not extended to the Sudanese government, despite its direct responsibility for human rights violations. The Security Council also declared an arms embargo in Côte d'Ivoire but again failed to ensure adequate monitoring.

As armed conflicts ended, large-scale repatriation of refugees proceeded or was planned. In Burundi and Liberia, the UN High Commissioner for Refugees facilitated voluntary returns. In Angola, the repatriation of thousands of refugees continued. In countries with long-term refugee populations, such as Tanzania, refugees often faced deteriorating living conditions, host governments reluctant to accept further refugees, and increased pressure to repatriate.

Conflicts such as in Darfur caused extensive displacement of people. The attack in August on Congolese refugees in a transit centre in Burundi, which killed more than 150 people, further demonstrated the need for enhanced protection of refugees and civilian populations in general.

International justice

There were important developments in addressing impunity for human rights violations in armed conflicts through the use of international justice mechanisms.

The governments of the DRC and Uganda referred war crimes and crimes against humanity committed in armed conflicts to the International Criminal Court (ICC), in the first cases in which ICC prosecutors would initiate such investigations. As the ICC can investigate and prosecute only a limited number of individual cases, there was still a need for comprehensive plans to end impunity for all such crimes, regardless of which side committed them and the perpetrator's level of responsibility. Uganda subsequently suggested that war crimes and crimes against humanity in Northern Uganda would be addressed in traditional reconciliation procedures, although its referrals to the ICC could not be withdrawn.

Trials started before the Special Court for Sierra Leone of people indicted for crimes against humanity, war crimes and other serious violations of international law, including rape, other forms of sexual violence and sexual slavery. The Court had previously ruled that the general amnesty granted in the 1999 Lomé peace agreement was "ineffective" in preventing it from prosecuting crimes against humanity and war crimes, and that Charles Taylor, former President of Liberia, had no immunity from prosecution. Charles Taylor, indicted for "bearing the greatest responsibility" for killings, mutilations, rape and other abuses through active support of armed opposition forces in Sierra Leone, remained in Nigeria. He had been granted refugee status, with apparent guarantees that he would be neither surrendered to the Special Court nor brought before Nigeria's own courts.

A commission of inquiry investigated reports of violations of international humanitarian law and human rights in Darfur following a Security Council resolution. Its brief included determining whether acts of genocide had occurred, and identifying the perpetrators with a view to ensuring accountability.

The UN High Commissioner for Human Rights established an inquiry into reports of unlawful killings and excessive use of force against anti-government demonstrators in Côte d'Ivoire. Another international commission of inquiry, set up under the terms of the 2003 Linas-Marcoussis peace agreement in Côte d'Ivoire, had not yet reported publicly the findings of its investigations into human rights abuses since September 2002, which concluded during 2004. Its report was to be the basis for government prosecutions.

At the request of the Security Council, an assessment was made of the feasibility of establishing an International Judicial Commission of Inquiry in Burundi, as outlined in the 2000 Arusha peace agreement. Such an inquiry would investigate and determine responsibility for crimes under international law committed in the period between independence from colonial rule and signature of the peace agreement.

Violence against women
Women continued to be raped and subjected to other forms of sexual violence despite the ending of armed conflicts in the Central African Republic, Côte d'Ivoire and Liberia. In Darfur and eastern DRC, such abuse was used as a weapon of war against women and girls who had already experienced years of violence. There was no safe haven for women, even in refugee camps. In the DRC, the collapse of the health system left survivors of rape without health care for sometimes fatal injuries and infections. This lack of even basic health care was common to many other states.

There was increasing evidence that the violence against women in conflicts and post-conflict situations was gender-based and an extreme manifestation of the discrimination and inequalities women experienced in peacetime. Women's physical integrity was threatened and their basic rights eroded on a daily basis. The violence that women faced in peacetime also contributed to a broad acceptance of violence in the home. In Nigeria, as in other countries, discrimination within the family and community was compounded by the existence of discriminatory laws.

Many girls living below the poverty line remained at risk of being enrolled as child soldiers, beaten, forced into sexual slavery, and even killed. In the DRC, there was continued recruitment of child soldiers despite a planned demobilization of the army that was still largely to be implemented by the end of the year. Programmes of disarmament, demobilization and reintegration failed to include specific provisions for those who had suffered sexual violence.

Death penalty
Senegal formally abolished the death penalty. Many other states remained abolitionist in practice. In Nigeria, a National Study Group on the Death Penalty called on the government to impose a moratorium on executions and to commute to life imprisonment the sentences of all death row prisoners whose appeals had been concluded. In Sierra Leone, the Truth and Reconciliation Commission recommended the immediate repeal of all laws authorizing the use of capital punishment. Nevertheless, shortly afterwards, 10 people convicted of treason were sentenced to death.

However, prisoners remained under sentence of death in countries including Burundi, Equatorial Guinea, Kenya and Mauritania, the majority of them after unfair trials. In Sudan, several hundred people were sentenced to death in 2004.

Economic, social and cultural rights
Africa continued to face severe economic conditions. Massive corruption and illegal exploitation of natural resources contributed to denying many, especially the most marginalized sectors of the population, their economic, social and cultural rights — in particular the rights to food, water, health, housing and education — as well as enjoyment of their civil and political rights, such as the right to a fair trial and the effective administration of criminal justice.

In Zimbabwe, communities were routinely deprived of their right to food, in part because of discriminatory policies by the government, which used food as a tool of political repression. The adequate implementation of the right to health in Rwanda, South Africa and Swaziland, and of the right to housing in Angola, continued to be denied, especially to women, children, the elderly, minorities and migrants. There was growing awareness of the basic needs of people living with HIV/AIDS, and access to anti-retroviral drugs was gradually made available through government and Global Fund programmes. However, considerable efforts were still needed to address discrimination, the impact of poverty and the severe shortage of medical staff as obstacles to the enjoyment of the right to health.

Political repression

Freedom of expression and association continued to come under attack by governments and remained restricted under the law in Swaziland. In Côte d'Ivoire, the government intimidated journalists and human rights defenders through manipulation of the print media. In Cameroon, Mauritania and Zimbabwe, the security forces were deployed to curb dissent or opposition to governments.

The leader of the opposition in Zimbabwe, Morgan Tsvangarai, was acquitted by a tribunal on charges of treason against the state, but questions remained about the independence of the judiciary. Youth militia in Zimbabwe were allowed to attack those perceived as critical of the government with impunity.

In Eritrea thousands of government critics and political opponents, many of them prisoners of conscience, were detained in secret. Some had been sentenced by panels of military and police officers in closed proceedings that flouted basic standards of fair trial. Those convicted were not informed of the accusations against them, had no right to defend themselves or be legally represented before the panels, and had no recourse to an independent judiciary to challenge abuses of their fundamental rights.

In Sudan, political opponents, supposed government critics, students and activists were detained under the National Security Forces Act, which allowed incommunicado detention without charge or trial for up to nine months. Many detainees were reported to have been tortured or ill-treated while held incommunicado under the Act.

The failure by the authorities to bring to justice members of the security forces suspected or accused of serious human rights violations contributed to the climate of impunity in many countries. In addition, the absence of thorough and credible investigations into allegations of torture and extrajudicial executions effectively weakened the rule of law.

Human rights defenders

Several governments imposed severe restrictions on the work of human rights defenders. The Non-Governmental Organizations Act (NGO Act) in Zimbabwe gave the government sweeping powers to interfere with civil society and human rights groups through a government-appointed NGO Council. Under the NGO Act, Zimbabwean groups were prohibited from receiving foreign funding for human rights work, and foreign human rights organizations were banned from working in Zimbabwe.

In Rwanda, the work of a leading independent human rights organization, the Rwandese League for the Promotion and Defence of Human Rights (LIPRODHOR), was effectively closed down. It was among a number of Rwandese NGOs recommended for dissolution on the grounds that they had supported the genocide, after investigations by a Parliamentary Commission that were neither fair nor transparent.

In Sudan, the government continued to arrest human rights defenders who exposed human rights violations instead of bringing the perpetrators of abuses to

justice. The government of Eritrea did not allow national human rights organizations to operate, and denied international human rights organizations access to the country. In Côte d'Ivoire, human rights defenders came under attack for expressing views perceived to be critical of the government.

A positive development was the establishment of a Special Rapporteur on human right defenders by the African Commission on Human and Peoples' Rights. However the Commission continued to face many challenges, including lack of adequate resources to carry out its mandate.

AI regional reports

- Open letter to Permanent Representatives at the African Union (AU) regarding the case of Charles Taylor, former President of Liberia, indicted for crimes against humanity and war crimes (AI Index: IOR 63/007/2004)
- The Protocol on the Rights of Women in Africa: Strengthening the promotion and protection of women's human rights in Africa (AI Index: IOR 63/005/2004)
- Towards the Promotion and Protection of the Rights of Human Rights Defenders in Africa: Amnesty International's recommendations to the Focal Point on Human Rights Defenders of the African Commission on Human and Peoples' Rights (AI Index: IOR 63/004/2004)
- African Court on Human and Peoples' Rights: Checklist to ensure the nomination of the highest qualified candidates for judges (AI Index: IOR 63/001/2004)

AMERICAS REGIONAL OVERVIEW 2004

Respect for human rights remained an illusion for many as governments across the Americas failed to comply with their commitments to uphold fundamental human rights. Widespread torture, unlawful killings by police and arbitrary detention persisted. The US-led "war on terror" continued to undermine human rights in the name of security, despite growing international outrage at evidence of US war crimes, including torture, against detainees.

Democratic institutions and the rule of law were at risk throughout much of Latin America. Political instability – fuelled by corruption, organized crime, economic disparities and social unrest – resulted in several attempts to bring down governments. Most were by constitutional means but some, as in Haiti, by-passed the democratic process.

Political armed groups and criminal gangs, principally those engaged in drug trafficking, had an increasing impact on people's fundamental rights. Poverty and discrimination affected millions of people, particularly the most vulnerable groups – women, children, indigenous people and Afro-descendant communities.

Positive developments were seen in the vigorous campaigns maintained by human rights defenders, who held both governments and armed groups to account, in defiance of harassment and persecution. Courts in several countries gave rulings that brought closer the prospect of bringing to trial military and political leaders responsible for massive human rights violations in previous decades.

National security and the 'war on terror'
The blatant disregard for international human rights and humanitarian law in the "war on terror" continued to make a mockery of President George Bush's claims that the USA was the global champion of human rights. Images of detainees in US custody tortured in Abu Ghraib prison in Iraq shocked the world. War crimes in Iraq, and mounting evidence of the torture and ill-treatment of detainees in US custody in other countries, sent an unequivocal message to the world that human rights may be sacrificed ostensibly in the name of security.

President Bush's refusal to apply the Geneva Conventions to those captured during the international armed conflict in Afghanistan and transferred to the US naval base at Guantánamo Bay, Cuba, was challenged by a judicial decision in November. The ruling resulted in the suspension of trials by military commission in Guantánamo, and the government immediately lodged an appeal. The US administration's treatment of detainees in the "war on terror" continued to display a marked ambivalence to the opinion of expert bodies such as the International Committee of the Red Cross and even of its own highest judicial body. Six months after the Supreme Court ruled that the federal courts had jurisdiction over the Guantánamo detainees, none had appeared in court. Detainees reportedly considered of high intelligence value remained in secret detention in undisclosed locations. In some cases their situation amounted to "disappearance".

The "war on terror" and the "war on drugs" increasingly merged, and dominated US relations with Latin America and the Caribbean. Following the US elections in November, the Bush administration encouraged governments in the region to give a greater role to the military in public order and internal security operations. The blurring of military and police roles resulted in governments such as those in Brazil, Guatemala, Honduras, Mexico and Paraguay deploying military forces to deal with crime and social unrest.

The US doubled the ceiling on the number of US personnel deployed in Colombia in counter-insurgency and counter-narcotics operations. The Colombian government in turn persisted in redefining the country's 40-year internal conflict as part of the international "war on terror".

Conflict, crime and instability
Civilians continued to be the principal victims of political violence. The human rights situation in Colombia remained critical, its civilians targeted by all sides in the conflict: the security forces, army-backed paramilitaries and armed opposition groups. Despite an agreed ceasefire and demobilization of some combatants, paramilitary forces were again responsible for widespread abuses. Security policies introduced by the government drew civilians further into the conflict.

Further evidence of spill-over from Colombia's internal war was seen in neighbouring countries. Frequent border skirmishes were reported in Venezuela and Ecuador, where the number of Colombians seeking refuge grew.

Political polarization and instability continued to affect Venezuela for much of the year. Levels of violence and protests diminished briefly after a referendum failed to unseat President Hugo Chávez, but the death of a high-profile special prosecutor in a car bombing raised fears of renewed political violence.

Long-standing instability in Haiti reached crisis levels after a military uprising toppled the government of President Jean Bertrand Aristide. Political violence and widespread human rights violations persisted, despite the presence of a UN military and police force. The severe loss of life and structural damage caused by a hurricane in September exacerbated instability and the breakdown of the rule of law, hampering distribution of international aid.

In a report on Guatemala, the UN warned that failure to bring about effective social, economic and political reforms could promote conflict.

Public protests against violent crime, particularly kidnapping, spread throughout Latin America. Crime levels remained high in Mexican and Brazilian cities, and in parts of Central America where poverty combined with the easy availability of weapons and the legacy of civil wars. Governments responded with tougher legislation, which sometimes violated constitutional and human rights safeguards. Vigilantism and mob lynchings of suspected criminals were reported in countries including Guatemala, Mexico and Peru, where confidence in the security forces continued to evaporate.

Impunity for human rights violations

Despite setbacks, efforts across the region to combat impunity for gross human rights violations in previous decades continued to gain momentum.

A series of rulings and actions based on international jurisdiction showed that military and security chiefs whose forces were responsible for human rights violations could no longer escape trial. An Argentine court issued an international warrant for the arrest of former Paraguayan President Alfredo Stroessner for his alleged involvement in human rights violations committed under Operation Cóndor, a joint plan to eliminate opponents by military governments of the 1970s and 1980s in Argentina, Bolivia, Brazil, Chile, Paraguay and Uruguay. Spain's Supreme Court confirmed that the Spanish justice system had jurisdiction to try former Argentine navy officer Adolfo Scilingo for human rights violations under the military government of 1976-83. More than 20 years after the alleged crimes, a former Honduran intelligence chief faced a civil action in the US courts brought by relatives of Hondurans tortured and killed in the 1980s.

National courts also made significant, if slow, progress in shedding light on past human rights violations. The Chilean Supreme Court lifted former President Augusto Pinochet's immunity from prosecution, allowing proceedings to be opened against him for human rights violations during Operation Cóndor.

In Brazil, the Supreme Court ordered the federal government to open files on the military operations against armed opposition groups in the region of Araguaia, state of Pará, during the military dictatorship. These may enable relatives finally to locate the bodies of victims of military actions.

Military and police courts continued to claim jurisdiction, despite recommendations by international human rights bodies. In Bolivia, the military initially rejected a Constitutional Court ruling that officers charged with offences against civilians should be tried in civilian courts. In Peru and Colombia, cases of human rights violations continued to be transferred to military courts in spite of rulings by the respective Constitutional Courts that they had jurisdiction only over offences committed "in the line of duty". In Ecuador, police courts still claimed jurisdiction in cases involving abuses by police agents although the authorities had given assurances that they would be heard by civilian courts.

Trial before civilian courts was no guarantee of justice, however. In Colombia, against all the evidence, charges were withdrawn against former General Rito Alejo del Río, indicted for forming illegal paramilitary groups responsible for human rights violations in the 1990s.

The USA continued to pressure governments throughout the region to sign unlawful immunity agreements shielding US personnel from surrender to the International Criminal Court. Of 12 countries that had refused to sign, 10 had some military aid suspended as a result. In November the US Congress threatened to cut off development aid to countries that refused to sign.

Death penalty

The USA continued to flout international human rights standards by inflicting the death penalty on child offenders, people with mental disabilities, defendants without access to effective legal representation, and foreign nationals denied their consular rights. In 2004, 59 executions were carried out by a capital justice system characterized by arbitrariness, discrimination and error. Scheduled executions of a number of child offenders were stayed pending a Supreme Court ruling on the case of a death row prisoner aged 17 at the time of the crime.

No judicial executions were carried out in the Caribbean, but the Judicial Committee of the Privy Council — the final court of appeal for most of the English-speaking Caribbean — reopened the possibility of a resumption of executions in Trinidad and Tobago by overturning a decision that the mandatory death penalty was unconstitutional. It ruled that mandatory death sentences for capital murder violated the Jamaican Constitution, and ordered new sentencing hearings for Jamaica's death row inmates. It also ruled that the mandatory death penalty was constitutional in Barbados.

Economic, social and cultural rights

Economic indicators improved in Latin America after a prolonged period of stagnation. However, growth was insufficient to significantly affect poverty levels. Extreme disparities in wealth, and in access to basic rights such as education, health, water and electricity, continued. Inequalities were persistently driven by race and ethnicity, particularly for indigenous and Afro-descendant peoples, who are among the poorest in the region.

According to a UN study on the spread of HIV/AIDs, the Caribbean is the second most affected region in the world. Social attitudes such as homophobia and stigmatization are cited by the UN among factors contributing to the spread of the epidemic.

Severe political violence and instability in Haiti exacerbated the long-standing denial of basic rights, including access to health services as the breakdown in health provision reached crisis proportions.

Disputes over land and labour conditions on plantations continued to fuel protracted conflicts and human rights violations in countries such as Bolivia, Brazil, Chile, Guatemala and Paraguay. Both protesters and police officers were killed as claims for access to land by landless peasant families brought them into conflict with large landowners backed by the security forces or hired gunmen.

By the end of 2004, Central American governments and the Dominican Republic had approved a free trade agreement with the USA. Civil society groups raised concerns about the lack of guarantees on labour rights, on protection of the environment and on continued access to affordable medicines. In December, 12 South American countries signed an agreement to create a political and economic regional bloc.

Violence against women

Women and girls remained at serious risk of human rights violations across the Americas. The Inter-American Convention on the Prevention, Punishment and Eradication of Violence against Women – which marked its 10th anniversary – had received more ratifications than any other treaty on human rights in the region. Only Canada and the USA had failed to ratify. However, its provisions were largely ignored by governments across the region, and gender-related violence against women remained endemic in the home and the community.

A UN report on the state of the world's cities stated that Latin America had the highest risk of all types of sexual victimization, with approximately 70 per cent of reported incidents described as rapes, attempted rapes or indecent assaults. Despite efforts by the Mexican authorities, there were further killings of women in the state of Chihuahua, and the horrific brutality that characterized killings of women in Guatemala gave cause for growing international concern.

Women were particularly vulnerable in situations of conflict. In Colombia, all parties to the conflict subjected women and girls to sexual violence, including rape and genital mutilation. They were targeted to sow terror, wreak revenge on adversaries and accumulate "trophies of war".

There was a growing awareness of the impact of people trafficking in the Americas on human rights, particularly of women and girls. According to a study by the Organization of American States, over 100,000 men, women and children were "trafficked" across Latin America and the Caribbean each year, 80 per cent of them women and most for the purposes of sexual exploitation.

Human rights defenders

Human rights activists across the Americas campaigned vigorously to hold governments and armed groups to their obligations to respect international and domestic human rights standards.

Women's rights activists were acclaimed in Colombia for their work for thousands of innocent victims of conflict and for the meaningful involvement of women in peace negotiations and the political process. Indigenous activists in Ecuador championed their community's rights to defend their livelihoods during disputes over the extraction of natural resources. Despite public hostility and prejudice, the work of Jamaican and Honduran sexual rights activists to promote equal rights and HIV/AIDS prevention was increasingly recognized and supported by human rights organizations at the international level.

The difficulties and dangers faced by activists in the Americas ranged from intimidation and restrictions on travel, to unfounded accusations of "terrorist" links or other violent activities, arbitrary detention, false criminal charges, and even death. Activists working locally on rural poverty and development, often in isolated areas, and journalists covering issues such as corruption were killed in Brazil, Colombia, Guatemala and Mexico.

On the international stage, governments gave commitments to support the work of human rights activists. However, some undermined the integrity of these pledges by tolerating slanderous statements by high-ranking government officials against those working for human rights. Appeals by women's rights activists for the authorities to examine their concerns and proposals seriously were frequently dismissed or ignored.

Only one government, Brazil, responded to a request by both the UN Special Representative on Human Rights Defenders and by AI for governments to draft, publish and make operational plans to implement the UN Declaration on Human Rights Defenders.

Regional initiatives

During the European Union/Latin America and Caribbean Summit in May, AI highlighted its concerns about the use of the judicial system to persecute human rights defenders. Delegates from AI's International Secretariat and from AI sections in the region attended the Americas Regional Social Forum in Quito, Ecuador, in August. In the same month, AI also participated in the III Human Rights Defenders Consultation in São Paulo, Brazil.

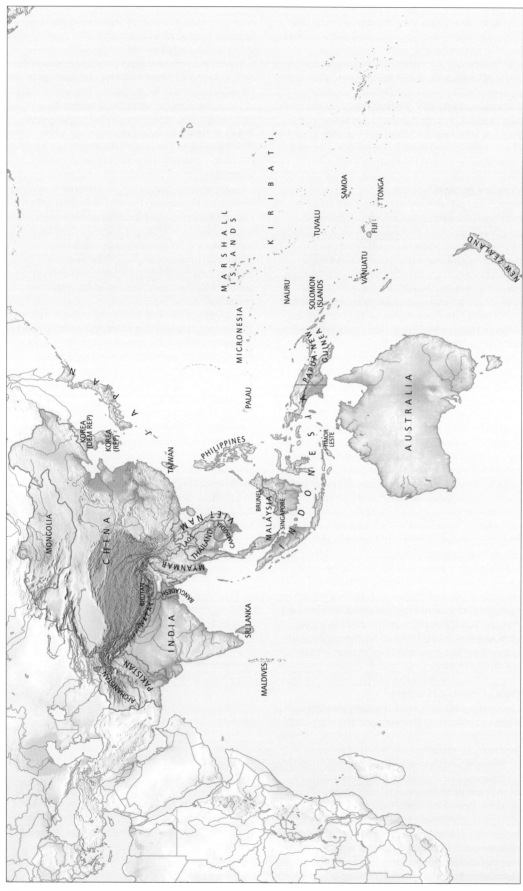

ASIA/PACIFIC REGIONAL OVERVIEW 2004

Human rights played a prominent role in elections in the region. The influence of issues such as poverty, the "war on terror" and impunity on political agendas raised hopes of renewed focus on human rights protection. Yet large pockets of repression remained, in which violations of the right to life and of freedom of expression and association were widespread. Grave human rights violations continued to take place as armed conflict raged in northeast India, Nanggroe Aceh Darussalam (NAD) province in Indonesia, and Nepal. A newly emerging conflict in southern Thailand raised concerns.

Even where opposing sides were pursuing attempts at conflict resolution, such as in India and Pakistan in relation to Jammu and Kashmir, in north-eastern Sri Lanka and in Mindanao province of the Philippines, there were frequent human rights abuses, including by armed political groups.

The "war on terror" continued to take a heavy toll in lives. Additional risks to human security arose from nuclear threats, the unrelenting arms race and widespread deprivation. Women, children, indigenous people and migrants faced impoverishment, discrimination and the politicization of aid. More than 1.5 million people were internally displaced.

At the end of the year, a massive earthquake and resulting tsunami killed more than 250,000 people in Indonesia, Sri Lanka, India, Thailand and other countries surrounding the Indian Ocean. There were grave concerns, particularly for the human rights of vulnerable groups affected by the tsunami.

Elections and denial of civil and political rights

Human rights shaped many political agendas during elections in Afghanistan, Australia, Cambodia, India, Indonesia, Philippines and South Korea. In India, rural poverty and the repeal of the Prevention of Terrorism Act were key issues in negotiations between coalition parties in the new government of the United Progressive Alliance. In Indonesia, the presidential candidacy of former armed forces chief General Wiranto attracted international criticism because of his indictment by the UN-sponsored court in Timor-Leste for crimes against humanity. He was not elected.

Bhutan, Brunei and the Maldives were among countries that made tentative moves towards democratization and increased human rights protection. Repression of human rights continued to be reported, however. In the Maldives, demonstrations in support of a faster pace of reforms resulted in the imposition of a state of emergency, the mass arrest and arbitrary detention of scores of political activists and

members of parliament, and allegations of sexual abuse and other ill-treatment.

Political dissent continued to be suppressed in countries including China, Laos, Myanmar, North Korea and Viet Nam. New, often draconian, regulations on use of the Internet restricted freedom of expression in China and Viet Nam. In Myanmar, despite the reconvening of the National Convention in May and a change of leadership in October, the political stalemate prevailing since 1988 offered little prospect of increased freedom of expression and association. Hundreds of prisoners, including National League for Democracy leaders Daw Aung San Suu Kyi and U Tin Oo, were wrongfully denied their liberty for peaceful acts that would not be considered crimes under international law. Thousands of prisoners were released in November, apparently because their imprisonment was the result of "improper deeds" by officials. Only about 40 political prisoners were believed to be among those released, and more than 1,300 remained behind bars. Sentenced after unfair trials, many of them had been convicted under security legislation and often solely for peaceful acts of dissent.

The legal framework for the protection of human rights in Asia remained weak. Ineffectual criminal justice systems provided little redress to the most vulnerable, including women and indigenous people, whose dominant reality continued to be hardship and discrimination. In countries such as Bangladesh, Malaysia, Pakistan and the Philippines, police corruption denied people the protection of human rights.

Armed conflict

Nepal slipped deeper into a security and political crisis. Despite scrutiny by the UN Commission on Human Rights, the authorities failed to put in place any meaningful mechanisms to increase respect for human rights. For the second successive year, the highest number of "disappearances" reported to the UN were in Nepal.

In Sri Lanka, during the run-up to parliamentary elections in April, the Liberation Tigers of Tamil Eelam killed several candidates and supporters of rival political parties.

In NAD province in Indonesia, where the military emergency was officially downgraded to a civil emergency, the pattern of grave abuses of civil, political, economic, social and cultural rights continued. The Indonesian security forces were primarily responsible for these violations, although the Free Aceh Movement (Gerakan Aceh Merdeka, GAM) also committed serious abuses, notably the taking of hostages and the use of child soldiers.

The death by suffocation of at least 78 demonstrators, piled on top of each other in lorries to be transferred to custody, brought to international attention the emerging conflict between the security forces and armed groups in the mainly Muslim part of southern Thailand. At the end of 2004, the death toll among both Buddhist and Muslim civilians was estimated to be around 500.

In India, particularly in Jammu and Kashmir and several states in the north-east, human rights abuses by the army and armed political groups continued, despite tentative moves towards political settlements. In Mindanao, the Philippines, a ceasefire agreement was periodically broken as forces of the separatist Moro Islamic Liberation Front (MILF) clashed with government forces. During fighting that often forced local people from their homes, both sides reportedly breached international humanitarian law, in indiscriminate attacks by the armed forces and in the use of "human shields" by MILF forces.

The International Atomic Energy Agency warned in November of a race against time to stop a "nuclear outrage" by "terrorist" groups in Asia. In South Asia, as relations improved between India and Pakistan, a moratorium on nuclear tests by both countries was announced in June.

'War on terror'
Human rights continued to be under attack in the global "war on terror". In Afghanistan, hundreds of people suspected of being sympathizers of the Taleban or al-Qa'ida were held in long-term arbitrary detention at Bagram airbase and other detention centres run by the US armed forces. Without access to judicial authorities, the detainees were effectively beyond the reach or protection of the law. Armed political groups attacked aid and election workers, killing 12 election staff and injuring more than 30 during the presidential election campaign. In Pakistan, the military carried out arbitrary detentions, possible extrajudicial executions and the deliberate destruction of houses during operations to remove from South Waziristan tribal area people suspected of association with the Taleban or al-Qa'ida. Armed groups were reported to have taken hostages and in some cases to have killed them.

In Southeast Asia, armed groups killed civilians in attacks in Indonesia and the Philippines. Six people were charged in connection with the killing of over 100 passengers in a bomb attack on a ferryboat in Manila Bay, the Philippines, in February. The six were alleged to be members of Abu Sayyaf, a Muslim separatist armed group involved in kidnappings and accused of links with al-Qa'ida. Most of the victims of a number of bomb attacks in Indonesia, including on the Australian Embassy, were Indonesian civilians.

Arbitrary detentions and unfair trials took place under security legislation in force in China, India, Malaysia, Nepal and Pakistan. In the Xinjiang Uighur Autonomous Region of China, members of the predominantly Muslim Uighur community continued to be detained as suspected "separatists, terrorists and religious extremists". Unofficial mosques were closed and certain Uighur language books and journals banned.

Violence against women
The impact on women and children of long-standing conflicts across the region was severe. In Jammu and Kashmir, a paramilitary unit, the Rasthriya Rifles, was reported to be responsible for a series of sexual assaults on women. In Manipur, northeast India, the alleged sexual assault and killing in custody of a young woman, Thangjam Manorama, sparked calls for the repeal of security legislation that had facilitated human rights abuses for decades. In Laos, in one of the worst single incidents of the 30-year conflict, five children on a foraging mission were reportedly ambushed by up to 40 soldiers, mutilated and killed. Four of the children, girls aged between 13 and 16, had apparently been raped before they were killed.

In Afghanistan, a new Constitution provided for gender equality. In practice, discrimination against women was still pervasive. Many women in prison had been accused of "running away" from home, adultery and other unlawful sexual activity outside marriage (*zina* crimes). Women who were raped did not complain to the authorities, primarily for fear that they would themselves be prosecuted for unlawful sexual activity.

Impunity for violence against women, both during armed conflict and in the domestic sphere, was pervasive. One example was the failure of the authorities in the Solomon Islands, despite assistance from a military-backed regional intervention force, to bring to justice those responsible for rape and other acts of sexual violence during the armed conflict of 1998-2003.

Refugees, internally displaced people and migrants
Millions of refugees and internally displaced people continued to be denied their rights. Refugees returning to Afghanistan faced prolonged insecurity, unemployment, inadequate shelter and a lack of access to land. The international community's attention was drawn to the plight of more than 1.5 million people displaced as a result of the tsunami. In contrast, the problems of hundreds of thousands of people in Myanmar, Nepal and Sri Lanka — driven from their homes as a result of internal conflicts and forced to find safety within their own countries — went largely unnoticed.

The conflict in NAD province of Indonesia forced refugees to flee to Jakarta and abroad, particularly to Malaysia, a destination of choice for many Indonesians seeking employment. The Malaysian authorities threatened to deport hundreds of thousands of migrants in a mass operation. An amnesty period, granted to allow migrants to return voluntarily to their home countries, was extended in November and again following the tsunami disaster.

In South Korea, Japan and many other countries in Asia, migrants frequently faced discrimination in accessing their rights to equality, housing, health care and labour rights.

Death penalty
Asia remained the continent with the highest number of reported executions, with China, Singapore and Viet Nam heading the list. In China, with few effective safeguards to protect the rights of defendants, large numbers of people continued to be executed after unfair trials. In October, the authorities announced reforms aimed at upholding the rights of criminal

suspects and defendants, including reinstatement of Supreme Court reviews in death penalty cases. It remained unclear, however, when these measures would be introduced.

Countries that resumed executions after intervals of several years included Indonesia, where three people were put to death in the first executions since 2001. In April, Afghanistan conducted the first execution known to have taken place since the fall of the Taleban. In India, the first known execution since 1997 was carried out amid public protests across the country and the subsequent resignation of the hangman. The outcry drew attention to the commutations that had previously been granted in similar cases.

Bhutan, one of the few countries to go against this negative trend, abolished the death penalty in law. There was further hope that emerging public debate might result in reduced use of the death penalty in the Philippines, Singapore, South Korea and Tonga.

Human rights defenders

Human rights defenders in the region risked harassment, arbitrary detention and threats to their lives. In Nepal, the lives of activists and their families were often in danger from both sides in the armed conflict. In the course of their work, lawyers and members of human rights organizations and the National Human Rights Commission received threatening telephone calls from unidentified people believed to be members of or closely associated with the army.

In China, the authorities continued to bring charges of subversion or vaguely defined national security offences against peaceful civil society activists and advocates of reform. Lawyers, journalists, HIV/AIDS activists and housing rights advocates were among those harassed, detained or imprisoned for documenting human rights abuses, campaigning for reform, or attempting to obtain redress for those whose rights had been violated. Li Dan, an AIDS activist, was briefly detained and beaten up after his release by unidentified assailants. His school for AIDS orphans in Henan province, where up to one million people reportedly became HIV-positive after selling their blood plasma to state-sanctioned blood collection stations, had recently been closed down by the local authorities.

Human rights activists in the region mobilized across national boundaries, particularly to counter the impact of the "war on terror" on human rights. Asia hosted several international meetings on human rights. At the World Social Forum in January in Mumbai, India, tens of thousands of activists debated the impact of the "war on terror" and globalization on human rights and human dignity. In September in Seoul, South Korea, national human rights institutions (NHRIs) from around the world considered the need to protect human rights in the context of the "war on terror". At a regional gathering of such institutions in February in Kathmandu, Nepal, members of the Asia Pacific Forum of NHRIs considered the issue of "terrorism and the rule of law", including an interim report of its Advisory Council of Jurists.

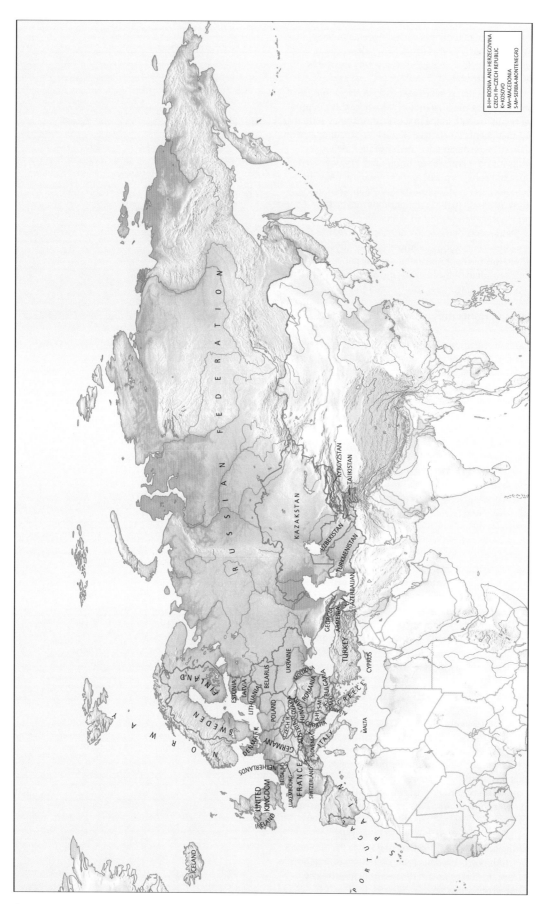

B-H=BOSNIA AND HERZEGOVINA
CZECH R=CZECH REPUBLIC
K=KOSOVO
MA=MACEDONIA
S-M=SERBIA-MONTENEGRO

EUROPE/ CENTRAL ASIA REGIONAL OVERVIEW 2004

Human rights continued to be casualties in the "war on terror". Entrenched racism, discrimination and intolerance were seen in attacks on members of Arab, Jewish and Muslim communities, in interethnic violence, and in failures to afford dignity to people with mental disabilities. All too often, those responsible for human rights abuses such as torture and ill-treatment continued to enjoy impunity. The European Union (EU) – expanded in May with the accession of 10 new states – continued to show a lack of political will to confront human rights violations within its own borders.

'War on terror'

Armed opposition groups brought death and destruction across the region – in suicide attacks in Uzbekistan, in bombings on rush hour trains in Spain, and in the school hostage-taking and siege in Beslan, Russia – claiming hundreds of lives.

Governments, in their turn, continued to roll back rights under the auspices of the "war on terror". Although the highest court in the UK ruled in a landmark decision that indefinite detention without charge or trial of foreign "suspected international terrorists" was unlawful, 11 men still remained in detention – and one under effective house arrest – at the end of 2004. Earlier the Court of Appeal of England and Wales had ruled that "evidence" obtained by torture of a third party would be inadmissible in court proceedings only if UK agents had been directly involved in, or connived at, the torture. Throughout the year the UK also sought to circumvent its obligations under domestic and international human rights law by asserting that international human rights law did not bind its armed forces in Iraq and Afghanistan.

In Russia, parliament extended to 30 days the period that someone suspected of "terrorism-related" offences could be held without charge. Uzbekistan conducted sweeping arbitrary detentions of hundreds of men and women said to be devout Muslims or their relatives, and sentenced scores of people accused of "terrorism-related" offences to long prison terms after unfair trials. Russian federal security forces continued to enjoy virtual impunity for violations in Chechnya.

Refugees and asylum-seekers

On asylum provisions and the challenges of migration, governments continued to emphasize control and deterrence rather than protection, in breach of international human rights standards. In Greece, for example, coastguards and police may have engaged in practices aimed at discouraging migrants from entering Greek territory in ways that endangered their lives. Italy, which has long lacked an adequate and comprehensive asylum procedure, expelled large numbers of people to Libya, most of them of North African origin and including asylum-seekers. The hasty and summary expulsions raised suspicions that the government was determined to act, regardless of the cost to human rights. Such flagrant abuses were compounded by the failure of the EU to balance its overarching emphasis on curbing the influx of asylum-seekers and migrants with a clear refugee protection perspective.

Racism and discrimination

Manifestations of racism, discrimination and intolerance continued to plague the region.

Discrimination appeared in many forms, including in the barriers that prevented people from accessing their basic rights. In countries from Finland to Cyprus, Roma remained severely disadvantaged in key areas of life such as housing, employment, education and medical services. In countries of the former Yugoslavia, large numbers of people seeking to rebuild their lives after being displaced by war continued to face discrimination on ethnic grounds, particularly in obtaining employment, education and health care. The treatment of people with mental disabilities remained a disgrace in many areas. In Bulgaria and Romania, the living conditions and lack of care in some hospitals and social care homes were so deplorable they amounted to inhuman and degrading treatment. In Slovakia and the Czech Republic, cage beds continued to be used in some institutions as a method of restraint. Discrimination persisted elsewhere, as in Ireland, where disability legislation introduced in 2004 was not rights-based, despite previous government pledges.

Racism by law enforcement officials continued as a backdrop to human rights violations in the administration of justice. Members of the Roma community, immigrants and asylum-seekers were among targets of racist abuse and ill-treatment. The perpetrators were rarely brought to justice.

Intolerance of others and their identities was also evident in the behaviour of private individuals and organizations. In France, people perceived to be immigrants or Muslims were subjected to waves of racist violence in Corsica. Individuals of Jewish origin and the symbols of their identity were attacked in countries such as Belgium, France and Ukraine. "Skinhead" groups in Russia subjected foreign students to race-hate attacks. Lesbian, gay, bisexual and transgender people in Poland were assaulted at marches calling for greater respect for the rights of sexual minorities.

Many governments lacked the political will to prevent, investigate and prosecute such attacks actively and with due diligence. In Georgia, hundreds of people who attacked religious minorities went unpunished. In Kosovo, some local police were accused of official complicity in incidents during the widespread inter-ethnic attacks that erupted throughout the province in March. The authorities – including international security contingents – failed to provide adequate protection to minority communities in some areas during the clashes. At the EU level, there was a persistent failure to put the criminalization of racism and xenophobia back on the legislative agenda.

Abuses by officials and impunity

Torture and ill-treatment, often race-related, were reported across the region, including in Belgium, Greece, France and Spain. From east to west, states often failed to implement or respect rights that could provide a safeguard against abuses in police custody or pre-trial detention. Authorities in a number of states did not allow detainees access to a lawyer from the moment of arrest, or did not ensure an effective, properly resourced and independent system to investigate complaints. Failure to conduct prompt, thorough and impartial investigations resulted in continued impunity for those responsible for torture and ill-treatment reported to be widespread in countries such as Albania, Georgia, Moldova, Romania, Russia, Tajikistan, Ukraine and Uzbekistan. In Turkey, torture and ill-treatment remained a serious concern despite positive changes to detention regulations. Turkey and many other states lacked independent scrutiny mechanisms to investigate such patterns of abuse. Reports continued that police in Bulgaria, Poland and Romania used firearms in violation of international standards on excessive force, sometimes with fatal results. In many countries, conditions in prisons, as well as in detention centres for asylum-seekers and unauthorized migrants, were cruel and degrading.

In the western Balkans, although there were some domestic prosecutions for war crimes, lack of political will and deficiencies in domestic justice systems led to continued and widespread impunity for wartime violations. Some war crimes suspects were transferred to the custody of the International Criminal Tribunal for the former Yugoslavia, but others continued to evade arrest, some apparently protected by authorities in Bosnia and Herzegovina, Croatia and Serbia and Montenegro. Thousands of "disappearances" that occurred during the 1991-95 war, and others from the conflicts in Kosovo and Macedonia, remained unresolved – as did those of opposition figures and journalists in Belarus and Ukraine.

Repression of dissent

Civil, political and religious dissent was systematically and often brutally repressed in Belarus, Turkmenistan and Uzbekistan. Demonstrations were banned, and peaceful protesters detained and often ill-treated in a range of countries including Turkey and Ukraine. Human rights defenders continued to face obstruction, intimidation and threats in Belarus, Turkey, Turkmenistan and Uzbekistan. In Russia, human rights activists and others seeking justice through the European Court of Human Rights in connection with the Chechen conflict experienced harassment and torture. Some paid with their lives. In Turkmenistan, some critics were forced into exile and their relatives targeted in efforts to silence dissent.

As in previous years, some states showed scant tolerance for the conscience of those who objected to compulsory military service. In violation of international obligations, Armenia, Finland and Turkmenistan imprisoned those whose conscience would not allow them to serve. Other states such as Cyprus, Greece and Lithuania retained legislation that made alternative service a punitive option.

Violence against women

The human rights of women and girls remained under attack across the region. Violence in the family was still regarded by many governments as residing in the "private sphere" – a convenient excuse in many instances for failures to define domestic violence as a human rights issue and resource it as such. From west to east, there were documented failures to provide support to women who had survived violence in the home, or to ensure their effective access to justice, redress and reparation. Some states did not introduce or implement adequately such basic provisions as comprehensive protection and restraining orders against abusers, or appropriate shelters for survivors of violence.

Trafficking of human beings, including women and girls for enforced prostitution, continued to afflict most countries throughout the region. In UN-administered Kosovo, the clients reportedly included international police and troops, and the women and girls – beaten, raped and effectively imprisoned by their owners – were often too afraid to escape. Survivors of this form of slavery were ill-served by many states with the power, and obligation, to do better. While many voices continued to press for state action against trafficking to be grounded in human rights protection, rather than through an agenda driven by organized crime and illegal migration, trafficked women were still failed by the authorities and judicial systems in countries of origin, transit and destination. Moldova, for example, remained a source country for women and girls trafficked for forced prostitution – the most vulnerable reportedly being women escaping domestic violence and children leaving institutional care. However, women were only exempted from prosecution in Moldova for crimes arising from being trafficked if they agreed to cooperate with law enforcement agencies. In Belgium, a destination country where trafficking for enforced prostitution reportedly continued to rise, the granting of residence permits was contingent on such cooperation – in accordance with EU legislation.

One potentially positive step to enhancing respect for the human rights of trafficked persons was the Council of Europe's draft Convention against Trafficking in Human Beings, which was discussed during 2004. Non-governmental organizations continued campaigning to strengthen its provisions.

Death penalty

There were some positive moves on the death penalty, reinforcing the regional trend towards abolition. The Greek parliament approved the abolition of the death penalty for all crimes. Tajikistan declared a moratorium on death sentences and executions. In Belarus, the Constitutional Court ruled that a number of provisions in the Criminal Code relating to the death penalty were inconsistent with
the Constitution and international law, paving the way — should the political will exist — for abolition or at least a moratorium.

However, Belarus — together with Uzbekistan and Tajikistan before its moratorium — remained the region's last executioners. In addition, both Uzbekistan and Tajikistan flouted their international commitments during the year by ignoring requests from the UN Human Rights Committee to stay executions. In Tajikistan, four men were executed in secret just days before the moratorium. In two of these cases the Committee had urged a stay while it considered allegations of unfair trials and torture. Uzbekistan executed at least four men whose cases were under consideration for similar reasons. The total number of those executed annually in Uzbekistan — within a criminal justice system seriously flawed by widespread corruption and the failure of the courts to investigate allegations of torture — remained secret but was believed to be scores. As in previous years, the post-Soviet shroud of secrecy in executing states covered not just statistics, but blanketed the lives of those on death row and their relatives: neither were informed in advance of the date of executions. Families were denied the bodies of their executed relatives and even the knowledge of where they were buried.

Action for human rights

While many governments continued to ignore the concerns and recommendations of regional and other international organizations charged with a role in human rights protection, such bodies continued to strengthen human rights safeguards. As part of their contribution to combating racism, the Organization for Security and Co-operation in Europe carried on highlighting the issue through a series of specific meetings, and the European Committee against Racism and Intolerance issued general policy recommendations on the struggle against anti-Semitism and on combating racism while fighting "terrorism". Regional bodies and mechanisms, including the Council of Europe's Commissioner on Human Rights, also took action against states' failure to improve or respect human rights. The Parliamentary Assembly of the Council of Europe rejected a request by Belarus for reinstatement of special guest status on these grounds, and the European Bank for Reconstruction and Development decided to cut aid and investment in Uzbekistan because it had not met the bank's human rights benchmarks.

The EU incorporated its Charter of Fundamental Rights into the new constitutional treaty and decided to set up an EU human rights agency. These developments should be an incentive to change the EU's complacent attitude to observing human rights within its own borders. A European Commission proposal for legislation on procedural rights in criminal proceedings was also a positive note, although it was feared that the content of the proposal might be watered down in negotiations between EU member states.

A powerful political will to drive reform in a positive direction was seen during the year in Turkey. Although implementation was uneven and at times resisted, the government pushed through many significant constitutional and legal changes to secure agreement to start negotiations on accession to the EU. The power of civil society to mobilize for change was also evident, from the platform for activism offered by the European Social Forum in London in November, to the streets of Ukraine during the presidential elections the following month. Human rights defenders, in the face of threats, intimidation and detention, remained resolute in continuing their work, inspiring others and achieving results.

AI regional reports

- Open letter to the Irish Presidency of the European Union (AI Index: IOR 61/002/2004)
- Amnesty International's Comments on the Interim Activity Report: Guaranteeing the Long-Term Effectiveness of the European Court of Human Rights (AI Index: IOR 61/005/2004)
- Concerns in Europe and Central Asia, July-December 2003 (AI Index: EUR 01/001/2004)
- Europe and Central Asia: Summary of Amnesty International's Concerns in the Region, January-June 2004 (AI Index: EUR 01/005/2004)
- Open letter: On the occasion of the EU Summit 4-5 November 2004 adopting the Hague Programme 'strengthening freedom, security and justice' in the EU (AI Index: EUR 01/006/2004)
- Belarus and Uzbekistan: The last executioners — The trend towards abolition in the former Soviet space (AI Index: EUR 04/009/2004)

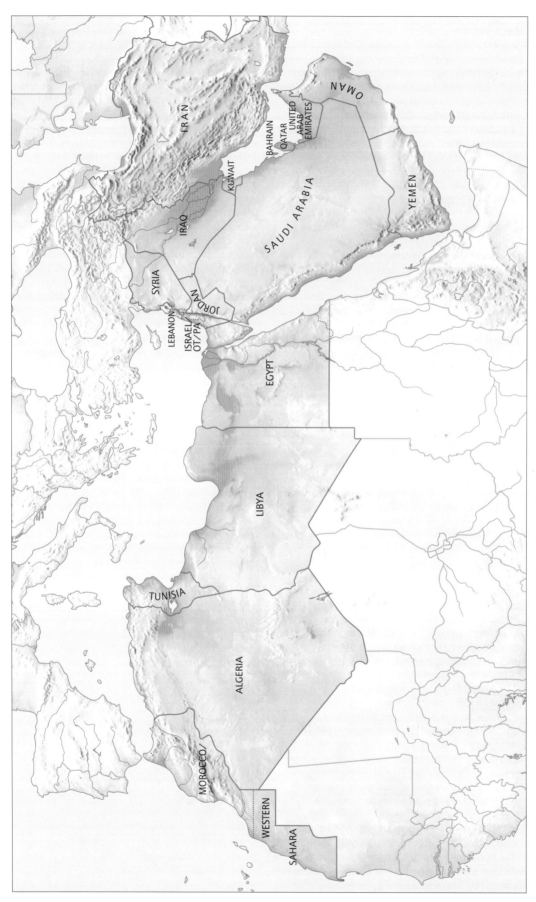

MIDDLE EAST/ NORTH AFRICA REGIONAL OVERVIEW 2004

Grave and multiple human rights violations, including the killing of hundreds of civilians in armed conflicts and political violence, continued with impunity throughout the region. Political and human rights reforms were debated at national and regional levels, with significant input from civil society groups, writers and journalists. The League of Arab States adopted a revised version of the Arab Charter on Human Rights.

The political and human rights situation continued to receive international attention. In June the G8 summit of major industrialized states endorsed a US-sponsored "partnership" plan, the Broader Middle East and North Africa Initiative, which pledged support for "democratic, social and economic reform emanating from [the] region" and "effective guarantees in the areas of human rights and fundamental freedoms". The Initiative was met with a mixture of scepticism and interest among governments and civil society. Non-governmental organizations (NGOs), at a gathering held in parallel to a follow-up G8 meeting in December in Morocco, pushed for a more effective mechanism to achieve reform. The NGOs recommended that reform be genuine and inclusive and that the G8 take a strong stand, collectively and as individual states, on progress towards democracy in the region. They called for the G8 to participate in monitoring elections and put pressure on the region's governments to stop harassing NGOs.

The European Union (EU) remained engaged with states in the region through the Euro-Mediterranean Association Agreements and through dialogue with Iran, Libya and the Gulf states. At the UN, the General Assembly adopted a resolution on human rights in Iran in November. In an advisory opinion, the International Court of Justice ruled that the construction by Israel of a fence/wall inside the occupied West Bank was unlawful under international law.

Armed conflict and impunity

Civilians bore the brunt of the casualties as the war in Iraq intensified and the death toll rose. Tens of thousands of men, women and children were reported to have been killed or injured since the armed conflict began in March 2003. Both the US-led occupying forces and armed groups operating in Iraq — often with the declared objective of resisting foreign occupation — continued to violate international human rights and humanitarian laws with impunity.

Throughout the year there were reports that scores of civilians had been killed unlawfully by the US-led forces during bombardments of Fallujah, Najaf and Samarra', and in various operations in Baghdad. Before the transfer of power to an interim Iraqi government in June, and in the run-up to general elections scheduled for January 2005, armed groups stepped up attacks against US-led forces, Iraqi police and army recruits, government personnel and professionals. Hundreds of civilians were killed in indiscriminate or direct attacks by armed groups, as in the attacks on Shi'a visitors to the holy shrines in Baghdad and Karbala in February. Scores of hostages, including Iraqis, foreign aid workers, journalists and security contractors, were abducted by armed groups, and dozens were killed. Although in several hostage cases political demands were made, for the withdrawal of foreign troops or companies for example, other hostages appeared to have been abducted to extract ransom payments.

Increasing numbers of Palestinians were killed and homes destroyed by the Israeli army in the Palestinian Occupied Territories. Some 700 Palestinians died, including about 150 children. Most were killed unlawfully, in reckless shootings, shellings or air strikes on refugee camps and other densely populated areas throughout the West Bank and Gaza Strip. Israeli forces continued to carry out extrajudicial executions of members and leaders of Hamas and other Palestinian groups, in which bystanders were frequently killed or injured. Some 109 Israelis, most of them civilians and including eight children, were killed by Palestinian armed groups in suicide bombings, shootings and mortar attacks inside Israel and in the Occupied Territories.

Routine destruction of Palestinian homes, land and property in the West Bank and Gaza Strip was stepped up in the biggest wave of house demolitions in the Gaza Strip since the beginning of the intifada (uprising). In May the Israeli army destroyed some 300 homes and damaged about 270 others in a refugee camp in Rafah, leaving close to 4,000 Palestinians homeless. In the West Bank, Israel continued to build a 600-kilometre fence/wall encircling and cutting off Palestinian towns and villages, despite the ruling by the International Court of Justice. The fence/wall and hundreds of Israeli army checkpoints and blockades throughout the Occupied Territories continued to hinder or prevent Palestinians' access to their land, their workplaces and to education, health and other crucial services.

Political violence and the 'war on terror'

Human rights violations continued to be justified by the global "war on terror" as security forces across the region responded to attacks by armed groups they accused of links with al-Qa'ida. Dozens of people, including children, were killed in Saudi Arabia as armed groups carried out bomb attacks, hostage-takings and targeted killings of Western nationals. Bomb attacks claimed the lives of over 30 civilians and injured more than 100 others, most of them Israeli tourists, in Taba, in the Sinai region of Egypt. In Yemen, there were reports that hundreds of people were killed, most of them as a result of excessive force by the security forces, in clashes with followers of Hussain Badr al-Din al-Huthi, a cleric from the Zaidi community.

Scores of people were detained in countries across the region on suspicion of "terrorist" acts or links to opposition armed groups. Hundreds remained in detention, denied their basic rights, after being arrested in previous years on similar grounds. Unfair trials of scores of suspects on "terrorist" charges were reported in Morocco, Saudi Arabia, Tunisia and Yemen. In Algeria, Libya and Tunisia, torture remained a concern as the "war on terror" was used to justify arbitrary detentions and unfair trials.

States continued cooperating on security operations, also as part of the "war on terror". Suspects held on grounds of security were reportedly transferred between Iran, Saudi Arabia, Yemen and other Gulf countries without due regard to risks of human rights violations in the receiving countries. Those held or extradited within the "war on terror" framework were at risk of arbitrary detention, torture, ill-treatment and unfair trial. States in the region continued to implement the 1998 Arab Convention on the Suppression of Terrorism, which lacked safeguards against torture, unfair trial and other human rights violations. Dozens of detainees released from US custody at Guantánamo Bay, Cuba, and in other countries were returned to their countries of origin, including Kuwait, Morocco and Yemen.

Women's rights and violence against women

Debate on women's rights increased at official levels and within civil society. A new Family Code issued in Morocco significantly improved the legal framework for women's rights. Women's groups and NGOs continued to press for the increased participation of women in public affairs, and a more robust approach to violence against women.

In Iraq, Israel and the Occupied Territories, violence against women was directly linked to conflict, or was exacerbated by the easy availability of arms and the social disruption of war. Across the region, violence within the home and family was perpetuated by state inaction, inadequate or discriminatory legislation, and social prejudice. Women in Iran faced discrimination in the courts and, in at least one case in 2004, a girl under the age of 18 was executed after a flagrantly flawed trial.

Refugees and migrants

In most countries in the region, there was no legal regime for the protection of refugees and asylum-seekers. Ratification of the 1951 Refugee Convention or its 1967 Protocol remained limited, the only countries that were party to them being Algeria, Egypt, Iran, Israel, Morocco, Tunisia and Yemen.

Restrictive immigration policies in many European countries resulted in migrants and asylum-seekers employing the help of criminal people-smugglers. Numerous would-be immigrants and asylum-seekers died in boat accidents, trying to cross the Mediterranean. In October and December, hundreds of people, most of North African origin, were deported from Italy to Libya under a bilateral agreement. They had no access to the protection of the UN High Commissioner for Refugees (UNHCR), in either Italy or Libya. On several occasions throughout 2004, Libya expelled large numbers of individuals to countries where they might have been at risk of serious human rights violations, without giving them access to the UNHCR. The Algerian security services reported that they had arrested some 3,500 suspected illegal immigrants in the first 10 months of 2004, the majority from African countries. Most were apparently deported to neighbouring countries or to their home countries without any consideration of their protection needs. In Iran, the introduction of primary education fees and the non-renewal of residency cards for Afghan refugees pressured many of them to return to Afghanistan, where the preconditions for a sustained, safe and dignified return might not be guaranteed.

Palestinian refugees, one of the largest refugee groups in the world, continued to suffer hardship in their host countries, while their right to return remained unfulfilled. Many were prevented from receiving the assistance they needed because the resources of the UN Relief and Works Agency for Palestine Refugees in the Near East (UNRWA) were overstretched. Palestinian refugees continued to undergo particularly severe hardship in Lebanon, where discriminatory policies undermined their ability to earn their livelihoods and effectively restricted their access to economic and social rights.

Justice, impunity and the death penalty

Throughout the region, states continued to pay little regard to their obligations under international human rights law. Arbitrary arrests and detentions, torture and ill-treatment, and unfair trials – sometimes before exceptional courts – were routine. In Algeria, Iran, Libya, Syria, Tunisia, Yemen and other countries, the authorities regularly placed restrictions on freedom of expression and association, or carried out sporadic clampdowns, often resulting in the detention of prisoners of conscience. Political activists continued to face arbitrary detention or prolonged imprisonment after unfair trials in countries such as Iran, Libya and Syria.

Perpetrators of human rights violations continued to enjoy complete impunity in most countries in the region. However, in Morocco, in an unprecedented measure in the region, an Equity and Reconciliation Commission was inaugurated to look into cases of "disappearances" and arbitrary detention in previous decades.

Death penalties continued to be imposed and carried out throughout the region. In Libya and other countries, death sentences were handed down after unfair trials, and in Iran, the execution of children under the age of 18 was still permitted. There was a setback in Lebanon, where capital punishment was reintroduced following a five-year de facto moratorium, when three executions were carried out at the beginning of the year. Human rights activists launched a campaign against the reintroduction of executions in Lebanon. There were public debates about the death penalty in Egypt and within the regional human rights NGOs.

The Arab Charter on Human Rights

In May the League of Arab States adopted a revised version of the Arab Charter on Human Rights, a redraft of a 1994 document. Submissions from international and regional NGOs, made to a Committee of Experts established by the League, were utilized in the Charter. AI submitted recommendations on restrictions and derogations of rights, the death penalty, torture, women's rights, the independence of the judiciary, and freedom of expression, many of which were reflected in the final text adopted by the League. However, concerns remained over provisions in the new Charter that were inconsistent with international human rights law. These included, among other things, provisions for death penalties to be passed and carried out on minors if allowed under national laws, and for the right to life to be subject to derogations in states of emergency. In addition, the Charter was silent on the subject of cruel, inhuman and degrading punishment, although it contained a prohibition of torture.

Human rights defenders

Human rights activists throughout the region continued their efforts to defend and promote human rights. As public debate on human rights spread, new human rights groups emerged in Saudi Arabia and the United Arab Emirates, and human rights organizations received official recognition in Kuwait.

Yet human rights defenders and bodies continued to be restricted in their activities and freedom of movement. In most states, they were at risk of intimidation and harassment. In Egypt, the authorities denied human rights organizations official registration, then prosecuted their members for pursuing "illegal activities". Several governments continued to use the criminal justice system to harass, threaten and restrict the activities of human rights defenders. In 2004 human rights defenders in Algeria, Bahrain, Iran, Saudi Arabia and Syria were arbitrarily detained. Many of them were brought before courts that failed to meet international standards for fair trial. In certain cases, for example in Iraq, the authorities provided no protection to women's rights activists and other human rights defenders who received death threats from private individuals or organizations because of their human rights work.

Regional initiatives

In March, AI carried out a regional launch of its global Stop Violence Against Women campaign in Amman, Jordan. A symposium brought together participants from across the region to discuss legal reform strategies on strengthening women's rights and ending violence against women. AI raised concerns about the effect of reservations entered by the majority of countries in the region to the UN Women's Convention, which reinforced discrimination against women and undermined their protection and freedom from violence.

In April, AI organized a Conference, Human Rights for All, in Sana'a, Yemen, in cooperation with the National Organization for the Defence of Rights and Freedoms, a Yemeni organization. The participants included regional and international lawyers, human rights activists, and relatives of the victims of abuses. The Conference called on the US and Gulf governments to end the legal limbo of "terrorist" suspects in US custody, including those held in undisclosed locations, and to grant them full access to lawyers, doctors, families and the International Committee of the Red Cross. A Sana'a Committee was subsequently established to follow up the conference and to coordinate information exchange between detainees, lawyers and families in different countries.

AI regional reports

- Reservations to the Convention on the Elimination of All Forms of Discrimination against Women: Weakening the protection of women from violence in the Middle East and North Africa region (AI Index: IOR 51/009/2004)
- The Gulf and the Arabian Peninsula: Human rights fall victim to the "war on terror" (AI Index: MDE 04/002/2004)

AFGHANISTAN

AFGHANISTAN
President of the Transitional Administration: Hamid Karzai
Death penalty: retentionist
International Criminal Court: ratified
UN Women's Convention: ratified
Optional Protocol to UN Women's Convention: not signed

Lawlessness and insecurity increased, hampering efforts towards peace and stability. Anti-government forces killed civilians involved in the electoral process, making large parts of the country inaccessible to humanitarian organizations. US forces continued arbitrary and unlawful detentions and failed to conduct independent investigations of reports that Afghan prisoners had been tortured and ill-treated. Armed groups committed abuses against civilians with impunity, including the abduction and rape of girls. Justice and redress were unobtainable for women who experienced widespread discrimination and violence in the community, including abduction, rape and forced marriage. Refugees were pressured into returning to Afghanistan despite continuing threats to their safety. A military commander was secretly executed after an unfair trial.

Background

A new Constitution was adopted in January by the Constitutional *Loya Jirga*. It contained human rights guarantees but lacked specific safeguards against abuses. For example, it did not provide equal marriage rights for women and men.

The transitional government slowly began to impose its rule outside the capital, Kabul. It removed the self-appointed governor of Herat. In the south and east there was a resurgence of anti-government forces, and the US-led coalition stepped up military operations. In areas controlled by armed factions ostensibly loyal to the government, the national armed forces and police, still seriously under strength, were deployed on several occasions to suppress outbreaks of fighting between factions. The economy, dominated by the opium trade, was under the control of faction commanders and there was no significant improvement in the country's infrastructure. Progress was made in disarming tens of thousands of former combatants who remained linked to factions and armed groups.

Hamid Karzai, incumbent President of the Afghan Transitional Authority, won presidential elections held amid violence and insecurity in October. The elections were reportedly marred by fraudulent voter registration and forcible confiscation of voter identification cards by faction leaders and local officials.

In September the UN Security Council extended the mandate of the International Security Assistance Force (ISAF) to October 2005. Under NATO command since 2003, ISAF's troops were expanded to 9,000 just before the elections.

Abuses by armed groups

Armed groups across the country consolidated their control over the local population and were responsible for killing civilians, aid workers, election officials and potential voters. By the third quarter of 2004, at least 21 aid workers, mostly Afghan nationals, had been killed.

In January, a bomb intended for US Coalition Forces killed 15 schoolchildren in Kandahar. Taleban officials, who had originally denied involvement in the incident, later issued an apology after public outrage.

In June, 16 passengers on a bus were deliberately killed by armed men, reportedly because they were carrying voter registration cards.

Three UN election workers, two women and one man, were taken hostage in Kabul by the armed group, Jaish-e-Muslimeen (Army of Muslims), on 28 October and held until 23 November.

There were several reports that gunmen attached to armed groups abducted and raped girls, and forced some into marrying them. Girls were increasingly sold into early marriages to alleviate poverty or in an attempt to guarantee their security.

One 17-year-old was abducted by three armed men from her aunt's home in Kapisa province in May after she refused to marry one of them. Her uncle was shot and wounded. The girl was returned to her parents in Kabul after they filed a complaint with the authorities and the Afghan Independent Human Rights Commission (AIHRC).

Violence against women

Women continued to face systematic and widespread violence, and public and private discrimination. Fear of abductions by armed groups forced women to restrict their movements outside the home. In the family, extreme restrictions on women's behaviour and high levels of violence persisted. Election officials registering women voters were among those killed by armed groups.

A woman was detained in mid-2004 in Kandahar and held without charge for several weeks while the prosecutor considered accusations against her of adultery and attempted murder of her "husband", a member of an armed group who had abducted her at the age of seven. He had routinely beaten and abused her, and by the age of 20 she had three children by him. No charges against him were considered.

A campaigner against violence against women was attacked in September because of her human rights work. She was outside her home in Kabul when three men drove up in a car. One jumped out and threw acid at her, burning her neck.

Most acts of violence against women were not reported for fear of reprisals or harsh judicial punishment of the victim, and very few were subject to investigation or prosecution. Tradition and social codes of behaviour governed judges' decisions on cases involving violence against women. Many women were imprisoned for alleged crimes such as running away from home, adultery and other sexual activity outside marriage – known as *zina* crimes. In some cases, despite lack of evidence, they were imprisoned to protect them from their families. Outside Kabul, refuges, counselling and health care for women were almost non-existent. In all regions, but particularly in Herat, hundreds of women set fire to themselves to escape violence in the home or forced marriage.

Ineffective justice system

The judiciary remained ineffective, corrupt and susceptible to intimidation from armed groups. Courts barely functioned in rural areas. Judges and lawyers were frequently unaware of the law and allowed severe discrimination against women. Rape, forced marriage and the exchange of girls to settle disputes were frequently not treated as crimes. There remained widespread confusion among officials in the criminal justice system, including judges, as to the exact legal basis of the "crime" of "running away". Such an offence does not exist in the Afghan Penal Code. Detainees were held for prolonged periods of time without legal basis and denied a fair trial.

Abuses by police officers were not investigated, and the effectiveness of the force was hampered by a lack of oversight mechanisms, affiliation to regional armed groups, non-payment of salaries and lack of equipment. Despite internationally supported police training programmes few women were recruited. Progress in the reform of the judiciary and police was particularly slow outside Kabul.

Insufficient attention was paid to the prisons service by the Afghan government and donor community. Inhumane conditions and gross human rights violations were reported, especially outside Kabul where provincial prisons remained under the control of armed groups.

Abuses by US forces

Evidence emerged that US forces had tortured and ill-treated detainees in the "war on terror" in Afghanistan. Former detainees reported being made to kneel, stand or maintain painful postures for long periods, and being subjected to hooding, sleep deprivation, stripping and humiliation. Suspects were detained without legal authority and held incommunicado, without access to lawyers, families or the courts.

▭ On 13 December, US officials acknowledged that eight prisoners had died in US military custody in Afghanistan, five more than previously disclosed in a Department of Defense briefing in May. Only the basic details of the cases were released. They included an investigation into a death in military custody on 28 August 2002, the earliest known death of a prisoner in US custody.

▭ On 14 October the US Army's Criminal Investigation Division recommended that 28 US soldiers be charged in connection with the beating to death of two prisoners at the US air base at Bagram in December 2002. Autopsies found "blunt force injuries" on the bodies of Mullah Habibullah and Dilawar. By the end of 2004 only one soldier had been charged – with assault, maltreatment and dereliction of duty.

▭ The US Department of Defense announced an investigation into a report in September that US Special Forces beat and tortured eight Afghan soldiers over a two-week period in March 2003 at a base near Gardez. One detainee reportedly died as a result.

Reports continued of civilian deaths as a result of US air strikes. There were reports that 11 civilians were killed by US bombing in the village of Sawghataq, Uruzgan province, in January, although US military officials claimed only to have killed five armed militants. US officials initially denied but later confirmed reports that at least five civilians died in air raids on Weradesh, eastern Afghanistan, in August. On election day at least 14 civilians were reportedly killed or wounded in Uruzgan province during US bombing of opposition forces.

Impunity

Regional officials and commanders with a record of human rights violations flaunted their impunity, some of them maintaining links with armed groups responsible for abuses. Little progress was made in bringing to justice those responsible for war crimes, including mass killings and rape, committed during the armed conflicts since 1978.

Despite repeated calls for independent investigations of deaths in custody and reports of torture by US forces, investigations were conducted under the auspices of the US Department of Defense. Requests for access to detainees by UN human rights experts and by the AIHRC and other non-governmental bodies continued to be refused.

Afghan government forces were not held to account for violating international law on the treatment of prisoners. No action was known to have been taken against soldiers who reportedly beheaded prisoners in southern Afghanistan in June.

Right to return in safety

Afghan refugees in Iran and Pakistan faced growing harassment and many returned to Afghanistan. In October, Iran declared its intention to repatriate most Afghans in Iran over the next 16 months. Other countries returned rejected Afghan asylum-seekers without ensuring that they could return in dignity and safety.

The number of refugees who had returned to Afghanistan from Iran and Pakistan since early 2002 reached just over three million by September. More than 32 per cent settled in Kabul because of insecurity and continuing human rights abuses in the provinces, or because there was insufficient work and shelter in their areas of origin. Others were unable to recover stolen land and property.

Death penalty

At least nine men were sentenced to death in 2004. Military commander Abdullah Shah was secretly executed in April after a trial by a special court in which he was denied basic rights of defence. Charged in connection with multiple murders, he had no legal counsel and was not allowed to cross-examine witnesses. The court failed to investigate allegations that he had been tortured or visible evidence of his injuries, and reportedly imposed the death penalty under political pressure. The trial was not open to the public.

AI country reports/ visits
Report
- Afghanistan: Abduction and rape at the point of a gun (AI Index: ASA 11/013/2004)
- Afghanistan: Women failed by progress in Afghanistan (AI Index: ASA 11/015/2004)
- USA: Human dignity denied – Torture and accountability in the "war on terror" (AI Index: AMR 51/145/2004)

Visits
AI delegates visited Afghanistan in February and in August and September 2004. They met senior government officials, UN officials, human rights defenders and representatives of non-governmental organizations. They also visited women's prisons in Kabul, Mazar-e-Sharif and Kandahar.

ALBANIA

REPUBLIC OF ALBANIA
Head of state: Alfred Moisiu
Head of government: Fatos Nano
Death penalty: abolitionist for ordinary crimes
International Criminal Court: ratified
UN Women's Convention and its Optional Protocol: ratified

There were complaints that detainees were ill-treated immediately on arrest or in police custody and, more rarely, in prison. Investigations into some complaints were started, but tended to be delayed and inconclusive. Detention conditions, particularly for remand prisoners held in police stations, remained harsh, although steps were taken to reduce overcrowding. Domestic violence was common. The trafficking of women and children for forced prostitution and cheap labour continued, although arrests and prosecutions for trafficking markedly increased.

Background
Poverty, unemployment, widespread corruption and official indifference undermined efforts to promote the rule of law. In November the UN Human Rights Committee called on Albania to eradicate ill-treatment by law enforcement officials; to ensure that perpetrators "are punished in a manner proportionate to the seriousness of the crimes committed; and to grant effective remedies including compensation to the victims". The Committee also urged Albania to reinforce remedies against trafficking, domestic violence and the abuse and exploitation of children. The Committee further called for guarantees for the independence of the judiciary, and for protection of minority rights.

Torture and ill-treatment
Police officers were alleged to have tortured or ill-treated detainees during arrest and in police custody. Such practices were facilitated by violations of legal procedures, in particular the denial of the detainee's right of access to a lawyer from the moment of arrest.

On 29 July, Klajdi Yzeiri and two relatives were detained overnight in police custody in Vlora. The three men were refused access to a lawyer and Klajdi Yzeiri was severely beaten by one or more police officers. On release he underwent a medical forensic examination which confirmed that he had severe bruising behind both ears, and on his neck and shoulders.

Complaints of ill-treatment by remand and convicted prisoners were less frequent, but in September a group of prisoners held in Prison 302 in Tirana complained of ill-treatment by prison guards, and there were similar complaints by remand prisoners held in Laç, Kukës and Fier police stations.

There were also several incidents in which police appeared to have used excessive force during operations to capture criminal suspects.

Gentian Pollo, a schoolteacher, alleged that police beat and kicked him while driving him, handcuffed, to Gjirokastër police station, and again at the police station. He was among a number of people who were injured and required hospital treatment after masked police units entered two bars in the village of Lazarat to arrest a convicted criminal in October.

Impunity
Prosecutors did not always investigate complaints of ill-treatment or did so only after delay. Even when an investigation was formally opened, it was often inconclusive. Prosecutors were reluctant to apply articles of the Criminal Code dealing with torture and "any other degrading or inhuman treatment", preferring to invoke lesser charges, such as "arbitrary acts".

On 13 May Beqir Kaba was arrested and held overnight in Peshkopi police station after he was wrongly accused of theft. He alleged that police officers beat his back, legs and hands with rubber truncheons, twisted and pulled his beard and his ears with pliers, and threatened to kill him. He was released the following day. A forensic medical examination later confirmed injuries inflicted by a "heavy instrument". Two police officers were reportedly later referred for investigation on a charge of "arbitrary acts".

In July Eriguert Ceka, aged 17, a remand prisoner in Rrëshen police station, suffered an injury to his head; three days later he died in Tirana military hospital. Shortly after, two police officers were arrested in connection with his death on charges of "arbitrary acts", "abuse of duty" and infringing the rules of service. In separate trials in November and December the officers were convicted of contravening service rules and sentenced to seven months' and eight months' imprisonment respectively. The court failed to establish how Eriguert Ceka came to be injured.

🗁 In May, two former state security officers were released. They had been arrested in 2003 in connection with the "disappearance" in 1995 of Remzi Hoxha, an Albanian from Macedonia then living in Tirana, and the torture of two other men. Investigation proceedings found that they had committed the offences of "abuse of office" and torture, but these offences were covered by a 1997 amnesty law. The prosecution did not find evidence to support charges of murder or "torture with serious consequences" – crimes not covered by the amnesty. The fate of Remzi Hoxha remained unknown at the end of 2004.

Conditions of detention

In July all prisoners convicted in final instance held in police stations were transferred to prisons to serve their sentences. This temporarily reduced the severe overcrowding in police stations, although it increased overcrowding in prisons. In other respects the conditions of detention in police stations, with very poor sanitation and diet, and no heating or access to television, radio or reading materials, remained largely unchanged and often could be considered as inhuman and degrading. A European Union-assisted prison reform plan for the construction of new remand and prison facilities was announced in September.

Trafficking

Poverty, lack of education, family breakdown and crime networks at home and abroad contributed to the continuing trafficking of women and children for sexual exploitation and cheap labour. In March a law on witness protection was adopted, although lack of supporting legislation and funding meant it could not be implemented. Most victims of trafficking did not report their traffickers for fear of reprisal.

🗁 In February a woman who claimed that she had been trafficked for forced prostitution at the age of 14 withdrew her previous testimony after being confronted with the defendant at his trial by Shkodër district court. He had reportedly earlier openly threatened her. She was immediately arrested in court and charged with perjury.

Nonetheless, prosecutions for the trafficking of women and children for forced prostitution, cheap labour or use as beggars, doubled by comparison with the previous year, and heavy sentences were imposed. Official zeal to obtain convictions may sometimes have resulted in police and courts using or condoning coercion or other illegal means to obtain evidence of trafficking.

🗁 In March Gjergj Bedulla was convicted by Korça district court of trafficking three children to Greece for cheap labour. However, before testifying in court, the children had reportedly been illegally detained by police for five days or longer and questioned without the presence of a lawyer or a guardian. The children subsequently withdrew their testimony, alleging they had given it under police coercion. In June the case was sent back for retrial on appeal.

Violence against women

Independent studies concluded that domestic violence was common. The law did not adequately protect victims, for whom there were limited support services provided by non-governmental organizations. The Criminal Code did not specifically criminalize domestic violence. Under the Family Code, adopted in 2003, a spouse who has been subjected to domestic violence may ask a court to ban the perpetrator from the home, but this measure could not be applied by courts for lack of supporting legislation. In October an initiative was launched by 10 Albanian non-governmental organizations to draft legislation against domestic violence.

AI country reports/visits
Reports
- Albania: Inhuman and degrading detention conditions in police stations – steps towards reform (AI Index: EUR 11/001/2004)
- Albania: What happened to Remzi Hoxha? (AI Index: EUR 11/004/2004)
- Albania: Disability and the right to marry (AI Index: EUR 11/005/2004)

Visit
In June, AI representatives visited Albania to conduct research.

ALGERIA

PEOPLE'S DEMOCRATIC REPUBLIC OF ALGERIA
Head of state: Abdelaziz Bouteflika
Head of government: Ahmed Ouyahia
Death penalty: abolitionist in practice
International Criminal Court: signed
UN Women's Convention: ratified with reservations
Optional Protocol to UN Women's Convention: not signed

Despite a scaling down of the internal conflict that has raged since 1992, dozens of civilians were killed. Impunity continued to be a key obstacle to addressing the legacy of the conflict. Tens of thousands of cases of killings, abductions, "disappearances" and torture committed by security forces, state-armed militias and armed groups remained without investigation. Torture continued to be reported, particularly during secret detention. Freedom of expression and assembly was markedly restricted. Human rights activists and journalists risked arrest and imprisonment. The state of emergency imposed in 1992 remained in place. Dozens of suspected members of armed groups were sentenced to death in their absence. A moratorium on executions remained in place.

Background
President Abdelaziz Bouteflika was re-elected in April. According to official figures he won nearly 85 per cent of the votes cast.

In August, General Mohamed Lamari resigned as chief of staff of the army. He had been a key figure in command while the armed forces were committing wide-ranging human rights violations in the context of the internal conflict, including torture, extrajudicial executions and "disappearances".

Amari Saïfi, also known as Abderrezak El Para, was extradited to Algeria from Libya. He was accused of having led an armed group that abducted 32 European tourists in the Algerian Sahara in 2003. He had been captured in Chad and subsequently handed over to Libya.

Demonstrations, strikes and protests remained widespread. People protested over a range of social, economic and political issues, including water, job and housing shortages, public mismanagement and corruption. Water reportedly reached households in the capital, Algiers, only one day out of three. According to official figures one third of the adult population was unemployed.

Killings
According to press reports, some 500 people were killed during the year. The majority were members of the security forces and armed groups. Some of the deaths reportedly occurred during armed confrontations. In other cases suspected armed group members were reportedly killed in operations by the security forces. There were concerns that some of these were extrajudicial executions. Dozens of civilians were killed in attacks, presumed to have been committed by armed groups but not known to have been independently and impartially investigated.

Impunity
In November, President Bouteflika announced plans for a general amnesty in a stated effort to turn the page on more than a decade of conflict. Although no details were provided, statements indicated that the proposal was to grant exemption from prosecution to security forces, state-armed militias and armed groups, thus preventing members of any party to the conflict being prosecuted for human rights abuses.

No full, independent or impartial investigations were carried out into the gross human rights abuses committed since 1992, including thousands of cases of civilians killed in targeted or indiscriminate attacks, extrajudicial executions, torture, ill-treatment and "disappearances". Members of armed groups who surrendered to the authorities reportedly continued to benefit from clemency or exemption from prosecution. The authorities again denied that state agents had been responsible for systematic and widespread human rights violations. The remains of victims of killings discovered in mass graves were generally not identified, and the available evidence was not used to establish responsibility for the killings.

◻ In January human remains were exhumed from a mass grave in the western province of Relizane in an apparent attempt to conceal or destroy evidence of human rights abuses. Between 1993 and 1998 over 200 civilians "disappeared" in the region at the hands of a state-armed militia. The site had been discovered in November 2003 by a local human rights activist who also collected evidence indicating that it contained the remains of some of the "disappeared". The authorities failed to prevent the apparent destruction of evidence and no investigation into the incident was known to have been opened by the end of 2004.

◻ Fouad Boulemia, a former member of an armed group, was sentenced to death in August after being convicted of the killing of hundreds of civilians in Bentalha near Algiers in 1997, an incident which had not been fully and independently investigated. Eyewitness accounts suggested that the armed group that carried out the killings had operated in conjunction with, or with the consent of, certain army and security forces units. Fouad Boulemia had been detained since 1999 and sentenced to death in 2001 for the killing of Abdelkader Hachani, a leader of the banned Islamic Salvation Front. At the time of the 2001 trial he claimed he had been tortured and threatened with death during his detention. The allegations were not known to have been investigated by the court.

In November, the Permanent People's Tribunal – an international panel of experts set up to examine human rights issues in the absence of formal commissions of inquiry – met in Paris to examine evidence on human rights abuses committed in Algeria since 1992. Written evidence was submitted by a coalition of non-governmental organizations (NGOs) and activists. The tribunal heard from over a dozen experts and victims of human rights abuses. In its concluding observations the tribunal underscored the importance of truth and justice for lasting peace and called on the government to allow access to UN human rights mechanisms.

'Disappearances'

No concrete steps were taken to establish the fate or whereabouts of thousands of people who "disappeared" between 1992 and 2003, or to allay the suffering of their families, many of whom continued to endure economic hardship. In August and September, many families of the "disappeared" were summoned by a special commission – commonly referred to as the ad hoc mechanism – set up by presidential decree in September 2003 to serve as an interface between the families and the authorities. The families were asked whether they would accept compensation payments for the "disappearance" of their relatives. They were not given any indication of how compensation payments would be allocated, nor of the amount of money that might be paid. The commission is not bound by the results of the consultation and it does not report publicly on the outcome or the methods used. Organizations working on behalf of the "disappeared" publicly protested against the lack of transparency. The commission's mandate does not empower it to view information held in the archives of the security forces.

Complaints filed in Algerian courts for abduction and illegal detention were not followed up. The authorities continued to deny that state agents had been responsible for a pattern of "disappearances". The UN Working Group on Enforced or Involuntary Disappearances expressed its "deep concern that there have been no clarifications of the more than 1,100 outstanding cases" which it had transmitted to the government.

Torture

Amendments to the Penal Code introduced a specific crime of torture, carrying severe penalties. However, allegations of torture were generally not investigated by the authorities. The UN Special Rapporteur on torture reported that the Algerian authorities had denied without investigation all allegations of torture submitted to them. The Special Rapporteur was unable to visit Algeria, despite his long-standing request to the authorities, reiterated in 2003.

There were concerns that secret detentions, which continued in violation of national and international law, facilitated torture. Allegations of torture continued to be reported, particularly in cases involving what the government described as "terrorist" activities.

▭ In June, brothers Toufik and Smail Touati were arrested in Algiers within three days of each other by Military Security officers and held in secret detention for 13 and 10 days respectively. They alleged that they were tortured while they were being interrogated. They were charged with belonging to a "terrorist" organization. The allegations of torture were not known to have been investigated.

Freedom of expression and assembly

Human rights defenders, journalists and others who criticized representatives of the state were at risk of arrest and imprisonment.

There was a sharp increase in the number of cases brought against journalists and newspaper editors in an apparent attempt by the government to discourage unfavourable coverage in the privately owned press. Many were defamation cases filed against individual journalists for reporting allegations of corruption or publicly criticizing representatives of the state and security forces. Some were imprisoned, others were given suspended sentences or were sentenced and remained at liberty pending the result of an appeal. Several newspapers were suspended indefinitely, officially for owing money to state-run printing firms. In June the authorities indefinitely suspended the activities of the Algiers office of the Arabic television channel Al-Jazeera, apparently in response to critical reporting. Neither Al-Jazeera nor any of the newspapers was operating again before the end of 2004.

Anti-government protests were widespread, including in the predominantly Amazigh (Berber) region of Kabylia. Several led to violent clashes between security forces and protesters who voiced their anger about public mismanagement, price rises, and lack of housing and access to basic services. Two demonstrations by families of the "disappeared" in Constantine and Algiers were forcibly prevented by the security forces. A ban on demonstrations in Algiers, in force since October 2001, remained in place.

Dozens of people were arrested for organizing anti-government meetings and protest activities. Political dissent was particularly repressed in the southern provinces of Djelfa, Laghouat and Ouargla, where scores of people were sentenced to prison terms of up to eight months for membership of unauthorised organizations. The UN Special Representative on human rights defenders remained concerned at the restrictions on freedom of assembly imposed on human rights defenders.

▭ Hafnaoui Ghoul, a human rights activist, journalist and spokesperson of an unofficial political group, the Movement of Citizens of the South, was arrested in May in the province of Djelfa. He was subsequently sentenced to a total of eight months' imprisonment in a series of court cases, the majority of which were defamation cases filed by local officials after he reported allegations of torture, public mismanagement and corruption. In October he was acquitted of membership of an unauthorized organization, but nine other defendants in the same trial were sentenced to between six and eight months' imprisonment. He was released in November following a national and international campaign.

Women's rights

Women continued to be subjected to discrimination in law and practice. Twenty years after the introduction of the discriminatory Family Code, women's organizations reinforced their campaigning activities for women's legal equality. A government-appointed commission proposed amendments to the Family Code, but these had not been adopted by the end of 2004. Proposed changes included the abolition of certain provisions – such as women requiring a "marital tutor" (a male relative) to conclude their marriage contract on their behalf – but fell far short of ensuring women's equality before the law. The proposed changes did not affect discriminatory divorce laws. The authorities did not act with due diligence to prevent, punish and redress acts of sexual violence against women or violence against women in the family. An amendment to the Penal Code made sexual harassment by people in positions of authority a crime punishable by up to one year's imprisonment, or two years in the event of a second offence.

AI country reports/ visits

Reports
- Algeria: "Disappearances" must be on presidential election agenda (AI Index: MDE 28/004/2004)
- Algeria: Newly discovered mass grave must be fully investigated (AI Index: MDE 28/010/2004)
- Algeria: Briefing to the Committee on the Elimination of Discrimination against Women (AI Index: MDE 28/011/2004)

Visits

AI was not given access to Algeria during 2004.

ANGOLA

REPUBLIC OF ANGOLA
Head of state: José Eduardo dos Santos
Head of government: Fernando da Piedade Dias dos Santos
Death penalty: abolitionist for all crimes
International Criminal Court: signed
UN Women's Convention: ratified
Optional Protocol to UN Women's Convention: not signed

Refugees continued to return from neighbouring countries. The provision of judicial, social and other services in war-damaged rural areas remained inadequate. There were reports of politically motivated violence and suppression of non-violent demonstrations. Human rights violations by soldiers and police in Cabinda and in the diamond-mining areas continued. There were also many reports of human rights violations by police in other parts of the country. At least 500 families were forcibly evicted from their homes.

Background

The Government of National Unity, which included representatives of the former armed opposition National Union for the Total Independence of Angola (União Nacional para a Independência Total de Angola, UNITA), made progress in reducing inflation and proposed to combat poverty. Over one million people remained dependent on food aid.

The government, in cooperation with the UN, began in January to develop a national plan of action on human rights: work on this continued at the end of 2004. An independent press flourished in Luanda but access to information outside the capital was mainly through state-controlled radio. The UN Special Representative on Human Rights Defenders, Hina Jilani, visited Angola in August. She acknowledged improved respect for human rights but urged the government to rebuild its judicial system and to be more open to civil society.

Refugee returns

Over 90,000 refugees were repatriated or returned spontaneously from neighbouring countries. Weak government structures in reception areas, lack of schools and clinics, and insufficient funds for food, seeds and tools made resettlement difficult. An inadequate system for issuing identity documents left many returnees without access to social services and vulnerable to extortion and ill-treatment by police and soldiers carrying out identity checks.

Political violence

UNITA complained that members of the ruling People's Movement for the Liberation of Angola (Movimento Popular de Libertação de Angola, MPLA) attacked its members and offices in several areas.

In July, after UNITA tried to set up party offices in Cazombo, Moxico province, a mob burned or looted about 80 houses belonging to UNITA supporters and others who did not speak the local language. The crowd, allegedly encouraged by the municipal authorities, also wounded about 10 people. Unarmed police were reportedly deployed but did nothing to stop the violence.

Cabinda

The government said that fighting had ended in Cabinda, an Angolan enclave situated between the Democratic Republic of the Congo (DRC) and the Republic of the Congo. However, an estimated 30,000 government soldiers reportedly maintained a repressive presence, detaining and assaulting people suspected of supporting the Front for the Liberation of the Cabinda Enclave (Frente de Libertação do Enclave de Cabinda, FLEC), looting goods and crops, and causing villagers to flee to other areas.

Human rights workers reported that soldiers based in Nkuto, Buco-Zau municipality, frequently detained people suspected of supporting FLEC. More than 60 women were reportedly briefly held in January and accused of taking food to FLEC. Some were beaten. Mateus Bulo, aged 66, and his daughter were among a group of people arrested in May. Mateus Bulo was subjected to a mock execution, then he and his daughter were both beaten with sticks before being allowed to return to their fields.

Members of a civil society organization, Mpalabanda, presented a petition for peace with thousands of signatures to the authorities in Cabinda city in July. In August, the two armed factions of FLEC – Renewed FLEC (FLEC Renovada) and FLEC-Armed Forces of Cabinda (FLEC-Forças Armadas de Cabinda, FLEC-FAC) – announced that they had united under the name FLEC and were ready for peace talks with the government.

Police

Efforts to improve police-community relations and training programmes formed part of the Modernization and Development Plan 2003/2007. However, there were many reports of police committing human rights violations. Senior officials admitted that excesses had occurred but it appeared that in many cases no disciplinary or criminal action was taken.

Three men – Manuel do Rosario, Laurindo de Oliveira and Antonio Francisco – reportedly "disappeared" in April after being arrested in Luanda in possession of a stolen car. Relatives searching for the men saw this car parked in a police station. In May they found the bodies of the three men in an unofficial cemetery in Cazenga suburb. Police exhumed the bodies and opened an investigation, but no results were reported by the end of 2004.

Police reportedly used excessive force to control both violent and non-violent demonstrations.

A violent protest in February concerning electricity supplies in Cafunfo, a diamond-mining town in northern Angola, left at least three people dead, according to official sources. Unofficial sources said that police fired indiscriminately, killing more than 10 people, including two teenage girls and 12-year-old David Alexandre Carlos, and wounding some 20 others. Seventeen protesters were subsequently detained and accused of disobeying the authorities, a crime punishable by up to seven months' imprisonment. Applications for bail were not granted. The trial began in July but was suspended and not concluded by the year's end. One of the defendants, a 15-year-old boy, was held with adult prisoners for several months before being given separate accommodation. There was apparently no inquiry into the reports that police had used excessive force.

The police authorities expressed concern about lack of respect for human rights, particularly after five people suffocated to death in an overcrowded police cell in Capenda-Camulemba municipality in northern Angola in December. Police shot dead two members of a crowd of protesters which had gathered outside the police station. A police inquiry was initiated.

In October, paramilitary police dispersed a peaceful demonstration by the Angolan Party for Democratic Support and Progress (Partido do Apoio Democrático e Progresso de Angola, PADEPA) calling for publication of oil revenues. In November, police dispersed another peaceful gathering and briefly arrested dozens of demonstrators. Seven were taken to police cells and complained of being beaten for refusing to sign confessions. They were charged with resistance to the authorities, tried and acquitted.

Hundreds of people were reportedly abused by paramilitary police and soldiers in December 2003 and January 2004 during the first phase of an operation to expel foreign nationals who had entered Angola's diamond fields after the war ended. Victims reported being held in harsh conditions for up to three months. Many complained of beatings, humiliating and unhygienic body cavity searches and theft. Some women were allegedly raped. In February the Interior Minister acknowledged that there had been abuses. Police said that by September 2004 more than 300,000 foreigners had been expelled.

Police said that the Civil Defence Organization (Organização da Defesa Civil, ODC), set up during the war, had been abolished. However, there were detailed reports of ODC cells continuing to operate, sometimes assisted by police, and abuses were attributed to some personnel.

Availability of weapons

Crime rates remained high, fuelled by widespread unemployment and the availability of weapons. One million civilians were estimated to hold firearms illegally. In July a national commission was set up to prevent the trafficking of light weapons and small arms. Non-governmental organizations (NGOs) and churches encouraged people to surrender weapons and the police and army seized thousands.

Economic, social and cultural rights

The Luanda Provincial Government's plans to close informal and unclean markets near the city centre and replace them with others, mostly in outlying suburbs, threatened many people's livelihoods. Traders protested after the Estalagem market was closed in March, reportedly without consultation and before alternative space had been prepared. Some demonstrators used violence and police reacted with what appeared to be excessive force, killing three people.

The National Assembly approved laws on urban development and land in March and August respectively. NGOs had submitted detailed recommendations during the drafting process and expressed concern that the new laws failed to provide adequate security of tenure for disadvantaged groups living in informal urban settlements and traditional communal areas.

At least 500 families living in areas designated for development in Luanda were evicted without adequate consultation or compensation. Hundreds of others were threatened with eviction. Many were rehoused in remote areas without amenities, schools or clinics. Some families had to share houses and some lost vegetable gardens. The last of about 4,000 families housed in tents since their eviction from Boavista in 2001 were allocated new houses in Viana.

▢ Over 1,100 people were evicted from 340 houses in Cambamba and Banga Ué in South Luanda in September without prior consultation. A civil construction firm and a military construction brigade demolished the houses, guarded by about 50 heavily armed police. Most of those evicted remained in the area without shelter.

Shortage of land and drought in south-east Angola led to a conflict between two groups of nomadic cattle herders in September which reportedly resulted in four deaths. The enclosure of large areas of land for commercial farming had increased pressure on remaining land and water sources.

Women and children

The government's report on women's rights submitted to the UN Committee on the Elimination of Discrimination against Women in June admitted that the legal protection for victims of domestic violence was inadequate and that the police lacked sensitivity towards them.

In September the UN Committee on the Rights of the Child examined Angola's initial report on children's rights. The Committee welcomed progress in some areas but urged, among other things, further legal protection for children and the establishment of an independent national human rights institution.

ARGENTINA

ARGENTINE REPUBLIC
Head of state and government: Néstor Kirchner
Death penalty: abolitionist for ordinary crimes
International Criminal Court: ratified
UN Women's Convention: ratified with reservations
Optional Protocol to UN Women's Convention: signed

There were numerous complaints of torture and ill-treatment by law enforcement and prison officers. Treatment of detainees amounted to cruel, inhuman and degrading treatment. Progress was made in bringing to justice those responsible for past human rights violations in the context of Operation Cóndor.

Background

Despite some recovery from the recent economic crisis, poverty and unemployment remained high. According to the Statistics and Census Institute the unemployment rate in 2004 was 19.1 per cent and 70 per cent of the working people earned less than the minimum required to cover an average family's food expenses.

Ill-treatment of demonstrators

Protests by *piqueteros* (unemployed workers) continued during the year, some turning violent. *Piqueteros* set up roadblocks and in some cases occupied workplaces. Demonstrators and popular leaders were arrested and charged. Several of them were released but most were charged and awaiting trial at the end of the year. Arrested demonstrators complained of ill-treatment.

▢ In October, more than 30 people detained by the police and army following demonstrations in Caleta Oliva, Santa Cruz Province, filed judicial complaints stating that members of the provincial police and the gendarmerie hooded them, kicked and punched them and beat them with sticks. According to reports some sustained fractures as a result of blows to the face.

Ill-treatment

Ill-treatment of detainees, including minors, in police stations was reported. There were repeated reports of cruel, inhuman and degrading treatment of prisoners in provincial jails, including in Buenos Aires and Mendoza Provinces. Investigations into such allegations were subject to long delays and there were concerns that they were not independent or exhaustive.

Seventeen prisoners died in Mendoza prison in suspicious circumstances. There were reports that prisoners were kept in extremely overcrowded conditions with poor sanitary facilities and inadequate medical care. Inmates also complained that prison guards beat them and imposed harsh and degrading punishments, such as making detainees stand naked for hours. In September reports appeared in the press of statements made by the Mendoza provincial authorities criticizing the work of human rights lawyers who provided legal advice to prisoners' families and submitted official complaints at the provincial, national and international level about deteriorating prison conditions and the ill-treatment of prisoners.

In November the Inter-American Court of Human Rights called on Argentina to protect the lives and physical integrity of all detainees. It urged the authorities to investigate complaints of ill-treatment, identify those responsible and apply the appropriate punishments.

In November, following its examination of Argentina's periodic report, the UN Committee against Torture issued its conclusion and recommendations. These highlighted how the discrepancy between the large number of torture and ill-treatment complaints and the very few convictions in such cases "contributes to the prevailing impunity" on this issue.

Operation Cóndor

Positive steps were taken during the year to investigate past human rights violations committed in the context of Operation Cóndor, a plan jointly organized by six South American military governments in the 1970s and 1980s. In July, a federal judge ordered the arrest of 12 former members of the armed forces. In August the Supreme Court ruled, in the case of the killing of Chilean General Carlos Prats and his wife in Buenos Aires in 1974, that there was no statute of limitations for crimes against humanity.

AI country reports/ visits
Reports
- Open letter from Amnesty International to the Governor of Santa Fe Province, Sr. Jorge Obeid (AI Index: AMR 13/003/2004)
- Argentina: Journalists: Press accreditation — the wrong credentials? Threats, attacks and intimidation against members of the press (AI Index: AMR 13/005/2004)
- Argentina: Concrete action is required to end torture (AI Index: 13/010/2004)
- Argentina: Letter to Julio Cobos, Governor of the Province of Mendoza (AI Index: AMR 13/012/2004)

ARMENIA

REPUBLIC OF ARMENIA
Head of state: Robert Kocharian
Head of government: Andranik Markarian
Death penalty: abolitionist for all crimes
International Criminal Court: signed
UN Women's Convention: acceded
Optional Protocol to UN Women's Convention: not signed

The police reportedly used excessive force when they detained scores of protesters calling for the resignation of President Robert Kocharian. Dozens of opposition activists and supporters, including women, were reportedly beaten and ill-treated by police. Journalists, opposition political activists and a human rights defender were assaulted by unknown assailants. Conscientious objectors to compulsory military service continued to be imprisoned, despite Armenia's commitments to the Council of Europe.

Background

From February onwards, opposition party deputies boycotted parliament in protest at its refusal to approve a referendum of confidence in the President. Opposition political parties then launched a two-month campaign of mass public protests, including street demonstrations, demanding the President's resignation. The authorities described the campaign as a coup attempt and opened a criminal investigation into the opposition Artarutyun (Justice) alliance. This investigation reportedly ended in September without any charges being brought. The opposition denied calling for the violent overthrow of the constitutional order. During their campaign, hundreds of opposition supporters were detained and dozens were sentenced to 15 days' administrative detention after trials that reportedly fell far short of international fair trial standards.

In October the Justice Ministry finally registered the Jehovah's Witnesses, which had sought registration for nine years.

Police ill-treatment and excessive use of force

Scores of people were injured and detained when special police units used water cannons and stun grenades to break up a peaceful opposition demonstration in the capital, Yerevan, on 13 April. Four journalists covering the demonstration were reportedly severely beaten by police. Dozens more opposition activists and supporters, including women, were reportedly ill-treated during armed police raids on the head offices of the main opposition parties that same night. According to reports most of these activists were detained in police cells for up to 48 hours. According to human rights groups and opposition parties, those detained at the demonstration and at party offices continued to be beaten and ill-treated at police stations.

On 28 April the Parliamentary Assembly of the Council of Europe (PACE) issued a resolution condemning the use of force by police during the opposition protests in Armenia and calling on the authorities to investigate alleged human rights violations and to release opposition members. Vagharshak Harutiunian, a member of the opposition Hanrapetutiun (Republic) party and a former Defence Minister, was held in pre-trial detention for two months on charges of calling for the "violent overthrow of the constitutional order" and "publicly insulting senior government officials". He was released following international pressure. In an address to PACE in June President Kocharian defended the use of force by police against opposition activists during the 13 April demonstration.

In May Edgar Arakelian, a 24-year-old opposition activist, was sentenced to 18 months' imprisonment for "attacking a state official performing their duties" during the 13 April demonstration. He admitted hitting a police officer with an empty plastic bottle but claimed he had acted in self-defence after the police officer had hit him, breaking his front teeth. He alleged in court that he had been tortured in pre-trial detention. In August the Appeals Court upheld his sentence. He was released in September after serving a third of his sentence.

In July the Council of Europe's Committee for the Prevention of Torture (CPT) published its first report on Armenia. The report concerned the CPT's visit to Armenia in 2002. It concluded that people detained by police ran a significant risk of being ill-treated, and recommended professional training for police officers as a priority. The report also raised concerns about overcrowding in prisons, conditions of detention for people sentenced to life imprisonment, and shortcomings at a psychiatric hospital.

Assaults on activists

At an opposition rally on 5 April police reportedly refused to intervene when around two dozen men, described as athletically built with shaven heads, disrupted the event and attacked journalists, kicking and beating them and breaking their equipment. In June a Yerevan court ordered two men to pay a small fine for their part in the incident. Three men of a similar description allegedly assaulted and critically injured opposition politician Ashot Manucharian in Yerevan on 22 April. Police reportedly suspended the investigation into the assault in June after failing to identify the perpetrators. In September police questioned a man identified by Ashot Manucharian as one of the perpetrators. However, no charges were brought.

Human rights activist Mikael Danielyan was attacked outside his home by four unknown assailants on 30 March. He was reportedly punched in the head and kicked after he fell to the ground. He believed that the attack was related to his human rights work. President Kocharian reportedly ordered an investigation into the attack. However, the investigation failed to identify any perpetrators.

Conscientious objectors imprisoned

Conscientious objectors continued to be sentenced to prison, despite parliament's adoption in December 2003 of a law providing for unarmed military service or alternative civilian service, and despite Council of Europe requirements to free all those so imprisoned. The law, which provides terms of service of punitive length for conscientious objectors, entered into force in July.

As of the end of 2004 prison sentences of between one and two years had been imposed on 13 men, all Jehovah's Witnesses, as a result of their conscientious objection. Another was fined, and a further 11 had been released on parole.

AI country reports/visits

Reports

- Europe and Central Asia: Summary of Amnesty International's concerns in the region, January-June 2004: Armenia (AI Index: EUR 01/005/2004)
- Belarus and Uzbekistan: The last executioners – The trend towards abolition in the former Soviet space (AI Index: EUR 04/009/2004)

AUSTRALIA

AUSTRALIA
Head of state: Queen Elizabeth II, represented by Michael Jeffery
Head of government: John Howard
Death penalty: abolitionist for all crimes
International Criminal Court: ratified
UN Women's Convention: ratified with reservations
Optional Protocol to UN Women's Convention: not signed

The rights of indigenous Australians remained a concern. Measures to combat "terrorism" led to legislative amendments with implications for civil rights. Limited options for permanent residency were introduced, although thousands of refugees remained in limbo. Refugee families were kept separated by the government's policy of mandatory and indefinite detention.

Indigenous people

In October, the Council of Social Services reported that the gap between indigenous and non-indigenous people in health, education, employment and housing remained a concern. The Aboriginal and Torres Strait Islander Commission, an elected body represented at the UN Permanent Forum of Indigenous People, was dismantled and replaced with a government-appointed advisory council.

In February, riots broke out in Sydney after the death of a young indigenous man, T. J. Hickey, who fell from his bicycle and was impaled on a fence during a police operation. In August the coroner exonerated the New South Wales police of any responsibility for his death. In November, riots broke out on Palm Island, Queensland, following the death of an indigenous man, Cameron Doomadgee, while in police custody. A specialist commission was appointed to conduct a full inquiry into the death.

Violence against women

The government recognized violence against women as an issue with the launch of its "Australia says NO" campaign. In October, the results of a UN-coordinated survey revealed that 36 per cent of Australian women with a current or former partner had experienced violence in a relationship. In October it was reported that domestic violence was the leading cause of premature death and ill-health in women aged 15 to 44.

In December, James Ramage was convicted in the Supreme Court of Victoria of the lesser charge of manslaughter, rather than murder, of his wife Julie Ramage, based on her allegedly provocative words. The Victorian Law Reform Commission and women's groups questioned the continued availability of the defence of provocation.

Human rights and security

New "counter-terrorism" laws extended the period of detention without charge for "terrorism-related" offences and further restricted choice of legal representation. New legal provisions enabled the Attorney-General to keep information with security implications secret from an accused in federal criminal trials if a magistrate agreed.

The government did not seek the transfer or release of two Australian detainees – David Hicks and Mamdouh Habib – held at Guantánamo Bay and acquiesced to the operation of the US Military Commissions. The preliminary hearing before a military commission of David Hicks took place in August. The government dismissed allegations of torture and ill-treatment of Mamdouh Habib, detained without charge.

Refugees and asylum-seekers

The High Court of Australia ruled that legislation providing for the mandatory detention of asylum-seekers was consistent with Australia's Constitution.
⬚ Indian national Peter Qasim, from the state of Jammu and Kashmir, entered his seventh year in indefinite detention.

The Human Rights and Equal Opportunity Commission reported in May on the physical and psychological harm suffered by children in detention and called for all children and their families to be released from immigration detention centres. As of November, at least 212 asylum-seekers remained in detention. The remaining 22 Afghans rescued by the MV Tampa in 2001 and detained on Nauru were recognized as refugees, leaving 54 still detained.

The government amended Temporary Protection Visa regulations, enabling selected refugees to apply for other permits or visas, but thousands of refugees remained in a state of uncertainty.

AUSTRIA

REPUBLIC OF AUSTRIA
Head of state: Heinz Fischer (replaced Thomas Klestil in July)
Head of government: Wolfgang Schüssel
Death sentence: abolitionist for all crimes
International Criminal Court: ratified
UN Women's Convention and its Optional Protocol: ratified

There were concerns that the new Asylum Law, which entered into force on 1 May, could increase the risk of refugees being sent to "safe third countries" from which they could be returned to countries where they could face human rights violations. Allegations of police brutality resulting in serious injury continued to be received. At least one person died in custody in disputed circumstances. Two human rights lawyers were harassed and criminal proceedings were initiated against them, apparently because of their human rights work.

Refugees and asylum-seekers

On 15 October, the Constitutional Court declared three articles of the 2004 Asylum Law unconstitutional. One article allowed asylum-seekers to be deported before a decision had been taken on their appeal. The second limited the possibility of presenting new evidence during a hearing, and the third allowed detention to be prolonged if an application was resubmitted.

There were continuing concerns about asylum-seekers' lack of access to translators during medical examinations which failed to offer proper care. It was unclear who under the new asylum law had responsibility for the representation of unaccompanied minors seeking asylum.

There were reports of ill-treatment of asylum-seekers held in refugee camps. There were concerns that mechanisms had not been put in place to ensure proper monitoring and accountability regarding facilities housing asylum-seekers; day-to-day responsibility for such facilities had been outsourced to private companies in 2003.
⬚ A Georgian asylum-seeker in the Traiskirchen Refugee Camp was allegedly ill-treated in February when he refused to leave the camp during asylum

procedures. According to reports, he was wrestled to the ground by officials and had cigarettes stubbed out on his shoulder.

Allegations of police ill-treatment and harassment

◻ A young man was reportedly beaten by police officers in August at a garden party in Vienna. Despite severe injuries, the police refused to allow an ambulance to be called and detained him without charge overnight. A hospital examination the following day revealed that he was suffering from a fractured skull and a cerebral haemorrhage. After the young man submitted a complaint to the Independent Administrative Tribunal, counter-charges were brought against him of resisting state authority and causing grievous bodily harm.

◻ In October, two human rights lawyers, Georg Bürstmayr and Nadja Lorenz, were charged with trafficking in human beings and incitement to break the law. However, the charges were withdrawn within days because of lack of evidence. At the time the charges were laid by officials of the Ministry of the Interior, Georg Bürstmayr was about to be re-appointed as head of the Commission of the Human Rights Advisory Board. The Minister of the Interior opposed the appointment, but gave no reasons for his objections. Following widespread protests, Georg Bürstmayr was reappointed.

Death in custody

◻ On 29 January the Independent Administrative Tribunal issued its conclusions concerning the death of Cheibani Wague, from Mauritania, during a police operation in the Vienna City Park in July 2003. Police had been called to Cheibani Wague's workplace following a dispute between him and a colleague. Video footage of the incident showed six police and medical officials surrounding Cheibani Wague as he lay handcuffed, face-down on the ground, apparently unconscious. An autopsy indicated lack of oxygen to the brain and irreversible failure of the circulatory system as the causes of death. The Tribunal established that the methods used to immobilize Cheibani Wague could have caused his death. The police officers involved in the incident had not been suspended during the investigation and no one had been charged in connection with Cheibani Wague's death by the end of 2004.

Extradition of asylum-seekers

There was continuing concern at the lack of monitoring by the Austrian authorities to ensure that guarantees given prior to extradition were in fact adhered to by the receiving government. The willingness of the Austrian authorities to consider extradition requests before applications for asylum had been properly processed was also a cause of concern.

◻ In February, Akhmet A., a Russian citizen, was extradited to Russia, despite pending asylum determination procedures. There were concerns that the investigation by the Austrian authorities into the offences he allegedly committed in Russia — which were the basis of the extradition request — was inadequate. There were reports that Akhmet A. may have been ill-treated in pre-trial detention by Russian law enforcement officers following his return to Russia.

Unequal age of consent

Austria refused to provide compensation and rehabilitation to all those convicted in previous years under an article of the Penal Code which discriminated against gay men by setting a higher age of consent than that set for heterosexuals and lesbians; the article had been repealed in 2002. The European Court of Human Rights had ruled on numerous occasions that convictions under this article were in breach of human rights law — namely the prohibition of discrimination and the right to respect for private life — and had ordered the Austrian government to pay compensation in a number of cases.

AI country reports/ visits
Reports
· Europe and Central Asia: Summary of Amnesty International's concerns in the region, January-June 2004: Austria (AI Index: EUR 01/005/2004)
· The EU Code of Conduct fails to prevent Austria transferring rifle production to Malaysia (AI Index: ACT 30/018/2004)

AZERBAIJAN

REPUBLIC OF AZERBAIJAN
Head of state: Ilham Aliev
Head of government: Artur Rasizade
Death penalty: abolitionist for all crimes
International Criminal Court: not signed
UN Women's Convention and its Optional Protocol: ratified

More than 100 political opposition activists were tried for their alleged participation in post-election violence in October 2003: at least 40 men received prison sentences following trials which reportedly did not meet international fair trial standards. Courts reportedly failed to exclude evidence allegedly extracted under torture. Political prisoners were among hundreds released during the year.

Trials of opposition activists

By the end of April, over 100 opposition activists had been tried in separate court cases for their alleged participation in violent clashes between supporters of the opposition and law enforcement officers in the wake of presidential elections in October 2003. During their trials, evidence reportedly based on confessions extracted under torture was admitted in court. Thirty-three men received prison sentences of between three and six years. The rest received suspended sentences. Among those who received a suspended sentence was human rights activist and imam of the independent Juma mosque Ilgar Ibrahimoglu. He was released on 2 April.

On 7 May, seven leading members of the political opposition went on trial at the Court for Grave Crimes in Baku for their alleged participation in the violence. International and national organizations called on the authorities to ensure that they received a fair trial in line with international standards. The seven were: Rauf Arifoglu, a deputy chairman of the Musavat (Equality) party and editor-in-chief of the *Yeni Musavat* opposition newspaper; Ibrahim Ibrahimli and Arif Hajili of Musavat; Panah Huseynov of the Khalq (People) party; Etimad Asadov of the Karabakh Invalids' Association; Sardar Jalologlu of the Azerbaijan Democratic Party; and Igbal Agazade of the Umid (Hope) party. They were reportedly accused of having masterminded the violence and were charged with organizing mass disturbances. They had consistently denied the charges since their arbitrary detentions in October 2003. Some of the seven were allegedly tortured by members of the Ministry of Internal Affairs' Organized Crime Unit. Others were reportedly detained in cruel, inhuman and degrading conditions.

At the end of May the seven refused to attend further preliminary court hearings in protest over what they believed to be the court's failure to conduct a fair and open trial according to international standards. Following this protest, the defendants' lawyers resigned and the court appointed new defence lawyers who attended the court session in the defendants' absence. Following calls from supporters and human rights groups, the seven resumed attending court hearings on 22 June.

In court several witnesses reportedly retracted earlier testimony, stating that law enforcement officials had pressured them – including by the use of force – to make statements incriminating the seven defendants. Individual officials denied in court all allegations of having tortured or ill-treated any of the defendants. The court reportedly did not order any investigations into the allegations of torture and ill-treatment.

On 22 October the court handed down sentences of between two and a half and five years' imprisonment to the seven. The Organization for Security and Co-operation in Europe, which had monitored the trial, expressed dismay at the harshness of the sentences. The Parliamentary Assembly of the Council of Europe had earlier called the seven defendants "presumed political prisoners" and asked for their release or pardon as part of Azerbaijan's obligations as a member state of the Council of Europe. On 19 November the Court of Appeals upheld the original verdict. An appeal to the Supreme Court was pending at the end of 2004.

Amnesty for convicted political prisoners
In March, May, September and December, President Ilham Aliev pardoned a total of close to 1,000 prisoners. Among those subsequently released were a number considered political prisoners by the Council of Europe, which had required Azerbaijan to release or retry them as one of its obligations on joining the organization. They included former Prime Minister Suret Huseynov and the leader of the self-proclaimed Talysh-Mugan Republic, Alikram Hummatov.

Police ill-treatment and conditions of detention
In December the Council of Europe's Committee for the Prevention of Torture and Inhuman or Degrading Treatment or Punishment (CPT) published its first report on Azerbaijan. The report, which concerned the CPT's visit to Azerbaijan in 2002, concluded that people detained by the police ran a significant risk of being ill-treated. Among the CPT's recommendations were that professional training for police officers become a priority and that legal safeguards against ill-treatment in custody be applied from the moment of detention. The report also highlighted serious shortcomings in the conditions of detention at several police detention centres. While acknowledging efforts made by the authorities to improve prison conditions, the CPT reported overcrowding in some prisons.

Nagorno-Karabakh
Death penalty – update
The status of the self-proclaimed Nagorno-Karabakh Republic (NKR), which is not recognized by the international community, remained unresolved. In August 2003 the NKR adopted the criminal code of neighbouring Armenia, thereby abolishing the death penalty. The three prisoners who remained on death row had their death sentences commuted to 15 years' imprisonment.

There had been no executions in Nagorno-Karabakh since 1997.

Torture and unfair trial – update
On 21 September former Defence Minister Samvel Babaian was released from prison after serving a third of his sentence. He was one of 35 prisoners pardoned by President Arkadi Ghukasian on 17 September. Samvel Babaian had been sentenced to 14 years' imprisonment in 2001 after an unfair trial and amid allegations that he had been tortured in police custody.

AI country reports/ visits
Reports
- Belarus and Uzbekistan: The last executioners – The trend towards abolition in the former Soviet space (AI Index: EUR 04/009/2004)
- Europe and Central Asia: Summary of Amnesty International's concerns in the region, January-June 2004: Azerbaijan (AI Index: EUR 01/005/2004)

BAHAMAS

COMMONWEALTH OF THE BAHAMAS
Head of state: Queen Elizabeth II, represented by
Ivy Dumont
Head of government: Perry Gladstone Christie
Death penalty: retentionist
International Criminal Court: signed
UN Women's Convention: ratified
Optional Protocol to UN Women's Convention: not signed

Instances of brutality by police and prison staff were reported. Asylum-seekers were deported without access to adequate asylum procedures. Death sentences were imposed; no executions were carried out.

Death penalty

At the end of 2004 there were at least 26 people on death row. Death sentences continued to be imposed by the courts; no executions were carried out.

In July, the Court of Appeal ruled that Ricardo Lockhart's 2003 murder conviction was unsatisfactory and unsafe. It substituted a conviction for manslaughter and commuted his death sentence to a prison term of 25 years.

Prison conditions

Conditions in Fox Hill Prison remained poor. Concerns included inadequate sanitation, food, water and medical care and some instances of ill-treatment.

In August an inquest heard evidence that Sidney McKenzie had been beaten before his death in September 2000. A prisoner alleged in court that prisoners had been beaten and threatened before coming to court to give evidence.

In October an inquest ruled that neglect and failure to provide medical attention contributed to the death of Kazimierz Kwasiborski, who died in prison on 28 August 2003.

Refugees

Asylum-seekers from countries including Haiti and Cuba were forcibly returned without access to a full and fair refugee determination procedure, in violation of international law. There were reports of inadequate medical attention, food and water at the Carmichael Detention Centre. At least five children were detained in violation of international standards.

Violations by the security forces

There were several reports of ill-treatment. At least three people were fatally shot by police.

The inquest into the fatal shooting by police of Jermaine Alexander Mackey in December 2002 had not concluded by the end of 2004.

In October several Haitian and Cuban detainees were reportedly beaten at the Carmichael Detention Centre. The report of a police investigation into the allegations was presented to Parliament in December. On 9 December, at least nine detainees and 11 guards were injured during a fire and confrontation at the Carmichael Detention Centre.

BAHRAIN

KINGDOM OF BAHRAIN
Head of state: King Hamad bin 'Issa Al Khalifa
Head of government: Shaikh Khalifa bin Salman Al Khalifa
Death penalty: retentionist
International Criminal Court: signed
UN Women's Convention: ratified with reservations
Optional Protocol to UN Women's Convention: not signed

Four political associations organized a petition calling for constitutional amendments, which led to the arrest of 17 people. The Bahrain Centre for Human Rights was closed by ministerial order and its executive director arrested. In response, hundreds of demonstrators took to the streets. The death sentence against a young Ethiopian woman was commuted.

Background

In April, the first woman government minister was appointed. Nada 'Abbas Haffadh, member of the Supreme Council for Women, became Health Minister. The long-serving Interior Minister Shaikh Muhammad bin Khalifa Al Khalifa was replaced in May by Major General Shaikh Rashid bin 'Abdullah bin Ahmad Al Khalifa.

In October King Hamad bin 'Issa Al Khalifa called for the enactment of laws that would end all forms of discrimination against women.

Arrests

'Abdul Ra'uf al-Shayeb, a board member of the National Committee for Martyrs and Victims of Torture, was arrested on 30 March. The arrest reportedly related to his entering a house without permission and having an "illicit relationship" with an Indonesian housemaid. However, 'Abdul Ra'uf al-Shayeb's arrest was believed to be connected with his call a few days earlier for a demonstration on behalf of victims of torture to take place on 4 April, the day of the first Formula One Grand Prix to be held in Bahrain. He was released on 3 April. At the end of the year he still faced charges of entering a house without the owner's permission.

Seventeen people, including juveniles, were arrested on 30 April for organizing a public petition calling for constitutional amendments. The petition was said to have been initiated by four political associations: the National Democratic Action Society, the Islamic National Reconciliation Association (al-Wifaq), the National Democratic Society and the Islamic Action Society. By 20 May all detainees had been released by order of the King.

Human rights defender detained

'Abdul Hadi al-Khawaja, a human rights activist and executive director of the Bahrain Centre for Human Rights (BCHR), was arrested on 25 September and ordered to be detained for 45 days by the public prosecutor. The day before, he had made a personal attack on the Prime Minister and voiced strong criticisms of the government's economic and human rights record while speaking at a BCHR-convened seminar on poverty. On 28 September the Minister of Labour and Social Affairs ordered the BCHR's closure.

'Abdul Hadi al-Khawaja appeared in court on 16 and 20 October and on 7 November, and was charged under Articles 165 and 168 of the 1976 Penal Code which include the offence of "inciting hatred of the state, defamation, spreading false information designed to destabilize public security". He denied all charges on the basis that the 1976 laws were "unconstitutional". On 21 November he received a one-year prison sentence but was released the same day, having been pardoned by the King. Hundreds of people demonstrated calling for his release, many of whom were arrested and remained in detention until their release also on 21 November by order of the King.

Torture and ill-treatment

◻ Hasan 'Abd al-Nabi Hassan, an unemployed man from Sitra, was arrested on 20 November by four men in civilian clothes as he stood near the royal palace holding banners, one of which said: "I am a Bahraini citizen and I demand a job". The men, said to be from the Royal Guard, ordered him to get into their car. When he refused three of them reportedly kicked and beat him with batons all over his body. The driver was reported to have deliberately reversed the car into him, hitting him on the side and arm. Hassan 'Abd al-Nabi Hassan lost consciousness and was taken to Rifa'a al-Gharbiya police station. He was handcuffed and put in a cell. When he asked for medical treatment and to see a lawyer, a duty officer beat him with a baton and metal handcuffs. He was released on 21 November and ordered to stop his protests near the palace.

Violence against women

There were reports of domestic violence against female migrant workers and Bahraini women. State inaction and discriminatory legislation left women vulnerable to gender-based violence.
◻ A Bahraini woman was divorced from her husband after she suffered regular beatings. No action against him was taken despite the availability of medical evidence and complaints. The husband kept custody of the couple's two children.

In May the Migrant Workers' Group, a local non-governmental organization (NGO) working under the umbrella of the BCHR, rescued Tushari Ramyalatha, a 19-year-old Sri Lankan maid. She was reportedly the victim of regular beatings and sexual harassment by her employer's family who also refused to pay her salary. She returned to Sri Lanka after her sponsor reportedly agreed to pay for her flight and six months' salary.

In August the Shura (advisory) Council announced that it had initiated a draft law to combat violence against women.

Death penalty

In January the Supreme Court commuted the death sentence of Yoshork Dostazudi, a 23-year-old Ethiopian woman, to life imprisonment. She had been found guilty of beating to death her female employer in December 1998.

AI country reports/ visits
Visit

AI visited Bahrain in August and September to carry out research for the Gulf Stop Violence Against Women project (see Middle East/North Africa Regional Overview 2004) and promote human rights. Workshops were organized and partnerships with local NGOs and human rights activists were established. AI delegates visited a women's prison in 'Issa Town.

BANGLADESH

PEOPLE'S REPUBLIC OF BANGLADESH
Head of state: Iajuddin Ahmed
Head of government: Begum Khaleda Zia
Death penalty: retentionist
International Criminal Court: signed
UN Women's Convention: ratified with reservations
Optional Protocol to UN Women's Convention: ratified

Impunity was a key factor in the government's failure to stem a tide of violence. Among the main victims of the violence were members of minority communities and politicians. Human rights defenders continued to be harassed and attacked. Thousands of opposition activists were arbitrarily detained. At least seven people were executed.

Background

The nexus between criminals and politicians appeared to reinforce institutionalized corruption, violence, and impunity for human rights abuses. Corruption, including in the criminal justice system, remained a major problem. In April a judge was removed from office following an unprecedented investigation by the Supreme Judicial Council, which considered allegations that he had taken a bribe to be "not totally baseless". The Anti-Corruption Commission was established in November.

At least 147 people reportedly died during the year in what the government portrayed as deaths in crossfire between the special security force known as the Rapid Action Battalion (RAB) and suspected criminals. There were concerns that the deaths, which usually occurred in desolate locations after the arrest of suspects, were deliberate killings by the RAB. Opposition parties alleged their members were most frequently targeted.

The 1999 High Court order for the judiciary to be separated from the executive was not implemented. The formation of the Bangladesh Judicial Service in November was seen as a step forward.

Growing tide of violence

The year was marked by violent attacks on members of the opposition and on public venues, including cinemas and places of worship. Investigations lacked the rigour to identify the motives. Members of the ruling coalition parties, including the Bangladesh Nationalist Party (BNP) and Jamaat-e-Islami, were allegedly responsible for a series of attacks on opposition rallies.

A grenade attack on the leaders of the opposition Awami League during a rally on 21 August left 22 people dead and hundreds injured. The opposition blamed Islamist groups in the BNP-led coalition for the attack. The government instituted a judicial inquiry. There were concerns about the inquiry's impartiality after the Prime Minister suggested that the opposition might have carried out the attack themselves in order to tarnish the government's image. The inquiry judge submitted his report to the authorities on 2 October. He told journalists that he had identified the perpetrators and a link to "foreign enemies" but gave no details. The content of the report and the government's response had not been made public by the end of 2004.

Three people were killed in a bomb attack at Hazrat Shahjalal shrine in Sylhet in January. In May another blast at the same shrine, a moderate Islamic place of worship not favoured by conservative Islamic groups, killed two people and injured dozens.

In October, BNP members reportedly attacked a public meeting in the northern town of Rangpur.

Attacks on human rights defenders

Human rights defenders continued to receive death threats and to be at risk of attacks. Perpetrators were believed to be linked to Islamist groups or armed criminal gangs whose conduct the defenders had criticized.

▭ In February, Dr Humayun Azad of Dhaka University was stabbed by unidentified assailants. The attack followed several death threats and was believed to be related to the publication of his novel about Islamist groups. No one was brought to justice for the attack. Humayun Azad recovered after several months of medical attention but died — reportedly of natural causes — in August.

▭ Sumi Khan, the Chittagong correspondent for the magazine *Weekly 2000*, was stabbed by unknown assailants on 27 February while travelling in a rickshaw on her way to send an article to her editor. The attack was believed to relate to her investigative articles about the involvement of local politicians and Islamist groups in attacks on members of Hindu communities. She continued to receive death threats. No one was brought to justice for the attack.

Non-governmental organizations (NGOs) perceived to oppose government policies were at risk of harassment.

▭ Dr Qazi Faruque Ahmed and David William Biswas, the president and vice-president of the NGO *Proshika*, were arrested on 22 May. Their arrest appeared to be politically motivated, coming amid allegations that *Proshika* had engaged in political campaigning against the current ruling alliance during the last general elections. They were released on bail in July and June respectively but charges against them remained pending.

Violence against minorities

Impunity for violence against minorities, including members of the Hindu and Ahmadiyya communities, was endemic.

No independent inquiry was conducted into the attacks on tribal people in the Chittagong Hill Tracts in 2003, which involved killing, rape, sexual assault, and the burning of hundreds of homes. No one was brought to justice for the killing of an Ahmadi preacher or for the chanting of hate slogans or for attacks against the Ahmadiyya community's places of worship. Although several people were arrested on charges of involvement in the burning of a Hindu home in Banskhali Upazila in 2003, there were concerns that the main alleged culprits were not among them.

Violence against women

Violence against women was widely reported, including acid attacks and cases of women killed in dowry disputes. Women accounted for the large majority of acid attack victims. According to the Acid Survivors Foundation, at least 153 women were attacked between January and October, and in cases that went before the courts, only one in nine ended in successful prosecution. In some cases the matter was reportedly "settled" out of court between the families of the victim and the perpetrator. Reasons for most attacks were reportedly disputes between families or refusal by women of marriage or sex.

Mass arrest of opposition activists

In several waves of mass arrests, thousands of people were detained, usually for weeks. Thousands were detained in April during a campaign of general strikes and anti-government protests organized by the Awami League. Thousands more were detained in September. Bangladeshi human rights organizations challenged the lawfulness of the arrests before the High Court, which sought but did not receive an explanation from the government.

Past abuses

On 20 October a court in Dhaka gave its verdict in the trial of 11 men accused of killing four Awami League leaders in Dhaka Central Jail in November 1975. Three were sentenced to death in absentia; another three – already sentenced to death for the killing of President Sheikh Mujibur Rahman in August 1975 – were given life imprisonment; and five were acquitted. The Awami League claimed the acquittals were politically motivated.

Death penalty

Over 120 people were sentenced to death. Seven people, including three policemen, were executed for rape and murder.

AI country reports/ visits
Reports
- Bangladesh: Government must stem growing tide of violence (AI Index: ASA 13/015/2004)
- Bangladesh: The Ahmadiyya Community – their rights must be protected (AI index: ASA 13/005/2004)
- Bangladesh: Chittagong Hill Tracts: A Call for Justice at Mahalchari (AI Index: ASA 13/003/2004)

BELARUS

REPUBLIC OF BELARUS
Head of state: Alyaksandr Lukashenka
Head of government: Sergei Sidorsky
Death penalty: retentionist
International Criminal Court: not signed
UN Women's Convention and its Optional Protocol: ratified

No progress was made in investigating four cases of "disappearance". Death sentences and executions continued. Human rights defenders were subjected to intimidation and harassment. The government continued to restrict freedom of expression and assembly; opposition activists were arbitrarily detained and allegedly ill-treated by police. Non-governmental organizations including human rights groups continued to be subjected to restrictions and closures.

Background

There was increasing international concern about Belarus' failure to improve human rights. In January the Parliamentary Assembly of the Council of Europe (PACE) rejected Belarus' request for the reinstatement of its special guest status with PACE. In April the UN Commission on Human Rights appointed a Special Rapporteur to examine the human rights situation in Belarus and to report back to the Commission in 2005. The Special Rapporteur was also mandated to monitor the development of a programme of human rights education for all sectors of society, in particular the judiciary, law enforcement and prison officials and civil society. He was refused a visa to visit Belarus in December.

In parliamentary elections on 17 October government candidates were elected to all seats. The elections were overshadowed by a referendum in which President Alyaksandr Lukashenka won the right to lift the constitutional limit of two presidential terms. Observers for the Organization for Security and Co-operation in Europe (OSCE) commented that the elections and the referendum fell significantly short of OSCE commitments.

Death penalty

In March the Constitutional Court concluded its assessment of the compliance of death penalty provisions in the Criminal Code with the Constitution and international standards. The Court found that a number of articles of the Criminal Code were inconsistent with the Constitution. The Court ruling made it possible for the head of state and parliament to abolish the death penalty or, as a first step, introduce a moratorium, should the political will exist. However, during 2004, at least five people were reportedly sentenced to death and executed.

'Disappearances'

In March the department for organized crime and corruption of the Procuracy announced that the investigation into the "disappearance" of television cameraman Dmitry Zavadsky in July 2000 had been stopped "because of the failure to discover the disappeared person". There was no progress in the cases of leading opposition figures Yury Zakharenko and Viktor Gonchar and businessman Anatoly Krasovsky, who all "disappeared" in 1999 and 2000.

In April PACE called on the authorities to carry out an independent investigation into the "disappearances" and to launch criminal investigations into the alleged involvement of high-ranking officials in the events and their cover-up.

Human rights defenders

A pattern of deliberate obstruction, harassment and intimidation of human rights defenders persisted. In June the Special Representative of the UN Secretary-General on human rights defenders, Hina Jilani, expressed serious concern at the reported curtailment of the freedom of association in Belarus. She expressed particular alarm at the threatened closure of the Belarusian Helsinki Committee (BHC), reportedly the last nationally operating human rights non-governmental organization.

In January the tax inspection office of the Minsk Moskovskaia District accused the BHC of using a European Union (EU) grant without registering it and of not paying taxes in accordance with national legislation. The EU programme that provided the grant was in fact exempted from tax, as recorded in a 1994 memorandum between the Belarusian authorities and the EU. In June, the BHC was cleared of all charges by the Minsk Economic Court, a decision upheld by the Appellate Court at the end of July. The decision confirmed that the organization's activities were lawful and complied with all procedures as required by the Belarusian authorities. Despite this, a criminal investigation into alleged tax evasion against the chair and the head accountant of the BHC continued until 28 December, after which the charges against them were dropped.

Freedom of expression

Peaceful protesters continued to be detained solely for exercising their rights to freedom of expression and assembly.

In September, Valery Levonevsky and Alexander Vasiliev, respectively the president and deputy president of the national strike committee of market traders, were each sentenced to two years in prison by the Leninsky district court in Grodno after being convicted of publicly insulting the President. They had distributed a leaflet containing a satirical poem and calling on people to take part in 1 May demonstrations and "to come and say that you are against 'somebody' going on holiday skiing in Austria and having a good time at your cost". President Alyaksandr Lukashenka was known to have spent his holidays in Austria.

Mikhail Marinich, a prominent member of the opposition, was detained on 26 April, originally for a traffic offence. The charge was then changed to possession of foreign currency and he was finally charged with illegal use, possession and transfer of arms after a pistol was found at his dacha. On 30 August he was charged with theft of computers from the organization Delovaia Initsiiativa, of which he is president. The computers were on loan from the US Embassy, which stated it had made no complaint. Members of the organization informed his lawyer that they had agreed to him storing the computers in his garage temporarily. On 20 December Mikhail Marinich was sentenced to five years' imprisonment by the Minsk district court for "abuse of an official position for the purpose of theft". The theft in question referred to the computers on loan to Delovaia Initsiiativa. The charge of possession of arms was dropped.

Opposition activists who held peaceful demonstrations to protest at the results of the October elections and referendum were subjected to arbitrary arrest and ill-treatment by the police. After demonstrations on 19 October about 50 demonstrators were reportedly detained and beaten. Anatoly Lebedko, leader of the United Civil Party, suffered concussion, broken ribs and possible kidney damage as a result of beatings. Forty people were charged with participation in or organization of unsanctioned public demonstrations and sentenced to up to 15 days' imprisonment or fined.

Violation of trade union rights

There was continuing pressure on trade unions to conform to government policies. Trade union members were constantly harassed.

In October, Sergei Antonchik was sentenced to 15 days' administrative detention by the Partizansky District Court in Minsk for holding a meeting on the premises of the Free Trade Union of Belarus. The meeting, which had been agreed with the chair of the union, was to organize the setting up of a new non-governmental organization.

Long-term prisoner of conscience

The Central District Court of the City of Minsk eased Yury Bandazhevsky's conditions of detention and transferred him to a "corrective labour settlement" in Grodno Region. Professor Yury Bandazhevsky was sentenced to eight years' imprisonment in June 2001 for alleged bribe-taking but AI believes that he was convicted because he had criticized official responses to the Chernobyl nuclear reactor catastrophe of 1986. The new terms of detention allowed him to receive visitors and request leave for family visits.

AI country reports/ visits
Reports
- Belarus: Stifling the promotion of human rights (AI Index: EUR 49/004/2004)
- Belarus and Uzbekistan: The last executioners – The trend towards abolition in the former Soviet space (AI Index: EUR 04/009/2004)
- Europe and Central Asia: Summary of Amnesty International's concerns in the region, January-June 2004: Belarus (AI Index: EUR 01/005/2004)
Visit
An AI delegate attended a human rights forum near Minsk in January.

BELGIUM

KINGDOM OF BELGIUM
Head of state: King Albert II
Head of government: Guy Verhofstadt
Death penalty: abolitionist for all crimes
International Criminal Court: ratified
UN Women's Convention and its Optional Protocol: ratified

There were further attacks on Jews and Muslims. Detainees, many of them foreign nationals, allegedly suffered police brutality and other cruel, inhuman and degrading treatment. Reports of prison overcrowding continued, accompanied by a high suicide rate among prisoners. There was concern that aspects of the asylum determination process and related appeals procedures were not in line with international standards on the rights of asylum-seekers. The entry into force of legislation passed in 2003, establishing a guardianship service to protect the rights of unaccompanied foreign children, was widely welcomed, but the treatment of some such children continued to fall short of international standards. The government announced a national action plan running between the end of 2004 and 2007 to combat domestic violence against women, but there were fears that the plan was insufficiently funded. Trafficking in people, in particular women and girls for sexual purposes, continued to increase.

Scrutiny by intergovernmental organizations
A report published in January by the European Commission against Racism and Intolerance (ECRI) said that Belgium had made progress but that a number of ECRI's recommendations had "not, or not fully, been implemented."

In July the UN Human Rights Committee expressed concerns relating to, among other things, reports of racist acts; police ill-treatment; failure to guarantee or fully respect the rights of asylum-seekers, unauthorized migrants, detainees, prisoners and the mentally ill; and insufficient assistance for victims of trafficking. It stated that changes to Belgium's universal jurisdiction legislation introduced in 2003 had negative repercussions for victims of serious violations of international humanitarian law. It also expressed concern that the definition of "terrorism" in the Terrorist Offences Act of December 2003 was not fully in line with the International Covenant on Civil and Political Rights.

Racism and xenophobia in the community
There were numerous accounts of Jews, including children, suffering verbal insults, harassment and violent attacks. There were also racist incidents directed against Arabs and Muslims, including asylum-seekers.

In January ECRI called for "a more determined institutional reaction against the use of racist or xenophobic discourse in politics" and for "concerted efforts of Belgian society as a whole" to address "manifestations of anti-semitism and Islamophobia."

In July the Human Rights Committee noted with concern the number of "racist, xenophobic, anti-Semitic and Anti-Muslim acts" and urged Belgium to take all necessary steps to protect communities resident in the country. The federal government strongly condemned such acts and a number of initiatives were taken by federal, regional and community authorities to protect vulnerable communities, combat racism and promote intercultural dialogue. In July, following a sudden upsurge in racist attacks, the government adopted a detailed federal action plan to combat racism, anti-Semitism and xenophobia.

In June, four young teenage students at a Jewish rabbinical school in an Antwerp suburb said that they were confronted in the street by a group of young men of North African appearance who were armed with knives and blunt instruments. One of the students, a 16-year-old boy, was stabbed in the back and suffered a punctured lung. The authorities said that every step would be taken to safeguard the school, and a criminal investigation was opened to track down the attackers.

In July several masked individuals armed with batons and a knife broke into Broechem open centre for asylum-seekers near Antwerp in the early hours of the morning. They entered the residents' rooms, terrorizing them and selecting three men for physical attack. The aggressors asked their victims questions of a racist nature, wanting to know, in particular, if they were Muslims. It later emerged that the victims, one of whom needed hospital treatment as a result of the attack, were of Russian, Israeli and Serbian origin. The police and the Federal Agency for the Reception of Asylum-Seekers (Fedasil) announced additional security measures to protect residents of the Broechem and other similar centres for asylum-seekers. Fedasil also lodged a criminal complaint against persons unknown and a criminal investigation was opened. The attackers – all teenagers, including minors – were arrested within days.

Police ill-treatment, racism and impunity
There were further reports of ill-treatment and racist abuse by police. The Standing Police Monitoring Committee stated that complaints of police racism were increasing and that most came from areas with large immigrant populations such as Brussels and Antwerp. The perpetrators of such abuses frequently enjoyed impunity. A number of the fundamental safeguards against ill-treatment in police custody were still not in place.

The Human Rights Committee called on Belgium to amend its Code of Criminal Procedure and "guarantee the rights of individuals in detention to notify their immediate families that they have been detained and to have access to a lawyer and a doctor within the first few hours of detention". The Committee expressed concern about the persistence of "allegations of police violence, often accompanied by racial discrimination", and about reports that relevant investigations were not always thorough and judgments, when handed down, were still "mostly of a token nature." It called for more thorough inquiries and for routine linking of actions alleging police ill-treatment and actions brought against alleged victims by the police.

ECRI called for "further efforts to prevent racist or discriminatory behaviour" by the police. It reiterated the need to implement existing domestic legislation against racism and racial discrimination to ensure that the legislation was applied also to police officers responsible for any such acts.

Abuses during deportation

There were further allegations that foreign nationals, both men and women, suffered excessive force and cruel, inhuman and degrading treatment in the context of deportation operations. In July the Human Rights Committee recommended that those responsible for carrying out deportations be better trained and monitored.

Some foreign nationals, who had been denied access to Belgian territory on arrival at the airport and then held in detention centres for aliens by administrative order awaiting deportation, were released on the orders of the court mandated to rule on the legality of their continued detention. In some cases such people were transferred directly to the transit zone of the national airport under police escort, on the orders of the Aliens Office attached to the Interior Ministry. They were then left for days or weeks, and occasionally months, effectively confined, without passports and access to legal advice, and without some of the basic means of survival such as food, fresh air and proper washing facilities. As a result, they were frequently forced to rely on the charity of passengers and airport staff. Among the victims were people whose asylum applications had been rejected.

The Ministry maintained that, although released by court order, the foreign nationals in question had no right of residence in Belgium and were still subject to deportation orders issued by the Aliens Office. It said that by being placed in the transit zone, the individuals were not being detained, but were simply being escorted to Belgium's border and were free to leave by catching a flight to their country of origin or a third country, with the costs being borne by the airline which had carried them to Belgium.

AI joined a number of domestic non-governmental organizations in public and direct appeals to the government calling for an end to the practice. In July the Human Rights Committee also expressed concern about foreigners being held in the transit zone "under questionable sanitary and social conditions". It considered such practices "akin to arbitrary detention which can lead to inhuman and degrading treatment" and said that Belgium should end them immediately.

◻ A teenager from Guinea-Bissau who arrived at Brussels airport in November 2003 and made an immediate but unsuccessful asylum application, spent some eight months in detention centres for aliens. During this period he was subject to several deportation attempts. The courts twice ruled that he should be released, allowed to enter Belgian territory, and provided with a guardian and appropriate care in an institution where he would be protected as a minor. The Aliens Office disputed that he was a minor, as he maintained, and eventually transferred him to the transit zone in the airport in July, where he spent several days without food and sleeping facilities. Following interventions and publicity by domestic non-governmental organizations and the media, the Interior Minister ordered the boy's transfer to an open centre for asylum-seekers.

During the year, at the request of the Interior Minister, an independent commission re-evaluated the techniques used in forcible deportation operations. AI drew the commission's attention to its continuing concerns as well as to the recommendations it had submitted to the Belgian government in 2003. The commission's final report and recommendations had not been published by the end of the year.

AI country reports/ visits
Reports and statements
- Europe and Central Asia: Summary of Amnesty International's concerns in the region, January-June 2004: Belgium (AI Index: EUR 01/005/2004)
- Stop Violence against Women: Belgium – breaking the cycle of violence (AI Index: EUR 14/001/2004)
- Belgium: Prompt action needed to address human rights concerns (AI Index: EUR 14/002/2004)

BHUTAN

KINGDOM OF BHUTAN
Head of state: King Jigme Singye Wangchuck
Head of government: Yeshey Zimba (replaced Jigmi Thinley in August)
Death penalty: abolitionist for all crimes
International Criminal Court: not signed
UN Women's Convention: ratified
Optional Protocol to UN Women's Convention: not signed

There was little progress towards a durable solution for more than 100,000 refugees from southern Bhutan living in camps in eastern Nepal. Nepali-speaking people in southern Bhutan continued to face discrimination. In March Bhutan abolished the death penalty.

Background
The government continued drafting Bhutan's first Constitution, a process that began in 2002. A draft Constitution was expected to be made public in early 2005 and form the basis for public consultations at *Dzongkhag* (district) level.

On 16 January Bhutan announced the end of a month-long operation to expel from its territory three armed separatist groups from north-east India – the United Liberation Front of Assam, National Democratic Front of Bodoland and Kamtapur Liberation Organization. It was reported by Bhutanese and Indian officials that 30 camps were destroyed and 650 combatants killed or taken into custody during the operation. Bhutanese authorities also said that up to 65,000 local people had been moved for their safety. In March the Bhutanese authorities launched a further operation against remaining members of India-based armed separatist groups. There were unconfirmed reports that Bhutanese civilians suspected of supporting these groups had been arrested and tortured.

In January Bhutan presented its first report to the UN Committee on the Elimination of Discrimination Against Women. The Committee identified access to education and political involvement as areas where women continue to be disadvantaged and called on Bhutan to include the principle of gender equality in its draft Constitution.

Refugees
Efforts to resolve the situation of Bhutanese refugees in eastern Nepal remained blocked during 2004. There was no progress in the first few months of the year, after Bhutan suspended talks following a violent incident during a visit by Bhutanese officials to Khudunabari refugee camp in December 2003. Only after Nepal issued a report into the incident in May did Bhutan accept in principle that the process could restart. However, there was no resumption of official bilateral talks or implementation of the agreement reached between Nepal and Bhutan in 2003 on the return of some refugees. Moreover, there were serious concerns about the conditions under which refugees might be required to return, and about the lack of monitoring of the process, since the UN refugee agency UNHCR continued to be denied access to Bhutan.

Following an announcement in 2003 of plans to reduce assistance in the camps, UNHCR planned to re-register the refugees. However, by the end of 2004, the Nepal government had not agreed to this.

In October, a US Assistant Secretary of State visited India, Bhutan and Nepal in a high-level initiative aimed at resolving the stalemate.

Death penalty
On 20 March the King issued a Royal Decree abolishing capital punishment. Although Bhutan is not known to have carried out an execution since 1964, the death penalty had previously been retained as a punishment for treason.

Education
Children in southern Bhutan continued to face discrimination in access to education, in violation of the UN Children's Convention. It was reported that children from the Nepali-speaking community, especially those whose relatives were living in refugee camps in Nepal, as well as some Christian children, faced difficulties obtaining the Security Clearance Certificate required to enrol in school and sit exams.

Possible prisoners of conscience
A number of possible prisoners of conscience from southern and eastern Bhutan remained in prison, although there were unconfirmed reports that some had been released on completion of their sentences.

AI country reports/ visits
- Amnesty International's concerns at the 55th Session of the Executive Committee of the United Nations High Commissioner for Refugees (AI Index: IOR 41/031/2004)
- Death Penalty News, June 2004 (AI Index: ACT 53/001/2004)

BOLIVIA

REPUBLIC OF BOLIVIA

Head of state and government: Carlos Mesa Gisbert
Death penalty: abolitionist for ordinary crimes
International Criminal Court: ratified
UN Women's Convention and its Optional Protocol: ratified

Torture and ill-treatment of detainees continued to be reported and prison conditions remained harsh. There was concern at delays in the investigations of confrontations between protesters and the security forces in 2003 which left over 100 people dead and hundreds more injured.

Background

2004 was dominated by political instability and social unrest.

In July, a referendum was held on the future of Bolivia's natural gas resources, the second largest in South America. The referendum, which was seen as a vote of confidence in the current administration, took place amid discontent, calls for a boycott and threats to burn ballot boxes. The government won the referendum.

A number of judicial complaints were filed against former President Gonzalo Sánchez de Lozada and members of his administration in connection with the killings of scores of demonstrators by members of the security forces in October 2003. Congress gave its authorization for legal proceedings to go ahead in October 2004.

Impunity

In May the Senate approved a bilateral agreement with the USA granting absolute immunity from international prosecution to US nationals accused by the International Criminal Court of committing genocide, crimes against humanity or war crimes. The agreement was awaiting ratification by the Chamber of Deputies by the end of the year.

Ill-treatment in detention

Conditions in many prisons amounted to cruel, inhuman and degrading treatment. Overcrowding and a lack of recreation, medical and rehabilitation facilities were commonplace. There were reports of ill-treatment of detainees.

In April, Francisco Javier Villanueva, a Spanish national, was detained in Santa Cruz, by plain-clothes police officers. He alleged that the officers, who failed to produce an arrest warrant, took him to an unidentified location where they beat him and threatened to kill him; put his head under water until he nearly drowned; and gave him electric shocks in an attempt to make him confess to involvement in the killing of a provincial prosecutor in the city of Santa Cruz in February.

Investigations into killings of demonstrators in 2003

Investigations into the killings of more than 100 people by the security forces in February and October 2003 made slow progress. Concerns intensified during the year about the impartiality, independence and thoroughness of the investigations. In February the Military Court acquitted four members of the armed forces accused of killing two civilians during a demonstration in February 2003 in La Paz. In July prosecutors in charge of the investigations into the October killings announced that they intended to close the investigations because it was "technically" impossible to identify those responsible for the deaths. However, in May, the Constitutional Court ruled that the four armed forces members should be tried by the ordinary courts and investigations were continuing under the jurisdiction of the ordinary courts at the end of the year.

AI country reports/ visits
Reports

- Bolivia: Crisis and justice – Days of violence in February and October 2003 (AI Index: AMR 18/006/2004)
- Bolivia: Ill-health of Francisco Cortés, peasant leader (AI Index: AMR 18/001/2004)
- Bolivia: New open letter to all Honourable Deputies of the Bolivian National Congress urging them to reject the bilateral agreement with the United States on the International Criminal Court (AI Index: AMR 18/002/2004)

BOSNIA AND HERZEGOVINA

BOSNIA AND HERZEGOVINA
Head of state: rotating presidency – Dragan Čović,
Sulejman Tihić and Borislav Paravac
Head of government: Adnan Terzić
President of the Federation of Bosnia and
Herzegovina: Niko Lozančić
President of the Republika Srpska: Dragan Čavić
Death penalty: abolitionist for all crimes
International Criminal Court: ratified
UN Women's Convention and its Optional Protocol:
ratified

Impunity for war crimes and crimes against humanity committed during the 1992-95 war continued to be widespread. Thousands of "disappearances" were still unresolved. While perpetrators of wartime violations continued to enjoy impunity, victims and their families were denied access to justice and redress. Lack of cooperation with the International Criminal Tribunal for the former Yugoslavia (Tribunal), particularly by the Republika Srpska (RS), was a major obstacle to justice. The efforts of the authorities to tackle impunity in proceedings before domestic courts remained largely insufficient, although some war crimes trials were conducted. According to the UN High Commissioner for Refugees (UNHCR), the number of people displaced by the war who had returned to their homes reached one million in July. However, many returns were not sustainable as returnees continued to face discrimination and, in some cases, violent attacks.

Background

Bosnia and Herzegovina (BiH) remained divided in two semi-autonomous entities, the RS and the Federation of Bosnia and Herzegovina (FBiH), with a special status granted to the Brčko District. The international community continued to exert significant influence over the country's political process, in particular through a High Representative with executive powers, nominated by the Peace Implementation Council, an intergovernmental body that monitors implementation of the Dayton Peace Agreement.

In December the peacekeeping Operation Althea/EUFOR, led by the European Union (EU), was launched as the direct descendant, under the Dayton Peace Agreement, of the NATO-led Stabilisation Force (SFOR). In addition to approximately 7,000 EUFOR troops, about 150 NATO troops remained, reportedly to assist the authorities in combating "terrorism" and in defence reform. The EU Police Mission, which included approximately 500 police officers, remained to monitor and supervise the activities of the local police.

A special Human Rights Commission within the Constitutional Court was established in January, to deal with the backlog of cases registered with the Human Rights Chamber before its closure in December 2003. As of December 2004, the Commission had resolved 3,231 applications, while 5,710 remained pending.

Wartime human rights violations
International prosecutions

The Tribunal continued to try alleged perpetrators of serious violations of international humanitarian law, but faced increasing financial constraints.

In March the Tribunal indicted Jadranko Prlić, Bruno Stojić, Slobodan Praljak, Milivoj Petković, Valentin Ćorić and Berislav Pušić, former commanders in the Croatian Defence Council (HVO), the Bosnian Croat armed forces. They were charged with crimes against humanity and war crimes against the non-Croat population. All the accused surrendered voluntarily to the Tribunal.

In March, Ranko Češić, a former member of the RS Army (VRS) and police reserve in Brčko, was sentenced to 18 years' imprisonment after he admitted 12 counts of crimes against humanity and war crimes. Miroslav Deronjić, former President of the Bratunac Municipal Board of the Serbian Democratic Party, received a 10-year sentence after pleading guilty to crimes against the non-Serbian population in the village of Glogova. Darko Mrđa, a former Prijedor police officer, was sentenced to 17 years in prison after he admitted his role in the murder in 1992 of over 200 non-Serbian civilians.

In April the Tribunal's Appeals Chamber found that genocide was committed in Srebrenica in 1995, and sentenced Radislav Krstić, a former general in the Bosnian Serb army, to 35 years' imprisonment for aiding and abetting genocide.

In June judges in the trial of Slobodan Milošević, former President of the Federal Republic of Yugoslavia, rejected a motion that genocide and other charges be withdrawn.

In October, Ljubiša Beara, former Chief of Security in the VRS, indicted for alleged crimes against the non-Serbian population in Srebrenica, was transferred to the Tribunal's custody. The Tribunal unsealed an indictment against Miroslav Bralo, a former HVO member, charging him with crimes in 1993 against Bosnian Muslims in the Lašva Valley. He voluntarily surrendered in November and was transferred to the Tribunal's custody.

In December Dragomir Milošević, who had been indicted for his alleged role, as a VRS commander, in the shelling of Sarajevo, voluntarily surrendered to the authorities of Serbia and Montenegro. He was subsequently transferred to the Tribunal's custody.

Cooperation between the RS authorities and the Tribunal remained inadequate. Most of the 19 publicly indicted suspects at large at the end of 2004 were Bosnian Serbs thought to be in neighbouring Serbia and Montenegro or in the RS. In April the RS police raided the family homes of Milan Lukić and Sredoje Lukić, indicted by the Tribunal for alleged crimes against the non-Serbian population near the town of Višegrad. The raid did not result in any arrest, and Milan Lukić's brother Novica was killed.

Domestic investigations and prosecutions

In September and October legislation was passed to regulate the functioning of a War Crimes Chamber to become operational within the State Court of Bosnia and Herzegovina in early 2005. There was some progress in making fully operational the new national criminal investigation agency (SIPA). In July the Office of the High Representative set up a police restructuring commission to develop reform policies and draft legislation, which in December proposed that SIPA, the State Border Service and local police forces be united in a single national police structure.

In a joint action in October, SIPA and SFOR officers arrested a man suspected of war crimes against the Bosnian Muslim population in Foča. He was reportedly shot and wounded after opening fire to resist arrest.

The domestic criminal justice system persistently failed to actively prosecute alleged war criminals as the judiciary and police services in the FBiH and the RS failed to cooperate with each other. In November the RS police arrested eight men alleged to have committed war crimes against the Bosnian Muslim population, but high-level suspects continued to evade arrest.

Victims, witnesses and courts remained without adequate protection from harassment, intimidation and threats, pending implementation of a comprehensive witness protection programme.

The trials for war crimes that did take place before local courts were mostly in the FBiH.

▭ In January the Mostar Cantonal Court acquitted Željko Džidić, Mate Aničić, Ivan Škutor and Erhard Poznić of war crimes charges, including their alleged involvement in the "disappearance" of 13 Bosnian Serb soldiers in Mostar in 1993, reportedly for lack of evidence.

▭ In February, Ratko Gašović, a former member of a Serbian paramilitary group, was sentenced to 10 years' imprisonment by the Sarajevo Cantonal Court for war crimes against the civilian population, including the rape of a non-Serbian woman. In November the sentence was reduced to eight years on appeal.

▭ In May the trial of 11 former police officers from Prijedor opened at the Banja Luka District Court. They were accused of the abduction and murder of Father Tomislav Matanović, a Roman Catholic priest, and his parents in 1995. The trial was continuing at the end of 2004.

▭ In June proceedings resumed at the Zenica Cantonal Court against Dominik Ilijašević, a former Bosnian Croat military commander accused of war crimes committed against Bosniak civilians in Stupni Do in central Bosnia. The trial reportedly had to be restarted after a suspension of the proceedings exceeded 30 days. It had not concluded by the end of the year.

▭ In December, Zoran Knežević, a former VRS member, was sentenced to 10 years' imprisonment by the Sarajevo Cantonal Court for raping two non-Serb women in the Sarajevo district of Grbavica in 1992 and 1994.

Srebrenica Commission

In January a Commission of Inquiry established by the RS authorities began investigating the massive human rights violations after the fall of Srebrenica in July 1995. In 2003 the Human Rights Chamber had ordered the RS authorities to conduct a full, meaningful, thorough and detailed investigation into the human rights violations which took place in and around Srebrenica between 10 and 19 July 1995. After the Commission's preliminary report in April highlighted systematic obstruction by the RS military, police and intelligence authorities, the High Representative ordered a number of measures to support the work of the Commission, including the dismissal of the Commission's Chairman and other RS officials.

In October the Commission's final report contained evidence of the participation of the RS police and armed forces in the killing of 7,800 non-Serbs after the fall of Srebrenica. It identified the location of mass graves, some of which were previously unknown. In November the RS government for the first time apologized for the human rights violations in and around Srebrenica.

'Disappearances' and missing persons

According to data from the International Committee of the Red Cross, almost 17,000 persons who went missing during the conflict are still unaccounted for. Many of them "disappeared" after being taken into custody by the military and security forces; those responsible have continued to enjoy impunity.

The exhumation of mass graves identified by the Srebrenica Commission began in June. By the end of 2004, the bodies of approximately 1,300 people killed after the fall of Srebrenica had been exhumed and identified.

Between August and November the remains of 456 people were exhumed from a mass grave in Kevljani, near Prijedor. The bodies are believed to be of former Bosnian Muslim inmates of the Omarska and Keraterm detention camps run by the Bosnian Serb authorities.

Right to return in safety and with dignity

Some 18,900 people returned to their pre-war homes between January and October, according to the UNHCR field mission in Bosnia and Herzegovina. Although just over one million displaced people are estimated to have returned to their homes since the end of the conflict, hundreds of thousands have not returned or have not been able to stay in their pre-war communities. In many cases, they have been deterred by the lack of jobs or access to employment. As well as the effects of a weak economy and the difficulties of economic transition and post-war reconstruction, returnees have faced discrimination on ethnic grounds when trying to find work. In some cases, they have been subjected to ethnically motivated violence.

Violations by peacekeeping forces

SFOR troops continued to arbitrarily detain people suspected of providing support to suspected war criminals indicted by the Tribunal. No arrest warrants were known to have been issued against such SFOR detainees, who were sometimes detained without charge or trial for several weeks.

In April, SFOR troops raided a Serbian Orthodox church and a neighbouring priest's home in Pale, reportedly in an attempt to apprehend former RS leader Radovan Karadžić, indicted by the Tribunal on charges of genocide, crimes against humanity and war crimes. The operation did not result in an arrest, but the priest and his son were seriously wounded, reportedly as a result of an explosive charge used in the forced entry of the priest's residence.

'War on terror'

In February, Amgad Fath Allah Yusuf 'Amir was released from custody in the FBiH. He had been arrested in July 2003 for allegedly carrying forged documents. The authorities in Egypt subsequently requested his extradition, claiming that he was a member of an armed Islamist group. AI was concerned that he would face the death penalty if extradited.

In May the wife of one of six men of Algerian origin who were illegally transferred to US custody in 2002 by the FBiH authorities and detained in Guantánamo Bay, Cuba, was reportedly beaten by three unidentified assailants at her flat in Sarajevo. A criminal investigation was opened. In July the cases of two of the men were included in a petition for a writ of habeas corpus by the New York-based Center for Constitutional Rights, seeking to challenge the lawfulness of their detention.

Human trafficking

In March the State Court imposed prison sentences of up to nine years on four members of an organized criminal network for trafficking women and girls who were forced into prostitution in a chain of nightclubs in Prijedor. The accused were convicted of organized crime and human trafficking. In July the State Court sentenced two men, including the owner of a nightclub in Kiseljak, near Sarajevo, to up to 15 months' imprisonment for offences related to the trafficking of women for forced prostitution.

AI country reports/ visits
Reports
- The apparent lack of accountability of international peacekeeping forces in Kosovo and Bosnia-Herzegovina (AI Index: EUR 05/002/2004)
- Europe and Central Asia: Summary of Amnesty International's concerns in the region, January-June 2004: Bosnia and Herzegovina (AI Index: EUR 01/005/2004)

BRAZIL

FEDERATIVE REPUBLIC OF BRAZIL
Head of state and government: Luiz Inácio Lula da Silva
Death penalty: abolitionist for ordinary crimes
International Criminal Court: ratified
UN Women's Convention: ratified with reservations
Optional Protocol to UN Women's Convention: ratified

Levels of human rights violations continued to be extremely high, despite a number of initiatives by the federal government's Special Secretariat of Human Rights. Reports of ineffective, violent, and corrupt policing raised doubts about the effectiveness of government proposals for reform. Hundreds, possibly thousands, of civilians were killed by police in alleged gun battles. Few if any of the cases were fully investigated. There were consistent reports of police participation in "death squads". The use of torture was widespread and systematic. The prison system was characterized by overcrowding, riots and corruption. Federal and state authorities provided limited protection for human rights defenders under threat. Rural and indigenous activists continued to be threatened, attacked and killed. Human rights violators remained largely unpunished. Following national and international condemnation the federal government promised to begin opening files detailing violations by the former military regime.

Background

The government maintained a tight fiscal policy ensuring payment of its foreign debt. While the country saw record growth rates for the first half of the year this came at the expense of large parts of its social spending. Combating hunger continued to be central to the government's social policy although it suffered criticism for its failure to meet promised land reform targets, among other things.

The Special Secretariat of Human Rights launched a number of projects, including a new campaign against torture. The government pushed through legislative proposals such as the reform of the judiciary, which included mechanisms for dealing with human rights crimes at federal level. Human rights groups were concerned that these proposals would not be effectively implemented due to insufficient political and financial support.

In addition to enacting gun control legislation the government launched a disarmament campaign, which included cash payments for handing in guns. However, it failed to follow up on the support, expressed by the President, for an international campaign for an arms trade treaty to control sales of small arms.

Following his visit in October the UN Special Rapporteur on the independence of judges and lawyers condemned the slowness of the judicial system, its exclusion of certain groups and the vulnerable position of children and adolescents within the system.

Public security and police killings

There were consistent reports from around the country of corrupt, violent and discriminatory policing. In shanty towns policing operations were usually seen as invasive and repressive. Military and civil police often contributed to violence and crime in poor and marginalized areas, which remained focal points for extreme levels of armed violence, often related to drug trafficking.

Official figures cited 663 killings by police in the state of São Paulo and 983 in Rio de Janeiro state. Both figures were lower than in recent years. The vast majority of the victims were young, poor, black or mixed-race men. While investigations were opened into some of these cases, few progressed very far.

Members of state police forces were attacked or killed both on and off duty. Eighty-two police officers were killed in São Paulo and Rio de Janeiro while on duty.

The government's national public security plan to reform state police forces, reportedly based on human rights principles, failed to live up to expectations. While some states began to implement elements of the plan, few adopted its fundamentals. Demands from elements of the media and public for more repressive policing in response to violent crime further hindered reform. The new national security force, created as part of the plan, was first used in the state of Espírito Santo in November, following reported attacks by drug gangs.

The Rio de Janeiro state government repeatedly failed to provide protection for marginalized communities facing invasion by drug gangs. Response by the military police to the violent invasions of two shanty towns, Rocinha in April and Vigário Geral in October, were belated and, in the case of Rocinha, violent. Following one of the invasions the state governor requested federal authorization to deploy the army on the streets. The request was effectively denied when the Rio de Janeiro government refused to adhere to stipulations requested by the federal government.

⌂ On 3 February, Flávio Ferreira Sant'Ana, a black dentist from São Paulo, was reportedly extrajudicially executed after being detained by military police officers searching for a shoplifter. Officers were reported to have planted a gun by his body, stating that he was killed in a shootout. There were strong indications that the killing was racially motivated. An investigation was opened.

'Death squads'

Across the country "death squads" continued to participate in the extrajudicial executions of criminal suspects in situations sometimes described as "social cleansing" as well as in the context of organized crime, often with the direct involvement of former and active police officers.

⌂ Between 19 and 22 August, seven homeless people were beaten to death in the centre of São Paulo. Two military police officers and a private security guard were subsequently charged with the killings. However, the charges were dropped on grounds of insufficient evidence.

There were some initiatives to curb the problem. In Bahia a state government task force dismantled several "death squads" throughout the year. In December a federal judge ordered the dissolution of Scuderie Detetive Le Cocq, a police benevolence organization with paramilitary characteristics long implicated in "death squad" activity, organized crime and corruption in Espírito Santo. In Pernambuco a military policeman, a prominent "death squad" member, was sentenced to 14 years' imprisonment for the 1999 killing of Josenildo João de Freitas Junior.

Torture and ill-treatment

Torture continued to be widespread and systematic in prisons, police stations and at point of arrest. The federal government stated that since 1997 a total of 240 people had been convicted for torture, pending further appeals.

However, there was concern at the continued failure to effectively implement recommendations made in 2000 by the UN Special Rapporteur on torture.

⌂ On 21 January, Rômulo Batista de Melo, a student, was arrested, accused of stealing a car that belonged to his friend. He died after suffering severe cranial injuries while in custody. The civil police alleged that the injuries were self-inflicted. Three policemen were charged with his killing.

In São Paulo's prisons, numbers of riots reportedly fell, following the introduction of new punishment systems – the Differentiated Disciplinary Regime and the Special Disciplinary Regime. Detainees informed AI that these regimes were abusive and used arbitrarily by prison directors. One prison director was unable to explain to AI what legal safeguards existed in such circumstances.

Severe overcrowding, insanitary conditions, riots, prisoner-on-prisoner violence and the systematic use of torture and ill-treatment pervaded the detention system. Extensive corruption and an ineffective criminal justice system added to the pressures.

⌂ In May, seven adolescents aged between 15 and 17 died in a fire they had started in Complexo de Defesa da Cidadania, a juvenile detention centre in Teresina, Piauí state. Police reportedly poured water over the boys through the cell window but refused to let them out. Charges were brought against the mother of one of the detainees for providing him with matches and against one military policeman for failing to find the matches during a routine search. Charges against the State Social Security Secretary, responsible for the centre, were dropped following a judicial ruling.

⌂ On 31 May, 30 detainees were killed when members of Rio de Janeiro's drug gangs rioted in the Casa de Custodia de Benfica, in the state capital. The riot took place following a decision to mix gang members together in the prison.

⌂ The Urso Branco prison, in the northern state of Rondonia, was again the scene of riots, abuse and torture. In April, 14 detainees were killed by other prisoners during a riot. This brought the number of killings in the prison to 78 since May 2001, underlining the failure of federal and state authorities to comply with measures issued by the Inter-American Commission on Human Rights in 2002. As a result of the failure to comply the case was sent before the Inter-American Court of Human Rights, the first case that Brazil has had to face there, and upheld.

Human rights defenders

Human rights defenders suffered threats, attacks, defamation and killings. Existing protection mechanisms continued to be weak. In October the federal government launched its first programme for the protection of human rights defenders, which aimed to use special units of the state police to protect those under threat. The project was welcomed as a first step, but many non-governmental organizations (NGOs) expressed concern that it transferred responsibility from federal to state authorities, often the very source of the threat.

In May the federal police appealed against orders to provide protection to Roberto Monte, Ruy dos Santos and José Veras Junior. They argued that as the three were not federal employees they should be protected by the state, not the federal authorities. Roberto Monte, an employee of the Centre for Human Rights and Collective Memory in Natal, Rio Grande do Norte, continued to receive threats for denouncing local "death squads" which included members of the state police.

In November an internal memo was made public instructing civil police in São Paulo to monitor trade unions, NGOs and social movements such as the Landless Workers' Movement. The state civil police chief reportedly stated that the order to monitor these organizations had come from the National Secretariat of Public Security in Brasília. An official investigation into the memo was launched by the state Public Prosecutor's Office.

Land and indigenous rights

The number of land activists and union leaders threatened and killed remained a serious concern. The Pastoral Land Commission (Commissão Pastoral da Terra, CPT) cited 29 killings up to November, 15 in the south of Pará state.

◻ On 29 January, Ezequiel de Moraes Nascimento, president of a rural workers' association, was shot in front of his family by two men in Redenção, south of Pará. Eight days later Ribamar Francisco dos Santos, treasurer of the Rural Workers' Union, was shot in front of his house in Rondon, south of Pará. The union president, Maria Joelma da Costa, continued to receive death threats. Proposals to withdraw her police protection were discarded following intervention by the CPT.

◻ On 20 November, five members of the Landless Workers' Movement were killed and 13 injured by masked gunmen in Felisburgo, Minas Gerais. Four men were later arrested, including a local landowner.

Indigenous peoples continued to face threats, attacks and violent evictions in their struggle for land rights. Failures to ensure their entitlement to their lands left them vulnerable to attacks and land invasions by illegal settlers, loggers and diamond miners among others.

◻ In January settlers invaded a Catholic mission in the indigenous reserve of Raposa Serra do Sol in Roraima state, following a government announcement that indigenous land claims would finally receive presidential approval. They held three missionaries hostage for three days, reportedly subjecting them to psychological torture and humiliation. The settlers, apparently coordinated by local landowners, also blocked roads in the area and threatened further attacks against indigenous communities. The process of granting the land to the indigenous inhabitants was postponed. It was subsequently further delayed by legal appeals and at the end of 2004 attacks and threats were ongoing.

In April police opened an investigation into the killings of 29 men who had been illegally mining on land belonging to the Cinta Larga indigenous people in the state of Rondônia. In December 2003 an investigative commission formed by members of the Rondônia legislative assembly warned of impending violence and called for federal intervention, including the presence of the army, in order to prevent conflict and illegal mining in the region. This was not provided. In November police announced they were charging 10 members of the indigenous community with the killings.

According to reports, the problem of slave labour continued to grow. However, the government brought in important legislation which allowed for the confiscation of lands on which slave or indentured labour was used. State officials and human rights activists working to combat the problem were threatened, attacked and killed.

◻ On 28 January, three Ministry of Labour inspectors and their driver were killed in Unaí, Minas Gerais, while inspecting farms in the region for slave labour. Four men, including a local landowner, were charged in relation to the killings.

Past human rights violations

Efforts to improve the human rights situation in the country continued to be undermined by the failure to punish those responsible for past violations, although some notable convictions were achieved.

◻ Eight years after the killing of 19 land activists in Eldorado dos Carájas by members of the Pará state military police, the two commanding officers involved in the killings had their prison sentences upheld in November. A request for a retrial of 145 other military policemen involved in the incident was rejected. They had all been acquitted previously. Appeals were pending on all decisions.

◻ Twelve years after the killing of 111 detainees in the Carandiru detention centre nobody had been imprisoned for the crimes. The military police colonel in charge of the operation, who was awaiting an appeal hearing against his conviction and sentence of 632 years, was working as a São Paulo state deputy. None of the 105 military police officers charged had yet stood trial.

In November a court in Pernambuco sentenced a man to 19 years' imprisonment for involvement with ordering the 1998 killing of indigenous leader Chicão Xucuru.

In response to a photograph published in a national newspaper in October, the army released a statement defending the repressive actions of the 1964-1985 military regime, stating that it had laid the foundations for a democratic Brazil. Although the statement was later withdrawn, the subsequent uproar led to the Minister of Defence resigning. No military officers resigned. In December, a federal court ordered the government to open files held on resistance against the dictatorship.

AI country reports/ visits
Visit
In July and August AI delegates visited São Paulo, Rio de Janeiro, Brasília, Espírito Santo, Minas Gerais, Mato Grosso do Sul and Pernambuco.

BRUNEI DARUSSALAM

BRUNEI DARUSSALAM
Head of state and government: Sultan Haji Hassanal Bolkiah
Death penalty: abolitionist in practice
International Criminal Court: not signed
UN Women's Convention and its Optional Protocol: not signed

The Internal Security Act (ISA), which allows for detention without trial, was used against people suspected of "subversive activities" and money counterfeiting. The death penalty was applied for drugs offences. Criminal suspects were sentenced to caning. Amendments to the Immigration Act introduced mandatory caning for some immigration offences.

Background
Under a 1962 state of emergency, constitutional provisions safeguarding fundamental liberties remained suspended. The monarch, Sultan Haji Hassanal Bolkiah, continued to exercise a wide range of executive powers, holding the offices of Prime Minister, Defence Minister, Finance Minister and head of the police. In July the Sultan ordered the reconvening of an appointed Legislative Council (last convened in 1984). The Council approved a constitutional amendment opening the way for the creation of a 45-member parliament, including 15 elected representatives.

Internal Security Act
People continued to be arrested under the ISA, which allows the Minister of Home Affairs, with the approval of the Sultan, to detain anyone deemed to be a threat to national security or public order. The Minister is empowered to sign two-year detention orders renewable indefinitely. ISA detainees are denied the rights to a trial, to legal counsel and to be presumed innocent. Those arrested were at risk of ill-treatment or torture during prolonged interrogation while held in isolation.

In July, three men were detained under the ISA. One, a former police officer, was accused of treason for leaking sensitive or classified documents. The two others, a former police Special Branch officer and a businessman, were accused of disseminating "subversive propaganda" after posting secret or sensitive information on the Internet.

In July, six alleged former members of the Al-Arqam Islamist group detained in September 2003 were released after they had sworn loyalty to the Sultan. Following months of religious "rehabilitation" while in detention, the men reportedly "confessed" and expressed remorse for attempting to revive the banned group.

Sixteen men were detained under the ISA between late 2003 and early 2004 accused of involvement in the distribution of counterfeit currency.

Death penalty and corporal punishment
In October the High Court sentenced a Malaysian national to death for possession of cannabis. Although death sentences have been imposed for drugs and other serious criminal offences in recent years, no executions were known to have been carried out since 1957.

Caning continued to be carried out as a mandatory punishment for a range of criminal offences. In February amendments to the Immigration Act introduced stiffer penalties, including mandatory caning, for those found guilty of immigration offences such as illegal entry or overstaying.

BULGARIA

REPUBLIC OF BULGARIA
Head of state: Georgi Parvanov
Head of government: Simeon Saxe-Coburg-Gotha
Death penalty: abolitionist for all crimes
International Criminal Court: ratified
UN Women's Convention: ratified
Optional Protocol to UN Women's Convention: signed

Living conditions and lack of adequate care in many institutions for people with mental disabilities continued to amount to inhuman and degrading treatment. Placement of adults in social care homes was in violation of the right to be free from arbitrary detention. There were reports of ill-treatment and torture by law enforcement officials; few perpetrators were brought to justice. Many of the victims were Roma who also suffered discrimination in other walks of life. Law enforcement officials continued to use firearms in circumstances prohibited by international standards, resulting in deaths and injuries.

Background
The National Assembly failed to take measures that would have contributed to greater respect for basic human rights. In May and October it failed to elect an Ombudsman although the law establishing this office came into force in January. It also failed to appoint an independent body to monitor implementation of the anti-discrimination law adopted in September 2003. In October the Assembly rejected the Draft Law for Establishment of a Fund for Educational Integration of Minority Children, which aims to resolve the problem of segregated schools for Roma children.

People with mental disabilities
The living conditions and lack of appropriate care and treatment in the majority of 12 social care homes visited by an AI delegate in June were so inadequate that they amounted to inhuman and degrading treatment. The rules regarding placement of adults in social care homes had still not been brought into line with international standards to ensure an independent review of the placement decision and provide effective legal safeguards for the people concerned. The staffing in institutions was, to varying degrees, inadequate, particularly at night when lack of appropriate supervision and care endangered residents' physical well-being.

Little improvement was observed in the provision of medical, including psychiatric, care, and other therapies and activities. The process of transferring residents to institutions more appropriate for their needs, initiated in 2002 by the Ministry of Labour and Social Policy, had not been carried out thoroughly and systematically.

The authorities failed to exercise their supervisory function appropriately and effectively. They also failed to put in place legal safeguards to protect residents from abuse and to establish independent mechanisms for investigating incidents of abuse.

◻ On 24 February, in the early morning, Yoncho Filipov Lazarov, a resident of Govezhda, died after he was reportedly pushed by an agitated fellow resident. There were only two people on duty to care for more than 65 residents. The staff apparently made no risk assessment when returning the agitated resident to the dormitory and did not supervise him following his return.

It appeared that the order of the Ministry of Labour and Social Policy prohibiting seclusion of residents was not being strictly enforced in all institutions. Also, there were no detailed guidelines regulating the use of restraint and seclusion methods in line with international standards and best professional practices.

No attempt was made to revise civil law regarding guardianship to bring it in line with international standards and to rectify the practice whereby an institution's director or another staff member is appointed as guardian of residents in their care.

Some effort was directed at arrangements to reintegrate into the community people who had been placed in institutions. In October, six women from "Kachulka village", a social care home for women with mental disabilities, were placed in a sheltered home in Sliven.

Other progress related to the care of children formerly in Fakia institution. In December 2003, 31 children were transferred to an institution in Mezdra, where living conditions and care, particularly medical care, were considerably better. However, inadequate staffing levels particularly affected children with complex needs in Mezdra and most other children's institutions.

In May the UN Committee against Torture expressed concern about poor conditions in homes for people with mental disabilities and the insufficient measures taken by the authorities to address the situation. Similar concerns were expressed by the European Committee for the Prevention of Torture and Inhuman or Degrading Treatment or Punishment in a report published in June on its visits to Bulgaria in April 2002 and December 2003.

Torture and ill-treatment
There were reports of ill-treatment by law enforcement officials that in some instances amounted to torture. Many of the incidents took place when the authorities failed to respect other rights of detainees, including the right to be questioned in the presence of a lawyer.

◻ In March, when Boris Daskalov refused to make a statement without his lawyer present, police at the Second Police Station in Plovdiv reportedly handcuffed his arms around his legs, inserted a wooden stick between his arms and knees, and suspended him between two chairs. According to reports, Boris Daskalov was gagged and beaten on the soles of his feet with rubber truncheons. He subsequently signed a statement written by the police and was released. In April it was reported that the Ministry of the Interior Inspectorate had initiated disciplinary proceedings against four police officers involved.

Investigations into most complaints of police ill-treatment were not prompt, thorough and impartial. In May the European Court of Human Rights made a ruling in the case of Girgina Toteva who alleged she had been beaten in a police station in Sevlievo in 1995 when aged 67. Following her complaint about the ill-treatment, she was charged with causing a police officer bodily injury and sentenced to six months' suspended imprisonment. The Court found that Girgina Toteva had suffered inhuman and degrading treatment by police officers and that the investigation into her allegations had been ineffective.

In May the UN Committee against Torture expressed concern about "numerous allegations of ill-treatment of persons in custody that may amount to torture, in particular during police interviews, which disproportionately affect the Roma, and the lack of an independent system to investigate complaints..." It recommended the establishment of an effective, reliable and independent complaint system.

Roma

In addition to the police ill-treatment of Roma, there were several reports of racist assaults on Roma, most of them carried out by skinhead groups. Roma also suffered discrimination in other walks of life. In a report published in January the European Commission against Racism and Intolerance (ECRI) concluded that there was still discrimination against minority groups, particularly Roma, and expressed concern about the excessive use of firearms and force by the police against Roma. ECRI also highlighted the problem of segregation of Roma children in schools.

In January, two police officers with a dog approached Assen Zarev, a Romani man who was playing with his five children in the Fakulteta neighbourhood in Sofia, according to the Romani Baht Foundation and the European Roma Rights Center, both non-governmental organizations. When Assen Zarev said he did not know the whereabouts of men being sought by the police, the officers reportedly set their dog on Assen Zarev, who was bitten twice. The officers reportedly hit Assen Zarev all over his body, threatened to shoot him, and took him to nearby woods where the ill-treatment continued. A group of people from the neighbourhood, mostly women, followed the police to protest against Assen Zarev's treatment. The officers reportedly fired warning shots to disperse the crowd and then released Assen Zarev. Four days later, 16 police officers returned to the Roma neighbourhood and arrested 17 men, saying that after the incident in the woods some of the Roma had assaulted the police. The 17 were verbally abused while being taken to the Third Police Station for questioning. They were released later the same day. An investigation into these incidents was initiated by the Sofia Regional Prosecutor, but its results were not known by the end of the year.

Unlawful use of firearms

At least two people were shot dead and several others were injured by law enforcement officials using firearms in breach of international standards. The authorities failed to revise legal provisions on the use of firearms or to ensure that investigations into reported incidents were carried out independently and impartially.

In February the European Court of Human Rights published its ruling in the case of *Nachova v Bulgaria*. The case concerned the July 1996 killing by a major in the military police of two unarmed Romani men in the village of Lesura. The Court found the state responsible for the deaths as well as the failure to conduct an effective official investigation. The Court also found a violation of the provision of Article 14 (prohibition of racial discrimination), concluding that the Bulgarian authorities had "failed in their duty... to take all possible steps to establish whether or not discriminatory attitudes may have played a role" in the shooting of the two Romani men.

In March in Plovdiv, a 25-year-old Romani man was shot in the head by a police officer from the Sixth District Police Station, according to the local non-governmental Human Rights Project. The police stated that an officer, who had pursued and then caught a suspect who refused to stop for an identity check, shot the suspect in the head after he was threatened with a knife. The victim's family stated that he had never been involved in violence and was not known to carry a knife. The Interior Ministry reportedly initiated an investigation into the incident and temporarily suspended two officers from duty. The results of the investigation were not known by the end of the year.

Attack on freedom of religion

On 21 and 22 July police raided about 250 places of worship, monasteries and other properties linked to the Alternative Synod of the Bulgarian Orthodox Church, and closed them down. Many priests and laymen arrested during the action were reportedly ill-treated and arbitrarily detained. The official Synod received additional state endorsement in the Denominations Act adopted in 2002, which had been criticized by the Council of Europe for imposing unacceptable restrictions on the right to freedom of religion.

AI country reports/ visits
Reports
- Europe and Central Asia: Summary of Amnesty International's concerns in the region, January-June 2004: Bulgaria (AI Index: EUR 01/005/2004)
- Bulgaria: Children of Dzhurkovo denied life of dignity and respect (AI Index: EUR 15/002/2004)

Visit

AI delegates visited Bulgaria in June and went to 12 social care homes for children and adults with mental disabilities.

BURKINA FASO

BURKINA FASO
Head of state: Blaise Compaoré
Head of government: Ernest Yonli
Death penalty: abolitionist in practice
International Criminal Court: ratified
UN Women's Convention: ratified
Optional Protocol to UN Women's Convention: signed

Opposition activists were arrested and held in incommunicado detention. No progress was made in bringing to justice those responsible for political killings in 1998 or the alleged extrajudicial execution of more than 100 people in 2001 and 2002.

Background

Burkina Faso was accused by the governments of Côte d'Ivoire and Mauritania of fuelling instability in the region by protecting and training armed opposition groups. In turn, the Burkinabè authorities accused several members of the opposition National Union for Democracy and Development (Union Nationale pour la Démocratie et le Développement, UNDD) of supplying information to Mauritania, Côte d'Ivoire and Guinea.

Trial before military court

Seven people were sentenced to up to 10 years' imprisonment in April following trials before a military court; there were concerns about the fairness of the trial. The seven were among several people, most of them military officers, who were arrested in October 2003 following an alleged coup attempt. They were accused of plotting against the state. One detainee died in custody two days after his arrest; the authorities claimed he had hanged himself in his cell.

Arrest of UNDD politicians

Noël Yaméogo, a member of UNDD, was arrested in September on his return from Côte d'Ivoire and reportedly kept in incommunicado detention for six days. He remained held at the National Security (Sûreté nationale) headquarters in Ouagadougou at the end of the year awaiting trial on treason charges.

Hermann Yaméogo, leader of UNDD, was held at Ouagadougou airport for four hours in September for questioning. The authorities announced that his parliamentary immunity would be lifted so that he could stand trial for supplying information to Mauritania, Côte d'Ivoire and Guinea.

In November, Mathieu N'do, UNDD spokesperson and director of the weekly newspaper *San Finna*, was detained incommunicado for six days at the National Security headquarters in Ouagadougou. He was questioned about his links with Côte d'Ivoire.

Impunity

No progress was reported in the investigation into the alleged extrajudicial executions of 106 people between October 2001 and January 2002. No one was brought to justice for the killings of journalist Norbert Zongo, Ablassé Nikiema, Ernest Zongo and Blaise Ilboudo in 1998.

BURUNDI

REPUBLIC OF BURUNDI
Head of state and government: Domitien Ndayizeye
Death penalty: retentionist
International Criminal Court: ratified
UN Women's Convention: ratified
Optional Protocol to UN Women's Convention: signed

Conflict was largely restricted to the province around the capital and a precarious calm prevailed in other parts of the country. Serious human rights abuses by all parties were reported, including unlawful killings, torture including rape and other sexual violence, abductions and unlawful detentions. Some 4,788 people remained in detention without trial. At the end of 2004, at least 95,000 people remained internally displaced. At least 90,000 refugees returned home, largely from Tanzania, although people continued to flee Burundi. Over 150 Congolese refugees were killed in an attack on a transit camp close to Bujumbura. At least 44 death sentences were passed.

Background

Little was done to organize elections scheduled for October 2004 under the August 2000 Agreement for Peace and Reconciliation in Burundi (Peace Agreement). The second phase of the transition, due to be ended by the elections, was extended for six months in October. An interim constitution was adopted and adhered to by virtually all political parties, narrowly avoiding a constitutional vacuum. Despite rising political and ethnic tension as October drew near, manipulated by some political leaders, widespread violence did not break out. Local, legislative and presidential elections were postponed until 2005. A national referendum on the constitution was postponed on several occasions and had not taken place by the end of the year.

Armed conflict continued throughout the year in Rural Bujumbura between one armed group, PALIPEHUTU-FNL (Rwasa), commonly referred to as the FNL, and government armed forces and the CNDD-FDD

(Nkurunziza). In June the UN Operation in Burundi (ONUB) took over from the African Union mission. A UN programme to address sexual exploitation by its peacekeepers was initiated.

Progress in implementing agreements between armed groups and the government continued to be slow. Members of various armed groups continued to return from exile, in preparation for demobilization, disarmament and reintegration (DDR). All armed groups recruited fighters, including some child soldiers, to boost their numbers prior to demobilization. Some were also reported to be training for combat, both in southern Burundi and outside the country. Fighters were slow to join pre-assigned cantonment sites. The CNDD-FDD (Nkurunziza) set up a parallel administration in other parts of the country as well as taking part in pro-government military operations. There were a number of clashes between rival armed groups, in particular between the CNDD (Nyangoma) and the CNDD-FDD (Nkurunziza). A DDR programme was launched in December.

Arms were reportedly distributed by various factions to the population, raising fears of further violence. The government took no action to counter the proliferation of small arms.

Between May and August, at least 80 people were arrested in northern Burundi, allegedly on their way to or from Rwanda, and accused of belonging to an armed movement aiming to destabilize the state. Around 30 of them were members of a Tutsi movement, PA Amasekanya, frequently accused of inciting violence. Others were linked to the Tutsi-dominated PARENA party of former President Bagaza. A former Minister of Youth, Sports and Culture, Bonaventure Gasutwa, was arrested in Rwanda and handed over to the Burundian authorities in connection with PA Amasekanya. Over 30 alleged members of the movement were provisionally released in October.

Burundi's economic crisis continued, and the country relied heavily on outside assistance and aid, although many donor pledges did not materialize or fell short of the target. Armed crime increased. Access to health care was extremely difficult for the majority of the population.

Human rights abuses in conflict zones

Government armed forces were responsible for serious human rights abuses against the civilian population in Rural Bujumbura, including routine looting and the destruction of property, rape and extrajudicial executions. Civilians were caught in cross-fire as well as deliberately attacked. CNDD-FDD (Nkurunziza) fighters, who maintained separate bases in Rural Bujumbura operating under an ambiguous command structure, were repeatedly accused of rape, beatings, looting and killings of civilians in the area.

An unknown number of suspected FNL sympathizers were killed by government forces and members of the CNDD-FDD (Nkurunziza), often in arbitrary or reprisal attacks following or during military operations.
◻ A five-year-old boy, a 72-year-old man, Ncahonankwa, and two others were killed by soldiers

from Mubone military position in Kabezi commune on 28 July. The soldiers ordered people to come out from their houses in Gakungwe before opening fire. Two of those killed, including Ncahonankwa, were reportedly bayoneted to death.

In Rural Bujumbura, low-level government officials and civilians suspected of collaborating with the CNDD-FDD (Nkurunziza) were killed by the FNL. The FNL also reportedly recruited child soldiers and continued to administer a parallel justice system, with punishments including beatings and killings.
◻ On 13 August, more than 150 Congolese refugees were killed and more than 100 others injured in an attack on Gatumba transit camp in Rural Bujumbura. The refugees had arrived in Burundi in June and were almost all from the Banyamulenge ethnic group. Nearby Burundian returnees were not harmed. The FNL claimed sole responsibility for the attack. Despite investigations by the UN, the government, Burundian and international human rights groups, at the end of 2004 there was still doubt over whether the FNL had in fact acted alone.

Arrests and abductions by CNDD-FDD (Nkurunziza)

Throughout 2004, the CNDD-FDD (Nkurunziza) operated a parallel "police" force which issued summonses, conducted searches and detained scores of people. Most of those detained appeared to be suspected by local CNDD-FDD (Nkurunziza) commanders of armed robbery or links with the FNL. Some were made to pay "fines" before being released. Others were beaten and had their property looted. All were unlawfully detained and outside the protection of the law. Many suspects were beaten, often severely, and several were reported missing or killed.
◻ Three men – Apollinaire Ndayiziga, Augustin Barakamfitiye and Ntabatamwaka – were beaten to death by members of the CNDD-FDD (Nkurunziza) in June.
◻ Zacharie Ndiwenumuryango, alias Hussein, aged 23, reportedly died on 24 September in a CNDD-FDD (Nkurunziza) place of detention after being badly ill-treated.

Child soldiers

A DDR programme for child soldiers in government forces and two minor armed groups was launched in January. More than 2,300 child soldiers, some as young as 11, had been demobilized by November. Provisional figures for the number of child soldiers to be demobilized under a general DDR programme due to start in November were submitted by other armed groups but the combined figure of approximately 500 was considerably lower than expected. The Ministry of Human Rights acknowledged that child soldiers were probably still within government ranks.

Rape and other sexual violence

Despite increasing awareness and condemnation of widespread rape, both within the home and by combatants, numerous cases of rape and sexual violence were reported. The victims included very young girls, men and young boys. Some women were forced into military barracks before being raped; others were raped as they fled attacks or while collecting firewood or working in their fields.

Partly as a result of collaboration between national human rights groups, international non-governmental organizations (NGOs) and the judiciary, an increasing number of victims received medical care and more cases were brought to court. A medical centre run by Médecins sans Frontières (MSF) in Bujumbura was reportedly receiving over 100 cases a month of sexual violence by November 2004.

Administration of justice

The justice system continued to suffer from inadequate resources and training, corruption, lack of belief in the rule of law and a lack of political will to end impunity. Lynchings and cases of ill-treatment continued to be reported. Some 4,788 people remained in detention without trial. Trials of people accused of participating in the violence which followed the 1993 assassination of former President Melchior Ndadaye continued. In April, 36 people, of whom two were civilians, were convicted of participating in an attempted coup in July 2001. Sixty-four others were acquitted.

At least 2,202 detainees held for long periods without trial, or detained in relation to certain offences linked to the conflict, were released. These included six CNDD-FDD (Nkurunziza) prisoners who had been sentenced to death. There was a series of strikes by prisoners in July over the issue of which detainees were selected for release.

In November, the Senate adopted legislation reforming the Supreme Court, and allowing it to review earlier court verdicts. The criteria for review included rulings by a national or international jurisdiction on errors in the original trial. The President had not approved the law by the end of 2004.

The new legislation could potentially assist hundreds of defendants who were tried, often after unfair trials and without legal assistance, by courts of appeal from 1996 until September 2003. A plea, on technical grounds, to the cassation chamber of the Supreme Court, was the only appeal mechanism available. If successful, the case was sent back for retrial. Since many defendants had no legal assistance, virtually no such pleas were deemed admissible.

Kassi Manlan trial

The trial of those accused of the November 2001 murder of the head of the World Health Organisation (WHO) in Burundi, Dr Kassi Manlan, re-opened in May. Four security guards detained since November 2001, who were originally charged with the murder, appeared on a lesser charge. Eight new defendants (one of whom subsequently died) were charged with planning or executing the murder. They included senior intelligence officials and the heads of two police forces at the time of the murder. Two defendants, both convicted murderers serving sentences in Mpimba central prison at the time,

stated in court that they had carried out the murder after being promised a large sum of money and release from prison. A verdict had not been reached by the end of 2004.

Death penalty

At least 44 death sentences were passed. At the end of 2004, 533 people were under sentence of death. No executions took place. However, in February 2004, during the trial of four men accused of a bank robbery in Bujumbura, President Ndayizeye raised fears that executions might resume. The men were subsequently sentenced to death and the sentence confirmed on appeal.

In November, the President ordered new legislation to be drawn up to tackle an apparent increase in violent crime including armed robbery and rape. He made clear his own preference for wide application of the death penalty. In the same month legislation was submitted to parliament providing a special radically shortened procedure for people caught committing such crimes. The new procedures fell far short of international standards for fair trial. They allowed a maximum of 40 days between arrest and execution or clemency, including a retrial. By the end of 2004, Parliament had not debated the draft legislation.

International and transitional justice

In September, Burundi ratified the Rome Statute of the International Criminal Court. Legislation establishing a National Truth and Reconciliation Commission (NTRC) was adopted by the National Assembly and Senate. Concern was expressed by Burundian human rights groups that the law did not provide mechanisms to protect the independence of commission members, and that lack of clarity over the roles of the NTRC and an international judicial commission of inquiry provided for under the Peace Agreement could jeopardize the work of both.

Refugees and the internally displaced

Pressure from the Tanzanian authorities and Burundian government on refugees to return increased. More than 90,000 refugees returned from Tanzania during 2004. While some refugees genuinely wanted to return, others returned because of increasingly harsh conditions in the camps and fear of being forcibly returned by the Tanzanian authorities. Some feared that they would lose their land in Burundi if they did not repatriate. Many returnees appeared to have been ill-informed about the situation in Burundi, some because they had received false assurances from Burundian government officials visiting the camps. Land disputes increased. Government bodies to assist in the rehabilitation of refugees and resolve land issues were inadequate and did not function properly.

At least 95,000 people remained internally displaced at the end of 2004, some since 1993, although about 160,000 returned to their home areas during 2004. The population of Rural Bujumbura continued to face short-term conflict-related displacement, repeatedly disrupting their lives. In several parts of the country people, including returnees, were too frightened to spend the night in their homes.

The killing in August of more than 150 refugees at Gatumba transit centre underlined the government's failure to protect refugees. Only after the massacre did the government agree to move the refugees away from the border with the DRC. The Burundian army, which has several nearby bases, did not intervene at the camp to protect the refugees.

AI country reports/ visits
Reports
- Burundi: Commitment to human rights is essential (AI Index: AFR 16/001/2004)
- Burundi: A critical time – Human rights briefing on Burundi (AI Index: AFR 16/002/2004)
- Burundi: Rape – the hidden human rights abuse (AI Index: AFR 16/006/2004)
- Burundi: Child soldiers – the challenge of demobilization (AI Index: AFR 16/011/2004)
- Burundi: Amnesty International's recommendations on the deployment of UN peacekeeping forces (AI Index: AFR 16/015/2004)

Visits
An AI delegate attended the launch of the Burundi network of the Coalition to Stop the Use of Child Soldiers in April.

AI delegates visited refugee camps housing mainly Burundian refugees in western Tanzania in October and a settlement of Burundian refugees from 1972 in Tabora region in December.

CAMBODIA

KINGDOM OF CAMBODIA
Head of state: King Norodom Sihamoni (replaced King Norodom Sihanouk in October)
Head of government: Hun Sen
Death penalty: abolitionist for all crimes
International Criminal Court: ratified
UN Women's Convention: ratified
Optional Protocol to UN Women's Convention: signed

Human rights violations continued to be reported against a background of political instability. A weak and corrupt judicial system remained a serious obstacle to human rights protection. A prominent trade union leader and political activist was assassinated. Vietnamese (Montagnard) asylum-seekers continued to arrive from neighbouring Viet Nam; some were forcibly returned. The Cambodian legislature ratified a UN agreement for the establishment of a criminal tribunal to bring to justice Khmer Rouge leaders.

Background
In July the Cambodian People's Party (CPP) and the National United Front for an Independent, Neutral, Peaceful and Cooperative Cambodia (FUNCINPEC) formed a coalition government, ending almost a year of uncertainty following inconclusive national elections in July 2003. Allegations that the opposition Sam Rainsy Party were planning to overthrow the government were widely perceived as an attempt to discredit political opposition.

In October, 82-year-old King Sihanouk abdicated unexpectedly and was succeeded by his son Prince Sihamoni.

In July Cambodia joined the World Trade Organization (WTO), amid concerns at the implications for the poorest sector of society. Cambodia remained one of the world's poorest countries, with 36 per cent of the population living in poverty and a high mortality rate among under-fives. Land disputes increased, with members of the wealthy elite and military involved in land grabbing and speculation. The number of reported injuries caused by landmines rose dramatically as poor people seeking land moved into affordable areas that had not yet been de-mined. The prevalence of HIV/AIDS continued to be a serious problem; Cambodia was reported to have the highest infection rate in Asia.

In September Cambodia acceded to the Optional Protocol to the International Covenant on Civil and Political Rights and international conventions on migrant workers and trafficking.

Impunity
Concerns remained about the weak and corrupt judicial system. High-profile cases were marked by

political interference and, more broadly, there was a failure to adhere to procedures laid down in national law and international standards.

🗁 Four Muslim men arrested in May and June 2003 remained in pre-trial detention at the end of 2004, well in excess of the period permitted under domestic law. They were accused of membership of Jemaah Islamiyah, an Islamist group reportedly linked to al-Qa'ida. The four were initially charged with the "commission of acts of international terrorism" under Article 2 of the vaguely worded Anti-Terrorism Law. Although these charges were dropped in February, the judge ordered that the men remain in detention while prosecutors brought new charges under the same law for attempted murder. The conduct of the case was marked by political interference with the judiciary and lack of evidence.

Many politically motivated killings from previous years remained unresolved and there was an alarming increase in mob killings of suspected thieves for which no one was brought to justice. Several people were the victims of what were believed to be politically motivated killings.

🗁 Chea Vichea, an internationally renowned trade union leader and Sam Rainsy Party activist, was shot and killed in January. He had received numerous death threats. The investigation into his murder was marked by judicial irregularities. Two men arrested five days after the killing initially confessed, but later claimed on national television that they had been tortured during interrogation. The case generated widespread domestic and international criticism. By the end of the year no one had been brought to justice for the killing.

Torture

Torture of prisoners in police custody was reported to be widespread. In June, the Deputy Director-General of the National Police, Sau Phan, asserted publicly that torture during interrogation was sometimes necessary to force suspected criminals to provide information. He was reported to have retracted his comments following extensive media coverage and criticism, including an intervention by the UN Special Representative of the Secretary-General on the situation of human rights in Cambodia. Local non-governmental organizations (NGOs) also reported the continuing use of torture in prisons as a punishment. According to reports, no one accused of torture was successfully prosecuted in 2004.

Refugees

There was an increase in new asylum-seekers from Viet Nam after demonstrations in the Vietnamese Central Highlands were violently suppressed in April (see Viet Nam entry). Cambodian and Vietnamese police increased border cooperation which led to many newly arrived asylum-seekers being forcibly returned to Viet Nam.

Following mounting international concern and pressure, the authorities allowed the UN High Commissioner for Refugees (UNHCR) limited access to border areas from July onwards and several hundred asylum-seekers were taken to Phnom Penh where their requests for refugee status could be processed. Those recognized as refugees by UNHCR were permitted to leave Cambodia under UN auspices for safe third countries.

Khmer Rouge tribunal

The new government passed legislation allowing for the establishment of a criminal tribunal to bring to justice suspected perpetrators of gross human rights violations during the period of Khmer Rouge rule (1975-1979). Serious flaws remained which threatened the integrity of the legal process and set a dangerous precedent for other future international or "mixed" tribunals. Concerns included the feasibility and inherent weakness of the proposed "mixed" tribunal consisting of Cambodian and international judicial officials, and inadequate provision for victim and witness protection. By the end of the year only a fraction of the necessary funding for the establishment of the tribunal had been forthcoming from the international community.

Freedom of assembly

Severe restrictions on public demonstrations, imposed following violent anti-Thai riots in Phnom Penh in January 2003, remained in force. Protests that did proceed without official sanction were often met with excessive use of force by the police.

Human rights defenders

Local human rights organizations played an increasingly crucial role in providing protection to asylum-seekers from Viet Nam. Several staff members of one organization based in Ratanakiri and Mondulkiri provinces faced harassment, threats and arrest by the authorities. Villagers in these provinces, some of them belonging to the same ethnic minority groups as the asylum-seekers, also took considerable risks in providing shelter and food to new arrivals from Viet Nam and assisting their passage to Phnom Penh. Many faced arrest, harassment and restrictions on movement as a result. Intimidating language used by senior politicians fostered an atmosphere of fear for local NGO staff and Cambodian staff of UN agencies working in the human rights field.

Violence against women and children

No progress was made on the draft law against domestic violence. NGOs reported that rape and violence against women and children were growing to "epidemic" proportions, and that the number of reported rape cases was increasing, with inadequate legal redress for victims in the courts. Trafficking of women remained of concern although several high-profile prosecutions of paedophiles involved in sex tourism marked a greater determination by the authorities and NGOs to address this issue.

AI country reports/ visits
Reports
- Cambodia: Jemaah Islamiyah suspects must all be brought to trial now (AI Index: ASA 23/006/2004)

- Cambodia: The killing of trade unionist Chea Vichea (AI Index: ASA 23/008/2004)

Visit

An AI delegation visited Cambodia in February.

CAMEROON

REPUBLIC OF CAMEROON
Head of state: Paul Biya
Head of government: Ephraim Inoni (replaced Peter Mafany Musonge in December)
Death penalty: retentionist
International Criminal Court: signed
UN Women's Convention: ratified
Optional Protocol to UN Women's Convention: not signed

The government held on to power in presidential elections after using violence to disrupt peaceful opposition meetings. Political leaders were detained to prevent public meetings and demonstrations. One political prisoner died in prison, apparently from medical neglect. The government failed to investigate reports of torture, "disappearances" or deaths in police custody independently or openly.

Background

Paul Biya, head of state since 1982, was re-elected in presidential elections in October amid allegations by opposition parties and the Catholic Bishops' Conference of Cameroon of vote-rigging and law-breaking. A Commonwealth Observer Group concluded that the electoral process lacked the necessary credibility in a number of key areas, including denying some voters the right to vote. However, the Group believed that the intention of those who voted was reflected in the result.

The oil-rich Bakassi peninsula remained under the control of Nigerian forces, despite a 2002 ruling by the International Court of Justice in The Hague that it be handed over to Cameroon. Nigerian forces had not vacated the area by deadlines set for May and September.

Critics gagged

Opposition parties continued to operate under severe constraints. Their supporters were arbitrarily detained and their public gatherings obstructed by the security forces.

▭ Jean-Jacques Ekindi and other leading members of the opposition Front of Alternative Forces (Front des forces alternatives, FFA) were briefly detained by the paramilitary mobile police on 12 January in Douala. They were prevented from publicly launching a petition for free and fair presidential elections.

Protest marches by a coalition of opposition parties were forcibly obstructed. The National Coalition for Reconciliation and Reconstruction (Coalition nationale pour la réconciliation et la reconstruction, CNRR) was calling for the electoral register to be computerized to prevent vote-rigging in favour of the ruling party, the Cameroon People's Democratic Rally (Rassemblement démocratique du peuple camerounais, RDPC).

▭ On 6 July a peaceful march in the capital, Yaoundé, was blocked by hundreds of anti-riot gendarmes. Among the demonstrators said to have been assaulted were John Fru Ndi, leader of the Social Democratic Front (SDF), and SDF members of parliament. On 3 August police officers and gendarmes reportedly surrounded and assaulted about 50 protesters near the central market in Yaoundé. On 10 August the police and gendarmes surrounded a group of CNRR supporters for several hours to stop them from marching, and allegedly punched and whipped a demonstrator who escaped the cordon.

▭ A march in Douala on 17 August was halted at its rallying point by police and gendarmes and Jean-Jacques Ekindi and other opposition leaders were detained.

John Kohtem, an SDF leader, was beaten to death on 20 August near Bamenda, the capital of North-West province, reportedly by followers of a local RDPC leader and member of parliament. Following mass protests by SDF supporters, 11 people were arrested in September in connection with the killing. The 11 and the member of parliament had not been formally charged by the end of the year.

Some human rights defenders faced official harassment.

▭ Judicial officials in Maroua, the capital of Extreme North province, seized property from the Movement for the Defence of Human Rights and Freedoms and returned it only after the group paid the officials.

Continued denial of press freedoms reflected the government's long-standing fear of uncensored news reporting. A ban imposed during 2003 on a number of radio and television stations accused of transmitting without licence remained in force. The government refused to grant them the licences.

▭ On 11 July, two local correspondents for the British Broadcasting Corporation (BBC) were arrested by soldiers in the Bakassi peninsula. Despite having government authorization to be in the area, they were accused of espionage, had their equipment and documents briefly seized, and were detained under house arrest in the town of Limbe until 16 July.

Political imprisonment

Political prisoners continued to be held. Several were in poor health, and were denied adequate medical care.

▭ Martin Cheonumu died in July, days after complaining of abdominal pain. He was the second prisoner to die since he and 17 other defendants were convicted in 1999 after an unfair trial by a court controlled by the Ministry of Defence. The defendants were denied access to legal counsel in pre-trial detention. The government announced in December that the right to appeal had been granted, but it had not occurred by the end of 2004. The 18 were members of the Southern Cameroons National Council (SCNC), a group advocating independence for the English-speaking provinces of Cameroon. They were convicted on charges including murder, robbery and illegal possession of firearms in connection with armed attacks in North-West province in 1997.

Torture in custody

Detainees in police custody remained at risk of torture. No procedures were in place to ensure that unexplained deaths or reports of torture or "disappearance" were independently or thoroughly investigated.

▭ Bruising and injuries on the body of Laurent Kougang, who died in police custody on 23 April, appeared to have been caused by severe beatings. After his arrest on 15 April, allegedly on suspicion of trafficking firearms, he was held at two police stations before being transferred to the central police station in Douala's Brazzaville district where he died. No investigation was known to have been carried out into the circumstances of his death.

▭ Police officers were reported to have handcuffed, assaulted and set fire to Afuh Benard Weriwo, aged 27, in Ikiliwindi on 12 May, as gendarmes stood by. He had been arrested after being accused of stealing a bicycle. He died from his injuries on 10 July. There was no official response to calls by witnesses and local activists for an investigation and for the suspected perpetrators to be brought to justice.

▭ There was still no investigation into the alleged "disappearance" of nine adolescents from the Bépanda Omnisports district of Douala in February 2001. Arrested on suspicion of stealing a gas cylinder and stove, the nine were reportedly tortured at the Gendarmerie Operational Command headquarters known as "Kosovo" before they "disappeared".

Death penalty

In July a Justice Department official said that death sentences were no longer carried out and that they were usually commuted to life imprisonment in response to petitions for presidential clemency. He said that 27 petitions were under examination, but provided no information about those still under sentence of death. Death sentences were last carried out in 1997.

AI country reports/visits
Visits

AI representatives sought to visit Cameroon to investigate reports of pre-election human rights violations, but, as in previous years, the government refused to grant them access.

CANADA

CANADA
Head of state: Queen Elizabeth II, represented by Adrienne Clarkson
Head of government: Paul Martin
Death penalty: abolitionist for all crimes
International Criminal Court: ratified
UN Women's Convention and its Optional Protocol: ratified

Indigenous women and girls continued to suffer a disproportionately high incidence of violence. There were continuing concerns about the use by police of Taser guns.

Violence against Indigenous women

Indigenous women and girls, who have long been socially and economically marginalized in Canada, continued to suffer a disproportionately high incidence of violence. The authorities failed to implement measures to reduce the marginalization of these women and ensure that police understand and are accountable to Indigenous peoples. AI urged the authorities to institute comprehensive plans of action to ensure that Indigenous women and girls receive the protection needed.

Police abuses

Six men died in separate incidents after they were subdued by police using a Taser gun. Autopsies were pending in some cases. The authorities announced reviews of the use of Taser guns, but failed to suspend their use until an independent study was carried out.

In June in Ontario, the public inquiry opened into the 1995 killing of Dudley George, an unarmed Indigenous man shot by police during a land rights protest.

In October the public inquiry into the 1990 freezing to death in Saskatchewan of Neil Stonechild, a 17-year-old Indigenous youth, concluded that there had been a police role in his death. The Saskatchewan provincial government subsequently announced that a new process for investigating complaints against the police would be established.

There was no response to AI's call for an inquiry into allegations of racially motivated violence against Albert Duterville, a prisoner at Port-Cartier penitentiary.

Security and human rights

A public inquiry opened in June into Canada's role in the case of Maher Arar, a Canadian citizen of Syrian origin who was deported from the USA to Syria in 2002, where he was detained without charge or trial for a year and allegedly tortured. The role of Canadian authorities in the cases of at least three other Canadian citizens who alleged they were tortured while in detention abroad remained unclarified.

Six men remained in detention pending deportation, pursuant to security certificates issued under the Immigration and Refugee Protection Act. In five of the cases the individuals faced a serious risk of torture if deported. Under security certificate proceedings, detainees only have access to summaries of the evidence against them and have no opportunity to challenge key witnesses.

Refugee protection
The Canada/USA "safe-third country" deal was implemented in December. Under the deal, most refugee claimants passing through the USA on their way to Canada will be required to make refugee claims in the USA. AI was concerned that asylum-seekers turned away from Canada will face arbitrary and harsh detention in the USA in contravention of international standards, and that many women fearing gender-specific forms of persecution will face *refoulement*.

The government continued to fail to enact the provisions under the Immigration and Refugee Protection Act that would provide asylum-seekers with a full appeal against a decision denying them refugee status.

Impunity and justice
In June the Ontario Court of Appeal ruled, in the case of *Bouzari v Iran*, that Canada's state immunity laws protect a foreign government from civil suits in Canadian courts for damages for torture suffered abroad.

Other concerns
There were no further negotiations regarding the long outstanding land claim of the Lubicon Cree in northern Alberta. The failure to reach a just resolution continued to contribute to violations of the rights of the Lubicon.

AI country reports/ visits
Report
· Stolen Sisters: Discrimination and Violence against Indigenous Women in Canada (AI Index: AMR 20/001/2004)
Visit
In October AI's Secretary General met federal government officials to discuss a range of issues, including violence against Indigenous women.

CENTRAL AFRICAN REPUBLIC

CENTRAL AFRICAN REPUBLIC
Head of state: François Bozizé
Head of government: Célestin Gaombalet
Death penalty: abolitionist in practice
International Criminal Court: ratified
UN Women's Convention: ratified
Optional Protocol to UN Women's Convention: not signed

Hundreds of women raped in late 2002 and early 2003 by combatants received no redress and those responsible were not brought to justice. Journalists who criticized influential individuals or the government were detained; some were sentenced to prison terms and fined. Several former government officials arrested in 2003 remained in custody without trial; one was acquitted and released.

Background
Insecurity remained a major concern, although the country was more politically stable than in previous years. In April, armed clashes occurred in the capital, Bangui, between government forces and former combatants awaiting demobilization. There were reports of Chadians in the national army deserting to join the insurrection. At least six people were killed and 16 others injured during the fighting. The former combatants were demanding adequate remuneration for their role in the war that brought President François Bozizé to power in 2003. They were removed from Bangui in May and sent to the north of the country. Some Chadian former combatants were reportedly returned to Chad. Their removal from Bangui was carried out with the support of the peacekeeping force backed by the Monetary and Economic Community of Central Africa (Communauté Economique et Monétaire d'Afrique Centrale, CEMAC).

President Bozizé appointed an electoral commission composed of representatives of political parties, civil society organizations and government officials to organize and supervise the elections. A national census was carried out in October. A new constitution, which limits the presidential term of office to two five-year terms, was adopted by referendum in December. Soon after the referendum, President Bozizé issued a decree slating presidential and legislative elections for February 2005. At least 15 people, including former President Patassé and President Bozizé, declared their candidature for the presidency.

French military experts remained in the country supporting CEMAC, as well as training specialized units of the Central African security forces.

In November, a new law on freedom of the press, drafted with the financial and logistical support of the UN Office in the Central African Republic, was adopted by the transitional parliament known as the National Transitional Council (Conseil national de transition, CNT). Under the new law libel and slander would not be punishable by imprisonment.

Violence against women

The government took no action to bring to justice combatants who systematically raped hundreds of women in late 2002 and early 2003 during the armed conflict which culminated in the overthrow of the government in March 2003. The conflict was between an armed political group led by François Bozizé and the forces of the then President Ange-Félix Patassé. Their respective foreign supporters from Chad and the Democratic Republic of the Congo (DRC) were also involved in the fighting. According to most survivors, witnesses and human rights and humanitarian representatives, most of the perpetrators were members of the Movement for the Liberation of Congo (Mouvement de libération du Congo, MLC), an armed political group from the neighbouring DRC which had entered the Central African Republic in October 2002, at former President Patassé's request.

Some women were reportedly killed after being raped; others died of their injuries. Children and elderly women were among the victims.

Female genital mutilation continued to be practised, despite a 1966 law banning it.

▢ Five members of the Presidential Guard who raped a woman in custody in October 2003 were tried by a military court, which found them guilty and sentenced them to five years' imprisonment in January 2004.

Journalists and press freedom

Before a new press law was adopted by the CNT, a number of journalists who published articles critical of the government or of people in positions of power were arrested and detained; some were held for several months. The government's action appeared to contradict President Bozizé's declaration in 2003 that press offences would be decriminalized.

▢ Jude Zossé of L'Hirondelle newspaper was arrested in February accused of insulting the head of state. The newspaper had published an article alleging that President Bozizé had personally collected and diverted taxes. Jude Zossé was found guilty and sentenced to six months' imprisonment in March. He was released following a presidential pardon in May.

▢ Alexis Maka Gbossokotto was arrested in July and detained after his newspaper, Le Citoyen, published an article alleging that a director of a state company had been involved in mismanagement of the company's funds. President Bozizé removed the director from his position soon after the article was published. In August, Alexis Maka Gbossokotto was found guilty of insulting the former director and given a one-year suspended sentence and fined US$920. He was released soon after his trial.

Detention of government opponents

Several former government officials detained in 2003 remained in custody at Ngaragba central prison in Bangui. Noël Nditifei Biangaye and Evelyne Loudégué were awaiting trial while on provisional release, while Simon Kulumba was allowed out of prison for medical treatment. Gabriel Jean-Edouard Koyambounou was tried in December and released after the Court of Appeal acquitted him of the charge of embezzling public funds. Tobi Kozo, also charged with embezzlement, was still awaiting trial at the end of the year.

Releases

Two brothers, army Colonel Danzoumi Yalo and Sani Yalo, who were arrested in December 2003 after they were accused of involvement in a plot against the government, were released in March without charge.

AI country reports/ visits
Report
- Central African Republic: Five months of war against women (AI Index: AFR 19/001/2004)

CHAD

REPUBLIC OF CHAD
Head of state: Idriss Déby
Head of government: Moussa Faki Mahamat
Death penalty: retentionist
International Criminal Court: signed
UN Women's Convention: ratified
Optional Protocol to UN Women's Convention: not signed

Nearly 100,000 new refugees, fleeing conflict and widespread systematic human rights violations in the Darfur region of Sudan, arrived in eastern Chad. Chadian civilians as well as refugees were attacked during cross-border incursions by a militia allied to the Sudanese government. Freedom of expression remained under threat. Investigations into human rights violations and other crimes allegedly committed by former President Hissein Habré and his associates appeared to have stalled. Nineteen death sentences were passed. No executions were reported.

Background

An apparent attempted coup, reportedly involving officers and several hundred troops from the Zaghawa ethnic group of President Idriss Déby as well as members of President Déby's close family, took place in May. Later that month, an amended constitution allowing President Déby to stand for a third term was adopted by the National Assembly, dominated by Idriss Déby's Patriotic Salvation Movement (Mouvement patriotique du Salut, MPS).

The Movement for Democracy and Justice in Chad (Mouvement pour la Démocratie et la Justice au Tchad, MDJT), the most active of a plethora of largely inactive armed political groups, did not appear to engage in significant military activity in Tibesti, northern Chad, its area of operation, during 2004. In October, the National Resistance Alliance, which groups together several armed political groups, announced that it was pulling out of a January 2003 peace agreement with the government of Chad. However, it apparently did not resume conflict.

In March, the Chadian armed forces, which received renewed US military support, clashed in Tibesti with an Algerian armed political group, the Salafist Group for Preaching and Combat (SGPC), which had retreated into northern Chad from Niger. The SGPC leader was captured by the MDJT, which handed him over to Libya in October for extradition to Algeria, where he was considered to be at risk of torture. He was likely to face trial on serious charges and could face the death penalty (see Algeria entry). The fate of at least 10 other SGPC fighters reportedly detained by the MDJT was not clear.

In October, President Déby accused a consortium of international corporations involved in a major oil exploitation project in southern Chad of failing to respect their agreements with the Chadian government.

Outbreaks of intercommunal violence between local farmers and nomadic herders, particularly in southern Chad, led to scores of deaths and the theft of livestock and destruction of property.

The spread of conflict from Sudan

In January, the Sudanese air force reportedly bombed Tiné close to the border with Chad, killing two civilians and injuring at least 10 among the refugee population on the Chadian side of the border. Chad continued to mediate in the conflict. However, fighting continued despite the signing of a new ceasefire agreement in N'Djaména in April.

Numerous incursions by the Janjawid militia from Sudan into Chad took place, with regular reports of looting and the killing of civilians. Relations between the Chadian and Sudanese governments deteriorated and there were clashes in Chad between Chadian security forces and the Janjawid in which civilians were reportedly killed. Reports of recruitment of Chadians by the Janjawid, and allegations of links between key figures of the Chadian government and the Sudan Liberation Movement/Army (SLM/A) and the Justice and Equity Movement, armed political groups operating in the Darfur region, in which many Zaghawa were involved, highlighted the risk that the Darfur conflict could spread.

Refugees from Sudan

There were more than 200,000 Sudanese refugees in Chad, nearly 100,000 of them arriving in 2004. Throughout the year, the UN High Commissioner for Refugees (UNHCR) attempted to relocate refugees to more accessible camps and to camps further from the border.

The huge influx of refugees, combined with the poverty of the local community as well as the increase in insecurity due to militia attacks, led to increasing tensions between the refugees and host communities. Late in the year at least one refugee girl was raped and other refugees were attacked as they collected wood.

Two refugees were shot and killed by members of the Chadian security forces in unclear circumstances following disturbances in the Forchana refugee camp. Arms were seized from the camp and at least 19 refugees arrested. Some of those arrested were reported to have been badly beaten. Following the disturbances in two refugee camps in July, humanitarian organizations were temporarily denied access to the camps by government authorities. Further violence and threats against humanitarian workers were reported in November 2004.

Freedom of expression under attack

Journalists were arbitrarily arrested, beaten and threatened. In February, Tchanguis Vatankhah, director of a private local radio station, *Radio Brakos*, in Moissala, southern Chad, was summoned for questioning at Moissala police station where he was reportedly beaten severely. The attack followed the broadcast of an interview with the leader of the opposition National Union for Development and Renewal Party. He was released without charge two days later.

In May, another private radio station, *FM Liberté,* was threatened with closure after broadcasting a call by activists for people to protest against the constitutional amendment allowing President Déby to restand for president. In June, *FM Liberté* was awarded six million CFA francs (approximately US$12,300) by the administrative chamber of the Supreme Court in damages following its suspension in 2003. The radio had been suspended on the orders of the Minister of Territorial Administration, after it criticized President Déby, although the constitutional authority to take such action rests with the Higher Communication Council. Tracts containing death threats against two *FM Liberté* journalists were delivered to the radio in July.

Impunity

No formal charges had yet been brought in Chad against people suspected of committing human rights violations and other crimes during the presidency of Hissein Habré (1982-1990) despite judicial investigations. The progress of investigations was not clear.

Possible 'disappearance'

Colonel Abdoulaye Sarwa, a former leader of an armed political group who had rejoined the government armed forces in 2003, "disappeared" following his arrest in October by members of the National Security Agency. The official reason for his arrest was given as "lack of military discipline". His family and human rights groups were unable to confirm his whereabouts. In November he was reported to be detained in Tanoua, close to the Libyan border, but this could not be confirmed.

Death penalty
In July, 19 men were sentenced to death by N'Djaména criminal court for murder or complicity in the murder of 21 peasant farmers in southern Chad in March, as well as the wounding of 10 other farmers and the theft of livestock. The killings followed a conflict between local farmers and nomadic herders. One other person was known to be under sentence of death. No executions were reported.

AI country reports/ visits
Statement
- Chad: Death penalty/Fear of imminent execution (AI Index: AFR 20/001/2004)

Visit
AI visited Sudanese refugee camps in eastern Chad in May.

CHILE

REPUBLIC OF CHILE
Head of state and government: Ricardo Lagos
Death penalty: abolitionist for ordinary crimes
International Criminal Court: signed
UN Women's Convention: ratified with reservations
Optional Protocol to UN Women's Convention: signed

Progress in ending impunity for past human rights violations continued to be slow, despite some positive developments. Torture and ill-treatment remained matters of concern. Indigenous Mapuche activists were subjected to human rights violations.

Past human rights violations
In January, in the first case of a conviction for "disappearance", the Santiago Appeals Court confirmed the prison sentences imposed on former secret police chief Manuel Contreras and four others in the case of Miguel Angel Sandoval Rodríguez who "disappeared" in 1975. In September another court hearing to decide whether the five should benefit from the 1978 Amnesty Law upheld the sentences. In November the Supreme Court ruled that the Amnesty

Law did not apply. The lawyer representing the State Defence Council had argued that cases of "disappearance" from the era of the military government (1973-1990) should be treated as murder rather than "permanent kidnapping". Treating "disappearance" as murder would have allowed the Amnesty Law to be applied. The proposal brought sharp condemnation from human rights groups.

During the judicial investigation into the "disappearance" of 10 members of the Chilean Communist Party in 1976, known as the Conference Street case, several train rails were found in the sea off the Chilean coast. The discovery supported allegations that the 10 had been tied to rails and dropped into the sea from helicopters by the secret police.

In August, the Supreme Court voted to lift former President Augusto Pinochet Ugarte's immunity from prosecution. This allowed proceedings to be opened against him for human rights violations committed under "Operation Cóndor", a joint plan by military governments in the Southern Cone to eliminate opponents during the 1970s and 1980s. On 13 December a judge ordered the indictment and house arrest of Augusto Pinochet on nine counts of kidnapping and one of murder. On 20 December the Santiago Appeals Court upheld the order. The lawyers representing Augusto Pinochet appealed to the Supreme Court, which had not ruled by the end of 2004.

Torture and ill-treatment
Chile submitted its third periodic report on the implementation of the UN Convention against Torture. In response, the UN Committee against Torture, while noting a number of positive developments, expressed concern that certain legislation, including the Amnesty Law, jeopardized the full exercise of fundamental human rights and entrenched impunity. It also criticized the definition of torture used in Chilean legislation and several aspects of the mandate of the National Commission on Political Imprisonment and Torture, set up by the government in 2003 to identify victims of torture under the military government and propose reparation measures. The National Commission's own report was published in November. Containing testimonies from nearly 28,000 torture victims, the report acknowledged that political detention and torture had been institutional state practices, and recommended reparation levels for the victims. However, no measures were proposed for obtaining justice.

Indigenous people
Human rights violations continued to occur in the context of land ownership disputes, affecting the Mapuche community especially.
🖆 Throughout the year Mapuche community leader Juana Calfunao Paillalef and her family suffered repeated intimidation, including death threats and an apparent arson attack on Juana Calfunao's home, in the context of their community's dispute with local landowners. Numerous complaints about the incidents had been made to the authorities since 2000, but there

was no official information on the progress of the investigations and no action appeared to have been taken to provide the family with adequate protection.

AI country reports/ visits
Report
· Chile: Concerns on torture and other cruel, inhuman or degrading treatment (AI Index: AMR 22/006/2004)

CHINA

PEOPLE'S REPUBLIC OF CHINA
Head of state: Hu Jintao
Head of government: Wen Jiabao
Death penalty: retentionist
International Criminal Court: not signed
UN Women's Convention: ratified with reservations
Optional Protocol to UN Women's Convention: not signed

There was progress towards reform in some areas, but this failed to have a significant impact on serious and widespread human rights violations perpetrated across the country. Tens of thousands of people continued to be detained or imprisoned in violation of their fundamental human rights and were at high risk of torture or ill-treatment. Thousands of people were sentenced to death or executed, many after unfair trials. Public protests increased against forcible evictions and land requisition without adequate compensation. China continued to use the global "war on terrorism" to justify its crackdown on the Uighur community in Xinjiang. Freedom of expression and religion continued to be severely restricted in Tibet and other Tibetan areas of China.

Background
The new administration, which had taken office in March 2003, consolidated its authority, particularly following the resignation of former president Jiang Zemin as chair of the Central Military Commission in September. Some legal reforms were introduced, including new regulations aimed at preventing torture in police custody and an amendment to the Constitution in March stating that "the state respects and protects human rights." However, the failure to introduce necessary institutional reforms severely compromised the enforcement of these measures in practice.

The authorities took a more proactive approach towards dealing with China's HIV/AIDS epidemic, including a new law in August aimed at strengthening AIDS prevention and stopping discrimination against those living with AIDS or other infectious diseases. However, grassroots activists campaigning for better treatment continued to be arbitrarily detained.

Political crackdowns continued on specific groups, including the Falun Gong spiritual movement, unofficial Christian groups, and so-called "separatists" and "religious extremists" in Xinjiang and Tibet.

The authorities continued to engage in "human rights dialogue" with other countries, but suspended their dialogue with the USA after the latter proposed a resolution on China at the UN Commission on Human Rights in March. China lobbied the European Union (EU) to lift its arms embargo, imposed after China's crackdown on the pro-democracy movement in June 1989, and won support from some EU states. However, the embargo remained in place at the end of the year.

China postponed the visit of the UN Special Rapporteur on torture, scheduled for June, but the UN Working Group on Arbitrary Detention (WGAD) visited China in September. International human rights non-governmental organizations (NGOs) continued to be denied access to the country to conduct independent research.

Human rights defenders
The authorities continued to use provisions of the Criminal Law relating to "subversion", "state secrets" and other vaguely defined national security offences to prosecute peaceful activists and advocates of reform. Lawyers, journalists, HIV/AIDS activists and housing rights advocates were among those harassed, detained or imprisoned for documenting human rights abuses, campaigning for reform, or attempting to obtain redress for victims of violations.

🗀 Ding Zilin, who set up the "Tiananmen Mothers" group to campaign for justice following the killing of her son in Beijing on 4 June 1989, was detained by the police in March to prevent her from highlighting her concerns. She was also placed under a form of house arrest a few days before the 15th anniversary of the crackdown to prevent her from filing a legal complaint on behalf of 126 others who also lost relatives in 1989.

🗀 Li Dan, an AIDS activist, was detained by police in Henan province in August in an apparent attempt to prevent him from protesting against the government's handling of the AIDS epidemic. He was released one day later but then beaten up by two unknown assailants. Li Dan had founded a school for AIDS orphans in the province where up to one million people are believed to have become HIV-positive after selling their blood plasma to unsanitary, state-sanctioned blood collection stations. The school had been closed down by the local authorities in July.

Violations in the context of economic reform
The rights of freedom of expression and association of workers' representatives continued to be severely curtailed and independent trade unions remained illegal. In the context of economic restructuring, large numbers of people were reportedly denied adequate reparations for forcible eviction, land requisition and

job layoffs. Public and largely peaceful protests against such practices increased, leading to numerous detentions and other abuses.

Beijing was often the focus for such protests due in part to house demolitions during the city's preparations for the Olympics in 2008. People also travelled to Beijing from other parts of the country to petition the central authorities after failing to obtain redress at the local level. Tens of thousands of petitioners were reportedly detained by Beijing police during security operations in advance of official meetings in March and September.

▢ Ye Guozhu was detained on suspicion of "disturbing social order" in August after applying for permission to hold a mass protest against forced evictions in Beijing. He was sentenced to four years in prison in December. Ye Guozhu and his family had been forcibly evicted from their home in Beijing last year to make way for construction reportedly related to the 2008 Olympics.

Violence against women
Numerous articles about domestic violence appeared in the national media, reflecting widespread concern that such abuses were not being effectively addressed.

Serious violations against women and girls continued to be reported as a result of the enforcement of the family planning policy, including forced abortions and sterilizations. In July the authorities publicly reinforced a ban on the selective abortion of female foetuses in an attempt to reverse a growing gap in the boy-girl birth ratio.

Women in detention, including large numbers of Falun Gong practitioners, remained at risk of torture, including rape and sexual abuse.

New regulations were introduced in January preventing the police from issuing on-the-spot fines to prostitutes. However, "Custody and Education" continued to be used to detain alleged prostitutes and their clients without charge or trial.

▢ Mao Hengfeng was sent to a labour camp for 18 months' "Re-education through Labour" in April for persistently petitioning the authorities over a forced abortion 15 years earlier when she became pregnant in violation of China's family planning policy. She was reportedly tied up, suspended from the ceiling and severely beaten in the labour camp. She had been detained several times in the past in psychiatric units where she had been forced to undergo shock therapy.

Political activists and Internet users
Political activists, including supporters of banned political groups, or those calling for political change or greater democracy continued to be arbitrarily detained and in some cases sentenced and imprisoned. By the end of the year, AI had records of more than 50 people who had been detained or imprisoned after accessing or circulating politically sensitive information on the Internet.

▢ Kong Youping , a leading member of the Chinese Democratic Party and former union activist in Liaoning province, was sentenced to 15 years' imprisonment in

September for "subversion". He had been detained in late 2003 after posting articles on the Internet attacking official corruption and urging a reassessment of the 1989 pro-democracy movement.

Repression of spiritual and religious groups
The Falun Gong spiritual movement remained a key target of repression, which reportedly included many arbitrary detentions. Most of those detained were assigned to periods of "Re-education through Labour" without charge or trial, during which they were at high risk of torture or ill-treatment, particularly if they refused to renounce their beliefs. Others were held in prisons and psychiatric hospitals. According to overseas Falun Gong sources, more than 1,000 people detained in connection with the Falun Gong had died since the organization was banned in 1999, mostly as a result of torture or ill-treatment.

Other so-called "heretical organizations" and unofficial religious groups were also targeted. Reports increased of arrests and detentions of unregistered Catholics and members of unofficial Protestant "house churches". Those attempting to document such violations and send reports overseas were also at risk of arrest.

▢ Zhang Shengqi, Xu Yonghai and Liu Fenggang, three independent Protestant activists, were sentenced to one, two and three years in prison respectively by the Hangzhou Intermediate People's Court for "leaking state secrets" in August. The charges related to passing information abroad about crackdowns on Protestants and the closure of unofficial churches in the area.

Death penalty
The death penalty continued to be used extensively and arbitrarily, at times as a result of political interference. People were executed for non-violent crimes such as tax fraud and embezzlement as well as drug offences and violent crimes. The authorities continued to keep national statistics on death sentences and executions secret. Based on public reports available, AI estimated that at least 3,400 people had been executed and at least 6,000 sentenced to death by the end of the year, although the true figures were believed to be much higher. In March, a senior member of the National People's Congress announced that China executes around 10,000 people per year.

A lack of basic safeguards protecting the rights of defendants meant that large numbers of people continued to be sentenced to death and executed after unfair trials. In October, the authorities announced an intention to reinstate Supreme Court review of death penalty cases and to introduce other legal reforms aimed at safeguarding the rights of criminal suspects and defendants. It remained unclear, however, when these measures would be introduced.

▢ Ma Weihua, a woman facing the death penalty on drugs charges, was reportedly forced to undergo an abortion in police custody in February, apparently so that she could be put to death "legally" as Chinese law prevents the execution of pregnant women. She had been detained in January in possession of 1.6kg of heroin. Her trial, which began in July, was suspended after her lawyer provided details of the forced abortion. She was eventually sentenced to life imprisonment in November.

Torture, arbitrary detention and unfair trials

Torture and ill-treatment continued to be reported in a wide variety of state institutions despite the introduction of several new regulations aimed at curbing the practice. Common methods included kicking, beating, electric shocks, suspension by the arms, shackling in painful positions, and sleep and food deprivation. Political interference in the rule of law, restricted access to the outside world for detainees, and a failure to establish effective mechanisms for complaint and investigation continued to be key factors allowing the practice to flourish.

The authorities officially announced an intention to reform "Re-education through Labour", a system of administrative detention used to detain hundreds of thousands of people for up to four years without charge or trial. However, the exact nature and scope of reform remained unclear.

People accused of political or criminal offences continued to be denied due process. Detainees' access to lawyers and family members continued to be severely restricted and trials fell far short of international fair trial standards. Those charged with offences related to "state secrets" or "terrorism" had their legal rights restricted and were tried *in camera*.

⌷ In October, Falun Gong organizations abroad publicized video footage of Wang Xia, a woman who had recently been released from prison in Hohhot, Inner Mongolia where she had served two years of a seven-year sentence for distributing materials promoting Falun Gong. She appeared emaciated and her body bore several scars. She had reportedly been tied to a bed, hung up, beaten, injected with unknown substances and shocked with electric batons after going on hunger strikes to protest against her detention.

North Korean asylum-seekers

Hundreds, possibly thousands, of North Korean asylum-seekers in north-east China were arrested and forcibly returned during the year. China continued to deny North Koreans access to any refugee determination procedures despite evidence that many had a genuine claim to asylum and in breach of the UN Refugee Convention to which China is a state party.

Those assisting North Korean asylum-seekers, including members of foreign aid and religious organizations, ethnic Korean Chinese nationals, and journalists attempting to raise awareness of their plight, were detained for interrogation, and some were charged and sentenced to prison terms.

⌷ Noguchi Takashi, a Japanese NGO activist helping North Koreans in China flee to a third country, was deported in August after being detained in the Guangxi Zhuang Autonomous Region. He had been charged with human trafficking and sentenced to eight months' imprisonment and a 20,000 yuan fine (US$2,400).

Xinjiang Uighur Autonomous Region (XUAR)

The authorities continued to use the "global war on terror" to justify harsh repression in Xinjiang, resulting in serious human rights violations against the ethnic Uighur community. The authorities continued to make little distinction between acts of violence and acts of passive resistance. Repression resulted in the closure of unofficial mosques, arrests of imams, restrictions on the use of the Uighur language and the banning of certain Uighur books and journals.

Arrests of so-called "separatists, terrorists and religious extremists" continued and thousands of political prisoners, including prisoners of conscience, remained in prison. Many of those charged with "separatist" or "terrorist" offences were reportedly sentenced to death and executed. Uighur activists attempting to pass information abroad about the extent of the crackdown were at risk of arbitrary detention and imprisonment.

China continued to use "counter-terrorism" as a means to strengthen its political and economic ties with neighbouring states. Uighurs who had fled to Central Asia, Pakistan, Nepal and other states, including asylum-seekers and refugees, remained at serious risk of forcible return to China. China continued to put pressure on the USA to return 22 Uighurs held in the US detention camp in Guantánamo Bay, Cuba. In June, the US authorities stated that the Uighurs would not be returned to China due to fears that they would be tortured or executed.

⌷ Abdulghani Memetimin, a 40-year-old teacher and journalist, continued to serve a nine-year prison sentence in Kashgar after being convicted of "leaking state secrets" in June 2003. He had been charged in connection with sending information to a Uighur-run NGO based in Germany about human rights violations against Uighurs in the XUAR and making translations of official speeches.

Tibet Autonomous Region and other ethnic Tibetan areas

Freedom of religion, expression and association continued to be severely restricted and arbitrary arrests and unfair trials continued. Over 100 Tibetan prisoners of conscience, mainly Buddhist monks and nuns, remained in prison. Contacts between the Chinese authorities and representatives of the Tibetan government in exile continued, with some signs that progress was being made. However, this failed to result in any significant policy changes leading to improved protection for the basic human rights of Tibetans.

⌷ Topden and Dzokar, two monks from Chogri Monastery, Drakgo (Luhuo) County, Sichuan province, together with Lobsang Tsering, a layman, were all reportedly sentenced to three years in prison in August for putting up posters advocating Tibetan independence. They had been detained in July together with numerous others who were released several days later. Some said they were beaten in detention.

Hong Kong Special Administrative Region

There were no attempts to reintroduce legislation under Article 23 of the Basic Law prohibiting acts of treason, sedition, secession or subversion – a proposal which had sparked public protests in 2003. However, a mainland ruling in April restricting Hong Kong's freedom to push ahead with political reform heightened concerns about an erosion of human rights in Hong Kong.

Fears about restrictions on freedom of expression were fuelled by the resignation of three radio talk show hosts in May after they allegedly received threats for calling for greater democracy in Hong Kong. The administrative detention of a Hong Kong Democratic Party candidate in China in advance of Hong Kong elections in September was also viewed by many as politically motivated. In November an appeal court reversed convictions for "public obstruction" against 16 Falun Gong practitioners who were detained after holding a demonstration in March 2002. Other convictions for obstructing and assaulting police were upheld.

Death sentences continued to be imposed on Hong Kong residents in other parts of China and there was still no formal rendition agreement between Hong Kong and China.

In June, the Hong Kong Court of Final Appeal ruled that the regional authorities must assess individual asylum-seekers' claims that they had fled torture before issuing a deportation order. However, asylum-seekers and other groups, including migrant workers, victims of domestic violence, and lesbians and gay men, remained vulnerable to discrimination. A positive move in this direction came with the issuing of a public consultation document on proposed legislation against racial discrimination in September.

AI country reports/ visits

Reports
- Executed "according to law"? – The death penalty in China (AI Index: ASA 17/003/2004)
- Uighurs fleeing persecution as China wages its "war on terror" (AI Index: ASA 17/021/2004)
- People's Republic of China: Human rights defenders at risk (AI Index: ASA 17/045/2004)

COLOMBIA

REPUBLIC OF COLOMBIA
Head of state and government: Álvaro Uribe Vélez
Death penalty: abolitionist for all crimes
International Criminal Court: ratified
UN Women's Convention: ratified
Optional Protocol to UN Women's Convention: signed

Negotiations between the government and the United Self-Defence Forces of Colombia, (Autodefensas Unidas de Colombia, AUC), an army-backed paramilitary umbrella organization, led to the reported demobilization of over 2,500 AUC combatants in 2004. Serious concerns remained about the process, principally over the issue of impunity, violations of the AUC ceasefire and continuing serious and widespread human rights violations by paramilitaries. The process also raised fears that paramilitaries were being "recycled" into the conflict. AI continued to document strong links between the security forces and paramilitaries. Despite a fall in certain indicators of political violence such as kidnappings and massacres, reports of extrajudicial executions carried out directly by the armed forces increased in 2004. Cases of "disappearances" and torture remained high. Civilians were targeted by all sides in the armed conflict – the security forces, paramilitaries and armed opposition groups. In the first half of 2004, at least 1,400 civilians were killed or "disappeared". Around 1,250 people were kidnapped and 287,000 were forced to flee their homes. Hundreds of civilians were subjected to mass and often irregular detentions by the security forces. The government continued to make statements equating the defence of human rights with the promotion of "terrorism". In December the government pardoned 23 prisoners belonging to the armed opposition group Revolutionary Armed Forces of Colombia (Fuerzas Armadas Revolucionarias de Colombia, FARC), but the FARC refused to release any of its hostages in return. Talks to initiate peace talks with the smaller National Liberation Army (Ejército de Liberación Nacional, ELN) continued. The FARC and ELN were responsible for serious and widespread breaches of international humanitarian law, including hostage-taking and the killing of civilians.

Paramilitaries

Negotiations between the government and the AUC, which purportedly aimed to demobilize up to 20,000 AUC combatants by the end of 2005, continued despite the fact that the whereabouts of AUC leader Carlos Castaño, missing since 16 April, remained unknown. On 13 May, the AUC and the government signed the Santa Fe de Ralito agreement, under which a "concentration zone" was set up in Tierralta, Córdoba Department. Security forces were withdrawn from the zone and arrest warrants against AUC leaders residing in the zone were suspended. An Organization of American States (OAS) mission, set up in January to verify the AUC ceasefire, oversaw the concentration of paramilitaries in the zone.

Over 2,500 paramilitaries were reportedly demobilized in 2004 in various parts of the country. But concerns remained that paramilitaries were being "recycled" into the conflict. On 31 August, the government published Decree 2767, which enabled demobilized paramilitaries to "cooperate" with the security forces in return for payment.

After national and international criticism, the government withdrew the Justice and Reparation Bill, which would have created a legal framework for the demobilization of illegal armed groups. The Bill, which failed to respect the right of victims to truth, justice and reparation, could have guaranteed impunity for human rights violators. The government objected to a new draft presented by Congress members which addressed some of these concerns and said it would present a new draft in 2005. Most paramilitaries who reportedly demobilized benefited from Decree 128, which may have granted de facto amnesties to human rights abusers. Its continued application raised doubts about the government's commitment to confronting impunity.

The paramilitaries also continued to violate their self-declared ceasefire, announced in December 2002. More than 1,800 killings and "disappearances" carried out since the ceasefire were attributed to the paramilitaries. Paramilitaries were also responsible for serious human rights violations in areas where they had reportedly demobilized and continued to operate with the support and collusion of the armed forces.

▢ On 19 May, some 11 peasant farmers were killed, reportedly by paramilitaries, in Tame Municipality, Arauca Department.

▢ On 18 April, at least 12 people from the indigenous Wayúu community were killed by suspected paramilitaries in Bahía Portete, La Guajira Department. Although the security forces were informed about the possibility of a paramilitary incursion and were alerted during the incursion, no attempt appeared to be taken to intervene. Reports suggested that some of the victims were handed over to paramilitaries after their abduction by army soldiers.

Impunity

The Office of the Attorney General failed to advance criminal investigations into human rights violations implicating high-ranking officers. In January it closed the investigation of General Álvaro Velandia Hurtado, accused of the "disappearance" and killing of Nydia Erika Bautista in 1987; in 2003, the Office of the Procurator General had ruled that criminal investigations against the former general should continue. In March, the investigation of General Rito Alejo del Río, accused of links with paramilitarism, was also closed.

The military justice system continued to claim jurisdiction over cases of potential human rights violations committed by members of the security forces, despite the 1997 ruling of the Constitutional Court that such cases must be investigated by the civilian justice system.

'Anti-terrorism' – activists targeted

In August, the Constitutional Court declared the Anti-Terrorist Statute, approved at the end of 2003, null and void. The statute would have allowed the military to arrest individuals, raid homes and offices and intercept communications without judicial warrant.

The government continued to undermine human rights defenders through statements equating their work with the promotion of "terrorism". On 16 June, President Uribe said that by "not having the courage to denounce Amnesty International, we have allowed it to legitimize terrorism internationally". These accusations were publicly rejected as unfounded and unacceptable by AI, other human rights non-governmental organizations and members of the international community.

As part of the government's "war on terror", hundreds of civilians, especially peasant farmers, human rights defenders, community leaders and trade unionists, were subjected to mass and often irregular detentions by the security forces. Many of these detentions were carried out solely on the basis of information provided by paid informants. The use of mass detentions was questioned by the Office of the Procurator General, the Human Rights Ombudsman, and the Office in Colombia of the UN High Commissioner for Human Rights.

Judicial officials who released those detained in mass arrests were themselves investigated. In May, the Office of the Attorney General ordered the arrest of Judge Orlando Pacheco. In November 2003 he had released over 120 people detained in Sucre Department on conflict-related charges due to lack of evidence. In June, the Office of the Attorney General ordered the recapture of those freed by Judge Pacheco.

Many of those detained and subsequently released were threatened or killed.

▢ On 6 October, community leader Teresa Yarce was shot dead by suspected paramilitaries in the Comuna 13 neighbourhood of Medellín. She had been detained without charge by the security forces in November 2002, and subsequently threatened, after she reported human rights violations committed during a security force operation in the area.

▢ On 17 September, sociologist Alfredo Correa was killed by alleged paramilitaries in Baranquilla, Atlántico Department. He had been detained by the security forces in June and released in July after claims that he was a member of the FARC proved unfounded.

Trade unionists continued to be targeted. Although the number of killings fell in 2004, over 60 trade unionists were killed. Death threats against trade unionists continued unabated. In August reports emerged of an alleged plot, known as Operation Dragon, to kill trade unionists and left-wing political leaders. An investigation into the alleged plot by the Office of the Attorney General led to the discovery of an intelligence document reportedly written by the army's III Brigade labelling trade unionists in Cali as subversive.

Armed forces

The security forces continued to kill, torture, and "disappear" civilians, either directly or in collusion with paramilitaries. There were increased reports of extrajudicial executions carried out directly by the army, with victims often portrayed as guerrillas killed in combat.

On 5 August, three trade unionists were killed by soldiers of the XVIII Brigade in Saravena Municipality, Arauca Department. The army claimed they were guerrillas killed in combat, but evidence emerged that they were unarmed and shot in the back.

On 10 April, five civilians, including a six-month-old baby, were killed in Cajamarca Municipality, Tolima Department, by soldiers of the Pijaos Battalion. The soldiers claimed the victims died in combat. Reports suggested that no combat took place and that at least one of the victims was shot at point-blank range.

On 19 March, seven police officers from the Unified Action Group for Personal Freedom and four civilians were killed by soldiers of the Boyacá Battalion in Guaitarilla Municipality, Nariño Department. The army claimed the police failed to stop at a checkpoint and opened fire forcing them to return fire. There was evidence that at least one of the victims had been shot at point-blank range.

In October, the government announced it had destroyed all the military's stockpile of anti-personnel landmines, in accordance with the 1997 Convention on the Prohibition of the Use, Stockpiling, Production and Transfer of Anti-Personnel Mines and on their Destruction.

Armed opposition groups

Armed opposition groups were responsible for repeated and serious breaches of international humanitarian law, including hostage-taking and the killing of civilians.

On 15 June, the FARC allegedly killed 34 coca gatherers in Tibú Municipality, Norte de Santander Department.

On 15 February, the ELN reportedly killed a teacher, Janeth del Socorro Vélez Galeano, and a peasant farmer, Robeiro Alfonso Urrego Ibarra, in Remedios Municipality, Antioquia Department.

The FARC also carried out attacks using disproportionate and indiscriminate weapons which resulted in the deaths of numerous civilians.

On 19 September, four civilians were killed and 17 others injured, including 10 children, when the FARC allegedly detonated a mine and opened fire on a civilian vehicle in San Carlos Municipality, Antioquia Department.

In October, President Uribe offered to begin negotiations on a humanitarian agreement with the FARC which could lead to an exchange of FARC prisoners for hostages held by the armed opposition group. No agreement had been reached by the end of the year, although in December the government pardoned 23 FARC prisoners. There was a lack of clarity about how the government had ensured that those pardoned were not implicated in human rights abuses.

The ELN and the government reportedly established contact to discuss opening formal peace talks. In May, President Uribe asked Mexican President Vicente Fox to act as "guarantor" for any future process. In July, Mexican officials held talks with jailed ELN commander Gerardo Bermúdez, alias "Francisco Galán".

Violence against women

Women and girls were raped, killed, "disappeared" and mutilated by all parties to the conflict. They were targeted for a variety of reasons, including to sow terror, wreak revenge on adversaries and accumulate "trophies of war".

On 15 July, two girls aged 16 and 17 were allegedly gang raped by more than 10 army soldiers attached to the IV Brigade in Sonsón Municipality, Antioquia Department. The girls and their families were reportedly threatened by some of the soldiers involved after they reported the rape to the Office of the Attorney General.

On 8 October, the FARC allegedly killed four women, one of whom was pregnant, and a man in a house in Colosó Municipality, Sucre Department. The FARC had reportedly accused the women of having relations with security force members.

Kidnappings

Armed opposition groups and criminal gangs accounted for most kidnappings; paramilitary groups were also responsible. There was a further fall in the number of kidnappings in 2004; from at least 2,200 in 2003 to around 1,250 people in 2004. Over 400 of these kidnappings were carried out by armed opposition groups, at least 120 by paramilitaries and around 350 by criminal gangs; those responsible could not be identified in over 300 cases.

On 24 July, the ELN reportedly kidnapped the Bishop of Yopal in Morcote on the border of Boyacá and Casanare Departments. He was released a few days later.

On 27 June, paramilitaries reportedly kidnapped former senator José Gnecco and members of his family on a highway in Santa Marta Municipality, Magdalena Department. They were all released a few days later.

On 21 May, the FARC allegedly kidnapped 11 people, including four women, in Algeciras Municipality, Huila Department. They were released on 10 June.

Abuses against civilians

Peasant farmers, internally displaced people and Afro-descendent and indigenous communities living in areas where armed groups were active and with a heavy military presence were at particular risk of attack. Over 287,000 people were forced from their homes in 2004, compared to some 207,000 in 2003. Moreover, there were increasing reports that armed groups in control of particular areas sought to prevent people from leaving their communities, often blocking access to food and services.

Certain government security measures continued to drag civilians further into the conflict. These included the network of civilian informants which, according to the government, involved more than 2.5 million people by August, and the army of peasant soldiers, who unlike regular soldiers often operated in their own communities and sometimes lived at home, thus placing their families at increased risk of revenge attacks by armed opposition groups.

On 22 August, the FARC allegedly killed a peasant soldier and his mother at their home in Corinto Municipality, Cauca Department.

Indigenous communities continued to face a serious human rights crisis.

On 3 August, suspected paramilitaries killed a Kankuamo leader, Freddy Arias Arias, in Valledupar, Cesar Department.

On 6 November, the FARC allegedly killed an Arhuaco leader, Mariano Suárez Chaparro, in the Sierra Nevada de Santa Marta, Magdalena Department.

US military aid

US security assistance amounted to an estimated US$550 million in 2004. The US Congress also approved an additional US$629 million in security assistance for 2005, including training for the security forces, weapons, and spare parts. In October the US Congress increased the ceiling on US troops in Colombia from 400 to 800, and on private contractors from 400 to 600. Congress also renewed the annual human rights certification process whereby the Secretary of State is required to certify Colombia's progress on specific human rights practices such as investigations and prosecutions of alleged human rights violations by security forces, and efforts to sever ties between the Colombian armed forces and paramilitary forces. Congress did not include specific limitations on US assistance for the paramilitary demobilization process, but did note that current US law prohibits assistance to "foreign terrorist organizations", such as the AUC.

Intergovernmental organizations

The UN Commission on Human Rights condemned the failure of the security forces, paramilitaries and guerrillas to respect international humanitarian law and condemned the recruitment of children by armed groups. It reiterated its concern regarding the climate of hostility generated by government officials regarding the work of human rights defenders; condemned reports of continued collusion of state agents with paramilitary groups; and noted the increase in complaints about forced "disappearances", mainly by paramilitaries, but also by the security forces. The Commission also expressed concern at increased reports of arbitrary and mass detentions. It called for the implementation of UN human rights recommendations.

AI reports/visits
Reports
- Colombia: A laboratory of war: Repression and violence in Arauca (AI Index: AMR 23/004/2004)
- Colombia: "Scarred bodies, hidden crimes" – Sexual violence against women in the armed conflict (AI Index: AMR 23/040/2004)

Visits
AI delegates visited Colombia in March, May, August and October.

CONGO
(DEMOCRATIC REPUBLIC OF THE)

DEMOCRATIC REPUBLIC OF THE CONGO
Head of state and government: Joseph Kabila
Death penalty: retentionist
International Criminal Court: ratified
UN Women's Convention: ratified
Optional Protocol to UN Women's Convention: not signed

The transitional power-sharing government made little progress in advancing laws and reforms essential to building security and respect for human rights. Government authority remained weak or non-existent in parts of eastern Democratic Republic of the Congo (DRC) which were under the de facto control of armed groups. Insecurity, ethnic tension and human rights abuses continued, including unlawful killings, widespread rape, torture and the recruitment and use of child soldiers. The government and international community made little concerted effort to address the immense needs of the war-scarred civilian population. According to the International Rescue Committee, an estimated 31,000 people died every month as a result of the conflict. Survivors of human rights abuses had little or no access to medical care.

Background

The transitional government, established in July 2003 and composed of all former belligerent groups who signed the 2002 All Inclusive Peace Agreement, was beset by factionalism and a series of political and military crises. It made only limited advances in improving security and respect for human rights and failed to extend its authority to many areas of eastern DRC, where instability and localized violence continued, threatening on occasion to reignite into wider conflict.

Slow progress was made on reforms essential for improved security and national unification. Plans for the integration of former combatant forces into a unified national army, and the disarmament, demobilization and reintegration (DDR) into civilian life of an estimated 200,000 other combatants were established, but few of these programmes, to be backed by international financial and technical assistance, had started by the end of 2004. Only the army chief of staff and other senior army command positions, and one army brigade, were integrated in 2004. In May the provincial governor posts were redistributed along party lines. In September a pilot DDR programme was launched in Ituri. However, by the end of the year very few of the estimated 15,000 combatants in that district had been demobilized. Armed group leaders reportedly intimidated combatants to prevent them joining the DDR process in Ituri.

Key laws relating to a new constitution and the organization of nationwide elections were substantially delayed and had not been approved by parliament by the end of 2004. A law defining Congolese nationality was promulgated in December.

There were reports of coup attempts in Kinshasa in March and June, although doubts remained about their authenticity. The first attempt was attributed to Mobutist officers of the former Zairian Armed Forces (Forces armées zaïroises, FAZ), who had fled to Congo-Brazzaville in 1997. The second attempt was reportedly the work of a Special Presidential Security Guard (GSSP) officer.

A prolonged military and political crisis, centred on the strategically important Kivu provinces bordering Rwanda, threatened to derail the transition process. In February in South-Kivu soldiers of the Goma-based Congolese Rally for Democracy (Rassemblement congolais pour la démocratie-Goma, RCD-Goma) forcibly opposed the authority of the government-appointed regional commander. The resulting impasse culminated in June in a military confrontation between pro-government and renegade RCD-Goma forces for control of the provincial capital, Bukavu. Civilians were targeted by both sides. Violent demonstrations nationwide, directed mainly at UN peacekeeping and government installations, followed the seizure of Bukavu by the renegade RCD-Goma forces. Ethnic tension between different groups in the region, deliberately manipulated by some leaders, escalated markedly. In August more than 150 mainly Congolese Tutsi refugees were massacred in Gatumba, Burundi (see Burundi entry). In August, the RCD-Goma temporarily suspended its participation in government. The bulk of the renegade RCD-Goma forces later regrouped in North-Kivu, where they continued to operate in defiance of central authority. The crisis had not been resolved by the end of 2004 when new fighting erupted in Kanyabayionga (North-Kivu) between pro RCD-Goma soldiers and the national army.

In October the DRC, Rwanda and Uganda, the major protagonists of the DRC conflict, signed a tripartite security agreement, establishing a commission to deal with common security issues. Mistrust between these states remained the prevailing regional dynamic, however. Rwanda threatened three times to renew its military operations in eastern DRC, citing (in June) the need to protect Congolese Tutsi from ethnic violence and (in April and November) the need to counter the threat posed to Rwanda by Rwandan insurgent forces based in eastern DRC. There were credible reports that Rwandan army units entered DRC in each of these months, although this was denied by the Rwandan government. Rwanda also appeared to exercise a degree of control over RCD-Goma armed forces in North and South-Kivu.

The UN peacekeeping force, MONUC, continued to struggle to contain violence and protect civilians in eastern DRC. An increase in the size of the force from 10,700 to 16,600 was authorized by the UN Security Council in October, but many areas of the east remained beyond MONUC's operational capacity. An arms embargo, imposed by the UN in July 2003 and monitored by MONUC, was only partially effective. In July 2004 the UN-appointed Group of Technical Experts on the Democratic Republic of the Congo reported that direct and indirect assistance, which included the supply of arms and ammunition, was provided in violation of the embargo to armed groups operating in eastern DRC by neighbouring countries and from within the DRC.

By the end of 2004 the MONUC-supervised programme of voluntary repatriation of combatants (mainly Rwandan insurgents) had repatriated around 11,000 combatants and their dependants to Rwanda, Burundi and Uganda, according to MONUC sources. However, several thousand Rwandan and to a lesser extent Burundian and Ugandan insurgents remained in eastern DRC, where they continued to commit abuses.

Human rights abuses were reported nationwide. The situation in eastern DRC remained especially alarming, where armed groups and militia perpetrated grave human rights abuses against civilians in the provinces of North-Kivu, South-Kivu, Maniema, Orientale (notably the Ituri district), Kasai Oriental and Katanga.

Unlawful killings

All armed forces and groups were responsible for unlawful killings of civilians in 2004. Killings were reported on an almost daily basis.

In late May and early June 2004, dozens of civilians were unlawfully killed and many rapes were committed by renegade RCD-Goma forces in Bukavu, South-Kivu province, after they took control of the city. Government loyalist forces, who later retook the city, also committed abuses. Many killings were perpetrated during looting of private homes. Those killed included Lambert Mobole Bitorwa, shot at home in front of his children; Jolie Namwezi, reportedly shot in front of her children after she resisted rape; Murhula Kagezi; and a 13-year-old girl, Marie Chimbale Tambwe, shot dead on the balcony of her home, apparently because she pulled a face at a soldier while he was looting in the street below.

Child soldiers

Tens of thousands of children remained in the ranks of armed groups and militia, who continued to recruit new child soldiers. In some cases former child soldiers who were being assisted by local NGOs in eastern DRC were forcibly re-recruited. Other children were reportedly tempted to return voluntarily to armed groups by the prospect of receiving payments from the DRC government to combatant forces, pending integration.

🗁 Jim, aged 13, was recruited in February by an armed group in South-Kivu province with the promise of a government payment. Two weeks later he received 5,000 Congolese francs (FC) – around $11 US – of which he had to give his commander 3,000 FC. A few days later, Jim was badly wounded in his right arm during weapons training. His arm was later amputated.

Violence against women

In the course of the DRC conflict, tens of thousands of women and girls have been victims of systematic rape committed by combatant forces. Throughout 2004 women and girls continued to be attacked in their homes, in the fields or as they went about their daily activities. Many suffered gang rapes or were taken as sex slaves by combatants. Rape of men and boys was also reported. Rape was often preceded or followed by the deliberate wounding, torture or killing of the victim. Some rapes were committed publicly or in front of family members, including children. Some MONUC civilian, police and military personnel were responsible for rape and sexual exploitation of women and girls.

Rape survivors' rights were further violated in the aftermath of the rape, deepening their suffering. Women suffering injuries or illnesses caused by the rape – some of them life-threatening – were denied medical care. The DRC's health care system, completely broken down in many areas, was unable to offer even the most basic treatment. Because of prejudice, many women were abandoned by their husbands and excluded by their communities, condemning them and their children to extreme poverty. Because of an incapacitated judicial system, there was no justice or redress for the crimes they endured.

🗁 In March AI delegates visited Odette, a girl of six, in hospital in the city of Kindu, Maniema province. She had been raped several weeks before by a mayi-mayi combatant as she played in front of her home. The man dragged her into the grounds of the local school where he raped her. The attack left her with extensive wounds to her vagina.

🗁 In early 2004 Lotsove, aged 12, was raped by combatants as she sought shelter from fighting between two armed groups for control of the gold mining area of Mongbwalu, Ituri district. During the attack, she lost track of six of her friends and her two sisters who had been with her. She found her sisters, Lolo and Vita, 13 and 14, three days later in a nearby village. Both had also been raped. Despite having pain in her lower abdomen, Lotsove was never seen by a doctor.

Torture and illegal detention

Arbitrary arrest and illegal detention remained frequent across the DRC. Many people spent long periods in detention without charge or trial. A number

were reportedly ill-treated or tortured. Human rights defenders and journalists engaged in legitimate investigation and criticism were also threatened and unlawfully detained.

🗁 In October a man named Musimbi was detained by the security services in Uvira, South-Kivu, and repeatedly beaten with wooden sticks, reportedly because he had accused local authorities of fomenting insecurity. After losing consciousness he was taken to his home, where security agents demanded a "fine" from his family.

Death penalty

Around 200 people were reportedly held on death row. At least 27 people were sentenced to death. No executions were reported.

International and transitional justice

In October the International Criminal Court (ICC) and the DRC government signed a cooperation agreement allowing the ICC to begin investigations into war crimes and crimes against humanity committed within the country. ICC investigators visited Ituri, where initial ICC enquiries were concentrated.

Impunity for the perpetrators of human rights abuses, and lack of redress for the victims, remained almost absolute. The effectiveness of the Congolese justice system continued to be undermined by a lack of basic material and human resources, suitable protection mechanisms for victims and witnesses, and devastated infrastructures. In one exceptional case in July, an armed group commander in Ituri, Rafiki Saba Aimable, was sentenced to 20 years' imprisonment by a Bunia court for torture.

Refugees and the internally displaced

Around 2.3 million civilians remained displaced by the end of 2004, mainly in eastern DRC. Many were cut off from humanitarian aid. In some areas armed groups refused relief workers access, attacked aid deliveries, looted stocks of food aid, or commandeered relief agencies' vehicles.

The Congolese authorities failed to make provision for the safety and dignity of people returning to the DRC, including refugees.

Between December 2003 and April 2004, tens of thousands of Congolese were forcibly expelled to DRC from Angola. Many were extremely weak from dehydration, hunger and days on the move. Those expelled reported human rights abuses on both sides of the border, including being detained and ill-treated by DRC security forces. Around 40,000 remain displaced in DRC at the year's end.

In September and October Congolese Tutsi refugees, including women and children, returning to South-Kivu province from Burundi were attacked with stones by members of the local non-Tutsi population.

AI country reports/ visits
Reports

• Democratic Republic of the Congo: Mass rape – time for remedies (AI Index: AFR 62/018/2004)

- Democratic Republic of Congo: Surviving rape – voices from the east (AI Index: AFR 62/019/2004)
- Democratic Republic of Congo: Public appeal: Still under the gun – more child soldiers recruited (AI Index: AFR 62/009/2004)
- Democratic Republic of Congo: Comments and recommendations of the July 2003 draft law implementing the Rome Statute of the International Criminal Court (AI Index: AFR 62/008/2004)

Visits

In February/March AI delegates visited North-Kivu, South-Kivu and Maniema. In May/ June, AI delegates visited Ituri and the capital, Kinshasa. In October, AI delegates launched a report and met government authorities in Kinshasa.

CONGO
(REPUBLIC OF THE)

REPUBLIC OF THE CONGO
Head of state and government: Denis Sassou-Nguesso
Death penalty: abolitionist in practice
International Criminal Court: ratified
UN Women's Convention: ratified
Optional Protocol to UN Women's Convention: not signed

The government repeatedly promised to bring to justice members of the security forces accused of involvement in "disappearances" in 1999, but failed to do so. Members of the security forces killed at least three people; one of the victims was accused of witchcraft. The authorities used the courts and administrative measures to silence journalists.

Background

A peace agreement signed between the government and the armed opposition National Resistance Council (Conseil national de résistance, CNR) continued to hold but it was not fully implemented. The CNR leader, Frédéric Bitsangou, and many of his combatants remained in their bases in the Pool region, giving rise to fears that conflict might resume. The government rejected CNR demands for a government of national unity, the return of exiled former leaders, clarification of its leader's legal status and a binding agreement to integrate combatants into government security forces. Humanitarian workers expressed concern that the population of the Pool region faced a dire situation with little or no access to medical, educational and food assistance. The infrastructure destroyed during the armed conflict remained largely unrepaired.

In July the country was suspended from the Kimberley Process Certification Scheme, which traces the origin of diamonds, because it failed to account for the origin of large quantities of rough diamonds that it was exporting.

Impunity

In a case lodged in a French court in 2001, senior Congolese officials were accused of responsibility for the May 1999 "disappearance" of at least 353 refugees returning from the neighbouring Democratic Republic of the Congo. In March a French court issued an international arrest warrant for army inspector General Norbert Dabira, but he was not arrested. In April Jean-François Ndenguet, the director of the Congolese police, was arrested in Meaux on the orders of the French Procuracy. He was released within 24 hours after he claimed diplomatic immunity.

In April the Congolese government promised to prove that the "disappearances" had not occurred and threatened to bring prosecutions against organizations that continued to claim that it was responsible. No such proof was given or prosecutions occurred. Killings of people suspected of practising witchcraft continued to be reported. In July several officials claimed that they had been charged with involvement in the "disappearances" at their own request – a claim denied by the Procurator General of the Supreme Court.

⮡ Sixty-year-old Mbon Pô was beaten to death in November by soldiers who accused him of responsibility for the death of his daughter, who was a soldier. The victim's son, also a soldier, was reportedly severely beaten by his colleagues when he tried to protect his father. Although there were reports of judicial investigations into the killing, no further action was reported by the end of 2004.

Unlawful killings

The authorities issued orders to the security forces to eliminate violent criminals, which led to unlawful killings of civilians. In January Bienvenu Feignand died after being shot by a special police unit set up to fight violent crime. The victim had not been involved in any criminal activity. No investigation was known to have been carried out into the shooting. The same month a young boy trying to stow away in an Air France passenger plane undercarriage was shot dead by members of the security forces.

Silencing the media

The government imposed restrictions on freedom of the press. Several national radio journalists who hosted broadcasts critical of government policies were either suspended or had their programmes stopped. They included Toudikissa Massanga and Dulcine Pambou.

In November government ministers threatened to cancel accreditations for foreign radio correspondents who presented a negative image of the government. For example, the accreditation for Saïd Penda, a correspondent for the London-based British Broadcasting Corporation (BBC), was cancelled after he interviewed a government opponent who described the President as a dictator.

Gislin Simplice Ongouya, the publication director of *L'Observateur*, had six charges of libel filed in court against him by directors of the state oil company. The newspaper had published articles in November 2003 accusing the directors of mismanagement. In January, Gislin Simplice Ongouya was informed that in July 2003 he had been found guilty of libel in his absence, without being asked to appear in court. He was ordered to pay damages of more than US$8,000, which threatened the newspaper with closure.

CÔTE D'IVOIRE

REPUBLIC OF CÔTE D'IVOIRE
Head of state: Laurent Gbagbo
Head of government: Seydou Diarra
Death penalty: abolitionist for all crimes
International Criminal Court: signed
UN Women's Convention: ratified
Optional Protocol to UN Women's Convention: not signed

Two years after the January 2003 Linas-Marcoussis Agreement sought to end the internal conflict, no real sign of a political solution was noticeable. In November government forces broke the 18-month ceasefire with an attack in which dozens of civilians and nine French soldiers died, leading to armed reprisals by French peacekeeping forces. Reliable sources indicated that French troops used excessive force against government supporters. Violent anti-French protests, which included looting and alleged rapes, led to the departure of more than 8,000 foreign nationals from the country. Xenophobic hate speech in the broadcast and print media supportive of President Laurent Gbagbo continued to fuel tensions between Ivorian and foreign nationals. In the north of the country held by former armed opposition groups, renamed New Forces (*Forces nouvelles*), human rights abuses continued, particularly in the context of fighting between rival factions. By the end of the year, an arms embargo and the threat of individual sanctions imposed by the UN, as well as mediation by the African Union, led to a calming of the situation which nevertheless remained very tense.

Background
After a three-month boycott the New Forces resumed participation in the National Reconciliation Government in January and talks were held in preparation for the disarmament of combatants. In February the UN Security Council adopted a resolution establishing a 6,000-strong peacekeeping force, the United Nations Operation in Côte d'Ivoire (UNOCI), with a mandate to oversee the disarmament and reconciliation process in conjunction with the French forces. However, the situation seriously deteriorated in March after government forces violently broke up a banned demonstration organized by opposition parties. As a result, some opposition parties pulled out of the government and in May President Gbagbo dismissed three opposition ministers including one of the leaders of the New Forces, Guillaume Soro.

Under heavy pressure from the international community – including the UN, France and key African countries – a new agreement was reached in Accra, Ghana, at the end of July. Under the terms of the deal, the New Forces were to start disarming by 15 October after certain political reforms agreed to previously had been adopted, including laws on land ownership, the eligibility of presidential candidates and a new code of nationality. However, these conditions were not met by the deadline, leading to political deadlock.

At the beginning of November, government warplanes broke an 18-month ceasefire and bombed the New Forces stronghold of Bouaké, killing dozens of civilians and nine French soldiers. The African Union and the Francophonie strongly condemned the strikes. The French forces retaliated by destroying most of the government air force. This in turn provoked anti-French protests in Abidjan, during which foreign businesses were looted and French and other non-Ivorian civilians were attacked in their homes and in some cases reportedly raped. French troops opened fire on the protesters, killing at least 20 and injuring several hundred in what appeared to be an excessive use of force. In the wake of these violent anti-French protests more than 8,000 foreign citizens, mostly French nationals, left the country. The Ivorian government reportedly contemplated filing a suit against France before the International Court of Justice, although this was denied by President Gbagbo. The November outbreak of violence led to pressure by the UN and mediation by the African Union. As a result, key laws on nationality, naturalization and presidential eligibility were adopted by the National Assembly in December. However, disagreement remained between the President and some opposition parties and the New Forces over the rules on eligibility for presidency.

Extrajudicial executions and 'disappearances'
On 25 March security forces broke up a banned demonstration in Abidjan with excessive force by using automatic weapons and heavy ammunition, including guns mounted on vehicles. In the nights following the demonstration there were a number of extrajudicial executions and "disappearances".

On the night of 26 March security forces raided houses in Abobo, a district on the outskirts of Abidjan. They shot at several people, including a pregnant woman and a young Hausa from Niger, Abdou Raouf, who was shot at point-blank range and later died from his wounds. Several people were arrested at their homes and subsequently "disappeared", including Koné Abdoulaye, known as Diaby, and Soumahoro Mustafa, a taxi driver.

Abuses by the New Forces

Armed elements of the New Forces were responsible for human rights abuses including deliberate and arbitrary killings and the abduction of a journalist.

▱ In June, following gun battles between two rival New Forces factions, at least 100 people were arbitrarily killed in Korhogo in the north of the country. Their bodies, some riddled with bullets, were found in July in three mass graves by a UN human rights team. They had reportedly been arrested by Guillaume Soro's armed supporters and put in containers where some of them died from suffocation. Others appeared to have been decapitated or killed with their hands bound behind their backs.

▱ In August, Amadou Dagnogo, the Bouaké correspondent of the Abidjan-based daily *L'Inter,* was held in Bouaké and reportedly beaten and tortured by supporters of Guillaume Soro. He managed to escape after six days and flew back to Abidjan.

Allegations of excessive use of force by French troops

On 6-7 November French troops allegedly used excessive force against civilians in Abidjan. The events occurred against a backdrop of anti-French protests following the destruction of the Ivorian air force. Senior members of the Ivorian security forces accused French troops of firing directly at an unarmed crowd without warning. They said that 57 civilians were killed and more than 2,200 injured. The French authorities acknowledged that troops may have been responsible for at least 20 casualties but stated that the soldiers had acted in totally legitimate self-defence and that they had fired warning shots. However, independent sources indicated that during the night of 6 November French troops fired from helicopters in an attempt to deter protesters from crossing a bridge in Abidjan. Other sources mentioned cases of injured people who had feet and hands torn off, probably by grenade explosions.

Attacks on journalists

Ivorian and foreign journalists and media organizations were harassed and attacked by security forces and pro-government militias.

▱ At least 10 journalists covering the banned demonstration in March were physically assaulted by security forces and civilian supporters of President Gbagbo.

▱ On the same day in November that government forces broke the ceasefire, supporters of President Gbagbo set fire to the offices of three opposition newspapers, including *Le Patriote,* a paper supportive of former Prime Minister Alassane Ouattara. International radio networks had their transmissions cut and were unable to resume broadcasting for some three weeks.

Refugees and humanitarian concerns

The two-year conflict in Côte d'Ivoire continued to destabilize the humanitarian situation in the country and the region.

▱ After breaking the ceasefire in November, the government cut off water and power supplies in the opposition-held north. Humanitarian non-governmental organizations and UN agencies expressed fears that there would be outbreaks of water-borne diseases such as cholera and diarrhoea. The supplies were restored after a week.

▱ Following the outbreak of violence in November an estimated 19,000 people, mostly women and children, fled to Liberia. They began returning from the end of November.

UN response

Throughout the year, the UN condemned human rights abuses in Côte d'Ivoire and denounced the xenophobic hate speech disseminated by some parts of the media. The UN also set up two missions of inquiry. The first, in April, concluded that security forces and pro-government militia were responsible for killing at least 120 people during the banned demonstration in March. The second led a three-month investigation into human rights abuses committed by all sides since the armed uprising in September 2002. The report of this commission was delivered in October to the UN Secretary-General and the High Commissioner for Human Rights but had not officially been made public by the UN by the end of 2004.

After the end of the ceasefire in November the UN Security Council unanimously adopted a resolution imposing an immediate 13-month arms embargo and calling for selected individuals to have assets frozen and travel bans imposed. A list of the people to be sanctioned was reportedly prepared but had not been published by the end of the year. A UN expert on the prevention of genocide also called on the authorities to condemn hate speech and put an end to broadcasts of hate messages on national television and radio.

AI country reports/ visits
Report
· Côte d'Ivoire: The indiscriminate and disproportionate repression of a banned demonstration (AI Index: AFR 31/004/2004)
Visit
In July, an AI delegation visited Burkina Faso to collect information about planters who had been expelled from or had to flee Côte d'Ivoire.

CROATIA

REPUBLIC OF CROATIA
Head of state: Stjepan Mesić
Head of government: Ivo Sanader
Death penalty: abolitionist for all crimes
International Criminal Court: ratified
UN Women's Convention and its Optional Protocol:
ratified

The legacy of the 1991-95 armed conflict continued to overshadow human rights in Croatia. Many of those responsible for human rights violations during the conflict continued to evade justice. Despite the Croatian government's pledge to cooperate fully with the International Criminal Tribunal for the former Yugoslavia (Tribunal), on occasion the Croatian authorities adopted an ambivalent attitude. Less than a third of the 300,000 Croatian Serb refugees who fled the fighting had returned by the end of 2004. The Croatian judicial system overwhelmingly failed to address wartime human rights violations and courts applied discriminatory criteria when investigating and prosecuting war crimes and crimes against humanity.

Background

In June, Croatia was officially granted European Union (EU) candidate status at the European Council summit in Brussels. In April the European Commission had noted that further progress was needed in the areas of minority rights, refugee returns, judicial reform, regional cooperation and the fight against corruption. In December the EU Council decided to open membership talks in March 2005, on condition that Croatia fully cooperates with the Tribunal.

Wartime human rights violations
International prosecutions

The authorities failed to arrest Ante Gotovina, a former Croatian Army General charged by the Tribunal with crimes against humanity and war crimes against the Krajina Croatian Serb population in 1995 during "Operation Storm". Croatian forces had committed widespread human rights violations including the killing of hundreds of civilians, "disappearances", torture including rape, and massive and systematic house destruction during "Operation Storm" and "Operation Flash". Despite formal assurances, the Croatian authorities continued to maintain an ambiguous attitude towards cooperation with the Tribunal and Ante Gotovina's arrest. In October Prime Minister Ivo Sanader reportedly publicly stated his belief in Ante Gotovina's innocence.

In February Ivan Čermak, former Commander of the Knin Garrison of the Croatian Army and Mladen Markač, former Commander of the Special Police of the Ministry of the Interior, were indicted by the Tribunal for crimes against humanity and violations of the laws or customs of war committed in 1995 against the non-Croat population during "Operation Storm". The suspects voluntarily surrendered to the Tribunal in March.

In May the Tribunal indicted former Croatian Army General Mirko Norac for crimes against humanity and violations of the laws or customs of war committed in 1993 against the non-Croat population in the Medak Pocket. Mirko Norac was already serving a prison sentence in Croatia after being convicted in 2003 by the Rijeka County Court of war crimes against non-Croat civilians. In September the Tribunal appointed a trial chamber to consider an application by the prosecutor to refer the case of Mirko Norac and Rahim Ademi, whose indictments were joined in July, to the authorities of Croatia for trial by the Zagreb County Court.

In June the Tribunal indicted Goran Hadžić, President of the self-proclaimed autonomous Republic of the Serbian Krajina (Republika Srpska Krajina, RSK) between early 1992 and late 1993. Goran Hadžić was charged with crimes against humanity and violations of the laws or customs of war committed against the non-Serbian population. He had not been arrested by the end of the year.

In March the Tribunal sentenced former Yugoslav Navy Admiral Miodrag Jokić to seven years' imprisonment for his role in the shelling of Dubrovnik's old town in 1991. Miodrag Jokić had pleaded guilty to all charges of war crimes.

In June Milan Babić, former RSK President, was sentenced by the Tribunal to 13 years' imprisonment for crimes against humanity committed against the non-Serbian population in 1991-1992.

In March the trial of six people accused of war crimes against the ethnic Croat population in Vukovar in 1991 began before the Special War Crimes Panel within the Belgrade District Court in the Serbian capital, Belgrade. After Vukovar fell to the Yugoslav Army and Serbian forces, more than 250 non-Serbs were removed from the Vukovar hospital and executed at the Ovčara farm. In May, 12 new suspects were indicted in connection with these crimes.

Domestic prosecutions

Most of those on trial for war crimes and crimes against humanity before local courts were Croatian Serbs. The Croatian judiciary continued to discriminate along ethnic lines in its investigations and prosecutions of wartime human rights violations. In some cases trials for war crimes and crimes against humanity conducted before domestic courts did not meet internationally recognized standards of fairness. Members of the Croatian Army and police forces generally continued to enjoy impunity for wartime human rights violations, despite initial efforts by the Croatian authorities to investigate and prosecute such crimes.

In a number of cases the Croatian Supreme Court overturned earlier acquittals in trials for war crimes and crimes against humanity allegedly committed by members of the Croatian Army and police forces.

⊂ In April the Osijek County Court sentenced former member of the Croatian Army Nikola Ivanković to 12 years' imprisonment for the killing of 19 Croatian Serb and Hungarian civilians in Paulin Dvor near Osijek in December 1991. No one was brought to justice for the subsequent attempt to cover up this crime by transporting the bodies to another location.

⊂ In May the Croatian police arrested a Bosnian Croat on suspicion that in 1993 he committed war crimes against the Bosniak (Bosnian Muslim) population in the village of Ahmići, in central Bosnia and Herzegovina.

⊂ In March the Croatian Supreme Court quashed the acquittal of a former member of the Croatian special police by the Karlovac County Court. He was accused of killing 13 disarmed Yugoslav Army reservists. Reportedly, the Karlovac Court had ruled that the accused had acted in "self-defence". The retrial began in September.

⊂ In May the Croatian Supreme Court quashed the acquittal of three former Croatian police officers and one serving police officer by the Bjelovar County Court. They were accused of killing six captured Yugoslav Army reservists in 1991. The Supreme Court reportedly ordered a retrial during which additional witnesses should be heard.

⊂ In August the Croatian Supreme Court overturned the acquittal of eight former members of the Croatian Military Police by the Split County Court. The eight were accused of killing two non-Croat civilians and torturing others in the Lora military prison in Split in 1992. The trial had reportedly been marked by the intimidation of witnesses, public demonstrations of support for the accused, and a lack of impartiality by the court. At the end of the year, only four of the accused were detained. A new trial was expected to begin in early 2005.

Unresolved 'disappearances' and missing persons

According to official data approximately 1,200 people who went missing during the conflict remained unaccounted for. This figure did not include the hundreds of people – mostly Croatian Serbs – missing since "Operation Storm" and "Operation Flash" in 1995 (see above). Efforts by the Croatian authorities to clarify the fate and whereabouts of missing Croatian Serbs were generally insufficient, leading to considerable delays in the identification process. Many of the missing were believed to be victims of "disappearances"; most of those responsible continued to enjoy impunity.

Right to return

Approximately 300,000 Croatian Serbs left Croatia during the 1991-95 conflict. According to the UN High Commissioner for Refugees, more than 200,000 Croatian refugees, mostly Croatian Serbs, remained displaced in neighbouring countries and beyond. Tens of thousands of Croatian Serbs could not return and many returns were not sustainable.

While the Croatian authorities had pledged to return illegally occupied property to returning Croatian Serbs by the end of June 2004 and other occupied property by the end of 2004, the repossession rate remained slow. Many Croatian Serbs, especially those who formerly lived in urban areas, could not return because they had lost their tenancy rights to socially owned apartments. Lengthy, and in some cases unfair, proceedings, particularly in lower level courts, remained a major obstacle for returnees pursuing their rights in court.

Croatian Serbs continued to face discrimination in employment and access to other economic and social rights.

AI country reports/visits
Reports
· Croatia: Briefing to the United Nations Committee against Torture, 32nd Session, May 2004 (AI Index: EUR 64/001/2004)
· Croatia: Briefing to the United Nations Committee on the Rights of the Child, 37th Session, September 2004 (AI Index: EUR 64/003/2004)
· Croatia: A shadow on Croatia's future – Continuing impunity for war crimes and crimes against humanity (AI Index: EUR 64/005/2004)
Visits
An AI delegate visited Croatia in February and in June.

CUBA

REPUBLIC OF CUBA
Head of state and government: Fidel Castro Ruz
Death penalty: retentionist
International Criminal Court: not signed
UN Women's Convention: ratified with reservations
Optional Protocol to UN Women's Convention: signed

By the end of 2004 there were at least 70 prisoners of conscience, most of them held since the 2003 crackdown on the dissident movement. However, 18 prisoners of conscience were released and many were moved to prisons nearer their homes. Dissidents and their relatives continued to be threatened and harassed. The US embargo and related measures continued to have a negative effect on the enjoyment of the full range of human rights in Cuba.

Prisoners of conscience
Seventy prisoners of conscience remained imprisoned at the end of the year, although the true number could be higher. All but two had been sentenced to prison terms ranging from 26 months to 28 years. The two had not been tried or sentenced.

Harsh prison conditions and health concerns

There were continuing concerns about the health of many prisoners of conscience. Some were reportedly denied access to appropriate medical attention and were held in harsh conditions, which reportedly contributed to their illnesses. However, by early December all but two of the remaining prisoners of conscience detained in the 2003 crackdown had undergone a medical examination.

◻ Omar Pernet Hernández, a 59-year-old librarian sentenced to 25 years' imprisonment in March 2003, was reportedly suffering from liver, kidney and lung problems, causing him extreme pain, as well as severe weight loss, dehydration, high blood pressure and gastritis. Normando Hernández González, a journalist sentenced to 25 years' imprisonment in March 2003, was reportedly suffering from anal bleeding, a stomach ulcer and gastritis. The families of both men said that the lack of medical attention and harsh prison conditions contributed to their illnesses.

Most prisoners were held in prisons far from their homes, making family visits extremely difficult. However, in August approximately 35 prisoners were moved to prisons in or nearer to their home provinces.

◻ Alfredo Manuel Pulido López, sentenced to 14 years' imprisonment in March 2003, was moved in August from Combinado del Este Prison in Havana to Kilo 7 Prison in his home province of Camagüey.

For the first time in 10 years, Cuba opened some sections of two prisons to the foreign press in response to criticisms concerning the treatment of prisoners.

Ill-treatment

There were several reports of ill-treatment of prisoners, including kicking and beating.

◻ In November prisoner of conscience Néstor Rodríguez Lobaina was reportedly pushed to the floor and beaten and scratched by prison guards. Subsequently a process to charge him with disrespect, disobedience and resistance was reportedly begun.

Releases

Four prisoners of conscience arrested in February 2002 and held without trial were released: Leonardo Bruzón Avila, Carlos Alberto Domínguez González, Emilio Leyva Pérez and Lázaro Miguel Rodríguez Capote. Fourteen prisoners of conscience arrested in the March 2003 crackdown were granted conditional release, which meant they could serve the rest of their sentences outside prison for health reasons. They were Osvaldo Alfonso Valdés, Margarito Broche Espinosa, Juan Roberto de Miranda Hernández, Carmelo Díaz Fernández, Oscar Espinosa Chepe, Orlando Fundora Alvárez, Edel José García Díaz, Marcelo López Bañobre, Jorge Olivera Castillo, Raúl Rivero Castañeda, Marta Beatriz Roque Cabello, Miguel Valdés Tamayo, Julio Valdés Guevara and Manuel Vázquez Portal. The government reportedly said the releases were part of a policy to free inmates early for reasons of health, age and good behaviour, while welcoming efforts by Spain's new government to revise the European Union policy on Cuba and reopen contacts.

Death penalty

No new death sentences were passed. Between 40 and 50 prisoners reportedly remained on death row at the end of the year.

International community
United Nations

A UN human rights envoy, appointed by the UN High Commissioner for Human Rights to probe alleged abuses in Cuba, reported that dozens of Cuban dissidents were being held in alarming conditions following their imprisonment in the 2003 crackdown.

In April the UN Commission on Human Rights passed a resolution deploring the verdicts against political opponents and journalists arrested in 2003. It called for Cuba to cooperate with the UN envoy and to "refrain from adopting measures which could jeopardise the fundamental rights, the freedom of expression and the rights to due process of its citizens".

In November, for the 13th consecutive year, the UN General Assembly passed a resolution calling on the USA to end its embargo on Cuba.

USA

In June tough new sanctions by the US government on Cuba were introduced, restricting Cuban-Americans' cash remittances to relatives on the island and limiting family visits between the USA and Cuba to 14 days once every three years. On 8 November US dollars ceased circulation in Cuba and were replaced by Cuban convertible pesos, following a decree by the Cuban Central Bank.

The dissident movement

An illegal coalition of dissident groups – All United (Todos Unidos) – coordinated by former prisoner of conscience Vladimiro Roca Antúnez presented a plan called "Proposal to Resolve Cuban Society's Grave Problems", based on interviews with 30,000 Cubans.

In May, Oswaldo Payá Sardiñas, leader of the Christian Liberation Movement (Movimiento Cristiano Liberación), launched a new national dialogue aiming to chart a course for political and economic transition.

Restrictions on travel outside Cuba continued to be applied to dissidents. In May, Blanca Reyes, the wife of prisoner of conscience and journalist Raúl Rivero Castañeda, was refused permission to go to Serbia-Montenegro to collect a UNESCO prize on behalf of her husband. Oswaldo Payá was not granted permission to travel to Belgium to attend a human rights ceremony in January or to attend a meeting in Spain that he was invited to by the Spanish government.

Dissidents continued to be threatened, harassed and detained.

◻ Members of the Christian Liberation Movement involved in collecting signatures for the Varela Project – a petition for a referendum on political and economic reforms – were repeatedly harassed and detained. Among those targeted were Daniel Pereira García, Flora María Echevarría, Eric Isabel Arriera Reynoso, José Lorenzo Pérez Fidalgo and Alexis Triana Montesinos.

AI country reports/ visits
Reports
- Cuba: Newly declared prisoners of conscience (AI Index: AMR 25/002/2004)
- Cuba: One year too many – prisoners of conscience from the March 2003 crackdown (AI Index: AMR 25/005/2004)

Visits
AI last visited Cuba in 1988 and has not been permitted into the country since then.

CYPRUS

REPUBLIC OF CYPRUS
Head of state and government: Tassos Papadopoulos
Death penalty: abolitionist for all crimes
International Criminal Court: ratified
UN Women's Convention and its Optional Protocol: ratified

There were continuing concerns about conditions of detention, discrimination against Roma and the provisions covering conscientious objection to military service.

Background
The de facto separation of the north and south parts of the island persisted, with the northern part remaining unrecognized by the international community. Prospects of a solution to the long-standing dispute were briefly rekindled by the intensification, prior to the island's accession to the European Union (EU), of UN-brokered peace talks. The talks culminated in referenda held in both parts of the island to endorse a UN-proposed plan. The plan was accepted in the north and rejected in the south. During the pre-referendum period in the south, the government was accused of failing to show due diligence in carrying out its duty to protect the rights to freedom of expression, and there were allegations of attempts to intimidate individuals into rejecting the plan.

In August the Committee for Missing Persons reconvened after five years in an attempt to discover the fate of about 2,000 people missing during ethnic strife in the island since 1963.

Conditions of detention
In a report published in February, the Council of Europe's Commissioner for Human Rights expressed concern about, among other things, the conditions of detention for foreign nationals in the main Nicosia prison.

On 12 May, Ionis Ambrosiades, aged 29, died in custody at the Limassol police offices. In July the Deputy Minister to the President informed AI that the death was attributed to suicide. The Deputy Minister did not indicate whether prison rules were being revised to prevent further suicides.

Imprisonment of refugees
A Palestinian couple who feared persecution in the Israeli Occupied Territories were sentenced to eight months' imprisonment in October for possession of false identification documents. They had been arrested earlier in the month while trying to board a plane to another European country where they allegedly planned to seek asylum. They subsequently applied for protection in Cyprus and their applications were under review when they were tried and convicted. The couple were reportedly not given access to adequate translation services during their trial.

Discrimination against Roma
On 30 June the Ombudsperson of Cyprus, a post appointed by the President, released a report on the living conditions in the Roma settlement of Makounta village. The report expressed concerns about the failure of the authorities to implement policies decided in March 2000 that were designed to tackle homelessness and unemployment among Roma. The report also noted that Roma had problems accessing medical and education services in Makounta. The report criticized the authorities' refusal to grant Roma the rights that they should enjoy as Cypriot citizens. One example given was the policy of detaining Roma in prison without a court order, a practice applied to undocumented migrants. Another report, published by the Ombudsperson's office on 5 July, noted problems of access to education faced by Roma children in Limassol.

Conscientious objection to military service
The length of alternative civilian service for conscientious objectors to military service remained punitive at 42 months. AI was also concerned that the determination of conscientious objector status fell under the jurisdiction of the Ministry of Defence, which breaches international standards that stipulate that the entire institution of alternative service should have a civilian character.

AI country reports/ visits
Report
- Europe and Central Asia: Summary of Amnesty International's concerns in the region, January-June 2004: Cyprus (AI Index: EUR 01/005/2004)

Visits
AI delegates visited southern Cyprus in September and December.

CZECH REPUBLIC

CZECH REPUBLIC
Head of state: Václav Klaus
Head of government: Stanislav Gross (replaced Vladimir Spidla in August)
Death penalty: abolitionist for all crimes
International Criminal Court: signed
UN Women's Convention and its Optional Protocol: ratified

There were reports of police ill-treatment; one man died as a result. Roma continued to suffer from racist violence and inadequate protection. Cage beds were used to restrain children and adults in social care homes for people with mental disabilities.

Police ill-treatment

Several cases of police ill-treatment were reported, relatively few of which were effectively investigated. Some of the victims were foreign nationals. The authorities failed to fulfil recommendations by the UN Committee against Torture and the UN Human Rights Committee to make the system for investigating complaints against police officers independent and impartial.

In April a UK national and a New Zealand national were taken by three municipal police officers to the Holešovice state police station after a dispute in a bar over a bill. After the state police said they would not pursue the case, the municipal police officers reportedly drove the men to a deserted area where they kicked them and beat them with truncheons. Both men needed hospital treatment as a result. In July an investigation against the officers was suspended "as no violation of the law took place". During the investigation the officers reportedly at first denied that their car had a global positioning satellite locator system, but subsequently stated that the system had not been working on the night in question. This issue was of importance in connection with the allegation that the two foreign nationals had been driven away from the police station.

In August a man died as a result of injuries suffered when he was kicked all over his body by a police officer in front of the police station in Olomouc. An investigation was initiated.

In May the UN Committee against Torture expressed concern that investigations into the alleged use of excessive force by police following demonstrations in Prague during the September 2000 International Monetary Fund/World Bank meeting had found that only one case qualified as a criminal offence.

Discrimination against Roma

In May the UN Committee against Torture expressed concern about "the persistent occurrence of acts of violence against Roma" and the alleged reluctance by police to adequately protect and investigate such crimes, despite efforts made by the government to counter such acts.

In June the European Commission against Racism and Intolerance expressed concern that a number of recommendations it had previously made to the Czech authorities had not been implemented, particularly in relation to combating discrimination and inequality. It also said that Roma children continued to be sent to schools for the mentally disabled and a disproportionately high number were removed from their families and placed in state institutions or foster care. Racially motivated violence and ill-treatment of Roma by police, including of children, continued to be reported.

Reports of racist assaults on Roma by members of the public continued. Some incidents were reportedly perpetrated by youths with extreme racist views who had previously been convicted for similar offences but received light or suspended sentences.

In January in Jeseník, Petr Blajze, Martin Jaš and Martin Stiskala each received a suspended sentence of three years' imprisonment for assaulting a Romani couple in their home in June 2003. The three youths had hit Lydie Žigová, who was 21 and pregnant, in the face with a cobblestone. As a result, she permanently lost sight in one eye. Jan Žiga suffered cuts to his face and chest after he was attacked with a broken bottle. Two weeks after the conviction, Martin Stiskala and several other youths reportedly chased the couple down the street shouting racist insults. In March, two of the same youths – Petr Blajze and Martin Jaš – shouted racist abuse at and assaulted Lukáš Tokár, a young Romani man with a mental disability. Martin Jaš reportedly punched Lukáš Tokár in the face, kicked him in the chest and threatened to kill him if he reported the incident to the police. Lukáš Tokár needed hospital treatment for a broken nose. Police subsequently detained Petr Blajze and Martin Jaš, who were reportedly charged in connection with the assault. In June the Jeseník district court reportedly sentenced Martin Stiskala to a two-year suspended prison sentence for assaulting and racially abusing a 19-year-old Romani man in Jeseník on 14 April. The Romani man had managed to hold Martin Stiskala until the police arrived and detained him.

In September the Ombudsman's office began an investigation into allegations that some Romani women had illegally undergone sterilization procedures. Information presented by the European Roma Rights Centre and local non-governmental organizations indicated that some women may have been subjected to sterilization procedures without their full and informed consent.

Cage beds in psychiatric and social care institutions

In July the Health Minister stated that he had instructed directors of all health institutions immediately to cease use of cage beds that are fitted with a metal-barred construction above the mattress. He called for the elimination of cage beds consisting of metal frames covered with netting by the end of 2004, and recommended replacement of these beds with seclusion rooms as well as increased staffing to improve care for people with mental disabilities. Although this decision was in line with recommendations of the European Committee for the Prevention of Torture and the UN Human Rights Committee, President Václav Klaus criticized the Health Minister and stated that the cage bed ban "was an unduly hasty step".

Cage beds continued to be used in institutions for children and adults with mental disabilities under the authority of the Ministry of Labour and Social Affairs. There was no official data available on the use of cage beds in social care homes. As there is no legislation governing the use of seclusion and other harmful restraints, there was concern that even if cage beds were eliminated, isolation and increased psychiatric medication would be used instead.

The authorities failed to introduce the much-needed reforms of the mental health care system. Such reforms would include the setting up of community-based alternatives to residential care in psychiatric and social care institutions.

AI country reports/ visits
Report
· Europe and Central Asia: Summary of Amnesty International's concerns in the region, January-June 2004: Czech Republic (AI Index: 01/005/2004)

DOMINICAN REPUBLIC

DOMINICAN REPUBLIC
Head of state and government: Leonel Fernández Reyna (replaced Hipólito Mejía in August)
Death penalty: abolitionist for all crimes
International Criminal Court: signed
UN Women's Convention and its Optional Protocol: ratified

Several people shot dead by police, principally during demonstrations over the economic crisis and power shortages, were apparently victims of unlawful killings. There were continuing allegations of torture and ill-treatment in detention centres. Concerns about the administration of justice persisted. Many women were subjected to domestic violence.

Background
The economic crisis caused by a 2003 banking scandal deepened. A 48-hour general strike was called in late January. In a pre-emptive move, the authorities arrested more than 40 popular movement leaders before the strike. Seven demonstrators were reportedly killed by police. The Dominican Liberation Party's candidate Leonel Fernández Reyna won the presidential elections in May and took office in August. Shortly after, he initiated a major purge of the police force and police presence on the streets was increased.

Alleged unlawful killings by police
Excessive use of force by police reportedly led to a number of deaths, particularly during demonstrations or as a result of shoot-outs.

☐ Arlene Pérez Simsar, aged 25, died after being shot in the head allegedly by a police patrol in Arroyo Hondo III, Santo Domingo, on 8 January. She was in a car with her boyfriend when four policemen approached the vehicle but, according to the boyfriend, failed to identify themselves. The boyfriend reportedly began to drive away, fearing a robbery, and the policemen opened fire on the car killing Arlene Pérez Simsar. Four policemen were later charged in connection with the killing.

☐ On 30 September, 21-year-old José Alfredo Méndez Diloné, a member of the Broad Front for Popular Struggle, was reportedly shot dead by a police officer while taking part in a demonstration against power shortages in Navarrete, Santiago province.

Prison conditions
Prison conditions often amounted to cruel, inhuman and degrading treatment. Poor living conditions, lack of medical attention and serious overcrowding were commonplace. Reports persisted of widespread abuse

by prison authorities. Safeguards to protect the right to life and prevent violence between prisoners were inadequate.

On 21 August, Robinson Michael Rosario Hernández was reportedly burnt alive at Mao detention centre, Valverde province, after a dispute broke out with other inmates over the control of drug trafficking. Two other prisoners died later, also as a result of severe burns.

Benito Simón Gabriel, 19, stated that he was suspended from a wall in the sun for seven hours at Monte Plata prison. Police captain Salvador López García was later arrested in connection with the torture.

Administration of justice

Scores of prisoners remained jailed after serving their sentences because they could not afford to pay administrative fees. Thousands of criminal cases were stagnant because the Public Ministry failed to refer them to the courts and the accused were released. In September, a new Penal Procedure Code came into force outlawing any arrest without a warrant issued by a judge.

Violence against women

Domestic violence was apparently widespread and affected women from all backgrounds. According to data collected by the Women and Health Collective, at least 89 women were killed in domestic disputes.

On 11 January, Siria Sena Ferreras, aged 33, died reportedly after being stabbed in the street by her husband in Villa Duarte, Santo Domingo.

AI country reports/ visits
Report
· Dominican Republic: Human rights violations in the context of the economic crisis (AI Index: AMR 27/001/2004)

ECUADOR

REPUBLIC OF ECUADOR
Head of state and government: Lucio Gutiérrez Borbua
Death penalty: abolitionist for all crimes
International Criminal Court: ratified
UN Women's Convention and its Optional Protocol: ratified

Police courts continued to claim jurisdiction over cases of police officers accused of violating human rights. Prison conditions were harsh. Indigenous and community leaders, as well as journalists, were attacked, threatened and intimidated.

Background

Throughout the year, indigenous groups, grassroots organizations, trade unions and opposition groups held protests against alleged government corruption and the government's socioeconomic policies.

The ongoing conflict in neighbouring Colombia (see Colombia entry), which has resulted in some 300,000 Colombians seeking refuge in the country, continued to have serious repercussions for Ecuador, particularly in the increasingly militarized border areas.

A law on transparency and access to information was passed allowing the media and citizens to gain access to information about state institutions.

In December, in an extraordinary session called by the President, Congress removed 27 of the 31 judges of the Supreme Court of Justice and nominated replacements. The reason given for this resolution was that the judges' contracts had actually ended in January 2003. The abrupt removal triggered serious concerns over the independence of the judiciary.

Economic, social and cultural rights

The UN Committee on Economic, Social and Cultural Rights expressed concern in June that the rights of indigenous communities were not being fully implemented and that concessions for the extraction of natural resources had been granted to international companies without the full consent of the communities affected.

The Committee was also concerned about discrimination against the Afro-Ecuadorian population and inequality between men and women.

Police courts

Police courts continued to claim jurisdiction over cases involving human rights violations despite promises made by the authorities that these would be heard by civil courts. Police courts are neither independent nor impartial and are a cause of impunity. Complainants and witnesses involved in such cases faced intimidation and death threats.

In October, 20 police officers who participated in a police operation related to an alleged robbery in which eight people died and three detainees "disappeared" after being taken into custody were acquitted by a Guayaquil police court. In April, journalist José Solís Solís received threatening telephone calls and was followed by unknown persons, apparently as a result of his reporting of the case.

Harassment of government critics

Journalists and indigenous and community leaders were subjected to armed attacks and threats after criticizing government policies.

◻ In January, Miguel Rivadeneira, from *Radio Quito*, received anonymous threatening telephone calls after reporting government corruption.

◻ In February, Leonidas Iza, President of the Confederation of Indigenous Nationalities of Ecuador (Confederación de Nacionalidades Indígenas del Ecuador, CONAIE), was shot at by unknown individuals in Quito. He was unharmed but four members of his family were injured.

Attacks and threats against indigenous activists in oil zones

Members of the Sarayaku indigenous community in Pastaza province and others campaigning to stop oil exploitation on their territory were subjected to physical attacks, death threats and other forms of intimidation. In 2003 the Inter-American Commission on Human Rights had ordered the Ecuadorian state to protect the Sarayaku community in the province.

◻ Marlon Santi, President of the Sarayaku Association, was attacked and beaten in Quito in February, the day before he was due to travel to Costa Rica to present his community's case before the Inter-American Commission on Human Rights.

Prison conditions

In January, President Gutiérrez declared Ecuador's overcrowded prisons to be in a "state of emergency" and promised extra funding to improve facilities. As of February, 11,000 inmates, about 1,000 of whom had been held for over a year pending trial, were reportedly held in harsh conditions in facilities built for 6,000. However, little effective action was taken and protests and riots took place in several prisons. On several occasions, visitors were held hostage to put pressure on the authorities to reduce sentences and improve conditions.

AI country reports/ visits
Report
- Ecuador: Broken promises – impunity in the police court system continues (AI Index: AMR 28/018/2004)

EGYPT

ARAB REPUBLIC OF EGYPT
Head of state: Muhammad Hosni Mubarak
Head of government: Ahmed Nazif (replaced 'Atif Muhammad 'Ubayd in July)
Death penalty: retentionist
International Criminal Court: signed
UN Women's Convention: ratified with reservations
Optional Protocol to UN Women's Convention: not signed

At least 34 people were killed and more than a hundred others injured in car bomb attacks in the Sinai region in October. Hundreds, possibly thousands, of people were arrested in connection with the attacks. Non-governmental organizations (NGOs) continued to operate under the restrictive NGO law introduced in 2002. Scores of members of the banned Muslim Brothers organization were arrested; several of them remained held awaiting trial at the end of the year. Thousands of suspected supporters of banned Islamist groups, including possible prisoners of conscience, remained in detention without charge or trial; some had been held for years. Torture and ill-treatment in detention continued to be systematic. Deaths in custody were reported. In the majority of torture cases, the perpetrators were not brought to justice. Death sentences continued to be passed and carried out.

Background

The state of emergency remained in place. In January the *Shura* Council, Egypt's Upper House, announced the creation of the National Council for Human Rights (NCHR) headed by former UN Secretary-General Boutros Boutros-Ghali. The body was mandated to receive complaints, advise the government and publish annual reports on the human rights situation in Egypt. It was received with scepticism by some national human rights groups. The NCHR communicated a number of complaints it received to the government and planned to issue its first annual report early in 2005 with recommendations on emergency legislation and amendments to preventive detention legislation, among other things.

In June the European Union-Egypt Association Council meeting took place within the framework of the Euro-Med Association Agreement, which entered into force earlier in the month. The Agreement contains, under Article 2, a legally binding clause obliging the contracting parties to promote and protect human rights.

The ruling National Democratic Party won the vast majority of seats in mid-term elections to the *Shura* Council in May. In July President Mubarak appointed a new government, including a new prime minister. The government approved the creation of two new political parties (al-Ghad and al-Dusturi), but refused to approve at least two others (al-Wasat and al-Karama).

Several hundred alleged members of the armed Islamist group al-Gama'a al-Islamiya were reportedly released in November. The releases were believed to have followed public renunciation of acts of violence, particularly by leading members of the group. Most of those released had reportedly been serving prison terms of between five and 10 years.

'War on terror'
Bomb attacks on the Hilton hotel in Taba and two backpackers' camps in Ras Shitani in Sinai region on 7 October killed at least 34 people and injured more than a hundred. Following the attacks, a large number of people were arrested in North Sinai in the latter half of October. Estimates of those arrested in connection with the attacks differed sharply; while official reports limited the number to 800, some national NGOs put the number of arrests at 3,000. Many of those released in November reported that they were tortured. Allegations of torture included beatings, suspension by the wrists or ankles and electric shocks. The vast majority of those still in custody at the end of the year were reportedly held incommunicado in State Security Intelligence (SSI) centres, including the SSI headquarters in Lazoghly Square, Cairo, where torture was frequently reported. Scores of complaints about the detention order of those arrested were addressed to the Public Prosecutor; 15 people received a ruling ordering their release in December, but only six were known to have been freed by the end of the year.

Prisoners of conscience
Prisoners of conscience continued to be arrested and sentenced for their peacefully held views.

In March the (Emergency) Supreme State Security Court in Cairo sentenced 26 prisoners of conscience, including three Britons, to prison terms of between one and five years. They were charged in connection with their alleged affiliation with the Islamic Liberation Party (Hizb al-Tahrir al-Islami), which was not registered. Following their arrest in April and May 2002, several of the men were held incommunicado for weeks and reportedly tortured. The (Emergency) Supreme State Security Court is an exceptional court that violates international fair trial standards and denies defendants the rights of appeal.
Update: Ashraf Ibrahim
In March prisoner of conscience Ashraf Ibrahim, an active member of the anti-war movement formed to oppose the war on Iraq, was acquitted of all charges by the (Emergency) Supreme State Security Court. He had been detained in April 2003.

Torture and ill-treatment
Torture continued to be used systematically in detention centres throughout the country. Several people died in custody in circumstances suggesting that torture or ill-treatment may have caused or contributed to their deaths.

Several members of the banned Muslim Brothers organization were reportedly tortured for several days after being taken from Mazra'at Tora Prison, where they were held in preventive detention, to the SSI branch in Madinat Nasr, Cairo. They were reportedly beaten, suspended by the wrists or ankles and given electric shocks; some of them reportedly sustained broken bones and ribs as a result. They were among 60 members of the organization arrested in the run-up to the May elections to the *Shura* Council. They were accused of affiliation to an unauthorized organization, possession of anti-government leaflets and working to overthrow the government by force, among other offences. Several others were also apparently denied medical attention in prison; one prisoner reportedly died as a result.

Akram Zohairy, aged 42, who had diabetes, reportedly sustained a broken foot while being transported back to prison in a police van after interrogation. Despite his condition, he was reportedly denied adequate medical attention for several days and died hours after being moved to hospital late on 8 June. Following his death, members of a parliamentary committee visited the detainees to investigate allegations of torture and later confirmed these allegations. The detention order for the group was renewed several times before all of them were released without charge in November.

Inadequate investigations
In the vast majority of cases of alleged torture, no one was brought to justice because the authorities failed to conduct prompt, impartial and thorough investigations. However, some trials of alleged torturers did take place, but only in criminal, not political cases. Compensation was provided in some cases of torture.
Update: Muhammad Badr al-Din Gum'a Isma'il
In March, the Alexandria Criminal Court sentenced three police officers to one year's imprisonment and dismissal from their functions for a period of two years. Following an appeal by defence lawyers, they were referred to a disciplinary court, which issued an additional order for their complete dismissal. Three others were acquitted. They were all tried in connection with the arrest, detention and torture of school bus driver Muhammad Badr al-Din Gum'a Isma'il in 1996.

Human rights defenders
Several organizations, including the Egyptian Association Against Torture and the Egyptian Initiative for Personal Rights, continued legal proceedings to appeal against the Ministry of Social Affairs' decision to refuse them registration as NGOs. Under a 2002 law regulating NGO activities, NGOs have to apply to the Ministry of Social Affairs to officially register. Those whose applications are rejected and who continue to operate are liable to prosecution.

The Cairo-based Nadim Centre for the Psychological Treatment and Rehabilitation of Victims of Violence was apparently targeted by the authorities because of its human rights work. The Centre was visited by two inspection committees from the Ministry of Health in July and August and accused of a number of breaches, including carrying out unauthorized activities as a medical institution. Under the Law on Medical Institutions, the Centre had 30 days to rectify these breaches or face closure. However, the authorities did not take any action following the visit of the second committee in August and at the end of the year the Centre was continuing to work, uncertain of its future.

Restrictions on freedom of expression

People continued to be at risk of detention, trial and imprisonment in violation of their right to freedom of religion and expression. In June al-Azhar Islamic Research Council, the country's leading religious institution, was granted wide-ranging powers to ban and confiscate material it considers violates religious principles, raising concerns of further curtailment of freedom of expression. Despite President Mubarak's introduction in February of a Bill abolishing prison terms for publishing offences, journalists continued to be imprisoned, threatened and beaten.

▢ 'Abd al-Halim Qandeel, editor of the opposition newspaper al-'Araby and known critic of the government, was reportedly assaulted by men in civilian clothes as he was returning home early on the morning of 2 November. He reported that he was gagged and blindfolded, beaten and stripped before being dumped on the main motorway between Cairo and Suez. The attack was believed to be an attempt by the authorities to silence his criticisms as part of the "popular movement for change" which called, among other things, for constitutional reform and the lifting of the state of emergency.

Unfair trial

Trials of civilians before courts established under emergency legislation, including state security courts, continued to take place. Cases involving national security or "terrorism"-related charges were often tried before military courts. These courts deny the right to an independent and impartial trial as well as the right of full review before a higher tribunal.

▢ In April, Ahmed Hussein Agiza was sentenced to 25 years in prison after an unfair trial before the Supreme Military Court. He had been forcibly returned to Egypt from Sweden in December 2001. After his return, he was held for more than a month in incommunicado detention and reportedly tortured, despite assurances allegedly given to the Swedish government by the Egyptian authorities that he would not be ill-treated. In June, President Mubarak reduced the sentence to 15 years. In December, the Swedish government reportedly admitted having received information that Ahmed Hussein Agiza had been tortured in Egypt. Ahmed Hussein Agiza was initially convicted in absentia in 1999 for his alleged links with an armed Islamist group; his second trial in 2004 constituted a retrial.

Extraditions

The authorities reportedly requested the extradition of Egyptian nationals from several countries, including Bosnia and Herzegovina, Uruguay and Yemen. As a result, some people were threatened with extradition or were forcibly returned to Egypt, where they were at risk of human rights violations, including torture or ill-treatment.

▢ In February, the Yemeni authorities handed over 15 Egyptian nationals including Dr Sayyid 'Abd al-Aziz Imam al-Sharif, Muhammed 'Abd al-Aziz al-Gamal and Uthman al-Samman. The last two had been sentenced to death in absentia in 1999 and 1994 respectively. The fate and whereabouts of those returned were not known to AI or, reportedly, to their families and friends. Their extradition was reportedly in exchange for the return of the Yemeni opposition figure, Colonel Ahmed Salem Obeid. They had been held in Sana'a, Yemen, by Political Security, the branch of the security forces which deals with political and security suspects (see Yemen entry).

Death penalty

Death sentences continued to be passed and carried out. Many people remained under sentence of death. The local NGO community started a debate on the future of the death penalty in the country.

▢ Six members of a family known as 'Abd al-Halim were reportedly hanged in Qina Prison in Qina, Upper Egypt, in September. They had been sentenced to death for the killing of 22 members of a rival clan in August 2002 in Sohag, Upper Egypt.

Refugees

With the deterioration of the situation in Darfur in western Sudan and the ongoing peace negotiations regarding southern Sudan, UN High Commissioner for Refugees (UNHCR)-Cairo decided to freeze individual determination status for Sudanese asylum-seekers for six months starting on 1 June, pending developments in Sudan. In August, 23 Sudanese refugees were reportedly arrested following a demonstration to protest against this decision. Those arrested were accused of rioting and damaging public property; they were all released in September. UNHCR-Cairo continued to provide protection against forcible return and provided all Sudanese asylum-seekers with temporary protection cards.

AI country reports/ visits
Visits

In May AI delegates met refugee and asylum-seeking families, UNHCR representatives and organizations working on behalf of refugees and asylum-seekers. The visit focused on access to primary education for refugee and asylum-seeking children.

AI organized a regional consultative workshop in Cairo on media and violence against women in the Middle East and North Africa.

EL SALVADOR

REPUBLIC OF EL SALVADOR
Head of state and government: Elías Antonio Saca
(replaced Francisco Flores in June)
Death penalty: abolitionist for ordinary crimes
International Criminal Court: not signed
UN Women's Convention: ratified with reservations
Optional Protocol to UN Women's Convention: signed

Attempts to make permanent an unconstitutional law penalizing "*mara*" (gang) members were abandoned following widespread criticisms. Impunity continued in cases of human rights violations committed during the 1980-1991 armed conflict and in relation to more recent cases, including violence against women.

Background

In the presidential election in March, Elías Antonio Saca, from the ruling Nationalist Republican Alliance (Alianza Republicana Nacionalista, ARENA), was elected and took office on 1 June. During the campaign he promised tougher measures to quell criminal violence.

Impunity

The government persisted in its stance that seeking to bring to justice those responsible for human rights violations perpetrated during the 1980-1991 armed conflict should not be done as it would reopen the wounds of the past. This was despite recommendations by the UN Truth Commission and the Inter-American Commission on Human Rights that the violations should be investigated. However, civil organizations continued their efforts to get justice.

In June the UN Committee on the Rights of the Child called on the authorities to assume an active role in efforts to trace children who "disappeared" during the armed conflict. In October the government unexpectedly issued an Executive Decree to form an "Inter-institutional Commission for the Search of Children who disappeared as a result of the armed conflict in El Salvador". Pro-Búsqueda, an organization working to find those children, had been seeking the creation of such an entity for many years. However, it considered that the government decision fell short of its proposal as the decree did not have the force of a legislative decision and did not include the participation of relatives.

◻ In September the Inter-American Court of Human Rights heard the case of Ernestina and Erlinda Serrano Cruz, two girls aged seven and three respectively when they "disappeared" in 1982 during an army operation in Chalatenango Department. A decision was pending at the end of the year. Their mother, who worked tirelessly to find them, died in March.

◻ In September a judge in California, USA, held Alvaro Saravia, a former captain in the Salvadorean army now resident in California, responsible for the assassination of Archbishop Oscar Romero in March 1980 in San Salvador. The judge said it was a "crime against humanity". Alvaro Saravia was ordered, in absentia, to pay US$10 million in compensatory damages to a relative of the Archbishop.

Violence against women

Few efforts to obtain justice for murdered women succeeded and more women were murdered. Only two of around a dozen cases involving the murder, decapitation and mutilation of women in early 2003 were investigated and those responsible for the crime sent to prison.

In February the UN Special Rapporteur on violence against women visited El Salvador and recommended that the government exercise due diligence to prevent, investigate and punish acts of violence against women and end impunity for perpetrators of such violence. Her final report was due in early 2005.

At least 159 women were murdered during the year as a result of domestic or social violence. Some of the killings were particularly brutal.
◻ In May the burned remains of two young women were found on the side of a road in Aguilares, Chalatenango.
◻ The body of a pregnant 17-year-old girl found in June in an open space in Apastepeque, San Vicente, had 150 wounds inflicted with a knife or similar weapon. The government blamed *mara* members for the violence, but there was no proper evidence to support this assumption.

Anti-gang legislation

The controversial temporary Anti-*Maras* Act (AMA) to deal with the crimes of youth gangs, which was approved in October 2003, was not renewed. In April the Constitutional Division of the Supreme Court of Justice found all articles to be in breach of the Constitution because they violated basic principles of equality before the law. In a report issued in June, the UN Committee on the Rights of the Child considered the AMA to be in breach of the UN Children's Convention and recommended its suspension. Attempts were made to have the legislation approved permanently but, in the face of strong criticisms from the judiciary and civil society, a consultation exercise was begun instead. It included judges, police, attorneys, members of parliament and representatives of civil society. It resulted in proposals to amend the Penal Code, Penal Procedure Code and legislation on juvenile crime. The reforms were approved in July by the Legislative Assembly.

Deaths in prison

◻ In August, 31 prisoners died in the La Esperanza Prison (previously known as Mariona) allegedly as a result of disputes among prisoners, some of them members of *maras*. Most of the victims had been stabbed. In October, two prison guards and one prisoner were charged with offences including homicide, attempted homicide, illegal association and allowing forbidden materials (which were used in the murders) to be brought into the prison.

AI country reports/ visits
Statements
- El Salvador: Pressing commitments for the government (AI Index: AMR 29/003/2004)
- El Salvador: Unconstitutional law should be repealed and new approaches to public security considered (AI Index: AMR 29/005/2004)

EQUATORIAL GUINEA

REPUBLIC OF EQUATORIAL GUINEA
Head of state: Teodoro Obiang Nguema Mbasogo
Head of government: Miguel Abia Biteo Borico (replaced Cándido Muatetema Rivas in June)
Death penalty: retentionist
International Criminal Court: not signed
UN Women's Convention: ratified
Optional Protocol to UN Women's Convention: not signed

Several alleged plots to overthrow the government led to waves of arrests. Several of those arrested were sentenced to long prison terms after unfair trials. Dozens of soldiers and former military personnel as well as political opponents of the government were detained without charge or trial. Many appeared to have been tortured in detention and at least one reportedly died as a result. One person was sentenced to death.

Background
The authorities alleged there were coup attempts in March, May and October.

In January, some 100 soldiers and former soldiers arrested in late 2003 were tried by a military court in Bata. Eighty were convicted of plotting to overthrow the government and given prison terms ranging from six to 30 years.

About 1,000 immigrants living in the capital, Malabo, some of whom had entered the country illegally, were rounded up, beaten and sometimes imprisoned before being expelled from the country in March.

In April, the ruling Democratic Party of Equatorial Guinea (Partido Democrático de Guinea Ecuatorial, PDGE) won legislative elections with 95 per cent of the vote. The opposition Convergence for Social Democracy (Convergencia para la Democracia Social, CPDS) won two seats in Parliament.

In July, a US Senate investigation into lax controls on money laundering at a bank in Washington, USA, revealed the misappropriation of at least US$35 million of oil revenue by the President of Equatorial Guinea and his relatives. The President denied the accusation and threatened to sue the foreign media for their reporting of the issue.

Unfair trials
In November, 11 Armenian and South African nationals and nine Equatorial Guineans were convicted of crimes against the head of state and crimes against the government and sentenced to between 14 and 63 years' imprisonment. The foreign nationals had been arrested in March in connection with an alleged plot to overthrow President Teodoro Obiang Nguema Mbasogo and replace him with Severo Moto, the exiled leader of a banned opposition party, the Progress Party of Equatorial Guinea (Partido del Progreso de Guinea Ecuatorial, PPGE).

Severo Moto and eight members of his "government in exile" were charged half way through the trial and tried in absentia. They were convicted of treason. Two other Equatorial Guineans arrested in March and April and tried on the same charges received sentences of 16 months' imprisonment each for reckless behaviour.

The trial was grossly unfair. No evidence was presented in court to substantiate the charges, other than the defendants' own statements which were in Spanish, a language they do not understand, and which the defendants stated were extracted under torture. The court ignored their claims and did not allow defence lawyers to raise the issue of torture. The defendants had no access to their lawyers until two days before the trial, which started on 23 August, and their lawyers were not given sufficient time to prepare their defence. The defendants complained that their statements had not been taken by an investigating judge, as required by national law, but by the Attorney General, who acted for the prosecution in court. Defence lawyers lodged an appeal which was pending at the end of the year.

Since their arrest, the foreign nationals had been held incommunicado and handcuffed and shackled 24 hours a day. They were deprived of adequate food and medical care and had only sporadic and limited access to their families.

Corisco Island
In May, the security forces on Corisco Island reportedly extrajudicially executed between 12 and 15 Equatorial Guineans resident in Gabon, who, they claimed, had invaded the island and attacked the military garrison there, killing one soldier. The authorities acknowledged the killing of four alleged attackers. Those who died were reportedly killed as they tried to flee the island or as they surrendered.

Five survivors were arrested and were allegedly tortured; one woman was reportedly raped. Some of the survivors appeared on television with cuts to their ears. One reportedly lost the use of his hands. They were held incommunicado and constantly handcuffed in the main police station in Bata for several months. In December they were tried by a military court, from which there is no right of appeal, and convicted of treason, "terrorism" and espionage, for which they received prison terms ranging from 22 to 28 years.

Five others who had managed to escape were illegally extradited from Gabon in June. They remained detained in Black Beach prison in Malabo without charge at the end of the year.

Arbitrary detention, torture and ill-treatment

Scores of political opponents of the government were arrested throughout the year. Most were released within a few days or weeks, but many remained in detention without charge or trial at the end of the year. Most were tortured or ill-treated at the time of their arrest. Former members of the PPGE were targeted. The authorities often arrested their relatives as hostages.

🗀 In March, Weja Chicampo, leader of the Movement for the Self-determination of Bioko Island (Movimiento para la Auto-determinación de la Isla de Bioko, MAIB), was arrested in the early hours of the morning by at least 10 hooded police officers who forced their way into his home in Malabo. He was severely beaten and sustained injuries to his jaw and left shoulder for which he did not receive treatment. He was taken to Black Beach prison and kept incommunicado for several months. He remained detained without charge at the end of the year. Weja Chicampo had returned from exile in Spain in August 2003 and was in the process of getting his party legally recognized at the time of his arrest.

🗀 Pedro Ndong and Salvador Bibang were detained in Malabo in March and remained held without charge or trial at the end of the year. Their detention was believed to be connected to their former membership of the PPGE.

🗀 In June, Marcelino Nguema Esono was arrested at his brother-in-law's house with three others as they watched a football match on television. None of the men was armed. Four security officers entered the house and one opened fire on Marcelino Nguema Esono, injuring his right thigh. Marcelino Nguema Esono was taken to a doctor and then taken with the others to the police station in Bata where they were beaten. The next day they were flown to Malabo where they remained detained without charge at the end of the year. They were reportedly severely beaten on the plane on their way to Malabo.

🗀 In October, dozens of military personnel and former military personnel were arrested throughout Rio Muni. They were taken to a police station in Bata where they were reported to have been ill-treated and tortured. They were accused of trying to overthrow the government. Most if not all were still held without charge or trial at the end of the year.

🗀 In November, Pío Miguel Obama, a member of CPDS and a Malabo local councillor, was arrested and accused of holding an "illegal meeting" in Basupú, his home town, although he was not there the day in question. He was released without charge on 24 December.

Deaths in detention

At least three prisoners died in detention, reportedly as a result of torture, harsh prison conditions and lack of medical treatment.

🗀 In January, Francisco Abeso Mba, a prisoner of conscience convicted following an unfair trial in 2002 of plotting to overthrow the government, died as a result of an illness. One month before his death, the authorities had allowed him to be cared for at home, but he was refused permission to travel abroad for treatment as recommended by doctors.

🗀 Gerhard Eugen Merz, a German national, died in detention nine days after his arrest in March in connection with an alleged coup attempt. The authorities said he had died of "cerebral malaria with complications". However, his body reportedly bore marks consistent with torture and those arrested with him testified in court in November that he had been tortured to death.

Death penalty

In December a military court in Bata sentenced a soldier, Francisco Neto Momo, to death for the killing of a colleague a few months earlier when both were on sentry duty. There is no right of appeal from a military court. It was not known whether the execution had been carried out by the end of the year.

AI country reports/ visits
Report
· Equatorial Guinea: Trial of alleged coup plotters seriously flawed (AI Index: AFR 24/017/2004)
Visits
In August and November AI delegates observed the trials of those accused of involvement in an alleged coup attempt in March.

ERITREA

ERITREA
Head of state and government: Issayas Afewerki
Death penalty: retentionist
International Criminal Court: signed
UN Women's Convention: ratified
Optional Protocol to UN Women's Convention: not signed

Hundreds of people were arrested for the peaceful expression of their opinions or religious beliefs. Political prisoners were held indefinitely without charge or trial, many incommunicado and in secret detention places. Thousands had been held since a major crackdown on dissent in 2001. Torture was reported, including of people fleeing or evading military conscription.

Background

The government and ruling People's Front for Democracy and Justice made no move towards multi-party elections as required by the 1997 Constitution. No opposition activity or criticism was tolerated and no independent non-governmental organizations were allowed. A Special Court continued to convict defendants in secret trials without defence representation or the right of appeal.

The UN made an emergency appeal on behalf of some 50 per cent of the population facing food shortages as a result of drought and the 1998-2000 border war with Ethiopia.

The government continued to support Ethiopian armed opposition groups fighting in Ethiopia, as well as Sudanese armed opposition groups. Sudan and Ethiopia supported the opposition Eritrean National Alliance (ENA), which included Eritrean Liberation Front (ELF) and Islamist groups. It was unclear whether there was armed activity inside Eritrea by ENA groups.

Border tensions

The UN Security Council and others expressed fears that the continuing border dispute could result in a new war between Eritrea and Ethiopia. In November Ethiopia accepted in principle the Eritrea-Ethiopia Boundary Commission's ruling that the border town of Badme was Eritrean territory according to colonial treaties, which it had previously rejected. However, agreement on a final settlement of the border issue by both sides was expected to take some time. The mandate of the UN Mission in Ethiopia and Eritrea, administering a buffer-zone along the border, was extended.

The Claims Commission, set up through the December 2000 Peace Agreement, judged in April and December that both sides were liable for violations of international humanitarian and human rights law regarding material destruction, rape, abductions, killings, ill-treatment, expulsions and deprivation of citizenship or properties of civilians during the 1998-2000 war.

Prisoners of conscience

Scores of people suspected of opposing the government or supporting armed opposition groups were detained in secret and held without charge or trial. They included forcibly returned asylum-seekers and former refugees now holding foreign citizenship who were detained after returning voluntarily to the country.

▭ Nothing was known of the whereabouts or condition of 11 former government leaders detained since September 2001. They included former Vice-President Mahmoud Ahmed Sheriffo, former Foreign Minister Haile Woldetensae and former Eritrean People's Liberation Front intelligence chief Petros Solomon. Dozens of others also remained in incommunicado detention, including Aster Yohannes, Petros Solomon's wife, who was detained on her return to Eritrea from the USA in December 2003. The few releases reported in 2004 included Abdulrahman Ahmed Yunis, aged 75, and Sunabera Mohamed Demena, aged 82, both seriously ill due to harsh prison conditions.

Journalists

Private media remained banned. Fifteen journalists from the private, international and state media were still held incommunicado at the end of the year, most detained in the September 2001 crackdown.

Long-term political prisoners

Thousands of government critics and opponents arrested during the first decade of independence after 1991 were believed to be still detained in secret military and security detention centres throughout the country. Some were feared to have been extrajudicially executed.

Military conscription

National service, compulsory for all men and women aged between 18 and 40, continued to be extended indefinitely, as it had been since the war with Ethiopia. The right to conscientious objection was not recognized by the authorities. There were frequent round-ups to catch evaders and deserters. Torture and indefinite arbitrary detention were used to punish conscripts accused of military offences.

▭ Paulos Iyassu, Isaac Moges and Negede Teklemariam, all members of the Jehovah's Witnesses, who oppose the bearing of arms, remained in incommunicado detention since 1994 in Sawa military training centre without charge or trial.

On 4 November, Eritrean security forces in Asmara indiscriminately arrested thousands of people suspected of evading military conscription. People were arrested at places of work, in the street, at roadblocks and at home. Prisoners were taken to Adi Abeto army prison near Asmara. That night, a prison wall was apparently pushed over by some prisoners, killing four guards. Soldiers opened fire and shot dead at least a dozen prisoners and wounded many more.

Religious persecution

A 2002 ban on religions other than the Eritrean Orthodox Church, the Catholic and Lutheran Churches and Islam remained in force. Police targeted minority Christian churches, broke up home-based worshipping, arrested and beat church members and tortured them in military detention centres to try to make them abandon their religion. Muslims suspected of links with Sudan-based armed Islamist groups were also targeted for secret detention.

The government claimed there was no religious persecution and in October the leaders of the four government-permitted faiths issued a statement condemning "subversive activities against the religious institutions of the country" by "alien and externally driven" Christian and Islamic groups.

⮒ In February, 56 members of the Hallelujah Pentecostal Church in Asmara were arrested, including children. They were taken to Adi Abeto and Mai Serwa military prisons and tortured. Many were still held at the end of the year.

⮒ Haile Naizgi, a former accountant for the non-governmental organization World Vision, and Dr Kiflu Gebremeskel, a former mathematics lecturer, both leaders of the Full Gospel Pentecostal Church, were arrested at their homes in Asmara in May. They were still held incommunicado at the end of the year.

⮒ Dozens of Muslim teachers arrested in Keren and other towns in 1994 remained "disappeared".

Torture and ill-treatment

Torture continued to be used against many recent political prisoners and as a standard military punishment. Army deserters, conscription evaders and forcibly returned asylum-seekers were held incommunicado and tortured in military custody. They were beaten, tied hand and foot in painful positions and left in the sun for lengthy periods (the "helicopter" torture method) or were suspended from ropes from a tree or ceiling. Religious prisoners were among many detainees held in Sawa and other military camps, beaten and forced to crawl on sharp stones. Many prisoners were kept in overcrowded metal shipping containers in unventilated, hot and unhygienic conditions and denied adequate food and medical treatment. Conditions in military prisons around the country were extremely harsh.

Violence against women

Female genital mutilation was widely practised, despite government and UN education programmes. Domestic violence against women was reportedly common.

Refugees

Several hundred Eritreans fled to Sudan and other countries, most of them army deserters or those fleeing conscription. In July, some 110 people who had fled to Libya were forcibly returned to Eritrea. On arrival they were detained and placed in incommunicado detention in a secret prison. In August the Libyan authorities attempted to forcibly return a further 76 Eritrean asylum-seekers, including six children. However, some of them hijacked the plane carrying them and forced it to land in the Sudanese capital, Khartoum, where all the passengers, except the hijackers, were given refugee protection. The hijackers surrendered to the Sudanese authorities and were sentenced to four years' imprisonment on appeal; their refugee status had not been determined by the end of 2004.

⮒ Some 232 Eritreans who were forcibly returned to Eritrea from Malta in 2002 continued to be detained incommunicado without charge or trial on the main Dahlak Island in the Red Sea or at other military detention centres.

AI country reports/ visits
Report
· Eritrea: "You have no right to ask" – Government resists scrutiny on human rights (AI Index: AFR 64/003/2004)

ESTONIA

REPUBLIC OF ESTONIA
Head of state: Arnold Rüütel
Head of government: Juhan Parts
Death penalty: abolitionist for all crimes
International Criminal Court: ratified
UN Women's Convention: ratified
Optional Protocol to UN Women's Convention: not signed

Estonia was the subject of a report by the Council of Europe's Commissioner for Human Rights which identified a number of human rights concerns, including violence against women.

Violence against women in the home

Domestic violence continued to be widespread, according to the report of the Commissioner for Human Rights, published in February. The number of cases reported to the police remained only a fraction of the total. Fear of retaliation was among the reasons for low reporting: at the time of the Commissioner's visit to Estonia in October 2003 there was only one shelter specifically for women survivors of domestic violence, and one for women with their children. In addition, police and prosecutors reportedly often viewed domestic violence as a private matter rather than a crime deserving particular attention. The Commissioner recommended strengthening the legislative framework for combating domestic violence; ensuring that the legal definition of domestic violence covers both physical and psychological aspects; improving provisions for the protection of survivors; and sensitizing the police and judiciary to this issue.

The Commissioner welcomed the fact that in December 2003 parliament adopted a law that enlarged the system of victim support services and increased the amount of compensation paid by the state. He noted that the authorities had defined the fight against domestic violence as one of the priorities in the field of criminal law for 2004.

Trafficking in women

Internal trafficking of women for forced sexual exploitation continued to be of considerable concern. The Commissioner for Human Rights reported that, according to the Estonian authorities, the number of women trafficked abroad for sexual exploitation had declined in recent years. However, no government statistics on the extent of trafficking existed. He stated that there was a clear need to conduct research and analysis in order to address the issue effectively. He also noted that the provision of protection and assistance for survivors of trafficking appeared insufficient. In response, the authorities reported that a national Round Table had been established, one of its tasks being to draft a National Action Plan against trafficking in human beings.

ETHIOPIA

FEDERAL DEMOCRATIC REPUBLIC OF ETHIOPIA
Head of state: Girma Wolde-Giorgis
Head of government: Meles Zenawi
Death penalty: retentionist
International Criminal Court: not signed
UN Women's Convention: ratified with reservations
Optional Protocol to UN Women's Convention: not signed

Widespread arbitrary detentions, torture and excessive use of force by police and soldiers were reported. A new media law, which would put journalists in the private media at risk of arrest, was proposed. Several thousand people remained in long-term detention without charge or trial; most were accused of supporting armed opposition groups. Prison conditions were harsh. Some prisoners "disappeared". A parliamentary inquiry into killings of members of the Anuak (Anywaa) ethnic group in Gambela town in December 2003 reported that 65 people had been killed; other reports put the number of dead in the hundreds. Trials continued of over 2,000 members of the former Dergue government

detained since 1991 on charges including genocide. Several death sentences were imposed; no executions were reported.

Background

Food scarcity continued to affect seven million people and a new famine crisis threatened those living in the Somali region in the east. A large part of Ethiopia's foreign debt was waived. International aid agencies expressed concern about the government's controversial three-year plan to resettle 2.2 million people to alleviate food insecurity. There were reports of food shortages, malnutrition, a high child mortality rate, and of inadequate health facilities and water in the resettlement camps.

A National Human Rights Commissioner was appointed in July, but his office had not opened by the end of the year.

Women's organizations worked to improve women's access to justice. They held public meetings against female genital mutilation and forced and early marriage of girls.

The government continued to face armed opposition in the Oromia region from the Eritrea-based Oromo Liberation Front (OLF) and in the Somali region from the Ogaden National Liberation Front (ONLF). Preparations continued for the May 2005 elections which 67 national and regional parties were scheduled to contest, including opposition parties.

Border tensions

The UN Security Council and others expressed fears that the continuing border dispute could once again result in a new war between Ethiopia and Eritrea. In November Ethiopia accepted in principle the Eritrea-Ethiopia Boundary Commission's ruling that the border town of Badme was Eritrean territory according to colonial treaties, which it had previously rejected. However, final settlement of the border issue by both sides was expected to take some time. The mandate of the UN Mission in Ethiopia and Eritrea (UNMEE), administering a buffer-zone along the border, was extended. A Claims Commission, set up through the December 2000 Peace Agreement, judged in April and December that both sides were liable for violations of international humanitarian and human rights law regarding material destruction, rape, abductions, killings, ill-treatment, expulsions and deprivation of citizenship or properties of civilians during the 1998-2000 war.

Freedom of the media

Debate continued throughout the year on the government's proposed new media law. International media organizations criticized it as being even harsher than the existing Press Law under which hundreds of journalists working for the private media had been imprisoned. In December a court overruled a government ban imposed in 2003 on the Ethiopian Free Press Journalists Association, a private media group documenting media abuses and opposed to the new media law.

Dozens of journalists arrested in previous years for their published articles, but provisionally released, faced court cases. By the end of the year only two journalists were believed to be in prison.

▢ Dabassa Wakjira, deputy news editor of the state television service, was arrested in May and charged with conspiracy to overthrow the government and membership of the OLF. He was refused bail and was still detained at the end of the year.

▢ Tewodros Kassa, editor of *Etiop* newspaper, was released in September on completion of a two-year prison term for publishing false information likely to incite violence.

Justice and rule of law

Although there were some improvements in the administration of justice, arbitrary and indefinite detention without charge or trial of suspected government opponents remained widespread. Thousands of political detainees arrested several years earlier remained held without charge. Police officers responsible for shooting demonstrators and suspected government opponents were not brought to justice. There were reports of unfair and long-delayed political trials; torture and ill-treatment of prisoners; and "disappearances".

▢ Imru Gurmessa Birru, a former employee of the Ministry of Coffee and Tea Development, was arrested in Addis Ababa in March. He was accused of links with the OLF, and allegedly tortured in the police Central Investigation Bureau (Maikelawi). He was denied medical treatment for diabetes and injuries sustained as a result of torture until June and returned to prison while treatment was continuing. He remained imprisoned without trial at the end of the year.

▢ Some 28 members of the opposition Gambela People's Democratic Congress Party arrested in 1998 remained imprisoned without trial in Addis Ababa. Among them was the former regional governor Okello Nyigelo.

▢ In September, in Dire Dawa town in the east, armed police attempting to disperse a crowd angry at customs confiscations killed six people and wounded 19 others. A government investigation into the incident had not reported by the end of the year.

Oromo demonstrations and arrests

More than 100 people were briefly detained in January at a demonstration organized by the Mecha Tulema Association, a long-established Oromo welfare organization. The protest was called to oppose the federal government's relocation of the Oromia region capital and administration from the national capital of Addis Ababa, where there is a large Oromo population, to Adama (also known as Nazareth) in eastern Oromia.

Eight Oromo students at Addis Ababa University were arrested for criticizing the Oromo regional government at a student cultural event on 18 January. Some 300 other students who demonstrated for their release were also arrested on campus. While in detention they were reportedly beaten and forced to do painful exercises. Most were released without charge after a few days. The university administration suspended most of the students and expelled others.

Between February and April there were further demonstrations by thousands of students and teachers in most towns in Oromia region protesting at the regional capital relocation; most of the region's schools were closed. In some places, police used live ammunition to disperse demonstrators, killing several school students. Demonstrators were detained for several months; some were beaten and made to do strenuous physical exercises while in custody. The government accused the OLF of organizing the demonstrations.

In May police arrested three leading officials of the Mecha Tulema Association, including Diribi Demissie, its president. They and 25 others, including several university students arrested in January, were charged with armed conspiracy and membership of the OLF. The three were released on bail in November.

More than 300 people were arrested in Agaro town in western Oromia in August in a continuing pattern of mass arrests of members of the Oromo ethnic group suspected of supporting the OLF. Most were released in October but some were charged. It was alleged that detainees were tortured and that some "disappeared"; some were believed to be held in secret detention centres.

Gambela region killings and detentions

A Commission of Inquiry headed by the President of the Supreme Court was set up by parliament in April following numerous killings of members of the Anuak ethnic group in Gambela town in December 2003. In July the Commission reported that 65 people were killed – 61 Anuak people and four members of highland ethnic groups – and 75 wounded, and that nearly 500 houses had been burned down and plundered. The Commission noted a background of ethnic conflict in the region. Three days of killings starting on 13 December 2003 were sparked off by the public display of the bodies of eight people allegedly killed by an Anuak armed group. The Commission criticized the regional authorities for not taking steps to prevent violence and acknowledged that federal soldiers were involved in the killings alongside highlanders. The Commission made no recommendations regarding prosecution of those responsible, whether police, military or civilians. To AI's knowledge, no one had been brought to justice by the end of 2004 for the killings of Anuak people.

According to unofficial sources and survivors, the number of people killed was several hundred and many women were raped. The violence also spread to other towns and villages in the region. Hundreds of people were detained and tortured, including civil servants and students, supposedly on suspicion of involvement in the murder of the eight. They were still detained without charge or trial at the end of 2004.

There were further arbitrary killings and arrests by the army in other towns and villages in Gambela region in 2004. In January, 300 people were killed by the army in a gold-mining area around Dimma town.

Human rights defenders

Professor Mesfin Woldemariam, former Chair of the Ethiopian Human Rights Council, and Berhanu Nega, Chair of the Ethiopian Economic Association, remained free on bail pending trial on charges of instigating violence at demonstrations at Addis Ababa University in April 2001. They denied the charges.

Dergue trials: update

The trial continued of 33 senior officials of the former government of Mengistu Hailemariam accused of genocide, murder, torture and other crimes. Others were on trial in absentia, including former President Mengistu. Ethiopia again unsuccessfully requested his extradition from Zimbabwe. Trials continued of several hundred less senior officials, most detained since 1991; several had been sentenced to death in 2004.

Death penalty

Several death sentences were imposed, but no executions were reported. In October, three OLF fighters detained since 1992, including Asili Mohamed, were sentenced to death after being convicted of killing and torturing civilians in Bedeno town in 1992. They denied the charges and their appeal to the Supreme Court was pending at the end of the year.

AI country reports/ visits
Visit
AI representatives visited different parts of Ethiopia in March.

FIJI

REPUBLIC OF THE FIJI ISLANDS
Head of state: Ratu Josefa Iloilovatu Uluivuda
Head of government: Laisenia Qarase
Death penalty: abolitionist for ordinary crimes
International Criminal Court: ratified
UN Women's Convention: ratified
Optional Protocol to UN Women's Convention: not signed

Political leaders failed to agree the implementation of a court ruling on constitutional power-sharing provisions. The authorities intensified investigations into people who participated in a coup in 2000 or were involved in subsequent human rights abuses. The Vice-President and the Deputy Speaker of Parliament were jailed for their role in the coup. Judges and witnesses in cases related to the coup were threatened and some were given police protection.

Background

The government continued its policy of favouring indigenous Fijians over the mainly Indo-Fijian non-indigenous community.

Military trials, criminal investigations and civil court cases showed unresolved tensions within and between the major ethnic groups in relation to the 2000 coup and the post-coup political dominance of indigenous Fijians. Political power struggles continued among the indigenous civilian and military elite. Nationalist indigenous Fijians sought the early release of imprisoned rebels.

Disputes over the cabinet's ethnic composition continued. A Supreme Court ruling in July again found that the Constitution required a multi-party (effectively multi-ethnic) cabinet which Fiji had not had since the coup. The opposition Labour Party rejected a government offer to participate in the cabinet.

In July the government replaced Ratu Epeli Ganilau as chairman of the indigenous Great Council of Chiefs after he advocated views that differed from government policy on human rights and social issues. Three government ministers and Fiji's UN representative in New York were accused by Senator Adi Koila Mara Nailatikau of assisting the coup.

In August the High Court sentenced Vice-President Ratu Jope Seniloli, Deputy Speaker of Parliament Ratu Rakuita Vakalalabure and three supporters to prison terms of up to six years on charges of treason relating to the 2000 coup. In November the Attorney General released the Vice-President on medical grounds.

In December, five politicians, including the Information Minister and the Lands Minister, were charged for their role in the coup.

Post-coup legal developments

Judges, state witnesses and journalists were anonymously threatened because of their work on high-profile coup trials. One witness lost her job at a government newspaper.

The police again failed to question four Fijian soldiers, now serving as peacekeepers overseas, over the beating to death of at least four military prisoners in November 2000.

Court martial proceedings against suspected rebels implicated senior officers in weapons transfers to coup leaders. In November and December, 43 rebel soldiers were sentenced to prison terms and another 29 admitted their role in the coup. Although a military witness in another court martial gave evidence that rebels had been ill-treated by soldiers arresting them, no officer was known to have been charged for such ill-treatment.

The High Court overturned the acquittal of six men and sentenced them to prison terms of between one and seven years for human rights abuses committed against Indo-Fijian farmers at Muaniweni during the coup.

Law and order

The police service improved its accountability for abuses of power. At least 10 officers were suspended from duty awaiting disciplinary or criminal charges.

Police intensified investigations into 55 officers who facilitated the coup, including former Police Commissioner Isikia Savua, who became Fiji's ambassador to the UN in January 2003. Officers had implicated Isikia Savua in a number of incidents including human rights violations against Indo-Fijian farmers and their families. However, the Director of Public Prosecutions declined to bring his case to trial on grounds of insufficient evidence.

Inhuman prison conditions

In January, the government fined the prison department for obstructing health inspections at Suva's Korovou Prison. Judges requested the advice of the Fiji Human Rights Commission (FHRC) on conditions at Korovou and released three prisoners who were held in cruel, inhuman or degrading conditions. The government again declined to improve conditions on grounds of financial constraints.

Violence against women

Prison terms of up to five years were imposed for rape. Several men accused of other serious abuses of women and children were merely given warnings by courts or released on bail.

By May the Fiji Women's Crisis Centre reported that violence against women and children had increased by 25 per cent compared to the same period in 2003. The centre's advocacy resulted in the prioritization by police of combating domestic violence and sexual abuse.

Racial discrimination

Discrimination against ethnic minorities was evident in plans for an indigenous Trust Fund and in the appointment of indigenous Fijians to almost all chief executive posts in the public service.

Human rights and law reform

The Fiji Law Reform Commission began extensive reviews of laws covering prisons, and certain crimes including violence against women in the home.

In September, the President published an FHRC handbook for the security services on Fiji's Bill of Rights and international human rights standards.

FINLAND

REPUBLIC OF FINLAND
Head of state: Tarja Halonen
Head of government: Matti Vanhanen
Death penalty: abolitionist for all crimes
International Criminal Court: ratified
UN Women's Convention and its Optional Protocol: ratified

Nine conscientious objectors to military service were adopted as prisoners of conscience. International monitoring bodies expressed concern about aspects of Finland's human rights record.

Conscientious objection to military service

The length of alternative civilian service remained punitive and discriminatory: all conscientious objectors were required to perform 395 days of alternative civilian service, 215 days longer than the majority of military recruits. AI continued to urge the authorities to reduce the length of alternative civilian service in line with internationally recognized standards and recommendations. Despite repeated assurances by the relevant minister that she would do everything in her power to shorten the length of alternative service, AI was not aware of any recent government proposal to review the legislation.
▢ Nine conscientious objectors were adopted as prisoners of conscience during 2004. They received prison sentences of between 169 and 197 days for refusing to perform alternative civilian service. They all cited the punitive length of service as a reason for their refusal.

International scrutiny of human rights record

In June the Council of Europe's Committee for the Prevention of Torture and Inhuman or Degrading Treatment or Punishment (CPT) published a report on its September 2003 visit to Finland. The government had previously authorized publication, in October 2003, of the CPT's preliminary observations.

The CPT found that there was no coherent set of regulations on the use of force and means of restraint authorized during the deportation of foreign nationals, and recommended that detailed instructions on the procedures to be followed be issued without delay.

🗁 The CPT detailed the case of a Ukrainian family, a married couple and two children aged 11 and 12. In 2002 they were deported back to Ukraine at the third attempt after an operation lasting three days. Before being deported, they were held in a custody unit for aliens in Helsinki where sedative drugs were administered without proper examination by a doctor and without proper records being kept. The CPT described the approach taken in this case as unacceptable.

In November the UN Human Rights Committee (HRC), after considering Finland's periodic report, noted with concern that Roma still faced discrimination in housing, education, employment and access to public places. It also reiterated its concern over the failure to settle the question of Sami rights to land ownership.

The HRC expressed concern about people held in pre-trial detention in police stations, noting a lack of clarity about their right of access to lawyers and doctors.

The HRC regretted that the right to conscientious objection was acknowledged only in peacetime, and that the civilian alternative to military service was punitively long. It reiterated its concern at the fact that the preferential treatment accorded to Jehovah's Witnesses had not been extended to other groups of conscientious objectors.

AI country reports/ visits
Report
- Europe and Central Asia: Summary of Amnesty International's concerns in the region, January-June 2004: Finland (AI Index: EUR 01/005/2004)

FRANCE

FRENCH REPUBLIC
Head of state: Jacques Chirac
Head of government: Jean-Pierre Raffarin
Death penalty: abolitionist for all crimes
International Criminal Court: ratified
UN Women's Convention and its Optional Protocol: ratified

Complaints about police violence and abuse rose sharply. Reports of ill-treatment by state agents, mainly police officers, showed that people of foreign origin were the predominant targets of abusive identity checks. Acts of racist violence, intimidation and vandalism were directed at members of Jewish and Muslim communities, and North African immigrants were the main focus of racist attacks in Corsica. Thousands of people took to the streets in November to protest against the high incidence of violence against women in general and, in particular, at the stoning to death of a young woman, Ghofrane Haddaoui, in Marseilles a month earlier. Conditions in prisons, as well as in holding centres for foreign nationals, deteriorated to below international standards. There were frequent reports that people had been physically ill-treated in holding areas and reception centres or during forcible deportation, and that unaccompanied children were detained in holding areas before being deported.

Ill-treatment by state agents
According to figures published in May by the police and prison oversight body, the National Commission of Deontology and Security (CNDS), complaints of police abuse or violence almost doubled in the previous year. The CNDS urged major structural reforms. Police bodies that investigate complaints against police officers in Paris and in the rest of the country recorded an increase in complaints of over nine per cent in 2003, the sixth consecutive year in which the number had risen. Officers continued to enjoy effective impunity: frequently, no action was taken against officers following complaints, or cases were slow to come to court. By contrast, police prosecutions of people charged with insulting state agents or resisting arrest usually came before the courts promptly.

In October the CNDS criticized the police complaints body for the Paris area, the General Inspection Services (IGS), for an ineffective inquiry into a racist police attack on members of the Kabyle ethnic community during New Year celebrations in Paris. In December a commission composed of human rights groups and judges, Citoyens-Justice-Police, reported that foreign nationals were victims in 60 per cent of police violence cases studied between July 2002 and June 2004. The remaining 40 per cent were French nationals, but many seemed to have been targeted because they appeared of foreign origin.

In a report in March covering visits in 2003, the Council of Europe's Committee for the Prevention of Torture and Inhuman or Degrading Treatment or Punishment (CPT), reiterated its disagreement with official refusal to grant access to a lawyer in some cases for the first 36 hours in police custody. The CPT stressed that all detainees should have access to a lawyer from the outset of custody, and also during police questioning — which is not currently permitted.

◻ In April an asylum-seeker and unauthorized street trader, Sukwinder Singh, was reported to have been brutally beaten by a police officer in the Goutte d'Or area of Paris. The officer allegedly banged his head against a car and punched him on the face and body after taking him in handcuffs to the police station. Sukwinder Singh later collapsed in the street and required hospital treatment. The same officer was said to have demanded money and to have ill-treated him earlier in the year. A complaint was submitted to the IGS, but no developments were reported by the end of 2004.

◻ In November, Abdelkader Ghedir suffered a fractured skull, fell into a coma and had to be hospitalized after he was questioned by police officers and officers of the security services of the state railways (SUGE) in connection with allegations of stone-throwing at trains. Three SUGE officers were placed under judicial investigation on a charge of "voluntary acts of violence" and one, alleged to have kneed Abdelkader Ghedir in the head, was provisionally imprisoned. Demands for a national police inquiry were rejected, although the police officers at the scene had reportedly been present during the alleged assault.

◻ Update: In December the correctional court of Nanterre (Hauts-de-Seine) sentenced two police officers from Asnières police station to eight-month and four-month suspended prison terms respectively for acts of violence "well in excess of the reasonable use of force" against 16-year-old "Yacine" in 2001. The state prosecutor had requested their acquittal. Yacine required emergency surgery to have a testicle removed. The police appealed against the convictions.

Ill-treatment in border areas

Conditions in reception centres or holding areas for foreign nationals were reported to have fallen below international standards in many areas. These included a number of administrative holding centres in Metropolitan France and similar centres in overseas departments and territories such as Cayenne (French Guiana) or Mayotte. People held at a reception centre for foreign nationals in Paris were allegedly subjected to acts of violence as well as inhuman and degrading conditions.

The Ombudsperson for Children expressed "extreme concern" about the situation of unaccompanied children placed in waiting zones before they were deported. Associations that assist refugees and asylum-seekers in border areas noted that the entry of such children was often systematically blocked. In a number of cases, children had been prevented from rejoining parents already in the country. In November such associations reported that conditions in a holding area at Roissy-Charles-de-Gaulle airport (ZAPI 3) had improved, but criticized a continuing pattern of excessive violence during forcible deportations.

In December, in a landmark decision, the Court of Appeal of Paris stated that holding areas should, for legal purposes, be considered as part of French territory and therefore that judges had competence to examine cases.

◻ Four passengers on board a flight at Roissy in August faced charges of interfering with air traffic and disturbing the peace after protesting about police brutality. They reported seeing French officers hitting a national of Mali who was being forcibly deported. As a result of their protests, they were escorted off the aircraft in handcuffs and held for several hours in police custody.

◻ Update: In September the Court of Appeal of Paris ordered that there was no case to answer in the death of Ricardo Barrientos, an Argentinian national, while being forcibly deported in December 2002. On an aircraft destined for Buenos Aires, he had reportedly been bent double, his hands cuffed behind his back, and his torso, thighs and ankles bound with Velcro tape, while two police officers and three gendarmes applied continuous pressure to his shoulder blades. He had a mask over his face and was covered with a blanket, which hid him from other passengers and prevented him appealing for help. He collapsed before the aircraft's doors were closed. The court decided that Ricardo Barrientos had not been subjected to "acts of violence leading unintentionally to death", as the charge maintained, because the officers had only been obeying orders to keep him under restraint. The court found that his death was attributable exclusively to natural causes arising from a heart condition. The judgment did not alleviate concerns that the methods of restraint used during the deportation failed to comply with international standards. The CPT, in its 13th General Report in 2003 on detentions under aliens legislation, pointed out the risk to a deportee who is obliged to "bend forward, head between the knees, thus strongly compressing the ribcage", and noted that "the use of force and/or means of restraint capable of causing positional asphyxia should be avoided wherever possible".

Racist violence

Numerous racist acts of violence and vandalism were directed against mosques, Jewish schools and synagogues, and Jewish, Muslim and Christian cemeteries. In July, President Jacques Chirac made a national appeal for racial and religious tolerance, calling for urgent action against a rise in the "despicable and odious acts of hatred soiling our nation". Up to 192 people were questioned by police, and judicial inquiries were opened into several acts of violence, racial abuse and incitement to racial hatred.

Corsica, which has a large immigrant population, was the focus of a wave of attacks against people of North African origin and their properties. Responsibility for several such attacks was claimed by a small armed political group, Clandestini Corsi. In September, during a wave of racist acts, the group congratulated the "anonymous underground movement" for an attack on the home of a North African resident in Biguglia, and made threats against anti-racist and human rights groups for condemning the violence. In November, AI reiterated its concerns and stated that Corsican nationalists or autonomists had a particular responsibility to be firm and consistent in their condemnation of such attacks, irrespective of the identity or aims of the perpetrators. Over 40 such attacks had been reported by the Corsican authorities by the end of 2004.

◻ In November the home of Moroccan imam Mohamed al Akrach in Sartène (Corse-du-Sud) came under fire after he refused to open his door to knocking and racial abuse. An arson attack had been made on the house in 2003. A week earlier assailants fired on the home of a Tunisian woman and her four children, and left racist graffiti at the scene. Some immigrants reportedly left Corsica because of xenophobic violence.

◻ In December, four minors were arrested for throwing acid into a hostel for immigrants in Ajaccio. Another such hostel and a Moroccan restaurant were also targeted.

◻ In December Oueda Bouatti lodged a complaint against two men who allegedly attacked her for wearing the Muslim headscarf in Mulhouse. One of the men reportedly referred to her scarf as "merde" (shit) before punching her and beating her with a stick.

Prisons crisis
The CPT report in March expressed concern at the "recent and alarming" rise in the prison population, which had resulted in serious overcrowding, an inhuman and degrading environment, and a high rate of suicides. The report concerned in particular the prisons of Loos (Nord Pas-de-Calais), Toulon (Provences-Alpes-Côte d'Azur) and Clairvaux (Aube), visited by the CPT in June 2003. It detailed unhealthy and unsafe conditions, the lack of activities for a large number of prisoners, a sense of exhaustion and frustration among prison officers, and the absence of an effective policy to prevent suicides. These problems were not only, or even mainly, caused by lack of infrastructure, the report found, but originated in a more repressive penal policy that would not be addressed by simply building new prisons. The CPT's recommendations stressed the need for prompt and radical action to cut overcrowding and obtain humane conditions.

Torture sentence
In December the Court of Cassation, the highest court in the legal system, rejected the appeal lodged by General Paul Aussaresses following his conviction on a charge of "justifying torture". His memoirs, published in 2001, described acts of torture and summary executions by French army officers in Algeria in the 1950s, and maintained that they had been necessary. In

April 2003 the Court of Appeal of Paris had fined him 7,500 Euros and his editors, Plon, 15,000 Euros. The Court of Cassation upheld the prosecution view that freedom of expression should not be confused with the right to say "anything anyhow".

Religious symbols in schools
In March parliament adopted a civil law (No. 2004-228) banning conspicuous religious symbols in state schools, such as large crosses, headscarves, skullcaps and turbans. The law, which reinforced similar existing measures, raised tensions between those who advocated a single national identity and a secular state, and those who believed it infringed principles of multiculturalism and the fundamental right to expression of conscientiously held beliefs. AI expressed concern that the law could have negative implications for the exercise of freedom of religion, expression and other basic rights, to education for example. The organization believed that concern for the protection of the secular nature of the French Republic should not override the fundamental rights to express conscientiously held beliefs or identity, and that the law could have a disproportionate and particular impact on Muslim girls if applied strictly. According to the French authorities, of more than 600 girls who returned to school in September wearing headscarves, a small number were expelled out of the 100 who refused to remove them and who were invited to talks with school officials. Nine Sikh students were said to have been refused entry to courses in September for wearing turbans. The law was to come under review in 2005.

AI country reports/visits
Reports
- Europe and Central Asia: Summary of Amnesty International's concerns in the region, January-June 2004: France (AI Index: EUR 01/005/2004)
- Corsica (France): Perpetrators of new wave of racist violence must be brought promptly to justice (AI Index: EUR 21/001/2004)

GEORGIA

GEORGIA
Head of state: Mikhail Saakashvili (since January)
Head of government: Zurab Zhvania (since February)
Death penalty: abolitionist for all crimes
International Criminal Court: ratified
UN Women's Convention and its Optional Protocol: ratified

Police used excessive force on several occasions. Hundreds of perpetrators of attacks on religious minorities remained unpunished. Chechens sought by the Russian Federation continued to be in danger of extradition.

Background

Mikhail Saakashvili was elected President in January in elections that were assessed as largely positive by observers from the Organization for Security and Co-operation in Europe (OSCE).

In February amendments to the Constitution were adopted that increased presidential powers. There was widespread criticism both of the amendments themselves and of the speed with which they were passed.

In March the pro-government National Movement won a partial rerun of the much-criticized parliamentary elections conducted under the previous government in November 2003. From the opposition, only the New Right/Industrialists bloc gained enough votes to have any representatives in parliament, giving the government a virtually unopposed majority. The OSCE described the elections as "the most democratic since independence", while also noting irregularities.

Arrests and investigations as part of the government's anti-corruption campaign were in many cases characterized by procedural violations.

Journalists critical of the authorities reportedly risked reprisals including beatings and dismissal from their work.

After the so-called "Rose Revolution" of November 2003, tensions increased between the central government and the autonomous republic of Ajaria. In May, the Ajarian leader, Aslan Abashidze, stepped down following a series of public protests against his leadership. The central government took direct control of the region for an interim period and elections on 20 June resulted in an overwhelming victory for President Saakashvili's supporters.

Shortly after the collapse of Aslan Abashidze's government, tensions increased between the central government and the internationally unrecognized breakaway region of South Ossetia. The conflict escalated from June for several weeks with frequent shoot-outs that led to casualties, including civilians, on both sides. No resolution to the disputed status of the region was in sight by the end of 2004.

In October disputes over the results of presidential elections in the internationally unrecognized breakaway region of Abkhazia led to hundreds of supporters of the two main candidates taking to the streets. Raul Khadzhimba, protégé of the outgoing President, protested against the declaration by the Central Election Committee and the Supreme Court of the opposition candidate Sergey Bagapsh as the winner by a small margin. In November supporters of both candidates occupied government and state television station buildings. In December an agreement was reached whereby Sergey Bagapsh and Raul Khadzhimba would run for President and Vice-President respectively in new elections planned for January 2005.

In June the Council of the European Union included Georgia along with Armenia and Azerbaijan in the European Neighbourhood Policy.

The new government received substantial international aid. At a joint European Commission/World Bank conference in June, individual countries and international organizations pledged around US$1 billion for the period 2004-2006.

In July the European Union launched a one-year programme aimed at assisting the authorities with the reform of the country's criminal justice system.

Torture and ill-treatment

Reports of torture and ill-treatment in pre-trial detention continued. In at least two cases suspects died allegedly as a result of torture or excessive use of force by police.

On 1 September, seven men were reportedly detained in the western town of Zugdidi, accused of membership of a paramilitary group and possession of firearms and explosives. One of them, Geno Kulava, was said to have been tortured and ill-treated in the police station of Khobi district. The report described how he was suspended from a pole between two tables, kicked and beaten, including with truncheons, and dropped on the floor. A burning candle was held against his forearm. After his lawyer complained to the court that his client had been tortured, Geno Kulava was examined by forensic experts on two occasions. They found traces of severe beatings and haemorrhages in several parts of his body. One of Geno Kulava's co-defendants, Levan Dzadzua, was allegedly beaten by police at another police station in Zugdidi. On 15 November Geno Kulava was released from prison following a court ruling, reportedly because of procedural violations. However, he was immediately rearrested, accused of abducting a resident of Zugdidi. Geno Kulava and Levan Dzadzua were still detained at the end of 2004. The authorities had reportedly not opened a thorough and impartial investigation into the allegations of torture and ill-treatment, and none of the alleged perpetrators had been brought to justice.

Excessive use of force by police and prison officers

Police used excessive force on several occasions. Concern was heightened by government statements that apparently encouraged the use of force by police and prison personnel or endorsed police operations where excessive force had been used.

🗁 In January police used excessive force while breaking up an unauthorized demonstration that blocked a main road in the west of the country. Some 200 demonstrators were peacefully protesting against the detention of Zaza Ambroladze, a resident of Imereti region charged with illegal possession of firearms. Television news footage showed dozens of people being kicked and beaten by police, including with truncheons. The following day *Imedi TV* broadcast a statement by President Saakashvili applauding the police operation. He stated that anyone who "defends criminal bosses" would be "dealt a very hard blow in the teeth".

Religious minorities

Hundreds of perpetrators of attacks on religious minorities remained unpunished.

🗁 In March police detained Basil Mkalavishvili, a defrocked Georgian Orthodox priest, and eight of his supporters in connection with a series of violent attacks on religious minorities. AI welcomed the detention of the nine, while expressing concern about the excessive force used in the police operation. The arrest, however, was not a clear signal in favour of religious freedom. Immediately after the police operation President Saakashvili publicly stated that "the Georgian state, not some local extremist who beats and raids people, should protect Georgia from harmful alien influence and extremism". The trial opened in Tbilisi in August. There were allegations that at least four victims who had suffered particularly severely from the attacks – Leila Kartvelishvili, Beniamin Bakuradze, Otar Kalatozishvili and his son Zaza Kalatozishvili – were dropped from the list of those called to testify in court.

Risk of extraditions

Chechens accused of "terrorism" continued to be in danger of extradition to the Russian Federation where they risked serious human rights violations. The Russian authorities frequently stated that Chechens wanted by them for "terrorism" were hiding in the Georgian Pankisi gorge, a charge that Georgia denied. In February, President Saakashvili told the Russian radio station *Ekho Moskvy* that people suspected of "terrorist" attacks in Moscow had already been extradited, adding an invitation to the Russian authorities to help find anybody remaining so that they could "throw them out of Georgia together". In October, the Georgian Interior Minister announced that Georgia would be prepared to provide the Russian authorities with lists of those living in the gorge. As a member of the Council of Europe and a party to the UN Refugee Convention and its Protocol, Georgia is obliged to refrain from deportations or extraditions that put people at risk of serious human rights violations.

🗁 Several local human rights activists alleged that the Georgian authorities facilitated the detention of the Chechens Khusein Alkhanov and Bekhan Mulkoyev

by officers of the Russian Federal Security Service in North Ossetia in Russia on 19 February. This was categorically denied by senior government officials. The two men had been detained by Georgian border guards when crossing into Georgia in August 2002. They were held in detention until 6 February 2004 when they were released by Tbilisi regional court. On 16 February local groups reported the two men had "disappeared", only one week before a delegation from the European Court was due to interview them in Tbilisi.

Allegedly fabricated charges

🗁 Merab Mikeladze and Lasha Chakhvadze, two supporters of the then Ajarian leader Aslan Abashidze, were detained by police in Tbilisi in February. Police charged them with illegal possession of weapons, a charge that AI believed to be fabricated. The two were released from custody on 27 February in what many termed a "deal" between the central authorities and the Ajarian authorities involving the subsequent release of two members of the youth movement *Kmara!* who had been detained in Ajaria. After their release, Merab Mikeladze and Lasha Chakhvadze left for Ajaria and refused to return to Tbilisi for further investigations. Shortly after the change of government in Ajaria, Lasha Chakhvadze was detained in Batumi. He was additionally charged with putting up resistance to the police in relation to his detention in February. He had not gone on trial by the end of 2004. Merab Mikeladze was believed to be in hiding at the end of the year.

Clampdown on dissent in Ajaria

The government of Aslan Abashidze intensified its clampdown on dissent following the "Rose Revolution" of November 2003. This included the detention and in some cases ill-treatment of activists critical of Aslan Abashidze and his policies, and ill-treatment and intimidation of independent journalists. AI received numerous reports of excessive use of force by Abashidze supporters against demonstrators critical of the Ajarian authorities.

🗁 In February, Gocha Khvichia and Imeda Tavdgeridze, two members of the youth movement *Kmara!*, which was particularly vocal in criticizing the Ajarian authorities, were allegedly beaten by Ajarian law enforcement officers at a checkpoint. The two young men, together with another *Kmara!* member, Sofiko Pataraia, and her sister, had been taken off a bus travelling from Tbilisi to Batumi after the officers had found *Kmara!* leaflets in their bags. All four were detained in a house near the checkpoint. Reportedly, the young women were forced to watch the two men being beaten and kicked by some 20 men, some of whom were masked. They were threatened and warned not to contact journalists or human rights organizations. The four were released later that day.

AI country reports/visits
Reports
· Georgia: President Saakashvili should put human rights at the heart of his policies (AI Index: EUR 56/001/2004)

- Europe and Central Asia: Summary of Amnesty International's concerns in the region, January-June 2004: Georgia (AI Index: EUR 01/005/2004)
- Belarus and Uzbekistan: The last executioners – The trend towards abolition in the former Soviet space (AI Index: EUR 04/009/2004)

Visit

AI delegates conducted research in Tbilisi and Batumi in March.

GERMANY

FEDERAL REPUBLIC OF GERMANY
Head of state: Horst Köhler (replaced Johannes Rau in July)
Head of government: Gerhard Schröder
Death penalty: abolitionist for all crimes
International Criminal Court: ratified
UN Women's Convention and its Optional Protocol: ratified

There were allegations of ill-treatment and excessive use of force by police. There was continued debate about whether there were circumstances in which law enforcement officials were permitted to use torture.

Background

In July, after a long delay, the Ministers of the Interior of the 16 Länder (regional states) recommended ratification of the Optional Protocol to the UN Convention against Torture. The Optional Protocol requires, among other things, an independent monitoring mechanism for detention facilities at the national level. Its establishment was under discussion.

The Bundestag (parliament) ratified the Optional Protocol to the UN Children's Convention on the involvement of children in armed conflicts. Regrettably, it ordered a reservation to be made to allow minors from the age of 17 to join the armed forces.

Police ill-treatment and excessive use of force

In January AI published a report on police ill-treatment and excessive use of force, highlighting 20 cases as examples, and citing a series of similar allegations. In the report, AI urged the federal government and the governments of the 16 Länder to ensure that allegations were investigated promptly and impartially, to keep statistics on incidents of possible police ill-treatment and to establish an independent body to investigate such cases. AI discussed the report and the recommendations with police representatives, government officials and other experts, but by the end of 2004 neither the federal government nor any Länder government had officially put AI's recommendations into action.

In many of the cases AI investigated, criminal proceedings against police officers were either discontinued or ended with acquittals. In only one case, that of Aamir Ageeb (see below), were police officers convicted.

◻ Svetlana Lauer, a 44-year-old German national originally from Kazakstan, alleged that several police officers ill-treated her at her home in Hallstadt, Bavaria, in February 2002. Criminal proceedings against the officers were discontinued and an appeal by Svetlana Lauer's lawyer was rejected in April 2003. However, proceedings initiated by the Bamberg Public Prosecutor's Office in September 2003 against Svetlana Lauer for resisting law enforcement officials, causing bodily harm to the officers and slander ended in an out-of court settlement after she agreed to pay 210 Euros. The case was officially closed in May 2004.

◻ Josef Hoss was allegedly ill-treated by police officers of the Special Deployment Command in December 2000 in St. Augustin near Bonn. Proceedings against the police officers were discontinued in June 2003. An appeal against the discontinuation of the proceedings was rejected by the Prosecutor's Office in Cologne in February 2004. A final appeal by Josef Hoss' lawyer was rejected in April 2004. The Special Deployment Command was reportedly disbanded. By the end of 2004, Josef Hoss' compensation case had not been decided.

◻ Sixty-two-year-old community activist Walter Herrmann was allegedly ill-treated after he was arrested by police in Cologne in September 2001. Walter Herrmann sustained multiple injuries, allegedly as a result of ill-treatment by police officers at the point of arrest and at Cologne Police Headquarters. In February 2004 the three policemen accused of ill-treating Walter Herrmann were acquitted by a court in Cologne. The judge found that there was not enough evidence to prove that Walter Herrmann's injuries were inflicted deliberately. Walter Herrmann's appeal against this decision was rejected in November and the acquittal confirmed.

◻ Thirty-year-old René Bastubbe was shot dead by a police officer in July 2002 in Nordhausen, Thuringia, when he resisted arrest and threw one or more cobble stones at the police officer. As René Bastubbe bent down to pick up another cobble stone, the police officer shot him in the back from a distance of several metres. René Bastubbe died as a result of massive blood loss. In October 2003 Mühlhausen District Court acquitted the police officer and ruled that he had shot René Bastubbe in self-defence. The Federal Supreme Court in Karlsruhe rejected an appeal in June 2004 by the prosecution to revise this judgment.

◻ Miriam Canning, a Kenyan national, was allegedly ill-treated by police officers in Stuttgart, Baden-

Württemberg, in July 2001. Police officers had entered her home in the early hours to check the identification of her 19-year-old son and her cousin, who had been stopped and searched by the police earlier that night. The Canning family lodged a complaint but the prosecuting authorities discontinued criminal proceedings against the police. A number of important issues were apparently not addressed by the prosecuting authorities, particularly the cause of Miriam Canning's injuries, which, according to a doctor, were perfectly consistent with her allegations. Nevertheless, in October 2004 Miriam Canning's claim for damages was dismissed on the ground that her injuries were caused by negligence or careless handling and not by a deliberate attack.

◻ Aamir Ageeb, a Sudanese national, died during forced deportation from Frankfurt to Khartoum via Cairo on 28 May 1999. According to experts he died of asphyxiation as a result of the manner in which he was restrained on the aeroplane. On 18 October 2004, the District Court of Frankfurt am Main convicted three officers of the German Border Police (Bundesgrenzschutz) of manslaughter. It imposed on each of them a suspended sentence of nine months with probation and a fine of 2,000 Euros to be paid to Aamir Ageeb's family. The presiding judge stated that not only the three officers sentenced but also their supervisors were responsible for the death of Aamir Ageeb, because they had failed to give clear instructions and to intervene during the deportation. Moreover, the directives for deportations were insufficient. Some of these had been changed and clarified as a result of Aamir Ageeb's death.

Torture debate
Public debate continued about whether there were circumstances, including "terrorism", in which law enforcement officials were permitted to use torture. It arose from a report that in 2002 Wolfgang Daschner, Vice-President of the Frankfurt am Main police, had ordered a subordinate officer to use force against a criminal suspect while investigating the kidnap of an 11-year-old boy. Wolfgang Daschner publicly defended his actions. In June 2004 the Regional Court in Frankfurt ordered Wolfgang Daschner to be tried on a charge of severe intimidation. On 20 December Wolfgang Daschner and a subordinate police officer were convicted of threatening a suspect with torture but the Regional Court found mitigating circumstances in their cases and therefore they were penalized only with a caution. However, the presiding judge stated that torture was a crime which violates international and constitutional law.

Many leading figures were quick to condemn torture, but the debate also gave rise to attempts by some to justify it and to argue that in some cases there should be exceptions from the fundamental prohibition of torture. AI remained concerned about the lack of an active, unequivocal response from senior politicians reaffirming Germany's commitment to upholding its international obligations on the prohibition of torture.

New Immigration Act
After about four years of discussion, a new Immigration Act was passed, most of which was due to come into force in January 2005. Under the new regulations, victims of human rights abuses committed by non-state actors and victims of gender-based human rights violations would be eligible for recognition as refugees. However, many of the new provisions appeared to undermine the rights of asylum-seekers and of people without residence permits.

AI country reports/ visits
Reports
- Back in the spotlight: Allegations of police ill-treatment and excessive use of force in Germany (AI Index: EUR 23/001/2004)
- EU arms embargoes fail to prevent German engines being incorporated into military vehicles available in Burma/Myanmar, China and Croatia (AI Index: ACT 30/016/2004)
- Europe and Central Asia: Summary of Amnesty International's concerns in the region, January-June 2004: Germany (AI Index: EUR 01/005/2004)

GHANA

REPUBLIC OF GHANA
Head of state and government: John Agyekum Kufuor
Death penalty: retentionist
International Criminal Court: ratified
UN Women's Convention: ratified
Optional Protocol to UN Women's Convention: signed

No death sentences were passed and there were no executions, although the death penalty remained on the statute books. A National Reconciliation Commission reported on human rights violations during Ghana's periods of unconstitutional government since 1957. A woman was imprisoned for practising female genital mutilation. A draft Domestic Violence Bill was still not tabled in parliament.

Background
After elections in December, President Kufuor was re-elected.

The National Reconciliation Commission
The National Reconciliation Commission (NRC) ended its hearings in July. Established by the government in 2002, initially for one year, its task was to compile a

record of human rights violations committed during Ghana's periods of unconstitutional rule since independence in 1957, and to recommend reparations and reforms. Most of the witnesses were victims of human rights violations under the military governments headed by former President J.J. Rawlings. Many of the 2,000-plus testimonies that were heard spoke of summary executions, "disappearances", torture and ill-treatment.

The NRC's report and recommendations were submitted to President Kufuor on 12 October but had not been made public by the end of 2004. The recommendations reportedly included reparations for about 3,000 victims and reforms of institutions including the security agencies.

Women's rights

Despite being made a criminal offence in 1994, female genital mutilation continued to be practised, particularly in the north. In January, a 70-year-old woman from Koloko, Upper East Region, who had performed female genital mutilation on seven girls, was convicted and sentenced to five years' imprisonment.

A draft Domestic Violence Bill had not yet been tabled in Parliament by the end of 2004, despite wide support from women's organizations and other civil society groups. The bill aimed to strengthen official responses to complaints of violence against women and to broaden remedies available to the courts.

GREECE

HELLENIC REPUBLIC
Head of state: Constantinos Stephanopoulos
Head of government: Constantinos Karamanlis (replaced Constantinos Simitis in March)
Death penalty: abolitionist for all crimes
International Criminal Court: ratified
UN Women's Convention and its Optional Protocol: ratified

Ill-treatment of migrants by border guards and by police officers in urban centres was reported. Conditions of detention for undocumented immigrants and asylum-seekers were poor. Trials relating to police ill-treatment of women, minorities and foreign nationals took place. Concerns were raised about conditions of detention in Korydallos prison. Discriminatory treatment of Roma by the authorities continued. Conscientious objectors continued to face the threat of imprisonment. In November the Greek parliament approved the ratification of Protocol No. 13 of the European Convention on Human Rights, thereby abolishing the death penalty for all crimes.

Background

Elections in March were won by the New Democracy party, ending 11 years of rule by the Pan-Hellenic Socialist Movement (PASOK).

In August, Greece hosted the 2004 Summer Olympic Games. There were reports of forced evictions of Roma families from sites designated for infrastructure and building projects linked to the Olympics, and concerns that security measures implemented in connection with the event undermined human rights.

Treatment of refugees and migrants

There were concerns that practices by coastguards and police, including border police, aimed at discouraging undocumented migrants from entering Greek territory, violated international standards. Such practices included interception on the Turkish border and immediate expulsion, refusal to accept applications for asylum, and failure to make available such applications to migrants.

In August migrants who had been detained for three months on the island of Samos reported conditions of detention that contravened international standards. Concerns were also raised by the UN High Commissioner for Refugees (UNHCR) following a visit to the detention centre. In September, 10 migrants were reportedly ill-treated by members of commando forces on Farmakonisi.

On 15 October, five coastguards were found guilty of torturing a group of immigrants on the island of Crete in June 2001, and received suspended prison sentences of between 12 and 30 months.

▢ A Sudanese national was at risk of forcible return to the conflict-torn Darfur region of Sudan from where he had fled in 2003 because the Ministry of Public Order refused to re-examine his case. He had been detained on his arrival in Greece in June 2003 and released three months later. He lived without welfare support in Greece until October 2003, when he travelled to the UK and claimed asylum. The UK authorities determined that Greece was responsible for deciding on his asylum claim and he was returned to Greece in June 2004. His new asylum application was rejected on the grounds that he had left Greece. The review of his original application had been cancelled. A decision to deport him was issued. A new application based on fresh information about the situation in Darfur was declared inadmissible. It was not known whether he had been deported by the end of the year.

☐ In November, AI expressed concern about reports that 502 children, the majority from Albania, had gone missing between 1998 and 2002 from a state-run children's home in Athens, where they were being sheltered after being taken off the streets by police. Many of the children were apparently victims of traffickers who forced them to sell trinkets or beg. AI was concerned that the children had reportedly not been adequately protected at the home and that little or no effort was made by the Greek authorities to find them. Despite the intervention of several non-governmental organizations and the Albanian Ombudsman, the Greek authorities had not undertaken a thorough and impartial judicial investigation into the case, although a preliminary police inquiry was launched in May.

☐ There were reports in December that police officers tortured and ill-treated a group of around 60 asylum-seekers from Afghanistan, at least 17 of whom were under 18 years old. Police reportedly punched, kicked, sexually abused and threatened them with guns both in their homes and at the local police station in Athens. Although a preliminary investigation was opened in the case, AI called for a prompt, thorough, independent and impartial investigation to be carried out under Article 137 of the Penal Code.

☐ There were reports that 186 children aged between 13 and 16 were among the approximately 700 refugees held in the Reception and Temporary Accommodation Centre for illegal immigrants in the Pagani area of Lesbos in extremely overcrowded conditions. As many as 200 people were reportedly crowded into rooms meant to accommodate 80. Most of the refugee children were believed to come from Iraq and Afghanistan and had arrived in Greek territory unaccompanied.

Update: Vullnet Bytyci
☐ The trial of a police officer accused of shooting dead 18-year-old Albanian Vullnet Bytyci in September 2003 at the Greek-Albanian border was postponed until February 2005.

Conditions of detention

The National Commission of Human Rights reported in May on the poor conditions of detention in high security facilities at Korydallos prison where convicted members of the "November 17" group were being held. The prisoners had been held separately from all other prisoners in two isolated groups of seven since their conviction in November 2003 of murder and causing bomb explosions. They continued to be denied participation in regular prison activities, such as using the library, and were denied access to fresh air, daylight in the cells and exercise in a larger space in violation of international standards. It was also reported that all visits to the prisoners were "closed" (a glass screen separated the prisoner from the visitor). Lawyers and prisoners said that conversations they held over the telephone during these visits were taped, a practice that violates international standards. The Ministry of Justice stated to AI in July that the "November 17" prisoners enjoyed better conditions than other prisoners in Korydallos and that possible violations of international human rights standards would be examined.

Impunity for human rights violations

Police investigations into allegations of ill-treatment by police officers failed to meet international standards of impartiality and independence.

☐ In February AI raised its concerns with the Public Order Ministry that investigations into the alleged ill-treatment of two young Romani men in August 2001 had been assigned to the same police departments whose officers allegedly committed the offences. In addition, some of the statements made by police officers in this investigation contained derogatory remarks about the Roma, suggesting that the ill-treatment suffered by the youths might have been the result of discriminatory treatment based on their identity.

☐ After protests at the failure of the judicial authorities to call Olga B., a Ukrainian national, as a witness in the 2003 trial of a police officer accused of raping her, the retrial took place in March. On 30 March the officer was acquitted. The Patras Appeals Prosecutor appealed. However, the officer was acquitted once again in December. Olga B. had also filed a complaint in Patras in September 2003 against two bailiffs who falsely claimed to have served her with a summons to appear in the initial trial. In June, the Amaliada Misdemeanours Court recommended that the bailiffs be acquitted, but this was overturned on 21 September by the Patras Appeals Prosecutor, who launched criminal proceedings against them. The case was to be heard in 2005.

Eviction of Romani families

Romani communities were reportedly evicted from three locations in Athens designated for transformation into Olympic facilities. The authorities, by failing to facilitate their move to appropriate alternative accommodation, violated the International Covenant on Economic, Social and Cultural Rights which Greece has ratified. Such evictions also contravened the government's "Integrated Action Plan for the Social Integration of the Greek Gypsies", which states that "it is anticipated that by the end of 2005 no Greek Rom will be living in tents or makeshift accommodation".

Conscientious objection

Legislation and practice relating to civilian alternatives to military service remained punitive in nature, although new legislation which came into force in 2004 reduced the length of such alternative service. The Special Committee, which makes recommendations on applications for conscientious objection, proposed a blanket rejection of applications based on ideological grounds where applicants do not declare particular beliefs.

AI called for a re-evaluation of the Committee's methods and for the authorities to establish an alternative to military service of a purely civilian nature, outside the authority of the Ministry of Defence.

⌷ On 5 April the claim of Kyriacos Kapidis of conscientious objection to military service on ideological grounds was rejected because the applicant "did not present his views about why he opposes military service convincingly as part of a general outlook on life and did not present evidence of activities and lifestyle characteristically led by ideological convictions that would prevent him from carrying out his military duties".

⌷ Professional soldier Giorgos Monastiriotis was sentenced to 18 months' imprisonment for desertion after his refusal on grounds of conscience to follow his unit to the Middle East in May 2003. He also resigned from the Navy for the same reason. On 6 October he was released pending appeal.

⌷ Conscientious objector Lazaros Petromelidis was tried on 16 December on two insubordination charges in the Naval Court of Piraeus. He was convicted in absentia and sentenced to two and a half years' imprisonment.

UN Committee against Torture

In November Greece's fourth periodic report to the UN Committee against Torture was examined. Concerns raised by the Committee included those previously raised by AI, namely the failure to investigate allegations of torture and ill-treatment promptly and impartially and the lack of an effective independent monitoring system to investigate complaints. The treatment of Albanian migrants, the low rates of refugee status recognition, the forced evictions of Roma, the failure to investigate the disappearance of children from the Aghia Varvara institution and the excessive use of force and firearms by the police were among the issues highlighted by the Committee.

AI country reports/ visits
Report

- Europe and Central Asia: Summary of Amnesty International's concerns in the region, January-June 2004: Greece (AI Index: EUR 01/005/2004)

GUATEMALA

REPUBLIC OF GUATEMALA
Head of state and government: Óscar Berger Perdomo (replaced Alfonso Portillo in January)
Death penalty: retentionist
International Criminal Court: not signed
UN Women's Convention and its Optional Protocol: ratified.

Forced violent evictions in rural areas increased sharply. Human rights defenders continued to suffer intimidation and persecution. Violence against women, in particular murders, increased. Impunity remained endemic, including for past human rights violations.

Background

Óscar Berger took office as President in January. In his inaugural speech he promised to strictly adhere to the 1996 Peace Accords. The Vice-President promised to prioritize the exhumation of massacre sites where hundreds of victims of past human rights violations were buried in clandestine graves during the internal armed conflict.

In February the UN Verification Mission in Guatemala (MINUGUA) called on the government to reaffirm its commitment to implementing recommendations made in 1999 by the Historical Clarification Commission. The government subsequently took some positive measures including modernization of the army and establishing a National Reparations Commission. MINUGUA's mandate and presence in Guatemala ended in November.

Throughout the year former members of the Civil Defence Patrols pressured Congress, including by the use of threats, to pay them compensation for services rendered during the internal armed conflict. Congress agreed in August, despite a June ruling by the Constitutional Court that such payments would be unconstitutional. During the conflict, which ended in 1996, members of the Civil Defence Patrols were implicated in hundreds of cases of human rights violations. Very few have ever been brought to justice.

In August the Constitutional Court delivered its opinion on the creation of a UN-backed Commission for the Investigation of Illegal Bodies and Clandestine Security Apparatus, which had been approved by the previous government. It stated that significant parts of such a commission would be unconstitutional. The government announced it would present alternatives to carry the process forward. By the end of the year discussions were still ongoing.

A proposed Office of the UN High Commissioner for Human Rights was delayed due to the government's reluctance to allow it to submit a "detailed and analytical public report on the country's human rights situation". An agreement, which would still require ratification by Congress, was due to be signed by the government and the UN in January 2005.

Economic, social and cultural rights

According to the UN, 56 per cent of the population were living below the national poverty line.

MINUGUA's final report concluded that, despite advances in the political sphere, fundamental reforms envisaged in the 1996 Peace Accords had not been implemented. It noted the persistence of problems of severe racism and vast social inequality. It warned that if left unchecked, the problems could lead to social conflict, stunted economic development and the corrosion of democratic government.

An unofficial government policy of using forced evictions to resolve ongoing agrarian disputes was widely implemented. There were reportedly 31 forced evictions in the first six months of the year. Many were violent and contravened international norms on the use of force and guidelines for carrying out evictions. Following nationwide protests in June, the President promised to take specific action on the issue but in August another forced eviction cost the lives of four policemen and eight rural workers. According to the Human Rights Ombudsman's Office, the police allegedly extrajudicially executed five rural workers.

Violence against women

According to press reports, the national police recorded more than 527 women murdered in Guatemala, a significant increase from 2003. Many of those killed, mainly from the poorer sectors of society, were raped prior to death. Some were also mutilated.

The UN Special Rapporteur on violence against women found that the Guatemalan government was failing in its international obligations to effectively prevent, investigate and prosecute violence against women. In March a special police unit was established to investigate and prevent crimes against women but was reportedly insufficiently resourced to deal with the scale of the problem.

Impunity

There was minor progress in trying past cases of genocide or crimes against humanity.

The Inter-American Court of Human Rights ordered the Guatemalan state to pay compensation to victims' relatives in a number of prominent cases of past human rights violations for which the state had recognized its responsibility. In a landmark ruling in April, the Court found the Guatemalan state responsible for the massacre of 268 people in Plan de Sánchez, Rabinal, Baja Verapaz, in 1982.

◻ In January, the Supreme Court confirmed a 30-year prison sentence imposed on Colonel Juan Valencia for ordering the murder of anthropologist Myrna Mack in 1990 and ordered his rearrest. He had been released in May 2003 after being acquitted on appeal and his whereabouts remained unknown.

◻ In July, an army lieutenant and 13 soldiers were sentenced to 40 years' imprisonment for the extrajudicial execution of 11 returned indigenous refugees in Xamán, Alta Verapaz, in 1995. They had been found guilty of manslaughter in 1999 but the lieutenant had been acquitted on appeal.

Both the UN Special Rapporteur on the independence of judges and lawyers and the Inter-American Commission on Human Rights expressed concern about the state of the justice system and warned that if appropriate steps were not taken, the rule of law would be in danger.

Threats and intimidation

Human rights activists, witnesses and members of the judiciary involved in investigations of past human rights violations were subjected to persistent intimidation, death threats and attacks. Trade unionists and journalists were also targeted. Such attacks were frequently commissioned or perpetrated by quasi-official groups allegedly acting in collusion with members of the security forces.

◻ In July, a cousin of one of the key witnesses in the 1992 abduction and killing of guerrilla commander Efraín Bámaca Velasquez was killed in what appeared to be an attempt to intimidate the family.

◻ In December, Florentín Gudiel, auxiliary mayor of a small town in the south-east of the country, was shot dead. He had been campaigning against corruption and had previously been commended by the UN for his community work.

Death penalty

No executions took place but 34 people remained on death row.

AI country reports/visits

Visits

AI delegates visited Guatemala in May and October.

GUINEA

REPUBLIC OF GUINEA
Head of state: Lansana Conté
Head of government: Cellou Dalein Diallo (appointed in December; Louceny Fall, February-April; Lamine Sidimé, January-February)
Death penalty: retentionist
International Criminal Court: ratified
UN Women's Convention: ratified
Optional Protocol to UN Women's Convention: not signed

Several political activists and dozens of students were arbitrarily arrested and detained briefly. Twelve people arrested in 2003 were released after more than 10 months in detention.

Background
In January, President Lansana Conté was sworn in for another seven-year term after the Supreme Court confirmed the results of the December 2003 presidential elections. The Guinean Human Rights Organization accused the election organizers of serious and massive violations of the law. In February former Minister of External Affairs Louceny Fall replaced Lamine Sidimé as Prime Minister. However, in April he resigned. In a letter sent from the French capital, Paris, he denounced the lack of dialogue between the President and the government. In December, Cellou Dalein Diallo was appointed Prime Minister.

Release of military officers
In October the former commander of the airport security service, Cheick Adelkader Doumbouya, and 11 other prisoners held on suspicion of plotting to overthrow President Lansana Conté were released. They had been held without charge, trial or access to lawyers for almost 10 months. Other prisoners arrested at the time were reportedly still in detention at the end of 2004. During his detention, Cheick Adelkader Doumbouya, who suffers from diabetes and glaucoma, was denied access to medical treatment.

Arrest of opposition members
Kaba Rogui Barry, Ibrahima Capi Camara and Baidy Aribot, all members of the Union of Republican Forces, UFR, were arrested on 29 March and charged with plotting a coup. They were released on probation more than two weeks later. They were not allowed to leave the country. In April, Sidya Touré, former Prime Minister and leader of the UFR, was detained for one day at police headquarters. He was charged with plotting against the authority of the state, along with a high-ranking officer whose whereabouts were unknown at the end of the year.

Arrest of students
In February at least 15 students were arrested in Conakry. They were released without charge or trial a few days later. In September police broke up a student strike which had forced the closure of the campus at an agrarian institute in Faranah. Some of the students were beaten and dozens were arrested. The students in both Conakry and Faranah were protesting against poor living conditions.

GUINEA-BISSAU

REPUBLIC OF GUINEA-BISSAU
Head of state: Henrique Pereira Rosa (interim)
Head of government: Carlos Gomes Júnior (replaced Artur António Sanhá in April)
Death penalty: abolitionist for all crimes
International Criminal Court: signed
UN Women's Convention: ratified
Optional Protocol to UN Women's Convention: signed

Human rights activists were arrested and beaten on account of their work. Several soldiers and civilians arrested following the September 2003 coup were held uncharged for several months in poor prison conditions. Soldiers arrested in December 2002 and accused of attempting to overthrow the government were released in June pending trial. Police used excessive force or firearms when dispersing demonstrations. Despite legislative elections in March, political instability continued and increased in October following a military revolt in which the Chief of Staff of the Armed Forces was killed.

Background
Dire economic and social conditions persisted. There were strikes in protest at unpaid salaries in the first half of the year. Further strikes were averted by an agreement between the government and the trade unions after the World Bank and other donors agreed to provide emergency aid, and workers began to receive part of their salaries.

Steps were taken to restore the independence of the judiciary with the appointment of the Supreme Court president in January. The appointment marked a return to constitutional rule, which had been severely undermined under former President Kumba Ialá.

In February the army clashed near the northern border with an armed group, believed to be a faction of the Movement of the Democratic Forces of Casamance (Mouvement des Forces Démocratiques du Casamance, MFDC). Four Guinea-Bissau soldiers were reportedly killed and at least a dozen injured.

Although political tension diminished slightly early in the year, the political situation remained fragile, undermining the democratization process. The African Party for the Independence of Guinea-Bissau and Cape

Verde (Partido Africano da Independência da Guiné e Cabo Verde, PAIGC) won legislative elections in March. However, it did not obtain a majority and after more than a month of unsuccessful negotiations with other parties, a government made up exclusively of PAIGC members took office in May.

In June, the UN Peace-building Support Office in Guinea-Bissau (UNOGBIS) warned of the danger of escalating tensions. In October, a group of soldiers revolted and killed the Chief of Staff of the Armed Forces and another officer. The soldiers were demanding full payment of salaries owed to them for serving in a peacekeeping mission to Liberia. They also called for the restructuring of the armed forces. The revolt ended after they reached an agreement with the government on both issues. The agreement also included an amnesty for offences committed by soldiers since 1980, and the appointment of a new Chief of Staff proposed by the soldiers.

Attacks on human rights defenders

Members of the Guinea (Bissau) Human Rights League (Liga Guineense dos Direitos Humanos, LGDH) were targeted by the authorities for denouncing human rights violations by the security forces.

▢ In March, João Vaz Mané, the LGDH vice-president, was detained for several hours. He had reported on a radio programme that a young man had been shot by a police officer in the Belem neighbourhood of Bissau, the capital, some days earlier and that three others had been arrested and ill-treated (see below). He was arrested without a warrant at the LGDH headquarters by police officers who reportedly beat and threatened to kill him and taken to two police stations in Bissau before being released uncharged.

▢ In June, Carlos Adulai Djaló, an LGDH activist in Bafatá, in the east of the country, was reportedly beaten by the former Vice-Chief of Staff of the Army, apparently on account of his LGDH activities.

Detention without charge or trial

At least 10 people, including military officers and civilian supporters of former President Kumba Ialá who were arrested in the aftermath of a coup in September 2003, were held throughout the year without charge or trial. They were detained in the Mansoa army barracks, in the north of Bissau, and were held incommunicado. Kumba Ialá, who had been placed under house arrest, was released in March.

Excessive use of force and firearms by police

In March police used excessive force to disperse a peaceful demonstration by secondary school students in Bissau who were protesting against a strike by their teachers. Dozens of students were reportedly arrested after they went on the rampage after the police charged into them, using tear gas and firing into the air.

Also in March a police officer deliberately shot a young man in the legs, reportedly for refusing to take a taxi he had flagged down. The officer reportedly hit and pushed the young man to the ground, as he tried to explain that the taxi was not going his way, and then shot him in the legs. Three people who tried to intervene, Leonel Pereira João Quade, Nestó Fonseca Mandica and Malam Sani, were arrested and held in the Second police station for five days, where they were reportedly beaten.

Updates

Eleven soldiers held since December 2002, accused of attempting to overthrow the government, were conditionally released in June pending trial. Their trial was postponed indefinitely in October following a military revolt.

GUYANA

REPUBLIC OF GUYANA

Head of state: Bharrat Jagdeo
Head of government: Samuel Hinds
Death penalty: retentionist
International Criminal Court: ratified
UN Women's Convention: ratified
Optional Protocol to UN Women's Convention: not signed

Death sentences continued to be imposed. There were reports that a "death squad" had abducted, tortured and killed dozens of people, and reports of killings by police in circumstances suggesting that they were extrajudicial executions. Torture, ill-treatment and severe overcrowding in detention were reported. Violence against women, including trafficking, was a significant problem.

Background

There were continued reports of high levels of violent crime, although no official statistics were published. At least four police officers were killed on duty.

Death penalty

Death sentences for murder were imposed by the courts. At the end of 2004, there were at least 25 people on death row, including two women. There were no executions.

In December jurors failed to reach a unanimous verdict in the trial of Mark Benschop for treason, a capital offence. A new trial was ordered.

'Death squad'

There were reports that a "death squad", whose members allegedly included serving and former police officers, had abducted, tortured and killed dozens of people since 2002. In May, the President announced a commission of inquiry into the alleged involvement in the "death squad" of the Minister of Home Affairs. Although the inquiry had not been completed by the end of 2004, AI raised concerns about its limited scope and about the lack of safeguards for witnesses. In November the commission of inquiry announced the establishment of a witness protection programme.

Three people were charged with the murder of Shafeek Bacchus on 5 January, of whom two were former police officers. His brother, George Bacchus, a self-confessed "informant", alleged that the "death squad" had killed Shafeek by mistake. One of those charged, Mark Thomas, died in February in police custody in disputed circumstances. In June, George Bacchus was killed two days before he was to give evidence. The magistrate presiding over the case resigned, citing reports that she was on a "death squad" hit list.

Law enforcement officials
In May the final report of the Disciplined Forces Commission, established in 2003 to investigate the operations of the security forces, was presented to parliament. It contained 164 proposals for reform of the police and army.

A number of police officers were charged in connection with fatal shootings, but none was convicted. There were at least 29 fatal shootings by the police, some of which were alleged extrajudicial executions. There were at least two deaths in police custody. Some criminal suspects were allegedly tortured or ill-treated immediately after arrest.
⊡ On 8 September, Kelvin Nero was shot dead by police. Police stated that he was shot during an armed confrontation and died on the way to hospital. Eyewitnesses alleged that he was shot while unarmed, with his back to police, then driven away and shot again. Police appealed for witnesses to come forward, but a national newspaper claimed that police failed to interview witnesses or to preserve forensic evidence.
⊡ Criminal proceedings against a police corporal charged with manslaughter in connection with the 1996 fatal shooting of Jermaine Wilkinson remained pending. In March, depositions from the 1996 preliminary inquiry were sent to the Director of Public Prosecutions after a seven-year delay. The officer remained free on bail.
⊡ In February, two police constables were committed to stand trial for murder, in connection with the fatal shooting of Yohance Douglas in March 2003.
⊡ Emron Hossein died on 10 April, reportedly as a result of beatings by police during his arrest. The Director of Public Prosecutions ordered three police officers to be charged with murder.

Conditions in detention
Conditions in detention remained harsh and amounted in some cases to cruel, inhuman and degrading treatment. The final report of the Disciplined Forces Commission made recommendations to address a range of issues, including rape and ill-treatment in detention.

Violence against women
In October, the Guyana Human Rights Association expressed concern about the prevalence of violence against women. It denounced the legal system's treatment of victims of sexual violence as systematically and intentionally humiliating. It called for a major campaign, involving government, religious and civic institutions, to hold perpetrators accountable.

Trafficking in human beings
A number of measures to address trafficking were announced. These included draft anti-trafficking legislation, with provisions for penalties, restitution and witness protection, and awareness campaigns. Human rights groups welcomed these but stressed that resources were needed for implementation. The Guyana Human Rights Association reported that Amerindian girls from mining communities were being trafficked for forced prostitution.

AI country reports/ visits
Statement
- Guyana: Need for immediate inquiry into death squad killings (AI Index: AMR 35/001/2004)

HAITI

REPUBLIC OF HAITI
Head of state: Boniface Alexandre (replaced Jean Bertrand Aristide in February)
Head of government: Gérard Latortue (replaced Yvon Neptune in March)
Death penalty: abolitionist for all crimes
International Criminal Court: signed
UN Women's Convention: ratified
Optional Protocol to UN Women's Convention: not signed

Scores of people were killed before, during and in the aftermath of a rebellion that toppled President Jean Bertrand Aristide. There were numerous reports of unlawful killings, torture and ill-treatment by police forces. Dozens remained in detention without charge or trial including members of Jean Bertrand Aristide's government and high-profile supporters of his Fanmi Lavalas Party. The judicial system continued to fall short of international standards, leaving the population without judicial safeguards and hindering the fight against impunity. There was no significant effort to recapture prison escapees convicted of grave human rights violations. The UN Security Council authorized international intervention in Haiti to deal with the political crisis after the rebellion and support the transitional government.

Background

In January, Haiti celebrated the bicentenary of its independence from France amid growing discontent and protest against Jean Bertrand Aristide's government. Repression of government opponents was harsh, carried out by police forces and armed gangs known as *chimères*, reportedly in the pay of the administration. On 5 February, conflict broke out in the city of Gonaïves and the insurgency quickly spread to other regions. Insurgents were mainly officials of the former Haitian Armed Forces, disbanded in 1995, members of the disbanded paramilitary organization Revolutionary Front for the Progress and Advancement of Haiti (Front Révolutionnaire pour l'Avancement et le Progrès d'Haïti, FRAPH) and a criminal gang based in Gonaïves that called itself Cannibal Army (Armée cannibale). The armed rebels operated under the leadership of Guy Philippe, former Haitian National Police (HNP) commissioner, and Louis-Jodel Chamblain, former second in command of the FRAPH and convicted perpetrator of human rights abuses. As the rebels advanced they helped detainees to escape.

On 29 February, President Aristide left the country in disputed circumstances while the rebels were threatening to march into Port-au-Prince. Boniface Alexandre, President of the Supreme Court, was immediately sworn in as the new transitional President. The same day, a Multinational Interim Force (MIF) was deployed in the country on a three-month mission authorized by the UN Security Council. On 9 March, Gérard Latortue was appointed interim Prime Minister after being chosen by a seven-member Council of the Wise acting in the absence of the parliament.

In June the UN Stabilization Mission in Haiti (MINUSTAH) took over from the MIF with a mandate, among other things, to support the transitional government in ensuring security and stability and to assist in the reform of the HNP.

In September, Hurricane Jeanne hit Haiti, causing flash floods that left thousands dead or missing in and around the city of Gonaïves. In the aftermath, distribution of international humanitarian aid was hindered by general violence and lawlessness. Armed gangs reportedly stole distributed foodstuffs from peoples' hands and sold them at high price, increasing humanitarian and security concerns.

Political violence increased dramatically in the capital after 30 September when there was a march by Fanmi Lavalas supporters. After that, numerous abuses, including the decapitation of three policemen, were allegedly committed by members of the HNP and armed gangs supposedly linked to the Fanmi Lavalas Party. In October, UN Civilian Police and HNP agents began joint operations in poor neighbourhoods in an attempt to curb endemic violence. No disarmament plan had been implemented by the end of the year and civilians continued to be killed by firearms on a daily basis. Demobilized soldiers and former rebels were acting as de facto authorities in several regions of the country, posing a serious threats to human rights.

Human rights abuses before the change of government

Human rights abuses committed during increasingly frequent street demonstrations continued 2003's political violence well into 2004. Police officers and armed government supporters were reportedly active in repressing anti-government demonstrations.

⬭ On 7 January, Maxime Desulmant, a university student, was reportedly shot dead by government supporters during a demonstration. During his funeral on 16 January, student demonstrators carrying his coffin clashed with HNP agents and pro-government demonstrators in front of the National Palace. Police used tear gas to disperse the students and at least five demonstrators were injured.

Human rights abuses under the transitional government

Human rights abuses committed by the HNP continued to be reported under the transitional government. Demobilized soldiers and former rebels who gained control of most of the country before Jean Bertrand Aristide's departure acted unchallenged as de facto authorities in some areas even under the transitional government. In some communities human rights abuses were also reportedly committed by reinstated rural police, known as "section chiefs". "Section chiefs", officially disbanded since 1994, were formerly recruited from among landed peasant families to carry out police functions and were the local representatives of the government. During 2004 many of them reinstated themselves or were reinstated by demobilized soldiers.

Unlawful killings by police

There were several unlawful killings allegedly by police officers.

⬭ On 26 October, according to witnesses, at least seven people were extrajudicially executed in Fort National, a deprived neighbourhood of Port-au-Prince, by men wearing black uniforms and balaclavas in police-marked vehicles. The police reported that no operation had been carried out in the area, despite strong evidence to the contrary. MINUSTAH's civilian police component established a commission to investigate the incident but no further information was made available.

⬭ In similar circumstances, police agents allegedly extrajudicially executed four adolescents in broad daylight at a road intersection at Carrefour Péan, Port-au-Prince, on 27 October. One of the victims had his hands tied behind his back.

Torture and ill-treatment

There were numerous reported incidents of ill-treatment, sometimes amounting to torture, at the time of the arrest and in police custody. Some of the victims were children.

In October, 13-year-old R.S. (full name withheld) was reportedly kicked in the stomach and chest by police officers while detained at a police station in Martissant, Port-au-Prince. During the assault, he was sitting on the ground handcuffed and blindfolded and repeatedly asked to denounce the whereabouts of *chimères*. R.S. was transferred to Martissant police station where he was detained for a day before being released.

At the end of October there were at least 10 people in police custody in Cap-Haitian, Haiti's second largest city, who had reportedly been ill-treated and beaten by the police.

Unlawful killings by 'section chiefs' and armed rebels

On 30 June, in Ranquitte, Central Department, a man accused of theft was reportedly detained and beaten to death by the "section chief" who had been reinstated by demobilized soldiers.

On 1 April in Savanette, Central Department, Plaisius Joseph was reportedly killed by members of an armed group associated with the demobilized military while they were executing an arrest warrant issued against people involved in a land conflict.

Arbitrary and illegal arrests

There were numerous reports of arbitrary and illegal arrests which violated constitutional provisions. Scores of people were taken into custody without a warrant issued by a judge or without having been caught in the act of committing a crime. Some arrests occurred outside the hours of 6am to 6pm permitted by the Constitution. In November, AI delegates visiting Petite-Goâve found that demobilized soldiers – acting as law enforcement agents with the complicity of the judiciary – were illegally holding four prisoners at the police station, used as their quarters after the police deserted the city.

Former Senators Yvon Feuillé and Gérard Gilles, and former Deputy Rudy Hérivaux were arrested without a warrant on 2 October at *Radio Caraïbes* after they took part in a radio show. Gérard Gilles was released the following week but the other two remained in jail until 23 December.

Prison conditions

Conditions in prisons and other places of detention were harsh and in many cases amounted to inhuman and degrading treatment. Overcrowding was commonplace. Several prisons across the country had not been repaired after they were attacked and partially or totally destroyed during the rebellion earlier in the year.

In Hinche, at the end of October, 19 male detainees were held in a 5m x 4m cell built in a private house used by the police after the police station was burned by rebels in February. All the prisoners escaped on 1 December.

Human rights defenders and journalists under attack

Human rights defenders continued to be harassed and sometimes threatened.

Rénan Hédouville, Secretary General of the Lawyers' Committee for the Respect of Civil Liberties, received several anonymous death threats by phone after the organization denounced human rights violations involving HNP officers and demobilized soldiers.

Mario Joseph, a lawyer working for the International Lawyers' Office, received numerous death threats by phone. He represented several people detained without charge, all supporters of the former President.

Journalists continued to face intimidation and harassment for criticizing the transitional government or demobilized military and for reporting on human rights abuses. A number of journalists had to exercise self-censorship in relation to certain subjects to avoid politically motivated repression. Radio stations vocally denouncing human rights violations were targeted.

Transitional authorities repeatedly changed *Radio Solidarité*'s broadcasting frequency in an attempt to stifle its condemnation of human rights violations and criticism of the government's administration.

Defenders of workers' rights faced intimidation, harassment and death threats from police.

On 24 January, 11 trade unionists were arrested and charged with conspiracy against state security.

On 28 October, Paul-Loulou Chéry, General Coordinator of the Haitian Workers' Confederation, the largest workers' union in Haiti, was visited by six police officers who searched his house without a warrant and reportedly threatened to kill him if he did not present himself at a police station. Police vehicles were posted in front of the Confederation's premises for several days and the premises' security guard was arrested without charge. After the incident Paul-Loulou Chéry changed his address and restricted his movements.

Impunity for past human rights abuses

Impunity for past abuses continued. Before and during the rebellion, numerous detainees convicted of human rights abuses escaped from prisons. The transitional government made no significant effort to recapture them.

Jean-Pierre Baptiste, also known as "Jean Tatoune", a former FRAPH commander, was sentenced to forced labour for life in 1994 for his involvement in a massacre in Raboteau, a poor neighbourhood in Gonaïves. He escaped from prison in August 2002 and was reportedly living in Raboteau itself.

In September, Louis-Jodel Chamblain and Jackson Joanis, both convicted in absentia for participation in the 1994 Raboteau massacre and for the murder in 1993 of Antoine Izméry, a human rights defender and businessman, were hastily brought to court for a retrial of the latter case. The prosecutor reportedly failed to present the evidence or summon key witnesses from the first trial in 1995. The two men were acquitted of the murder but at the end of the year remained imprisoned awaiting retrial on the Raboteau massacre charges.

Violence against women

Many women were raped or gang-raped by members of armed gangs, demobilized soldiers and police officers. Several women told AI that they were too afraid of the police to report the crimes. Some women who had been raped during the military rule in 1991-1994 were in hiding after the perpetrators of such abuses were back in public life and freely circulating in the streets.

On 13 September, D.P. (full name withheld), aged 19, was raped in her house in the presence of her two brothers by five men wearing black clothes and hoods. After the attack she did not receive any medical attention. In fear for her life or of being raped again, she left her home and lived on the streets.

MINUSTAH

MINUSTAH's deployment was slow. The military and civilian police contingents had not been fully deployed by the end of the first term of its mandate in November, thereby hindering the implementation of the mandate, particularly with regard to the protection of civilians and the monitoring of human rights. By the end of 2004, none of the human rights observers had been appointed. Little progress was made in setting up a comprehensive disarmament, demobilization and reintegration programme for armed groups.

AI country reports/ visits
Reports
- Haiti: Breaking the cycle of violence – a last chance for Haiti? (AI Index: AMR 36/038/2004)
- Haiti: Perpetrators of past abuses threaten human rights and the reestablishment of the rule of law (AI Index: AMR 36/013/2004)
Visits
AI delegates visited Haiti in March and April and in October and November.

HONDURAS

REPUBLIC OF HONDURAS
Head of state and government: Ricardo Maduro
Death penalty: abolitionist for all crimes
International Criminal Court: ratified
UN Women's Convention: ratified
Optional Protocol to UN Women's Convention: not signed

Violent deaths of children and young people continued at alarmingly high levels. Members of human rights groups, indigenous groups and the lesbian, gay men, bisexual and transgender people (LGBT) community suffered intimidation, harassment and death threats. Two indigenous activists were political prisoners.

Background
There were public protests against state corruption, illegal logging and other socio-economic issues.

In November the Public Ministry announced that corruption charges against former President Rafael Callejas were to be dropped. This generated a crisis in the Ministry as the prosecutors involved were dismissed or suspended and demanded in turn the removal of the Attorney General.

Children and young people
The authorities again failed to take effective measures to prevent or investigate killings of children and young people. More than 350 violent deaths of children and young people were reported during the year. Although progress was made in investigating a small number of cases, only three convictions resulted.

The anti-gang law introduced in 2003 to deal with crimes committed by youth gangs, which was criticized by human rights groups for severely restricting the right to freedom of association, reportedly led to the arrest of some 1,500 alleged gang members, often simply for having tattoos. The majority of those arrested had not been charged or tried by the end of the year.

In an incident in San Pedro Sula Prison in May, 104 young people were killed after a fire broke out in a cell. All the dead and injured were members of the Salvatrucha gang who remained locked in their cells during the fire. A formal complaint for negligent homicide was presented against the then director of the prison, but the charges were later dropped due to lack of evidence.

Fifty-one people, including police officers, soldiers and prisoners, were indicted for their involvement in the deaths of 68 people, including 61 imprisoned members of the M-18 gang, at El Porvenir prison in April 2003. According to the prosecution, the killings were planned by the authorities in the context of a dispute over the supply of drugs within the prison. In December the man who was Prison Director at the time of the incident was found guilty of the deaths; he was to be sentenced in February 2005. Trials were pending for the other accused.

Human rights defenders

Members of human rights organizations faced harassment and intimidation. Andrés Pavón Murillo, President of the Committee for the Defence of Human Rights in Honduras (known by its Spanish acronym CODEH), received threatening phone calls and was verbally attacked on television and radio after alleging that members of the government were implicated in human rights violations, negligence and denial of justice following the fire at San Pedro Sula prison in May. Staff at the non-governmental Centre for the Prevention, Rehabilitation and Treatment of Victims of Torture (CPTRT) received death threats in the context of a break-in at their offices.

Despite reports that two of those responsible for the murder of journalist Germán Antonio Rivas in November 2003 had been identified, the authorities failed to apprehend them.

Indigenous people

Indigenous activists were subjected to threats and harassment and two were held as political prisoners.
◻ In May, leaders of the Regional Coordination of Popular Resistance (CRRP) and the Civic Council of Indigenous and Popular Organizations (COPINH) in the department of Intibucá were harassed and received death threats. CRRP leader José Idalecio Murillo and seven members of his family escaped unhurt when four men fired shots at their home.
◻ Despite evidence of serious procedural irregularities, an appeal court confirmed the 25-year prison sentence imposed on brothers and COPINH leaders Marcelino and Leonardo Miranda, both of whom were repeatedly tortured in pre-trial detention in 2003. However, in November an appeal to the Supreme Court was upheld and the case was referred back to the Santa Rosa de Copán appeal court. AI was concerned that the two did not receive a fair trial and that the charges against them had been filed in order to punish them for their human rights work.

Lesbians, gay men, bisexual and transgender people

There was continuing concern about the climate of intimidation facing the LGBT community in Honduras. In September, at the instigation of the Evangelical Church, the National Congress recommended that the legal status granted in August to three LGBT organizations be revoked on the grounds that it constituted an attack on "the family, public order and decency". However, government officials defended their decision to grant the organizations legal status, stating that it did not violate domestic legislation and was in line with international treaties signed by Honduras.

No progress was made in the police investigation into the killing of Erick David Yáñez (Ericka) in 2003. Members of the Comunidad Gay Sampedrana, a non-governmental LGBT group based in San Pedro Sula where the killing took place, were harassed and intimidated even though the Inter-American Commission on Human Rights had in 2003 ordered the authorities to adopt precautionary measures to protect four members of the group.

HUNGARY

REPUBLIC OF HUNGARY
Head of state: Ferenc Mádl
Head of government: Ferenc Gyurcsány (replaced Peter Medgyessy in October)
Death penalty: abolitionist for all crimes
International Criminal Court: ratified
UN Women's Convention and its Optional Protocol: ratified

There was continued concern about police ill-treatment, including of Roma, and conditions in detention. Protection for women in violent relationships remained inadequate. The use of cage beds to restrain people with mental disabilities was banned.

Police ill-treatment

On at least one occasion excessive use of force by police officers appeared to contribute to the death of a suspect who was reportedly resisting arrest.
◻ In June, Svetoslav Martov, a 27-year-old Bulgarian national, was arrested for rowdy behaviour on a flight from Amsterdam to Budapest. Allegedly experiencing drug withdrawal symptoms, he was later being transported from a Budapest court to a detention centre when he reportedly assaulted the officers. The officers stopped the car and used a routinely practiced method of restraint: pushing the detainee to the ground, kneeling on the lower back, holding the neck and twisting an arm behind the back. Svetoslav Martov lost consciousness and died on the way to the hospital. An autopsy apparently established that his death had been caused by suffocation as a result of being held by the neck. The two officers involved in the incident were reported to have been suspended from duty. No independent inquiry was initiated into the safety of the method of restraint.

Violence against women

Data collected by the local non-governmental organization Women Together Against Violence Against Women showed that on average at least one woman per week was killed by her partner.

A parliamentary resolution in April 2003 required the government to draft a law on restraining orders for abusive partners by the end of March 2004 and to establish a network of shelters for battered women. However, the government failed to implement these and nine other requirements contained in the resolution.

Protection for women in violent relationships remained inadequate. The government failed to introduce legislation which would provide for restraining orders in line with best international practice.

There were no government-run shelters for women fleeing violence. Women with children requiring shelter had to go to "mother homes" – centres designed for poor mothers. Apart from only providing shelter to women with children, these centres had long waiting lists and were publicly listed, making them easy for the abuser to find. In October the minister responsible announced that rather than building a network of new shelters the ministry would be looking to extend the function of existing "mother homes".

Discrimination against Roma

In June the European Commission against Racism and Intolerance (ECRI) published its third report on Hungary, welcoming some legislative and policy measures aimed at reducing racism, intolerance and discrimination. However, it remained concerned about continuing reports of racially motivated violence, including police ill-treatment. ECRI assessed that the Roma minority continued to be "severely disadvantaged in most areas of life". ECRI was also concerned about racist feelings expressed in the media and by some politicians and about negative attitudes towards migrants and asylum-seekers. It appealed for better implementation and extension of anti-racism laws and for a stronger response to incidents of police ill-treatment of minorities.

Conditions in detention

In June the government published the report of the Council of Europe's Committee for the Prevention of Torture and Inhuman or Degrading Treatment or Punishment (CPT), following the CPT's visit in May and June 2003. The CPT found that people held in detention pending trial were frequently remanded in police establishments, often for several months, rather than in remand prisons where conditions were better. Some detainees stated that they had been offered a transfer to a remand prison as an inducement to provide information. The CPT was also concerned that staff in the fourth District Police Station in Budapest openly carried truncheons and tear gas canisters in detention areas.

A study of pre-trial detention published by the Hungarian Helsinki Committee in November echoed the CPT's findings. The entry into force of a provision of the Penal Procedure Code mandating pre-trial detention in remand prisons was delayed.

In the prison system the CPT found serious overcrowding. Allegations of ill-treatment by staff were received from detainees at Unit III of the Budapest Remand Prison.

Rights of people with mental disabilities

In March the Mental Disability Advocacy Center, a regional non-governmental organization, published a report on the trial rights of people with mental disabilities sentenced to psychiatric detention by criminal courts. Annual court reviews determining the need for continued detention did not meet national and international standards. Court-appointed lawyers apparently failed to probe evidence presented to the court. They rarely met their clients before the reviews or explained to them the contents of psychiatric reports. In some cases they recommended that their client be further detained, contrary to the client's stated wishes. The court decision to continue detention appeared to rest solely on the opinion of the treating psychiatrist whose findings were not challenged. The average review lasted less than eight minutes.

In July the Minister for Health, Social and Family Affairs issued a decree banning the use of cage beds. However the decree fell short of international standards regarding the use of restraint. Individual hospitals were left to determine for how long restraints could be used. The decree included no provision for monitoring its implementation.

AI country reports/ visits
Report
- Europe and Central Asia: Summary of Amnesty International's concerns in the region, January-June 2004: Hungary (AI Index: EUR 01/005/2004)

INDIA

REPUBLIC OF INDIA
Head of state: A.P.J. Abdul Kalam
Head of government: Manmohan Singh (replaced Atal Bihari Vajpayee in May)
Death penalty: retentionist
International Criminal Court: not signed
UN Women's Convention: ratified with reservations
Optional Protocol to UN Women's Convention: not signed

Perpetrators of human rights violations continued to enjoy impunity in many cases. Gujarat state authorities failed to bring to justice those responsible for widespread violence in 2002. Security legislation was used to facilitate arbitrary arrests, torture and other grave human rights violations, often against political opponents and marginalized groups. In the north-eastern state of Manipur, local groups opposed human rights violations under the Armed Forces Special Powers Act and called for its repeal. In numerous states, human rights defenders were harassed. The new United Progressive Alliance (UPA) government made a number of promises that, if implemented, could improve human rights. Socially and economically marginalized groups, such as *dalits*, *adivasis*, women and religious minorities, continued to face discrimination at the hands of the police and the criminal justice system.

Background

Relations between India and Pakistan improved during the year with talks and a series of confidence-building steps taking place. In July the government of Andhra Pradesh revoked an eight-year ban on the Maoist (naxalite) People's War Group (PWG) and six associated organizations. In October the first ever peace talks were held between state officials and PWG representatives. In other areas of low intensity conflict, including in Assam and Manipur, tensions intensified.

In May the ruling National Democratic Alliance, led by the Bharatiya Janata Party (BJP), suffered a surprise defeat in national elections which brought the UPA coalition government, led by the Congress Party, to office. Manmohan Singh was appointed Prime Minister after party leader Sonia Gandhi declined the post.

The BJP retained power in several states and the party returned to a more overtly Hindu nationalist agenda.

More than 15,000 people were killed or remained missing, and over 112,000 were displaced by the 26 December tsunami that caused extensive damage to coastal districts of Andhra Pradesh, Kerala and Tamil Nadu states and two Union Territories – the Andaman and Nicobar Islands, and Pondicherry. National and local relief efforts began immediately.

Violence against women

Despite the efforts of women's rights advocates to address the widespread problem of violence in the home, India still lacked comprehensive legislation addressing domestic violence.

The government failed to submit overdue periodic reports to the UN Committee on the Elimination of Discrimination against Women.

Impunity continued for most perpetrators of widespread rape and killing in Gujarat in 2002. During the communal violence Muslim women were specifically targeted and several hundred women and girls were threatened, raped and killed; some were burned alive (see Gujarat below).

Impunity

Members of the security forces continued to enjoy virtual impunity for human rights violations.

In April women members of the Association of the Parents of Disappeared Persons were beaten by police when they demonstrated in Srinagar against continuing impunity for those responsible for "disappearances" in the state of Jammu and Kashmir. While the state admitted in 2003 that 3,744 persons had "disappeared" since insurgency began in 1989, human rights activists believed the true figure to be over 8,000. No one had been convicted by the end of 2004.

In Punjab the vast majority of police officers responsible for serious human rights violations during the period of militancy in the mid-1990s continued to evade justice, despite the recommendations of several judicial inquiries and commissions. In response to 2,097 reported cases of human rights violations, the National Human Rights Commission had ordered the state of Punjab to provide compensation in 109 cases concerning people who were in police custody prior to their death. The culture of impunity developed during that period continued to prevail and reports of abuses including torture and ill-treatment persisted.

Gujarat

In August the Supreme Court issued a key decision in connection with communal violence in Gujarat state in 2002. The violence followed a fire on a train in which 59 Hindus died in February 2002; right-wing Hindu groups blamed the fire on local Muslims. In the ensuing violence more than 2,000 people, mostly Muslims, were killed. The Court directed that more than 2,000 complaints closed by the police and some 200 cases which had ended in acquittals be reviewed.

Bilqis Yakoob Rasool was five months pregnant when she was gang-raped and saw her three-year-old daughter killed by a mob in March 2002. She reported the rape and the killing of 14 relatives to the police. In January 2003 the police closed the case on the grounds that those responsible could not be found. A subsequent investigation by the Central Bureau of Investigation (CBI) found evidence of a police cover-up. In April, 12 people were arrested for rape and murder. In addition, six police officers were charged with involvement in the cover-up and two doctors were accused of distorting post-mortem investigations.

In August the Supreme Court directed that the case be tried outside Gujarat. The trial was ongoing at the end of 2004.

⊟ Several relatives of Zahira Sheikh died when the Best Bakery in Vadodara was burned down in March 2002. The case against 21 people accused of starting the fire collapsed in June 2003 when Zahira Sheikh and several witnesses withdrew their statements after receiving death threats. In April 2004 the Supreme Court ordered that the case be retried in Maharashtra state. The Court identified serious failings in the criminal justice system, but also accused the Gujarat government of ignoring the violence and protecting the perpetrators. The ruling was welcomed by the human rights community as a landmark judgment. In November, Zahira Sheikh again withdrew her statement. A petition was filed requesting a CBI investigation into this development.

Applications to transfer several other cases to courts outside Gujarat were pending at the end of 2004.

The new government made a commitment to enact a model comprehensive law to deal with communal violence.

Abuses by opposition groups

There were reports of abuses – including torture, attacks and killings of civilians – by armed groups in a number of states in the north-east as well as Andhra Pradesh, Bihar, Jharkhand, and West Bengal.

In Jammu and Kashmir, members of opposition groups were responsible for targeted killings of civilians. Victims included relatives of state officials and people suspected of working for the government. The use of explosives led to indiscriminate killings of civilians.

⊟ In April, Asiya Jeelani, a human rights activist, and her driver were killed when her car carrying a team of election monitors hit an explosive device apparently laid by opposition groups opposed to the elections. Another team member, Khurram Parvez, lost his leg in the incident.

Security legislation

In September the government fulfilled its election pledge to repeal the Prevention of Terrorism Act (POTA) which it said had been "grossly misused" and which had led to widespread human rights violations. The cases of all those held under the act were to be reviewed within a year.

However, there were concerns over amendments to the Unlawful Activities (Prevention) Act, which included provisions similar to those in the POTA. There were also concerns that the definition of "terrorist acts" in the bill remained vague and open to broad interpretation. Several states indicated that they would introduce legislation containing provisions similar to those in the POTA.

The 1958 Armed Forces Special Powers Act (AFSPA) remained in force in "disturbed areas" including large parts of the north-east. A number of provisions of the AFSPA breached international standards. For example, the Act empowered the security forces to arrest people without a warrant and to shoot to kill in circumstances where their lives were not in danger. It also granted members of the armed forces immunity from prosecution for acts carried out under its jurisdiction.

⊟ On 11 July, Thangjam Manorama (also known as Henthoi) died after being arrested under the AFSPA by members of the Assam Rifles in Greater Imphal, Manipur. Her body was found later the same day a few kilometres from her home; it reportedly showed signs of torture and multiple gunshot wounds. There were reports that she had been raped. Her death was followed by protests by community and women's groups which the security forces tried to suppress by detaining participants and firing on demonstrators, injuring scores of people. A judicial inquiry was ongoing at the end of the year.

The lapsed Terrorist and Disruptive Activities Act continued to be used by some state authorities to detain and harass human rights defenders and political opponents.

Death penalty

At least 23 people were sentenced to death and one person was executed. No comprehensive information on the number of people under sentence of death was available, but there was continuing concern that some prisoners had spent prolonged periods on death row, which could amount to cruel, inhuman or degrading punishment.

⊟ Dhananjoy Chatterjee was executed by hanging in August after spending 13 years in prison. He had been convicted of rape and murder in 1990. His was the first known execution in India since 1997.

Human rights defenders

Human rights defenders in many parts of the country were harassed and attacked.

⊟ On 21 August at least 13 members of the Association for Protection of Democratic Rights (APDR) were attacked in Greater Kolkata, West Bengal, allegedly by supporters of the ruling political party. A group of up to 60 people attacked a peaceful meeting, kicking and beating the participants. Although the police station was less than 50m away, the police reportedly failed to assist or protect the APDR members until the attackers dispersed several hours later. Several of the victims required hospital treatment for serious injuries.

Economic, social and cultural rights

Despite positive economic gains in recent years, approximately 300 million people remained in poverty.

In October a spokesperson from the Global Fund to Fight AIDS, TB and Malaria stated that AIDS/HIV infection rates were rising and that India possibly had the world's largest number of people living with HIV.

Bhopal 20 years on

Twenty years after the Union Carbide Corporation's (UCC) pesticide plant in Bhopal leaked toxic gases, the plant site had still not been cleared up and toxic wastes continued to pollute the environment and groundwater. More than 7,000 people died within days of the 1984 leak and 15,000 more died in the following years as a result of the toxins, while tens of thousands more were living with chronic and debilitating illnesses. Survivors continued to be denied adequate compensation, medical help and rehabilitation. No one had been held responsible for the leak. UCC and Dow Chemicals (which took over UCC in 2001) had publicly stated that they had no responsibility for the leak or its consequences. UCC refused to appear before a court in Bhopal and the Indian government agreed to a final settlement in 1989 which was inadequate and was not paid out entirely. In mid-2004 the Supreme Court ordered that the remaining compensation money for victims of the gas leak be paid out. AI joined with other campaigners and survivors to call for an immediate clean-up of the pollutants, site and the affected surroundings, a full remedy for the victims, and to demand that those responsible be brought to justice.

AI country reports/ visits
Reports
- Clouds of injustice: Bhopal disaster 20 years on (AI Index: ASA 20/015/2004)
- Open letter on human rights defenders attacked in West Bengal (AI Index: ASA 20/095/2004)
- India: Punjab — Twenty years on impunity continues (AI Index: ASA 20/099/2004)
Visit
AI delegates attended the World Social Forum in Mumbai in January to discuss issues including arms control, corporate accountability and violence against women.

INDONESIA

REPUBLIC OF INDONESIA
Head of state and government: Susilo Bambang Yudhoyono (replaced Megawati Sukarnoputri in October)
Death penalty: retentionist
International Criminal Court: not signed
UN Women's Convention: ratified with reservations
Optional Protocol to UN Women's Convention: signed

On 26 December an earthquake and tsunami devastated large parts of Nanggroe Aceh Darussalam (NAD) and surrounding areas, leaving more than 200,000 people dead or missing and displacing approximately half a million others. Even before the disaster, the human rights situation in the province had been grave. Prior to the massive international relief effort mounted in response to the tsunami, access to the province had been restricted. The downgrading in May of the military emergency to a civil emergency had little impact on the human rights situation. Cases of extrajudicial executions, arbitrary detention, torture, sexual violence and destruction of property continued to be reported. Hundreds of suspected members or supporters of the armed pro-independence group, the Free Aceh Movement (GAM), were imprisoned following trials which contravened international standards. Repression of pro-independence activists in other regions also resulted in human rights violations. Elsewhere, police resorted to excessive force in responding to protests and when carrying out arrests. Dozens of people were arrested, detained and tried under "anti-terrorism" legislation. Justice for past human rights violations remained elusive although a number of members of the security forces faced trial. At least one person was sentenced to a term of imprisonment and at least four others were facing trial for the peaceful exercise of their right to freedom of expression. After a three-year de facto moratorium on executions, three people were executed.

Background
Megawati Sukarnoputri was replaced in October by former army general Bambang Susilo Yudhoyono after Indonesia's first direct presidential election. Regional and national parliamentary elections were also conducted. For the first time no parliamentary seats were reserved for the security forces. The reform process moved incrementally forward with several important legislative initiatives. However, corruption remained endemic. Forced evictions and disputes over land and resources led to conflict. Ethnic and religious tensions also resulted in violence, including in Maluku and Central Sulawesi. In September, Munir, a prominent human rights defender, died of arsenic poisoning on a flight to the Netherlands. A police investigation into his death was continuing at the end of the year.

Repression of pro-independence movements
In NAD, the gravity and pervasiveness of human rights abuses committed by the security forces and GAM meant that virtually all aspects of life in the province were affected, even before the devastation caused by the earthquake and tsunami.

Reliable figures relating to the conflict remained difficult to obtain. By September, according to official sources, 2,879 members of GAM and 662 civilians had been killed since May 2003. More than 2,000 suspected members of GAM had been arrested. The security forces conceded the difficulty in distinguishing between GAM members and the civilian population.

Trials of hundreds of suspected GAM members or supporters contravened international standards for fair trial, with many suspects denied full access to lawyers and convicted on the basis of confessions reportedly extracted under torture. There were concerns that some may have been imprisoned solely on the basis of the peaceful expression of their political beliefs.

Disproportionate restrictions were placed on the freedom of expression and movement. Tight restrictions on access to NAD by international human rights monitors, humanitarian workers and journalists, combined with intimidation and harassment of local activists, effectively prevented independent human rights monitoring. In March, the National Human Rights Commission (Komnas HAM) reported that it had found indications that gross human rights abuses had been committed in NAD by both the security forces and GAM between March and November 2003.

GAM was responsible for human rights abuses including taking hostages and using child soldiers. The authorities also accused GAM of unlawful killings.

Hundreds of Acehnese fled to Malaysia and other countries (see Malaysia entry).

In Papua, operations by the security forces against the armed opposition group, the Free Papua Organization, reportedly resulted in extrajudicial executions. At least three men and two women were reportedly shot dead by police in Teluk Bintuni in April. Local human rights organizations said that those killed were civilians. Police stated that they fired after being attacked. Eleven police officers were disciplined as a result of the incident, but no criminal investigation or charges were known to have followed.

At least six civilians were reportedly killed and thousands displaced in Puncak Jaya during violence which started when the security forces began operations against the Free Papua Organization in August.

Excessive use of force by police
Police demonstrated a lack of restraint and continued to employ excessive force when responding to protests and during arrests. On several occasions police opened fire on demonstrators.

In March, six people were killed and 19 injured when police opened fire on protesters outside the police station in Ruteng, Flores. The protesters, whom police said attacked the station, were demanding the release of seven people arrested in the context of a dispute over the rights of indigenous people to grow coffee in protected forests. Twenty-one officers were disciplined and one officer was dismissed from his post. None faced criminal charges. An investigation by Komnas HAM was ongoing at the end of the year.

Prisoners of conscience and political prisoners
At least one prisoner of conscience was sentenced to a prison term during the year, at least 10 others were facing trial, and eight others sentenced in previous years remained in prison. They included peaceful political and independence activists in NAD, Papua and Maluku. In addition to known prisoners of conscience, hundreds of alleged pro-independence activists, the majority of them from NAD, were sentenced to imprisonment after trials reported to have fallen short of international standards. Among them were believed to be individuals sentenced for their peaceful activities. Charges against journalists and human rights organizations threatened to undermine freedom of expression.

Bambang Harymurti, editor of *Tempo* magazine, was sentenced to one year's imprisonment for libel after publishing an article citing allegations that a businessman stood to profit from a fire that had destroyed part of a textile market. The article included a statement from the businessman denying the allegation. Bambang Harymurti remained free pending appeal at the end of the year.

Holly Manuputty and Christine Kakisima, the wife and daughter of an independence activist in Maluku, were detained on charges of "rebellion". The charges against Holly Manuputty and Christine Kakisima focused on their presence at peaceful pro-independence meetings held at their house. Their trials were ongoing at the end of the year. They were among at least 66 people detained before and after a peaceful rally supporting independence in Ambon, Maluku. Many of those detained were reportedly sentenced to terms of imprisonment of up to nine years; trials involving the remainder were continuing at the end of the year. Although the rally itself was peaceful, it triggered communal violence in which at least 38 people were reportedly killed.

Impunity
The majority of human rights violations were not investigated and only a few investigations led to prosecutions.

By the end of the year only one person remained convicted for crimes against humanity committed in Timor-Leste in 1999. An appeals court upheld the conviction of Eurico Guterres, former militia leader, but halved his sentence to five years' imprisonment. He remained free pending final appeal to the Supreme Court. Four senior members of the security forces and the former provincial governor, Abilio Soares, had their convictions overturned on appeal. The Supreme Court confirmed the earlier acquittals of 12 others who had been indicted in relation to the 1999 violence.

Indonesia continued to refuse to transfer to Timor-Leste 304 people indicted by the Timor-Leste Prosecutor General. They included former general Wiranto who was head of the Indonesian armed forces in 1999. Wiranto had also not faced trial in Indonesia for his role in the violence of 1999. Although named as a suspect by Komnas HAM, he was never indicted by the Attorney General's Office and ran as a candidate in May's presidential elections, finishing third.

An ad hoc Human Rights Court in Jakarta convicted 12 military officials of charges arising from the killing, detention and torture of Muslim protesters in Tanjung Priok, Jakarta, in 1984. Major-General (retired) Rudolf Adolf Butar-Butar was sentenced to 10 years' imprisonment; the 11 other officers received sentences well below the statutory minimum of 10 years. They all remained free pending appeal. Two high-ranking officers, including the serving Commander of the Special Forces Command (Kopassus), Major-General Sriyanto, were acquitted. Other senior officials who were named as possible suspects by an initial investigation were not indicted.

After considerable delay, the trials of two senior police officers began in the Human Rights Court in Makassar in May. They were charged with command responsibility for the shooting of one person and torture of dozens of others in Abepura, Papua, in 2000. The trial was ongoing at the end of the year. The initial investigation, conducted in 2001, was marred by allegations of witness intimidation.

Investigations into other human rights violations progressed slowly. In September Komnas HAM reported that it had found initial evidence suggesting that security forces had committed crimes against humanity in two separate incidents in Papua: in Wasior in June 2001 and Wamena in April 2003. The report was submitted to the Attorney General's Office.

Other cases of human rights violations involving members of the security forces came before district and military courts. In many cases, police and military officers remained on duty during the investigation and trial and, when convicted, received sentences that did not reflect the gravity of the offence.

A law passed in September provided for the establishment of a Truth and Reconciliation Commission to resolve, outside the court system, cases involving grave human rights violations committed prior to the enactment of the Law on Human Rights Courts (Law 26/2000). The Commission can conduct investigations, grant reparations to victims and recommend presidential amnesties.

Security legislation
In the wake of further bomb attacks, including two in Sulawesi and one outside the Australian embassy in Jakarta, dozens of people were arrested, interrogated and detained under the Law on Combating Criminal Acts of Terrorism. At least 28 people were tried and convicted, many under the same legislation, for their involvement in bomb attacks in previous years. Most of those arrested and tried were suspected members of Islamist groups.

Concerns about the Law remained, including the inadequate definition of acts of "terrorism" and provision for up to six months' detention without access to judicial review.

The newly established Constitutional Court ruled that the retroactive application of the 2003 security legislation was unconstitutional. This placed in doubt the convictions of several people charged and tried under the legislation in relation to bombings in Bali in 2002.

Death penalty
Ayodhya Prasad Chaubey, Namsong Sirilak and Saelow Prasert were executed by firing squad, the first executions since 2001. The three had been convicted of drug trafficking in 1994. There were concerns that their trials may not have met international fair trial standards.

At least eight people were sentenced to death during the year, bringing to 54 the total number of people known to be under sentence of death. Thirty of those facing execution had been convicted of drug-related offences.

Violence against women
According to data collected by the National Commission on Violence Against Women (Komnas

Perempuan), the number of cases of violence against women was on the rise. In September, the Law on the Elimination of Domestic Violence (Law 23/2004) was passed, which provides a framework for government, police and community responses to domestic violence. The Law defines domestic violence to include physical, sexual and psychological violence and neglect, and, for the first time in Indonesian legislation, criminalizes marital rape. The family is defined to include residential domestic staff.

AI country reports/visits
Reports
- Indonesia: New military operations, old patterns of human rights abuses in Aceh (Nanggroe Aceh Darussalam, NAD) (AI Index: ASA 21/033/2004)
- Indonesia: A briefing on the death penalty (AI Index: ASA 21/040/2004)
- Indonesia and Timor-Leste: Justice for Timor-Leste — the way forward (AI Index: ASA 21/006/2004)

IRAN

ISLAMIC REPUBLIC OF IRAN
Head of state: Leader of the Islamic Republic of Iran: Ayatollah Sayed 'Ali Khamenei
Head of government: President: Hojjatoleslam val Moslemin Sayed Mohammad Khatami
Death penalty: retentionist
International Criminal Court: signed
UN Women's Convention and its Optional Protocol: not signed

Scores of political prisoners, including prisoners of conscience, continued to serve prison sentences imposed following unfair trials in previous years. Scores more were arrested in 2004, many in connection with press articles or publications both in print and on the Internet which were alleged to "endanger national security" or defame senior officials or religious precepts. Many of the families of those arrested also faced intimidation. Independent human rights defenders were harassed. At least two individuals died in custody and 159 people were executed, including one minor. At least two of the 36 people who were flogged reportedly died following the implementation of the punishment; no investigations were carried out into these deaths. The true number of those executed or subjected to corporal punishment was believed to be considerably higher.

Background

A new parliamentary session started in May, following controversial and flawed parliamentary elections in February which were marked by mass disqualification of sitting deputies. The elections resulted in a comprehensive victory for groups opposed to social and political reform. Some of the statements from the new parliamentarians included attacks on women said to be "improperly attired". Incoming women parliamentarians rejected previous policies aimed at gender equality.

The emerging political trend in parliament gave impetus to members of the semi-official Hezbollah, which occasionally attacked gatherings of people they believed supported opposition political movements. It also encouraged the judiciary and its security force to limit public dissent, resulting in arbitrary arrests and the detention of prisoners in secret centres. In the latter half of the year in particular, practices employed by the judiciary – including arbitrary arrest, denial of legal representation and detention in solitary confinement – were responsible for most of the human rights violations reported in the country.

International concern over Iran's obligations to the International Atomic Energy Agency (IAEA) dominated the year. IAEA reports throughout the year suggested that Iranian officials were not always presenting the entire scope of the country's nuclear programmes. In November, following an agreement with the European Union (EU), Iran committed itself to suspending uranium enrichment.

The ongoing Human Rights Dialogue process between the EU and Iran led to few lasting benefits. In March, the EU stated that it had seen little improvement in human rights and that violations remained widespread. Several Iranian human rights defenders criticized the process for its lack of transparency and effectiveness. In a concluding statement, the EU reiterated long-standing human rights concerns including the use of torture, unequal rights for women, the use of the death penalty, religious discrimination and the lack of an independent judiciary. Iran's judiciary rejected these comments, while newspaper interviews given by the deputy head of the judiciary, Mohammad Javad Larijani, expressed contempt for the process and human rights.

In November, the UN General Assembly passed a resolution condemning the human rights situation in Iran. It drew attention to Iran's "failure to comply with international standards in the administration of justice, the absence of due process of law, the refusal to provide fair and public hearings and right to counsel..." and forms of systematic discrimination. It urged the authorities to appoint an independent and impartial prosecutor in Tehran and to fulfil Iran's international commitments. A proposed visit by the UN Working Group on Enforced or Involuntary Disappearances was postponed at the government's request.

Discriminatory law and practices

Discriminatory laws and practices continued to be the source of social and political unrest and of human rights violations. People continued to be denied state employment because of their religious affiliation and political opinions under *gozinesh*, or "selection" provisions which serve to prohibit individuals from working for state bodies. Analogous laws applied to professional bodies such as the Bar Association or trades unions.

In January, *gozinesh* criteria were deployed by the Guardians' Council, which reviews laws and policies to ensure that they uphold Islamic tenets and the Constitution, in order to disqualify around 3,500 prospective candidates from standing in the February parliamentary elections. The exclusion of around 80 incumbent parliamentarians attracted domestic and international condemnation.

The *gozinesh* provided the legal basis for discriminatory laws and practice. Religious and ethnic groups which were not officially recognized – such as the Bahai's, Ahl-e Haq, Mandaeans (Sabaeans) and Evangelical Christians – were automatically subject to *gozinesh* provisions and faced discrimination in a range of areas, including access to education.

Freedom of expression and association

Freedoms of expression and association came under attack throughout the year as a result of flagrant flaws in the administration of justice, coupled with a deeply politicized judiciary. Journalists faced politically motivated and arbitrary arrest, prolonged detention, unfair trials and imprisonment. The laws used to arrest and imprison journalists, relating to defamation, national security and disturbing public opinion, were vaguely worded and at variance with international standards. 2004 saw an increase in the harassment or intimidation of the relatives of detainees or people under investigation.

A report published in January by the UN Special Rapporteur on the promotion and protection of the right to freedom of opinion and expression concluded that there was a "climate of fear induced by the systematic repression of people expressing critical views against the authorized political and religious doctrine..."

⬚ In October and November, scores of journalists, particularly Internet journalists, were arbitrarily detained in connection with their work and especially following publication of an appeal by around 350 signatories, calling for political reform. Those detained were expected to face trial in the following months. They included Javad Gholam Tamayomi, Shahram Rafihzadeh Rouzbeh and Mir Ebrahimi. In December many of those arrested reportedly confessed while in detention, but later told a government body that these confessions were extracted under duress.

⬚ Taqi Rahmani, Alireza Alijani and Hoda Saber, intellectuals and writers associated with the National Religious Alliance (Melli Mazhabi), remained arbitrarily detained without any prospect of release. For over a year, the court where they had lodged their appeal had refused to issue a verdict. This effectively prevented the families from taking any form of follow-up action. Despite an announcement in November that they would be released and the payment of substantial bail, the prison authorities prevented them from being released and they remained in detention at the end of the year.

📁 The death sentence passed in 2002 on Professor Hashem Aghajari for statements he made that were construed to be blasphemous was overturned by the Supreme Court in June. However, new charges were brought against him of insulting religious precepts, and "spreading false information". In July, Professor Hashem Aghajari was sentenced to five years' imprisonment, with two years suspended, and barred from practising his profession for five years. His appeal was still pending before a Tehran court at the end of the year.

Impunity

Impunity for human rights violations resulted in political instability and mistrust of the judiciary, which was perceived by many human rights activists as unwilling to uphold the law in an impartial manner.

📁 In July, Mohammad Reza Aqdam Ahmadi, a Ministry of Intelligence official, went on trial for participating in the "quasi-intentional murder" of Zahra Kazemi, a photojournalist who died in custody in 2003. He was acquitted following a two-day trial. Following his acquittal, a spokesperson for the judiciary stated that Zahra Kazemi's death must have been an accident, despite forensic reports prepared following her death which indicated that she was murdered. International observers – including UN Special Rapporteurs on freedom of opinion and expression; on the independence of judges and lawyers; and on torture – condemned the flagrantly flawed proceedings. The court ordered the state to pay the family of the deceased the legally required monetary compensation as no culprit had been found. The family lodged an appeal which was pending at the end of the year.

📁 Brothers Manuchehr and Akbar Mohammadi, and Ahmadi Batebi, who were among the students detained, tortured and sentenced after unfair trials following student demonstrations in 1999, continued to face violence while in custody. The brothers required medical treatment in the course of the year for their injuries. No investigations were carried out into their allegations of ill-treatment in custody.

📁 Six years after the murders of two political activists and three writers – a case known in Iran as the "Serial Murders" – no steps had been taken to bring those who ordered the killings to justice. In 1999 it had been acknowledged that the killings had been committed by state officials. During the year, former Intelligence Minister Qorbanali Dorri Nafafabadi, who had been "excused" from taking part in earlier hearings in the case, was reportedly appointed state prosecutor. Nasser Zarafshan, a human rights defender and the lawyer for the families of the two political activists, remained incarcerated following an unfair trial in 2002.

Human rights defenders

The award of the Nobel Peace Prize to human rights defender Shirin Ebadi in 2003 contributed to the growth and increasing self-confidence of civil society. Nevertheless, independent non-governmental organizations were hampered by a registration process that was open to undue influence. Human rights defenders also faced limitations on their movements.

Defenders of women's rights protested against discrimination against women in the justice system and in some criminal cases secured last-minute suspensions of executions or pardons.

📁 In July, the Society for Defence of the Rights of Prisoners was granted permission to operate. The organization aimed to inform prisoners and their families of their rights and to provide material support to detainees, through training and education. However, members of the Society's Board faced politically motivated criminal charges. For example, Emaddedin Baqi was sentenced to one year's imprisonment by an appeals court in October on charges of spreading anti-state propaganda. Earlier in the month his passport had been confiscated as he prepared to leave the country to address a number of human rights conferences in North America.

📁 Journalists and human rights defenders Mahboubeh Abbasgholizadeh and Omid Me'mariyan were arrested for a period of several weeks each on 28 and 10 October respectively, possibly in connection with their Internet writings and the support they had given to independent non-governmental organizations. Tens of other civil society activists faced harassment though summons and interrogation. Those detained had "confessed" while in custody although later reported to a governmental commission that these were extracted under duress.

Legal reform

In March, following repeated rejection, President Khatami withdrew bills that proposed extending the powers of the President and prohibiting the Guardians' Council from disqualifying parliamentary candidates. In May, parliament again voted to ratify the UN Convention against Torture. Parliament's previous attempt to ratify the Convention had been rejected by the Guardians' Council in August 2003.

In April the Head of the Judiciary issued a judicial directive reportedly prohibiting the use of torture. In May, a little known law concerning "respect for legitimate freedoms and preservation of civil rights" was enacted. This also contained provisions against forms of torture.

Laws giving recognized religious minorities and women more rights were enacted in 2004 but in June the incoming parliament rejected the previous parliament's passage of a bill granting women equal inheritance rights with men. In August, the Guardians' Council rejected a proposal to make Iran a state party to the UN Women's Convention.

Death penalty, torture and other cruel, inhuman and degrading punishments

At least 159 people were executed in 2004, including at least one minor. Scores of others, including at least 10 people who were under 18 at the time the crime was committed were sentenced to death. It was not known how many of these sentences had been upheld by the Supreme Court. The true figures were believed to be considerably higher. The death penalty continued to be handed down for charges such as "enmity against God" or "morality crimes" that did not reflect internationally recognizable criminal charges.

⌐ On 15 August, Atefeh Rajabi, reportedly aged 16, was hanged. She was sentenced after a grossly unfair trial during which she was publicly insulted and doubts regarding her mental state appeared to be ignored.

At least 36 people were sentenced to flogging, although the true figure was thought to be significantly higher.

⌐ Mohsen Mofidi died in February in Tehran following the imposition of a flogging sentence. No investigation was carried out by the authorities to establish whether he died as a result of the flogging.

⌐ In November and December Leyla Mafi, who was reported to be a child offender with mental disabilities, and Hajieh Esmailvand were sentenced to death, the latter reportedly by stoning. They were convicted of prostitution and other acts of immorality (a'mal khalaf-e 'ofat). Following domestic and international protests both women were granted a stay of execution. Afsaneh Norouzi, who was sentenced to death in 2003, had her case transferred to a conciliation council.

Torture continued to be routine in many prisons.

⌐ In July, the head of a prison in Dezful, southern Iran, was dismissed in connection with an incident in which his staff tied an inmate to a ceiling fan, severing circulation to his hands, which then had to be amputated.

AI country reports/ visits
Reports
- International Labour Organization: Amnesty International's concerns relevant to the 92nd International Labour Conference 1 to 17 June 2004 – Discrimination in Iran (AI Index: IOR 42/008/2004)
- Iran: Prisoner of conscience appeal case – Siamak Pourzand: a case study of flagrant human rights violations (AI Index: MDE 13/025/2004)
- Iran: Five years of injustice and ill treatment – Akbar Mohammadi: case sheet (AI Index: MDE 13/027/2004)
- Iran: Sentenced to death for killing abusive husband (AI Index: MDE 13/041/2004)
- Iran: Emaddedin Baqi – Human rights defender at risk (AI Index: MDE 13/044/2004)

Visits
AI did not receive replies to a request to send a trial observer to Iran. In June, an AI delegate took part in a session of the EU-Iran Human Rights Dialogue in Tehran, despite the initial opposition of the Iranian authorities.

IRAQ

REPUBLIC OF IRAQ
Head of the Coalition Provisional Authority: (until June) Paul Bremer
Head of the interim government: (from June) Iyad 'Allawi
Head of state: (interim, from June) Shaikh Ghazi al-Yawar
Death penalty: retentionist
International Criminal Court: not signed
UN Women's Convention: ratified with reservations
Optional Protocol to UN Women's Convention: not signed

US-led forces in Iraq committed gross human rights violations, including unlawful killings and arbitrary detention, and evidence emerged of torture and ill-treatment. Thousands of Iraqi civilians were killed during armed clashes between US-led forces and Iraqi security forces on the one side, and Iraqi armed groups on the other. Armed groups committed gross human rights abuses, including targeting civilians, hostage-taking and killing hostages. Women continued to be harassed and threatened amid the mounting daily violence. The death penalty was reinstated in August by the new interim government.

Background
At the start of 2004 Iraq was occupied by US-led Coalition forces and governed by the Iraqi Governing Council (IGC), which had been appointed in 2003 by the Coalition Provisional Authority (CPA) headed by Paul Bremer.

On 8 March the IGC agreed an interim constitution. Among its main provisions were that the three Kurdish provinces in the north would remain autonomous, freedom of speech and religious expression would be guaranteed, elections to a National Assembly, mandated to draft a constitution, would be held by January 2005, and at least a quarter of the National Assembly should be women. Many Shi'a clerics, especially Grand Ayatollah Ali al-Sistani, expressed reservations about the interim constitution, in particular provisions allowing for US-led multinational forces to remain in Iraq after the formal end of occupation, the right of three provinces to veto a referendum on a permanent constitution and a three-quarter majority requirement to amend the constitution.

On 1 June the IGC was dissolved and an interim government was announced. Iyad 'Allawi, a Shi'a Muslim, was appointed Prime Minister. Shaikh Ghazi al-Yawar, a Sunni Muslim, was appointed President, a largely ceremonial position.

On 8 June the UN Security Council adopted Resolution 1546, which declared that Iraq's occupation would end on 30 June and called for National Assembly elections by 31 January 2005. The resolution gave the UN a greater role in helping the Iraqis in the political and human rights fields during the transitional period, including the convening of a national conference, held in August, to select a consultative council to advise the interim government, with the power to veto its orders. Resolution 1546 stated that the US-led multinational force would remain in Iraq until the end of 2005 (unless asked to leave earlier by the Iraqi government) with the authority to "take all necessary measures to contribute to the maintenance of security and stability in Iraq".

On 28 June, the Iraqi interim government replaced the CPA, formally ending the occupation of Iraq. However, the US-led multinational force of around 150,000 troops continued to exercise control over security-related matters.

The dire security situation deteriorated further throughout 2004. There was intense fighting between the US-led forces and Iraqi armed groups opposed to their presence. Attacks by Iraqi insurgents on Iraqi police stations, US and UK troops and other targets, including civilian targets, steadily mounted. Thousands of Iraqis as well as US soldiers and other nationals died as a result.

In April, US Marines launched a military operation in Falluja after the killing of four US security guards. A ceasefire was agreed, US troops left the city and for the next few months Falluja was reportedly controlled by insurgents.

Also in April fighting erupted in Baghdad and in southern Iraq between Coalition forces and Iraqi troops on one side and the "Mahdi Army", a militia of the Shi'a Muslim cleric Muqtada al-Sadr, on the other. The fighting began after the CPA closed down the newspaper of Muqtada al-Sadr's group, ordered his arrest, and detained one of his closest aides. Clashes between the Mahdi Army and US troops continued for weeks in al-Najaf, Kufa and Karbala.

In August these clashes erupted again in al-Najaf, Basra and Baghdad. They lasted for more than two weeks before an agreement to end the fighting was reached, with the involvement of Grand Ayatollah Ali al-Sistani.

In November US Marines and Iraqi forces launched an all-out attack on Falluja. Between 1,200 and 1,600 insurgents and 71 Marines were reportedly killed, as well as an unknown number of Iraqi civilians, and the city was devastated. Most of Falluja's population fled before the military operations.

On 7 November a 60-day state of emergency was declared throughout Iraq (except in the Kurdish provinces) following widespread bomb and suicide attacks by insurgents. Towards the end of the year, after the interim government announced that elections would be held on 30 January 2005, insurgents stepped up their attacks.

Detention without charge or trial

A letter by the US Secretary of State annexed to UN Security Council Resolution 1546 lists "internment" among the tasks of the "Multinational Forces" after 28 June, but fails to mention what legal framework or safeguards would apply. On 27 June, the CPA issued a memorandum setting out the process of arrest and detention by US-led forces after 28 June. Criminal suspects held by the US-led forces had the right to remain silent, to consult a lawyer and to be brought before a judicial authority no later than 90 days. "Security internees" could be held for up to 18 months, but in special cases this could be extended further; they were entitled to periodic reviews of their continued detention.

Thousands of people were held without charge on suspicion of anti-Coalition activities and their legal status at the end of the year was not clarified. Many were held in harsh conditions, including in unacknowledged centres, for months and were denied access to lawyers and families for long periods.

🗁 Mohammad Jassem 'Abd al-'Issawi, who was arrested on 17 December 2003, was first held incommunicado in Abu Ghraib prison and then transferred to Camp Bucca in Um Qasr. US soldiers reportedly kicked and punched him during arrest at his home in Baghdad. His family only discovered where he was being held in mid-2004.

🗁 Al-Shaikh 'Adnan al-'Unaibi was arrested in al-Hilla, Babel governorate, by US soldiers in May during a meeting organized by followers of Moqtada al-Sadr. By the end of 2004 his whereabouts remained unknown despite efforts by the Babel Human Rights Association to locate him.

Arrests of people suspected of involvement with insurgents or critical of the presence of foreign troops were reported daily. Many of those detained were picked up in indiscriminate and violent raids, often at night.

At the end of November a senior US military official announced that 8,300 people were being held by US-led forces in Iraq. These included about 4,600 held in Camp Bucca, about 2,000 in Abu Ghraib, and 1,700 in holding areas in the custody of field commanders. Both Camp Bucca and Abu Ghraib remained under the control of US forces after the June handover of power. Some detainees, known as "ghost detainees", were hidden to prevent the International Committee of the Red Cross (ICRC) from visiting them.

🗁 On 17 June, US Defense Secretary Donald Rumsfeld admitted that in November 2003 he had ordered military officials in Iraq to detain a suspected senior member of Ansar al-Islam, an armed Islamist group operating primarily in northern Iraq, without listing him in the prison's register. The prisoner was reportedly arrested in mid-2003, transferred to an undisclosed location outside Iraq, returned to Iraq and detained in secret until May 2004. It was not known whether the prisoner was still held at the end of 2004.

Releases

Hundreds of detainees were released during 2004. On 23 March Coalition forces announced the release of 494 detainees because they no longer posed a "security threat". On 15, 16 and 30 September, a total of 563 detainees were reportedly released from Abu Ghraib Prison. After August, cases were reviewed by the Combined Review and Release Board, including six Iraqi officials from the Ministries of Justice, Human Rights and the Interior and three colonels from the multinational force.

◻ On 14 February the CPA announced the release of Sa'adoun Hammadi, former speaker of the Iraqi parliament, who had been held without charge since May 2003.

Torture and ill-treatment by US-led forces

Torture and ill-treatment by US-led forces were widely reported. An ICRC report leaked in February identified several methods of torture and ill-treatment during arrest, internment and interrogation, including: hooding for up to four days; handcuffing that caused skin lesions and nerve damage; beatings with hard objects; threats of execution; solitary confinement; acts of humiliation with detainees being paraded naked; exposure while hooded to loud noise or music; and being forced to remain for long periods in painful "stress" positions.

A US military investigation, headed by Major General Antonio Taguba and conducted between August 2003 and February 2004, found "systemic and illegal abuse of detainees" in Abu Ghraib prison and that US military personnel had "committed egregious acts and grave breaches of international law at Abu Ghraib and Camp Bucca".

In April photographs of Iraqi detainees being tortured and ill-treated in 2003 by US soldiers in Abu Ghraib prison were published around the world. They showed groups of naked Iraqi detainees being forced to adopt humiliating and sexually explicit positions. Electric wires were attached to the body of one detainee. Others were seen threatened by dogs. Other evidence indicated that Iraqi prisoners were beaten severely, forced to eat pork and drink alcohol, made to masturbate in front of female US soldiers, and forced to walk on their hands and knees and bark like dogs. US officials stated that "abuse" in Abu Ghraib was the responsibility of a few soldiers and that charges would be brought against them. One US soldier was sentenced to a year's imprisonment in May after pleading guilty to abuse charges at a special court martial in Baghdad. In October another US soldier was sentenced to eight years' imprisonment after pleading guilty to several abuse charges. Other soldiers were awaiting trial by the end of the year.

In June the UK authorities announced that four members of the Royal Regiment of the Fusiliers would face court martial for abuse of detainees elsewhere in Iraq.

◻ Huda Hafez Ahmed, a businesswoman, was arrested in late 2003 when she went to a US base in al-'Adhamiya district of Baghdad to look for her sister, Nahla, who had been detained. Following her release in June she stated that she was left overnight in a cold room with only a wooden chair, hit in the face, made to stand for 12 hours with her face against a wall, and subjected to loud music and sleep deprivation for three days.

Killings of civilians

Hundreds of Iraqi civilians were killed by US-led forces when they launched major attacks against insurgents in Falluja, Baghdad, Mosul, Samarra and other cities and towns.

◻ In April at least 600 civilians, including many women and children, were reportedly killed in Falluja as a result of such attacks.

◻ On 12 September, 13 civilians, including a young girl and a television cameraman, were killed in Haifa street, Baghdad, when US troops fired from a helicopter at a crowd, allegedly in response to shots fired from the same area. Press reports contradicted the US account that shots had been fired at the helicopter from the area.

In February UK officials said that UK forces had been involved in the killing of 37 civilians since 1 May 2003, and acknowledged that the figure was not comprehensive.

◻ On 1 January Ghanem Kadhem Kati' was shot dead in Beit Asfar by UK soldiers. A neighbour reportedly tried to tell the soldiers that earlier gunfire was part of a wedding celebration. Ghanem Kadhem Kati' was unarmed and standing with his back to the soldiers. The UK military police apparently launched an investigation, but its findings were not published by the end of 2004.

Inadequate investigations by UK and US governments

US, UK and other foreign forces in Iraq continued to enjoy immunity from Iraqi criminal and civil law. They remained subject solely to the jurisdiction of their own states. Only a minority of killings of Iraqi civilians and other alleged abuses involving multinational forces were investigated, and those investigations that did take place were often inadequate and shrouded in secrecy. In many cases, victims' families were not told how to apply for compensation, or were given misleading information. In December the High Court in the UK ordered a full inquiry into the death in custody in Basra in September 2003 of an Iraqi detainee, Baha Dawood Salem al-Maliki (also known as Baha Dawood Salem).

Abuses by armed groups

Armed groups opposed to the presence of US-led forces in Iraq were responsible for gross human rights abuses which caused thousands of civilian casualties. These groups, thought to be a mixture of former Ba'ath supporters, former members of the various security services, Sunni radical Islamist groups and foreign fighters, were behind numerous attacks targeting civilians as well as indiscriminate attacks. Most of their attacks, including suicide bombings and explosions, targeted Iraqi security forces and police stations, members of the US-led forces, members of the government and Iraqis working for or cooperating with the Iraqi interim government and the US-led forces. Some attacks on government targets such as police stations left scores of civilians dead.

Hostage-taking rose dramatically after April. Many Iraqis and foreign nationals, including aid workers, journalists, truck drivers and civilian contractors, were kidnapped by armed groups to put pressure on their governments to withdraw their troops from Iraq, or to discourage foreigners from travelling to Iraq. Scores of hostages were executed by their captors. Other kidnappings were carried out by armed groups to extract ransoms from families or employers. Some kidnap victims, including children, were killed.

⌑ On 2 March more than 100 civilians were killed and over 400 injured when nine bombs were detonated in Karbala and Baghdad during 'Ashura, the holiest day in the Shi'a Muslim calendar.

⌑ On 21 April, 73 people, including 17 children, were killed when several bombs exploded at three police stations in Basra and a police academy in the Zubair area.

⌑ On 17 June, at least 41 people were killed and more than 138 injured in a car bomb attack outside an army recruitment centre in al-Muthana district, Baghdad. Most of the victims were civilians applying for jobs.

⌑ In August, 12 Nepalese men, taken hostage by the Iraqi armed group Army of Ansar al-Sunna, were killed.

⌑ On 30 September a series of bombs detonated in Baghdad as crowds gathered to celebrate the opening of a water treatment plant. At least 41 civilians, including 34 children, were killed. The al-Tawhid wal Jihad armed group led by Abu Mus'ab al-Zarqawi claimed responsibility on its website.

⌑ On 19 December, 66 people were killed when suicide bombers targeted a bus station in Karbala and a funeral procession in Najaf. At least 200 others were reportedly injured.

Violence against women
Women and girls continued to be harassed, injured and killed by armed groups and individuals, relatives, and members of the US-led forces. Many women lived under constant fear of being beaten, abducted, raped or murdered. The interim constitution and limited amendments introduced by the CPA, while being steps in the right direction, fell far short of the extensive reforms necessary to end discrimination against women in Iraqi legislation, including in the penal, personal status and nationality laws.

Several women political leaders were targeted in politically motivated attacks, and campaigners for women's rights were threatened.

⌑ In March, gunmen in Mosul opened fire on Nisreen Mustafa al-Burwari, the only woman member of the Iraqi cabinet at the time. She escaped unhurt, but two of her bodyguards were killed.

⌑ Yanar Mohammad, a member of the Organization of Women's Freedom in Iraq, was threatened with death in early 2004 unless she stopped her activities to protect women's rights. The threats appeared to come from an Islamist group known as the Army of Sahaba. She reportedly asked CPA officials for protection, but was told there were more urgent matters that needed attention.

⌑ In November Amal al-Ma'malji, a women's rights activist and adviser at the Ministry of Municipalities and Public Affairs, was killed in her car in Baghdad along with her secretary, bodyguard and driver. She was a co-founder of the Advisory Committee for Women's Affairs in Iraq and the Independent Iraqi Women Assembly.

There continued to be reports of "honour killings" in which women and girls were killed by male relatives in connection with alleged "immoral behaviour". These crimes were often ignored by the police. Several organizations began working in Iraq during 2004 to help women victims of violence. However, support facilities, such as shelters or rehabilitation centres, were not available for the vast majority of women victims of violence.

Death penalty
In August the Iraqi interim government reinstated the death penalty for a range of crimes including murder, drug trafficking, kidnapping and "endangering national security". Although the authorities justified the reimposition of the death penalty on grounds of the deteriorating security situation, there were indications that some Iraqi officials opposed its use.

⌑ In November the head of the Supreme Judicial Council stated that 10 people had been sentenced to death by Iraqi courts. The death sentences were upheld by an appeal court and were reportedly with the Iraqi President and the Prime Minister for final confirmation. At the end of 2004 it was not known if any executions had been carried out.

Judicial proceedings against former government leaders
On 1 July, former President Saddam Hussain and 11 senior members of his government appeared before the Iraqi Central Criminal Court and not the Iraqi Special Tribunal which was set up in December 2003 specifically to try Saddam Hussain and other former officials. They were charged with crimes punishable under Iraqi legislation. However, defence counsel was not made available to the accused. For months lawyers complained about the failure of the US and Iraqi authorities to authorize visits to the detainees who were held in a detention centre at Baghdad Airport.

At the end of 2004 Iraqi judicial authorities were still finalizing the rules of procedures and evidence for the Iraqi Special Tribunal. Twenty-one judges and prosecutors were reportedly selected as members of the Tribunal. In December 'Ali Hassan al-Majid, a former General and loyal relative of Saddam Hussain, and Sultan Hashem Ahmad, the former Defence Minister, appeared before an investigative judge for a pre-trial hearing. Charges against them reportedly included involvement in the 1988 gassing of Kurds in Halabja and the crushing of the Kurdish and Shi'a uprising in March 1991.

AI country reports/visits
Reports
- Iraq: One year on the human rights situation remains dire (AI Index: MDE 14/006/2004)
- Iraq: Killings of civilians in Basra and al-'Amara (AI Index: MDE 14/007/2004)
- Iraq: Human rights protection and promotion vital in the transitional period (AI Index: MDE 14/030/2004)

Visits
In February and March an AI delegation visited southern Iraq to investigate human rights violations, including killings of civilians.

IRELAND

IRELAND
Head of state: Mary McAleese
Head of government: Bertie Ahern
Death penalty: abolitionist for all crimes
International Criminal Court: ratified
UN Women's Convention: ratified with reservations
Optional Protocol to UN Women's Convention: ratified

Allegations persisted of ill-treatment by police officers, and such allegations were not investigated impartially. Concerns about the system for reporting, recording and prosecuting racist crimes continued. Conditions in psychiatric and other institutions for mentally disabled people remained unsatisfactory. Concerns were expressed about inadequate asylum-seeking procedures and discrimination against migrant workers. Provisions to protect women escaping violence in the family were insufficient.

Background

The European Committee of Social Rights issued its conclusions on Ireland's first report, finding 12 cases of non-conformity and requesting further information on nine cases.

The Ombudsman for Children began to investigate complaints against some public institutions.

Treatment of people with disabilities

The report of the Inspector of Mental Hospitals, published in September, criticized seriously unsatisfactory conditions for the care and treatment of patients in psychiatric hospitals, as well as gaps in provision for specific groups of vulnerable persons.

The severe shortage in psychiatric services for young people resulted in children being detained in adult psychiatric hospitals.

A National Disability Strategy was published in September. This included the Disability Bill 2004, which, despite prior government pledges, was not human rights-based, and did not adequately provide for the progressive realization of economic and social rights of people with disabilities. The Strategy and Bill were criticized by disability groups.

Policing

Allegations continued to be made of ill-treatment and other serious misconduct by members of the Garda Síochána (police force), which were not adequately investigated by the Garda Complaints Board.

The Tribunal of Inquiry (the Morris Tribunal) into complaints against Garda officers in the Donegal Division issued its first report in July. The tribunal found culpability ranging from instances of negligence to two officers corruptly orchestrating the planting of ammunition and hoax explosives. It made recommendations for improved management,

recording of incidents, an urgent review of policy on the handling of informants, and greater accountability.

Seven Garda officers were tried in connection with allegations of excessive use of force during a demonstration in Dublin in May 2002. Six were acquitted and the seventh was convicted of assaulting a teacher.

The Garda Síochána Bill 2004 was published in February, setting out for the first time in statutory form the functions of a police service. It also provided for the creation of an independent Garda Ombudsman Commission to deal with complaints, with powers of investigation, arrest and detention of Garda officers. The Irish Human Rights Commission voiced concern about certain provisions of the Bill. Its recommendations included: all interviews with suspects should be video-recorded; the Ombudsman Commission should have the right to inspect any Garda station; and all investigations, except the most minor, should be conducted by the Commission.

Places of detention

Detention conditions did not comply with international standards: many prisons were overcrowded, lacked adequate sanitation facilities and had insufficient education and employment programmes. People facing deportation were detained in prisons, rather than in special detention centres. Mentally ill prisoners continued to be held in padded cells in ordinary prisons rather than in specialized institutions.

The authorities failed to establish an independent and impartial individual complaints mechanism for prisoners, as recommended by the European Committee for the Prevention of Torture.

Asylum-seekers and migrants

The Immigration Act 2004 was fundamentally flawed in its lack of respect for internationally recognized human rights. There was no independent human rights monitoring of immigration controls at ports of entry.

Concern heightened throughout 2004 about the status and entitlement of migrant workers, including their rights to family reunion, and to be provided with a means of appeal against a deportation order.

The 27th Amendment to the Constitution was passed, removing the constitutional guarantee of citizenship for people born in Ireland who do not have a parent with Irish citizenship.

Family members of children with Irish citizenship, who were not themselves Irish nationals, faced the retrospective application of changed government policy to deny them automatic residency. Such families were not entitled to legal aid when applying to remain on humanitarian grounds. According to official figures, by October, 32 parents of Irish children had been deported, and another 352 had been issued with deportation orders. Concern remained that the best interests of the child were not sufficiently being taken into account in deportation decisions. In October a decision by the European Court of Justice confirmed the rights of children who are citizens of the European

Union (EU) to the care and company of their parents in the EU. In December, the government announced revised arrangements for processing claims from the non-national parents of Irish children born before 1 January 2005.

Racism and equality
There were inordinate delays in developing the National Action Plan against Racism. According to the National Consultative Committee on Racism and Interculturalism, there was an increase in the number of racially motivated incidents in the aftermath of a citizenship referendum in June. A number of human rights and Traveller groups condemned the erosion of travellers' rights and heavy-handed policing methods used in relation to Travellers. Concerns about the inadequacy of the system for reporting, recording and prosecuting racist crimes persisted.

The Equality Act 2004, ostensibly enacted to comply with EU Directives on equal treatment in relation to race, employment and gender, inadequately implemented the Directives' requirements, and undermined existing non-discrimination provisions. Of particular concern were provisions for differential treatment of non-EU nationals in access to education and to a number of state services, discrimination on the basis of nationality in the area of immigration and residency, and the continuing failure of the government to introduce a statutory duty on public authorities to ensure greater equality.

Violence against women
Voluntary organizations supporting victims of rape, sexual assault, domestic violence, and trafficking for sexual exploitation reported that they were seriously hampered by inadequate funding. There was also concern at the shortage of shelters for women and children leaving abusive situations, and at the vulnerability of immigrant women whose legal status prevented them from seeking help.

The only conviction for marital rape secured in Ireland was overturned in October.

Arms trade
In May, the government published a review of Ireland's export control system for military and dual-use goods. It subsequently committed itself to introducing new legislation which would include controls on arms brokering and the submission of an annual report to the Oireachtas (Irish parliament). There were gaps in the proposed legislative framework.

AI country reports/ visits
Report
- Ireland: Comments and recommendations on the International Criminal Court Bill 2003 (AI Index: EUR 29/001/2004)

ISRAEL AND THE OCCUPIED TERRITORIES

STATE OF ISRAEL
Head of state: Moshe Katzav
Head of government: Ariel Sharon
Death penalty: abolitionist for ordinary crimes
International Criminal Court: not ratified
UN Women's Convention: ratified with reservations
Optional Protocol to UN Women's Convention: not signed

The Israeli army killed more than 700 Palestinians, including some 150 children. Most were killed unlawfully – in reckless shooting, shelling and air strikes in civilian residential areas; in extrajudicial executions; and as a result of excessive use of force. Palestinian armed groups killed 109 Israelis – 67 of them civilians and including eight children – in suicide bombings, shootings and mortar attacks. Stringent restrictions imposed by the Israeli army on the movement of Palestinians in the Occupied Territories caused widespread poverty and unemployment and hindered access to health and education facilities. The Israeli army destroyed several hundred Palestinian homes, large areas of agricultural land, and infrastructure networks. Israel continued to expand illegal settlements and to build a fence/wall through the West Bank, confining Palestinians in isolated enclaves cut off from their land and essential services in nearby towns and villages. Israeli settlers increased their attacks against Palestinians and their property and against international human rights workers. Certain abuses committed by the Israeli army constituted crimes against humanity and war crimes, including unlawful killings; extensive and wanton destruction of property; obstruction of medical assistance and targeting of medical personnel; torture; and the use of Palestinians as "human shields". The deliberate targeting of civilians by Palestinian armed groups constituted crimes against humanity.

Background
In February Prime Minister Ariel Sharon announced the "disengagement plan", to evacuate all Israeli settlements in the Gaza Strip and four in the West Bank, while maintaining military control of all land and sea access to the Gaza Strip, and of its airspace. In October Prime Minister Sharon's bureau chief publicly stated that the evacuation of Israeli settlements in the Gaza Strip was intended to strengthen Israeli control of much of the West Bank, where more than 100 Israeli settlements are located. Israel started to build a

network of secondary roads and tunnels in the West Bank intended to keep existing main roads for the sole use of Israeli settlers. No steps were taken to implement the "road map" peace plan, agreed the previous year by Israel and the Palestinian Authority (PA) and sponsored by the USA, the UN, the European Union and Russia. After the death of PA President Yasser Arafat in November, the "road map" sponsors expressed renewed interest in its implementation and urged Israel and the PA to resume peace negotiations within its framework.

Killings and attacks by the Israeli army

The Israeli army killed around 700 Palestinians, including some 150 children, in the Occupied Territories, most of them unlawfully. Many were killed in deliberate as well as reckless shooting, shelling and bombardment of densely populated residential areas or as a result of excessive use of force. Some 120 Palestinians were killed in extrajudicial executions, including more than 30 bystanders, of whom four were children. Others were killed in armed clashes with Israeli soldiers. Thousands of others were injured.

▢ Four Palestinian schoolgirls were shot dead by the Israeli army in their classrooms or walking to school in the Gaza Strip in September and October. Raghda Adnan al-Assar and Ghadeer Jaber Mukhaymar, aged 10 and nine, were shot dead by Israeli soldiers while sitting at their desks in UN schools in Khan Yunis refugee camp. Eight-year-old Rania Iyad Aram was shot dead by Israeli soldiers as she was walking to school. On 5 October Israeli soldiers shot dead 13-year-old Iman al-Hams near her school in Rafah. According to an army communication recording of the incident and testimonies of soldiers, a commander repeatedly shot the child at close range even though soldiers had identified her as "a little girl... scared to death". The commander was charged with illegal use of his weapon, obstructing justice, improper use of authority and unbecoming conduct. He was not charged with murder or manslaughter.

▢ On 22 March, Hamas leader Sheikh Ahmad Yassin, a 66-year-old wheelchair-bound paraplegic, was assassinated in an Israeli air-strike as he was leaving a mosque in Gaza City after dawn prayers. Seven other Palestinians were killed in the attack and at least 17 were injured. His successor, 'Abd al-'Aziz al-Rantisi, was likewise assassinated by the Israeli army on 17 April.

▢ Ten-year-old Walid Naji Abu Qamar, 11-year-old Mubarak Salim al-Hashash, 13-year-old Mahmoud Tariq Mansour and five others were killed on 19 May in Rafah in the Gaza Strip when the Israeli army opened fire with tank shells and a helicopter-launched missile on a non-violent demonstration. Dozens of other unarmed demonstrators were also wounded in the attack.

'Human shields'

Israeli soldiers continued to use Palestinians as "human shields" during military operations, forcing them to carry out tasks that endangered their lives, despite an injunction by the Israeli High Court banning the practice. A petition against the use of "human shields" submitted by Israeli and Palestinian human rights organizations to the Supreme Court in May 2002 was still pending at the end of 2004.

▢ In April, Israeli soldiers used 13-year-old Muhammed Badwan as a "human shield" during a demonstration in the West Bank village of Biddu. The soldiers placed the boy on the hood of their jeep and tied him to the front windscreen to discourage Palestinian demonstrators from throwing stones in their direction.

Killings and attacks by Palestinian armed groups

Sixty-seven Israeli civilians, including eight children, were killed by Palestinian armed groups in Israel and in the Occupied Territories. Forty-seven of the victims were killed in suicide bombings, the others were killed in shooting or mortar attacks. Most of the attacks were claimed by the al-Aqsa Martyrs Brigades, an offshoot of Fatah, and by the armed wing of Hamas. Forty-two Israeli soldiers were also killed by Palestinian armed groups, most of them in the Occupied Territories.

▢ Chana Anya Bunders, Natalia Gamril, Dana Itach, Rose Bona and Anat Darom and six other Israelis were killed on 29 January when a Palestinian man blew himself up on a bus in Jerusalem. More than 50 other people were wounded in the attack. The suicide bombing was claimed by both the al-Aqsa Martyrs Brigades and the armed wing of Hamas.

▢ Tali Hatuel, who was eight months pregnant, and her four young daughters, Hila, Hadar, Roni and Meirav, aged between two and 11, were shot dead in the Gaza Strip while travelling by car near the Gush Katif settlement block where they lived. They were shot at close range by Palestinian gunmen who had opened fire on their car and caused it to career off the road.

▢ On 28 June, three-year-old Afik Zahavi and 49-year-old Mordechai Yosepov were the first victims of a rocket fired by Palestinian armed groups from the Gaza Strip into the nearby Israeli city of Sderot. On 29 September, four-year-old Yuval Abebeh and two-year-old Dorit Aniso were killed by another Palestinian rocket while playing outside their relatives' home in Sderot.

Attacks by Israeli settlers in the Occupied Territories

Israeli settlers stepped up attacks against Palestinians and their property throughout the West Bank and also increased attacks on international human rights activists. They destroyed and damaged trees owned by Palestinians and frequently prevented Palestinian farmers from harvesting their crops.

▢ On 27 September, an Israeli settler shot dead Sayel Jabara, a Palestinian taxi driver, as he was driving his passengers between Nablus and Salem. The settler claimed that he shot Sayel Jabara because he thought that he might attack him, even though Sayel Jabara was not armed. The settler was released on bail less than 24 hours after the killing.

In September and October Israeli settlers, wearing hoods and armed with stones, wooden clubs and metal chains, assaulted two US citizens, members of the Christian Peacemaker Teams (CPT), and AI delegates as they escorted Palestinian primary school children to school near Tuwani village in the Hebron area. CPT members Kim Lamberty sustained a broken arm and knee as well as bruising, and her colleague Chris Brown sustained a punctured lung and multiple bruises. The attackers came from the Israeli settlement of Havat Ma'on and returned there after the attacks. Israeli settlers from Havat Ma'on continued to attack Palestinian children on their way to school with impunity.

Impunity

Most members of the Israeli army and security forces continued to enjoy impunity. Investigations, prosecutions and convictions for human rights violations were rare. In the overwhelming majority of the thousands of cases of unlawful killings and other grave human rights violations committed by Israeli soldiers in the previous four years, no investigations were known to have been carried out.

Israeli settlers also enjoyed impunity for attacks on Palestinians and their property and international human rights workers. The Israeli army and police consistently failed to take steps to stop and prevent such attacks and routinely increased restrictions on the local Palestinian population in response to attacks by Israeli settlers.

Destruction of Palestinian property in the Occupied Territories

The Israeli army carried out large-scale destruction of Palestinian houses and property in the Occupied Territories, far exceeding the destruction of previous years. It demolished several hundred homes, mostly in the Gaza Strip, making thousands of Palestinians homeless, and destroyed large areas of agricultural land, roads and water, electricity and communications infrastructure. Such destruction was often a form of collective punishment on the local population in retaliation for attacks by Palestinian armed groups. The army usually gave no warning of the impending destruction and inhabitants were forced to flee their homes without being able to salvage their possessions. UN agencies and humanitarian organizations were unable to respond to the needs of tens of thousands of Palestinians whose homes had been destroyed by the Israeli army over the previous four years.

In May the Israeli army destroyed some 300 homes and damaged some 270 other buildings in Rafah refugee camp in the Gaza Strip, making nearly 4,000 people homeless in the space of a few days. Several people were trapped in their homes when Israeli army bulldozers began to tear down the houses and had to drill holes in the back walls to escape. Thousands of other residents also fled their homes, fearing imminent destruction. UN schools had to be used as temporary shelters for the homeless. The mass destruction came in the wake of an attack by Palestinian gunmen in which five Israeli soldiers were killed. Israeli officials claimed the destruction was intended to further widen the no-go area along the Egyptian border and to uncover tunnels used by Palestinians to smuggle weapons into the Gaza Strip from Egypt.

In October, after two Israeli children were killed by a Palestinian mortar fired from the Gaza Strip, the Israeli army launched a major attack in and around the Jabalya refugee camp in the northern Gaza Strip, and destroyed or damaged some 200 homes and buildings as well as roads and other vital infrastructure.

Collective punishment, closures and violations of economic and social rights

The Israeli army continued to impose stringent restrictions on the movements of Palestinians in the Occupied Territories. Military checkpoints and blockades around Palestinian towns and villages hindered or prevented access to work, education and medical facilities and other crucial services. Restrictions on the movement of Palestinians remained the key cause of high rates of unemployment and poverty. More than half of the Palestinian population lived below the poverty line, with increasing numbers suffering from malnutrition and other health problems.

Palestinians had to obtain special permits from the Israeli army to move between towns and villages within the West Bank and were barred from main roads and many secondary roads which were freely used by Israeli settlers living in illegal settlements in the Occupied Territories. Movement restrictions for Palestinians were routinely increased in reprisal for attacks by Palestinian armed groups and during Jewish holidays. Further restrictions were also imposed on the movement of international human rights and humanitarian workers throughout the Occupied Territories.

The Israeli army routinely used excessive and unwarranted force to enforce blockades and movement restrictions. Soldiers frequently fired recklessly towards unarmed Palestinians, ill-treated, humiliated and arbitrarily detained Palestinian men, women and children, and confiscated or damaged vehicles. Sick people needing to reach medical facilities were often delayed or denied passage at checkpoints.

Continued construction by Israel of a fence/wall through the West Bank left an increasing number of Palestinians cut off from health, education and other essential services in nearby towns and villages and from their farm land – a main source of subsistence for Palestinians in this region. Large areas of Palestinian land were encircled by the fence/wall and Palestinians living or owning land in these areas had to obtain special permits from the Israeli army to move in and out of their homes and land. Israeli soldiers frequently denied passage to residents and farmers in these areas. In July the International Court of Justice declared that Israel's construction of the fence/wall in the West Bank was illegal under international law and called for it to be dismantled.

In an exceptional ruling in June, the Israeli High Court ordered that some 30km of the fence/wall be re-routed. The Israeli army subsequently made minor adjustments to some five per cent of the route of the fence/wall.

Detainees and releases

Thousands of Palestinians were detained by the Israeli army. Most were released without charge. More than 3,000 were charged with security offences. Trials before military courts often did not meet international standards of fairness, and allegations of torture and ill-treatment of Palestinian detainees were not adequately investigated. Some 1,500 Palestinians were detained administratively without charge or trial during the year.

In January Israeli authorities and the Lebanese group Hizbollah concluded an exchange of detainees, hostages and remains of soldiers and combatants. Hizbollah released an Israeli businessman and the bodies of three Israeli soldiers captured in Lebanon in October 2000. Israel released some 400 Palestinians detainees, 35 detainees from other Arab countries, mostly Lebanese, and the bodies of 59 Lebanese killed by the Israeli army and buried in Israel. Among those released by Israel were four Lebanese men who had been held as hostages without charge or trial for several years.

Former nuclear technician and whistle-blower Mordechai Vanunu was released in April, having served his entire 18-year jail sentence, mostly in solitary confinement. Upon his release he was banned from leaving the country and from communicating with foreigners and his movements in the country were restricted. He was twice rearrested and interrogated in November and December.

Violence against women

The UN Special Rapporteur on violence against women visited the Occupied Territories in June to gather information on the impact of the occupation and conflict on women. She concluded that the conflict had disproportionately affected Palestinian women in the Occupied Territories, in both the public and private spheres of life. In addition to the women killed or injured by Israeli forces, Palestinian women were particularly negatively affected by the demolition of their homes and restrictions on movement, which hampered their access to health services and education, and by the sharp increase in poverty. The dramatic increase in violence as a result of the conflict also led to an increase in domestic and societal violence, while at the same time there were increased demands on women as carers and providers.

Discrimination

In August the UN Committee on the Elimination of Racial Discrimination called for the revocation of the Citizenship and Entry into Israel Law, passed the previous year and extended for six months in July. The law institutionalized racial discrimination. It barred Israeli Arab citizens married to Palestinians from the Occupied Territories from living with their spouses in Israel, and forced families to either live apart or leave the country altogether.

AI country reports/visits
Reports
- Israel and the Occupied Territories: The place of the fence/wall in international law (AI Index: MDE 15/016/2004)
- Israel and the Occupied Territories: Under the rubble – House demolition and destruction of land and property (AI Index: MDE 15/033/2004)
- Israel and the Occupied Territories: Torn apart – Families split by discriminatory policies (AI Index: MDE 15/063/2004)
- Israel and the Occupied Territories and the Palestinian Authority: Act now to stop the killing of children! (AI Index: MDE 02/002/2004)

Visits
AI delegations visited Israel and the Occupied Territories in May, September and October.

ITALY

ITALIAN REPUBLIC
Head of state: Carlo Azeglio Ciampi
Head of government: Silvio Berlusconi
Death penalty: abolitionist for all crimes
International Criminal Court: ratified
UN Women's Convention and its Optional Protocol: ratified

There were further allegations of excessive use of force, ill-treatment and racial abuse by law enforcement and prison officers, together with reports of detainee and prisoner deaths in disputed circumstances. Detention conditions in some facilities, including temporary holding centres for aliens, fell below international standards. Many asylum-seekers faced obstacles in exercising their right to claim asylum; some may have been returned to countries where they were at risk of human rights violations. Roma and a number of other ethnic minorities suffered discrimination in many areas including policing, housing and employment. Domestic violence against women remained prevalent, but the majority of victims did not report it to the authorities, leading to calls for more concerted efforts to educate the public about the assistance already available to women and for further research into this serious abuse. Trafficking in people, in particular women and children, for sexual exploitation and forced labour remained a problem, despite government efforts to combat it.

Background

In September, the Committee of Ministers of the Council of Europe deplored the fact that "no stable improvement" could yet be seen in tackling the excessive length of judicial proceedings in Italy. The Committee noted that "the situation generally worsened between 2002 and 2003."

There was continuing tension between the government and many magistrates who argued that proposed reforms to the justice system would undermine their independence. In December the UN Special Rapporteur on the independence of judges and lawyers expressed concern to the President of the Republic that the reforms represented "a worrying limitation" to the independence of the judiciary and welcomed the President's decision not to ratify the reforms and to return the relevant judicial reform bill to parliament.

Legislative initiatives to introduce a specific crime of torture into the Penal Code, as repeatedly recommended by UN treaty bodies, continued to suffer delays and setbacks.

Asylum and immigration

There was still no specific and comprehensive law on asylum. A draft law still awaiting parliamentary discussion at the end of the year fell short of relevant international standards. The protection for asylum-seekers offered under certain provisions of immigration legislation did not guarantee access to a fair and impartial individual asylum determination procedure. There were fears that many people in need of protection were forced to return to countries where they were at risk of grave human rights violations. Excessive delays in the asylum determination process, combined with inadequate provision for the basic needs of asylum-seekers, resulted in many people being left destitute while awaiting the outcome of initial asylum applications.

Thousands of migrants and asylum-seekers continued to arrive on southern shores by boat and hundreds of others perished in the attempt. Many such boats set out from Libya. The Office of the UN High Commissioner for Refugees (UNHCR), AI and other domestic and international organizations working for refugees' human rights expressed deep concern about a number of episodes where the fundamental rights of people arriving by sea were not respected.

☐ In July UNHCR expressed "strong concern over apparent disregard for accepted international and European standards and for fundamental elements of due process" in connection with the expulsion to Ghana of 25 asylum-seekers. They were among a group of 37 people who had been allowed, on humanitarian grounds and after considerable delay, to disembark from a boat belonging to a German non-governmental organization.

☐ In October UNHCR expressed "deep concern" over the fate of hundreds of new arrivals from Africa and the Middle East on the southern island of Lampedusa, following reports that many were being sent to Libya "without proper assessment of their possible protection needs." It said that lack of access to the individuals concerned, in both Italy and Libya, was preventing it from exercising its mandate to ensure that refugees are properly protected. AI called for such access to be granted immediately. UNHCR subsequently reported that some five days after requesting authorization, and "following the return by air of more than 1,000 persons to Libya", it was granted access to the Lampedusa processing centre where those arriving had been held initially. Its preliminary evaluation was that "the rushed method used to sort out the incoming persons by nationality" had "not allowed individual persons from all national groups concerned to claim asylum."

Temporary holding centres

Thousands of foreign nationals without a right of residence in Italy, or suspected of not having such a right, were detained in temporary holding centres where they could remain for up to a maximum of 60 days before expulsion from the country as illegal immigrants or release. Many inmates experienced difficulties in gaining access to the expert advice necessary to challenge the legality of their detention and of expulsion orders. Some inmates trying to pursue asylum claims were apparently unable to gain access to the asylum determination process.

Tension in the centres was high, with frequent protests, including escape attempts, and high levels of self-harm. There were reports of frequent overcrowding, unsuitable infrastructures, unhygienic living conditions, unsatisfactory diets and inadequate medical care. Several criminal investigations were under way into alleged physical assaults on inmates.

Updates

☐ In January, a Roman Catholic priest employed as the director of Regina Pacis temporary holding centre in Puglia province, two doctors, five members of the administrative personnel, and 11 *carabinieri* providing the centre's security service, were ordered to stand trial in connection with the physical assault and racial abuse of inmates in November 2002. The trial was continuing at the end of the year.

☐ The Bologna Public Prosecutor concluded a criminal investigation into allegations that some 11 police officers, one *carabiniere* and a member of the Red Cross administration running the via Mattei holding centre were involved in a physical assault on inmates in March 2003. The Prosecutor indicated that he would be requesting the committal for trial of at least four police officers.

In January the Prosecutor opened another criminal investigation, following complaints lodged by three former inmates who alleged that they and other detainees had regularly been given strong sedative drugs without their knowledge. The Prosecutor subsequently concluded that the food and drink taken from the centre for expert analysis had not revealed the presence of the drugs indicated in the inmates' complaints and supporting blood analyses, and that the latter were unreliable. However, his findings and request to the judge of preliminary investigation that no further action be taken were challenged by lawyers representing the inmates. The judge's decision was still awaited at the end of the year.

Police brutality

Allegations of ill-treatment by law enforcement officers often concerned Roma, immigrants from outside the European Union and demonstrators. Police shootings, some fatal, occurred in disputed circumstances. A number of criminal investigations were under way into such incidents. Some officers were brought to trial but in general law enforcement officers enjoyed considerable impunity.

⊡ In February the Supreme Court overturned an appeal court ruling which had acquitted a Naples police officer of the murder of 17-year-old Mario Castellano in 2000. A first instance court had sentenced the officer to 10 years' imprisonment. The boy, who was unarmed, was riding a motor-scooter but was not wearing a helmet, as required by law, when he apparently failed to obey a police order to stop. He was shot in the back by the police officer who maintained that he had shot him accidentally. Mario Castellano's family made an unsuccessful application for the president of the appeal court to be substituted, questioning his impartiality in view of opinions he had expressed in the media criticizing the lower court's verdict. The Supreme Court said that the appeal court's argument for acquittal had been "illogical" and ordered a retrial.

Updates: policing of 2001 demonstrations

Among the ongoing criminal proceedings were a number relating to policing operations surrounding the mass demonstrations which occurred in Naples in March 2001 and during the G8 Summit in Genoa in July 2001.

⊡ In July, 31 police officers on duty in a *carabinieri* barracks used as a detention facility on the day of the Naples demonstration, were committed for trial on charges ranging from abduction to bodily harm and coercion: some officers were additionally accused of abusing their position as state officers and of falsifying records. Their trial opened in December.

⊡ In February, a judge ruled that there were no grounds to prosecute 93 people accused of belonging to a criminal association intent on looting and destroying property. The accused had been detained during an overnight police raid on a building legally occupied by the Genoa Social Forum (GSF), the main organizer of the Genoa demonstrations. All the other accusations originally brought against them, including violently resisting state officers and carrying offensive weapons, had been dropped in 2003.

⊡ In December, 28 police officers involved in the GSF raid, including several high-ranking officers, were committed for trial on various charges, including assault and battery, falsifying and planting evidence and abusing their powers as state officers. Scores more law enforcement officers involved in the raid and believed to have participated in physical assaults apparently could not be identified because their faces were frequently hidden by riot helmets, masks or scarves during the raid and they displayed no other means of individual identification. The trial was due to open in April 2005.

⊡ The Genoa Public Prosecutor's Office requested the committal for trial of 12 *carabinieri*, 14 police officers, 16 prison officers and five prison doctors and nurses who were on duty inside Bolzaneto temporary detention facility at the time of the G8 Summit and through which over 200 detainees passed. The charges envisaged included abuse of authority, threats, assault, falsification of records and failure to officially report injuries. A judge of preliminary investigation was scheduled to start examining the request in January 2005.

⊡ In October a police officer became the first law enforcement officer to be sentenced in connection with the G8 Summit policing operation. The officer, who had opted to be tried using a fast-track procedure, which allows sentences to be reduced by a third, was given a 20-month suspended sentence and ordered to pay compensation for striking a 15-year-old demonstrator in the face with his truncheon. At the same time, five other officers accused of participating in assaults on the boy and six other demonstrators, who had opted to be tried using the ordinary criminal process, were committed for trial to answer charges including abuse of authority, threats, assault, perjury and falsification of records. The boy and the other six demonstrators had originally been accused of assaulting officers and resisting arrest, but the boy had already been cleared of the charges, while the prosecutors had already requested that no further action be taken against the other demonstrators.

Ill-treatment and poor conditions in prisons

Chronic overcrowding and understaffing persisted in prisons, along with high rates of suicide and self-harm. There were many reports of poor sanitary conditions and inadequate medical assistance. Infectious diseases and mental health problems were on the increase.

Numerous criminal proceedings, involving large numbers of prison staff, were under way into alleged ill-treatment of individual prisoners and sometimes large groups of prisoners. Some proceedings were marked by excessive delays, with a few dating back to the mid-1990s. The allegations related to prisons across the country. They concerned psychological and physical, including sexual, abuse of prisoners, in some cases carried out systematically and sometimes amounting to torture. The criminal proceedings included at least six into individual prisoner deaths which occurred in disputed circumstances between 1997 and 2004.

AI country reports/ visits

Reports

- Europe and Central Asia: Summary of Amnesty International's concerns in the region, January-June 2004: Italy (AI Index: EUR 01/005/2004)
- Italy: Government must ensure access to asylum for those in need of protection (AI Index: EUR 30/001/2004)

Visit

Two AI representatives visited Italy in October.

JAMAICA

JAMAICA
Head of state: Queen Elizabeth II, represented by
Howard Felix Cooke
Head of government: Percival James Patterson
Death penalty: retentionist
International Criminal Court: signed
UN Women's Convention: ratified with reservations
Optional Protocol to UN Women's Convention: not
signed

Reports of police brutality and excessive use of force
by police and the armed forces continued. The
number of police officers charged with murder
increased, but there were no convictions. At least
100 people were killed by the police, many in
circumstances suggesting they were extrajudicially
executed. Conditions of detention frequently
amounted to cruel, inhuman or degrading treatment.
At least two people were sentenced to death; there
were no executions.

Background
Large sections of the population continued to live in
poverty. The economy showed signs of improvement
but remained dire. The situation was exacerbated
by the devastation caused by Hurricane Ivan in
September. Jamaican society continued to suffer from
a high level of violence; at least 1,445 people were
reportedly murdered, including 12 police officers.

Unlawful killings
The authorities gave differing figures on the number
of people killed by the police. National human rights
groups believed the figure of 130 to be accurate.
Many of these killings may have been unlawful. For
the fifth consecutive year, no police officers were
brought to justice for their involvement in cases of
unlawful killing, although some were under
investigation.
    In March, Phillip Baker, Craig Vacianna and taxi
driver Omar Graham were killed by police in Burnt
Savannah. All were shot in the head. The police claimed
that they returned fire after the men got out of the taxi
and shot at them. Local residents claimed the three
men were killed one at a time after being forced to
kneel down. Omar Graham reportedly begged for his
life before he was shot.
    In September, Sandra Sewell and Gayon Alcott
were fatally shot in disputed circumstances in August
Town by members of the Jamaican Defence Force.
According to members of the local community, Gayon
Alcott was shot after being challenged for smoking
marijuana and then shot again as he tried to flee.
Sandra Sewell was killed as she crouched to avoid the
gunfire. Soldiers claimed they were fired upon and then
returned fire and that an automatic gun was recovered
from the scene of the crime.

Impunity
Investigations into alleged extrajudicial executions
remained inadequate. Police officers often failed to
protect crime scenes, allowing forensic evidence to be
destroyed, lost or damaged. Statements from officers
involved in fatal shootings were often taken after long
delays. A government pledge to strengthen
investigations into police killings failed to materialize.
    In March, the prosecution of a police officer
charged with the murder in 2000 of 13-year-old Janice
Allen collapsed after the state failed to present any
evidence and the prosecution told the court that a
police officer whose testimony was vital was not in the
country; this later transpired to be untrue and the
officer was available to give evidence. The family of
Janice Allen unsuccessfully appealed against the
officer's acquittal.
    In December, two police officers were acquitted of
the murder of seven-year-old Romaine Edwards who
died after the officers shot into the yard were he was
standing, allegedly at a wanted criminal. Romaine
Edwards' parents denied that any armed men were
present when he was shot.
    In April, the Prime Minister announced that the
Police Public Complaints Authority would be relocated
and its staffing increased. The office was relocated but
no significant increase in personnel was reported to
have occurred.
    There was an increase in the number of officers
charged with unlawful killings committed while on duty.
They included six police officers charged in April with the
murder of four people in Crawle in May 2003, and three
police officers charged in May with the murder of Jason
Smith in 2002. The trial of six officers in connection with
the murder of seven young men in Braeton in March 2001
was scheduled to begin in January 2005.

Death penalty
In July, the Judicial Committee of the Privy Council in
the UK, the highest court of appeal for Jamaica, ruled
that mandatory death sentences for capital murder
violated the Constitution. The ruling requires that all
those currently under sentence of death be given new
sentencing hearings in order to present mitigating
evidence to the court.

Torture and ill-treatment
There were continuing reports of ill-treatment,
possibly amounting to torture, in police custody.
Conditions in prison and other places of detention
were harsh and in many cases amounted to cruel,
inhuman or degrading treatment.
    Conditions at the Tower Street Correctional Centre
led to a hunger strike by prisoners. Inmates were
reportedly held six to a cell of approximately 3m x 2m.
    There was a reported drop in violence between
inmates, but numerous prisoners were killed during
the year.
    In September, Mark Frazier was allegedly killed by
other prisoners in Montego Bay Freeport police lockup.
However, local residents alleged that he was beaten by
police officers while being taken into custody.

Violence against women

According to government figures, at least 550 rapes of women were reported to the authorities between January and July. Many of those raped declined to report the assault. In November, a government minister stated that one in five women aged between 15 and 19 are subjected to forced sexual intercourse.

Human rights defenders, gay men and lesbians

Those involved in defending human rights continued to face hostility. In November, the Police Federation called for human rights groups to cease their "illegal interference" and urged the government to charge them with sedition.

In November, the human rights organization Human Rights Watch released a report on abuses against gay men and lesbians, *Hated to Death: Homophobia, Violence and Jamaica's HIV/AIDS Epidemic.* Following the publication of the report, the gay and lesbian community also reported a rise in attacks and threats against homosexuals.

AI country reports/ visits
Visits

In October AI sent a pathologist to observe the autopsies of Sandra Sewell and Gayon Alcott. In November an AI delegation visited Jamaica to hold talks with national human rights groups.

JAPAN

JAPAN
Head of government: Koizumi Junichiro
Death penalty: retentionist
International Criminal Court: not signed
UN Women's Convention: ratified
Optional Protocol to UN Women's Convention: not signed

Two men were executed in 2004 in secret by hanging. At least 61 prisoners remained on death row. Refugee recognition procedures failed to meet international standards. The issue of reparations for forced sexual slavery during World War II remained unresolved.

Background

Peru continued to seek the extradition of former Peruvian President Alberto Fujimori, wanted in Peru for masterminding "death squad" massacres in Peru between 1991 and 1992. Alberto Fujimori, in exile in Japan since 2000, is considered a Japanese citizen because of his Japanese parentage, and therefore not subject to extradition. Interpol issued a worldwide notice for Alberto Fujimori's arrest in March 2003. In response to a second formal extradition request from Peru in February 2004, the Japanese government asked for further information.

In June, Japan stated that it would link future aid to Viet Nam with improvements in human rights. Japan halted new aid to Myanmar in 2003, and resumed only limited aid in 2004.

Japan was involved in bilateral and multilateral talks to resolve the North Korean nuclear crisis. Bilateral talks were held with North Korea to settle the issue of the alleged abduction of several hundred Japanese citizens in the 1970s and 1980s. In August the Japanese government announced that it would give North Korea food aid as well as medical aid and in November, four Japanese government officials went to North Korea to monitor its distribution.

Death penalty

Japan executed two death row inmates in September. Both executions — by hanging — were carried out in secret. The prisoners were informed only a few hours before the execution and their families and lawyers were told after the executions had taken place. The executions were carried out while parliament was in recess in an attempt to avoid public debate or criticism.

📁 Mamoru Takuma, who murdered eight schoolchildren in Osaka in 2001, was executed with unusual speed, less than a year after his death sentence had been finalized. He was reported to have a history of mental illness.

Death row inmates were kept in solitary confinement and communication with the outside world was very restricted. At least 25 prisoners whose sentences have been finalized have spent more than 10 years on death row awaiting execution. Ten per cent of death row inmates were reportedly victims of miscarriages of justice.

◻ In August the Tokyo High Court rejected a request for retrial by Hakamada Iwao, who had spent over 38 years in detention and always protested his innocence.

Refugees and migrants

The crackdown on illegal immigrants was strengthened after the government announced its security policy at the end of 2003. Businesses reportedly employing undocumented migrants were raided. The government also manipulated fear of "terrorism" to facilitate the forcible repatriation of thousands of foreign workers.

This crackdown was followed by an amendment to the Immigration Control and Refugee Recognition Law which raised the maximum fine for undocumented migrants and extended the maximum re-entry ban on deported foreigners from 5 to 10 years.

The new law scrapped the requirement that refugees apply for refugee status within 60 days of arrival. However, concerns regarding the detention of asylum-seekers remained. Mentally ill asylum-seekers continued to be detained without appropriate medical care and reports of suicide attempts continued. Some asylum-seekers were detained and thereby separated from their children. Several people were detained for years and were suddenly forcibly repatriated while their appeals were still pending. In 2004, of 426 people who applied for refugee status, only 15 were granted asylum.

◻ In February, the Tokyo District Court upheld the decision to reject refugee status for a gay Iranian man known as Shayda, despite numerous reports of homosexuals being executed in Iran. Shayda was recognized as a refugee by the UN refugee agency UNHCR in 2001. The Tokyo Court acknowledged that under Iran's Islamic penal law, those accused of same-sex acts face punishment, including the death penalty. However, the Court stated that Shayda could live in Iran safely as long as he did not "overtly" engage in such activities and that a person could find ways to avoid persecution. Shayda's application for refugee status was rejected in 2000, and he was then detained for 19 months for overstaying his visa.

◻ In November, a Vietnamese woman was forcibly repatriated to Viet Nam even though her husband (a refugee) and baby remained in Japan.

In August Japanese officials, assisted by the Turkish police, visited Turkey to investigate the families of those seeking asylum in Japan. Such investigations exposed asylum-seekers and their families to increased danger as information regarding individual applications was given to Turkish authorities.

Violence against women

The issue of reparations for former "comfort women" – women forced into sexual slavery during World War II – remained unresolved. In February, Tokyo's High Court rejected compensation claims by seven Taiwanese former "comfort women". The women claimed that they were victims of systematic sexual abuse by the Japanese Imperial Army and suffered discrimination after the war. They had demanded compensation and an official apology from the Japanese government. There were originally nine plaintiffs, but two died during the case.

In May Japan enacted a law against domestic violence providing protection not only to spouses but also to former spouses and children. The law allowed courts to order perpetrators from their homes and to stay away from spouses, former spouses and children.

AI country reports/ visits
Report
- Japan: Government endangers refugees' families in Turkey (AI Index: ASA 22/004/2004)

JORDAN

HASHEMITE KINGDOM OF JORDAN
Head of state: King 'Abdallah II bin al-Hussein
Head of government: Faisal al-Fayez
Death penalty: retentionist
International Criminal Court: ratified
UN Women's Convention: ratified with reservations
Optional Protocol to UN Women's Convention: not signed

At least 16 people were sentenced to death and one was executed. One man died in custody in Jweideh prison. Scores of political arrests were made, including for suspected "terrorist" activity, and there were reports of torture and ill-treatment in custody. At least 20 people were victims of family killings. Perpetrators continued to enjoy lenient sentences for killing female relatives for reasons of "honour".

Death penalty

At least 16 people were sentenced to death, nine of them in absentia. Ibtisam Hussain, a 24-year-old woman, was executed in March, the only known execution in the year. She was convicted of murdering two children aged five and six in 2002; an earlier sentence of manslaughter was overturned on appeal. She was the first woman to be executed in Jordan since May 2002.

Death in custody

'Abdallah al-Mashaqbeh died in Jweideh prison in early September apparently following clashes between prisoners and prison staff. The incident was investigated by the government-funded National Centre for Human Rights (NCHR), which submitted a report to the government containing evidence that the victim had been physically abused by prison staff and that people held in Jordan's prisons were being beaten. On 10 October, 11 police officers assigned to Jweideh prison pleaded not guilty in court on charges relating to the death of 'Abdallah al-Mashaqbeh.

Arrests and the State Security Court (SSC)

Scores of people were arrested for alleged "terrorist" activity and at least 18 security-related cases proceeded before the SSC. The SSC invariably uses panels of military judges and fails to provide adequate safeguards for fair trial. In at least six of the trials, defendants alleged that their "confessions" were made under torture. At least one case was referred to the National Institute of Forensic Medicine which concluded that the defendant had not been tortured. AI remained concerned that no judicial and impartial investigations were initiated into torture allegations.

◻ In December the trial before the SSC began of 13 men charged in connection with alleged attempts to carry out a chemical attack and of belonging to an illegal organization linked to al-Qa'ida. Four, including Abu Mus'ab al-Zarqawi, were being tried in absentia. Some of the defendants faced the death penalty if convicted. Four men were reportedly killed in April during clashes with security services who were making arrests in connection with these allegations.

Jordanian national Wisam 'Abd al-Rahman was released from US detention in Guantánamo Bay, Cuba, in the first quarter of the year. Reportedly, on his return to Jordan, he was held by the General Intelligence Department for 55 days, then placed under house arrest.

In October the government denied reports that it was allowing a detention centre to be run by the US Central Intelligence Agency (CIA) in Jordan to interrogate "terror" suspects.

Violence and discrimination against women

The National Institute of Forensic Medicine said that around 750 women a year visit forensic medical clinics in Amman after suffering domestic violence, although it estimated that the actual number of victims could be 10 times higher. On 2 September the authorities announced plans for the opening in early 2005 of the long-awaited government "family reconciliation" centre for victims of domestic violence. The Jordanian Women's Union continued to run a small shelter for women needing temporary refuge from domestic violence.

At least 20 people were victims of family killings, including two 17-year old girls, a baby and two men. In July the Justice Ministry proposed amendments to Article 98 of the Penal Code. Article 98 is often invoked in defence of men who kill their female relatives in a "fit of rage" caused by "unlawful" or "dangerous" acts on the part of the victim. The proposals included heavier sentencing — at least five years in prison — for such crimes. During 2004, at least two men who said they had killed women for reasons of "honour" benefited from Article 98.

◻ A man who killed his 18-year-old daughter, Amal, for reasons of "honour" was sentenced to six months'

imprisonment, in line with Article 98. The sentence was overturned on appeal and the case went for retrial in October. Amal had gone missing from her home and when she returned she was held for her own protection by the authorities. She was subsequently released when her father signed a guarantee that she would not be harmed by her family. He killed her the same day.

Proposed amendments by the government to the Personal Status Law to allow women the right to divorce without their husband's consent were rejected by the Lower House of Parliament and remained pending before the Upper House.

A campaign focusing on violence against women — 16 Days of Activism against Gender Violence — was launched in November by Jordanian non-governmental organizations including the NCHR.

AI country reports/ visits
Visits

AI delegates visited Jordan in March to research violence against women. The same month AI's Secretary General visited Jordan for the regional launch of AI's Stop Violence Against Women campaign.

KAZAKSTAN

REPUBLIC OF KAZAKSTAN
Head of state: Nursultan Nazarbaev
Head of government: Danial Akhmetov
Death penalty: retentionist
International Criminal Court: not signed
UN Women's Convention and its Optional Protocol: ratified

Uighur asylum-seekers and refugees were at risk of detention and forcible return to China. An independent journalist was released early and an opposition leader's terms of imprisonment were eased.

Background

In April Kazakstan signed a first Mutual Cooperation Agreement with the Council of Europe pledging to encourage total abolition of the death penalty and to submit annual reports on progress towards the rule of law. A moratorium on executions had been introduced in December 2003.

The Organization for Security and Co-operation in Europe (OSCE) said the September parliamentary elections, which saw the pro-presidential party Otan win over 60 per cent of the votes, fell short of OSCE and Council of Europe standards.

In November the National Security Committee (KNB) announced that it had arrested 13 men – nine from Kazakstan and four from Uzbekistan – in connection with a series of explosions and attacks on police checkpoints in March and April and three suicide bombings in July in neighbouring Uzbekistan. Four Kazak women were also detained, accused of having been trained as suicide bombers. All were described as members of a previously unknown organization, the Mujahedin of Central Asia, allegedly linked to the banned Islamic Movement of Uzbekistan and al-Qa'ida.

Uighur asylum-seekers and refugees

Members of the Uighur ethnic group who were returned to China were at risk of grave human rights violations.

In November the KNB announced that Kazakstan had extradited 14 Uighurs to China and Kyrgyzstan in the past six years. All were allegedly members of the East Turkestan Liberation Party and had been accused of "extremist" activities.

There was concern that increasing cooperation between Kazakstan and China could result in greater restrictions on freedom of expression, association and assembly for Uighur nationals in Kazakstan. Local Uighur activists expressed alarm at a series of racist media reports which described Uighurs as "separatists" or "terrorists".

Uighur asylum-seekers faced an ever-present risk of being detained by the police as "illegal immigrants", which put them in greater danger of being forcibly returned to China. Kazakstan did not allow Uighurs access to the national asylum procedure, reportedly because of the delicate relationship with China. Local non-governmental organizations (NGOs) working with Uighur asylum-seekers also reported growing numbers of cases where Uighurs "disappeared" and were presumed to have been forcibly returned to China.

Some NGOs were reportedly threatened, intimidated and harassed in order to prevent them from working with Uighurs.

Political prisoners – update

🗁 In August Galymzhan Zhakiyanov, one of the leaders of the opposition Democratic Choice of Kazakstan, was transferred from prison to a more relaxed regime at a so-called colony settlement in Pavlodar region. He had been sentenced to seven years' imprisonment in 2002 for "abuse of office" and financial crimes. The real reason for his imprisonment appeared to be his peaceful opposition activities.

🗁 Sergei Duvanov, an independent journalist, was conditionally released in August after serving half of his sentence. He had been sentenced in January 2003 to three and a half years in prison for rape after a trial which according to international observers fell far short of international fair trial standards and may have been politically motivated. On 29 December a court ordered his transfer to a colony settlement which allowed him to work and to live at home.

AI country reports/visits
Reports
· Europe and Central Asia: Summary of Amnesty International's concerns in the region, January-June 2004: Kazakstan (AI Index: EUR 01/005/2004)
· Belarus and Uzbekistan: The last executioners – The trend towards abolition in the former Soviet space (AI Index: EUR 04/009/2004)

KENYA

REPUBLIC OF KENYA
Head of state and government: Mwai Kibaki
Death penalty: abolitionist in practice
International Criminal Court: signed
UN Women's Convention: ratified
Optional Protocol to UN Women's Convention: not signed

Women and girls continued to be subjected to violence in the home, in the community and in the custody of the state. There were continuing reports of torture and ill-treatment by the police. Cases of excessive use of force and arbitrary shootings by police were also recorded. Conditions in detention frequently amounted to cruel, inhuman and degrading treatment. Death sentences continued to be imposed.

Background

The Constitutional Conference completed its work in March. However, despite attempts at consensus-building, the process of bringing the new constitution into force was repeatedly blocked. Contentious issues included chapters relating to the structures of the executive, the devolution of power, and the judiciary. The adoption of the new constitution, announced for 30 June, was again delayed, causing demonstrations around the country and engendering anti-government hostility. A new constitution was still pending at the end of 2004.

During a reshuffle of the National Rainbow Coalition (NARC) cabinet, in a bid to set up a government of national unity, members of the former governing party, the Kenya African National Union (KANU), were brought back into the government's ranks. NARC, a coalition of 14 different political parties, gained power following elections in December 2002.

Police struggled to respond adequately to the high level of violent crime recorded around the country, much of it committed using illicit firearms. There was a complete overhaul of the police force's top officers in March and the police high command presented a five-year strategic plan aiming at reforms.

In July, the Commission of Inquiry set up to investigate illegal or irregular allocation of land handed over its report to the government. Following public demand, the contents of the report were made public in December. In September police used tear gas to disperse members of the Maasai community who were demonstrating over land they lost in colonial times. Several protesters were arrested and one shot dead by police.

In October, Wangari Maathai, environmentalist and founder of the Green Belt Movement, received the Nobel Peace Prize for her contribution to democracy and sustainable development. An Assistant Minister for Environment in the present government, in the 1990s she was severely assaulted by riot police and jailed overnight for her leading role in campaigns against forest clearances and urban encroachment.

The trial of three men charged with the murder of 15 people in the Mombasa hotel bombing of 2002 was continuing at the end of 2004. They made new applications for bail in November, arguing that they could not be guaranteed that their trial would be conducted within a reasonable time as the prosecution had asked for an adjournment. Their application was rejected.

More people were arrested during "counter-terrorism" operations. The Attorney General announced in September that the Suppression of Terrorism Bill 2003 was being re-drafted to take into consideration comments received from the national and international human rights community.

The UN Security Council met in the capital Nairobi on 18-19 November. This was only the fourth time since 1952 that the full Security Council held a formal session outside its New York headquarters.

Violence against women

Violence against women was widespread, despite efforts to increase public awareness by the authorities and by civil society. Perpetrators included both state officials and private individuals.

◻ Margaret Muthoni Murage was six months pregnant when she was arrested on 4 May in Nairobi. Accused of stealing gold jewellery from her employer, the 17-year-old was taken to a police station for questioning. When AI delegates visited her in prison some two weeks later, she said that one of the officers repeatedly beat her, kicked her in the side and then knocked her, stomach-first, against the wall. She was taken to the counter and flung under it before being returned to the cell. Shortly afterwards she suffered a miscarriage in the police station. No action had been taken against the police officers by the end of 2004.

Women and girls were also subjected to domestic violence, sexual assault, rape, including of young children, incest, forced marriages and female genital mutilation. Gang rapes and rapes during robberies, burglaries and carjackings were frequently reported. Large numbers of women and girls were raped and murdered. From January to August, police recorded 1,895 rapes, but many more were not reported to police. In 2003 there were 2,308 rapes reported to

police. The Kenya Demographic Health Survey, released in August, indicated that more than half the women in Kenya had experienced violence since they were 15. The survey revealed that husbands inflicted 60 per cent of the beatings.

Women's rights groups attributed the low rate of convictions in sexual offences cases to a lack of trained police officers to carry out investigations, to difficulties in the preservation of forensic evidence in rape cases, and to a lack of lawyers with specialized training to prosecute such cases. Government institutions to support survivors of violence were inadequate and services such as shelters and counselling were lacking. There was no access to post-exposure prophylaxis against sexually transmitted diseases in rape cases.

The authorities announced several measures to address violence against women, including a special unit in the office of the Director of Public Prosecutions to handle sexual offences and a women-only police station (Kilimani Police Station, Nairobi) to deal exclusively with rape, domestic violence and child abuse cases. In October, the Kenya Women Parliamentarian Association sponsored a motion to allow the government to chemically castrate rapists. No debates had taken place on the issue by the end of 2004.

Torture

There were repeated public complaints that police officers tortured and ill-treated detainees. Although the law was amended in 2003 to prohibit the use of confessions made under duress as evidence in criminal proceedings, practices amounting to torture continued to be used as a means of investigation and to extract confessions. The authorities failed to investigate complaints of torture promptly and thoroughly.

◻ On 24 and 25 January, seven suspects were tortured at Matunda Police Station, Lugari District. They appeared before Kitale Court on 30 January. On seeing their condition, the magistrate ordered immediate medical treatment. A complaint about the torture was lodged with the relevant department within the police. No action had been taken against the offending police officers by the end of 2004.

Unlawful use of firearms by the police

Law enforcement officers used firearms in circumstances far wider than those allowed by international human rights standards, both during anti-crime operations and to disperse demonstrations. There were several reports of excessive use of force and killings by the police in disputed circumstances.

◻ On 7 July, police in the town of Kisumu fired live ammunition at unarmed demonstrators protesting against the delay in enacting the new constitution. Police killed one person and seriously injured at least 10. Several arrests were also made.

Harsh prison conditions and deaths in custody

Despite some reforms, prison conditions remained harsh. Chronic overcrowding continued to cause serious problems. An estimated 50,000-plus prisoners were held in the country's 92 prisons with a capacity of 19,000. The lack of basic health, nutrition and sanitation provision amounted to cruel, inhuman and degrading treatment. Understaffed and poorly trained prison wardens used excessive force to control inmates. Several people died in custody, allegedly as a result of ill-treatment.

📁 Five inmates died at Meru Prison on 26 September. According to a post-mortem, they died following injuries caused by blunt trauma and had multiple soft tissue injuries. They were reportedly kicked and struck with truncheons, mainly on the head and joints, on the day they died. They were then forced into a small cell which housed 18 prisoners on the fatal night. The five were discovered dead the next morning. Forty-five inmates reportedly died in suspicious circumstances in Meru prison during the first nine months of 2004, with 14 deaths recorded in September alone. Inquest files were opened at the Meru Court regarding the deaths of 26 September.

Death penalty

Death sentences continued to be imposed but the last executions were carried out in 1986. An important opportunity was lost to abolish the death penalty in Kenya during the constitutional review — the proposed draft constitution made no mention of abolishing it. A total of 101 death row prisoners were released following a court ruling that the prosecution's case had been led by officers below the rank of inspector, as required by the Penal Code. The legality of the release was questioned, as the law provides that death row convicts can be released only by the Court of Appeal or by presidential amnesty.

Statistics from Kamiti Maximum Security Prison in Nairobi indicated that by June 2004 there were 946 prisoners on death row of whom 66 had completed their appeal processes and were awaiting presidential pardon while 880 had appealed against their sentences.

AI country reports/visits

Reports
- Kenya: Memorandum to the Kenyan Government on the Suppression of Terrorism Bill 2003 (AI Index: AFR 32/003/2004)
- Kenya: The Government should fully investigate recent deaths in custody in Meru district (AI Index: AFR 32/006/2004)

Visit
AI delegates visited Kenya in May/June to conduct research.

KOREA
(DEMOCRATIC PEOPLE'S REPUBLIC OF)

DEMOCRATIC PEOPLE'S REPUBLIC OF KOREA
Head of state: Kim Jong-il
Head of government: Pak Pong-ju
Death penalty: retentionist
International Criminal Court: not signed
UN Women's Convention: ratified
Optional Protocol to UN Women's Convention: not signed

The government continued to fail in its duty to uphold and protect the right to food, exacerbating the effects of the long-standing food crisis. Chronic malnutrition among children and urban populations, especially in the northern provinces, was widespread. Fundamental rights, including freedom of expression, association and movement, continued to be denied. Access by independent monitors continued to be severely restricted. There were reports of widespread political imprisonment, torture and ill-treatment, and of executions.

Background
Relations between North and South Korea cooled during the year. In July South Korean navy ships fired at a North Korean ship that had crossed the western sea border. Notwithstanding, in October, South Korea pledged to support a World Food Programme (WFP) emergency operation in North Korea aimed at 6.5 million vulnerable people, most of them children and women. In addition, South Korea promised 1.2 million tons of rice in the form of concessional loans to North Korea.

The third round of six-party talks (involving North and South Korea, China, Japan, Russia and the USA) aimed at persuading North Korea to cease its nuclear weapons programme met in Beijing in June, but little progress was achieved. North Korea refused to attend a fourth round scheduled for September. North Korea warned in October that it would use "war deterrent force" if the USA brought the nuclear dispute before the UN Security Council.

In October, the US President signed into law the North Korean Human Rights Act of 2004, which provided humanitarian assistance and for North Koreans to be granted asylum in the USA.

International scrutiny of human rights record
In April, the UN Commission on Human Rights passed a resolution expressing deep concern about continuing reports of systemic, widespread and grave violations of human rights. A Special Rapporteur on the situation of human rights in North Korea was appointed in July.

In June, the UN Committee on the Rights of the Child (CRC) expressed concern at the limitations on civil and political rights of North Koreans, including children. It also expressed concern that the minimum age for voluntary enlistment in the armed forces was

16 and that school children were taught to assemble and dismantle weapons. The CRC raised concerns about the independence and impartiality of the authorities taking sentencing decisions in the juvenile justice system.

Denial of access

Information and access continued to be highly controlled. A three-member delegation of the CRC was allowed unprecedented access in April. However, despite repeated requests, the government continued to deny access to the UN Special Rapporteur on the human rights situation in North Korea and the UN Special Rapporteur on the right to food as well as to AI and other independent human rights monitors.

In October, the WFP announced that its staff in North Korea were not permitted free access to monitor aid distribution for "security reasons". This continued obstruction by the government and denial of access to monitors undermined accurate assessment of the population's need for food assistance.

Freedom of expression

Severe restrictions on freedom of expression and association persisted. The news media was controlled by a single political party, which journalists were coerced into joining. According to reports, at least 40 journalists since the mid-1990s have been "re-educated" for errors such as misspelling a senior official's name. Radio and television sets were tuned to receive only state broadcasts and those who listened to foreign radio stations risked being punished.

Freedom from hunger and malnutrition

Millions of North Koreans continued to suffer hunger and chronic malnutrition. Continued government restrictions on freedom of movement and information, lack of transparency and hampering of independent monitoring meant that food aid may not always have reached those most in need.

Rations from the Public Distribution System – the primary source of staple food for more than 70 per cent of the population – were reportedly set to decline from the already insufficient 319g per person per day in 2003 to 300g in 2004. Urban families reportedly spent up to 85 per cent of their incomes on food. Such households were heavily dependent on inflation-prone private markets, where staples cost 10 to 15 times more than in the government-run system.

Much of the population was afflicted by critical dietary deficiencies, consuming very little protein, fat or micro-nutrients. The CRC expressed concern about increasing infant and child mortality rates, high rates of malnourishment and stunting in children, and alarming increases in maternal mortality rates. It also expressed serious concern about lack of access to clean drinking water and poor sanitation.

The acute food shortages forced thousands to cross "illegally" to China's north-eastern provinces. Those repatriated faced detention, interrogation and imprisonment in poor conditions.

Torture and ill-treatment

North Koreans forcibly repatriated from China were detained and interrogated in detention centres or police stations operated by the National Security Agency or the People's Safety Agency.

▢ Three North Korean nationals – Chang Gyung-chul, his brother Chang Gyung-soo and their cousin Chang Mi-hwa – were arrested by Chinese Security Police in Shanghai, China, in August 2003. They were taken to Sinuiju City, North Korea, for interrogation, then transferred to the National Security Agency detention centre in North Hamgyung Province.

In September 2004 Chang Gyung-chul and Chang Gyung-soo were each sentenced to 10 years' imprisonment, apparently because of their unauthorized departure from North Korea. The unusually harsh sentence was attributed to the fact that their mother, Shin Jong-ai, who is now a South Korean citizen, was earlier imprisoned on similar charges.

Beatings were reportedly common during interrogation. If prisoners were caught communicating, they were beaten with wooden sticks or iron bars. After the beating, cold water was reportedly poured over the prisoners' bodies, even in the middle of winter. Some prisoners were reportedly subjected to "water torture", where they were tied up and forced to drink large quantities of water.

Conditions in detention centres and prisons (which were severely overcrowded) worsened, partly as a result of the lack of food. Food shortages also reportedly resulted in deaths from malnutrition in political penal labour colonies or "control and management places". Prisoners charged with breaking prison rules had their food cut even further.

In June, the CRC expressed concern at reports of institutional violence against juveniles, especially in detention and in social institutions.

Executions

Reports of public executions continued to be received, although fewer in number than in previous years. Executions were by firing squad or hanging. The UN Commission on Human Rights resolution on North Korea expressed concern at public executions and the imposition of the death penalty for political reasons. Reports also suggested that extrajudicial executions and secret executions took place in detention facilities.

Women in custody

Women detainees were reportedly subjected to degrading prison conditions. Women detained after being forcibly returned from China were reportedly compelled to remove all clothes and were subjected to intimate body searches. Women stated that, during pre-trial detention, the male guards humiliated them and touched them inappropriately. All women, including those who were pregnant or elderly, were forced to work from early morning to late at night in fields or prison factories. Prisons lacked basic facilities for women's needs.

North Korean asylum-seekers in Asia

Hundreds of North Koreans tried to enter foreign diplomatic missions and foreign-run schools in Beijing. More than 100 were in diplomatic missions, waiting for permission to leave China. In October, the Chinese government claimed that the diplomatic missions involved were too tolerant.

In July, at least 468 North Koreans flew from Viet Nam to South Korea, becoming the biggest single group of North Korean asylum-seekers to arrive there since the division of the peninsula. More than 5,000 North Koreans had reached South Korea and been granted South Korean nationality.

In October, Mongolian authorities detained two North Koreans seeking to reach the USA. They were attempting to fly to South Korea from where they hoped to take advantage of the US North Korean Human Rights Act of 2004.

The CRC expressed concern at reports of North Korean street children in Chinese border towns. It was also deeply concerned at reports that children (and their families) returning or deported back to North Korea were considered not as victims, but as perpetrators of a crime.

AI country reports/ visits
Report
· Starved of Rights: Human rights and the food crisis in the Democratic People's Republic of Korea (North Korea) (AI Index: ASA 24/003/2004)

KOREA
(REPUBLIC OF)

REPUBLIC OF KOREA
Head of state: Roh Moo-hyun
Head of government: Lee Hae-chan (replaced Goh Kun in June)
Death penalty: retentionist
International Criminal Court: ratified
UN Women's Convention: ratified with reservations
Optional Protocol to UN Women's Convention: not signed

Prisoners continued to be sentenced to death, but an unofficial moratorium on executions in place since 1998 continued. More than 60 prisoners were under sentence of death at the end of 2004. Prisoners of conscience continued to be held under the controversial National Security Law. Under a new work permit system, at least 180,000 undocumented migrant workers faced immediate detention and subsequent deportation. At least 758 conscientious objectors were imprisoned for refusing to perform compulsory military service.

Background
President Roh Moo-hyun was impeached in March — the first time a South Korean President had been impeached — on charges of incompetence and mismanagement. The impeachment was reversed by the Constitutional Court in May. During the interim, Prime Minister Goh Kun served as acting President. In National Assembly elections in April, the newly established Uri Party won a majority of seats.

Inter-Korean talks continued but were stalled when at least 468 North Koreans seeking asylum in Viet Nam went to South Korea in July.

Following investigations of unauthorized nuclear testing and other matters by an International Atomic Energy Agency (IAEA) team in August, the IAEA director-general expressed "serious concern" over South Korea's failure to report its nuclear experiments.

National Security Law
The NSL, which provides long sentences or the death penalty for loosely defined "anti-state" activities or espionage, was the subject of intense political debate. In August the Constitutional Court ruled that the NSL was not unconstitutional. In September, the National Human Rights Commission recommended the abolition of the NSL. President Roh also called for the law to be abolished.

As of December 2004, at least nine prisoners were held under the NSL. Six were members of the national students' organization, Hanchongnyeon, which was banned in 1997.

🗁 Professor Song Du-yul, a German national of South Korean origin, was sentenced in March to seven years' imprisonment by the Seoul District Court for "joining an anti-state organization" and supporting an "enemy-benefiting organization", under the NSL. He was a prisoner of conscience. Professor Song was released in July 2004 by the Seoul High Court which overturned the main charges and substituted a suspended sentence. Prosecutors appealed to the Supreme Court. Professor Song was allowed to leave the country.

Migrant workers
The Employment Permit System Act came into effect in August, giving the Ministry of Labour a legislative structure to control and monitor migrant workers for the first time. The Act allows migrant workers with visas to work for a maximum of three years, and gives some protection of basic rights. However, undocumented workers who have stayed longer than four years are liable to immediate detention pending deportation. Employers face large fines if they employ undocumented workers.

In October, there were at least 180,000 undocumented migrant workers not registered with the authorities, many of whom were unemployed. Others provided cheap labour, often in dangerous conditions.

Migrant workers faced widespread discrimination. Many were beaten by employers. They received less pay than Korean workers for the same work. Many were not paid regularly and most did not receive severance pay.

Leaders of migrant workers' unions were targeted by the authorities. At least five migrant union leaders were reportedly deported to their countries of origin in 2003-2004.

📁 Samar Thapa, a Nepali national, chief of the Emergency Struggle Committee of the Equality Trade Union – Migrants' Branch, was forcibly deported to Nepal in April. He had been detained by immigration authorities in February in Seoul while leading a demonstration. At the time, investigations were continuing into complaints he had submitted to the National Human Rights Commission of Korea concerning human rights abuses against migrant workers, and to the Ministry of Labour for non-receipt of his salary. He was detained in Yeosu detention centre where he went on hunger strike and was reportedly in poor health.

Conscientious objectors
As of June 2004, at least 758 conscientious objectors, mostly Jehovah's Witnesses, were detained for refusing to perform compulsory military service. The government consistently refused to make available the civilian alternative to military service to those objecting on grounds of conscience. Prison terms for conscientious objectors appeared to have reduced in length, but with criminal records their future employment prospects are damaged.

📁 Lim Taehoon, a 28-year-old gay rights activist, refused to perform military service because of his pacifist ideals and because of discrimination against gay, bisexual and transgender people by the military. He was arrested in February and at the end of 2004 was still detained in Seoul Detention Centre.

AI country reports/ visits
Reports
- Republic of Korea (South Korea): Open Letter to all Leaders of Political Parties (AI Index: ASA 25/009/2004)
- Republic of Korea (South Korea): Open Letter to newly elected Members of the 17th National Assembly (AI Index: ASA 25/004/2004)
- Republic of Korea (South Korea): Open letter to Acting President Goh Kun – Continued use of the draconian National Security Law (AI Index: ASA 25/003/2004)
Visit
An AI delegation visited Seoul between September and October.

KUWAIT

STATE OF KUWAIT
Head of state: al-Shaikh Jaber al-Ahmad al-Sabah
Head of government: al-Shaikh Sabah al-Ahmad al-Sabah
Death penalty: retentionist
International Criminal Court: signed
UN Women's Convention: ratified with reservations
Optional Protocol to UN Women's Convention: not signed

The effects of the ongoing US-led "war on terror" and the deteriorating security situation in Iraq were felt in Kuwait. Arrests were made of individuals suspected of involvement with alleged militant groups, including those fighting against US forces in Iraq. Demands grew for reforms, particularly for women's political enfranchisement, and the government consequently reintroduced a bill to amend the electoral law. At least nine executions were reported.

Human rights developments
The first official human rights non-governmental organization in Kuwait was established in August when the Ministry of Social Affairs and Labour granted a licence to the Kuwait Human Rights Society, some 10 years after it was formed.

In June, the Chair of the National Assembly's Human Rights Committee announced that, following a meeting of the Committee in which the *Amnesty International Report 2004* was discussed, a committee would be formed to prepare an annual report on human rights in Kuwait. Plans to create a women's issues committee were also announced.

Diplomatic relations with Iraq were resumed in August. Kuwaiti forensic teams continued to inspect mass graves in Iraq. By the end of the year the total number of Kuwaiti prisoners of war whose remains had been identified had reached 190.

Arrests on grounds of national security
Security measures were tightened following a surge of violence in neighbouring Iraq and bombings in Saudi Arabia. In May the Gulf Cooperation Council signed a "counter-terrorism" pact, strengthening cooperation and coordination among security agencies and improving the exchange of intelligence information.

At least 20 people were reportedly arrested in a crackdown on those suspected of involvement with networks apparently enlisting Kuwaitis to fight US forces in Iraq. Those arrested alleged that they were tortured and ill-treated, denied access to lawyers, and forced to make confessions. On 28 November, 22 men went on trial in Kuwait City, charged with taking part in an aggressive act against a friendly country; raising funds for Islamist activists engaged in fighting US-led forces in Iraq; and illegal possession of weapons. Six suspects who attended the hearing denied the charges against them. The session was adjourned. At the end of the year, two of the suspects remained in custody, 16 had been released on bail, and four others, named previously by the Interior Ministry as wanted for questioning, remained at large.

Hamad Nawaf al-Harbi, Mohamed Essa al-Asfour, Ahmed Abdullah al-Otaibi and Bader Hamlan al-Otaibi were arrested in July. They alleged that they were tortured by security forces, denied access to their lawyers during interrogation, and forced to make false confessions. The men reportedly went on hunger strike but ended it after they were threatened with being moved to a cell holding criminal prisoners where they could be at risk of violence from inmates. They were released on bail in August after being charged with supporting and recruiting on behalf of "terrorist" groups, including those fighting US forces in Iraq. They called for a reinvestigation of their cases on the grounds that they had been forced to make false confessions. In October, the Ministry of the Interior issued a statement denying allegations that those accused of links to the insurgency in Iraq had been tortured.

In April, the convictions of four men arrested in November 2002 were quashed on appeal. Mohsen al-Fadli, Adel Bu Hemaid, Maqboul Fahad al-Maqboul and Mohammed al-Mutairi had been convicted of "joining a foreign nation's military and endangering the security of Kuwait" and sentenced to five years' imprisonment in February 2003. They had been freed on bail in December 2003 pending the appeal.

Women's rights

In March, a parliamentary committee rejected a government proposal to grant women the right to vote and stand as candidates in municipal elections. In May a bill amending the electoral law to grant women the right to vote and run for political office was approved by the Cabinet and sent to the National Assembly for ratification. A similar measure was narrowly defeated in 1999 owing to opposition by Islamist members of parliament. In a speech before parliament in October, the Amir, al-Shaikh Jaber al-Ahmad al-Sabah, urged that the bill be ratified. Islamist members of parliament later announced that they would support the right of women to vote, but were undecided on women's right to run for political office.

Following Kuwait's submission of its combined initial and second periodic report issued in January, the UN Committee on the Elimination of Discrimination against Women criticized women's lack of political rights in Kuwait. It said this seriously limited their ability to enjoy other rights protected under the Convention, and was therefore contrary to its object and purpose. The Committee also "expressed concern at the continuing existence of *de jure* discrimination against women in various laws", including the Nationality Act, the Personal Status Act, the Civil Code and the Private Sector Employment Act.

There were several reports of the abuse, including rape, of migrant domestic workers, who number around 400,000 in Kuwait.

Freedom of expression

Arrests and trials took place in violation of the right to freedom of expression.

Yasser al-Habib, aged 21, who was arrested in November 2003, was sentenced in January to one year's imprisonment and fined US$3,340. He was reportedly charged with "insulting the Prophet Mohammed's companions, abusing a religious sect and distributing an audiotape without a licence", in connection with an audiotape recording of a closed lecture that he gave on Islamic historical issues. In February he was released under an annual pardon announced by the Amir of Kuwait on the occasion of the country's National Day, but his rearrest was ordered a few days later. The public prosecutor said the release had been an error. Yasser al-Habib went into hiding. An appeals court dismissed the original verdict and ordered a retrial, reportedly upgrading the charges. In May, Yasser al-Habib was sentenced in absentia to 10 years' imprisonment. According to unconfirmed information, charges against him included seeking to overthrow the state and belonging to an organization that seeks to overthrow the state.

AI country reports/ visits
Report
- The Gulf and the Arabian Peninsula: Human rights fall victim to the "war on terror" (AI Index: MDE 04/002/2004)

Visits
AI visited Kuwait in January to conduct research on detainees held in the context of the "war on terror" and in July to conduct research for the Gulf Stop Violence Against Women project (see Middle East/North Africa Regional Overview 2004).

KYRGYZSTAN

KYRGYZ REPUBLIC
Head of state: Askar Akaev
Head of government: Nikolai Tanaev
Death penalty: retentionist
International Criminal Court: signed
UN Women's Convention and its Optional Protocol: ratified

Uighur asylum-seekers and refugees faced the risk of being detained by police and of being forcibly returned to China. Conditions on death row were reported to be cruel and inhuman. Despite its own moratorium on executions, Kyrgyzstan continued to deport people to face execution in China and Uzbekistan.

Uighur asylum-seekers and refugees
In March, Kyrgyzstan formally ratified an extradition treaty with China. Local non-governmental organizations estimated that Kyrgyzstan had returned around 50 Uighurs to China in recent years, despite the risks they faced there of serious human rights violations. In 2001 the two countries had signed a bilateral agreement on fighting "terrorism", "extremism" and "separatism" under the Shanghai Cooperation Organization. There was concern that such agreements could also be used by Kyrgyzstan to restrict the rights of Uighur nationals to freedom of expression, association and assembly.

Local Uighur activists expressed alarm at a series of racist media reports, including generalized descriptions of Uighurs as "separatists" or "terrorists".

An Uighur asylum-seeker reported that the police had accused him of being a "separatist" and a "terrorist" when they arrested him in Bishkek. The officers ignored the official document issued to him by the UN High Commissioner for Refugees (UNHCR) and took him to a detention centre. He was only released following intervention by the UNHCR.

Deported to face execution
At least eight men were in danger of extradition to China and Uzbekistan where they were at high risk of torture and execution. Two Uighurs extradited to China in July 2002 were reportedly sentenced to death in January and executed in March.

On 19 February, Uzbek nationals Nodir Karimov (also known as Asadullo Abdullaev) and Ilkhom Izattulaiev were sentenced to death by the Military Court of Kyrgyzstan for involvement in violent crimes with a "religious extremist" basis, including a bomb attack on a market in Bishkek in December 2002. At the end of 2004 the two were believed to be on death row in Bishkek. If extradited to Uzbekistan they would be at imminent risk of torture and execution.

Death penalty
A moratorium on executions in force since 1998 was extended until the end of 2004. According to official information, 31 men were sentenced to death between 30 June 2003 and 30 June 2004.

Conditions on death row
At least 130 men were believed to be on death row at the end of 2004. The Kyrgyzstani Ombudsman reported problems with conditions, including overcrowding, on death row in two prisons. Dozens reportedly died from illnesses or by committing suicide and some who had been kept in single cells for a long time had lost the ability to move around unaided. He also reported that short visits by relatives and daily exercise periods had been banned.

AI country reports/ visits
Reports
- Europe and Central Asia: Summary of Amnesty International's concerns in the region, January-June 2004: Kyrgyzstan (AI Index: EUR 01/005/2004)
- Belarus and Uzbekistan: The last executioners – The trend towards abolition in the former Soviet space (AI Index: EUR 04/009/2004)

LAOS

LAO PEOPLE'S DEMOCRATIC REPUBLIC
Head of state: Khamtay Siphandone
Head of government: Bounyang Vorachit
Death penalty: retentionist
International Criminal Court: not signed
UN Women's Convention: ratified
Optional Protocol to UN Women's Convention: not signed

Serious human rights concerns persisted. The Lao military stepped up its offensive against the mainly ethnic Hmong rebel groups. Reports of torture and at least two deaths in custody lent weight to concerns about conditions of detention and the state of the judicial system. At least four prisoners of conscience remained in detention. Despite death sentences being handed down by the courts, there were no reports of executions. There was increased suppression of religious practice, especially of evangelical Christianity.

Background
The government made some efforts to increase transparency and its engagement with the international community on human rights issues.

Foreign journalists again covertly visited ethnic Hmong rebels, increasing international attention on the issue.

Laos played an increasingly active political role regionally. It became a member of the Asia-Europe Meeting and took on the rotating presidencies of both the Association of South East Asian Nations and the Mekong River Commission, with the Secretariat of this sub-regional grouping relocating to Vientiane in July.

Laos continued to delay ratification of the International Covenant on Civil and Political Rights and the International Covenant on Economic, Social and Cultural Rights, both of which it signed in 2000.

Ethnic Hmong conflict

The ongoing internal armed conflict with predominantly ethnic Hmong minorities continued unabated. Covert visits by international journalists to some of the rebel groups highlighted concerns about access to food and medicine. Reports emerged that in May, five children aged between 13 and 16 – four of them girls – were mutilated and murdered by members of the Lao military. The girls were apparently raped before being killed. The Lao authorities strongly denied these allegations of war crimes, denouncing evidence provided, including video footage, as a fraud. An unknown number of rebels and their families reportedly "surrendered" during the year. The authorities continued to refuse unrestricted access by the international community, including humanitarian agencies of the UN, to those who had "surrendered" or to areas where the conflict continued. During 2004 small numbers of refugees from the conflict began to emerge in neighbouring Thailand.

◻ Thao Moua and Pa Fue Khang, sentenced to 12 and 15 years' imprisonment respectively in June 2003 for assisting foreign journalists reporting on the conflict, were transferred to Samkhe prison in Vientiane. Reports indicated that they, along with other prisoners in Samkhe, were given arduous tasks impossible to complete, resulting in harsh punishment. Va Char Yang, who was originally arrested along with the two but escaped from police custody, fled the country and was resettled by the UN High Commissioner for Refugees (UNHCR). He reported that he was badly beaten in detention.

Political prisoners and conditions in detention

Prisoners of conscience Feng Sakchittaphong and Latsami Khamphoui, both 63-year-old former government officials jailed for advocating peaceful economic change, reached the end of their 14-year prison sentence in October. Both men were permitted to leave Laos for France in December to seek medical care and join family members.

During 2004 information emerged that Khamphouvieng Sisaath had died in custody in September 2001 as a result of punishment inflicted by prison guards. He had been among five members of the Lao Students' Movement for Democracy arrested after attempting to hold a peaceful demonstration in Vientiane in October 1999. He was reported to have been tied spread-eagle to a post in the prison grounds and left there for several hours in the hot sun. He died from heat exhaustion. The other confirmed members of the group – Thongpaseuth Keuakoun and Seng-Aloun Phengphanh – remained in Samkhe prison, where they were serving sentences for treason. The authorities continued to dispute the identity of Bouavanh Chanhmanivong and Keochay, two others reportedly detained with the group in 1999. The length of prison terms imposed on the group remained unclear.

◻ Sing Chanthakoummane and Pangtong Chokbengboun continued to be imprisoned at Prison Camp 7. They had been arrested in 1975 and detained without charge or trial for 17 years for "re-education" before being sentenced to life imprisonment after an unfair trial in 1992. They were believed to be the last two remaining prisoners detained at the end of the civil war after the establishment of the Lao People's Democratic Republic.

A group of 16 Lao nationals were finally deported to Laos from Thailand in July. The men, members of an opposition group, were involved in an armed attack in Champassak province in 2000. They were tried and sentenced in October. Their place of detention was not known and concerns persisted about their health and treatment by the authorities.

African prisoners detained in Phonthong prison, Vientiane, were subjected to racism and particularly harsh treatment by prison guards. There was no African diplomatic presence in Laos to offer consular assistance.

◻ Information emerged that Ibrahim Kalin, of Liberian origin, was severely beaten by guards in Phonthong prison, reportedly in October 2002 after a conflict with another inmate. He was hospitalized two days later and subsequently died from his injuries.

Freedom of religious practice

Numerous incidents of religious repression of evangelical Christians were reported, including several cases of people being imprisoned or put into wooden "stocks" for not renouncing their faith. The majority of reports emanated from district level. Their number and consistency indicated that official government policy on freedom of religion, reported to have been relaxed in recent years, had not been implemented uniformly.

Death penalty

At least seven people, including one woman, were sentenced to death for drug-related offences. The total number of people on death row remained unclear. No executions were reported. A number of offences remained punishable by the death penalty, but no executions were known to have been carried out for over 11 years.

◻ Mohammed Abubakari, a Ghanaian national, was sentenced to death in August on drugs-related charges. While it was reported that he was defended by a local lawyer, he did not receive any consular assistance.

Economic, social and cultural rights

The Nam Theun 2 dam project, supported by the World Bank, received a boost when France agreed to become a major investor. However, the project continued to face international criticism from environmental and human rights groups. There were concerns over the future resettlement of up to 6,000 people in the area to be flooded and over the impact the dam would have on the economic, social and cultural rights of around 40,000 people downstream.

Concern also continued about the reported high mortality rates of "upland Lao" involved in a government resettlement programme to lowland areas. The controversial programme was part of efforts to eradicate opium poppy cultivation – which reportedly dropped significantly during 2004 – and to address the poor provision of basic health and education services to upland Lao.

Access for human rights organizations

AI made its first visit to the country in February and met representatives from the Foreign Ministry and the Ministry of Justice. Official access within the country for human rights organizations, including AI, remained severely limited, however, hampering the collection of independent and impartial information about human rights.

AI country reports/ visits
Statements
- Laos: Mass surrender of ethnic minority rebels and their families (AI Index: ASA 26/001/2004)
- Laos: Military atrocities against Hmong children are war crimes (AI Index: ASA 26/004/2004)

LATVIA

REPUBLIC OF LATVIA
Head of state: Vaira Vike-Freiberga
Head of government: Aigars Kalvītis (replaced Indulis Emsis in December)
Death penalty: abolitionist for ordinary crimes
International Criminal Court: ratified
UN Women's Convention: ratified
Optional Protocol to UN Women's Convention: not signed

Concerns about violence against women, among other issues, were raised with the Latvian authorities by a UN monitoring committee and the Council of Europe's Commissioner for Human Rights after examination of Latvia's human rights obligations.

Violence against women in the home

In July the UN Committee on the Elimination of Discrimination against Women considered Latvia's initial, second and third periodic reports on its implementation of the UN Women's Convention. The Committee noted a number of positive aspects, including progress in legislative reform. However, among its areas of concern were the lack of sufficient data and information on the prevalence of violence against women, particularly domestic violence, and of comprehensive legislation on such violence. These deficiencies appeared to indicate that violence against women, particularly in the family, was considered a private matter between the individuals involved. The Committee was also concerned that marital rape was not a separate offence in the criminal code.

Among its recommendations, the Committee urged Latvia to adopt legislation on domestic violence and ensure that the perpetrators of violence against women were brought to justice. Women who had experienced violence should be provided with immediate means of redress and protection, including protection or restraining orders, and with access to legal aid. There should be sufficient numbers of shelters to meet the needs of women at risk of violence in the home. Marital rape should be criminalized as a separate offence. The Committee also recommended that law enforcement and other officials receive training to sensitize them to all forms of violence against women. The Committee additionally urged Latvia to ratify the Optional Protocol to the Convention, which provides a procedure for the submission of individual complaints to the Committee.

The Council of Europe's Commissioner for Human Rights also raised concerns about domestic violence in a report, published in February, of his visit to Latvia in October 2003. He noted reports that such violence was relatively common, and that the courts and police appeared to play down its seriousness, treating it as of private concern only.

Trafficking of women

Both the Committee and the Commissioner, while recognizing the legislative and other measures that the government had already taken, expressed concern about the continued trafficking of women and girls for the purposes of sexual exploitation. The Committee called, among a number of other recommendations, for the full implementation and funding of a national strategy to combat trafficking in women and girls. It urged that Latvia take action towards improving the economic situation of women, to eliminate their vulnerability to traffickers, and introduce rehabilitation and reintegration measures for women and girl survivors of trafficking, including special shelters.

LEBANON

LEBANESE REPUBLIC
Head of state: Emile Lahoud
Head of government: 'Umar Karami (replaced Rafiq al-Hariri in October)
Death penalty: retentionist
International Criminal Court: not signed
UN Women's Convention: ratified with reservations
Optional Protocol to UN Women's Convention: not signed

Scores of people, including Islamist activists and members of opposition groups, were arrested for political reasons. Most were released after short periods. Trials of Sunni Islamist activists accused of "terrorism" and other state security offences continued. There were reports of torture and ill-treatment, and at least two detainees died in custody. There was an apparent increase of violence against women. Attacks on freedom of expression and association continued. At least three people were sentenced to death and three executions were carried out. Human rights groups and members of parliament stepped up their campaign for the abolition of the death penalty.

Background

In September the authorities amended the Constitution to allow an extension of President Emile Lahoud's term of office. The government's proposed amendment was supported by a majority in parliament. Opponents rejected it as unconstitutional and linked it to undue interference by Syria in the internal affairs of the country. The amendment was passed one day after the UN Security Council issued Resolution 1559 sponsored by the USA and France calling for the respect of Lebanese sovereignty, the withdrawal of all foreign troops from the country and the disbanding of Lebanese and non-Lebanese militias. Four ministers resigned from the government in protest at the amendment. In October Marwan Hamadah, one of the ministers who resigned in September, escaped with injuries requiring surgery when a bomb planted in his car exploded. His bodyguard, Ghazi Abu-Karrum, was killed. The case was referred to the investigating military magistrate.

A new government led by 'Umar Karami was formed following the resignation in October of Prime Minister Rafiq al-Hariri, which included for the first time two women ministers.

Syria withdrew some 3,000 troops during the year.

A draft law calling for the abolition of the death penalty was presented to parliament by seven members of parliament as part of a national campaign to end the death penalty. A new "terrorism law" was passed in the context of the government's move to introduce a new Penal Code, a draft of which was being considered by parliament. A campaign led by human rights group Hurriyyat Khasah (Private Liberties) to promote respect for the rights of lesbians and gay men was stepped up during the year. It included calls for reform of provisions of the Penal Code that criminalize homosexuality.

Arrests

Scores of people, mostly Sunni Islamist activists and members of opposition groups, were arrested for political reasons. Among them were members of two banned opposition groups, the Free Patriotic Movement and the Lebanese Forces, most of whom were released after short periods. Dozens of members of the banned Islamist Hizb al-Tahrir (Liberation Party) were detained for days or weeks and released on bail pending trials including before the Military Court. They were arrested for the peaceful expression of their political and religious opinions, including organizing a sit-down in July in Tripoli, northern Lebanon, to protest against the visit to Lebanon of the interim Iraqi Prime Minister, Iyad 'Allawi.

▢ Dozens of Sunni Islamist activists arrested in September without due legal process and detained incommunicado in secret detention centres remained held without access to their lawyers and families. They were arrested following raids carried out by the security forces in different parts of the country, including the south and the Beqa' Valley. The former Interior Minister accused them of involvement in "terrorism" and plots to bomb embassies, the Justice Palace and other places. The detainees included Ahmad Salim al-Miqati, Nabil Jallul, Jamal 'Abd al-Wahid, Shafiq al-Banna and Isma'il al-Khatib. Two women — Latifa al-Khatib, the sister of Isma'il al-Khatib, and An'am Jallul, the sister of Nabil Jallul — were released, apparently without charge, following public protests against the serious violations surrounding the arrests and the subsequent death in custody of Isma'il al-Khatib (see below).

Trials

Trials of Sunni Islamist activists before the Justice Council and other courts on charges of "terrorism" and other state security offences continued during the year. Trials before the Justice Council of dozens of Islamist activists, known as the Dhinniyyah detainees, charged with "terrorism" and other state security offences entered a fourth year. Proceedings fell short of international standards. There appeared to be no prospect of the detainees receiving a fair trial. The charges against them carry the death penalty.

▢ In March the Military Court sentenced a group of Islamist activists, including six Palestinians, a Yemeni national and a Lebanese national, to up to 20 years in prison on charges of "terrorism", including operating a "terrorist" network and involvement in bombing US fast-food restaurants. Mu'ammar 'Abdallah 'Al- 'Awami was sentenced to 20 years in prison with hard labour; Usamah Lutfi Salih, Usamah Amin al-Shihabi, and Amin Anis Dib were given 15 years in prison with hard labour; and 'Ali Musa Masri was sentenced to five years in prison. 'Ali Muhammad Qasim Hatim and Muhammad 'Abd-al-Karim al-Sa'di (also known as Abu-Muhjin), the alleged leader of the banned Sunni Islamist group 'Usbat al-Ansar or League of Supporters, were tried in absentia and sentenced to life imprisonment with hard labour and 15 years in prison with hard labour respectively.

Torture and deaths in custody

There were reports of torture and ill-treatment, and at least two detainees died in custody.

▢ In September Isma'il al-Khatib died in custody after more than 10 days' incommunicado detention at a secret location. Following his arrest (along with dozens of Sunni Islamist activists) he was described by the authorities as the leader of an al-Qa'ida network in the country. An official medical report stated that he died of a heart attack and that he had suffered, among other things, difficulty in breathing, swollen feet and liver problems. The report was repudiated by the family, including his sister who had been detained with him and said she heard him screaming in pain. Photographs taken of Isma'il al-Khatib after his death showed serious wounds on his body. The government ordered an investigation into his death.

Violence against women

There was apparently an increase in violence against women. At least six women were killed during the year, mostly by male relatives, as a result of family crimes or other forms of violence against women. Such crimes continued to be committed by men with near impunity facilitated by lenient sentences for killings carried out in a "fit of fury". Information was received on alleged torture, including rape, of Filipina maids working in Lebanon.

▢ A 27-year-old Palestinian man killed his sister by cutting her throat for allegedly having pre-marital sexual relations with her fiancé. The attack reportedly took place in October in a Beirut hospital where the woman worked. The man handed himself in to the authorities.

▢ Seventeen-year-old Fadela Farouq al-Sha'ar died on 5 February in Tripoli apparently after being strangled, allegedly by her brother. He was said to have confessed to the murder before disappearing. She was apparently killed for allegedly eloping with a man she wanted to marry without the consent of her family.

▢ A Filipina woman, Catherine Bautista, one of thousands of maids reportedly working in difficult conditions in Lebanon, died on 4 May. Her body was found almost naked in the garden of the building in Beirut where she worked. An investigation ordered by the authorities closed the case in July apparently after concluding that she had died after jumping out of her employers' apartment.

Freedom of expression and association

Attacks on freedom of expression and association continued during the year.

▢ In May at least five civilians were killed, including a photographer, and at least 27 others injured when the Lebanese army apparently used excessive force to suppress a demonstration organized by the General Workers' Union in al-Sallum neighbourhood in southern Beirut. Following an official investigation, the government promised compensation for those injured.

▢ In April a dozen people were injured during the peaceful build-up to a demonstration outside the UN Economic and Social Commission for Western Asia (ESCWA) offices in Beirut organized to submit a petition calling for the release of Lebanese political detainees held in Syria. The injuries were caused when security forces used batons against the demonstrators. Human rights defender Ghazi 'Aad, who uses a wheelchair, was beaten. No investigation was known to have been carried out.

▢ In March a professor at the Lebanese University, Adonis Akra, appeared several times before the Publications Court in Beirut in connection with the publication of a book that included details of his incarceration in a Syrian jail and the torture techniques used against him. He was charged with undermining Lebanon's relations with a friendly country and tarnishing the image of its leaders. In February 2003 Adonis Akra had been detained by the security forces for seven hours and forced to cancel the launching of the book. The book was subsequently banned in Lebanon, copies of it were confiscated, and charges were brought against its publishers, Dar al-Tali'ah.

Refugees

Palestinian refugees continued to be discriminated against despite calls by the UN Committee on the Elimination of Racial Discrimination (CERD) for their rights to be protected.

In March CERD expressed concern "with regard to the enjoyment by the Palestinian population present in the country of all rights stipulated in the Convention [on the Elimination of All Forms of Racial Discrimination] on the basis of non-discrimination, in particular access to work, health care, housing and social services as well as the right to effective legal remedies." CERD urged Lebanon "to take measures to ameliorate the situation of Palestinian refugees with regard to the enjoyment of the rights protected under the Convention, and at a minimum to remove all legislative provisions and change policies that have a discriminatory effect on the Palestinian population in comparison with other non-citizens."

Death penalty

At least three people were sentenced to death. Three men – Ahmad Mansour, Badea' Hamada and Remi Antoan Za'atar – were executed in Rumieh prison in Beirut in January. The executions were the first since 1998.

AI country reports/ visits
Report
- Lebanon: Samir Gea'gea' and Jirjis al-Khouri – Torture and unfair trial (AI Index: MDE 18/003/2004)
Visits
AI delegates visited Lebanon several times during 2004.

LIBERIA

REPUBLIC OF LIBERIA
Head of state and government: Charles Gyude Bryant
Death penalty: retentionist
International Criminal Court: ratified
UN Women's Convention: ratified
Optional Protocol to UN Women's Convention: signed

The peace process advanced slowly as political tensions and insecurity continued. The human rights situation progressively improved, but delays in deployment of UN peacekeeping forces, and in disarmament and demobilization, left civilians vulnerable to abuses by combatants. Despite the gravity of crimes committed during the armed conflict, including crimes against humanity and war crimes, impunity reigned. These crimes included widespread and systematic rape and other forms of sexual violence, and the recruitment and use of child soldiers. Lack of resources hampered post-conflict reconstruction, including rebuilding institutions for the protection of human rights, such as the national justice system. Refugees and internally displaced people slowly began to return to their homes.

Background
Implementation of the Comprehensive Peace Agreement of August 2003 was slow and fraught with difficulties. Commitment to the peace process was thrown into question by power struggles within the

National Transitional Government of Liberia, which comprised representatives of the former government of Liberia and of the two armed opposition groups, Liberians United for Reconciliation and Democracy (LURD) and the Movement for Democracy in Liberia (MODEL), as well as by internal leadership disputes within the LURD. The government's mismanagement of public resources further deterred donor governments from fulfilling pledges made at the International Reconstruction Conference on Liberia held in February. Progress towards the country's recovery after protracted conflict – including the provision of food, water, sanitation, health care and education – was consequently frustrated. By December some 70 per cent of the promised US$520 million had been made available.

Disarmament and demobilization of combatants resumed in April, after being promptly abandoned in December 2003. Delays in the process, however, coupled with slow deployment of UN peacekeeping forces throughout the country, resulted in continuing insecurity. Abuses against the civilian population continued in territory still under the control of combatants.

Some 101,500 combatants – far higher numbers than anticipated – were disarmed and demobilized. They included over 22,000 women and 11,000 children. The three parties to the conflict were subsequently formally disbanded. The comparatively small quantity and poor quality of arms and ammunition surrendered, however, raised concerns that they were hidden or transferred to neighbouring Côte d'Ivoire, where the political and security situation remained fragile. The UN Mission in Liberia (UNMIL) and UN peacekeeping operations in Sierra Leone and Côte d'Ivoire sought to strengthen cooperation on cross-border movements of combatants, arms and ammunition, and in disarmament and demobilization, but with limited effectiveness.

Insufficient funds for rehabilitation and reintegration of unemployed and restive former combatants threatened to undermine the peace process. In late October underlying volatility erupted into serious rioting in the capital, Monrovia, which was exploited by former parties to the conflict and combatants, and ignited religious and ethnic tensions. The violence, which included rape, resulted in 19 deaths and more than 200 injured. Some 200 people were arrested.

In December legislation for electoral reform was passed, after considerable delay, by the National Transitional Legislative Assembly. This paved the way for presidential and legislative elections scheduled for October 2005.

Former President Charles Taylor, who had relinquished power in 2003, remained in Nigeria. The Nigerian government had granted him asylum despite his indictment by the Special Court for Sierra Leone for crimes against humanity, war crimes and other serious violations of international law during Sierra Leone's armed conflict (see Nigeria and Sierra Leone entries).

In September, in a significant move towards the protection of human rights, the government signed or ratified 18 international treaties, including the Rome Statute of the International Criminal Court.

Continuing human rights abuses

Despite commitments in the peace agreement to respect international humanitarian and human rights law, combatants of all sides continued to commit human rights abuses against the civilian population. In areas where UNMIL forces had yet to deploy, civilians remained vulnerable to forced labour, harassment, intimidation, extortion and looting. These areas included south-eastern counties of Sinoe, Grand Kru, River Gee and Maryland, under control of MODEL forces, and large parts of Lofa, Grand Cape Mount, Gbarpolu and Bomi counties, controlled by LURD. While MODEL forces reportedly exploited timber resources, LURD controlled rubber plantations. Both former government and MODEL forces remained in Nimba County, preventing civilians from moving freely and extorting food and other possessions. It was, however, difficult to obtain corroborated information from more inaccessible areas. With progressive UNMIL deployment and disarmament and demobilization, the security and safety of civilians improved.

Crimes against humanity and war crimes during the conflict

Liberia's conflict had been characterized by crimes against humanity, war crimes and other serious violations of international law. Responding to these crimes, including rape and other forms of sexual violence and the recruitment and use of child soldiers, presented particular challenges.

Rape and other forms of sexual violence

In the conflict, rape and other forms of sexual violence against women and girls – by all sides but particularly forces of the former government – had been widespread and systematic. Thousands of women and girls were abducted by combatants, raped, and forced to become the sexual partners or "wives" of their abductors. Some 75 per cent of women and girls associated with fighting forces who presented for disarmament and demobilization reported that they had been sexually assaulted.

Severely deficient health facilities were unable to respond adequately to the serious physical and psychological consequences of sexual violence. Specific provisions for women and girls in the disarmament and demobilization process, including those affected by sexual violence, were compromised by lack of resources for rehabilitation and reintegration.

Although ended, the legacy of conflict exacerbated the risk of sexual violence. For example, the conditions for vast numbers remaining in camps for the internally displaced, and extreme poverty and loss of independence, increased vulnerability to sexual violence and exploitation.

Although women's participation at all levels of decision-making was necessary to ensure that

protection of their rights was central to Liberia's recovery, there were only three women in the government and four in the legislative assembly.

Use of child soldiers

Considerably fewer children disarmed and demobilized than the 21,000 initially estimated, in part because failure of parties to the conflict to provide information prevented accurate predictions. Many children had returned spontaneously to their homes. Others were unaware of the disarmament and demobilization process, or resisted inclusion because they feared being stigmatized as former child soldiers. The majority of children were successfully reunited with their families but concerns remained that inadequate rehabilitation and reintegration left them vulnerable to re-recruitment.

Some children remained under the control of commanders and were exploited as labourers, for example on the Guthrie rubber plantation controlled by the LURD. Others were reportedly encouraged by former MODEL commanders, including by cash incentives, to go to Côte d'Ivoire. When a ceasefire between the Ivorian government and armed opposition forces was briefly violated in early November, both former LURD and MODEL commanders were reported to have re-recruited former combatants, including children, in eastern Liberia to fight in Côte d'Ivoire.

Ending impunity

Despite the gravity of crimes under international law during the conflict, it remained unclear if, how and when those responsible would be held criminally responsible and reparations made to victims. The government took no action to bring the perpetrators to justice. Nor was there a resolute commitment by the international community to end impunity in Liberia.

The peace agreement made provision for the government to consider a general amnesty for those involved in military activities during the conflict. Although the government did not overtly pursue this option, its position remained ambiguous. Chairman Gyude Bryant and other government members had previously expressed preference for such an amnesty.

Although the peace agreement provided for a Truth and Reconciliation Commission, AI stressed that this could not be a substitute for a court of law to try alleged perpetrators of serious violations of international law. With UNMIL's assistance, legislation to establish the Commission was drafted but had yet to be passed.

While UNMIL, other UN agencies and non-governmental organizations investigated and documented crimes committed during the conflict, there were concerns that lack of coordination of these initiatives and failure to collect information at an early stage might jeopardize future criminal proceedings.

Strengthening institutions to protect human rights

As a result of the conflict, the judicial and legal systems had been all but destroyed and considerable challenges remained in establishing the rule of law and respect for human rights. Rehabilitation of some courts progressed, and cases were set for trial, but limited resources resulted in protracted delays. Detainees were routinely held in police custody beyond the legal limit of 48 hours before being brought before a court and charged or released. Access to justice for both suspects and victims remained extremely limited.

UNMIL, together with national and international stakeholders, developed plans for training judges, magistrates and justices of the peace, as well as a review of the seriously deficient juvenile justice system. A number of illegally detained children were released pending hearing of their cases.

Lack of resources and debilitated infrastructure resulted in dire conditions in all places of detention, including severe overcrowding, poor hygiene, and inadequate food and medical care. In August, 27 detainees in police custody in Monrovia were admitted to hospital suffering from severe malnutrition, dehydration and skin diseases. International agencies subsequently provided food and other services. Efforts to provide separate cells for detained women, men and children were thwarted by resource constraints. Assaults on detainees by police and prison officials highlighted the need for effective screening of recruits, training in international human rights standards, and adequate disciplinary measures.

Draft legislation to establish the Independent National Commission on Human Rights, provided for by the peace agreement, came before the legislative assembly but had yet to be passed.

Refugees and internally displaced people

Gradual improvements to the security situation following the peace agreement resulted in the spontaneous return of large numbers of the 340,000 refugees who had fled to other countries in West Africa. In October the UN High Commissioner for Refugees (UNHCR) officially began a three-year programme of facilitated voluntary repatriation, but less than half the funding needed to ensure safe and dignified returns was received. UNHCR expected some 100,000 Liberian refugees to have returned by the end of 2004, most spontaneously.

In October the government declared that internally displaced people, estimated to number as many as 300,000, could return in safety to Grand Cape Mount, Bomi, Gbarpolu, Margibi, Bong and River Cess counties. The viability of return was, however, compromised by continuing security concerns and lack of basic infrastructure. Provision of basic necessities for internally displaced people was frequently inadequate.

Renewed insecurity and tension in Côte d'Ivoire in early November forced some 10,000 people, mostly women and children, to flee to Liberia, exacerbating an already difficult humanitarian situation. Almost half had returned by the end of the year.

UN Mission in Liberia

Deployment of UNMIL forces across the country progressed during the year. The full complement of

15,000 troops and 1,115 civilian police officers had almost been reached by December – making UNMIL the largest UN peacekeeping operation worldwide.

During the year, complaints were made that some UNMIL personnel sexually exploited women through prostitution and economically exploited children as domestic help.

The UNMIL Human Rights and Protection Section developed comprehensive plans to protect and promote human rights. Initiatives included monitoring and reporting, with particular attention to women, children and internally displaced people, and training for UNMIL personnel, both military and civilian, as well as the Liberian police. The Section assisted in drafting legislation for the establishment of the Truth and Reconciliation Commission and the Independent National Commission on Human Rights. Some of its efforts were frustrated, however, by lack of funds and delays in recruitment of its full complement of staff. By December, human rights officers were based in 11 of Liberia's 15 counties.

The UNMIL Senior Gender Adviser and Gender Unit aimed to ensure that the protection of women and girls was incorporated into all aspects of UNMIL's operation, including rehabilitation and reintegration opportunities for women associated with fighting forces. It also sought to strengthen the capacity of the Ministry of Gender and Development to develop a strategy across government ministries to address specifically the protection of the rights of women and girls. The Gender Unit's work was, however, also hindered by limited resources.

UN sanctions on arms, diamonds and timber

Although the government urged the lifting of economic sanctions, the UN Security Council maintained bans on the export of rough diamonds and timber, as well as all sales or supply of arms and related *matériel* to any recipient in Liberia other than UNMIL. The Panel of Experts established by the Security Council to monitor compliance with sanctions concluded in December that conditions for ending sanctions on diamonds and timber, including controls to ensure that revenues from diamond and logging sales benefited the Liberian people, had yet to be met. The Security Council stressed the links between illegal exploitation of diamonds and timber, illicit trade in these resources and proliferation and trafficking of arms which fuelled and exacerbated conflicts in West Africa, particularly Liberia.

AI country reports/ visits
Reports
- Liberia: Recommendations to the International Reconstruction Conference, New York, 5 and 6 February 2004 (AI Index: AFR 34/002/2004)
- Liberia: The promises of peace for 21,000 child soldiers (AI Index: AFR 34/006/2004)
- Liberia: One year after Accra – immense human rights challenges remain (AI Index: AFR 34/012/2004)
- Liberia: No impunity for rape – a crime against humanity and a war crime (AI Index: AFR 34/017/2004)

Visit
AI delegates visited Liberia in July to carry out research and to meet members of the government and UNMIL personnel.

LIBYA

SOCIALIST PEOPLE'S LIBYAN ARAB JAMAHIRIYA
Head of state: Mu'ammar al-Gaddafi
Death penalty: retentionist
International Criminal Court: not signed
UN Women's Convention: ratified with reservations
Optional Protocol to UN Women's Convention: ratified

The country was reopened to international human rights monitors, namely AI. Over the course of the year, the authorities announced several reform initiatives, including the possible abolition of the People's Court and a restriction of the scope of the death penalty. However, limited progress was made in establishing the truth about how prisoners died in custody in past years. No significant steps were taken to shed light on other past human rights violations, including "disappearances". Prisoners of conscience detained in previous years remained in prison. Legislation criminalizing peaceful political activities remained in force. The security forces continued to arbitrarily arrest people for political reasons and to detain them incommunicado for long periods without charge. Migrants and asylum-seekers were not protected. Unfair trials before the People's Court continued to take place. The death penalty continued to be handed down.

Background
Libya restored diplomatic relations with the European Union (EU) and the USA following its announcement at the end of 2003 that it would dismantle its programmes for weapons of mass destruction. Normalization of relations was also enabled by the conclusion of negotiations with Germany and France on two separate bombings: the first of the *La Belle* nightclub in Berlin, Germany, in 1986, which killed three people and wounded about 250; and the second of UTA flight 772 over Niger in 1989, which led to 170 deaths. In April, in his first official trip to Europe for 15 years, Colonel Mu'ammar al-Gaddafi visited the European Commission in Belgium. In October the EU announced the lifting of its embargo on sales of weapons to Libya in the context of enhanced cooperation against illegal immigration.

In March a cabinet reshuffle took place and the Secretariat of the General People's Committee for Justice and Public Security was divided into two separate entities, one for Justice and the other for Public Security.

In April Colonel Mu'ammar al-Gaddafi called for a number of legal and institutional reforms. These included the abolition of the People's Court, a special court known to try political cases, and the transfer of its jurisdiction to ordinary criminal courts; a more stringent application of Libyan law; and a reduction in the scope of the death penalty to cover only the most serious crimes.

In June Libya ratified the Optional Protocol to the UN Women's Convention and in August the authorities informed AI that Libya was in the process of ratifying several other international and regional human rights treaties.

Amnesty International visit
In February an AI delegation went to Libya to research and discuss the human rights situation, the first such visit for 15 years. The organization was granted unprecedented access to prisoners of conscience and political prisoners. Delegates had lengthy meetings with Colonel Mu'ammar al-Gaddafi and senior Libyan officials as well as members of the judiciary and lawyers. At all levels, Libyan officials showed a willingness to discuss issues of concern to the organization.

In August the authorities provided a detailed response to AI's report, published in April, *Time to make human rights a reality*. The response showed the authorities' willingness to engage with concerns raised by AI. Positive indications in the letter included plans for legal and institutional reforms, many of which had already been signalled in April by Colonel Mu'ammar al-Gaddafi.

Freedom of expression and association
Legislation continued to prohibit the formation of associations or political parties outside the existing political system. With the exception of the Human Rights Society of the Gaddafi International Foundation for Charitable Associations, which is headed by Saif al-Islam al-Gaddafi, the son of Colonel Mu'ammar al-Gaddafi, human rights organizations or individuals wishing to carry out human rights work continued to be prevented from operating freely.

A draft Penal Code, which was announced by the authorities in 2003, was examined by a committee of legal experts assembled by the then Secretariat of the General People's Committee for Justice and Public Security. It was subsequently sent for discussion by Libya's local decision-making bodies, the Basic People's Congresses. The draft, which was obtained by AI in February, retained numerous provisions that contravene Libya's obligations under international law, including provisions that prescribe the death penalty for activities solely amounting to the peaceful exercise of freedom of expression and association.

Despite the authorities' categorical denial of the existence of prisoners of conscience, scores of prisoners of conscience continued to be held for their non-violent political views or activities.

◻ In December the People's Court of Appeal upheld the death sentences against Abdullah Ahmed 'Izzedin and Salem Abu Hanak, as well as prison terms ranging from 10 years' to life imprisonment against some 83 others, which were originally handed down in 2002. AI considered all 85 to be prisoners of conscience as they had not used or advocated violence. The Court also confirmed the acquittal of 66 men. According to Libyan law, the two death sentences will be considered by the Supreme Court and, if confirmed, will go before the Supreme Council for Judicial Bodies, Libya's highest judicial body, for final approval.

The sentences were reportedly pronounced in absentia after the accused apparently refused to attend the court as a mark of protest. This followed earlier protests in the form of hunger strikes in April and October 2004 that called for an end to their continued detention, among other things.

Those on trial were professionals and students arrested in and after June 1998 on suspicion of supporting or sympathizing with the banned Libyan Islamic Group (al-Jama'a al-Islamiya al-Libiya), also known as the Muslim Brothers. They were charged under Law 71 of 1972 banning political parties. They were sentenced, after a trial which fell short of international standards for fairness, solely on account of the peaceful expression of their ideas and for secretly meeting to discuss those ideas with others.

There were continuing reports of people being held incommunicado by the Internal Security Agency. Torture and ill-treatment were widely reported during incommunicado detention, apparently with the primary function of extracting confessions.

◻ In March prisoner of conscience Fathi al-Jahmi was released after the People's Court of Appeal handed down a suspended sentence of one year's imprisonment. He had been detained since 2002 in connection with his reported calls for reform at a session of the Basic People's Congress in al-Manshia, Bin Ashour, Tripoli.

Two weeks after his release, the authorities reportedly took him from his home in Tripoli along with his wife, Fawzia 'Abdullah Gogha, and eldest son, Muhammad Fathi al-Jahmi. Throughout their detention, they were reportedly denied access to the outside world, including to lawyers and relatives, and their exact whereabouts were unknown. The authorities told AI that Fathi al-Jahmi was being held for his own protection because of alleged public outrage generated by media interviews he conducted following his release from prison.

Muhammad Fathi al-Jahmi and Fawzia 'Abdullah Gogha were released in September and November respectively. However, Fathi al-Jahmi remained in detention. In November he reportedly appeared before the People's Court, charged with defaming the Leader of the Revolution and communicating with foreign entities.

Unfair trials

Cases continued to be heard by the People's Court, despite calls by Colonel Mu'ammar al-Gaddafi for its abolition. Trials before the court continued to fall short of minimum standards for fair trial. A draft law to abolish the People's Court was being examined by Libya's local and national legislative bodies.

◻ In December some 20 men were reportedly sentenced to death and some 158 others to life imprisonment by the People's Court in connection with their alleged affiliation to the Libyan Islamic Fighting Group. Those sentenced to life imprisonment included Mustapha Muhammad Krer, a Libyan national with Canadian citizenship. He allegedly first saw a lawyer when his trial opened, nearly two years after his arrest and detention. Subsequently, he was reportedly denied the right to a lawyer of his own choosing.

Mustapha Muhammad Krer had left Libya in 1989 because he was reportedly being sought by the authorities and following the arrest of his brother, al-Mukhtar Muhammad Krer. He returned to Libya in 2002 after his family was informed of the death in custody of al-Mukhtar Muhammad Krer.

Death penalty

Despite Colonel Mu'ammar al-Gaddafi's stated opposition to the death penalty, which he reiterated to AI in February, death sentences continued to be handed down, including after unfair trials.

◻ In May, six health professionals arrested in 1999 – five Bulgarian nurses and a Palestinian doctor – were sentenced to death by firing squad. They were accused of deliberately infecting 426 children with the HIV virus while working in al-Fateh Children's Hospital in Benghazi. A sixth Bulgarian defendant was sentenced to four years' imprisonment. Nine Libyan defendants were acquitted. The defendants had told AI delegates in February that their confessions, which they later retracted, had been extracted under torture, which included electric shocks, beatings and suspension by the arms. Their appeal case before the Supreme Court was expected to open in 2005. On the basis of the allegations of torture, eight members of the security forces and two others (a doctor and a translator) employed by them were charged. They had faced trial alongside the foreign and Libyan health professionals before the same criminal court in Benghazi. In May, the court pronounced that it was not competent to examine their cases. By the end of the year, the alleged torturers had not been tried.

Migrants and asylum-seekers

In a welcome step, Libya ratified the International Convention on the Protection of the Rights of All Migrant Workers and Members of Their Families in June. However, it had not ratified the 1951 UN Refugee Convention and its 1967 Protocol, nor had it established national asylum procedures by the end of 2004. In the absence of a legal protection framework, the effective guarantee of refugee rights was seriously undermined.

Widespread arrests of individuals from sub-Saharan Africa, including possible asylum-seekers, were reported. Some faced the threat of deportation to their countries of origin where they would be at risk of serious human rights violations. Ill-treatment of those detained was widely reported.

◻ In October, hundreds of individuals, predominantly of North African origin, were removed from Italy to Libya under a bilateral agreement. On arrival in Libya, they were reportedly detained and denied access to the UN High Commissioner for Refugees (UNHCR).

◻ In July the authorities forcibly returned over 110 individuals detained in Libya to Eritrea, where they were at risk of torture. On arrival in Eritrea, they were detained and held incommunicado in a secret prison.

◻ In August the authorities attempted to forcibly return to Eritrea 76 Eritrean nationals, including six children. Some of the Eritreans hijacked the plane that was carrying them and forced it to land in the Sudanese capital, Khartoum, where they all applied for asylum. Many said they had been ill-treated and denied medical attention in custody in Libya.

Update

◻ Seven Eritrean nationals, who were unlawfully detained after the expiry of their three-month prison sentences for illegal entry into Libya in 2002, were released. They had fled from Eritrea to Libya via Sudan and were arrested in 2002 as they attempted to travel by boat to Italy where they planned to seek asylum.

Legacy of past human rights violations

The authorities continued to fail to address human rights violations committed in previous years, including long-standing cases of political imprisonment, "disappearances" and deaths in custody.

◻ In August an investigation was opened in Lebanon into the "disappearance" of Imam Musa Sadr – a prominent Shi'a cleric who "disappeared" with two others in 1978 in Libya – after his family filed a lawsuit before the Lebanese courts. Lawyers working on behalf of Imam Musa Sadr's family called for the indictment of 18 senior Libyan officials. The Lebanese Public Prosecutor summoned the officials for questioning in March 2005.

The fate of many prisoners who were killed or "disappeared" in Abu Salim Prison in Tripoli in 1996 remained unknown. In February Colonel Mu'ammar al-Gaddafi told AI that there had been armed clashes between prisoners and guards – the first official recognition known to AI that any incident had taken place in the prison. In April Colonel Mu'ammar al-Gaddafi affirmed the right of families to know what happened to their relatives during the incidents. However, by the end of the year no thorough, independent and impartial investigations were known to have been opened into deaths in custody in the past, including those that allegedly took place in Abu Salim Prison in 1996.

AI country reports/visits
Report
· Libya: Time to make human rights a reality (AI Index: MDE 19/002/2004)

LITHUANIA

REPUBLIC OF LITHUANIA
Head of state: Valdas Adamkus (replaced Arturas Paulauskas in July)
Head of government: Algirdas Brazauskas
Death penalty: abolitionist for all crimes
International Criminal Court: ratified
UN Women's Convention and its Optional Protocol: ratified

Concerns about violence against women, "anti-terrorism" measures, protection for asylum-seekers and the rights of conscientious objectors were among those raised by international monitoring bodies.

Violence against women
In the home
In May the UN Human Rights Committee issued its concluding observations after examining Lithuania's second periodic report on implementation of the International Covenant on Civil and Political Rights. The Committee welcomed efforts to combat the rising incidence of violence against women and children in the home, but noted the lack of protection in law against domestic violence. It recommended the enactment of specific legislation, to include provision for restraining orders on violent family members. The Committee also urged Lithuania to continue its efforts to provide shelters and other support for survivors of domestic violence; to take measures to encourage women to report domestic violence; and to sensitize the police in their handling of such cases.

Similar concerns were expressed by the Council of Europe's Commissioner for Human Rights in a report of his November 2003 visit to Lithuania, issued in February. He said that domestic violence was reportedly widespread, and that the low levels of reporting to the police appeared to be because it was commonly seen as a private matter, not a human rights violation.

Trafficking of women
The Commissioner noted that Lithuania remained a country of origin, transit and destination for trafficked people, most of them women trafficked for sexual exploitation, but that it lacked a rehabilitation programme for women forced into prostitution.

Although trafficking was criminalized under existing legislation, the law did not sufficiently address criminal networks. It did not identify precise means of compensating victims of trafficking, he reported, or the possibility of exempting them from legal responsibility for acts, such as illegal entry, that resulted from being trafficked. Nor could they remain in Lithuania for a period while deciding whether to cooperate with police action against their traffickers.

'Anti-terrorism' measures

The Committee expressed concern about the draft law on the legal status of foreign nationals, which could allow those regarded as a threat to state security to be removed, without right of appeal, to a country where they were at risk of torture or other cruel, inhuman or degrading treatment. It recommended that any "anti-terrorism" measures conform to the International Covenant, and that Lithuania ensure protection for all from forcible return to countries where they risked such abuses.

Asylum-seekers

The Committee was concerned at information that asylum-seekers from certain countries were prevented from requesting asylum at the border; that the criteria for detaining asylum-seekers in "exceptional circumstances" remained unclear; and at the low percentage of applicants granted asylum in recent years. The Committee recommended that Lithuania ensure access to the domestic asylum procedure for all asylum-seekers, irrespective of their country of origin, and provide information on the criteria for detention.

Conscientious objection

The Committee reiterated its concern about the conditions of alternative service available to conscientious objectors to military service, "in particular the eligibility criteria and the duration of such service as compared with military service". It recommended that Lithuania clarify the grounds and eligibility for alternative service, permit an alternative service outside the defence forces, and ensure that the duration of such service is not punitive.

MACEDONIA

THE FORMER YUGOSLAV REPUBLIC OF MACEDONIA
Head of state: Branko Crvenkovski (replaced Boris Trajkovski in February)
Head of government: Vlado Buchkovski (replaced Hari Kostov in November, who replaced Branko Crvenkovski in May)
Death penalty: abolitionist for all crimes
International Criminal Court: ratified
UN Women's Convention and its Optional Protocol: ratified

There was an improvement in the human rights situation, although there were continuing allegations of ill-treatment by security officials. The trafficking of women and girls for forced prostitution continued, although some perpetrators were arrested and convicted. Domestic violence against women remained widespread but prosecutions were rare. Senior former officials were arrested and charged in connection with the extrajudicial execution of seven immigrants in 2002.

Background

On 26 February President Boris Trajkovski died in a plane crash in Bosnia and Herzegovina.

In August parliament adopted a new regional law to reduce the previous 123 municipalities to 80. Within each municipality, minorities constituting 25 per cent or more of the population would have their language recognized as an official language. The new internal borders provoked widespread demonstrations by ethnic Macedonians who saw the new boundaries, especially those relating to Struga and the capital, Skopje, as favouring ethnic Albanians. However, in November a referendum against the new law failed due to insufficient turn-out.

In October the European Union (EU) formally opened accession talks with Macedonia. At Prime Minister Kostov's invitation, the EU extended the mandate of Proxima (the EU police force tasked with advising the country's police force) for a further 12 months from 15 December.

Unemployment and poverty levels remained high. According to official figures, some 400,000 people (out of a population of around two million according to the 2002 census) were unemployed, and more than 30 per cent of the population lived on less than US$2.15 per day.

Members of the Romani community were especially disadvantaged, usually residing in substandard settlements lacking basic amenities and figuring disproportionately among the unemployed. Furthermore, only one in 10 Romani children completed elementary school: a precondition for registering for health and social insurance in later life. State health care for children is dependent on one parent completing elementary education.

Extrajudicial executions at Rashtanski Lozja

The authorities finally acknowledged that seven immigrants (six Pakistanis and one Indian) who were killed in March 2002 in Rashtanski Lozja had been extrajudicially executed. The authorities had previously claimed that the men were Islamic militants planning to attack western diplomatic targets in Macedonia, were connected to ethnic Albanian insurgents in the country, and that they had died after opening fire against the authorities. However, major inconsistencies in the government version pointed to extrajudicial executions. In April the authorities stated that the then Macedonian authorities had contacted the men while they were in Bulgaria, had brought them to Macedonia on false pretences, had murdered them and had planted false evidence against them.

The authorities charged a number of people with murder in connection with the killings, including three former police commanders, two special police officers and a businessman, as well as former Minister of Internal Affairs Ljube Boshkovski who fled to Croatia. He was arrested by the Croatian authorities in connection with the killings and remained in detention pending trial in Croatia.

The 'disappeared' and abducted

There was some progress in discovering the fate of 20 missing persons – 13 ethnic Macedonians, six ethnic Albanians, and one Bulgarian citizen – who "disappeared" or were abducted during the 2001 conflict between security forces and the ethnic Albanian National Liberation Army. DNA analysis carried out on bodies found in 2003 in a mass grave near the village of Trebos, Tetovo, identified four of the abducted ethnic Macedonians.

In May, police in Kichevo received an unsigned letter indicating burial sites in Zheleznec, Jama and Veles, and an anonymous phone call claiming that human bodies were buried in a pit in Jama, in the Bistra mountains. The Ministry of Internal Affairs disclosed that the writer of the letter, written in Serbian, claimed that he was a police instructor who had fought against Albanian "terrorists", and that the corpses were those of missing Albanians. Four bodies were exhumed from the site in Jama, an autopsy was ordered and relatives of the "disappeared" came forward to facilitate DNA identification. Among reports of official complicity in the "disappearances", a police officer reportedly claimed to have seen a missing ethnic Albanian, Ruzhdi Veliu, in Bitola prison after his "disappearance".

In September the Ministry of Internal Affairs stated that an arrest warrant had been issued in connection with the abducted ethnic Macedonians but that the suspect, a former local commander of the ethnic Albanians, was in hiding. However, no indictments in connection with the "disappeared" ethnic Albanians had been issued by the end of 2004.

Prisoner of conscience Zoran Vranishkovski

On 11 January Zoran Vranishkovski, also known as Bishop or Metropolitan Jovan, was arrested along with four monks and seven nuns after holding a religious service in his private apartment. All were released after about 30 hours, but Zoran Vranishkovski was re-arrested on 12 January and charged with "causing national, racial or religious hatred, discord and intolerance" under Article 319 of the Criminal Code. AI believed he was detained because he argued that the Serbian Orthodox Church should have control of the Macedonian Orthodox Church, from which he had been expelled. On 30 January he was released from custody. On 18 August he was sentenced to 18 months' imprisonment, confirmed on appeal, but remained at liberty pending a further appeal.

Police ill-treatment

There appeared to be fewer alleged instances of police ill-treatment, although cases continued to be reported.
In June Sashko Dragovich was allegedly beaten at Butel Police Station No. 1 in Skopje to force him to confess to theft. A medical certificate reportedly recorded injuries to his face, head and arms, inflicted by truncheon and fist. In October the Ministry of Internal Affairs informed the Macedonian Helsinki Committee that an investigation had failed to prove that the injuries had been inflicted by police, but that disciplinary proceedings would be instituted against the officer involved for other legal infractions connected to the arrest.

In March the Court of Appeal postponed for the 17th time the trial of four police inspectors who allegedly beat 12-year-old Isak Tairovski in 1994 so badly that he was permanently disabled. The hearing was postponed because one of the accused and a witness did not attend court.

Journalists punished for libel and slander

In April amendments to the Criminal Code removed the possibility of official prosecutions for slander and libel. However, private individuals could still bring cases, and slander and libel remained criminal offences carrying possible prison sentences. The Association of Journalists of Macedonia warned that this could intimidate and silence journalists. It pointed out that there were some 50 such charges each year, the majority against journalists, often initiated by officials in connection with investigative journalism.

Violence against women

Domestic violence against women remained widespread. Official figures released in November reported 98 criminal charges and 623 misdemeanour charges brought during the year for domestic violence.

Changes to the Criminal Code in April raised minimum prison sentences for human trafficking from five to eight years. Despite police raids against traffickers, prosecutions and convictions were low. Statistics for 2003 published by a daily newspaper showed that in the Tetovo region, 80 police raids on suspected brothels with trafficked women found 95 people "without regulated residence in Macedonia". The raids resulted in 38 people being charged in connection with trafficking and forced prostitution but only one conviction. The newspaper stated that the

Tetovo prosecution had difficulties in gathering evidence and that witnesses were often afraid to testify and were sometimes the subject of death threats. In December the police announced that in the previous nine months they had discovered 39 cases of trafficking involving 79 people.

Refugees and internally displaced people
About 2,400 registered internally displaced people remained after the 2001 conflict in Macedonia, of whom about half were accommodated in collective centres while the remainder were with relatives. In addition there were an estimated 1,500 refugees from Kosovo, predominantly Roma.

AI country reports/ visits
Reports
- Europe and Central Asia: Summary of Amnesty International's concerns in the region, January-June 2004: Macedonia (AI Index: EUR 01/005/2004)

MALAWI

REPUBLIC OF MALAWI
Head of state and government: Bingu wa Mutharika (replaced Bakili Muluzi in May)
Death penalty: retentionist
International Criminal Court: ratified
UN Women's Convention: ratified
Optional Protocol to UN Women's Convention: signed

The May 2004 general election dominated the year. There were reports of excessive force against protesters by the police, and of the torture of suspects in police custody. The state-controlled news media overwhelmingly favoured the campaign of the ruling United Democratic Front (UDF). Prison conditions and the rate of prison deaths remained a significant concern.

Background
Observers found the polling at the presidential and parliamentary elections on 20 May to have been largely free and fair, but the overall process unfair. State-controlled radio and television gave by far the most airtime and the most favourable coverage to the ruling UDF's campaign and presidential candidate, Bingu wa Mutharika.

In August former human rights lawyer Ralph Kasambara was appointed Attorney General.

Police abuses
Reports continued of excessive force by the police to disperse protesters.
▭ On 22 February the police reportedly used excessive force to curtail a peaceful rally organized by the opposition coalition. Several people were injured when live ammunition was fired to disperse the crowd.

Police used live ammunition to quell rioting that followed the announcement of the result of the presidential elections.
▭ On 23 May, 10-year-old Epiphania Bonjesi was shot when police used live ammunition on demonstrators in Blantyre. She was admitted to hospital and died on 24 May. According to eyewitnesses, a police officer took aim and fired at her as she sat on her veranda. Five other people reportedly died from bullet wounds during the same disturbances. No independent inquiry into the deaths was carried out, and the findings of any police investigation were not made public. No action was known to have been taken against any officer. Requests for information by the Malawi Human Rights Commission and human rights groups received no response. Compensation of the equivalent to US$2,700 was reportedly paid by the authorities to the family of Epiphania Bonjesi.

The torture or ill-treatment of suspects and deaths in police custody were reported to continue.
▭ Mabvuto Maguja died on 23 May, reportedly as a result of repeated beatings following his arrest the same day by Lilongwe police. The postmortem examination found that the cause of death was consistent with pressure on his chest from a blunt object such as a foot, and that injuries to his neck were consistent with strangulation. Wekha Maguja and Gift Chikani, arrested with him, were also allegedly beaten. During the course of the arrests, police officers were reported to have beaten Hannah Kapaluma with machetes and sexually assaulted her .

Prisons
More than 180 prisoners died in 2004 – up from 162 in 2003 – out of a prison population of 9,000. This rate of deaths required urgent remedial measures according to standards established by the International Committee of the Red Cross. Many of the deaths were HIV related; others were the result of preventable illnesses caused or exacerbated by overcrowding, poor diet, insanitary conditions and medical neglect.

Constitutional freedoms threatened
In June a presidential decree that no demonstration connected with the elections should take place was ruled unconstitutional by the High Court. Extensive political control of state media limited freedom of expression.

In July the President directed police to round-up women commercial sex-workers. However, the High Court subsequently ruled that the presidential decree was unconstitutional and in breach of the right of freedom of movement, as well as discriminatory on the basis of gender.

MALAYSIA

MALAYSIA
Head of state: Raja Tuanku Syed Sirajuddin
Head of government: Abdullah Ahmad Badawi
Death penalty: retentionist
International Criminal Court: not signed
UN Women's Convention: ratified with reservations
Optional Protocol to UN Women's Convention: not signed

A Royal Commission of Inquiry was set up to examine reported patterns of police abuses and make recommendations for institutional reform. The release of former Deputy Prime Minister Anwar Ibrahim, who had been convicted of sodomy after charges were filed against him that were politically motivated, helped to rebuild public confidence in judicial independence. At least 84 suspected Islamist activists remained held without charge or trial under the Internal Security Act (ISA). An array of restrictive laws curtailed enjoyment of freedom of expression, association and assembly. Suspected undocumented migrants, asylum-seekers and refugees were at risk of ill-treatment and poor conditions while detained prior to deportation. At least seven people were sentenced to death. Thousands of convicted prisoners, mostly undocumented migrant workers, were caned.

Background
In March the United Malay National Organization (UMNO)-led Barisan Nasional (National Front) ruling coalition won an emphatic election victory.

Addressing violations by police
An independent Royal Commission of Inquiry, with a one-year mandate, investigated patterns of abuses by police, including excessive use of force and unlawful killings during arrest of criminal suspects; torture and ill-treatment; and deaths in custody. Commenting on preliminary findings, the Commission's chairman stated that the inquiry found ill-treatment by police and poor conditions in police cells. He called for reform of remand laws and strengthening of police internal disciplinary procedures.

In April, the Human Rights Commission of Malaysia (Suhakam) released a report of its public inquiry into allegations of police abuses in Kundasang, Sabah, in 2003. It found severe overcrowding and inhumane conditions in police cells, and police misuse of remand laws to detain suspects longer than necessary.

▢ A body believed to be that of 24-year-old Francis Udayapan was found in a river in April. He had been arrested on suspicion of theft of a mobile phone in Kuala Lumpur. Police said he drowned after escaping, but relatives said he had been beaten and died in police custody. After public protests, a coroner's inquest was opened in August and was continuing at the end of 2004.

▢ In September human rights lawyer P. Utayakumar was arrested for allegedly defaming the police by saying that police officers had been involved in an assault on him in May. The lawyer had previously received death threats apparently connected to his high-profile work on behalf of victims of police abuses.

Detention without trial under the ISA
The ISA continued to allow for detention without trial for up to two years, renewable indefinitely, of anyone considered by the authorities to be a potential threat to national security or public order. The ISA fails to provide precise definitions or criteria for determining which individuals pose a threat. Attempts to seek judicial redress through habeas corpus petitions continued to prove ineffective. During an initial 60-day period of "investigative detention", detainees were held incommunicado and denied access to lawyers, family members and independent doctors. In the course of extended police interrogations, they remained at risk of physical intimidation, humiliation and intense psychological pressure at times amounting to torture.

The authorities failed to act on recommendations made by the National Human Rights Commission (Suhakam) in 2004 for the repeal of the ISA and its replacement by a comprehensive law balancing national security concerns and respect for human rights.

In July Suhakam Commissioners inspected police remand centres after receiving complaints from ISA detainees of ill-treatment and torture during their initial 60-day detention.

At least 84 alleged Islamist activists reportedly remained in detention under the ISA. They included 75 detainees accused of association with al-Qa'ida and the south-east Asian network Jemaah Islamiyah (JI), which was allegedly linked to the 2002 Bali bombings, as well as 12 alleged members of the Malaysia Mujahidin Group (Kumpulan Mujahidin Malaysia, KMM). At least 10 men were also under ISA detention for alleged passport forgery or other offences.

▢ In March, 16 alleged KMM detainees staged a three-week hunger strike to protest against the government's renewal of their two-year detention orders, despite the reported recommendation by the ISA Advisory Board for their release.

▢ In May, detainee Mohamad Abdul Rahman, an Indonesian national with permanent resident status in Malaysia suspected of links with JI, was deported to Indonesia a few hours before his scheduled habeas corpus hearing.

▢ Five alleged supporters of KMM or JI were released in July and a further four in November. However, they were subjected to restriction orders curtailing their freedom of movement.

The judiciary and restrictive laws
A number of judicial rulings assisted a gradual restoration of public confidence in the independence of the judiciary and in its willingness to scrutinize and check politically motivated prosecutions under

restrictive laws. However, such laws continued to impose unjustified curbs on the rights to freedom of expression, association and assembly of opposition figures, journalists and other members of civil society.

▭ In April the High Court upheld the appeal of youth leader Mohamad Ezam Mohamad Nor, a member of the opposition People's Justice Party, against his 2002 conviction under the Official Secrets Act (OSA). He had been found guilty of distributing classified documents about official corruption to journalists in 1999. In the appeal hearing, the judge stated that the prosecution had failed to establish adequately that the documents were classified, and that a specific section of the OSA was "draconian and repressive".

▭ In September the Federal Court upheld the final appeal of former Deputy Prime Minister Anwar Ibrahim and his adopted brother, Sukma Darmawan. Both men had been convicted of sodomy in 2000. The Court found that a key prosecution witness was unreliable and that Sukma Darmawan's "confession" had not been made voluntarily.

Opposition parties and civil society groups continued to express concern that police were not impartial in granting permits for public assemblies and used unnecessary or excessive force when dispersing demonstrations.

▭ In February, without giving sufficient warning, police fired water cannon laced with chemical irritant to disperse a crowd gathered at the national police headquarters in Kuala Lumpur to present a memorandum on police brutality.

Ill-treatment of migrant workers and asylum-seekers

There were periodic reports of ill-treatment of undocumented migrant workers and asylum-seekers in detention camps and during deportation. Conditions in detention camps, including the provision of adequate medical care, food and clean water, failed to meet international standards. Fears that conditions would worsen due to increased overcrowding mounted after the government announced plans in July to arrest and deport over 1.2 million suspected "illegal immigrants" by the end of 2005. Concerns about the planned mass deportations included the lack of fair individual assessment procedures for detained migrants, serious weaknesses in fair trial safeguards for those prosecuted under the Immigration Act, and inadequate protection for more vulnerable detainees, including women and children.

With the authorities repeatedly failing to distinguish between people seeking asylum (mostly from Myanmar and Nanggroe Aceh Darussalam in Indonesia) and suspected undocumented migrant workers, asylum-seekers and refugees remained at risk of detention and *refoulement*. In April, for example, 30 Burmese nationals were arrested outside the Kuala Lumpur office of the UN High Commissioner for Refugees (UNHCR) as they sought to register as asylum-seekers. In July, at least 60 asylum-seekers, mostly Acehnese, were arrested in Selayang and sent to Seminyih immigration detention camp. At least 20 were

subsequently reported to have been "voluntarily" repatriated. However, as the year progressed, recognition by police and immigration officials of documentation provided by UNCHR to asylum-seekers appeared to improve. In November, the government announced that Rohingya refugees (an ethnic minority from Myanmar) would be issued identity cards allowing them to stay and work in Malaysia.

Death penalty and corporal punishment

At least seven people were sentenced to death, mostly for drug trafficking offences. No executions were reported.

Caning, a cruel, inhuman or degrading punishment, was carried out throughout the year as an additional punishment to imprisonment. Thousands of people found guilty of breaches of the Immigration Act were among those caned.

AI country reports/ visits
Report
· Malaysia: Human rights at risk in mass deportation of undocumented migrants (AI Index: ASA 28/008/2004)
· Malaysia: Irene Fernandez defends rights of migrant workers despite conviction (AI Index: ASA 28/015/2004)

MALDIVES

REPUBLIC OF MALDIVES
Head of state and government: Maumoon Abdul Gayoom
Death penalty: abolitionist in practice
International Criminal Court: not signed
UN Women's Convention: ratified with reservations
Optional Protocol to UN Women's Convention: not signed

Mass arrests of opposition leaders and activists followed large-scale demonstrations in August to press for political reform. Detainees were reportedly ill-treated in police custody. Among those held without charge or trial for more than two months were several members of parliament. Government promises of reform were undermined by arrests of political opponents in February and August, and the imposition of a state of emergency between August and October.

Background
President Maumoon Abdul Gayoom, head of state since 1978, announced plans in June to introduce constitutional reforms, to allow the formation of political parties and to strengthen the judiciary.

However, the newly elected constitutional assembly (People's Special Majlis) was suspended in July after 24 members refused to take part in an open vote to elect the speaker. In October it held another session, but without opposition members who were in detention.

The government continued to state its commitment to the reform of the criminal justice system. A new penal code and police law were reportedly being drafted by the end of 2004. Existing legal safeguards, including access to lawyers and independent medical examinations, were ignored or withdrawn under emergency powers.

In January, regulations were issued for the Human Rights Commission of the Maldives, established and appointed by President Gayoom in December 2003. The regulations provided for the Commission to initiate investigations and prosecutions, and to publish an annual report of its activities. Statutory legislation had not been passed by the year's end.

Maldives acceded to the UN Convention against Torture in April.

At least 82 people were killed, 26 people remained missing and over 20 inhabited islands in the Maldives were destroyed as a result of the tsunami that struck countries around the Indian Ocean on 26 December.

Detentions and ill-treatment

The government declared a state of emergency following mass protests at the slow pace of democratic reform on 12 and 13 August in the capital, Malé. About 200 people were detained, most of them supporters of the opposition Maldivian Democratic Party (MDP). The authorities said that 128 detainees had been released without charge by mid-September. The emergency was lifted in October, when more than 50 detainees were reportedly still held without charge. By the end of 2004 all of the detainees, including members of the constitutional assembly, had been released.

Under emergency powers, the government suspended normal legal safeguards, including the right of detainees to have access to a lawyer. Detainees were allowed only limited visits from their families, weeks after their arrest. Some relatives were harassed and briefly detained.

There were consistent reports that some detainees were beaten after being transferred, handcuffed and blindfolded, to the police training island, Girifushi, and that at least three woman were sexually assaulted. Although some detainees received hospital treatment for their injuries, others were reportedly denied medical attention.

◻ At least four prisoners of conscience – Fathimath Nisreen, Mohamed Zaki, Ahmed Ibrahim Didi and Naushad Waheed – were serving long prison terms imposed in 2002 after unfair political trials. They had been transferred to house arrest in early 2004, but were taken into police custody after the imposition of the state of emergency. In October, they were transferred back to house arrest.

◻ Jennifer Latheef, a freelance filmmaker, and Mohamed Mahir, a businessman, who had both been prisoners of conscience on several previous occasions, were among those detained in August. Jennifer Latheef was reportedly punched in the face, held in tight handcuffs for several hours, sexually molested and kicked while blindfolded and shackled. She was transferred to house arrest in November. Mohamed Mahir was transferred to house arrest in November, reportedly after three months in solitary confinement. They were both released at the end of 2004.

Politically motivated charges and trials

At least 17 people were charged with criminal offences for attending mass rallies in August after they had been released or transferred to house arrest. They included four members of the constitutional assembly – Ibrahim Hussein Zaki, Mohamed Munawwar, Gasim Ibrahim, and Ibrahim Ismail – who were charged with treason. However, charges against them were withdrawn at the end of the year.

◻ Islamic preacher Ibrahim Fareed was arrested in August. He was reportedly sentenced to two years' imprisonment after a hasty trial in September on charges of attempting to overthrow the government.

Prison killings investigation

In January the report was published of an investigation into the death of prisoner Hassan Evan Naseem in September 2003 at Maafushi prison, and the deaths of four other prisoners and the injury of dozens more after police fired on a prison protest the next day. The investigators concluded that security personnel had violated procedures for the treatment of prisoners and the use of firearms. Subsequently, the government announced plans to reform police security, staff training and health care provision at the prison. Some 12 suspects arrested in 2003 in connection with the deaths had not been brought to trial by the end of 2004.

AI country reports/ visits
Statement
· Maldives: Yet another crackdown on peaceful political activity (AI Index: ASA 29/003/2004)
Visit
AI delegates visited the Maldives in October for meetings with government officials and non-governmental organizations. The delegates were given access to political detainees arrested in August.

MALTA

REPUBLIC OF MALTA
Head of state: Edward Fenech-Adami (replaced Guido de Marco in April)
Head of government: Lawrence Gonzi (replaced Edward Fenech-Adami in April)
Death penalty: abolitionist for all crimes
International Criminal Court: ratified
UN Women's Convention: ratified with reservations
Optional Protocol to UN Women's Convention: not signed

Asylum-seekers were automatically detained and held for prolonged periods. Conditions of detention in facilities holding asylum-seekers and migrants fell below international standards. Domestic violence against women remained a problem.

Asylum and immigration

Hundreds of asylum-seekers and migrants arrived by boat and an unknown number died in the seas around Malta while attempting to reach Europe. By the end of the year, over 800 people, including women and children, were held in detention centres run by the police and armed forces. Many were held on grounds beyond those permissible under international norms. Some were detained for between one and two years. Inmates frequently lacked access to appropriate legal advice. There were severe delays in the decision-making process regarding asylum applications, largely as a result of understaffing in the Refugee Commissioner's Office and the Refugee Appeals Board. There was a lack of transparency in the appeals process as the Board regularly failed to provide reasons for upholding first instance decisions rejecting asylum applications.

In February, the Council of Europe's Commissioner for Human Rights issued a report on his 2003 visit. He expressed concern about the policy of automatic detention until the conclusion of refugee determination proceedings or return to country of origin. He emphasized that in principle asylum-seekers should not be detained. He urged the authorities to develop alternatives and to ensure that the detention of irregular migrants was not "prolonged indefinitely." He called on the authorities to adopt a law permitting the detention of asylum-seekers only in exceptional circumstances and under judicial control. He also called on the authorities to ensure that legal aid was available to asylum-seekers during the appeals process; to provide decision-making bodies with sufficient staff; and to ensure appeal decisions were "motivated on the facts and merits."

Amendments to the Refugee and Immigration Acts in August provided for an increase in the resources available to the decision-making bodies and for inmates of detention centres to submit a request for conditional release on grounds that continued detention would be "unreasonable as regards duration or because there is no reasonable prospect of deportation within a reasonable time." However, no criteria were given for assessing what would constitute an "unreasonable" length of detention. The government continued to assert that it would not be in Malta's "national interest" to end the detention policy.

Conditions of detention

In the second half of the year, following a large number of arrivals by sea, some detention centres were severely overcrowded, with people housed in tents and provided with inadequate sanitary arrangements and diets. Tensions ran high and inmates staged a number of protests. Some detainees, including children, had little access to exercise in the open air and no recreational facilities. Children also experienced delays in gaining access to education.

A number of detainees suffered mental health problems. After examining the situation of those receiving treatment under police surveillance in Mount Carmel Psychiatric Hospital, the Ombudsman concluded that they did not suffer from chronic mental health problems but depression, mainly due to lack of information about their situation and their indefinite detention.

In July the government announced it was in the process of setting up a centralized social welfare service to address the needs of asylum-seekers and refugees. In December the government said that it had agreed on a policy document addressing all aspects of migration, including measures to improve accommodation facilities, to be discussed during a national conference on immigration in February 2005.

The European Committee for the Prevention of Torture visited Malta in January, principally to examine the treatment of foreign nationals detained on arrival, as well as the procedures and means of restraint applied in the context of forcible deportations by air. The report was not available by the end of the year.

Update: deportation of Eritreans in 2002

In May, AI issued a report describing the organization's grave concerns about the human rights situation in Eritrea (see Eritrea entry), including the treatment of some 220 Eritrean citizens deported from Malta to Eritrea in 2002. The Maltese government asserted that it had received no information prior to their departure indicating that the individuals would be at risk of human rights violations if returned. It subsequently set up an inquiry, apparently to examine whether the process leading to the deportations was regular and legal, and whether any individuals or authorities had exerted undue pressure for the Eritreans to be returned.

AI wrote to the Minister for Justice and Home Affairs and the magistrate conducting the inquiry seeking cooperation in providing AI with details of the inquiry's terms of reference and making a series of recommendations aimed at ensuring that the inquiry was thorough and impartial. AI recalled the correspondence which it had addressed to the Minister both before and after the 2002 deportations warning that Eritrea could not be considered a safe country for

Eritrean asylum-seekers and pointing out specific categories of Eritreans at particular risk of serious human rights violations if returned.

The authorities declined to provide AI with the terms of reference. In September the media reported the publication of the magistrate's findings. She apparently criticized the Refugee Appeals Board for failing to supply the reasons for rejecting the asylum applications lodged by some of the deportees, but concluded that this failure did not affect the legality of the whole process leading to deportation and that no undue pressure had been exerted. It was unclear to what extent the inquiry had examined the deportations in the light of Malta's obligations regarding the principle of *non-refoulement* contained in the UN Refugee Convention and AI's warnings to the government before the deportations were carried out.

Violence against women

Women were frequently subjected to domestic violence which was still not defined in Malta as a specific crime in law. The UN Committee on the Elimination of Discrimination against Women and the UN Committee on Economic, Social and Cultural Rights expressed concern at the delay in passing a Domestic Violence Bill, under discussion since March 2000, and urged Malta to expedite its adoption.

AI country reports/ visits
Reports
- Malta: Amnesty International's concerns with the International Criminal Court Act 2002 (AI Index: EUR 33/001/2004)
- Open Letter to the Maltese Minister for Justice and Home Affairs (AI Index: EUR 33/002/2004)
- Europe and Central Asia: Summary of Amnesty International's concerns in the region: January-June 2004: Malta (AI Index: EUR 01/005/2004)

MAURITANIA

ISLAMIC REPUBLIC OF MAURITANIA
Head of state: Maaouiya Ould Sid 'Ahmed Taya
Head of government: Sghaïr Ould M'Bareck
Death penalty: abolitionist in practice
International Criminal Court: not signed
UN Women's Convention: ratified with reservations
Optional Protocol to UN Women's Convention: not signed

Dozens of people were arrested in connection with two alleged plots to overthrow the government. More than 180 people appeared before the Criminal Court in a trial which did not meet international standards for fair trials. Torture of detainees continued. Slavery and forced labour persisted.

Background
On two occasions, in August and September, the authorities claimed to have uncovered plots to overthrow President Maaouiya Ould Taya. The authorities accused Libya and Burkina Faso of supporting the plotters and providing them refuge. Libya and Burkina Faso denied the accusations and Burkina Faso asked the African Union to open an inquiry into them. Between August and October the authorities arrested a number of civilians and soldiers in connection with a failed coup attempt in June 2003 and the alleged plots in August and September 2004.

In May the African Commission on Human and Peoples' Rights decided that the dissolution of the opposition coalition Union of Democratic Forces-New Era (Union des forces démocratiques-Ere nouvelle) in October 2000 constituted a violation of the African Charter on Human and Peoples' Rights.

In August the UN Committee on the Elimination of Racial Discrimination expressed concerns about the persistence of slavery-like practices, 23 years after the abolition of slavery. It also expressed concern that some human rights organizations had been denied official recognition by the authorities.

Mauritania strengthened its military cooperation with the USA in the context of the "war on terror".

Prisoners of conscience and political opponents
In April the Supreme Court confirmed the sentences of former President Mohamed Khouna Ould Haidalla and eight of his supporters. In November 2003 the former President had been given a five-year suspended sentence, fined and deprived of civil and political rights. His son, Sid'Ahmed Ould Haidalla, detained since November 2003, was released on bail in January.

In October, Jemil Ould Mansour, Cheikh Mohamed El Hacen Ould Dedew and El Moctar Ould Mohamed Moussa were held incommunicado for six days in Nouakchott, then released without charge. They were rearrested in November and detained incommunicado for 14 days in an unknown place. They were later charged with "complicity in the fabrication and forgery of documents that might cause a disturbance to public order and prejudice internal and external security" and remained in detention at the end of the year. AI considered them to be prisoners of conscience. On the first day of the trial nine women, all relatives of the defendants, were arrested while trying to attend the trial and accused of distributing leaflets. One of them was provisionally released after a week and the others were still in detention at the end of 2004.

Incommunicado detention, torture and ill-treatment
There were reports of torture and ill-treatment of detainees, mainly of those held in connection with the failed coup attempt of June 2003 and the alleged August and September 2004 plots.

Dozens of military officers and civilians were arrested and detained incommunicado for weeks in unknown places following the August and September plot allegations. Some detainees alleged that they suffered various forms of physical and psychological torture, including being beaten and suspended by the feet from an iron bar.

⬁ Abderrahmane Ould Mini and Saleh Ould Hannena, accused of being the masterminds of the attempted coup in June 2003, were reportedly held in solitary confinement and kept in handcuffs and leg-irons. The two went on hunger strike in November in protest at their conditions of detention. During the trial Saleh Ould Hannena said that he had been tortured during his detention.

Unfair trial
In November more than 180 people including military officers were tried on charges of threatening the security of the state in connection with the alleged coup plots in August and September and the failed coup in June 2003. Their trial before the Criminal Court at Ouad Naga did not meet international standards for fair trials.

AI was particularly concerned that the defendants were detained incommunicado for months and that some of them were tortured. The right to a fair hearing was not respected and defence lawyers were subjected to serious intimidation by the president of the court. Two defence lawyers were arrested and held for a short time. Families of the detainees had their right to visit their relatives restricted.

Slavery
While the government continued to deny that slavery existed, people were believed to be held in forced labour or slavery.

⬁ In January, a local human rights organization, SOS Slaves, wrote to the Minister of the Interior to express its concern about Matalla, a man who had escaped from slavery in the region of Tiris Zemour. Matalla had told the authorities that 11 members of his family remained in conditions of slavery in Tiris Zemour.

Freedom of expression and association
In April the Minister of the Interior refused to officially recognize the Party for Democratic Convergence, a party newly created by associates of former President Mohamed Khouna Ould Haidalla.

AI country reports/ visits
Reports
- Mauritania: Urgent Action appeal in case of Mohamed Khouna Ould Haidalla and others (AI Index: AFR 38/002/2004)
- Mauritania: Urgent Action appeal in case of Abderrahmane Ould Mini and others (AI Index: AFR 38/008/2004)

MEXICO

UNITED MEXICAN STATES
Head of state and government: Vicente Fox Quesada
Death penalty: abolitionist for ordinary crimes
International Criminal Court: signed
UN Women's Convention and its Optional Protocol: ratified

Human rights violations persisted, particularly at state level where arbitrary detention, torture and ill-treatment and the misuse of the judicial system were common. The federal government maintained its commitment to protect and promote human rights nationally and internationally. Legislation was proposed to strengthen human rights protection in the Constitution and the federal criminal justice system. A National Human Rights Programme was drawn up. Federal intervention to combat violence against women in Ciudad Juárez continued with limited success. Two prisoners of conscience were released after more than a year in custody. A number of human rights defenders were threatened and three journalists were murdered. Progress in the prosecution of those responsible for past human rights violations was limited. Political violence surrounded local elections in various states.

Background
The federal government presented and supported human rights initiatives at the UN Commission on Human Rights and at the Organization of American States. The government cooperated openly with international human rights mechanisms, including the Office of the UN High Commissioner for Human Rights, analyzing the domestic situation and promised to address 400 outstanding recommendations made by these mechanisms.

The Government Policy Commission on Human Rights and its subcommittees continued to develop a range of initiatives, including the harmonization of domestic legislation with international human rights standards. Training programmes took place on the prevention and documentation of torture. However, without a working majority in the legislature, advances in most areas were limited and there was increasing doubt over the government's capacity to deliver substantial improvements. The majority of state governments continued to resist significant reforms.

Congress lacked commitment to human rights reforms. Despite this, the long-delayed ratification of the Rome Statute of the International Criminal Court was brought a step closer with the approval of enabling legislation. The Senate selected the president of the National Human Rights Commission for a further five-year term. However, a lack of effective and transparent prior consultation with prominent human rights organizations undermined the Commission's credibility.

Crime, particularly kidnapping, increased public security concerns for many sectors of society.

In October demonstrations on both sides of the border with the USA marked the 10th year of Operation Gatekeeper, the US government initiative to restrict the flow of illegal migrants. The operation had reportedly led to an increased number of deaths as migrants tried to cross the border in remote and dangerous areas.

Human rights policy and legislation

In March and May the government proposed reforms to the Constitution and the criminal justice system, in part to strengthen human rights protection. While the proposals included many positive elements, they were not adequately consulted and fell short of recommendations by international human rights mechanisms, particularly those made by the Office of the UN High Commissioner for Human Rights in its 2003 diagnostic report. At the end of the year Congress had not made any progress in agreeing the reforms.

In December the government published its long awaited National Human Rights Programme, drawn up in discussion with sectors of civil society.

Human rights organizations in Guerrero campaigned for "disappearance" to be made a specific criminal offence in the state. At the end of 2004 the state congress had not voted on the proposal.

Violence against women in Chihuahua

The federal government continued to intervene to tackle the murder of women in Ciudad Juárez, Chihuahua State. Although the number of reported cases was lower than in previous years, there were still at least 18 murders of women in Ciudad Juárez, at least four of which involved sexual violence.

The Special Federal Prosecutor for Ciudad Juárez from the Federal Attorney General's Office reviewed more than 150 flawed investigations by the Chihuahua state authorities into the murders . At least seven more cases were taken over directly by the Prosecutor.

Possible criminal or administrative negligence was identified in the conduct of at least 100 state officials involved in the original murder investigations. However, since the same state authorities had the task of investigating these offences, there was serious concern that those responsible would not be held accountable.

Representatives of the Federal Attorney General's Office continued to deny the pattern of violence against women in the state and did not take any action on cases in the city of Chihuahua. Long overdue reforms to the state criminal justice system to address deep flaws in investigative and judicial practices, including the use of torture to extract confessions from suspects, did not occur. The election of a new state governor raised some hopes that the situation might finally be addressed.

▭ In October, Víctor Javier Garcia Uribe was sentenced to 50 years' imprisonment for the murder of eight women in 2001, despite compelling evidence that he had confessed under torture.

▭ In November, 16-year-old Martha Lizbeth Hernández was raped and murdered near her home in Ciudad Juárez. Investigations were continuing at the end of the year.

Arbitrary detention, torture and ill-treatment

Arbitrary detention, torture and ill-treatment by police remained widespread, particularly at state level. The authorities failed to combat these practices effectively or to ensure judicial remedy to victims.

▭ In May, during the European Union and Latin American and Caribbean Summit in Guadalajara, Jalisco State police used arbitrary detention and torture against scores of demonstrators. The state government refused to investigate the abuses despite compelling evidence and a recommendation of the National Human Rights Commission.

▭ In January, an 18 year-old indigenous Tlapaneco man, Socrates Tolentino González Genaro, was detained and tortured by municipal police in Zapotitlan Tablas, Guerrero State. The following day his mother was informed that he had committed suicide and told to sign a form for the release of his body. His mother, who was unable to read, discovered later that she had unknowingly signed a statement accepting that her son had committed suicide. Through the combined efforts of the family and a local human rights organization, Socrates González's body was exhumed. An autopsy confirmed that he had been tortured and unlawfully killed. Four police officers were under investigation for his death at the end of 2004.

Misuse of the justice system

The justice system continued to be misused, particularly at state level. The lack of impartiality of the judiciary and the prosecution services resulted in malicious prosecutions and unfair judicial procedures.

▭ In August, two lawyers, María del Carmen Grajales and Heriberto Gómez, acting in defence of a murder suspect in Chiapas, were detained by police and charged with fabricating evidence. The two were later released on bail. AI believed they were being prosecuted in reprisal for their efforts to prove that police had tortured their client and fabricated evidence.

◻ National and international pressure led to charges against two indigenous environmental activists being dropped. Hermenegildo Rivas and Isidro Baldenegro had been arrested in their homes in Colorados de la Virgen, Chihuahua, in 2003.

◻ In November, Felipe Arreaga, a long-standing peasant environmental activist in the mountains of Petetlan, Guerrero State, was detained and charged in connection with the murder of the son of a *cacique* (local political boss) in 1998. Despite presenting evidence to prove his innocence, he remained in custody as prosecution witnesses failed to appear before the court. AI believed Felipe Arreaga was being prosecuted in reprisal for his efforts to protect local forests from logging.

Human right defenders

Human rights defenders continued to suffer threats, intimidation and smear campaigns. State authorities failed to effectively prevent or investigate such incidents. In two states where the local Human Rights Commissions exposed human rights violations, the Commissions' presidents were harassed by local authorities and removed from office.

◻ In September a man identifying himself as a member of the Federal Investigation Agency entered the office of the Fray Pedro Lorenzo de la Nada Human Rights Committee in Ocosingo, Chiapas State, intimidating staff and threatening to arrest them.

◻ In September the Governor of Guerrero and a senior military commander made unsubstantiated allegations against human rights organizations in order to undermine the legitimacy of their work.

◻ The family of human rights defender Digna Ochoa, who died in 2001, appealed against an investigation into her death which concluded that she had committed suicide. Two appeals were rejected by federal judges, despite grave shortcomings in the investigation.

Attacks on journalists and freedom of speech

At least three journalists were murdered, apparently in reprisal for investigating drug traffickers and links to local authorities and businesses.

◻ In June, journalist Francisco Ortiz Franco was gunned down in Tijuana, Baja California, in front of his children. Five suspects were detained in connection with the killing, including a former police officer.

In Chiapas, the passing of excessively restrictive legislation on defamation undermined freedom of speech in the state.

Past human rights violations

There were limited advances in the prosecution of those accused of committing serious human rights violations during Mexico's "dirty war" between the 1960s and 1980s. The Special Prosecutor on past human rights violations, appointed in 2002, requested a number of indictments against senior members of former administrations. Eleven arrest warrants were granted but a number were rejected, including one requested for the former President, Luis Echeverría. These were rejected on the grounds that the crimes, which included murder and genocide, had expired under Mexico's statute of limitations. An appeal on this case was pending in the Supreme Court at the end of the year. There was serious concern that senior military and civilian officials would not be successfully prosecuted. The Minister of Defence and other senior military figures publicly called for amnesty legislation to protect those accused of abuses.

◻ Two former officials were detained for the "disappearance" of Jesús Piedra Ibarra in 1975. An arrest warrant was also issued for the former director of the Federal Security Directorate, Luis de la Barreda.

◻ A military tribunal closed the case against army General Arturo Acosta Chaparro, accused of the "disappearance" of 143 people in Guerrero in the 1970s, after deciding that evidence against him was no longer valid and accepting that senior official witnesses could no longer recall the facts. He remained in prison on unrelated criminal charges.

◻ Military jurisdiction ensured that there was still no progress in securing justice for two indigenous women raped by members of the Mexican army in Guerrero in 2002. The two women's cases were before the Inter-American Commission of Human Rights.

Indigenous peoples

Political violence surrounded local elections in Chiapas and Oaxaca, particularly in conflict-afflicted indigenous communities. The failure of the authorities to address underlying issues affecting many indigenous communities, such as marginalization and indigenous rights, frequently resulted in increased tensions and violence. Likewise, the tendency of the authorities to favour *caciques* often resulted in increased violence and impunity for abuses.

◻ In September the mayoral candidate, Guadalupe Avila Salinas, in the community of San José Estancia Grande, Oaxaca State, was murdered. She was reportedly murdered by the municipal president of the governing party, who subsequently evaded arrest. Two days later in the municipality of Loxicha, Lino Antonio Almoraz was murdered the day before community elections in which he had been campaigning. He was a member of the organization Union of Communities against Repression and Militarization in the Loxicha Region. Members of this organization were among 40 victims of political killings in Loxicha since 1997 when large sections of the community were detained and tortured, accused of belonging to an armed opposition group.

◻ In April a protest about access to water by hundreds of members of the community of Zinacantán, Chiapas, sympathetic to the Zapatista political movement was attacked by supporters of the governing party of the municipal council. Many members of the community were injured and many temporarily fled their homes fearing further attacks, only returning days later.

AI country reports/ visits
Reports
- Mexico: Ending the brutal cycle of violence against women in Ciudad Juárez and the city of Chihuahua (AI Index: AMR 41/011/2004)
- Mexico: Memorandum to the Mexican Federal Congress on reforms to the Constitution and criminal justice system (AI Index: AMR 41/032/2004)
- Mexico: Indigenous women and military injustice (AI Index: AMR 41/033/2004)
- Mexico: Allegations of abuse dismissed in Guadalajara – reluctance to investigate human rights violations perpetuates impunity (AI Index: AMR 41/034/2004)

Visit
In June an AI delegation visited Mexico City and the states of Veracruz, Oaxaca and Guerrero.

MOLDOVA

REPUBLIC OF MOLDOVA
Head of state: Vladimir Voronin
Head of government: Vasile Tarlev
Death penalty: abolitionist for all crimes
International Criminal Court: signed
UN Women's Convention: ratified
Optional Protocol to UN Women's Convention: not signed

Torture and ill-treatment in police custody continued to be a major problem and conditions in temporary detention facilities amounted to cruel and inhuman treatment. Moldovan women continued to be trafficked abroad for sexual exploitation. Tensions continued between the self-proclaimed Dnestr Moldavian Republic (DMR) and Moldova.

Ill-treatment and torture in custody
Torture and ill-treatment in police custody continued to be a major problem, aggravated by the high number of detentions resulting from the failure to use alternative methods such as provisional release and from a system of quotas and rewards for police based on the number of crimes resolved. The criminal code passed in July 2003 did not include an article criminalizing torture; however, two draft articles addressing torture were being considered by the Ministry of Justice at the end of 2004. Conditions in temporary holding facilities, where detainees can be held for up to 30 days, remained well below international standards. All such facilities were underground, inadequately ventilated and detainees did not have access to adequate toilet facilities. The penal code does not include a prohibition of torture.

⌑ In March the central court in the capital, Chişinău, ruled that the Ministry of the Interior was in breach of Article 3 of the European Convention on Human Rights in the case of Veceslav Drugaleov, because it had detained him in inhuman and degrading conditions from August 1999 to 2001. Veceslav Drugaleov had contracted tuberculosis as a result of a previous period of detention in 1996. He was detained again in 1999 and spent 18 months in the temporary detention facility of Călăraşi police station. This was the first ruling of its kind on conditions of detention in the country.

⌑ Oleg Talmazan was detained in March in connection with a financial crime and accused of failing to repay a bank loan under Article 123 of the Criminal Code. He was detained at the Chişinău Department for Organized Crime for over one month. The ventilation system in the underground temporary holding facility was periodically turned off, depriving the prisoners of adequate air. Sanitary conditions were inadequate and the prisoners were allowed into the exercise yard for only 30 minutes once a week. He was not allowed correspondence or to see his family. On 27 March he suffered a heart attack, but was not hospitalized despite the fact that an ambulance had been called out and had recommended his hospitalization. On 8 April he was transferred to a prison hospital and held for a further 30 days until 7 May. Oleg Talmazan lodged a complaint, but no action was known to have been taken on his case.

Violence against women
Moldova was a source country for women and girls trafficked for forced prostitution. Moldova continued to be one of the poorest countries in Europe, with a significant proportion of its population living below the poverty line. Out of a population of 4.3 million, up to one million people worked in other countries.

The groups of women most vulnerable to being trafficked were women escaping domestic violence and children leaving institutional care. According to the International Organization for Migration, 80 per cent of the women and girls trafficked for forced prostitution from Moldova were victims of domestic violence before being trafficked and after their return. Most women and girls were trafficked to Turkey and Macedonia, but a rising number were trafficked to Pakistan and the Middle East.

Article 165 of the Criminal Code establishes trafficking as an offence, defining it in line with Article 3 of the UN Protocol to Prevent, Suppress and Punish Trafficking in Persons, especially Women and Children (the Trafficking Protocol). The government set up a National Committee, but by the end of 2004 a National Plan of Action to combat trafficking was not yet in place. In particular, trafficked women and girls were not necessarily treated as victims of crime and were only exempted from criminal liability for acts that they may have committed as a result of being trafficked if they agreed to cooperate with law enforcement agencies. Preventive and support services were offered by non-governmental organizations and the International Organization for Migration, but there was no coherent national referral mechanism involving government bodies. Witness protection was hampered by lack of funding.

Self-proclaimed Dnestr Moldavian Republic (DMR)

There was no progress in resolving the status of this internationally unrecognized, breakaway region. Tensions escalated in June around the issue of Moldovan schools in the DMR that teach Moldovan/Romanian in the Latin script. The DMR authorities refused to register the schools in question, despite an agreement brokered by the Organization for Security and Co-operation in Europe (OSCE) in mid-2003, and teachers, pupils and parents were harassed by police. In June a high-level OSCE delegation visited the DMR and called for a more constructive stance on the part of the authorities; an end to harassment; and for the schools to be registered. In September, the authorities of the DMR agreed to register the schools in Tiraspol and Rîbniţa for one year, but the students' education continued to be disrupted by repair work on the school buildings.

On 2 June Alexandru Leşco, who had served 12 years in prison in the DMR, was released. Alexandru Leşco and the other members of the "Tiraspol Six" had been convicted in 1993 of "terrorist acts" including the murder of two DMR officials. Andrei Ivanţoc and Tudor Petrov-Popa remained in detention.

In July the European Court of Human Rights ruled that both Moldova and the Russian Federation were responsible for the unlawful detention and torture and ill-treatment suffered by Ilie Ilaşcu, Alexandru Leşco, Andrei Ivanţoc and Tudor Petrov-Popa. The court ruled that all had been detained arbitrarily and that Tudor Petrov-Popa and Andrei Ivanţoc were still being detained arbitrarily in breach of Article 5 of the European Convention on Human Rights.

AI country reports/ visits
Report
· Europe and Central Asia: Summary of Amnesty International's concerns in the region, January-June 2004: Moldova (AI Index: EUR 01/005/2004)
Visit
AI delegates visited Moldova in June.

MONGOLIA

MONGOLIA
Head of state: Bagabandi Natsagiin
Head of government: Elbegdorj Tsahiagiin (replaced Enkhbayar Nambariin in August)
Death penalty: retentionist
International Criminal Court: ratified
UN Women's Convention and its Optional Protocol: ratified

Journalists exposing corruption and abuse of power and lawyers defending victims of torture were at risk of intimidation and criminal charges because of their work. Detention conditions remained harsh. Violence against women was widespread.

Background
Neither the government party, the Mongolian People's Revolutionary Party, nor the opposition Motherland Democratic Coalition gained a majority in elections in June. They formed a "Grand Coalition" government.

Attacks on freedom of expression
Journalists, particularly those reporting on abuse of power or corruption, were at risk of investigation by the police on charges of criminal defamation.
🗀 In April, Erdenetuya Altangerel, a journalist, was detained for 23 days in a pre-trial detention centre. She was sentenced to three months' imprisonment by a district court for using the media to defame a member of parliament. Around 1,000 journalists protested against the court decision. On appeal, her sentence was reduced to a fine.

Human rights defenders
Human rights lawyers were at risk of intimidation and criminal proceedings.
🗀 In November, L. Sanjaasuren, lawyer for Enkhbat Damiran, who was forcibly returned from France to Mongolia in 2003, was sentenced to 18 months' imprisonment in a closed trial. He was convicted of revealing a state secret while defending his client.

Detention conditions
Conditions in the holding cell in the City Police Department were cruel and inhuman. Throughout 2004, around 300 people were held together in the cell, which has a normal capacity of 120. Access to medical treatment and sanitary facilities were inadequate. Tuberculosis was reportedly on the increase among prisoners, although this was contradicted by an official statement in March.

Death penalty
According to a National Human Rights Action Plan adopted in December 2003, the practice of delaying executions for three years was to be reviewed at an unspecified date.

There were no published statistics about the death penalty, but according to media reports the number of people on death row was increasing.

Impunity

The state failed to provide reparations to individuals wrongly imprisoned.

⌔ A district court awarded compensation to a herdsman, Erdene-Ochir, after seven years' wrongful imprisonment, but did not compensate him for the damage to his health. Due to poor prison conditions, most of his teeth were broken and he had arthritis and kidney disease.

Violence against women

According to a study carried out by the National Centre Against Violence, domestic violence was the third most common cause of death and injury in Mongolia. The police lacked training on how to handle such cases. Impunity for sexual violence was widespread; 88 per cent of rape cases taken to court were dismissed.

Media reports of women being trafficked to China increased, and the police apparently took little action to deal with such cases.

AI country visits/ reports

Visit

AI delegates visited detainees in the holding cell in the City Police Department in April and October.

MOROCCO/ WESTERN SAHARA

KINGDOM OF MOROCCO
Head of state: King Mohamed VI
Head of government: Driss Jettou
Death penalty: abolitionist in practice
International Criminal Court: signed
UN Women's Convention: ratified with reservations
Optional Protocol to UN Women's Convention: not signed

An Equity and Reconciliation Commission was inaugurated to look into hundreds of cases of "disappearance" and arbitrary detention in previous decades. The authorities continued their clampdown on suspected Islamist activists, sentencing more than 200 people to prison terms. Several of those sentenced had allegedly been tortured during questioning by the security forces. Other breaches of

the right to a fair trial were reported. The authorities drafted a law to combat torture and said in July that allegations of torture reported in 2002 and 2003 would be investigated. The legal framework for women's rights was significantly improved. A royal pardon was granted to 33 people, including political prisoners and prisoners of conscience.

Background

The USA accorded Morocco the status of "major non-NATO ally" in June, apparently in acknowledgement of what a senior administration official described as "Morocco's steadfast support in the global war on terror". The status lifted restrictions on arms sales. The USA also signed a free-trade agreement with Morocco.

The Personal Envoy of the UN Secretary-General for Western Sahara, James Baker, resigned in June after seven years of failed efforts to resolve the dispute over the territory's status. Morocco's efforts to convince the international community of its sovereign rights over Western Sahara suffered a setback in September when South Africa formally established diplomatic ties with the Polisario Front, which calls for an independent state in Western Sahara and operates a self-proclaimed government-in-exile in refugee camps near Tindouf, south-western Algeria. A new war of words subsequently flared up between Morocco and neighbouring Algeria.

Equity and Reconciliation Commission

On 7 January an Equity and Reconciliation Commission was inaugurated by King Mohamed VI to "close the file on past human rights violations". One of its tasks is to complete payment of compensation to victims of "disappearances" and arbitrary detention that occurred between the 1950s and 1990s. The Commission is also charged with providing other forms of reparation to enable victims to be rehabilitated and reintegrated into society, and with proposing measures to prevent recurrence of such human rights violations. To this end, it consulted with victims and associations representing them on a range of ideas. By December the Commission had received requests for reparations concerning more than 16,000 victims.

Another main task of the Commission is to establish the fate of hundreds of people who "disappeared" in previous decades and, in the case of those who died in detention, to locate their remains. During the year the Commission collected testimonies from relatives of the "disappeared" and began preparing a report, due in April 2005, that would set out the reasons and institutional responsibilities for grave violations up to 1999. In December it began organizing public hearings, broadcast on radio and television, in which dozens of witnesses and victims would present their testimonies.

However, the Commission's statutes categorically excluded the identification of individual perpetrators and rejected criminal prosecutions, prompting the UN Human Rights Committee in November to express concern that no steps were planned to bring to justice those responsible for "disappearances". Some perpetrators were alleged to remain members or even high-ranking officials of the security forces.

Abuses during the 'counter-terrorism' campaign

The authorities continued their clampdown on suspected Islamist activists, a campaign that began in 2002 and intensified following the killing of 45 people in bomb attacks in Casablanca on 16 May 2003. Over 200 people were sentenced to prison terms ranging from several months to life imprisonment, convicted of belonging to "criminal gangs" or of involvement in planning violent acts. Those sentenced to death in 2003 remained in custody at the end of the year. No executions have taken place in Morocco/Western Sahara since 1993. Several of those sentenced in 2004 were allegedly tortured to extract confessions or to force them to sign or thumbprint statements they rejected. Other breaches of the right to a fair trial were reported, such as the frequent rejection by courts of requests by defence lawyers to call defence witnesses.

In February, AI sent a memorandum to the authorities detailing the findings of its research into the alleged torture in 2002 and 2003 of dozens of suspects held in secret detention by the Directorate for the Surveillance of the Territory (the internal intelligence service), allegations the authorities had dismissed as baseless at the time. Subsequently, the authorities acknowledged that a limited number of abuses may have occurred, and in July the Prime Minister declared that investigations would be carried out and "appropriate measures" taken against those responsible. Several investigations were started and a law to combat torture was drafted.

The UN Human Rights Committee expressed concern in November about the large number of alleged cases of torture or ill-treatment in detention and the lack of independent investigations into them.

Women's rights

On 3 February a new Family Code was promulgated which significantly improved the legal framework for women's rights. Husbands and wives were accorded equal and joint responsibility for running the family home and bringing up children, and the wife's duty of obedience to her husband was rescinded. The minimum age of marriage for women was raised from 15 to 18, the same as for men, and the requirement of a male marital tutor (*wali*) for women to marry was eliminated. Severe restrictions were imposed on male polygamy. The right to divorce by mutual consent was established and unilateral divorce by the husband was placed under strict judicial control. However, provisions governing inheritance rights, which widely discriminate against women, remained almost entirely unchanged.

Confirming the findings of local women's rights organizations, the UN Human Rights Committee expressed its concern in November about the high level of domestic violence against women.

Pardon of political prisoners

On 7 January a royal pardon was granted to 33 people, including political prisoners and prisoners of conscience. Among them were human rights defenders, journalists and Islamist activists, including Ali Lmrabet, a Moroccan journalist sentenced to three years' imprisonment in June 2003, and Ali Salem Tamek, a human rights defender from Western Sahara sentenced to two years' imprisonment in October 2002.

Rights of migrants

Hundreds of migrants, most from sub-Saharan Africa, were arrested and deported. Several alleged that the security forces used excessive force during arrest or tortured or ill-treated them in custody. In April, two Nigerian nationals died reportedly after being shot by the security forces near the border with the Spanish enclave of Melilla. The authorities launched an investigation into the incident.

The UN Special Rapporteur on the human rights of migrants published a report in January following a visit to Morocco in October 2003. She expressed particular concern about the situation of sub-Saharan migrants who often "live in the most appalling conditions". She noted that "many of them, fleeing from conflict in their own countries, have no assurance that they will be granted refugee status or that their asylum applications will be considered before they are escorted to the border" for deportation. The Special Rapporteur reported that "neither the authorities responsible for law and order and for control of air, sea and land borders, nor the judicial authorities, have clear information regarding refugee status". She recommended, among other things, that "a plan of action be drawn up to protect migrants' rights through training for judicial authorities, access to appeal procedures, awareness-raising and information campaigns."

Expulsion of journalists

At least five foreign journalists reporting on Western Sahara were expelled, apparently as part of an attempt by the authorities to prevent independent reporting on the territory. The expulsions were not preceded by judicial rulings and the journalists were not allowed to submit reasons against their expulsion or to have their cases reviewed by a judicial authority.

🖙 Catherine Graciet and Nadia Ferroukhi, respectively a French journalist and a French-Algerian photographer, were arrested at a police roadblock by men in plain clothes on 27 January as they were travelling to Western Sahara to report on living conditions there. They were detained overnight in a hotel and then taken to Agadir, where they were reportedly questioned by police in plain clothes and then obliged to take a flight to France. They said that the authorities accused them of not having notified the Moroccan authorities that they planned to report on Western Sahara before travelling to the region. Official sources said that they were expelled because they were suspected of undertaking "propaganda" activities in favour of the Polisario Front and were found in possession of "large amounts of documentation" favourable to the Polisario Front's position.

Polisario camps

The Polisario Front freed 200 Moroccan prisoners of war whom it had captured between 1975 and 1991 and detained ever since in its camps near Tindouf, south-western Algeria. One hundred were released in February and another 100 in June. They were then repatriated under the auspices of the International Committee of the Red Cross. However, 412 remained in detention at the end of the year. Under international humanitarian law, the Polisario Front was obliged to release the prisoners without delay after the end of armed hostilities in 1991 following a ceasefire brokered by the UN.

Those responsible for human rights abuses in the camps in previous years continued to enjoy impunity. The Polisario authorities failed to hand over perpetrators still resident in the camps to the Algerian authorities to be brought to justice, and the Moroccan government failed to bring to justice perpetrators of abuses in the Polisario camps who had left the camps and were present on its territory.

AI country reports/ visits
Reports
· Morocco/Western Sahara: Torture in the "anti-terrorism" campaign – the case of Témara detention centre (AI Index: MDE 29/004/2004)

MOZAMBIQUE

REPUBLIC OF MOZAMBIQUE
Head of state: Armando Guebuza (replaced Joaquim Chissano in December)
Head of government: Luisa Diogo (replaced Pascoal Mocumbi in February)
Death penalty: abolitionist for all crimes
International Criminal Court: signed
UN Women's Convention: ratified
Optional Protocol to UN Women's Convention: not signed

Armando Guebuza, the candidate of the ruling Mozambique Liberation Front (Frente da Libertação de Moçambique, Frelimo), became President following peaceful elections in December. President Joaquim Chissano, after 18 years in office, did not contest the election. A plan to modernize the police was approved but discipline and control systems remained weak. There were reports of deaths in police custody and excessive use of force and firearms. Investigations into alleged people trafficking continued. Steps were taken to address violence against women.

Background
Frelimo gained 160 seats in the legislative elections, held simultaneously with the presidential poll. The opposition coalition, Mozambique National Resistance – Electoral Union (Resistência Nacional Moçambicana – União Eleitoral, Renamo-UE), obtained 90 seats, but said that it would not take them up as the elections had been unfair. European Union observers said there had been serious irregularities which may have affected some parliamentary seats.

Efforts to eradicate corruption continued. An Anti-Corruption Law was published in June. Seven people were convicted of involvement in a US$14 million bank fraud, also in June. They included two men convicted in 2003 of the murder in 2000 of journalist Carlos Cardoso, who had been investigating the fraud. Another person convicted of the murder escaped from the maximum security prison in Maputo in May, apparently with the aid of corrupt police, and sought asylum in Canada. Police said they had no new information concerning the murder in 2001 of António Siba-Siba Macuácua who had been investigating another bank fraud.

The National Statistics Institute announced in July that, unless checked, HIV/AIDS could be responsible for one in every three deaths by 2010.

Political violence
There were several instances of politically motivated violence in the run-up to elections, some involving members of the bodyguard of Renamo leader, Afonso Dhlakama, in Sofala province. This prompted calls for the 200 former Renamo soldiers, authorized to

continue as an armed unit as a temporary measure under the 1992 peace agreement, to be disbanded.

In April, bodyguard members reportedly arrested and beat at least six people, including Frelimo supporters and one police officer, and burned the Frelimo office in Maringuè. In August, 25 armed bodyguard members invaded the Inhaminga police station and set free Renamo-UE party activists arrested on suspicion of assaulting a Frelimo official. In October, Renamo-UE activists attacked Frelimo offices in Mozambique Island, Nampula province, injuring several people, one of them seriously.

Policing

Crime remained a serious problem, particularly in some densely populated areas of Maputo where there were high rates of unemployment and inadequate police presence.

In May, the government adopted the Strategic Plan of action and modernization of the Police of the Republic of Mozambique (Polícia da República de Moçambique, PRM), for the years 2003 to 2012. The plan had been developed after consultation with government and non-governmental stakeholders. Respect for human rights was reflected in seven of its nine Guiding Principles. However, while the plan acknowledged the problem of abuse of police powers, it made no specific provision for ensuring greater accountability for human rights violations.

Human rights violations attributed to the police included beatings and other ill-treatment, deaths in custody and excessive use of force and firearms. In most cases the authorities apparently failed to take appropriate action to investigate such reports and bring the perpetrators to justice, thus reinforcing a sense of impunity. However, dozens of officers were expelled for disciplinary offences and some also faced criminal charges, including for rape.

There were a few reports of police being prosecuted for human rights violations. For example, an officer was sentenced to three months' imprisonment in Xai-Xai in February for beating a 60-year-old widow and her daughter in December 2003. Another received a seven-year sentence and a fine in June for shooting dead 18-year-old Carlos Faruca in Beira in October 2003.

Abuses by community police

Members of the Community Policing Councils, non-statutory bodies set up by the PRM in many districts to assist police in preventing crime, received no salary and little training. In some areas they were said to have helped to reduce crime but in others to have resorted to beatings, bribery and theft. Although not authorized to do so, some reportedly carried firearms.

⬭ Community police reportedly arrested Cristóvão Francisco Manuel at his home in Beira in January and accused him of theft. They searched the house, handcuffed him and took him to their office where they beat him for several hours. Neighbours, hearing the victim's screams, protested and the beatings stopped. However, the community police had lost the keys to the handcuffs. He was released the following day. There was apparently no police inquiry into his treatment.

Death in custody

Procedures to determine the causes of deaths in custody appeared to be inadequate. Autopsies or medical examinations were not automatically carried out, or were not supported by inquiries by an independent official.

⬭ An autopsy was held at the request of the Mozambique Human Rights League (Liga Moçambicana dos Direitos Humanos, LMDH), a week after the death of Geraldo Celestino João in Chimoio, Manica province, in March. Police had allegedly arrested him at his home without a warrant, handcuffed him, thrown him on the ground, shot him twice in the thighs, hit and kicked him, then taken him to hospital, where he died. The provincial prosecutor investigated the case and, stated in October that the victim had been shot while trying to escape. The LMDH appealed against the finding, but received no reply before the end of 2004.

Excessive use of force and firearms

Reports of excessive use of force and firearms suggested inadequate training in the minimum use of force. There was little indication that police considered alternative tactics before resorting to the use of force and firearms.

⬭ Manjor António Manjor, the son of a local Renamo representative, was injured in Inhaminga in late August. Six paramilitary police went to his home allegedly to search for illegal weapons, but without showing a warrant. They reportedly fired in the air, questioned Manjor António Manjor, and then shot him in the leg, allegedly to stop him running away. The police subsequently took him to hospital. There was apparently no official inquiry into the shooting.

⬭ Paramilitary police beat two demonstrators in July, breaking the arm and collar-bone of one of them. The demonstrators, who had worked in the former German Democratic Republic and were known as "Majermane", were demanding payment of money they believed they were owed. Some had occupied the German Embassy. In May, the police had imposed a ban on demonstrations by the "Majermane", citing security concerns. The LMDH challenged the constitutionality of this ban in August but the Administrative Court had not decided the issue by the end of 2004.

Trafficking

Government and civil society representatives debated the need for a law on people trafficking in response to reports of women and children being taken to South Africa for forced labour or prostitution. Investigations continued into reports of missing persons, violent deaths and mutilations in Nampula province which fuelled fears of trafficking in people and in human organs in 2003 and early 2004. The Attorney General published a report in February which criticized the work of local police and procurators but found no proof of such trafficking. A further report concluded in August was not published, reportedly because it contained details of individuals being prosecuted.

There were reports of extraction of human organs for ritual purposes in Nampula and Niassa provinces. Four people were charged in connection with the mutilation of the penis of a nine-year-old boy in Manica province in 2003. They had not been tried by the end of 2004.

⬦ Marta Paita, aged 39, was killed in Mecuburi district, Nampula province, in March. Organs were extracted from her body. Her two-month old daughter was found dead at her side. She had been attacked while walking back to her home after a visit to a clinic. Six men were arrested in connection with the crime, but the case had not gone to trial by the end of 2004.

Violence against women and children

Offices for Attending to Women and Child Victims of Violence were established in all 10 provinces with police specially trained to deal with violence in the family. The government's Offices for Women and Children and Social Action and a range of non-governmental organizations (NGOs) also provided protection and assistance to victims of domestic violence. Cases reported in the media and to NGOs included forced marriage of girl children, sometimes as young as six years old.

AI country reports/ visits
Visits

AI delegates carried out research in Mozambique and met police and other government officials in April and May. NGOs from north and central Mozambique participated in a human rights workshop coordinated by AI in Nampula in April.

Following the research visit a memorandum containing recommendations on policing and human rights was sent to the government.

MYANMAR

UNION OF MYANMAR
Head of state: Senior General Than Shwe
Head of government: General Soe Win (replaced General Khin Nyunt in October)
Death penalty: retentionist
International Criminal Court: not signed
UN Women's Convention: ratified with reservations
Optional Protocol to UN Women's Convention: not signed

In October the Prime Minister was placed under house arrest and replaced by another army general. Despite the announcement of the release of large numbers of prisoners in November, more than 1,300 political prisoners remained in prison, and arrests and imprisonment for peaceful political opposition activities continued. The army continued to commit serious human rights violations against ethnic minority civilians during counter-insurgency operations in the Mon, Shan and Kayin States, and in Tanintharyi Division. Restrictions on freedom of movement in states with predominantly ethnic minority populations continued to impede farming, trade and employment. This particularly impacted on the Rohingyas in Rakhine State. Ethnic minority civilians living in all these areas continued to be subjected to forced labour by the military.

Background

In May the government convened the National Convention in order to draft a new Constitution. The Convention did not involve most political parties, including the National League for Democracy (NLD). Twenty-eight ceasefire groups participated, 13 of which raised issues about greater local autonomy. The Convention adjourned in July and did not reconvene.

In October Prime Minister General Khin Nyunt, who had also been head of Military Intelligence (MI), was removed from power and placed under house arrest. He was replaced by State Peace and Development Council (SPDC, the military government) Secretary 1 General Soe Win. Other cabinet members thought to be allied to General Khin Nyunt, including Home Minister Colonel Tin Hlaing, were also removed and held under house arrest. The same month the SPDC stated that they would carry out the seven-point "road map" to democracy announced by General Khin Nyunt in August 2003.

Ceasefire talks between the Karen National Union (KNU), a Karen armed opposition group, and the SPDC continued sporadically during the year but no ceasefire was agreed. Skirmishes between the KNU and the army continued in the Kayin State and Tanintharyi Division. Fighting between the army and the Shan armed opposition group, the Shan State Army-South (SSA-South), continued in south-eastern Shan State. The army expanded its presence in southern Ye township,

Mon State, where the Hongsawati Party, a breakaway faction of the ceasefire group, the New Mon State Party (NMSP), had fought against the central government.

Although the NLD headquarters reopened in May, all other NLD offices remained closed, amid reports of SPDC repression of NLD members. Such tactics included withdrawal of business licenses, short-term detention, and travel restrictions for members' peaceful political opposition activities.

Political arrests and imprisonment

Over 1,300 political prisoners remained in prisons throughout the country, including many who had already served their sentences. NLD General Secretary Daw Aung San Suu Kyi was held under house arrest throughout the year. NLD Vice-Chairman U Tin Oo was transferred to house arrest from Kalay Prison in February. Some prisoners were released after they had served their sentences.

At least 33 prison sentences were handed down for political reasons. Among those sentenced were NLD district officials from Mandalay and Ayeyarwaddy Divisions, and Shan State; former political prisoners; and student activists. At least two groups of political activists were given sentences of between seven and 22 years' imprisonment in April and May, reportedly for having contact with opposition political groups in exile.

◻ U Ohn Than, a former political prisoner, was arrested in September and sentenced in October to two years' imprisonment for disturbing public order. He had reportedly staged a peaceful one-man protest outside City Hall in Yangon, calling for political freedoms.

◻ At least 24 political prisoners remained in detention after they had served their sentences. They included six student leaders and around 10 alleged members of the Communist Party of Burma, the majority of whom had been imprisoned since 1989 or 1991. They also included two prisoners of conscience, Daw May Win Myint and Than Nyein, both NLD MPs elect, who suffered severe and chronic health problems during the year.

At least three people died in custody or shortly after being released from prison.

◻ Prisoner of conscience and lawyer Min Thu, arrested in 1998 in connection with the preparation of a history of the student movement, died in Insein Prison in June. He had reportedly been ill-treated in prison in 2001, when authorities held prisoners in cells normally used to keep military dogs while they investigated a prison hunger strike.

An unknown number of MI personnel and other government officials were arrested amid reports of widespread corruption. Colonel Hla Min, Information Division of the Defence Ministry, and several others were detained in Insein Prison at the end of the year.

Releases

Approximately 40 political prisoners, including prisoners of conscience and possible prisoners of conscience, were among 9,248 prisoners released in late November. The SPDC said they had been wrongfully arrested by the National Intelligence Bureau (NIB), which the SPDC abolished on 22 October. However, the SPDC did not clarify whether the releases were of criminal or political prisoners.

◻ Prisoner of conscience and prominent student leader Paw U Tun, alias Min Ko Naing, was released on 19 October after more than 15 years in prison.

Human rights violations against ethnic minorities

The vast majority of Rohingyas continued to be effectively denied the right to a nationality under the 1982 Burma Citizenship Law. Rohingyas in northern Rakhine State routinely had to receive permission and pay a fee in order to leave their villages, which greatly inhibited their ability to trade and seek employment. Rohingyas were also frequently subjected to forced labour.

◻ In January young single women from Kyong Kanya village, Khaw Za village tract, southern Ye township, Mon State were forced to serve and entertain army officers. Male villagers were forced to purchase alcohol for the army. This practice by the army was repeated in other areas of southern Ye township where the Hongsawati Party had been active.

◻ A Shan farmer from Murngkhun village, Non Laew village tract, Laikha township, Shan State, was forced to transport troops with his tractor so frequently that he did not have sufficient time to farm. In January troops accused him of not wanting to transport them, kicked him off his tractor, and broke his arm by stamping on it.

◻ A Rohingya man from northern Maungdaw township reported that villagers from nine village tracts had to build a road for the security forces beginning in February.

Impunity

No one was brought to justice for the attacks by government supporters against the NLD on 30 May 2003 in Depeyin, Sagaing Division, when an unknown number of people were killed or injured, nor did any independent investigation take place.

Death penalty

Nine people sentenced to death for high treason in November 2003 for conspiring to assassinate government officials and bomb government buildings had their sentences commuted during the year. Among them were prisoners of conscience Thet Zaw, editor of *First Eleven* sports magazine; U Aye Myint, a lawyer; and Min Kyi, a lawyer, who had their sentences commuted to three years' imprisonment in May. The same month Shwe Mann, a fourth prisoner of conscience in the same case, had his death sentence commuted to "transportation for life". U Aye Myint, Min Kyi and Shwe Mann were accused, among other things, of passing information about forced labour to the International Labour Organization (ILO). The ILO raised the cases of these three men with the SPDC in March after it had interviewed them at Insein Prison. The three said that they had been tortured during initial interrogation after their arrest in July 2003. In October, the four men had their sentences further reduced to two years in prison. Five other men sentenced to death in the same case had their sentences commuted to life imprisonment in May, and one of the five had his sentence further reduced to five years' imprisonment in October. No executions were reported.

International initiatives

The UN Special Envoy for Myanmar received permission for one trip to Myanmar in March, when he met NLD leader Daw Aung San Suu Kyi, who indicated her willingness to work with General Khin Nyunt's government. The UN Special Rapporteur on Myanmar was not allowed to visit the country.

In April the UN Commission on Human Rights extended the mandate of the Special Rapporteur on Myanmar for a further year. In December the UN General Assembly adopted a resolution expressing "grave concern at... the ongoing systematic violation of human rights" in Myanmar.

Following the Asia-Europe Meeting (ASEM) in October, which the SPDC attended as a member for the first time, the European Union Common Position that provides for some sanctions against Myanmar was strengthened on the basis of the lack of progress in lifting restrictions on political activity in the country.

In March the ILO Governing Body postponed implementation of a Plan of Action for Myanmar, which provided for a facilitator to hear complaints about forced labour and find a solution. The decision was taken in light of the death sentences handed down to three men who had passed information to the ILO (see above). In November the ILO Governing Body announced the reinstatement of measures originally adopted at the International Labour Conference in June 2000, which called on all ILO members and international organizations to examine their relations with the SPDC and their operations in Myanmar to ensure that they did not result in forced labour.

AI country reports/ visits
Reports
- Myanmar: The administration of justice – grave and abiding concerns (AI Index: ASA 16/001/2004)
- Myanmar: The Rohingya minority – fundamental rights denied (AI Index: ASA 16/005/2004)
- Myanmar: Facing political imprisonment – prisoners of concern to Amnesty International (AI Index: ASA 16/007/2004)

NAMIBIA

REPUBLIC OF NAMIBIA
Head of state: Samuel Nujoma
Head of government: Theo-Ben Gurirab
Death penalty: abolitionist for all crimes
International Criminal Court: ratified
UN Women's Convention and its Optional Protocol: ratified

The human rights situation showed improvement on the low point of 1999-2000 when there was a sharp rise in violations following an armed secessionist uprising in the north-east Caprivi region and Namibia's intervention in the Angolan civil war. However, threats to the independence of the judiciary were a cause for concern. New statistics on violence against women and children showed no slowdown in the rate of attacks. The Caprivi treason trial began: most defendants, many of whom were prisoners of conscience, had been in prison awaiting trial for five years.

Background
Elections in November saw the ruling Swapo party returned to power with 76 per cent of the vote. Swapo's candidate Hifikepunye Pohamba won the presidential election; he was due to replace President Samuel Nujoma, who had been the head of state since independence in 1990, in March 2005.

Trial of Caprivi detainees
The trial of some 120 people accused of high treason, murder and other offences in connection with a secessionist uprising in the Caprivi region in 1999 finally got under way in August, after most of the defendants had spent almost five years in custody.

The case was expected to continue well into 2005. The judge barred the media from identifying several state witnesses – the first such ruling since independence in 1990. Police officers accused of torturing suspects detained in the wake of the uprising had still not faced any formal charges or disciplinary action.

Legal issues
A new Labour Bill was passed that specifically outlaws discrimination in the workplace on the grounds of HIV status. The approval of a Stock Theft Amendment Bill, which makes the crime of stealing a goat punishable by a possible 30-year jail sentence, was criticized by opposition parties as draconian.

Leading politicians continued to verbally attack the judiciary, with Swapo youth leader Paulus Kapia accusing the judge in the Caprivi case of "sabotaging peace" in Namibia after he ordered the release of 13 suspects. The decision to release the 13 was later overturned by the Supreme Court. Swapo's election manifesto committed the party to changing the composition of the body that appoints judges so that it would "comply with the will of the people".

Violence against women and children
The police announced that during 2003 over 1,000 cases of rape were reported to Women and Child Protection Units compared to 814 in 2002. Interim figures released in 2004 indicated no decline in the rate of attacks on women and children. Despite concern over the high number of assaults, Women's Solidarity, a leading non-governmental organization offering counselling to victims of domestic violence, closed down in early 2004 due to a lack of funding.

Refugees
Six refugees from the Democratic Republic of the Congo were charged with inciting public violence after a demonstration on World Refugee Day at the Osire camp in central Namibia. The six had been protesting about delays in processing their applications for asylum. The voluntary repatriation of Angolan refugees continued throughout the year.

Freedom of expression
Although there were fewer reports of politicians using hate speech against minorities and political opponents than in previous years, in May President Nujoma made a vitriolic speech against Ben Ulenga, leader of the Congress of Democrats opposition party, during which he referred to him as a homosexual.

The government refused to insert election-related educational material in *The Namibian* because of its ban on advertising in the newspaper, a ban in place since 2001 because of *The Namibian*'s alleged anti-government reporting. Opposition parties complained that the *Namibian Broadcasting Corporation* showed a heavy bias to the ruling Swapo party during election campaigns.

NEPAL

KINGDOM OF NEPAL
Head of state: King Gyanendra Bir Bikram Shah Dev
Head of government: Sher Bahadur Deuba (replaced Surya Bahadur Thapa in June)
Death penalty: abolitionist for all crimes
International Criminal Court: not signed
UN Women's Convention: ratified
Optional Protocol to UN Women's Convention: signed

The conflict intensified and there was an increase in human rights abuses by government security forces and the armed opposition Communist Party of Nepal (CPN) (Maoist). The security forces were responsible for an unprecedented number of "disappearances", a rise in unlawful killings, and continuing arbitrary arrests and torture. The CPN (Maoist) abducted civilians and committed torture and unlawful killings. There was a growing culture of impunity and disregard for the rule of law among the security forces, who systematically obstructed the courts and the National Human Rights Commission (NHRC). In addition to the human rights abuses committed in the context of the conflict, incidences of discrimination and violence related to caste, gender, ethnicity and sexuality were reported.

Background
In March the UN Commission on Human Rights issued a Chairperson's Statement on the situation in Nepal, and the government made a high-profile commitment to respect human rights. Despite this, the conflict worsened and the human rights situation deteriorated. Many civilians were displaced by the fighting and women and children were particularly severely affected.

The five main political parties led mass demonstrations calling for a return to parliamentary democracy. In May the Prime Minister resigned and in June King Gyanendra reappointed Sher Bahadur Deuba, who had been Prime Minister when the King dissolved parliament in 2002.

In August the Maoists staged a week-long blockade of the capital, Kathmandu, stopping supplies from reaching the city.

Twelve Nepali hostages in Iraq were killed by their captors in late August, sparking violent protests. Angry crowds attacked the main mosque in Kathmandu and the offices of some Middle Eastern airlines.

The army continued to receive military equipment from abroad, including attack helicopters made in India with parts manufactured by European companies and thousands of rifles from India and the USA.

The mandates of the National Women's Commission and National Dalit Commission expired in March and were not renewed.

'Disappearances'

Hundreds of people "disappeared" after being arrested by members of the Royal Nepal Army (RNA), the Armed Police Force (APF) and the civilian police. AI recorded 418 "disappearances" between the end of the ceasefire in August 2003 and 30 August 2004, and the NHRC reported 707 cases over the same period.

Around one third of the "disappeared" were eventually released or located, sometimes after several months in secret detention.

"Disappearances" were facilitated by the Terrorist and Disruptive Activities (Control and Punishment) Act (TADA) 2002, which allowed the security forces to arrest suspects without warrant and detain them without charge. Following its expiry, the TADA was replaced in October by a new Terrorist and Disruptive Activities (Control and Punishment) Ordinance (TADO), which increased provision for detention without charge or trial from 90 days to one year.

Following public pressure, in July the government established a committee under the Home Ministry to locate the "disappeared". In September, in an effort to legalize detentions, a number of detainees were transferred from unacknowledged detention in army barracks to a special civilian detention centre in Kathmandu. The UN Working Group on Enforced or Involuntary Disappearances visited Nepal in December.

Mass arrests of peaceful demonstrators and excessive use of force

In April-May largely peaceful demonstrations calling for a return to parliamentary democracy were met with mass arrests and excessive use of force by the police. Well over 1,000 protesters were arrested and reportedly held in warehouses and other overcrowded and insanitary locations, sometimes for several days, before being released without charge. The NHRC and other human rights organizations were initially denied access to them.

⌂ Ujeer Magar, a journalist reporting on the demonstrations, and Mahamuniswor Acharya, a human rights observer with the Human Rights Organization of Nepal (HURON), were both badly beaten by police in early April.

Torture and ill-treatment by security forces

Torture and ill-treatment of people in the custody of the security forces continued to be regularly reported. In November it was reported that none of the 19 torture victims awarded compensation by courts in the last eight years had yet received any money.

⌂ A taxi driver was arrested without warrant by security forces in Kathmandu in August. He was taken to Singh Nath Gan army barracks, Bhaktapur, where he was reportedly punched, kicked, beaten with a stick and had water forced up his nose. He was held for four days, and warned that if he complained he would be killed.

Unlawful killings by security forces

Members of the security forces continued to kill unarmed civilians, often claiming that they had died in an "encounter" with CPN (Maoist) forces, or while trying to escape from custody.

⌂ Two women, 18-year-old Reena Rasaili and 17-year-old Subhadra Chaulagain, were shot dead by plain-clothes security force personnel in Pokhari Chauri village, Kavre District, on 13 February. Reena Rasaili was allegedly raped before her death. Four days later, 15-year-old Maina Sunuwar was arrested by soldiers searching for her mother, who had witnessed the earlier shootings. She was reportedly killed on the day of her arrest.

Impunity and the breakdown in rule of law

The security forces operated with growing impunity and disregard for the rule of law. In the face of Supreme Court orders to respond to habeas corpus petitions, military authorities consistently issued false denials or failed to respond in substance. They also obstructed the NHRC from fulfilling its monitoring and investigative duties. Many people were rearrested immediately after they had been released by the courts.

⌂ Krishna Khatri Chhetri (K.C.), a former student leader, "disappeared" in September 2003. A habeas corpus petition was dismissed when the authorities denied his arrest. Following reports that he was held in Bhairabnath Gan army barracks, Kathmandu, and had been tortured, a second habeas corpus petition was filed in February 2004. The RNA refused entry to NHRC representatives when they attempted to visit Bhairabnath Gan barracks in June to search for Krishna K.C. The RNA continued to claim that Krishna K.C. was not in their custody despite Supreme Court orders to cooperate and reliable information that he was held in the barracks.

Unlawful killings by CPN (Maoist) members

CPN (Maoist) members deliberately killed civilians, including local government officials, members of political parties, and those who refused to accede to extortion demands or were considered informants.

⌂ Ganesh Chiluwal, head of the Maoist Victims' Association, an organization working for the welfare of victims of Maoist abuses, was shot dead in Kathmandu on 15 February, reportedly by two armed Maoists.

Abductions and other abuses by CPN (Maoist)

Maoists reportedly abducted thousands of civilians, including large numbers of students and teachers who were forced to take part in "political education" sessions, lasting from a few days to several weeks. They also abducted, tortured and killed civilians, whom they accused of "spying" and other crimes, and security force personnel whom they had captured. Maoists also staged a number of blockades which prevented the free movement of food, medicines and other basic goods.

Eight members of the *dalit* community allegedly had their legs crushed with hammers by CPN (Maoist) members at a secondary school in Thalsa, Achham, in June, apparently as punishment for working for a local landlord.

Human rights defenders

Human rights defenders were attacked, and their work obstructed, by both sides to the conflict. Despite government pledges, support for the NHRC's human rights monitoring work was not forthcoming.

Jeetman Basnet, 28, former editor and publisher of *Sagarmatha Times* magazine, as well as a lawyer, was arrested by three RNA personnel from Tinkune, Kathmandu, on 4 February. He was held for more than eight months at Bhairabnath Gan army barracks and throughout his detention was blindfolded with his hands tied behind his back. For the first three days he was severely beaten and had his head held underwater in a dirty pond several times until he lost consciousness. He was released on 17 October without charge.

Dekendra Raj Thapa, a journalist, human rights activist and development worker, was abducted in Dailekh district on 27 June and killed two weeks later by the CPN (Maoist).

Violence against women

Gender-based violence, in particular rape of women by members of the security forces, was frequently reported. Violence against women in the family and in the community was also widespread. Women faced legal discrimination, especially in connection with issues of citizenship and inheritance. These laws were criticized in January by the UN Committee on the Elimination of Discrimination against Women when considering Nepal's periodic report, as were laws allowing for harmful traditional practices, in particular early marriage and bigamy.

Discrimination against minorities

A number of incidents of discrimination related to caste, ethnicity and sexuality were reported. Communities such as the Tharu and Badi continued to experience high levels of discrimination and violence, perpetrated by both the community and security forces.

On 25 July police in Kathmandu forced four *metis* (male transvestites) into a police van and allegedly robbed, beat and raped them. On 9 August, police arrested 39 *metis* in Kathmandu and reportedly gave them no food or water for 15 hours. All were members of the Blue Diamond Society, a support organization which faced a possible Supreme Court ban on its activities.

AI country reports/ visits
Reports
- Nepal: Escalating "disappearances" amid a culture of impunity (AI Index: ASA 31/155/2004)
- Nepal: Human rights defenders under threat (AI Index: ASA 31/141/2004)
- Nepal: Open letter regarding attacks on civilians by Communist Party of Nepal (Maoist) (AI Index: ASA 31/139/2004)
- Amnesty International's visit to Nepal: Official Statement (AI Index: ASA 31/014/2004)
Visits
AI visited Nepal in January/February and again in September/October. Delegates met the Prime Minister and other government officials, as well as local human rights groups, and a wide range of people in civil society.

NEW ZEALAND

NEW ZEALAND
Head of state: Queen Elizabeth II, represented by Silvia Cartwright
Head of government: Helen Clark
Death penalty: abolitionist
International Criminal Court: ratified
UN Women's Convention and its Optional Protocol: ratified

The detention of a refugee held for two years on the basis of a national security assessment by the intelligence services was the subject of various legal reviews and appeal processes. The first national action plan for human rights was prepared.

Detention of refugee without fair hearing

Ahmed Zaoui, an Algerian refugee, was released on bail on 9 December by order of the Supreme Court after being detained for two years. He was held on the basis of a national security assessment made by the intelligence services that relied on controversial convictions in Europe and classified intelligence information. He remained at risk of deportation on the basis of a security risk certificate issued in March 2003 under the Immigration Act.

In January, the Director of Security argued that New Zealand's reputation with "like-minded countries" would suffer if Ahmed Zaoui were allowed to remain in New Zealand, given that he had been convicted in Belgium and France on charges of criminal association and passport irregularities and had been expelled from Switzerland.

The Refugee Status Appeals Authority had granted Ahmed Zaoui refugee status in August 2003. It concluded that information supplied by the intelligence services was "limited" and some of its contents "questionable", that the European convictions were unsafe, and that Ahmed Zaoui had become "the victim of a self-validating legend" based on "an intentional strategy of the Algerian regime and its allies".

In March the Inspector General of Intelligence and Security, who was reviewing the security risk certificate, resigned following a finding by the High Court of "apparent bias". The review was further delayed as the government sought to appeal against a Court of Appeal decision in September that the review should include human rights considerations.

In September the High Court determined that the continued detention or deportation of Ahmed Zaoui could be justified "only if there are objectively reasonable grounds based on credible evidence that Zaoui constitutes a danger to the security of New Zealand of such seriousness that it would justify sending a person back to persecution."

AI campaigned for Ahmed Zaoui to be released, or for the reasons for his continued detention to be tested in a fair judicial hearing meeting international standards.

Action Plan for Human Rights

In September the Human Rights Commission published the first comprehensive assessment of the status of human rights in New Zealand. Amongst the concerns highlighted were the abuse of a significant number of children and the vulnerability to abuse of people in detention and institutional care. The Commission submitted a national Action Plan for Human Rights to the Attorney General on 10 December.

NICARAGUA

REPUBLIC OF NICARAGUA
Head of state and government: Enrique Bolaños
Death penalty: abolitionist for all crimes
International Criminal Court: not signed
UN Women's Convention: ratified
Optional Protocol to UN Women's Convention: not signed

Violence against women and girls was a major concern.

Background

Political tensions ran high after the Treasury Inspector's Office called on the National Assembly, which is dominated by opposition parties, to impeach President Enrique Bolaños on corruption charges for failing to disclose the sources of his funding during the 2001 presidential elections. The President had become increasingly isolated after backing efforts to prosecute his predecessor and former ally, Arnoldo Alemán, who was sentenced to 20 years' imprisonment in December 2003 for fraud and money-laundering.

The Human Rights Procurator's Office faced a crisis after the National Assembly failed to appoint new directors and other staff when the previous incumbents completed their term of office in June or later. Members of the Office were concerned by the damage the situation was causing to the defence of human rights.

Violence against women

There was concern at the high levels of violence against women and girls. The National Police reported that 77 women had been murdered during 2003 and during the first quarter of 2004, and that 164 complaints of domestic violence were received in one police district alone in the same period. In July, the Minister of Health stated that 95 per cent of rapes in Nicaragua take place within the home. The Supreme Court, with the support of the Inter-American Development Bank, began a consultation with state institutions and civil society with a view to setting up a cross-disciplinary programme of professional services to address the needs of victims of domestic and sexual violence.

NIGER

REPUBLIC OF THE NIGER
Head of state: Mamadou Tandja
Head of government: Amadou Hama
Death penalty: abolitionist in practice
International Criminal Court: ratified
UN Women's Convention: ratified with reservations
Optional Protocol to UN Women's Convention: not signed

More than 230 soldiers, arrested following a failed mutiny in 2002, remained in detention without trial. Journalists continued to be targeted in an attempt to restrict freedom of expression. Slavery remained widespread and unpunished.

Background
In July, the three political parties backing the head of state won local elections. In December, President Mamadou Tandja was re-elected for a second term and his party, the National Movement for the Development of Society (Mouvement national pour la société de développement, MNSD) won the legislative elections.

Detention without trial
In July a military prosecutor announced that more than 230 soldiers arrested after an attempted mutiny in 2002 would be tried by a military court, drawing protests from human rights organizations. However, the soldiers were still in detention without trial at the end of 2004.

Freedom of expression
▢ In January, Mamane Abou, the editor of *Le Républicain*, the leading newspaper in Niamey, was released on probation by the court of appeal. He had been sentenced to six months' imprisonment in November 2003 for publishing information critical of government officials.
▢ In August, Moussa Kaka, a correspondent for *Radio France Internationale*, was detained for questioning and held for four days after interviewing a suspected rebel who claimed responsibility for an attack in the north of the country.
▢ In December, police raided premises in Niamey where the private weekly, *Le Témoin*, was printed. No official explanation for the raid was given but according to the newspaper's management, it may have been in response to the publication of an interview with four soldiers and a gendarme who had been held hostage for three months by an armed opposition group.

Slavery
Hundreds of thousands of people reportedly remained in conditions of slavery despite the adoption of a new Penal Code in 2003 making slavery a punishable crime.

NIGERIA

FEDERAL REPUBLIC OF NIGERIA
Head of State and government: Olusegun Obasanjo
Death penalty: retentionist
International Criminal Court: ratified
UN Women's Convention and its Optional Protocol: ratified

People continued to be sentenced to death by stoning for sexually-related offences; no executions were carried out in 2004. Violent attacks, some involving members of the security forces, were reported from the Niger Delta. Violence against women was widespread and gender-based discrimination both in law and in practice remained a serious concern. The authorities failed to conduct independent investigations into human rights abuses and to bring those responsible to justice. Critics of the government faced harassment and intimidation.

Death penalty
No executions were carried out during 2004. Death sentences were imposed both by the high courts and by *Sharia* (Islamic law) courts in northern Nigeria.

Appellate courts overturned three death sentences passed by courts in northern states under new *Sharia* penal legislation. The new *Sharia* penal legislation continued to criminalize behaviour termed as *zina* (sexually-related offences) and changed the punishment for Muslims convicted of *zina* from flogging to a mandatory death sentence, applicable to people who are or have been married. Offences defined in this way were used to deny both women and men their rights to privacy and to freedom of expression and association, and in practice frequently to deny women access to justice. Rules of evidence discriminating against women continued to be applied, putting women at greater risk of conviction on charges of *zina*. Trials under the new *Sharia* penal legislation were in general grossly unfair, denying the poor and vulnerable basic rights such as the right to a lawyer. The new *Sharia* penal legislation also extended jurisdiction in capital cases to the lowest courts in the *Sharia* judicial system.
▢ In March, an Upper *Sharia* Court in Bauchi State, north-eastern Nigeria, acquitted Jibrin Babaji. He had been sentenced to death by stoning in September 2003 by a *Sharia* court in Bauchi, after being convicted of "sodomy". The main reasons given for his acquittal were that he had been denied his right to a fair trial and the lower court had committed procedural errors relating to the use of his "confession" as evidence.
▢ In September, the Upper *Sharia* court in Katanga, Bauchi State, sentenced Saleh Dabo to death by stoning after convicting him of rape.

In November, the Dass Upper *Sharia* Court in Bauchi State acquitted Hajara Ibrahim, who had been convicted of *zina* and sentenced to death by stoning earlier in the year. One of the reasons for her acquittal was that she had never been married and so should not have been given a mandatory death sentence.

In December, the Upper *Sharia* Court in Ningi, Bauchi State acquitted Daso Adamu, who had been convicted of *zina* and sentenced to death by stoning in September. One of the reasons for the acquittal was that the Lower *Sharia* Court had committed procedural errors in relation to the use of her confession as evidence. She had been detained in Ningi prison with her three-month-old daughter until she was released on bail. The man in the case reportedly denied the charges and was not convicted.

An appeal against a sentence of death by stoning for *zina* passed on Fatima Usman and Ahmadu Ibrahim in May 2002 was further adjourned in 2004 by the *Sharia* Court of Appeal in Minna, Niger State, and was still pending at the end of the year. The couple had been released on humanitarian grounds to await the appeal.

In October, the National Study Group on the Death Penalty, set up by President Obasanjo in November 2003, published its report, recommending the imposition of a moratorium on executions until the Nigerian justice system could guarantee fair trial and due process. The Federal Government had not imposed a moratorium by the end of the year.

The Niger Delta: oil, human rights and violence

There was continuing violence in the Niger Delta and reports of excessive use of force by the security forces or law enforcement officials. Many hundreds of people were reportedly killed in the Delta, Bayelsa and Rivers States in 2004. The economic, social and cultural rights of the people in the Niger Delta – the main oil-producing region in the country – continued in general to be unfulfilled, leading to increasing frustration and tension both within and between communities. The situation was exacerbated by the easy availability of guns in the region. Oil company employees and assets, such as pipelines, were frequently targeted for attack and sabotage.

In January the Ohoror-Uwheru community in Ughelli North Local Government Area in Delta State was attacked by armed men, reportedly including members of Operation Restore Hope, a joint military and police task force. An unknown number of civilians were killed in the attack and as many as 50 women and girls were reportedly raped.

In August, at least 20 civilians were known to have been killed in fighting between rival groups in a spate of violence in and around Port Harcourt, Rivers State, although national non-governmental organizations reported a considerably higher figure. Large numbers of people were believed to have fled the area around Port Harcourt to escape the violence.

Violence against women

Violence against women remained widespread and persistent. Gender-based violence reported in 2004 included sexual violence, violence in the family, female genital mutilation and forced marriage. Discriminatory legislation remained in place. For example, the Criminal Code, applicable in the southern states, prescribes three years' imprisonment for unlawful and indecent assault if the victim is a man, but two years' imprisonment if the victim is a woman. The Penal Code, applicable in the northern states, states that a man is empowered to "correct" an erring child, pupil, servant or wife, provided that it does not amount to serious physical injury.

Although statistics on violence in the family were not available, such violence was believed to be widespread. Abuses were reported against both men and women in 2004 involving physical assault, incest and rape of domestic workers. Economic hardship and discriminatory laws and practices regarding divorce, child maintenance and the employment of women meant that many women were forced to remain within violent relationships.

In Lagos State a draft Domestic Violence Bill, which had received two readings in the House of Assembly, continued to face resistance and was the subject of fierce debate about cultural values.

Violence in the family was often not reported because of the lack of a legal framework for the protection of victims and the practices and attitudes of law enforcement officials and religious leaders, among others. Very few perpetrators were brought to justice.

Impunity

Nigeria continued to fail to bring to justice not only those responsible for human rights violations in Nigeria but also individuals charged with grave offences under international criminal law.

There was no progress in investigations into human rights violations committed by the Nigerian armed forces under the present government, particularly the killing of civilians at Odi, Bayelsa State, in 1999 and in Benue State in 2001.

The findings of the Human Rights Violations Investigation Commission, known as the Oputa Panel, had still not been made public and the government had made no public statement about plans for implementing the recommendations by the end of 2004. Established in 1999 to investigate human rights violations committed between 1966 and the return to civilian rule in 1999, the Oputa Panel had reported the findings of its public hearings and investigations to President Obasanjo in May 2002.

The whereabouts of a District Police Officer implicated in the murder of 16-year-old Nnaemeka Ugwuoke and 17-year-old Izuchukwu Ayogu in Enugu State in March 2002 remained unknown. He allegedly escaped from police custody in Abuja. The mutilated bodies of the two students had been found dumped at a construction site two weeks after they had been arbitrarily detained by officers of the Enugu State police. Almost three years later, no one had been brought to justice for the killings.

Charles Taylor

In August 2003, Liberian President Charles Taylor relinquished power and left Liberia for Nigeria with implicit guarantees from the Nigerian government that he would be neither prosecuted in Nigeria nor surrendered to the Special Court for Sierra Leone. An international warrant for his arrest had been issued after the Special Court announced his indictment in June 2003 for war crimes, crimes against humanity and serious violations of international humanitarian law during Sierra Leone's internal armed conflict on the basis of his active support for the Sierra Leonean armed opposition. AI protested that the Nigerian government had violated its obligations under international law, but calls for Charles Taylor to be surrendered to the Special Court or investigated with a view to criminal or extradition proceedings in Nigerian courts were ignored.

On 31 May 2004, the Nigerian Federal High Court granted leave to two Nigerians who had been tortured by members of the armed opposition while in Sierra Leone to challenge the asylum granted by the Nigerian government to Charles Taylor on the basis that he did not qualify for asylum and that the correct asylum process had not been followed. In November, an *amicus curiae* brief submitted by AI to the Federal High Court was accepted. In it AI challenged the Nigerian government's decision on the grounds that it violates Nigeria's obligations under international law, including the 1951 UN Refugee Convention and the African Union's Convention Governing the Specific Aspects of Refugee Problems in Africa. At the end of the year proceedings were continuing.

Human rights defenders and journalists under attack

Human rights defenders and journalists who were critical of the government, and in particular of President Obasanjo, continued to face intimidation and harassment. A number of journalists and trade unionists were detained and interrogated by the police.

On 4 and 5 September the State Security Service (SSS) arrested two staff members and the security guard of the magazine *Insider Weekly* for allegedly publishing articles critical of the President. Copies of the forthcoming issue of the magazine were confiscated, and computers and files were seized. The three men were interrogated and held in incommunicado detention before they were released without charge on 10 September.

On 9 September the SSS arrested journalist Isaac Umunna when he went to seek the release of his wife on bail; she had been arrested by the SSS the previous day. Isaac Umunna was a former journalist for *Insider Weekly* and was working for the London-based magazine *Africa Today* and the Lagos-based weekly

Global Star at the time of his arrest. On 15 September, he was moved to an unknown location. He was released without charge on 17 September.

On 29 April the SSS arrested Buba Galadima, a member of the Conference of Nigerian Political Parties (CNPP) and chairman of the mobilization committee of the CNPP. He was held in incommunicado detention for some time before being released without charge on 13 May. His arrest effectively prevented him from taking part in an anti-government protest planned for 3 May.

AI country reports/visits
Reports
- Nigeria: The death penalty and women under the Nigerian penal systems (AI Index: AFR 44/001/2004)
- Open Letter to the Chairman of the African Union (AU) seeking clarifications and assurances that the establishment of an effective African Court on Human and Peoples' Rights will not be delayed or undermined (AI Index: IOR 63/008/2004)
- Nigeria: The security situation in Rivers State – an open letter from Amnesty International to Peter Odili, State Governor of Rivers State (AI Index: AFR 44/027/2004)
- Nigeria: Amicus Curiae brief submitted to the Federal High Court reviewing refugee status granted to Charles Taylor (AI Index: AFR 44/030/2004)
- Nigeria: Are human rights in the pipeline? (AI Index: AFR 44/031/2004)

Visits
AI delegates visited Nigeria in March and November.

PAKISTAN

ISLAMIC REPUBLIC OF PAKISTAN

Head of state: Pervez Musharraf
Head of government: Shaukat Aziz (replaced Chaudhry Shujaat Hussain in August, who replaced Mir Zafarullah Khan Jamali in June)
Death penalty: retentionist
International Criminal Court: not signed
UN Women's Convention: ratified, with reservations
Optional Protocol to UN Women Convention: not signed

Arbitrary arrests and detentions in the context of the "war on terror" continued. Several people reportedly "disappeared". In the tribal areas, arbitrary arrests and possible extrajudicial executions were reported during security operations. The government failed to control sectarian violence which cost hundreds of lives. The blasphemy laws continued to be used to prosecute members of minorities. Government initiatives to improve protection of rights of women and juveniles provided only limited relief. Some children continued to be prosecuted as adults. At least 394 people were sentenced to death and 15 were executed.

Background

The political role of the military was consolidated when in April the National Security Council was set up by an act of parliament. Chaired by the President, and with eight government representatives and five representatives of the army, it was given a consultative role in security matters. In November a law was passed allowing General Musharraf to remain president and chief of the army, contrary to his earlier promise that the two roles would be separated.

Relations between Pakistan and India improved during 2004. In June, a moratorium on nuclear tests was agreed and, in September, talks began on several issues including that of Jammu and Kashmir.

Security operations in the tribal areas

Security operations continued throughout 2004 in the tribal areas close to the border with Afghanistan, which are not accessible to journalists and other observers. The operations aimed to remove people suspected of "terrorist" activities seeking shelter with the tribal population.

In March, arbitrary arrests and detentions and possible extrajudicial executions were reported in South Waziristan. Tribal fighters who might have been associated with the Taliban or al-Qa'ida reportedly took hostages and committed unlawful killings.

⬜ On 26 March the bodies of eight members of the paramilitary Frontier Corps were found with their hands bound behind their backs, apparently shot at point blank range. Opposition fighters had detained the men four days earlier during an attack on a convoy.

Arbitrary arrests and 'disappearances'

The Anti Terrorism Act (ATA) was amended in October to provide life imprisonment for supporters of "terrorists" and to allow police to seize the passports of "terrorist" suspects. In April, the Supreme Court ruled that those convicted of "terrorism" could not benefit from provisions under the law relating to murder, which allow the heirs of the victims to forgive the offender at any stage, thereby ending criminal proceedings.

Scores of people were arrested during demonstrations or for allegedly belonging to banned organizations. Most were released after several hours but some were held for prolonged periods in arbitrary and incommunicado detention. Some remained "disappeared" for longer periods despite families' efforts to trace them through the courts.

⬜ Students Akdas Iqbal and Sujeel Shahid, British and Dutch nationals respectively, were detained by an unknown agency on 14 June in Lahore in a wave of arrests of people suspected of links to "terrorist" organizations. During hearings of habeas corpus petitions filed by their relatives, the authorities denied holding them. Both were released without charge after a month.

Several journalists were held incommunicado for exercising their right to freedom of expression.

⬜ Khawar Medhi Rizvi was arrested on 16 December 2003 in Karachi along with two French journalists on their return from Balochistan. In January the French journalists received suspended sentences under the Foreigners Act for travelling to the area without official clearance. However, government authorities repeatedly denied holding Khawar Medhi Rizvi. He was brought before a court in Quetta on 26 January and charged with sedition and criminal conspiracy for allegedly assisting in the preparation of a documentary falsifying events in the region. The trial had not concluded by the end of 2004.

Several people suspected of links to "terrorist" organizations who "disappeared" were non-Pakistanis.

⬜ Tanzanian national Ahmed Khalfan Ghailani "disappeared" after being arrested on 25 July in Gujarat, Punjab province, along with several other non-Pakistani nationals, including several women and children. He was alleged to have links to al-Qa'ida. He was not charged or tried and his whereabouts remained unknown at the end of the year.

At least some of those in arbitrary detention were tortured.

⬜ Afghan Islamic cleric Mohammad Noor who was arrested in Faisalabad in August for alleged links with "terrorists" died in police custody four days later. An autopsy reportedly found several wounds on his body.

Lack of protection of minorities

At least 25 people were criminally charged with blasphemy and at least six of them remained in detention at the end of 2004. Hostility to anyone charged with blasphemy endangered their lives.

Samuel Masih, a 27-year-old Christian, was arrested in August 2003 and charged with having thrown litter on the ground near a mosque in Lahore. This was deemed an offence under section 295 of the Pakistan Penal Code, which provides up to two years' imprisonment for defiling a place of worship. Samuel Masih was held in a Lahore prison but transferred to hospital in May, suffering from tuberculosis. He died after his police guard attacked him in the hospital. The police officer stated that he had done his "religious duty"; he was charged with murder.

The government did not take adequate measures to prevent attacks on religious congregations. In the month of October alone, some 80 people died in sectarian violence. There were frequent reprisal attacks. Following a bomb attack on a Shi'a gathering in Sialkot on 1 October which killed some 30 people, a bomb was thrown at a Sunni mosque in Multan which killed some 41 people. Scores of people were arrested after sectarian attacks but most were released due to lack of evidence.

Violence against women

Violence against women in the community, including crimes of "honour", continued to be reported. The Human Rights Commission of Pakistan reported that in 2003 more than 600 women had been killed for alleged breaches of "honour". Many cases went unreported and victims included very young girls.

In June a tribal council directed that seven-year-old Mouti be killed for an alleged illicit relation with an eight-year old boy. Her father refused to accept the verdict and approached the local district administrator who provided protection.

Legal provisions allowing those who commit "honour" killings to seek forgiveness from heirs of the victim continued to prevent criminal prosecution.

In June, Shamim Badshah forgave her husband for murdering their daughter Fozia, whom he had killed on suspicion of maintaining an illicit relationship. A court in Lahore where the murder case was being heard ordered his release.

Although women's groups demanded that the waiving of criminal prosecution for crimes of "honour" by the victims' heirs be banned in order to deter potential perpetrators, this provision remained unchanged. In October the National Assembly passed draft legislation making the handing over of a woman as compensation for murder a criminal offence punishable by up to three years' imprisonment. Under another amendment, criminal charges under the laws on blasphemy and *Zina* (unlawful sex) are to be investigated only by higher ranking police officers. However, the amendments had not been signed into law by the end of the year.

Despite the Sindh High Court's ruling in April that trials by *jirgas* (tribal councils) were unlawful, the provincial government was reported to be preparing legislation to legalize this private justice system. Trials by *jirga* continued to be reported and no steps were known to have been taken against those participating in them.

Violence against children

Implementation of the Juvenile Justice System Ordinance (JJSO) of 2000 was inadequate, so that juveniles continued to be held and tried along with adults. In April, the relevant minister said that plans had been made to ensure implementation.

The ban on imposing the death penalty on juveniles contained in the JJSO was sometimes ignored. Problems in determining the age of some juveniles also meant that some juveniles under sentence of death did not benefit from a commutation order issued in 2001.

In February, 17-year-old Shahzad Hameed was sentenced to death for murder in Sheikhupura, Punjab province.

Saifullah Khan was 16 when he allegedly murdered another boy in April 2001 in Chardassa. He was sentenced to death in 2002. On appeal, the Peshawar High Court in October 2004 set aside the conviction and directed that he should be tried under the JJSO.

In October, the JJSO was extended to the Provincially Administered Tribal Areas. It still did not apply in the Federally Administered Tribal Areas (FATA) which are governed by the Frontier Crimes Regulation (FCR) of 1901. Under the FCR, family members of a person suspected of a crime can be punished instead of or along with that person. At least 70 children, including some 16 under the age of 10, were believed to be held under the FCR.

In December, the JJSO was revoked by the Lahore High Court which considered the law "unconstitutional" and "impractical". Juvenile courts set up under the JJSO were to be abolished and cases pending before it transferred to the regular courts. As a result juveniles could once again be sentenced to death.

Death penalty

At least 394 people were sentenced to death. At least 15 executions were reported. In November Asif Mahmood, who had spent 15 years on death row for a murder committed in 1989, was found innocent and released. His appeal had been pending for 13 years.

In June, the death sentence of Rehmat Shah Afridi, chief editor of the *Frontier Post*, who was sentenced to death in July 2001 for alleged trafficking in hashish, was commuted to life imprisonment. The High Court said that the death penalty was a disproportionate punishment for trafficking in hashish. AI considered Rehmat Shah Afridi to be a prisoner of conscience who was tried and convicted solely for his journalistic work.

AI country reports/ visits

Reports

- Pakistan: Human rights abuses in the search for al-Qa'ida and the Taleban in the tribal areas (AI Index: ASA 33/011/2004)
- Pakistan: Open letter to President Pervez Musharraf (AI Index: ASA 33/003/2004)

PALESTINIAN AUTHORITY

PALESTINIAN AUTHORITY
President: Rawhi Fattouh (replaced Yasser 'Arafat in November)
Prime Minister: Ahmad Quray
Death penalty: retentionist

The internal security situation deteriorated significantly in the West Bank and Gaza Strip during 2004. Power struggles and disagreements between and within the Palestinian Authority (PA), and political factions and groups resulted in increasingly frequent armed confrontations, attacks on individuals and property, and abductions. Palestinian armed groups and members of various security services also killed some 18 Palestinians who allegedly "collaborated" with the Israeli security services. Members of Palestinian armed groups continued to carry out attacks against Israelis both in the Occupied Territories and inside Israel, killing 109 Israelis. The PA frequently condemned Palestinian attacks against Israelis and Palestinians, but the security forces and judicial authorities were unable or unwilling to prevent and investigate such attacks and bring those responsible to justice.

Background
The al-Aqsa intifada (uprising), which started on 29 September 2000, continued. Some 700 Palestinians were killed by Israeli security forces, many of them unlawfully (see Israel and the Occupied Territories entry). Palestinian members of armed groups killed 109 Israelis, including 67 civilians. About half of them were killed in suicide bombings, generally claimed by the al-Aqsa Martyrs Brigades (an offshoot of Fatah) and the 'Izz al-Din al-Qassam Brigades (the military wing of Hamas). Some of the attacks were claimed by Islamic Jihad and the Popular Front for the Liberation of Palestine. Palestinian armed groups also continued to launch mortar attacks from the Gaza Strip towards nearby Israeli cities and Israeli settlements inside the Gaza Strip, killing five Israeli civilians. Thousands of Palestinians and hundreds of Israelis were injured.

Palestinians were hindered or prevented from gaining access to their agricultural land, workplaces and education and health facilities by the Israeli army which set up blockades and imposed stringent restrictions on the movement of Palestinians in the Occupied Territories and carried out repeated military raids into Palestinian towns and villages. The continued construction of a 600km fence/wall through the West Bank also cut off towns and villages from each other. As a result unemployment and extreme poverty remained high, with some two thirds of Palestinians forced to rely on international aid.

President Yasser 'Arafat remained confined to his headquarters in Ramallah until he fell ill and was taken to France for medical care. He died on 11 November. The Speaker of the Palestinian Legislative Council (PLC), Rawhi Fattouh, took over as interim President for a 60-day period and presidential elections were scheduled for January 2005.

Increased lawlessness
The PA security and judicial institutions, whose infrastructure had been repeatedly targeted and largely destroyed by the Israeli army in previous years, became increasingly dysfunctional and were themselves involved in factional in-fighting. The PA security forces' operational capacity remained severely limited; the Israeli army continued to prevent them from carrying weapons and operating in most areas of the Occupied Territories.

As central authority and control were increasingly eroded, disagreements, rivalries and in-fighting between political factions, security services and armed groups resulted in an increase in violent confrontations. Incidents included demonstrations, armed protests, abductions of and attacks on members of the security forces, PA officials and foreign nationals. Attacks and confrontations often involved different factions of the al-Aqsa Martyrs Brigades, which increasingly acted independently of or against each other.

At least 13 people, among them international relief workers and PA security force officials, were abducted by armed Palestinians, most of them in the Gaza Strip. They were all released unharmed within hours. The kidnappers reportedly protested against widespread corruption, called for PA reforms, or demanded payment of their salaries. Journalists and media workers were threatened, beaten or abducted by armed men in what appeared to be an attempt to stifle independent and critical reporting, in particular concerning the internal political situation and allegations of corruption in the PA. In most cases, the attacks were not claimed by any group, but were believed to have been carried out by the al-Aqsa Martyrs Brigades.

▢ On 8 January the Gaza correspondent with the *al-Arabiyya* television station, Saifeddin Shahin, was attacked and beaten in Gaza City by five armed men who reportedly warned him not to criticize Fatah in his reports. One of the alleged attackers was arrested by Palestinian police but was subsequently released without charge.

▢ In February, gunmen burst into the offices of Chief of Police Ghazi al-Jabali in Gaza City and opened fire, killing one officer and wounding 11 others, one of whom later died.

▢ PLC member and former Information Minister Nabil 'Amr was shot in the leg by gunmen in Ramallah on 20 July; his right leg had to be amputated. He had criticized the PA's corruption, lawlessness and lack of accountability. No investigation was known to have been carried out, and no one had been arrested in connection with the attack by the end of the year.

Unlawful killings by Palestinians

Scores of Palestinians were killed in cases of political inter-factional fighting and score-settling. At least 18 others were killed by Palestinian individuals or members of armed groups because they were suspected of "collaborating" with the Israeli security services. At least five Palestinians were killed by gunmen while in PA custody. Most of the killings were attributed to the al-Aqsa Martyrs Brigades. The PA consistently failed to investigate these killings and none of the perpetrators was brought to justice.

▢ Nineteen-year-old Shafi 'Ali Ahmad was abducted on 8 May by a group of armed men outside the shop where he occasionally worked in Kafr al-Dik village in the West Bank. His body was found the following day on the outskirts of the village. A communiqué signed by an al-Aqsa Martyrs Brigades group stated that he had been killed because he had "collaborated" with the Israeli security services. However, the group subsequently apologized for the killing and publicly announced that Shafi 'Ali Ahmad was not a "collaborator" and should not have been killed.

▢ On 2 July Muhammad Rafiq Daraghmeh was killed in Qabatiya in the West Bank by members of the al-Aqsa Martyrs Brigades, who accused him of "collaborating" with the Israeli security services and of sexually abusing his daughters. He was killed in the town square in front of a large crowd which had gathered after gunmen reportedly announced through loudspeakers that he would be killed.

Use of children by armed groups

Several children were involved in attacks against Israelis; two of them carried out a suicide attack inside Israel. Others were arrested by the Israeli army for their alleged involvement in such attacks. Palestinian armed groups have no declared policy of recruiting children and claim to disavow the use of children; some blamed such abuses on local cells acting on their own initiative or "collaborators" seeking to discredit the armed groups.

▢ In March Hussam 'Abdu, a 16-year-old boy with mental disabilities, was arrested at Huwara checkpoint, near Nablus, while wearing a suicide belt. The Israeli army had advance information about the case and had closed the checkpoint. The boy remained detained in Israel awaiting trial at the end of the year.

Detention, torture and ill-treatment

Some 750 Palestinians were held in Palestinian prisons or detention centres. Most were detained without trial, apparently in relation to criminal offences. About 115 were detained on charges of "collaborating" with the Israeli intelligence services. Most had been arrested in previous years. There were reports of torture and ill-treatment, including beatings and sleep deprivation, by various Palestinian security forces, mainly the Police Criminal Investigation Department and the Preventive Security Forces.

Death penalty

No executions were carried out, but at least eight people were sentenced to death. Three had been convicted of "collaborating" with the Israeli security services; the others were found guilty of criminal charges. By the end of the year at least 21 Palestinians remained on death row.

▢ On 13 April, Ihab Abu al-'Umrein, Rami Juha and 'Abd al-Fattah Samur were sentenced to death in a Gaza court for the rape and murder of 16-year-old schoolgirl Mayada Khalil Abu Lamadi in 2003. A fourth defendant was sentenced to life imprisonment.

Violence against women

The UN Special Rapporteur on violence against women visited the Occupied Territories in June to gather information on the impact of the occupation and conflict on women. She concluded that the conflict has disproportionately affected Palestinian women in the Occupied Territories, in both the public and private spheres of life. In addition to the women killed or injured by Israeli forces, Palestinian women were particularly negatively affected by the demolition of their homes and restrictions on movement, which hampered their access to health services and education, and by the sharp increase in poverty. The dramatic increase in violence as a result of the occupation and conflict also led to an increase in domestic and societal violence, while at the same time there were increased demands on women as carers and providers.

AI country reports/ visits

Visits

AI delegates visited areas under the jurisdiction of the PA in May, September and October.

PAPUA NEW GUINEA

PAPUA NEW GUINEA
Head of state: Queen Elizabeth II, represented by
Governor-General Paulias Matane (replaced Acting
Governor-General Bill Skate in June)
Head of government: Michael Somare
Death penalty: abolitionist in practice
International Criminal Court: not signed
UN Women's Convention: ratified
Optional Protocol to UN Women's Convention: not
signed

Human rights violations by police, including against
women, continued as law and order deteriorated.
Ethnic violence left at least 30 people dead. Many
police enjoyed impunity for brutality and shootings.
The government prepared procedures for executions.
Refugees from Papua, Indonesia, were given
improved legal status and living conditions.

Background

Gun-related violent crime and inter-communal
violence dominated public debate. At least 30 people
were known to have been killed in armed clashes
between villages or ethnic groups. Provincial power
struggles, reprisal killings, corruption and government
mismanagement continued to fuel violence. The
violence adversely affected living standards and the
economy, and hindered government measures against
deteriorating infrastructure, education and health
services. Some businesses and banks closed because of
such violence.

Government mediation and security measures
helped to prevent the escalation of ethnic or politically
motivated violence in some provinces. At least 70 of
the planned 200-strong contingent of Australian
Federal Police and 50 civilians were deployed in
Bougainville, Port Moresby and Highland provinces,
under an agreement signed with Australia in August.

In October the government agreed the draft
Constitution for an autonomous provincial
administration in Bougainville. The UN extended its
observer mission.

Escalating rates of fatal malaria and HIV infection
prompted emergency interventions by aid
organizations. Port Moresby's General Hospital alone
reported 115 new HIV/AIDS cases a month.

Law and order problems

There were serious problems in the criminal justice
system, including long delays in bringing suspects to
trial, which observers saw as fuelling crime and
impunity. In September the former Chief Justice argued
that judicial processes were inefficient and ineffective,
and advocated a radical overhaul. The Chief Justice

complained that the government filled only 19 of 25
positions for judges, leaving the courts understaffed.
The Justice Minister expressed concern about violent
attacks on judges and break-ins in court houses.

There were concerns that the payment of court
awarded compensation and out-of-court settlements
to victims of police brutality significantly reduced the
police budget, affecting police capacity to address
crime.

Violence against women

Women's organizations recorded hundreds of rape
cases in addition to domestic violence. Although some
incidents of violence against women led to successful
convictions, perpetrators were often seen as enjoying
impunity.

◻ In March, police raided a guest house and then
gang-raped and brutally assaulted women staff and
guests. The police marched about 45 men and at least 42
women and girls to Boroko police station, humiliating
them publicly. After police filed prostitution and other
charges, the men were released but the women and
girls were detained. After their release, at least five
women were gang-raped by officers in the police car
park. All charges against those arrested were dismissed
in court, and no action was taken against any of the
officers responsible for sexually assaulting the women
and girls.

◻ Women's groups protested against the sentence –
a suspended seven-year prison term – given to a man
convicted in March of aggravated rape and assault of a
woman. Police then rearrested the man for an earlier
offence.

A new Family Support Centre assisting abused
women and children opened near Port Moresby
General Hospital in May. East New Britain province
established a Family Violence Committee in September
to assist the Police Sexual Offences Section.

There were reports of the torture and murder of
people accused of, or in some cases being victims of,
sorcery, particularly women. In Chimbu Province in
February, villagers reportedly kidnapped and bound four
women with ropes and slashed their bodies with knives.

Police use of excessive force

There were numerous allegations that police used
excessive force in carrying out their police duties.
Some incidents involved fatal shootings or rape. Port
Moresby's Police Commander warned criminals that
police would shoot to kill, fuelling the perception
that police officers would not be held accountable
for use of excessive force that resulted in fatal
shootings.

◻ In March, Wewak police beat two village elders
trying to serve the police with a court summons. The
summons alleged serious police brutality at Yangoru
Police Station in December 2003 when officers
allegedly forced a woman to undress and have sex with
her detained husband in his cell, and then tried to cut
off his genitals. The elders had also responded to
concerns raised by local villagers about widespread
police ill-treatment.

Death penalty

Despite public opposition to the death penalty, including by the former Chief Justice and churches, the Justice Minister prepared procedures in anticipation of a resumption in executions.

Refugees and children

The last person detained in an Australian-controlled camp on Manus Island was resettled in Australia. Australia extended its contract on the vacant camp.

The government registered children born to refugees after the UN Committee on the Rights of the Child recommended that efforts be increased to ensure all children were registered at birth. In January the Committee, in considering Papua New Guinea's initial report under the UN Children's Convention, expressed concern about violence against children by police and by staff in institutions.

At least 185 Papuan refugees were relocated from Vanimo in August with UN assistance after their refugee status was established. The move increased the refugees' access to economic opportunities.

AI country reports/ visits

Report

- Papua New Guinea: The state as killer? (AI Index: ASA 34/001/2004)

Visit

AI visited Port Moresby in May.

PARAGUAY

REPUBLIC OF PARAGUAY
Head of state and government: Nicanor Duarte Frutos
Death penalty: abolitionist for all crimes
International Criminal Court: ratified
UN Women's Convention and its Optional Protocol: ratified

Members of peasant farmers' organizations and indigenous groups were subjected to human rights violations in the context of disputes over land and social issues. There were continued reports of the torture and ill-treatment of army conscripts. The Truth and Justice Commission, which will document past human rights violations, was established.

Background

There was an increase in crime, including a wave of kidnappings, which led to some political sectors calling for the reintroduction of the death penalty.

More than 40 per cent of the rural population was reported to live in poverty. There were frequent protests over land reform and other socio-economic issues. Negotiations between peasant farmers' organizations and the authorities to resolve the land issue broke down in September. Subsequently, peasant leaders called for renewed protests and land invasions.

In September, parliament considered a constitutional amendment to make military service voluntary rather than obligatory.

Violence over land disputes

Members of peasant farmers' organizations and indigenous groups were reportedly subjected to attacks, death threats and harassment by armed civilians working for landowners or private companies. Two indigenous leaders were killed in unclear circumstances.

📁 In August scores of indigenous Enxet people living in the community of Puerto Colón, Department of Presidente Hayes, were forcibly evicted from their ancestral land by a private company. In October the Inter-American Commission on Human Rights ordered the government to protect the Enxet people and to allow them to return to their land while it examined the case.

Past human rights violations

In July, an Argentine court issued an international warrant for the arrest of former President Alfredo Stroessner for his alleged involvement in human rights violations committed under "Operation Cóndor", a joint plan by military governments in South America to eliminate opponents during the 1970s and 1980s. Alfredo Stroessner, living in exile in Brazil, was also wanted by the Paraguayan courts in connection with "disappearances" and other human rights violations committed under his rule (1954-1989).

Former General Lino Oviedo was arrested on his voluntary return to the country in June and taken to a military prison. He had been sentenced to 10 years' imprisonment in 1998 for his part in a 1996 coup attempt and faced three further criminal charges. Two of these related to his alleged involvement in the murder of Vice-President Luis María Argaña in 1999. There was concern that the investigations into these charges were being conducted under military jurisdiction that would not guarantee him a fair trial.

Truth and Justice Commission

The Truth and Justice Commission, created in 2003 to examine human rights violations committed between 1954 and 2004, was established in August. However, there were doubts about its ability to function after parliament more than halved the requested budget.

Torture and ill-treatment of conscripts

There were continued reports of torture and ill-treatment of conscripts. Little progress was made in investigating the deaths of more than 100 conscripts who had died since 1989.

In February, 20-year-old Miguel Angel Quintana Sánchez lodged an official complaint with the parliamentary Human Rights Commission alleging that he had been repeatedly beaten and threatened while doing military service.

Inter-American Court of Human Rights

In September, the Inter-American Court of Human Rights ordered Paraguay to pay damages in two human rights cases. One related to a fire at the Panchito López juvenile detention centre in 2000 in which 12 inmates died. The other was the case of former presidential candidate Ricardo Canese who was accused of defaming his opponent Juan Carlos Wasmosy during the 1993 election. The Court ruled that his freedom of expression had been violated.

PERU

REPUBLIC OF PERU
Head of state and government: Alejandro Toledo Manrique
Death penalty: abolitionist for ordinary crimes
International Criminal Court: ratified
UN Women's Convention and its Optional Protocol: ratified

Some of the Truth and Reconciliation Commission's recommendations were implemented. Military courts continued to claim jurisdiction over cases of human rights violations. Trade unionists and journalists were among those subjected to threats and attacks. There were reports of torture and ill-treatment of detainees and of excessive use of force by police. Prison conditions remained harsh.

Background

Throughout 2004 there were mass demonstrations and strikes to protest against government policies and demand better working conditions. According to the UN, over 50 per cent of Peruvians lived in poverty and almost 25 per cent in extreme poverty. In rural areas, widespread discontent with local authorities reportedly led to violent social unrest, including the murder by lynching of a mayor accused of corruption in Ilave, Puno. In two other districts in the same department a 30-day state of emergency was declared following violent clashes between police and protesters.

Small groups of members of the armed opposition group Shining Path reportedly continued to operate in some areas. In June there were reports of ambushes by Shining Path in the highlands and central jungle regions.

No progress was made over the extradition of former President Alberto Fujimori from Japan on charges of human rights violations, and a second extradition request was filed on corruption charges.

In October the Constitutional Court ruled that articles of military law criminalizing homosexuality were unconstitutional.

Past human rights abuses

The government established a system of prosecutors' offices and courts to investigate and try past human rights abuses. It also announced several initiatives to offer reparation to the victims of human rights abuses and their families and to assist development in areas affected by violence. However, by the end of 2004, very few people had received compensation. Trials had started in only three of 43 cases of human rights abuses presented by the Truth and Reconciliation Commission to the Attorney General's Office.

Military courts

Cases of human rights violations continued to be transferred to military courts, despite the

Constitutional Court's ruling in August that military courts should only try offences committed in the line of duty. However, there were positive developments in November and December when the Supreme Court of Justice ruled in favour of civilian courts over military courts in two such cases where the jurisdiction had been disputed.

In August the Supreme Council of Military Justice confirmed the dismissal of the charges by a military court in 1994 of the former presidential adviser on intelligence, Vladimiro Montesinos; the former Commander in Chief of the Armed Forces, Nicolás Hermoza Ríos; and the retired General Luis Pérez Documet for their alleged involvement in the killing and "disappearance" of nine students and a teacher in 1992.

Women's rights
Violence against women in the family remained a concern, despite implementation of legal reforms during the previous decade aimed at tackling the problem.

Draft legislation on equal opportunities and gender equality was still pending in Congress after more than two years.

No progress was made in over 500 cases documented by the Truth and Reconciliation Commission of women and girls raped, mainly by the military, during the internal armed conflict.

Prison conditions, torture and ill-treatment
Prison conditions remained harsh. Conditions in maximum security prisons in some cases amounted to cruel, inhuman and degrading treatment. Despite calls for the closures of Challapalca and Yanamayo prisons, in Tacna and Puno, both remained open.

Torture and ill-treatment of detainees by security officials remained a concern. Legislation introduced in 1998 to criminalize torture had led to only three convictions by the end of 2004.

Threats and intimidation
There were reports of threats and attacks against trade unionists, journalists, human rights defenders, and victims and witnesses of human rights violations. In two separate cases local authorities appeared implicated in the alleged murders of journalists.

The legacy of the counter-insurgency
Retrials began in the cases of scores of political prisoners after the Constitutional Court ruled in 2003 that life imprisonment and the use of military courts to try civilians were unconstitutional. The 2003 decree laws issued to conform with this ruling annulled sentences handed down by military courts for the crime of "treason" and ordered that cases be retried in civilian courts. They also ordered the retrial of all those tried between 1992 and 1997 by civilian "faceless judges" (judges whose identities were kept secret). Cases being retried included that of Abimael Guzmán, the former leader of Shining Path. Hundreds of people were awaiting retrial.

The National Terrorism Court began reviewing irregular or incomplete arrest warrants issued under the same 1992 legislation. During the year over 3,000 people reportedly had warrants withdrawn.

Prisoners of conscience and possible prisoners of conscience unfairly charged with "terrorism-related" offences remained in prison. There were serious concerns that they would remain in prison while awaiting retrial within a slow and inefficient judicial system.

Transnational companies
In February a Canadian mining company announced that it would begin arbitration proceedings over a 2003 government ruling to block a mining project in Tambogrande, Piura. The project faced strong opposition from local inhabitants who feared that mining in the area would result in water and soil contamination and endanger crops, threatening their social and economic rights.

In September the government withdrew permission from a transnational mining company to carry out gold exploration in Cerro Quilish, Cajamarca, following protests by local peasants who argued that mining would damage water supplies.

Economic, social and cultural rights
The UN Special Rapporteur on the right to health expressed concerns that a trade agreement with the USA would lead to essential drugs becoming unaffordable for millions of Peruvians. He stated that many Peruvians died from treatable medical conditions.

The UN Special Rapporteur on the right to adequate housing raised concerns that public housing programmes did not reach those living in extreme poverty.

AI country reports/ visits
Report
- Peru: The Truth and Reconciliation Commission – a first step towards a country without injustice (AI Index: AMR 46/003/2004)

PHILIPPINES

REPUBLIC OF THE PHILIPPINES
Head of state and government: Gloria Macapagal
Arroyo
Death penalty: retentionist
International Criminal Court: signed
UN Women's Convention and its Optional Protocol:
ratified

Peace talks between the government and armed
groups — Muslim separatists in Mindanao and
communist rebels — made some progress, although
armed clashes continued. Human rights violations,
including arbitrary arrests, extrajudicial executions
and "disappearances", were reported during military
operations. Armed opposition groups were
responsible for abuses, including killings and
hostage-taking. Serious defects in the
administration of justice, particularly the lack of
effective investigations and fair trial safeguards,
undermined the right of victims of human rights
violations to redress. There were reports of the ill-
treatment or torture of criminal suspects by police,
and a series of unsolved "vigilante" killings of
alleged criminals in Davao City. At least 88 death
sentences were imposed. Despite a threat of a
resumption of executions, none was carried out.

Background
President Arroyo received a six-year mandate after
winning national elections in May. She announced that
her policy priorities were to alleviate poverty, address
unemployment and education, and reach an end to
armed insurgencies by Muslim separatists and
communist rebels with a just conclusion to the peace
process.

Mindanao peace process
In March talks between the government and the
separatist Moro Islamic Liberation Front (MILF)
resumed in Kuala Lumpur, Malaysia. A ceasefire
agreement was periodically broken as MILF forces
clashed with Armed Forces of the Philippines (AFP)
units.

There were reports of breaches of international
humanitarian law by both sides, including apparently
indiscriminate use of force by AFP units and the use of
"human shields" by MILF forces.

The MILF leadership continued to deny assertions
that the group maintained links with a regional
"terrorist" network, Jemaah Islamiyah. In August the
authorities dropped criminal charges against MILF
leaders accused of involvement in "terrorist" bombings
in Davao City in 2003.

In October, 60 military monitors from Malaysia and
Brunei arrived in Mindanao to help oversee ceasefire
arrangements and facilitate a resumption of peace
negotiations.

Communist insurgency and peace process
In February peace talks between the government and
the National Democratic Front (NDF) representing the
Communist Party of the Philippines (CPP) and its armed
wing, the New People's Army (NPA), resumed in Oslo,
Norway. The two sides renewed commitments to
address the root causes of the conflict by addressing
social, economic and political reforms. They set up a
Joint Monitoring Committee to examine complaints of
human rights violations and breaches of international
humanitarian law. As a confidence-building measure,
the government pledged to expedite earlier
agreements to release rebel prisoners. At least 27
prisoners were reported released. In August the NDF
suspended talks, calling on the government to lobby
for the removal of the NPA's designation as a "Foreign
Terrorist Organization" by the USA and its allies.

NPA attacks on government targets and clashes
between AFP and NPA units continued throughout
2004. Suspected NPA members were subjected to
arbitrary arrest, "disappearance", torture and
extrajudicial execution. Also at risk were members of
legal leftist organizations.

⌐ In February, Juvy Magsino, a human rights lawyer
contesting local mayoral elections, and human rights
activist Leyma Fortu were shot dead by unidentified
assailants in Mindoro Oriental. The authorities claimed
the attacks were related to electoral tensions.
However, both women were affiliated with the left-
wing political party Bayan Muna, whose members had
suffered a series of attacks over recent years, allegedly
carried out by "vigilantes" linked to a local AFP brigade.

The CPP-NPA committed human rights abuses
including unlawful killings and hostage-taking.
⌐ In January a mayor, a vice-mayor and three others
were reported killed by NPA rebels in separate attacks
believed to be linked to NPA extortion demands.

In September NPA guerrillas reportedly kidnapped
and killed the police chief of a town in Abra province
after putting him on "trial" for rape and killing NPA
members.

Impunity and the administration of justice
During unlawfully extended periods of "investigative"
detention before the filing of charges, scores of
suspects were tortured or ill-treated by Philippine
National Police (PNP) officers or military personnel to
extract confessions or information.

Despite an extensive array of institutional and
procedural safeguards, suspected perpetrators of serious
human rights violations were rarely brought to justice.
Prolonged and frequently unfair trial proceedings placed
excessive burdens on people seeking judicial remedies
for human rights abuses. Victims from poor or
marginalized communities, when faced with physical
threats combined with "amicable" financial settlements,
frequently abandoned attempts to seek redress.

Women and minors continued to be at risk of
physical or sexual abuse and poor conditions in
detention. Children were at times detained with adults
in overcrowded facilities, exposing them to abuse by
other prisoners.

Killing of suspected criminal suspects

High crime rates and a lack of confidence in criminal justice institutions meant there was little public opposition to killings of suspected criminals by PNP officers or by "vigilantes", some allegedly linked to local officials and the PNP.

⌓ At least 100 alleged criminal suspects were shot dead in Davao City, reportedly by unidentified "vigilantes". The city's mayor made statements suggesting that extrajudicial executions were an effective means to combat criminality. The victims were often alleged drugs dealers and petty thieves, sometimes members of gangs or street children. PNP investigations remained ineffective and no prosecutions were known to have been launched by the end of 2004.

Violence against women

In January Congress enacted legislation criminalizing acts of violence against women and their children within intimate relationships. Despite this achievement, incidents of domestic violence remained endemic and women's groups continued to campaign for the effective implementation of legislation through adequately financed government monitoring programmes and training.

Death penalty

In January the Supreme Court, having examined new evidence, suspended the executions of convicted kidnappers Roberto Lara and Roderick Licayan and granted them a retrial. The two men were due to be the first prisoners to be executed since President Arroyo lifted a moratorium on the execution of convicted kidnappers and drugs traffickers in 2003.

Following President Arroyo's inauguration in July, there were reports that executions would again resume. However, the President granted a series of reprieves to those facing imminent execution. Bills calling for the repeal of death penalty legislation were filed before the new Congress. A total of 1,110 prisoners were on death row at the end of 2004.

At least 21 young offenders remained under sentence of death for offences committed when they were under the age of 18, even though the law makes clear that child offenders cannot be sentenced to death or executed. Seven were transferred off death row and their cases returned to the Supreme Court after lower courts reviewed evidence about their age. Fourteen other young offenders remained on death row pending a similar review.

POLAND

REPUBLIC OF POLAND
Head of state: Aleksander Kwaśniewski
Head of government: Marek Belka (replaced Leszek Miller in May)
Death penalty: abolitionist for all crimes
International Criminal Court: ratified
UN Women's Convention and its Optional Protocol: ratified

Three people died as a result of unlawful use of firearms by police officers. Domestic violence was not effectively investigated and prosecuted, and the victims frequently did not receive adequate protection. Lesbians and gay men were not adequately protected by the police. A march to promote the rights of lesbians, gay men, bisexual and transgender (LGBT) people in Warsaw was prohibited in violation of the right to freedom of assembly.

Unlawful use of firearms by police

Three people died in two separate incidents when police officers used firearms in circumstances that were in breach of international standards. Both incidents were being investigated. Some members of the Sejm (parliament) called for a thorough reform of the police force as well as of its recruitment and training, but their recommendations were not adopted.

⌓ On 29 April in Poznań, police officers shot dead a 19-year-old man and seriously injured another after they pursued a car they reportedly believed was occupied by criminal suspects. The two unarmed suspects attempted to run away after their car was blocked by an unmarked police car, reportedly believing that they were being pursued by carjackers.

⌓ On 9 May in Łódź, police officers intervened after a group of young men assaulted some students. In the ensuing clash, the officers used riot guns and fired six shots, killing a 19-year-old male student and a 23-year-old woman who were not involved in the violence. According to the police, the guns had been loaded with live ammunition by mistake. The incident prompted the Łódź police chief and his deputy to resign, and the province's police chief was dismissed.

Women's rights

In November a report by the UN Human Rights Committee expressed concern about the high number of cases of domestic violence against women. It reported that measures such as restraining orders and temporary arrests were not widely used, that appropriate protection was not afforded to victims, that shelters did not exist in many places, and that training for law enforcement officers was inadequate. The Committee recommended specific steps that Poland should take to address these problems.

The Committee was also concerned about the low number of women in senior positions in public services and the disparities in remuneration between men and women.

Expulsion of refugee

🗁 In May, Imam Ahmed Ammar, a Yemeni national who had lived in Poland for 14 years, was ordered by the Wielkopolski Voivodship (local administration) office to leave the country within a week because he was "a risk to security". The decision was apparently made on the basis of an opinion of the Internal Security Agency, which refused to reveal the grounds for its decision. Ahmed Ammar appealed against the decision. In June, after he was forced to obey another order to leave the country, Ahmed Ammar was reportedly arrested by Political Security officers on his arrival in Yemen and taken to prison in Aden. He was released a month later.

Identity-based violations

LGBT people were assaulted by groups of young men. In May in Krakow, around 3,000 participants in a demonstration – the March for Tolerance – were inadequately protected by the police when they were assaulted by 300 people, including some representatives of the Sejm and local authorities. In November, football supporters in Poznań assaulted several hundred participants in a demonstration calling for greater respect for the rights of sexual minorities. Subsequently, nine people suspected of violent conduct were arrested.

In June, Lech Kaczyński, the mayor of Warsaw, did not permit the holding of the Equality Parade, a march of LGBT people and their supporters. He reportedly stated that such an event would be "sexually obscene" and offensive to other people's religious feelings.

The UN Human Rights Committee was concerned that the right of sexual minorities not to be discriminated against was not fully recognized in Poland and that discriminatory acts and attitudes against people on the ground of sexual orientation were not being adequately investigated and punished. It recommended appropriate training for law enforcement and judicial officials, and for discrimination on the ground of sexual orientation to be specifically prohibited in Polish law.

PORTUGAL

PORTUGUESE REPUBLIC
Head of state: Jorge Fernando Branco de Sampaio
Head of government: Pedro Santana-Lopes (replaced José Manuel Durão Barroso in July)
Death penalty: abolitionist for all crimes
International Criminal Court: ratified
UN Women's Convention and its Optional Protocol: ratified

Disproportionate use of force and ill-treatment by police officers continued to give rise to concern about Portugal's failure to comply with international law and standards. There were reports of ill-treatment and other forms of abuse by prison officers. Systemic failures to ensure the protection of the human rights of detainees in Lisbon prison were exposed. The rate of deaths in prisons was alarmingly high. International human rights monitoring bodies expressed concern about Portugal's human rights record.

Background

In an opinion published in March, the Council of Europe's Commissioner for Human Rights expressed concern about long-standing procedural shortcomings in the exercise of the right to legally challenge detention on remand. The Commissioner concluded that such detention ought to be the exception and should, therefore, not be imposed without appropriate procedural guarantees.

In July the Sixth Revision of the Portuguese Constitution entered into force. It included a prohibition on discrimination on the basis of sexual orientation.

The government approved proposals for reform of the prison system in June. The objectives included achieving a humane, just and safe prison system aimed at social rehabilitation; protecting inmates' fundamental rights; improving detention conditions; fulfilling inmates' health needs; combating overcrowding; and regular oversight of the functioning and quality of the prison service by internal and external bodies.

Policing concerns

Disproportionate use of force and ill-treatment by police officers continued to be reported. No steps were known to have been taken to establish an oversight agency, independent of the Ministry of the Interior, with powers to investigate grave human rights violations by law enforcement officials and to enforce disciplinary measures, as recommended by the UN Human Rights Committee in August 2003. There also appeared to have been no response to the criticism of police use of firearms by the General Inspectorate of the Internal Administration (GIIA), made public in November 2003.

AI reiterated long-standing concerns about the arbitrary use of force, including lethal force, by the police to the Minister of the Interior in May. Concern arose, in particular, from reports that the police had used firearms and rubber bullets unnecessarily or disproportionately to the threat posed, if any, to the officers involved, and that individuals might have been unlawfully killed as a result. Police training and operational guidelines were reportedly inadequate, and insufficient measures had been taken to ensure implementation of international laws and standards in policing practices.

☐ In January the Minister of the Interior reportedly decided that the police officer involved in the killing of Nuno Lucas in August 2002 should be expelled from the police force. A disciplinary investigation by the GIIA had reportedly concluded that – irrespective of whether the discharge of fire had been intentional or unintentional – the use of a firearm in the circumstances had been improper (*indevido*).

☐ In March a police officer on trial for the homicide of António Pereira in June 2002 was acquitted after claiming he had not been aware that rubber bullets could kill and had not been trained in the use of the rubber bullet shotgun. Important questions remained about the circumstances of the killing, and about the accountability of all those involved in allowing police officers to use weapons without adequate training and in the reported absence of guidelines on the circumstances in which bullets could be discharged.

☐ In December the trial began in Lisbon of six people, three of them police officers reportedly accused of assaulting the other three defendants in 1995.

Prison concerns

Ill-treatment and other forms of abuse by prison officers were reported in a number of prisons. The Office of the Ombudsman appeared to have insufficient resources to discharge fully and effectively its tasks, including investigating detainees' complaints.

Concerns about the safety of detainees persisted. Safeguards to prevent self-harm, including through the identification of vulnerable inmates, remained inadequate in some prisons, as did systems to ensure detainees necessary assistance at night and in disciplinary cells. The incidence of reportedly self-inflicted deaths remained of concern, including in the prisons of Lisbon, Sintra and Coimbra. In Vale de Judeus prison, there were three reported suicides in January alone. An alarmingly high number of inmates, 70 in total and two thirds of them held on remand, were reported to have died in prison in 2004.

Conditions amounting to cruel, inhuman and degrading treatment continued in several prisons, frequently resulting from overcrowding and seriously inadequate sanitary facilities. In some prisons, conditions in disciplinary cells were extremely poor. In others, detainees were reportedly locked in their cells for up to 23 hours without access to fresh air, sometimes for several days at a time. Health care provisions continued to be inadequate, despite high rates of HIV and other serious medical conditions in the prison

population. The authorities continued to fail to ensure the separation of convicted prisoners from pre-trial detainees. Lawyers expressed concern that detainees did not receive copies of prison rules, leaving them unaware of their rights, including in relation to disciplinary proceedings.

☐ An inquiry by prison service inspectors into the beating of Albino Libânio in Lisbon Prison in November 2003 found that he had sustained multiple injuries. He had not received medical assistance, despite the injuries he sustained, reportedly as a result of an assault that may have amounted to torture. At the end of 2004, a criminal investigation was pending, and disciplinary proceedings against a number of prison officers had been opened. The circumstances of the attack and the refusal of virtually all the prison officers at Lisbon Prison to cooperate with the internal inquiry raised fears that it had not been an isolated incident, and that the inquiry had exposed systemic failures to ensure the protection of detainees' human rights.

Racism and discrimination

The unavailability of relevant data and statistical information was a significant obstacle to assessing the extent to which law enforcement was affected by racism and discrimination. There appeared to be no statistics available on the ethnicity of the individuals subjected to "stop and search" practices by the police, or on the ethnicity (and not just the nationality) of detainees.

In August, after considering Portugal's 10th and 11th periodic reports under the UN Convention against Racism, the Committee on the Elimination of Racial Discrimination (CERD) adopted Concluding Observations.

The government's reports under consideration by the CERD contained unsubstantiated assertions about the circumstances of the fatal shootings by police, in two separate incidents, of Ângelo Semedo and António Pereira in 2002, apparently to justify the conduct of the officers involved in the killings. The areas where the killings took place were described as "marginal neighbourhood[s]", and Bela Vista, in Setúbal, where António Pereira was killed, as "a kind of ghetto, where the police, who feel unwelcome, fear to enter". Reports continued of policing being carried out in a discriminatory manner in deprived areas, where people belonging to ethnic and other minorities often felt they were being targeted by officers but did not have sufficient trust in the police to lodge a complaint.

Among the CERD's concerns were the lack of statistical data on the ethnic composition of the population, the continuing occurrence of racially motivated acts and incitement to hatred, and the persistence of intolerance and discrimination towards minorities. It recommended the adoption of criminal legislation establishing racist motivations as aggravating circumstances in the perpetration of an offence. Concern was also raised about allegations of police misconduct – including excessive use of force and ill-treatment – towards ethnic minorities or people of non-Portuguese origin. The CERD recommended thorough, impartial and effective investigations of those incidents, bringing those responsible to justice, the provision of remedies and compensation to the victims, and intensive training for law enforcement officials to ensure they respect and protect the human rights of all, without discrimination. In addition, the CERD expressed concern about the isolation of some groups of immigrants and members of ethnic minorities in areas it described as "ghetto-like neighbourhoods", and highlighted the difficulties experienced by members of the Romani minority in areas such as employment, education and housing.

Finally, the CERD expressed concern about the non-suspensive effect of appeal in the admissibility phase of the asylum procedure, and recommended that Portugal respect the legal safeguards for asylum-seekers ensuring that its asylum legislation and procedures comply with relevant international obligations.

AI country reports/ visits
Reports
- Portugal: Attack on a prisoner in Lisbon Prison (AI Index: EUR 38/001/2004)
- Europe and Central Asia: Summary of Amnesty International's concerns in the region, January-June 2004: Portugal (AI Index: EUR 01/005/2004)
Visit
An AI delegate visited Portugal in March.

ROMANIA

ROMANIA
Head of state: Traian Băsescu (replaced Ion Iliescu in December)
Head of government: Călin Popescu Tăriceanu (replaced Adrian Năstase in December)
Death penalty: abolitionist for all crimes
International Criminal Court: ratified
UN Women's Convention and its Optional Protocol: ratified

People with mental disabilities were arbitrarily deprived of their liberty in psychiatric establishments. In some hospitals the conditions amounted to inhuman and degrading treatment. A number of patients died as a result of malnourishment, cold, inadequate care or abuse by staff and other patients. Ill-treatment by law enforcement officials, which sometimes amounted to torture, was widespread. Police resorted to firearms in circumstances prohibited by international standards, killing at least two men and injuring dozens of people. Many victims of police ill-treatment and misuse of firearms were Roma.

Conditions in prisons were sometimes inhuman and degrading, and there were reports of ill-treatment of detainees.

Background
Presidential and general elections held in November were marred by allegations of fraud. The rules allowed people to cast a ballot in any polling station without producing a voter registration card, and multiple voting was allegedly widespread. The second round of presidential elections on 12 December was won by Traian Băsescu, supported by the Justice and Truth Alliance which formed a coalition government at the end of 2004.

The government failed to curb widespread corruption in the management of public funds and organization of public services, particularly health care. In November, when transcripts of meetings of the ruling party's Executive Committee, chaired by the Prime Minister, were published, it emerged that they had discussed influencing the judiciary, manipulating the media and undermining the activities of civil society organizations.

A third of the population lived in poverty, which particularly affected children and the elderly. According to an official study published in July, 66,000 children were employed in conditions described as grave. Some children had been sold into bonded labour, others were trafficked abroad for sexual and other exploitation. Following a visit in September, the UN Special Rapporteur on the sale of children, child prostitution and child pornography stated that he was shocked by the situation and that state mechanisms did not effectively protect the most vulnerable.

The news media were subjected to political and economic pressures which imposed considerable restrictions on the freedom of journalists. A number of journalists who reported on organized crime or public funds mismanagement were assaulted. Investigations into such incidents appeared ineffective.

Detention in psychiatric hospitals
The placement, living conditions and treatment of patients in many psychiatric wards and hospitals were in violation of international human rights standards.
◻ In one hospital in Poiana Mare, 18 patients died in January and February, most of them reportedly as a result of malnutrition and hypothermia.

Confining people for involuntary psychiatric treatment without sufficient medical grounds and without charging them with a criminal offence amounted to arbitrary detention and denial of fair trial rights. Many people placed in psychiatric wards and hospitals apparently did not require psychiatric treatment. Many young adults were held in institutions because they had no family and there were no programmes to reintegrate them into the community.

The living conditions and diet in many psychiatric wards and hospitals were deplorable. Overcrowding resulted in patients having to share beds. Some patients shared beds as the only way to keep warm in unheated wards. Conditions were worst in wards for long-term patients and for those with the most severe disabilities.

Many patients were denied adequate medical treatment, including access to psychiatric medication, because of lack of allocated resources. Some were subjected to electroconvulsive therapy without anaesthetics and muscle relaxants. Few hospitals had staff and facilities to offer the full range of therapies and rehabilitation. Many patients apparently did not receive appropriate treatment for physical conditions in addition to their mental health problems.

Restraint and seclusion practices in many psychiatric wards and hospitals were not in line with international standards and in some instances amounted to cruel, inhuman and degrading treatment or punishment.

In May, in response to a memorandum from AI, the government adopted a list of measures to improve the mental health care system. However, some were ineffective. For example, hospitals were ordered to increase budgets for patients' food and staff salaries. However, many hospital directors stated that they received no additional funds. In November, reports from local monitors indicated that there had been no improvements in many of the hospitals visited.

Abuse of patients and residents continued and several died from gross negligence or from violence perpetrated by other patients.

⬜ In September in Braila, a 66-year-old patient with dementia was placed by an orderly under a scalding hot shower. He suffered extensive burns from which he died.

Torture and ill-treatment

Ill-treatment by law enforcement officials continued to be widespread and inadequately addressed by the authorities. Many victims were criminal suspects. A number of people were beaten and verbally abused when unable to produce an identity card. Some people were beaten by off-duty officers intervening in disputes.

Some people were deliberately intimidated by police at the behest of local authorities. For example, in February police raided a student dormitory in Bucharest after protests about the lack of hot water. In March, police searched the homes of members of a socially stigmatized yoga movement, MISA, and ill-treated some of them, capturing this inhuman and degrading treatment on film and broadcasting it on television.

⬜ In separate incidents in June and July, members of the Falun Dafa Romania, an organization of Falun Gong practitioners, were reportedly ill-treated by police and secret service officers in Bucharest. They were attempting to protest against the persecution of Falun Gong practitioners in China, but their requests to hold a demonstration were rejected.

Some victims were placed in psychiatric wards after being beaten by police. The editor of a Bucharest daily newspaper was confined in May but discharged following the intervention of family members.

Some people seriously injured by police were not given appropriate medical assistance. At least two people died as a result of ill-treatment by law enforcement officials.

⬜ In September in Constanța, following a dispute with a bar owner, Laurenţiu Capbun and two other men were reportedly assaulted by a police officer, the bar owner's friend, and four masked officers of a special intervention unit. The beating reportedly continued in the Fourth Section Police Station. The three men were released next morning without charge. Laurenţiu Capbun died five days later, apparently as a result of previous health problems aggravated by the beating. The police officers were reportedly to be disciplined for "not reporting the incident to the Constanța Municipal Police and not having an authorization to intervene" but were apparently not charged with any criminal offence.

Investigations into reported incidents were hardly ever independent and impartial. A police commissioner was dismissed because he revealed the identity of two officers of a special state security unit who were, unusually, charged for beating a man in August.

Many children were abused by police. Often they were suspected of a petty offence or happened to witness a police action.

⬜ In March, on one of the main streets of Bucharest, 15-year-old C.B. stopped to watch as police officers argued with some taxi drivers. A special intervention force team arrived, beat the taxi drivers and pushed them into police vans. Five officers wearing balaclavas then punched and kicked C.B. in the head and back and put him in one of their cars. He was taken to Police Station 14 and was released two hours later. C.B. was admitted to a children's emergency hospital where he received treatment for numerous injuries. The hospital released him two days later, reportedly under pressure from the police.

A number of reported victims of police ill-treatment or torture were women, some of whom were raped.

⬜ In February it was reported that two young women from Ţăndarei, Ialomiţa county, had been raped and beaten in December 2003 by three senior police officers who had offered to help one of them obtain a driving licence. They were reportedly beaten, repeatedly raped and held against their will for seven days. Their parents found out that they had left work in the company of the police officers. When this was reported to the Municipal Police, a senior official reportedly tried to remove the officers' names from the complaint. After the two women returned home, they were examined by a forensic medical doctor but were reportedly harassed and warned by the police not to complain. In February, their case was reported in the press and the Ministry of Interior suspended the suspected officers from duty pending an internal inquiry. No results were made public by the end of 2004.

Unlawful use of firearms by law enforcement officers

At least two men died as a result of shooting by law enforcement officers who resorted to firearms in circumstances that breach international standards. Shooting unarmed suspects who attempted to avoid arrest was considered legal and officially condoned. In January the Prime Minister stated that the Spanish police, who had shot a suspected Romanian car thief in the head, had "a more efficient regime of firearms use". Investigations were rarely impartial, independent and thorough. No official statistics were available, but dozens of people were injured in firearms incidents.

🗁 On 30 May, two police officers in the village of Jegălia, in Călărași county, chased Nicușor Șerban, in an attempt to arrest him on suspicion of rape. When he jumped over a fence, officer S. reportedly shot at him twice, hitting him in the back. He died on the way to hospital.

Assaults on the Roma

Many victims of police ill-treatment and unlawful use of firearms were Roma. Roma also suffered at the hands of security guards who were registered with the local authorities.

🗁 According to the European Roma Rights Center and the "*Tumende*" Association of Vale Jiului, a local Romani organization, on 11 March Bela Dodi died after being beaten by private security guards at the Coroiești mine in Vulcan, Hunedoara county. Bela Dodi and four other Romani men were collecting scrap metal when private security guards assaulted them. Bela Dodi, who was trying to run away, fell, hit his head, and died. The four other men were taken to a hospital for treatment for their injuries. In November 2003 employees of the same private security firm had reportedly beaten Olga David, a 42-year-old Romani woman, who subsequently died from her injuries.

Prison conditions

Poor living conditions, serious overcrowding and lack of activities or medical services in many prisons amounted to inhuman and degrading treatment. There were continued reports of ill-treatment by staff who also resorted to inappropriate means of restraint, including handcuffing prisoners in hospital.

🗁 In September in the Juvenile and Youth Penitentiary in Craiova, three minors died and two suffered severe injuries when a boy set fire to their cell in protest over a missing parcel. The staff, with only one psychologist and social worker in an institution holding 330 minors, failed to address the boy's complaint and confined him in the cell in an agitated state. The mattresses were highly inflammable and fire extinguishers and procedures were inadequate. The penitentiary director and head of security services were subsequently dismissed.

AI country reports/ visits
Reports
- Romania: Memorandum to the government concerning inpatient psychiatric treatment (AI Index: EUR 39/003/2004)
- The Romanian government fails to acknowledge the human tragedy unfolding in psychiatric hospitals (AI Index: EUR 39/005/2004)
- Romania: More ill-treatment of children (AI Index: EUR 39/008/2004)

- Europe and Central Asia: Summary of Amnesty International's concerns in the region, January-June 2004: Romania (AI Index: EUR 01/005/2004)

Visits
In February an AI delegate visited Romania to conduct research. In November an AI delegation met government officials to discuss concerns in psychiatric institutions. Together with the Center for Legal Resources, a local non-governmental organization, an international round-table discussion was organized on human rights protection for people with mental disabilities and reform of mental health services in Romania.

RUSSIAN FEDERATION

RUSSIAN FEDERATION
Head of state: Vladimir Putin
Head of government: Mikhail Fradkov (replaced Mikhail Kasianov in March)
Death penalty: abolitionist in practice
International Criminal Court: signed
UN Women's Convention and its Optional Protocol: ratified

Serious human rights violations continued to be committed in the context of the conflict in the Chechen Republic (Chechnya), belying claims by the authorities that the situation was "normalizing". The security forces enjoyed virtual impunity for abuses. Chechen armed opposition groups were responsible for abuses including bomb attacks and hostage-taking in which hundreds of people were killed. Human rights defenders and people pursuing justice for human rights violations through the European Court of Human Rights were harassed and assaulted; several were killed or "disappeared". Several thousand people displaced from Chechnya remained in Ingushetia, despite pressure from the authorities to return. The human rights situation in Ingushetia deteriorated, especially following an attack by a Chechen armed opposition group in Ingushetia in June. Torture and ill-treatment in places of detention continued to be reported throughout the Russian Federation. Attacks, some of them fatal, on members of ethnic and national minorities and on foreign nationals were reported in many regions but convictions for racist attacks were rare.

Background

In March, Vladimir Putin was re-elected President. International observers judged the elections to be "well administered" but criticized the overt pro-Putin bias of the state-controlled media. Around 25.5 million people were living below subsistence level, according to official statistics. There were mass protests over proposals to overhaul the social benefits system, replacing travel, housing and health care benefits with monthly cash payments.

A law was passed in June banning demonstrations in various public places including close to presidential residences, court buildings and prisons and placing severe restrictions on the organization of other demonstrations and public meetings. There were reports of demonstrations dispersed violently by law enforcement agencies.

The length of time that someone suspected of "terrorism-related" offences could be held without charge was extended to 30 days. In June the state Duma (parliament) approved legislation increasing penalties for "terrorism-related" offences; the maximum sentence was increased from 20 years to life imprisonment.

In December the Duma voted to abolish elections for the governors of the regions who would in future be appointed by the President, despite widespread criticism that this represented a curtailment of civil and political rights.

For the third time, the UN Commission on Human Rights failed to adopt a resolution on the human rights situation in Chechnya. In October the Committee on Legal Affairs and Human Rights, in its report to the Parliamentary Assembly of the Council of Europe, condemned the human rights situation in Chechnya as "catastrophic".

Chechen conflict

"Disappearances", killings, torture and ill-treatment of civilians were frequently reported in the context of the Chechen conflict. Many of the abuses occurred during targeted raids by Russian federal and Chechen forces. In most cases the Russian and Chechen authorities failed to conduct prompt, independent and thorough investigations into allegations of human rights violations against the civilian population.

Increasingly, reports suggested that violations, and in particular "disappearances", were being carried out by so-called *Kadyrovtsy*, Chechen security forces under the command of Deputy Prime Minister Ramzan Kadyrov.

◻ In February, over 80 relatives of Omar Khambiev, a former Chechen Minister of Health, were rounded up from various parts of Chechnya by the *Kadyrovtsy*. They were reportedly tortured and ill-treated in an attempt to stop Omar Khambiev speaking out about violations in Chechnya and to force his brother, Magomed Khambiev, a leader of a Chechen armed opposition group, to surrender.

◻ At 2am on 27 March, military vehicles carrying masked uniformed men entered the village of Duba-Yurt. Nineteen houses were raided and 11 men

detained. Three were released soon afterwards. The bodies of the remaining eight were found on 9 April several kilometres away, reportedly bearing marks of torture and multiple gunshot wounds.

◻ In April, a court in Rostov-on-Don found four members of a special Russian military intelligence unit not guilty of the murder of six civilians in Chechnya. Although the four admitted to the killings, the court ruled that their actions were not punishable as they had been following orders. The decision was widely criticized and the Supreme Court of the Russian Federation quashed the verdict. A new trial started in October.

Abuses by armed groups

In February bomb explosions on the Moscow metro during the rush hour resulted in up to 41 deaths and more than 100 injured. President Putin was quick to blame Chechen separatist leader Aslan Maskhadov for the attack, although this was denied; no other group claimed responsibility.

In May, Akhmad Kadyrov, President of the Chechen Republic, was assassinated in a bomb explosion while watching a Victory Day parade in the Dinamo stadium in Grozny. An eight-year-old girl was also among the casualties.

In August, two passenger aeroplanes exploded in mid-air over central Russia killing some 90 people.

In September, more than 1,000 people, several hundred of them children, were taken hostage in a school in Beslan, North Ossetia. Nearly 350 people are thought to have died when explosives were detonated in the school and in the ensuing shoot-out between hostage-takers, armed local civilians and security forces. Shamil Basaev, leader of a Chechen armed opposition group, claimed responsibility for the hostage-taking as well as for the explosion of the two aeroplanes. The events triggered fears of spreading instability throughout the volatile North Caucasus region.

Violence against women in Chechnya

Women were increasingly detained and tortured in order to make them confess to cooperating with Chechen armed groups. There were reports of rape in detention.

◻ "Madina" (not her real name) was detained in April by Russian federal forces. She was blindfolded and taken to the main Russian military base in Khankala. She was held there for two weeks and allegedly subjected to electric shocks every day. She was also allegedly stripped naked, beaten and sexually abused by groups of officers, and threatened with rape. Madina was reportedly released after two weeks and told that the officers had made a mistake in detaining her. She said she was threatened that she would be killed if she reported what had happened to her.

◻ Milana Ozdoeva, a widow from Kotar Yurt in the Achkhoi-Martan region of the Chechen Republic, was reportedly questioned by a member of the Russian federal forces on 5 and 9 January. According to her neighbours, on 19 January several men came to her home and took her away. They refused to let her take her two-month-old baby with her. Milana Ozdoeva subsequently "disappeared".

The UN Special Rapporteur on violence against women visited Chechnya in December. In a subsequent statement, the Rapporteur highlighted the climate of fear and insecurity in the region due to abuse of the civilian population by security forces and Chechen armed groups.

Conflict spreads beyond Chechnya

Human rights abuses characteristic of the Chechen conflict were increasingly reported in Ingushetia and other North Caucasus regions. Raids by Russian federal and Chechen security forces resulted in "disappearances" and killings. Attacks by Chechen armed opposition groups resulted in dozens of casualties in Ingushetia.

Tent camps for internally displaced people were closed down and the authorities put increasing pressure on displaced Chechens to return home, despite well-founded fears about the security situation in Chechnya.

☐ Rashid Ozdoev, Ingush Deputy Prosecutor, "disappeared" in March after his car was stopped by armed men reportedly identified as from the Federal Security Service (FSB). There were reports that he was taken to the Russian military base at Khankala and held under a false name, but his whereabouts had not been established by the end of 2004. In the course of his work, Rashid Ozdoev had previously raised concerns with the Ingush and Russian federal authorities about unlawful actions by the FSB.

☐ Two students were killed in March when a car they were sitting in with two other young people was fired on from a helicopter. The failure of the authorities to investigate the killing led to a demonstration in Nazran, Ingushetia, during which police detained a number of students, allegedly beat them and threatened them with expulsion from university.

☐ In June Ingush police and Russian federal security forces raided a settlement of people displaced from Chechnya on a former dairy farm in Altievo, Nazran district, Ingushetia. They reportedly ordered more than 1,000 of the occupants, including children, to vacate their living quarters while they carried out an inspection. Excessive force was reportedly used during the inspection, as shots were repeatedly fired in the air and into walls. Some of the women were reportedly made to partially undress in front of men. The displaced people were ordered to leave the camp within two days or the settlement would be burned down. Thirty-six men were arrested and held incommunicado; most were released after five days, nine were released a month later.

Racially motivated crimes

Ethnic and national minority groups and foreign citizens – including students and asylum-seekers – were targeted in racist attacks; the Sova Information-Analytical Centre reported 44 racist murders. There were also reports of attacks on Jewish places of worship and cemeteries. Any investigations into racist attacks were often ineffective and led to lesser charges of hooliganism rather than more serious race-hate charges.

☐ Nikolai Girenko – a prominent human rights defender and an expert on racism and discrimination in the Russian Federation – was shot dead on 19 June in his home in St Petersburg. He headed the Minority Rights Commission at the St Petersburg Scientific Union and had conducted several studies for the authorities of neo-Nazi and "skinhead" groups and had repeatedly warned that such groups were on the rise. Many people believed his murder was related to his human rights activity and anti-racism campaigning.

☐ In February, Antoniu Amaru Lima, a 24-year-old medical student from Guinea-Bissau, was stabbed to death by a gang in the city of Voronezh. In September, three young men were convicted of the killing on racial grounds and sentenced to between nine and 17 years' imprisonment. The conviction was hailed as an important precedent in the fight against racism in the Russian Federation.

☐ In February, verdicts were handed down in connection with an attack by some 150 "skinheads" on market traders, many of them from ethnic minority groups, at the Yasenevo market in Moscow in April 2001. Five of the 150 alleged attackers were brought to trial. Two were acquitted, two were given suspended sentences and one was sentenced to six months' imprisonment.

☐ Khursheda Sultanova, a nine-year-old Tajik girl, was stabbed to death in St Petersburg in February. She was travelling home with her father and 11-year-old cousin when they were attacked by a gang of youths armed with knuckle-dusters, chains, sticks and knives. The attackers reportedly shouted racist slogans. According to police reports, Khursheda Sultanova was stabbed 11 times in the chest. Although a number of youths were detained and charged in connection with the case, no one had been charged with murder by the end of the year. The Procuracy reportedly ruled out a racial motive for the murder.

☐ In December, seven teenagers were given prison sentences of between two and a half and 10 years for the killing of a Tajik girl, Nulufar Sangboeva, in the St Petersburg region in 2003.

Discrimination against Chechens remained commonplace throughout the Russian Federation. They were subjected to arbitrary document checks and searches by the authorities. Following the Moscow metro bombing in February, and the hostage-taking in Beslan in September, human rights groups reported an increase in the number and severity of attacks on Chechens and others from the Caucasus living in Moscow and other cities.

Despite statements by the authorities to the contrary, Meskhetians living in Krasnodar Territory continued to be denied citizenship and registration, resulting in discrimination in almost every aspect of daily life, including in education, employment and health care.

Roma were targeted by police in St Petersburg and subjected to racist attacks in other parts of the country.

☐ On 20 May police in St Petersburg launched "Operation *Tabor*" ostensibly to crack down on theft and begging. Several hundred people were detained during the Operation, most of them Roma. On 21 May uniformed men thought to be police raided a Romani settlement in Obukhovo district in St Petersburg. They reportedly ordered the Roma to leave immediately, took money from them, fired shots into the air and burned down two huts.

Human rights defenders

Human rights defenders and people seeking justice through the European Court of Human Rights were harassed; some were tortured and killed.

◻ Imran Ezhiev, head of the North Caucasus office of the Society for Russian-Chechen Friendship, was detained by a group of armed men in military uniform on 29 January. He was taken to a police station in Sleptsovskaia village, Ingushetia, where he was reportedly beaten and threatened with "disappearance" by police officers. He was released the next day following the intervention of the head of the Russian Presidential Human Rights Commission.

◻ Anzor Pokaev was detained, allegedly by federal troops, during a raid on his home in Starye Atagi in Chechnya in April. His body, bearing several gunshot wounds, was found at the roadside the next morning. His father and nine others had filed an application to the European Court of Human Rights in July 2003 concerning the "disappearances" in April 2002 of their relatives, who included Anzor Pokaev's brother, Amir.

◻ In August a Moscow court sentenced Uzbek human rights defender Bakhrom Khamroev to one and a half years' imprisonment for the illegal possession of drugs. There were allegations that the charges had been fabricated. In November a court in the Perm region, where he had been sent to serve his sentence, changed it to a conditional sentence and released him.

In May, President Putin made unprecedented criticism of the non-governmental community, questioning many organizations' real motivation. Draft amendments to the tax code passed a first reading in the Duma in August; the proposals included significant restrictions on sources of financing for non-governmental organizations.

Media freedom

Journalists were criticized by government officials and persecuted and harassed by the authorities and by non-state actors. Following the hostage-taking in Beslan, concerns were raised about the way the government had provided information on the event and how journalists had been prevented from gathering information.

◻ In September, Anna Politkovskaya, a journalist, reported that she lost consciousness after drinking a cup of tea on a flight to North Ossetia. On arrival in Rostov-on-Don, she was taken to hospital and put in intensive care. Doctors later told her that she may have been poisoned, but that medical staff had allegedly been ordered to destroy the initial tests. Anna Politkovskaya has been detained and threatened several times in connection with her reporting on Chechnya.

Torture and ill-treatment

Police routinely used torture and ill-treatment to extract confessions. Investigations into allegations of torture or ill-treatment were rare and often inadequate, contributing to a climate of impunity.

◻ In June, 15-year-old Victor Knaus from the Volgograd region was allegedly beaten and forced to confess to the murder of two children.

Riot police were reportedly responsible for beatings and other forms of ill-treatment in a number of prisons throughout the Russian Federation. Prisons continued to be overcrowded. Conditions in many pre-trial detention facilities were so poor that they amounted to cruel, inhuman or degrading treatment.

Conditions for prisoners serving life sentences also amounted to cruel, inhuman or degrading treatment or punishment, and in some cases possibly torture. Every aspect of their imprisonment was designed to ensure their isolation from the outside world and other prisoners.

Fair trial concerns

In April, Igor Sutiagin, a researcher at the Russian Academy of Sciences, was sentenced to 15 years in a strict regime penal colony after an unfair trial. He had been held in pre-trial detention since his arrest in October 1999 on charges of treason. The charges against him had been so vaguely formulated that in December 2001 the first court to consider his case had observed that they were "impossible to understand". He was accused of providing information to a foreign company but the trial failed to adequately examine his defence, including his claim that all the information was available in public sources. His imprisonment appeared to be part of an ongoing pattern of arbitrary persecution of independent scientists, journalists and environmentalists.

In March a Rapporteur was appointed by the Council of Europe's Committee on Legal Affairs and Human Rights to analyse the circumstances surrounding the arrests and prosecutions of Mikhail Khodorkovskii, former head of the Yukos oil company; Platon Lebedev, a business partner; and Aleksei Pichugin, a former security official for Yukos. There were allegations that the trials were politically motivated. The Rapporteur pointed to serious procedural violations committed by different law enforcement agencies and questioned the fairness, impartiality and objectivity of the authorities. There were also concerns about Platon Lebedev's and Aleksei Pichugin's health and lack of access to an independent medical examination and medical treatment.

Violence against women

Thousands of women were killed as a result of gender-based violence in the home or community. Those responsible for violence against women were rarely brought to justice. The Russian Federation had no law specifically addressing domestic violence. However, there was increased coverage in the media of issues such as violence in the home and abuses including rape by the security forces in Chechnya. Russia ratified the

Protocol to Prevent, Suppress and Punish Trafficking in Persons, Especially Women and Children, supplementing the UN Convention against Transnational Organized Crime (known as the Palermo Protocol). Thousands of Russian women are reportedly trafficked to countries around the world each year for forced sexual exploitation. Russia also ratified the Optional Protocol to the UN Women's Convention.

AI country reports/ visits
Reports
- Russian Federation: Amnesty International statement on the situation of Chechen asylum-seekers (AI Index: EUR 46/010/2004)
- Russian Federation: Chechen Republic — "Normalization" in whose eyes? (AI Index: EUR 46/027/2004)
- Joint NGO statement on the Beslan hostage tragedy (AI Index: EUR 46/050/2004)
- Russian Federation: The risk of speaking out — attacks on human rights defenders in the context of the armed conflict in Chechnya (AI Index: EUR 46/059/2004)
Visits
AI delegates visited the Russian Federation in March/April, June, October and December.

RWANDA

REPUBLIC OF RWANDA
Head of state: Paul Kagame
Head of government: Bernard Makuza
Death penalty: retentionist
International Criminal Court: not signed
UN Women's Convention: ratified
Optional Protocol to UN Women's Convention: not signed

Trials of people suspected of involvement in the 1994 genocide continued, both within Rwanda and at the International Criminal Tribunal for Rwanda (ICTR) in Arusha, Tanzania. Rwandese courts concluded fewer than 200 trials of genocide suspects in 2004. No executions were carried out. Approximately 80,000 people remained in detention, most suspected of participation in the genocide. Members of the political opposition, the independent news media and civil society were harassed, arrested and unlawfully detained.

Background
Rwanda's relations with neighbouring Burundi, Uganda and the Democratic Republic of the Congo (DRC) failed to improve as Rwanda continued to insist that it had the right to pursue members of Rwandese armed groups based in the DRC. The Rwandese Defence Forces (RDF) entered Burundi on 22 April, allegedly in search of members of these groups. There were also reports of Burundians being trained in Rwanda to destabilize Burundi (see Burundi entry). The Ugandan and Rwandese governments expelled two diplomats from each other's embassies in late November. Officials in the Ugandan government alleged that a member of an armed group operating in northern Uganda, the People's Redemption Army (PRA), had been trained in Rwanda (see Uganda entry). On 2 December, Ugandan troops clashed with soldiers suspected to be members of the RDF in transit to the eastern DRC. Rwanda continued to support armed groups opposed to the DRC government in eastern DRC (see DRC entry). Relations between Rwanda and the DRC worsened in June, November and December when Rwanda threatened to re-enter the DRC to defeat Rwandese armed groups operating there. There were numerous reports that the RDF was engaged in military operations within the DRC.

Suppression of political opposition
The government continued to suppress the political opposition and those critical of government policies or government officials. Members of the banned Democratic Republican Movement (Mouvement démocratique républicain, MDR) continued to be arrested and detained. At least one MDR member was extrajudicially executed. Family members of some alleged MDR members or supporters had their land confiscated or were denied social services by local

authorities. Some top officials who worked for Faustin Twagiramungu during his 2003 presidential campaign were arrested and unlawfully detained.

◻ David Habimana and his brother were detained on 6 October. They were held in a number of police stations before being taken to Department of Military Intelligence (DMI) facilities on 21 October. They did not appear before a judge within the time required by law and were detained clandestinely by the DMI. David Habimana was a top official in Faustin Twagiramungu's presidential campaign.

Suppression of civil society

On 30 June 2004, the Rwandese parliament accepted the recommendations of a parliamentary commission created to investigate the existence and spread of a "genocide ideology" in Rwanda following the assassination of three genocide survivors between April and November 2003. Several institutions, including religious institutions, schools and national and international non-governmental organizations (NGOs), were accused in the report of either supporting genocide or disseminating its principal tenets. The NGOs named included rural development organizations, a group for survivors of the conflict in the north-west in 1997 and 1998, and one of the few remaining credible human rights organizations operating within Rwanda. The allegations against these organizations and some of their staff, which were unsubstantiated, appeared to be politically motivated. They were working with populations perceived to be hostile to the government or, in the case of the human rights organization, held the government to account for human rights violations. In September, the government officially recognized the report and urged the judicial authorities to initiate legal proceedings.

None of the named organizations was dissolved as recommended by the National Assembly, but their ability to raise funds, employ qualified staff and carry out their work was seriously damaged. Some individuals named in the Commission's report were detained and many lost their jobs. Several sought asylum abroad.

In October, between 14 and 17 people were detained after the Ministry of Education dismissed 37 school officials and teachers and provisionally suspended 27 students. The government reportedly fabricated evidence against some of them and the alleged victims made false allegations against others.

Freedom of the press

Journalists continued to face intimidation and harassment for articles criticizing government policy or documenting the misdeeds of government officials. Several journalists were repeatedly detained and interrogated in early 2004. Three fled Rwanda in March after receiving death threats and one in September after being subjected to intimidation.

◻ Charles Kabonero, editor of the independent newspaper, *Umuseso*, was tried in November for "divisionism" and attacking the dignity of a high political authority. The district court acquitted him of the "divisionist" charge and sentenced him to a symbolic fine of one Rwandese franc.

Abuses in the criminal justice system

Most of the proposed legislation to address abuses in the criminal justice system became law in the first half of 2004. The results of this judicial reform remained unclear. Trials in the first half of 2004 did not meet international standards of fairness. There was a presumption of guilt, and standards of evidence for conviction were lowered. Government interference in judicial decisions was a constant threat.

◻ Pasteur Bizimungu was sentenced in June to 15 years' imprisonment for inciting civil disobedience, associating with criminal elements and embezzling state funds. During the 12-day trial, prosecution witnesses contradicted themselves and admitted giving false statements under considerable duress. The underlying motive for the trial was Pasteur Bizimungu's launch of a political opposition party in May 2001.

Genocide trials

On 7 April 2004, Rwanda commemorated the 10-year anniversary of the 1994 genocide. Within Rwanda, 80,000 detainees awaited trial for their alleged participation in the genocide. They were held in harsh conditions. Another 500,000 to 600,000 Rwandese were implicated in the genocide, largely through the pre-trial confessions of detainees. A reformed judiciary was established in mid-2004.

The nationwide establishment of the 8,140 gacaca jurisdictions — a community-based system of justice intended to try most genocide suspects — was delayed until 2005. The trial phase of the 746 gacaca jurisdictions in a pilot project which began in 2002 was similarly delayed. Few of these had completed the pre-trial phase by the end of 2004.

International Criminal Tribunal for Rwanda

Trials of leading genocide suspects continued at the ICTR, which held 63 detainees at the end of 2004. Up to 14 high-level indictees remained at large.

Four trials involving 18 defendants continued from preceding years. Four new trials involving seven defendants began in 2004. Six judgments were given: two defendants were conditionally released; two received substantial prison sentences and two received life imprisonment.

Three new suspects were arrested in the Netherlands, the DRC and South Africa. Another 40 suspects were identified for investigation.

The ICTR was working under a UN Security Council deadline to finish trials by the end of 2008 and appeals by 2010. The tribunal's chief prosecutor indicated that the 40 cases yet to be investigated would be transferred to other jurisdictions.

Defence lawyers went on strike for two days in January in protest at cost-cutting measures that they said harmed their ability to defend their clients. The ICTR argued that it was reacting to UN General Assembly demands to control expenses.

Sexual violence

Ten years after the 1994 genocide, hundreds of thousands of Rwandese women who were victims of sexual violence were still awaiting legal redress. Nearly 70 per cent of them contracted HIV as a result of rape and had not received medical care or other forms of assistance. Sexual violence against women and girls continued. According to officials, there were more than 2,000 reported cases of rape and defilement in 2004; 80 per cent of the victims were minors.

Refugees

Sixty thousand refugees remained outside Rwanda; most were unsure if they wanted to return and lived in fear of being forcibly returned.

According to the UN High Commissioner for Refugees (UNHCR), 8,457 Rwandese refugees were repatriated in the first six months of 2004 from African countries that had signed tripartite agreements with Rwanda and UNHCR. Despite vigorous promotion of voluntary repatriation, the number of Rwandese registering for repatriation remained small. UNHCR postponed until mid-2006 a decision on the application of "cessation clauses" which would terminate international protection for Rwandese refugees.

There were reports that hundreds of repatriated Rwandese had again left the country to seek asylum. There were also reports of young repatriated men being pressured into military training and transferred to military service in eastern DRC.

Government officials, members of the security forces and leaders of the Rwandese-backed Congolese Rally for Democracy (Rassemblement congolais pour la démocratie, RCD-Goma) reportedly entered camps housing Congolese refugees in Rwanda in March, April and May to recruit soldiers to serve in the DRC. Rwandese officials reportedly pressurized refugees to enlist by refusing to provide them with the appropriate refugee documents and threatening them with the loss of their Congolese citizenship.

AI country reports/ visits

Reports

- Rwanda: "Marked for Death" — rape survivors living with HIV/AIDS in Rwanda (AI Index: AFR 47/007/2004)
- Rwanda: The enduring legacy of the genocide and war (AI Index: AFR 47/008/2004)
- Rwanda: Protecting their rights — Rwandese refugees in the Great Lakes region (AI Index: AFR 47/016/2004)

Visits

AI delegates visited Rwanda in January. An AI delegate attended the Great Lakes regional meeting of the European Initiative for Democracy and Human Rights in May.

SAUDI ARABIA

KINGDOM OF SAUDI ARABIA
Head of state and government: King Fahd Bin 'Abdul 'Aziz Al-Saud
Death penalty: retentionist
International Criminal Court: not signed
UN Women's Convention: ratified with reservations
Optional Protocol to UN Women's Convention: not signed

Killings by security forces and armed groups escalated, exacerbating the already dire human rights situation in the country. Scores of people, including peaceful critics of the state, were arrested and over two dozen suspected in connection with the "war on terror" were detained following their forcible return by other countries. At least five possible prisoners of conscience were tried following hearings that failed to meet international standards, but the status of others, including the hundreds held from previous years, remained shrouded in secrecy. The debate on discrimination against women, which began in previous years, gained further momentum with a sharp focus on domestic violence and political participation. Allegations of torture were reported and flogging, which constitutes a cruel, inhuman and degrading punishment and may amount to torture, remained a routine practice. At least 33 people were executed. Approximately 600 Iraqi refugees remained as virtual prisoners in Rafha Military Camp. Optimism spread among foreign workers following measures announced by the government to protect their economic and social rights, and the country was deemed to have made progress in the alleviation of poverty. AI continued to be denied access to the country.

Background

The government continued to advocate political reform against a background of escalating violence and a dire human rights situation. In March it established the first ever officially sanctioned National Human Rights Association (NHRA) whose 41 members included 10 women. The NHRA's stated aims include protection of human rights and cooperation with international organizations.

Preparations for the first national (although partial) municipal elections announced in 2003 were completed. The elections were planned to take place in three stages with municipalities placed into regional groupings. The first stage began with registration of voters in the region of Riyadh where voting was scheduled for February 2005. The other two stages were planned to be completed by April 2005. The voting regulation issued in August stipulated the election of half of the members of each municipality and the appointment of the other half by the government. Women were not allowed to vote or stand for election (see below).

Killings

Killings by security forces and armed groups escalated, resulting in dozens of deaths. Most killings by security forces took place in Riyadh, Makkah and Jeddah. Some took place during clashes with armed groups and gunmen wanted by the authorities, such as Abdul Aziz Muqrin, alleged leader of al-Qa'ida in Saudi Arabia, who was killed in June in Riyadh. However, most took place following car or street chases and house raids by security forces. The government invariably announced that those killed were armed gunmen, but due to secrecy it was not possible to assess whether this was accurate.

Dozens of people were killed by armed groups and gunmen in different parts of the country. The killings were carried out during armed attacks and following hostage-taking operations.

In May, three gunmen entered offices and residential compounds of employees of oil companies in al-Khobar in the Eastern Province and took dozens of people hostage, mainly expatriate workers. They killed some of the hostages allegedly selected as non-Muslims. Security forces stormed the building where the hostages were held. By the end of the operation 22 civilians, seven members of the security forces and one gunman had reportedly been killed.

In June, Frank Gardner, a UK television journalist, and his cameraman, Simon Cumbers, were attacked by gunmen while filming in Riyadh. Simon Cumbers died in hospital; Frank Gardner was seriously injured.

Political prisoners and possible prisoners of conscience

Arrests were carried out throughout the year of suspected members and sympathizers of armed groups and, in some cases, peaceful critics of the state.

Scores of people were arrested in connection with armed groups, including some whose names appeared on a list of 26 wanted men published by the government in December 2003. The arrests were carried out following armed clashes, street chases, house raids, forcible handover by other countries, or after surrender by the suspects during a one-month amnesty announced by the government on 23 June. The legal status, places of detention and well-being of most of those detained remained shrouded in secrecy, in violation of international standards which prohibit incommunicado detentions and "disappearances".

Some of those arrested as critics of the state were released after a short period in detention. At least five were brought to trial. The legal status of the rest, numbering scores from 2004 and hundreds from previous years, remained unclear.

Five suspected critics of the state were brought to trial in three separate cases. One case involved two university professors, Dr Matrouk al-Falih and Dr Abdullah al-Hamid, and a writer, Ali al-Damayni. The three were among 11 academics and intellectuals arrested in March for calling for political reform and criticizing the government. Eight were released reportedly after signing an undertaking not to repeat such calls and criticisms. The three reportedly refused to sign the undertaking and remained in detention. In a rare departure from the usual practice of secrecy, the three men were allowed access to families and lawyers and in August were brought before a court whose hearings were scheduled to be public. AI planned to send an observer to the trial but its delegate was not granted a visa. The first session of the trial was held in public but was postponed half way through reportedly on the grounds that members of the public were disruptive. Subsequent court sessions were planned to revert to secret hearings. The other two cases involved Dr Said bin Zu'air and his son, Mubarak, both of whom were arrested in 2004. Dr Said bin Zu'air was convicted of vague charges that included disobeying the country's ruler, and sentenced to five years in prison. In a separate trial his son Mubarak was sentenced to 10 months in prison on similar charges. The legal status of another son, Sa'd, who was arrested in July 2002, remained unclear. Dr Said bin Zu'air had previously been detained without charge or trial for about eight years for being a critic of the state.

Ahmed Abu 'Ali, a 24-year-old US national, was arrested in June 2003 at the University of Madinah where he was studying. The US Federal Bureau of Investigation (FBI) reportedly interrogated him or attended his interrogation in relation to a US case – *US v Royer* – involving 11 people charged with "terrorism"-related offences. Ahmed Abu 'Ali had connections with one of the defendants, but that defendant was acquitted. Ahmed Abu 'Ali remained held in Saudi Arabia without charge, trial or access to lawyers.

Women's rights

The debate on women's rights continued with a strong focus on domestic violence and the right to political participation.

Domestic violence attracted national and international attention when in April Rania al-Baz, who had been beaten by her husband, made her ordeal public to raise awareness about violence suffered by women in the home in Saudi Arabia. A television presenter and mother of two, Rania al-Baz was attacked by her husband on 4 April at their home in Jeddah, apparently for having answered the telephone. She suffered 13 fractures to her face. Her husband then put her in his van and reportedly dumped her unconscious at a hospital in Jeddah, claiming that she was a victim of a traffic accident. He went into hiding before surrendering to the police on 19 April. He was reportedly charged with attempted murder but this was later reduced to severe assault for which he was convicted in May. He was sentenced to six months' imprisonment and 300 lashes. Rania al-Baz had the option of a civil action to seek retribution (*qisas*) in the form of compensation or corporal punishment commensurate with the harm she sustained, but apparently chose to pardon her husband in exchange for divorce and custody of her two sons. The husband served over half of his prison sentence. It was not known if he received the lashes.

When Rania al-Baz' disfigured face hit newspaper front pages it forced into the open the many severe forms of discrimination that facilitate and perpetuate violence against women in Saudi Arabia, and the issue of impunity. The case was the first of its kind in the country to proceed under the public eye in a criminal court and result in conviction and punishment. Rania al-Baz revealed that her husband had a history of violence against her but that she could not leave him for fear of losing custody of her children. When she had tried to leave him he prevented her from seeing her children for two months. Divorce in Saudi Arabia is primarily the man's prerogative. Women's rights in this regard are so limited that they are almost impossible to exercise. To gain a divorce, women, unlike men, must prove harm or fault by the spouse, be able to pay compensation, face the risk of losing custody of children, and be able to convince an all-male judiciary. The problems are compounded by severe restrictions on women's movement, total dependency on male relatives and social stigma attached to divorce. Women activists, writers, journalists and lawyers called for legal and judicial changes to end such discrimination and combat the impunity enjoyed by perpetrators of violence against women. It was reported in November that the Ministry of Social Affairs had proposed measures to combat domestic violence, which were awaiting approval by the Council of Ministers.

The government announced in October that women were excluded from participating in the municipal elections in 2005, even though the election regulations introduced in August did not explicitly rule out women's participation. This decision contradicted steps taken by the government to increase work opportunities for women and reduce the spheres of discrimination against women.

Torture and ill-treatment

The strict secrecy surrounding arrests and detention prevented assessment of the scale of torture and ill-treatment of people arrested during or after violent incidents or under the "war on terror" policy. However, there were concerns over televised "confessions" of some of these detainees. There were also reported allegations of torture.

▱ In September, three detainees were shown on state television as members of an armed group "confessing" details about the group, including its use of pictures of torture of detainees by security forces to recruit members and scare its recruits against surrendering to the police. Confessions of suspects televised in the past had often been obtained under torture, ill-treatment or deception.

▱ Six Yemenis reportedly alleged that they were subjected to beatings, sleep deprivation, and being chained together most of the time. All were reportedly arrested during a visit to the house of their employer in Jeddah where police apparently found weapons. They were reportedly released after 18 days of interrogation and then deported to Yemen in August without having been charged or tried.

▱ Brian O'Connor, a Christian Indian national aged 36, was allegedly beaten severely by the religious police following his arrest in March in Riyadh, reportedly for possessing a bible and other Christian literature. He was charged with selling alcohol and sentenced to 10 months' imprisonment and 300 lashes. However, in November he was deported to India.

▱ In May a group of UK nationals who alleged they had been tortured in Saudi Arabia in 2001 appealed in the UK against a 2003 ruling by the UK's High Court in a case brought by Ron Jones against his alleged torturers in Saudi Arabia. The High Court had dismissed the case on the grounds of sovereign immunity under the UK 1978 Act. In October the Court of Appeal ruled that claimants could sue the individual officials who tortured them but not the government.

Flogging

Flogging remained a routine corporal punishment imposed by courts as a main or additional sentence.

▱ Forty-two youths were reportedly flogged for rioting, destroying cars and harassing women in Makkah in August. The flogging was carried out as an additional sentence to imprisonment and a fine.

Refugees

Voluntary repatriation of some 3,500 Iraqi refugees from the Gulf war of 1991 was reportedly suspended in May following deterioration of the security situation in Iraq. Approximately 600 refugees reportedly remained as virtual prisoners in the Rafha Military Camp in the northern desert near the border with Iraq. They were denied the opportunity to seek asylum in Saudi Arabia.

Death penalty and executions

At least 33 people, including a Sri Lankan woman and 13 male foreign nationals, were executed. According to the government they were convicted of murder, rape or drug-related offences. The number of prisoners who remained under sentence of death was not known to AI, but they included Sara Jane Dematera, a Filipina, who was convicted in 1993 after a secret and summary trial of murdering her employer. In April she was allowed a visit by her mother.

Economic and social rights

Optimism spread among the more than seven million foreign workers about their economic and social rights, and the UN indicated that Saudi Arabia had made progress in the fight against poverty. The government announced plans to reform the labour law that would improve protection of the rights of foreign workers. It also announced that it had taken punitive measures against employment agencies and employers who mistreated workers. It said that it had strengthened labour complaints' mechanisms and urged abused workers to submit complaints. Some foreign workers reportedly formed associations to assist their compatriots to submit complaints. In one case, the workers were said to have established a refuge for abused female domestic workers.

AI country reports/ visits
Report
- The Gulf and the Arabian Peninsula: Human rights fall victim to the "war on terror" (AI Index: MDE 04/002/2004)

SENEGAL

REPUBLIC OF SENEGAL
Head of state: Abdoulaye Wade
Head of government: Macky Sall (replaced Idrissa Seck in April)
Death penalty: abolitionist for all crimes
International Criminal Court: ratified
UN Women's Convention and its Optional Protocol: ratified

There was a sharp fall in armed clashes in the Casamance region and in December a peace agreement aimed at putting a definitive end to the conflict was signed. Refugees and internally displaced people began returning home and there were efforts to rebuild destroyed infrastructure. Civil society groups protested publicly about arrests of journalists or political opponents. Senegal abolished the death penalty in December.

Background
In April, President Abdoulaye Wade dismissed Prime Minister Idrissa Seck's attempts to broaden the political base of the government. President Wade appointed Macky Sall as Prime Minister and the new government included Djibo Leïty Kâ, leader of the opposition Union for Renewal of Democracy (L'Union pour le renouveau démocratique, URD).

Reconstruction in Casamance
There was a sharp fall in clashes between the security forces and the armed opposition group claiming independence for Casamance, the Democratic Forces of Casamance Movement (Mouvement des forces démocratiques de Casamance, MFDC). Moreover, in September, the armed wing of the MFDC publicly committed itself to stop attacking civilians in Casamance. This encouraged former refugees and displaced people to return home. Noticeable efforts began to remove landmines, reconstruct demolished houses and revitalize the destroyed economy.

Negotiations to implement the peace agreements signed by the government and the MFDC in 2001 were reportedly hampered by internal divisions between rival factions of the MFDC. Leadership rivalries intensified between the MFDC's historic leader, Father Augustin Diamacoune Senghor, and the Secretary General, Jean-Marie Biagui. Jean-Marie Biagui was confirmed as Secretary General by a special MFDC general assembly in September and then called for the MFDC to be transformed into a political party called the Movement for Federalism and Constitutional Democracy (Mouvement pour le fédéralisme et la démocratie constitutionnelle, MFDC). However, in December, a peace agreement officially aimed at putting a definitive end to the conflict was signed by the Senegalese authorities and Father Diamacoune in Ziguinchor, the main city of Casamance.

Threats to freedom of expression
As in previous years, journalists and political opponents continued to be harassed and intimidated in an apparent attempt to restrict freedom of expression.

In January, Mamadou Lamine Diop, spokesperson of the Reform Party (Parti de la réforme), was detained and interrogated for some hours by police from the Division of Criminal Affairs (Division des affaires criminelles) for criticizing President Wade in a radio interview.

In July, Madiambal Diagne, managing editor of the daily newspaper, *Le Quotidien*, was detained and charged with "publishing confidential reports and correspondence, false information and news which could cause serious political problems". This arrest provoked a massive protest from human rights groups which accused the authorities of trying to muzzle the press. Most Senegalese private daily newspapers also pressed for his release. Madiambal Diagne was provisionally released after two weeks and by the end of 2004 no further judicial proceedings had been reported.

Impunity in Casamance
For many years members of the security forces responsible for massive human rights violations in Casamance had enjoyed impunity, as the authorities took no steps to investigate or bring them to justice. In June the government took a step further towards ensuring permanent impunity. It announced a general amnesty for members of the MFDC, a decision which will prevent the perpetrators of serious human rights abuses being brought to justice.

Abolition of the death penalty
In July, President Wade presented a bill to abolish the death penalty. It was unanimously approved by the Council of Ministers and was adopted in December by the National Assembly by an overwhelming majority.

As a result, the Minister of Justice announced that he would request the commutation of four pending death sentences. They included three death sentences passed in 2004 by the Dakar Criminal Court for robbery resulting in death.

SERBIA AND MONTENEGRO

SERBIA AND MONTENEGRO
Head of state: Svetozar Marović
Head of government: Vojislav Koštunica (Serbia, replaced Zoran Živković in March), Milo Đukanović (Montenegro)
International Criminal Court: ratified
Death penalty: abolitionist for all crimes
UN Women's Convention and its Optional Protocol: ratified

Cooperation with the International Criminal Tribunal for the former Yugoslavia (Tribunal) in The Hague deteriorated as the authorities failed to transfer almost all those indicted by the Tribunal believed to be in Serbia. There were allegations of extrajudicial executions, and trials continued of former officials accused of complicity in previous political crimes. Police torture and ill-treatment continued. Domestic violence and the trafficking of women and girls for forced prostitution remained widespread. Roma continued to be deprived of many basic rights. In Kosovo there were allegations of official complicity in inter-ethnic attacks in March, and the authorities failed to protect minority communities. Witnesses in war crimes trials were subjected to intimidation in Kosovo.

Background

Serbia and Montenegro continued to operate in a loose state union where most responsibilities remained with the separate republics. The UN Interim Mission in Kosovo (UNMIK) continued to administer Kosovo, with the Special Representative of the UN Secretary-General (SRSG) holding executive powers. Harri Holkeri was replaced as SRSG in June by Søren Jessen-Petersen.

War crimes

The trial of former President Slobodan Milošević, accused of responsibility for war crimes in Croatia, Bosnia and Herzegovina and Kosovo, continued before the Tribunal. The prosecution concluded its case. In June the Tribunal rejected defence calls for the charge of genocide to be dropped. It ruled that there was "a joint criminal enterprise" which committed genocide in Brčko, Prijedor, Sanski Most, Srebrenica, Bijeljina, Ključ and Bosanski Novi and that evidence implicated Slobodan Milošević in that joint criminal enterprise.

The Serbian authorities refused to transfer to the Tribunal several people indicted for crimes against humanity and war crimes in Kosovo in 1999, including: Serbian Assistant Interior Minister (dismissed in March) and former Kosovo police chief Sreten Lukić; former Yugoslav army chief Nebojša Pavković; and

former commander of Priština Corps Vladimir Lazarević. In July Goran Hadžić, former head of the Krajina Serbs in Croatia, fled his house in Serbia immediately after the Tribunal had forwarded a sealed indictment for him and before an arrest warrant was issued. In October another indictee, Ljubiša Beara, was transferred to the Tribunal – the sole transfer in 2004. About 20 suspects indicted by the Tribunal were believed to remain at large in Serbia and Montenegro.

In November Tribunal President Theodor Meron reported to the UN General Assembly that apart from the case of Ljubiša Beara, Serbia and Montenegro had virtually not cooperated at all with the Tribunal. Similarly, Tribunal Prosecutor Carla Del Ponte reported to the UN Security Council that Serbia was not willing to arrest indictees, that networks supporting people accused were so powerful that they could interfere with judicial proceedings, and that both in Serbia and in Kosovo aggressive nationalist rhetoric was being used against the Tribunal and herself.

⬚ In June Vladimir "Rambo" Kovačević, indicted in connection with the shelling of Dubrovnik, was given six months' provisional release by the Tribunal due to mental illness and transferred to the Belgrade Military Medical Academy.

⬚ In March the special War Crimes Panel within the District Court of Belgrade began to try six people indicted by Serbia's special war crimes prosecutor in connection with the Ovčara massacre near Vukovar, Croatia, in 1991. Another of the accused died in March after jumping from a hospital window in January. In May, 12 more suspects were indicted. However, there were concerns about the apparent selective nature of the indictment in that there was no mention of the responsibility of former Yugoslav National Army (JNA) officers in the crime, in spite of the testimony of many witnesses indicating this.

⬚ In March Saša Cvjetan, a member of Serbia's notorious "Scorpions anti-terrorist" police unit, was sentenced in Belgrade to 20 years' imprisonment for the murder of 19 ethnic Albanians in Podujevo in 1999.

Exhumations

Serbia continued to hand over to UNMIK the bodies of ethnic Albanians murdered in Kosovo and buried in mass graves in Batajnica near Belgrade, Petrovo Selo, and Bajina Bašta near Lake Perućac. By the end of 2004 a total of 378 of the 836 exhumed from these sites had been returned. In March the Serbian special war crimes prosecutor stated that "intensive investigations" were ongoing into the Batajnica and Petrovo Selo mass graves – both situated on Ministry of the Interior property – but no indictments had been issued by the end of 2004. In May, 55 bodies buried after the 1991-92 war with Croatia were exhumed from cemeteries in Belgrade and in Obrenovac.

Possible extrajudicial executions

There were allegations of extrajudicial executions.
⬚ In October, two conscript sentries – Dražen Milovanović and Dragan Jakovljević – were shot dead at a Belgrade military complex. The military claimed

that one had shot the other and then committed suicide but other sources alleged that both men had been murdered by a third party. In November a military commission of inquiry reaffirmed that they had shot each other after a quarrel. However, a non-military State Commission of Inquiry set up by President Marović to investigate the deaths announced in December that a third party was definitely involved. The contradictions between the findings of the military and civilian investigations remained unresolved by the end of 2004.

In May Duško Jovanović, editor-in-chief of the Montenegrin daily *Dan* and a critic of leading officials, was assassinated in Podgorica. The sole suspect arrested claimed connections with the security services, and there were allegations of official complicity in the murder.

Past political murders

In February, the trial began of Radomir Marković, former head of Serbian state security, and other security officials accused of involvement in a 1999 attempt on the life of leading politician Vuk Drašković in which four people died, and the murder of former Serbian President Ivan Stambolić in August 2000.

The trial of those accused of involvement in the murder in March 2003 of Prime Minister Zoran Đinđić continued. On 1 March an eyewitness to the assassination, Kujo Kriještorac, was shot dead. In May the prime suspect, Milorad "Legija" Ulemek-Luković, surrendered in Belgrade.

In April the Serbian Minister of Internal Affairs, Dragan Jočić, announced a special task force to investigate unsolved murders including those of journalists Slavko Ćuruvija and Milan Pantić in April 1999 and June 2001 respectively, and former secret policeman Momir Gavrilović in March 2004. The Minister also called for a new inquiry into the assassination of Zoran Đinđić and expressed doubts about the deaths in March 2003 of two suspects in the assassination, Dušan Spasojević and Mile Luković. The police had said that the two men were shot dead in an exchange of fire while resisting arrest. On 30 April the Belgrade weekly *NIN* published official autopsy findings which indicated that Dušan Spasojević had been shot in the back while on the ground, and that Mile Luković had been beaten and shot in the head at close range. In May an investigation into the deaths was announced but no results had emerged by the end of 2004.

Police torture and ill-treatment

The number of reports of police torture or ill-treatment apparently fell. However, allegations continued and in a number of trials testimony said to have been obtained under torture was admitted in court. Investigations into previous cases remained seriously flawed.

In April Dragan Jočić admitted that there had been human rights violations during "Operation Sabre" — the clampdown on organized crime following the assassination of Zoran Đinđić. In May the Assistant Minister of Internal Affairs, referring to a September 2003 report on "Operation Sabre" by AI, stated that there had been six cases of torture during the operation. In July, delegates from Serbia and Montenegro appearing before the UN Human Rights Committee in Geneva stated that investigations had been opened into the 16 cases featured by AI and reiterated that in six cases there had been ill-treatment or torture. However, no information was made available on the investigations, and the implication that these were the only cases was shown to be false. No proceedings were initiated against police officers suspected of using torture during "Operation Sabre", and in a number of trials testimony allegedly obtained under torture was admitted in court.

Attacks on minorities

In response to widespread attacks on Serb communities in Kosovo by Albanians in March, there were a number of attacks on minorities in Serbia and on mosques in Belgrade and Niš. The authorities announced a number of arrests in March: 88 for attacking the police in Belgrade; 53 for rioting in Belgrade; nine (later 11) in Niš for burning the Hadrović mosque; and, in May, 24 for attacking Albanian and Gorani business premises in the Vojvodina.

There was a rise in attacks against minorities in the multi-ethnic Vojvodina region. In June the non-governmental Helsinki Committee for Human Rights in Serbia reported that there had been 40 such attacks since the nationalist Serbian Radical Party won the most seats in Serbian general elections in December 2003.

Violence against women

Domestic violence remained widespread. Although there was a rise in proceedings against perpetrators in Serbia after criminal legislation was adopted in 2002, most cases were excluded from this legislation due to a restrictive legal definition of who constituted a "family member".

Serbia and Montenegro remained a source, transit and destination country for women and girls trafficked for forced prostitution. When those involved in trafficking were convicted, courts imposed lenient sentences.

On 5 March Belgrade District Court convicted Milovoje Zarubica and 12 others of involvement in trafficking women and girls from Moldova. They received sentences ranging from five months to three and a half years' imprisonment on charges which included rape. They were released from custody pending appeal.

In June the US State Department report on trafficking noted continuing official corruption in Serbia, with off-duty police officers caught providing security at venues where trafficking victims were located. It stated that only one had been charged with a criminal offence. In Montenegro, the report stated that although 15 cases had been submitted for prosecution since 2002, there had been no convictions.

In November the Organization for Security and Co-operation in Europe Mission in Kosovo expressed concern about the findings of a commission appointed by the Montenegrin government in April 2004 to investigate the actions of the Montenegrin police in a case involving a Moldovan woman. She had been trafficked into Montenegro for sexual exploitation and her statements had implicated a number of senior government officials. The commission's report denigrated the victim's character.

Discrimination against Roma

Economic hardship and unemployment affected many sections of society, but many Roma continued to be especially deprived. Most lived in sub-standard unhygienic settlements and they faced discrimination in education, employment and health.

Most Roma who fled Kosovo after July 1999 continued to face severe problems, exacerbated by difficulties in obtaining registration necessary for access to health and social welfare. In Montenegro they continued to be treated as refugees and not entitled to benefits of citizenship. Many Roma from both Serbia and Montenegro suffered similar deprivation because they were not officially registered at birth.

In Serbia the authorities began to implement strategies to improve the Roma's plight but with little effect; in Montenegro there was no such strategy.

Kosovo
War crimes, arrests, trials and retrials

Arrests, trials and retrials for war crimes and crimes against humanity continued, involving both Kosovo Albanians and Serbs. Tens of thousands of Kosovo Albanians continued to protest against the prosecution of ex-members of the Kosovo Liberation Army (KLA).

▭ Tribunal prosecutors stated that witnesses in the case of ex-KLA members Fatmir Limaj, Isak Musliu and Haradinaj Bala, whose trial began in November, were subjected to organized and systematic intimidation. Beqa Beqaj, a relative of Isak Musliu, was indicted by the Tribunal for attempting to interfere with witnesses and was arrested in November and transferred to the Tribunal in The Hague.

Accountability of KFOR

Troops from KFOR, the NATO-led international force in Kosovo, were accountable only to their national legislatures.

▭ On 7 April, in the first judicial case involving an alleged human rights violation by KFOR troops while on duty, the UK High Court ruled in civil proceedings that the UK government should pay compensation to Mohamet and Skender Bici for damages caused when in 1999 UK KFOR troops opened fire on their car. Two other passengers, Fahri Bici and Avni Dudi, were killed. An investigation by the UK Royal Military Police had cleared the three soldiers responsible but the presiding judge ruled that the soldiers had deliberately and unjustifiably caused the injuries.

Failure to solve inter-ethnic crimes

UNMIK failed to make significant progress in bringing to justice those responsible for ethnically motivated murders and attacks since 1999.

The violence of 17-19 March

From 17-19 March, inter-ethnic violence erupted throughout Kosovo. The authorities estimated that about 51,000 people were involved in 33 violent incidents. In most, Albanians attacked Serb enclaves and communities.

The UN Secretary-General reported that 19 people died – 11 Albanians and eight Serbs – and 954 were injured, as well as 65 international police officers, 58 Kosovo Police Service (KPS) officers and 61 KFOR personnel. Approximately 730 homes and 36 Orthodox churches, monasteries and other religious and cultural sites were damaged or destroyed. In less than 48 hours, 4,100 minority community members were newly displaced, of whom most were Serbs. The others were Roma, Ashkali and Albanians from the Serb majority areas of Mitrovica/Mitrovicë and Leposavić/Leposaviq.

In a number of places the security forces, including KFOR, failed to protect minority communities.

▭ Approximately 200 inhabitants from the long-settled Serb community of Svinjare/Frashër were forced from their homes, which were then burned, by a crowd of some 500 Albanians. Svinjare/Frashër is about 500 metres from a main French KFOR base. KFOR evacuated the inhabitants but did nothing to deter the arsonists.

There were also serious allegations of complicity by Albanian members of the KPS in a number of places including Vučitrn/Vushtrri, where the entire Ashkali community was forced out of their homes, which were then torched, by a crowd of some 300 Albanians.

In June UNMIK announced that police had arrested 270 individuals. International prosecutors were handling 52 serious cases involving 26 defendants, of whom 18 were in detention, and approximately 120 cases were being handled by local prosecutors. By October more than 100 trials had been completed. Eighty-three people had been convicted, with sentences including fines and imprisonment of up to five years, and more than 200 cases were still in process. However, UNMIK gave no details of cases involving alleged KPS complicity.

Trafficking of women and girls for forced prostitution

Trafficking of women and girls for forced prostitution remained a serious concern. Arrests and prosecutions of traffickers remained relatively low and measures to ensure witness protection had not yet been implemented. After three years' discussion, an Administrative Directive to implement provisions of the 2001 Trafficking Regulation and ensure support, protection and reparation for trafficking victims had not been agreed. Similarly, the Action Plan on Trafficking, due to be completed by the end of July, had not been finalized by the end of 2004.

AI country reports/ visits
Reports

- Serbia and Montenegro: Amnesty International's concerns and Serbia and Montenegro's commitments to the Council of Europe (AI Index: EUR 70/002/2004)
- Serbia and Montenegro (Kosovo): The legacy of past human rights abuses (AI Index: EUR 70/009/2004)

- Kosovo (Serbia and Montenegro): "So does it mean that we have the rights?"– Protecting the human rights of women and girls trafficked for forced prostitution in Kosovo (AI Index: EUR 70/010/2004)
- Serbia and Montenegro (Kosovo/Kosova): The March violence – KFOR and UNMIK's failure to protect the rights of minority communities (AI Index: EUR 70/016/2004)

Visits

AI delegates visited Kosovo in May, and Serbia in October/November.

SIERRA LEONE

REPUBLIC OF SIERRA LEONE
Head of state and government: Ahmad Tejan Kabbah
Death penalty: retentionist
International Criminal Court: ratified
UN Women's Convention: ratified
Optional Protocol to UN Women's Convention: signed

The human rights situation continued to improve with increased security and stability. Trials began before the Special Court for Sierra Leone but the government of Nigeria continued to refuse to surrender former Liberian President Charles Taylor to the court. Publication of the Truth and Reconciliation Commission's report was expected to contribute towards reconciliation and prevention of human rights violations. The trial of some 90 former combatants charged with murder and other offences in 2002 was stalled, but 18 others associated with the former armed opposition were released after prolonged detention without charge or trial. Effective administration of justice was seriously compromised by deficiencies in the national justice system.

Background information

Relative security allowed further advances of the peace process following the 10-year internal armed conflict. Disarmament, demobilization and reintegration of some 70,000 former combatants, including almost 7,000 children, were officially declared complete in February. Women associated with fighting forces, however, had not been adequately integrated into the process. The economic situation remained precarious and high unemployment hampered reintegration of former combatants, threatening renewed insecurity.

Restoration of local government following elections in May reinforced state authority. Government control

of and revenue from diamond mining increased. However, the armed forces and police still lacked capacity to assume full responsibility for security. The UN Mission in Sierra Leone (UNAMSIL), the International Military Advisory and Training Team and the Commonwealth police development team continued to provide training and support. The UN Security Council decided that a reduced UNAMSIL presence would remain in 2005 to monitor security and provide support to the army and police in border and diamond-producing areas. Illegal transfers of arms and ammunition into neighbouring Liberia were reported. UNAMSIL and UN peacekeeping operations in Liberia and Côte d'Ivoire sought to strengthen cooperation on issues such as cross-border movements of combatants, arms and ammunition, and disarmament and demobilization.

The Special Court for Sierra Leone

Trials began before the Special Court for Sierra Leone of some of those indicted for bearing the greatest responsibility for crimes against humanity, war crimes and other serious violations of international law committed after 30 November 1996. Charges included murder, mutilation, rape and other forms of sexual violence, sexual slavery, conscription of children to fight, abductions and forced labour.

In March the Appeals Chamber ruled that the general amnesty provided by the 1999 Lomé peace agreement and subsequently enacted in Sierra Leonean law did not apply to the Special Court, other international or foreign courts, and therefore did not prevent prosecution by such courts of crimes under international law. The general amnesty, however, continued to prevent prosecutions for such crimes in Sierra Leone's courts.

Nine of the 11 people indicted in 2003 remained in the Special Court's custody. The joint trial of three members of the pro-government Civil Defence Forces began in June, and that of three members of the former armed opposition Revolutionary United Front (RUF) in July. The trial of three members of the Armed Forces Revolutionary Council (AFRC), which seized power in a 1997 coup and subsequently allied itself to the RUF, had yet to start. Reports of the death of former AFRC leader Johnny Paul Koroma, also indicted in 2003 but still at large, were not confirmed. The appointment of judges to a second trial chamber was expected to accelerate the pace of trials.

Charles Taylor

In May the Appeals Chamber ruled that Charles Taylor, indicted for having actively supported the RUF and AFRC, had no immunity from prosecution for crimes against humanity and war crimes by virtue of his status as a head of state. He had relinquished power and left Liberia for Nigeria in August 2003, shortly before a peace agreement was signed. Nigerian President Olusegun Obasanjo argued that he was acting in the interests of peace in Liberia.

In September, AI applied to the Nigerian Federal High Court for leave to submit an *amicus curiae* brief demonstrating that Nigeria's granting of refugee status to Charles Taylor violated its obligations under international law, including the UN and Africa Union conventions on refugees. Proceedings were continuing at the end of 2004 (see Nigeria entry).

Truth and Reconciliation Commission

The Truth and Reconciliation Commission published its long-awaited report in October. It had been established in 2000 to create an impartial historical record of human rights abuses committed during the conflict, provide a forum for victims and perpetrators to recount their experiences, and facilitate reconciliation. Among issues covered in the report were the brutal nature of the conflict, the role of external actors, and factors such as mineral resources which had fuelled the conflict. Prominent among its recommendations were: defending the right to life, including through abolition of the death penalty; protecting human rights, including those of women and children; strengthening democracy, the rule of law and good governance; and providing reparations, including to people who had suffered sexual violence or amputation of limbs.

Strengthening institutions to protect human rights

Despite some progress, including appointment of additional High Court judges, effective administration of justice remained severely compromised by understaffed and poorly equipped courts, and a huge backlog of cases. Lack of access to justice was aggravated by poverty and illiteracy.

Responding to the acute shortage of judicial officials, the UN Development Programme and the Chief Justice's office elaborated plans to recruit additional magistrates. In December the UK committed £25 million (about US$50 million) to support judicial and legal reform.

Reactivated in 2003, the Law Reform Commission reviewed existing laws, including those relating to violence against women, to enhance conformity with international standards such as the UN Women's Convention. Despite an improved rate of prosecutions and convictions for sexual and gender-based violence and related offences against women and children, many cases were not reported to the police or were withdrawn before the start of criminal proceedings.

Female genital mutilation remained widespread and community-based initiatives to combat the practice were hampered by lack of resources.

Legislation to establish the Human Rights Commission of Sierra Leone, anticipated in the Lomé peace agreement, was passed by Parliament in July, after considerable delay.

Death sentences for treason

In late December, the High Court in the capital, Freetown, passed death sentences on nine former members of the RUF and AFRC and one civilian after convicting them of treason. Another defendant was sentenced to 10 years' imprisonment and four were acquitted. The charges related to an armed attack in January 2003 on the armoury at Wellington barracks, on the outskirts of Freetown, in an apparent attempt to overthrow the government. Johnny Paul Koroma was said to be implicated but had evaded arrest.

These death sentences came shortly after the Truth and Reconciliation Commission had recommended the repeal without delay of legislation authorizing the death penalty, a moratorium on executions pending abolition, and commutation by President Ahmad Tejan Kabbah of pending death sentences. None of these recommendations had yet been implemented. Fifteen other prisoners were reported to be under sentence of death.

Detention and trial of former combatants

The High Court trial of some 90 former RUF members and renegade soldiers known as the "West Side Boys" was repeatedly adjourned. In July they rioted in protest at the Maximum Security Prison, Pademba Road, in Freetown. Arrested in 2000 but not charged with murder and other offences until 2002, they remained without legal representation.

Of a group of 21 military personnel detained without charge or trial in Pademba Road prison since 2000, 18 were released without charge: two in May and another 16 in August. Three had died in 2003, one in March and two in December, apparently as a result of medical neglect.

Deaths in custody

At least two other prisoners died in Pademba Road prison in 2004, highlighting the life-threatening conditions which continued in prisons and police cells despite regular monitoring and some improvements.

Ibrahim Bah, aged 16, died in February after being severely beaten by staff at the Kingtom Remand Home for juvenile offenders in Freetown following an escape attempt. Two other boys required hospital treatment. Despite prompt investigation by the police, assisted by UNAMSIL, the suspected perpetrators remained at large.

Immediate measures were taken to protect children at the home and the incident prompted a review of the juvenile justice system by UNAMSIL and the UN Children's Fund (UNICEF), in cooperation with government authorities, aimed at reforms to include revised legislation, training and directives for the police and judiciary.

Freedom of expression

Paul Kamara, editor of the newspaper For di People, was convicted of seditious libel and sentenced to two concurrent two-year prison terms in October. In October 2003 the paper had claimed that a commission of inquiry in 1967 had "convicted" President Kabbah, then a ministerial official, of fraud. AI's protests against Paul Kamara's imprisonment highlighted the disproportionate sentence and undermining of the right to freedom of expression.

Refugees and internally displaced people

Repatriation of Sierra Leonean refugees from Guinea and Liberia had been completed by July and internally displaced people had returned to their areas of origin.

With improved security in Liberia, from October the UN High Commissioner for Refugees began a programme of voluntary repatriation for some 66,000 Liberian refugees in Sierra Leone.

Some 340 former Liberian combatants were interned at Mape, Port Loko District. Despite intervention by national agencies and the International Committee of the Red Cross, conditions remained poor and at least two internees were reported to have died as a result. Plans were made for their repatriation and inclusion in Liberia's disarmament, demobilization and reintegration programme.

UN Mission in Sierra Leone

The UNAMSIL human rights section continued to monitor police stations, prisons, the judicial system and national institutions, and to promote women's human rights through training and awareness-raising programmes. It also trained peacekeeping troops, judicial and law enforcement officials, human rights and other civil society groups in international human rights and humanitarian law.

In September the UN High Commissioner for Human Rights reported that allegations of sexual abuse and sexual exploitation by UNAMSIL peacekeeping forces persisted. The outcome of investigations by UNAMSIL into the alleged assault and killing of a 19-year-old woman by peacekeeping forces in April had not been made public by the end of 2004.

AI country reports/ visits
Reports
- The Special Court for Sierra Leone: An open letter from Amnesty International to President Olusegun Obasanjo (AI Index: AFR 44/002/2004)
- Sierra Leone: Statement at the official opening of the courthouse of the Special Court for Sierra Leone (AI Index: AFR 51/004/2004)
- Special Court for Sierra Leone: A historic decision to reject amnesty for crimes under international law (AI Index: AFR 51/006/2004)
- Nigeria/Sierra Leone: Special Court ruling – no immunity for former Liberian President Charles Taylor (AI Index: AFR 44/018/2004)
- Open letter to Permanent Representatives at the African Union regarding the case of Charles Taylor, former President of Liberia, indicted for crimes against humanity and war crimes (AI Index: IOR 63/007/2004)
- Nigeria: Amicus Curiae brief submitted to the Federal High Court reviewing refugee status granted to Charles Taylor (AI Index: AFR 44/030/2004)
- Sierra Leone: Amnesty International expresses dismay at 10 death sentences for treason (AI Index: AFR 51/009/2004)

Visits
AI delegates visited Sierra Leone in March and July, met officials of the government and the Special Court for Sierra Leone and non-governmental organizations, and observed trials before the Special Court.

SINGAPORE

REPUBLIC OF SINGAPORE
Head of state: S.R. Nathan
Head of government: Lee Hsien Loong (replaced Goh Chok Tong in August)
Death penalty: retentionist
International Criminal Court: not signed
UN Women's Convention: ratified with reservations
Optional Protocol to UN Women's Convention: not signed

Six people were executed between January and September, according to government figures. Freedom of expression continued to be curbed by restrictive legislation and the threat of civil defamation suits against political opponents. Seventeen men held without charge or trial under the Internal Security Act since 2002 had their detention extended for a further two years. Jehovah's Witnesses continued to be imprisoned for their conscientious objection to military service.

Background
In August there were indications of a possible relaxation of tight political and social controls as new Prime Minister Lee Hsien Loong called for an "open" and "inclusive" society. However, a broad array of restrictive laws remained in place, curtailing the rights to freedom of expression, association and assembly.

Death penalty
In October, the government reported that six people had been executed since January and that 19 people had been executed in 2003. Despite an apparent decrease in the number of executions, Singapore continued to have the highest rate of execution per capita in the world. The death penalty remained mandatory for drug trafficking, murder, treason and certain firearms offences.

Curbs on freedom of expression and assembly
Although some restrictions on indoor political meetings were lifted, strict government controls on civil society organizations and the press continued to curb freedom of expression and were an obstacle to the independent monitoring of human rights.

The threat of potentially ruinous civil defamation suits against opponents of the ruling People's Action Party (PAP) continued to inhibit political life and engendered a climate of self-censorship.

In September, a court awarded damages of 500,000 Singapore dollars (about US$305,000) against Chee Soon Juan, leader of the opposition Singapore Democratic Party, in a defamation suit originally lodged in 2001 by two leaders of the PAP. If Chee Soon Juan were unable to pay the sum he would be declared bankrupt, thus depriving him of his right to stand for election.

In April, the former leader of the opposition Workers' Party, J.B. Jeyaretnam, who was declared bankrupt and expelled from parliament in 2001 following a series of defamation suits, applied unsuccessfully for discharge from bankruptcy. In November the Court of Appeal dismissed his appeal.

Detention without trial

In September, the government released two detainees held without trial under the Internal Security Act (ISA) and placed them under orders restricting freedom of movement. It also extended for a further two years the detention orders of 17 other men. In total, 36 men accused of plotting to carry out bomb attacks continued to be held without charge or trial under the ISA. The authorities said that many of the men, who were arrested in 2001, 2002 and 2004, were members or supporters of an Islamist group, Jemaah Islamiyah. The ISA violates the right to a fair and public trial and the right to be presumed innocent until proven guilty according to law.

Conscientious objectors

At least four conscientious objectors to military service were imprisoned in 2004, and 20 others continued to serve prison sentences. All were members of the banned Jehovah's Witnesses religious group. There is no alternative civilian service in practice for conscientious objectors to military service in Singapore.

AI country reports/visits
Report
- Singapore: The death penalty – a hidden toll of executions (AI Index: ASA 36/001/2004)

SLOVAKIA

SLOVAK REPUBLIC
Head of state: Ivan Gasparovič (replaced Rudolf Schuster in April)
Head of government: Mikuláš Dzurinda
Death penalty: abolitionist for all crimes
International Criminal Court: ratified
UN Women's Convention and its Optional Protocol: ratified

There were reports that police ill-treated Roma and inadequately protected them from racist violence. One man died in suspicious circumstances. People with mental disabilities in psychiatric hospitals continued to be placed in cage beds, an inhuman and degrading method of restraint.

Roma

In February protests by members of the Roma minority in Eastern Slovakia, which were reportedly sparked off by changes in the social welfare policy, escalated in some instances into rioting and looting. In some cases police officers resorted to excessive use of force, verbal racist abuse and other deliberate acts of ill-treatment. Many of those arrested were not allowed to contact their family, a lawyer or anyone else, and were denied access to a doctor of their choice. Three women held in pre-trial detention reportedly had their hair cut off against their wishes.

On 24 February police reportedly intimidated and harassed members of the Romani community in Trebišov. According to the European Roma Rights Center (ERRC) and the Center for Roma Rights in Slovakia (CRRS), around 250 police officers went to the town in the early hours purportedly to arrest people suspected of theft, destruction of property and assaulting police in disturbances that had taken place in Trebišov the previous evening. In the next few hours, according to reports, police officers indiscriminately entered Romani homes without presenting search warrants and beat men, women and children with truncheons, prodded them with electric batons, and kicked and otherwise physically assaulted them irrespective of their age or health. Some of the officers reportedly addressed racist insults to the victims. At least 26 people were taken into custody, where they were said to have been beaten and subjected to degrading treatment.

The body of Radoslav Puky was found on 7 March in the Ondava river close to the Romani settlement. He had last been seen fleeing police officers on the day of the police action in Trebišov. An autopsy report reportedly established that he had died as a result of violence, not drowning. The results of an investigation had not been made public by the end of the year.

There were reports that Roma were not effectively protected from racist violence. Some incidents were said to have been organized by local authorities who engaged private security guards to beat and intimidate Romani families in order to force them to move to another community.

In July, Štefan and Olga Šarkozi, whose house in Záhorská Ves village had been burned down by a racist mob in December 2003, were reportedly ordered to leave their land and the village immediately by the local mayor, according to the League of Human Rights Advocates, a local human rights organization. The mayor later returned with four security guards who had baseball bats and assaulted Štefan Šarkozi, members of his family and Marián Rehák. In the evening, the Šarkozis took refuge under a bridge. The mayor reportedly arrived in the night with security guards and again assaulted the family. Štefan Šarkozi sustained a broken arm, his daughter Oľga suffered injuries to her legs, his son Jozef injuries to his face and chest, and his youngest daughter Adriana was thrown into the river. The incidents were reported to the Malacky District Police Department and the Ministry of the Interior in Bratislava, which reportedly initiated an investigation. In September, following the Šarkozis' refusal to sell their land, the police and private security guards demolished a shack built by the family and damaged or destroyed their belongings.

Reports on racism

A report published in January by the European Commission against Racism and Intolerance (ECRI) expressed concern about racially motivated violence, including police ill-treatment, and said that the Roma minority "remains severely disadvantaged in most areas of life, particularly in the fields of housing, employment and education."

A report published in August by the UN Committee on the Elimination of Racial Discrimination expressed concern about racially motivated crimes and incidents, and about police ill-treatment of Roma and other minority groups.

Use of cage beds in psychiatric hospitals

In January the National Council (parliament) amended the Social Aid Act in order to prohibit the use of physical and non-physical means of restraint in social services facilities for people with mental disabilities. The prohibition did not apply to hospitals and other establishments under the control of the Ministry of Health. A Ministry of Health official reportedly stated that the Ministry had no plans to deal with cage beds. A television programme filmed in September by the British Broadcasting Corporation (BBC) in a psychiatric hospital in Sokolovce showed eight patients held in cage beds. One of them had been restrained in this manner for about five weeks and the staff were unable to explain why the patient had sores and bruises.

The authorities failed to introduce the much-needed comprehensive reform of the mental health care system, which would include the setting up of community-based alternatives to residential care in psychiatric and social care institutions.

AI country reports/ visits
Report
· Europe and Central Asia: Summary of Amnesty International's concerns in the region, January-June 2004: Slovakia (AI Index: EUR 01/005/2004)

SLOVENIA

REPUBLIC OF SLOVENIA
Head of state: Janez Drnovšek
Head of government: Janez Janša (replaced Anton Rop in November)
Death penalty: abolitionist for all crimes
International Criminal Court: ratified
UN Women's Convention and its Optional Protocol: ratified

The status of thousands of former Yugoslav citizens (known as the "erased") who were removed from the Slovenian population registry in 1992 remained unresolved.

Denial of residency and citizenship

Approximately 18,300 people were removed from the Slovenian population registry in 1992, of whom most were citizens of other former Yugoslav republics who had been living in Slovenia and had not filed an application for citizenship after Slovenia became independent. Many became stateless as a result, and a few were reportedly expelled from Slovenia.

The Slovenian Constitutional Court had ruled that the removals from the population registry were unlawful. The Court stated that the removals violated the principle of equality and, in cases of expulsion, violated rights to a family life and to freedom of movement. AI was concerned that the removals also gave rise to violations of social and economic rights: some individuals lost their employment and pension rights. The Slovenian Constitutional Court also decided in April 2003 that previous provisions to resolve this issue were inadequate and ordered the Slovenian authorities to restore the permanent resident status of former Yugoslav citizens who were unlawfully removed from Slovenian registers.

In a referendum in April 2004, approximately 95 per cent of voters rejected the bill to implement the Constitutional Court's decision, which would have restored residency status to approximately 4,000 people. Several political leaders and Slovenian non-governmental organizations had called for a boycott of the referendum, which saw a turnout of around 31 per cent. The issue of the "erased" continued to be heavily politicized, and initiatives to hold a second referendum on the so-called "systemic bill", a second act aimed at addressing the issue of those removed from the population registry in 1992, were blocked by the Constitutional Court.

In the absence of a clear legal framework regulating the implementation of the Slovenian Constitutional Court's decision, the Slovenian Ministry of the Interior began issuing permanent residence decrees. By November, approximately 4,300 such decrees had been issued. AI was concerned at the slow pace of implementation of the Constitutional Court's decision, as well as the fact that individuals concerned might not be granted access to reparation, including compensation.

AI country reports/ visits
Reports
- Europe and Central Asia: Summary of Amnesty International's concerns in the region, January-June 2004: Slovenia (AI Index: EUR 01/005/2004)

SOLOMON ISLANDS

SOLOMON ISLANDS
Head of state: Queen Elizabeth II, represented by John Ini Lapli
Head of government: Allan Kemakeza
Death penalty: abolitionist for all crimes
International Criminal Court: signed
UN Women's Convention and its Optional Protocol: ratified

International efforts began to rebuild the country following five years of armed conflict that ended in 2003. Australia-led intervention troops escorted 1,600 indigenous Guadalcanalese villagers who had fled to the north coast during the conflict and who returned to rebuild their homes on Guadalcanal. The government discouraged Malaitan settlers from returning to rural Guadalcanal. Post-conflict arrests exceeded 4,000. Some former police, militants and a cabinet minister were jailed as the justice system struggled to keep up with its workload.

Post-conflict developments
The Regional Assistance Mission to Solomon Islands (RAMSI) reduced its military component after security improved. However, in December, 100 RAMSI troops returned after a suspected Malaitan militant shot dead an Australian RAMSI police officer.

By February, nearly 2,000 displaced Guadalcanal villagers had returned to the island's Weathercoast, the majority escorted by Australia-led intervention troops, but many were still sheltering in makeshift huts without access to safe water when visited by AI in April.

The human rights concerns of women and villagers in areas worst affected by the conflict were often sidelined as government and aid donors focused on rebuilding the economy and essential services.

By keeping parliamentary sessions to a minimum, the government evaded public scrutiny of its role during the conflict. It warned former Malaitan settlers displaced from their homes on Guadalcanal in 1999 not to reclaim their properties on Guadalcanal, but did not establish a promised commission of inquiry to resolve land disputes underlying the conflict.

Justice system
By December most militant leaders were awaiting trial either in custody or on strict bail conditions, including a former Foreign Minister.

By July more than a quarter of the police force, some 400 officers, had been removed from the service. Of those RAMSI said that 70 former police officers, including former deputy commissioners, had been arrested. A further 71 former officers were charged with human rights violations, including rape and other torture. The UN Development Programme helped to demobilize an additional 230 police special constables, most of them recruited from former militant groups.

Despite the opening of a new courtroom at the High Court, the judiciary remained overwhelmed by the post-conflict caseload. As a result, suspects spent up to 16 months in pre-trial detention, fuelling a prison riot in Honiara in August.

In February, Daniel Fa'afunua, a former militant and cabinet minister, was imprisoned for attacking a RAMSI policewoman during his arrest, but not for attacking his former wife, the action which had prompted his arrest. She had withdrawn her complaint despite being treated in hospital for her injuries. He was also jailed for ordering gunmen to force the publisher of the *Solomon Star* newspaper to pay US$800 after the newspaper published an article about an unnamed government minister publicly assaulting a taxi driver.

Violence against women
Women's groups raised concerns about violence in the family. A UN-funded workshop trained 20 women in data-collection on the impact of conflict on women. Police reported an increase in the number of women reporting rape, including cases from the conflict period. Of 55 women interviewed by AI in Weathercoast villages about the conflict, 19 reported that they had been raped by police or militant forces. The government failed to create a planned National Policy on Violence against Women and left the police service dependent on RAMSI for essential services. No funds were made available for a police unit to address abuses of women and children.

AI country reports/visits

Report
- Solomon Islands: Women confronting violence (AI Index: ASA 43/001/2004)

Visit

AI visited conflict-torn areas of Guadalcanal and Malaita islands in April/May.

SOMALIA

SOMALIA
Head of Transitional National Government (until October): Abdiqasim Salad Hassan
Head of state of Transitional Federal Government (from October): Abdullahi Yusuf Ahmed
Head of government of Transitional Federal Government (from December): Ali Mohamed Gedi
Head of Somaliland Republic: Dahir Riyaale Kahin
Head of Puntland Regional State: Mohamed Abdi Hashi (replaced Abdullahi Yusuf Ahmed in October)
Death penalty: retentionist
International Criminal Court: not signed
UN Women's Convention and its Optional Protocol: not signed

The first step towards establishing a new Transitional Federal Government was the swearing-in of a President in October, after 14 years of state collapse and political violence, and two years of peace talks in Kenya. A Charter for the five-year transition period included human rights guarantees. However, prominent "warlords" responsible for faction fighting, which continued in central and southern regions, became members of the new government, with impunity for human rights abuses. Thousands of civilians fled the country or were displaced. Journalists were arrested and human rights defenders threatened in several areas. Violence against women was widespread. There was no rule of law in the south. In Somaliland, there were unfair political trials, including the imprisonment of a 16-year-old girl for espionage, and reports of torture.

Background

Throughout Somalia's central and southern regions and the capital, Mogadishu, there was constant insecurity and frequent faction fighting. There had been no national government or administration, army, police or justice system since 1991. The Transitional National Government (TNG), set up in 2000, controlled only a small part of Mogadishu. Other areas were held by various armed clan-based faction leaders, some belonging to the Somalia Reconciliation and Restoration Council (SRRC), a coalition backed by Ethiopia.

Drought continued to create a humanitarian emergency in the north-west. Aid workers were often at risk. A UN staff member was kidnapped in January in Kismayu and held for several days, and a Kenyan and a Somali aid worker were killed in Somaliland in March. Following a visit by the UN Independent Expert for Somalia, the UN Commission on Human Rights passed a resolution in April calling on all parties to stop acts of violence and to respect human rights and international humanitarian standards. It extended the mandate of the Independent Expert for Somalia for one year: AI urged the Office of the UN High Commissioner for Human Rights to appoint a human rights adviser for Somalia.

In August a UN panel of experts monitoring the 1992 international arms embargo on Somalia issued its third report on illegal weapons transfers from governments in the region and private arms dealers.

The self-declared regional state of Puntland, formed in the north-east in 1998, supported the new federal Charter and Puntland's President became President of Somalia. Elections in Puntland were due in early 2005 but political parties had not been formed by the end of 2004.

The Indian Ocean earthquake and tsunami disaster in December caused more than 150 deaths and displaced thousands of people on the Puntland coast.

Somaliland

The Somaliland Republic, established in the north-west in 1991, was the only part of the former Somali Republic to have a government, a civil service, a multi-party system and a justice system. A National Human Rights Commission was in preparation, with the support of local non-governmental organizations (NGOs). Somaliland pursued its demand for international recognition and refused to participate in the peace talks in Kenya or to join a new federal Somalia. There was brief fighting between Somaliland forces and neighbouring Puntland in January and October over rival claims to eastern border regions.

Transitional Federal Government

In October the TNG ended with the swearing-in of a President for the incoming Transitional Federal Government (TFG), after two years of peace talks in neighbouring Kenya. Under a transitional Charter (interim constitution), a 275-member parliament was formed, with seats allocated to the four main clans and to minority communities. The parliament elected a national President, who appointed a Prime Minister to form a government to take office in early 2005 for the five-year transition period. The Charter requires the disbanding of the militias of the "warlords". A planned attack on the port of Kismayu by a warlord, General Mohamed Said Hersi "Morgan", was narrowly averted in September. The TFG was expected to relocate from Kenya to Somalia in early 2005 when security permitted.

The international community promised future assistance for reconstructing the collapsed state as part of an arrangement for international recognition and support for the TFG. Agreements designed to guarantee peace, good governance and protection of human rights were under discussion. An African Union peace-support force was being prepared to assist with security and demobilization of faction militias.

Rule of law

There was no effective or competent system of administration of justice to uphold the rule of law and provide impartial protection of human rights. The TNG and faction leaders failed to protect citizens. Abuses by faction militias, including child soldiers, were committed with impunity. Some *Shari'a* (Islamic law) courts functioned on a local basis, but did not meet international standards of fair trial.

Clan-based faction militias protected their own clan members, leaving unarmed minorities vulnerable to abuses.

Conditions in the TNG's central prison in Mogadishu were harsh.

In Somaliland there were arbitrary arrests, allegations of torture, and unfair political trials.

In January, Osman Mohamoud (known as "Bur-Madow"), a clan leader, was arrested and charged with insulting the president and demoralizing the army. He had attempted to mediate the Somaliland-Puntland conflict in Sool region. He was convicted on the first charge and sentenced to six months' imprisonment.

In June, 30 Ethiopian Somalis arrested in December 2003 and accused of being fighters of the Ogaden National Liberation Front (an Ethiopian opposition force) were sentenced to three and five-year prison terms. Their appeal had not been heard by the end of 2004.

In December, Zamzam Ahmed Dualeh, aged 16, was convicted of espionage and imprisoned for five years after a grossly unfair trial where her rights as a child were given no recognition. The judge summarily dismissed her allegations of rape and torture by police officers. He sentenced her four defence lawyers to three years' imprisonment for contempt of court, but they were released on appeal after payment of a fine.

Journalists

At least 17 journalists were arrested during 2004, mostly for short periods, and some of them were beaten, because they had reported human rights abuses or criticized "warlords" or political authorities.

In Puntland, Abdishakur Yusuf Ali, editor of *War Ogaal* newspaper, was arrested for the seventh time in April and sentenced to six months' imprisonment but released on appeal and payment of a fine in June.

In Somaliland, Hassan Said Yusuf, editor of *Jamhuuriya* (*The Republican*) newspaper, was arrested in August on account of an article about the peace talks. He alleged that police officers threatened to kill him. In October he was acquitted of

publishing a false report. This was said to be his 15th arrest on such charges.

Human rights defenders

Despite the risks, human rights defenders in Somalia and Somaliland campaigned for respect for human rights and reported on violence against women and minorities, faction killings, arbitrary arrests, kidnappings and political trials.

In the trial of Zamzam Ahmed Dualeh in Somaliland, human rights activists publicly criticized the trial and imprisonment of defence lawyers. Some were arrested outside the court but released uncharged after some hours.

Women's rights

The allocation of seats in the transitional parliament failed to meet the Charter's quota of 12 per cent women. Women had little access to public decision-making and justice in Somaliland and Puntland.

Women's organizations in all areas campaigned against violence against women, including female genital mutilation, which continued to be widespread. Women human rights defenders also campaigned against domestic violence and rape of internally displaced women.

Minority rights

Some progress towards recognition of minority rights was reflected in the allocation of 31 seats in the transitional parliament to minority communities. However, social discrimination and abuses by clan members persisted, particularly against the under-privileged Bantu group (also known as *Jarir*) and occupational groups such as the Midgan.

Refugees and internally displaced people

Refugees continued to flee from faction fighting, kidnappings, threats to human rights defenders and other abuses.

Over a third of a million internally displaced people survived in extremely poor conditions in camps, where food supplies were often diverted by clan militias, and rape of minority women was common. In Kismayu, minority families were forced to hand over a substantial proportion of relief supplies to clan members and many had to pay clan members to protect them from local factions.

Death penalty

Official courts, including Islamic courts and informal clan "courts", continued to impose the death penalty and executions were carried out in several areas. Compensation (*diya*) was paid in some murder cases as an alternative to execution.

In Somaliland in July, two men were sentenced to death (one in absentia) for involvement in an armed attack on Hargeisa airport in March 2003 in support of Jama Mohamed Ghalib, a government opponent who was briefly detained and then deported. The appeal against the death sentence and prison sentences imposed on 11 others had not been heard by the end of 2004.

Reports
- Somalia: Urgent human rights message to the peace talks in Kenya (AI Index: AFR 52/002/2004)
- Somaliland: 16-year-old girl jailed for five years in grossly unfair espionage trial should be released or retried (AI Index: AFR 52/005/2004)

SOUTH AFRICA

REPUBLIC OF SOUTH AFRICA
Head of state and government: Thabo Mbeki
Death penalty: abolitionist for all crimes
International Criminal Court: ratified
UN Women's Convention: ratified
Optional Protocol to UN Women's Convention: not signed

The government began its "rollout" treatment programme for people with HIV and AIDS, but thousands still remained without access to anti-retroviral (ARV) drugs. Despite reforms to improve access to justice and health care for rape survivors, complainants still faced obstacles. The number of reported deaths in police custody and arising from police action increased. Credible allegations of torture or ill-treatment were made by criminal suspects, refugees and political activists. Corrupt and discriminatory practices by officials obstructed access by asylum-seekers to determination procedures. Individuals suspected of "terrorist" offences were detained incommunicado, ill-treated or forcibly repatriated.

Political developments
In April the ruling African National Congress party won nearly 70 per cent of the seats in national parliamentary elections, as well as majorities in all nine provinces.

The trial of Deputy President Jacob Zuma's financial adviser, Schabir Shaik, began in October. He faced charges of corruption and fraud committed on behalf of Jacob Zuma and relating to an alleged bribe solicited from a French arms company. In May the Public Protector (ombudsman) concluded that the Deputy President's constitutional rights had been violated by the head of the National Prosecuting Authority (NPA) and the then Minister of Justice. They had announced in 2003 that, although there was a prima-facie case against the Deputy President, he would not face charges. The NPA head, who resigned in July, accused the Public Protector of joining an "orchestrated campaign" to discredit the NPA and jeopardize the trial.

A report by the UN Development Programme (UNDP) in May noted the persistence of massive unemployment;

a slight decline in the percentage of the population living in poverty but an increase to over 10 per cent of the population living in extreme poverty (on less than one US dollar per day); and a worsening rate of income inequality. An increasing number of black South Africans had no access to one or more basic services. The report suggested these trends resulted in part from government policies. Church-based, trade union and other civil society organizations made similar criticisms.

Limited access to health care
The government's "rollout" programme to provide care and treatment to people living with HIV and AIDS led to 28,743 people gaining access to anti-retroviral (ARV) drug treatment through 108 state-accredited facilities by December. This official total was just over a half of the government's revised target of 53,000 by March 2005. About 500,000 of the estimated 5.3 million people with the virus require ARV treatment. Women and girls under 30 years of age had the highest infection rates, according to the UNDP report and UNAIDS.

In several hospitals visited by AI in August, only a small proportion of patients needing ARV treatment were receiving it because of a severe shortage of medical staff and delays in the supplies of the drugs and equipment. The stigma associated with HIV and AIDS, widespread poverty, poor education, and limited, unreliable public transport were additional socio-economic factors hampering access to treatment. The Treatment Action Campaign (TAC), in its July report on implementation of the rollout, noted similar problems in most provinces.

In December the Pretoria High Court awarded costs against the Minister of Health in a case brought by the TAC in June to compel the Minister to make public the implementation timetable for the rollout. The Court found that the Minister had acted unconstitutionally in failing to respond properly to the application.

There was improvement in the access to HIV-prevention treatment for rape survivors who tested negative shortly after the rape. However, the availability of ARV drugs for women and girls who became HIV positive as a result of rape was severely limited.

Violence against women
Police statistics for the year 2003/2004 recorded 52,759 reported rapes, with the highest provincial ratio being recorded in the Northern Cape at nearly 190 incidents per 100,000 people. President Mbeki publicly minimized the concerns of service-providing and advocacy organizations about the high levels of rape and the link with the epidemic of HIV infection among younger women. In October the President's response was criticized in a parliamentary motion.

Child and adult rape survivors interviewed by AI in August, all of whom were HIV positive, had access to emergency medical care. However, they had considerable difficulties in obtaining further medical treatment or psychological care because of the social stigma, unemployment, and their lack of secure housing and access to affordable transport. In one case the survivor and her mother were threatened with violence by the perpetrators, who had been released on bail.

Reforms to improve access to justice for survivors continued during the year. The police Family Violence, Child Protection and Sexual Offences Unit, responsible for investigating these cases, was enlarged. Additional "victim-friendly facilities" were established at hospitals and at police stations, with the support of NGOs and business organizations. By December, 52 specialized sexual offences courts had been established. The conviction rate in rape cases in these courts was 20 per cent higher than cases brought to trial in ordinary courts. Complainants' access to justice was still limited by staff shortages, distances from the courts, poor police work and lack of social welfare support. Only about seven per cent of all the rape cases reported to the police resulted in convictions. The NPA launched a comprehensive training programme for police and criminal justice officials to improve their implementation of the 1998 Domestic Violence Act.

In December, South Africa ratified the Protocol to the African Charter on Human and Peoples' Rights on the Rights of Women in Africa.

Police violations

The police oversight body, the Independent Complaints Directorate (ICD), reported for the year ending March 2004 that it had received 47 per cent more complaints of "serious criminal offences" by the police. In the same period it received 714 reports of deaths in police custody or arising from police action, an increase of over 35 per cent on the previous year.

Suspects in criminal investigations, refugees, and members of organizations protesting against poor social and economic conditions were among the victims of alleged torture, ill-treatment or the unjustified use of lethal force.

◻ Charles Mabiya died on 25 September at Zonkizizwe police station near Johannesburg, one day after his arrest with two others, Sibusiso Lukhele and Bheki Khoza, on suspicion of armed robbery. The three men were beaten at the time of their arrest, and Charles Mabiya was allegedly denied medical care. Postmortem evidence indicated he had multiple injuries, including head injuries. In October one detective was arrested by the ICD and charged with murder and assault with intent to cause grievous bodily harm.

◻ In December three Serious and Violent Crime Unit members were charged in the Johannesburg Regional Court with theft, defeating the ends of justice and assault with intent to cause grievous bodily harm. The three, who were released on bail, were alleged to have tortured crime suspects and others to obtain information on stolen property which they then seized unlawfully. The police officer leading the investigation received threats.

◻ On 22 August, Joseph Kongolo, granted refugee status after fleeing the Democratic Republic of the Congo, was unlawfully detained and assaulted by

police in Johannesburg. He was head-butted, slapped in the face and had his genitals grabbed by two police officers who were searching the building where he lived for suspected illegal immigrants. He was released from Jeppe police station the following day after the senior public prosecutor declined to press charges.

◻ On 16 February two high school students, Dennis Mathibithi and Nhlanhla Masuku, were shot dead by a member of the Ekurhuleni Metro Police in Katlehong near Johannesburg. The police said they were responding to violent protests over court-ordered evictions. The students were unarmed and postmortem examinations confirmed that they had been shot in the back. Ballistics tests showed a link with one officer's weapon. He was arrested on 18 February and charged with murder, attempted murder and attempting to defeat the ends of justice. An internal inquiry by the Ekurhuleni Metro Police apparently cleared him of any unlawful actions.

◻ Four members of the Landless People's Movement (LPM) were tortured or ill-treated after they were arrested following a protest rally on 14 April and detained overnight at Protea South police station in Soweto. Samantha Hargreaves and Ann Eveleth were interrogated in the middle of the night about their political activities and subjected to suffocation torture by police Crime Intelligence officers. Moses Mahlangu was threatened with violence during interrogation. Maureen Mnisi, the Gauteng provincial chairperson of the LPM, was repeatedly slapped and kicked by officers during a cell search. Following their release the four LPM activists lodged complaints with the police and the ICD. No results from any internal police investigation were communicated to them. The ICD's investigation was hampered by lack of cooperation from the provincial police authorities, and no arrests were made by the end of the year.

◻ On 30 August, 17-year-old student Teboho Mkhonza died shortly after local police fired into a crowd of protesters near Harrismith, Free State province. The demonstrators, who were unarmed, were protesting at the municipal council's failure to provide basic services to the impoverished community. According to film, witness and forensic evidence, the police opened fire with birdshot, prohibited for use in controlling crowds. The police gave no warning and fired as people fled. Following investigation, in December the ICD recommended prosecution of three officers for murder and attempted murder and disciplinary action against the officers for a breach of standing orders on the use of force and firearms.

Violations of refugee rights

Asylum-seekers were at risk of arbitrary arrest or deportation because of officials' corrupt practices at refugee reception centres and borders, which obstructed, delayed or denied their access to determination procedures. Human rights lawyers and organizations expressed concern, particularly at the discriminatory treatment of Zimbabwean asylum-seekers. The South African Human Rights Commission and the Parliamentary Portfolio Committee on Foreign

Affairs held public hearings in November on xenophobia and allegations of human rights abuses against migrants and asylum-seekers. In September the Pretoria High Court ruled that the detention of unaccompanied foreign children was unlawful.

Joint operations by Home Affairs officials and members of intelligence and police services against individuals suspected of links with international "terrorist" organizations resulted in the incommunicado detention, ill-treatment or forcible repatriation of immigrants or asylum-seekers.

⌷ Mohammed Hendi, a Jordanian national who had applied for permanent residence, was detained by police and intelligence officers when they raided his home on 2 April. He was held for 22 days at police stations in the Pretoria area, shackled, denied access to a lawyer, and subjected to racial abuse during interrogation. On 14 April the police and immigration authorities attempted to deport him and arbitrarily deny his residence application. Lawyers secured his release on 23 April through a habeas corpus action in the High Court. Jamil Odys, detained at the same time, was deported to Jordan on 14 April despite having lodged an asylum application. In May the national Commissioner of Police told Parliament that the security services had in April arrested and deported a number of "terrorism" suspects, but he refused to give more details.

AI country reports/ visits
Visit
AI delegates visited South Africa in August for research and meetings with provincial authorities on concerns relating to access to justice and health care for survivors of sexual violence. AI raised with the national and provincial authorities its concerns about human rights violations by members of the security forces.

SPAIN

KINGDOM OF SPAIN
Head of state: King Juan Carlos I de Borbón
Head of government: José Luis Rodríguez Zapatero (replaced José María Aznar López in March)
Death penalty: abolitionist for all crimes
International Criminal Court: ratified
UN Women's Convention and its Optional Protocol: ratified

Multiple train bombings in March caused the deaths of 191 people and injured over 1,600. The massacre, attributed to a group with links to al-Qa'ida, was perpetrated during a general election campaign. The UN Special Rapporteur on torture found that torture and ill-treatment were "more than sporadic", and the European Court of Human Rights criticized Spain for lack of promptness or thoroughness in the investigation of complaints of torture and ill-treatment dating from 1992. There were a large number of allegations of torture and ill-treatment — many of them race related — and a reported increase in the ill-treatment of minors in detention centres. Racially motivated attacks were reported in El Ejido (Almería), Elche (Alicante) and elsewhere. An increase in official complaints of violence against women was registered in the first half of the year.

Madrid bombings
On 11 March an armed group reportedly linked to al-Qa'ida exploded 10 bombs on four commuter trains in Madrid, killing 191 people and injuring over 1,600. The bombs exploded on trains in the main station of Atocha and the suburban stations of El Pozo and Santa Eugenia. The then centre-right government immediately and persistently blamed the armed Basque group Euskadi Ta Askatasuna (ETA), which denied any involvement. By November police and judicial inquiries into the Madrid bombings had ruled out involvement by ETA (which, in August and September, had carried out a series of small blasts in Asturias, Cantabria and the Basque country and which exploded further bombs in December).

An increase in racist abuse and ill-treatment was reported in the aftermath of the Madrid massacre. In some police and prison ill-treatment cases Muslims were abused as "terrorists".

Throughout the year over 100 Muslims were arrested in connection with various judicial inquiries into the bombings and the alleged preparation of other crimes. Among those arrested was the *al-Jazeera* journalist Taysir Allouni, a Syrian-born Spanish citizen who had first been arrested in 2003. Like others arrested with him, Taysir Allouni denied any involvement in crimes linked to "terrorism". A parliamentary commission, established by the new minority government to investigate the events surrounding the bombings and the conduct of the security services and Spanish government, decided in September to prolong its investigation and took evidence from past and present prime ministers. In December the judge investigating the bombings criticized the lack of coordinated assistance to the victims.

☐ In March, Ángel Berroeta Legaz was shot dead in his bakery in Pamplona (Navarra) by an off-duty National Police officer who was also a neighbour. According to reports, the officer fired four shots at Ángel Berroeta after the latter had been engaged in a heated argument with the officer's wife. The baker had reportedly refused to display in his shop a poster denouncing ETA as the perpetrators of the bombings. The police officer and his son were arrested and police and judicial inquiries were opened into the death.

Torture and ill-treatment

There were a large number of allegations of torture or ill-treatment, many of them race related or connected with the practice of incommunicado detention. Several court sentences were passed for torture or ill-treatment.

In February the UN Special Rapporteur on torture reported on a 2003 visit to Spain to study safeguards for the protection of detainees in the context of "anti-terrorism" measures. The Rapporteur noted that: "the degree of silence that surrounds the subject and the denial by the authorities without investigating the allegations of torture have made it particularly difficult to provide the necessary monitoring of protection and guarantees". He concluded that the "internal consistency of the information received" and precise factual details provided in relation to a number of allegations suggested that they "could not be fabrications". Although not a regular practice, the occurrence of torture was "more than sporadic and incidental". The Rapporteur recommended that the government draw up a comprehensive plan to prevent and suppress torture and that the practice of holding people incommunicado be ended. The former government, which vigorously repudiated the report's conclusions, continued to refuse to introduce safeguards for incommunicado detainees and by the end of the year the new government had made no moves to implement the Rapporteur's recommendations.

☐ In November the European Court of Human Rights issued a judgment on the case of 15 Catalans who claimed they had been physically and mentally tortured while held incommunicado on the eve of the Olympic Games in Barcelona in 1992. While it did not find that Spain had violated the European Convention on Human Rights regarding the allegations themselves, the Court stated that its task had been hindered by a lack of detailed information and the "very long period" since the events. The Court found that Spain had violated Article 3 of the Convention by failing to hold a thorough and effective investigation into the allegations. The Court said the defendants had been denied a reasonable opportunity to establish the matters of which they complained. One of the problems was the lack of detail contained in medical reports.

☐ In June an officer of the Catalan autonomous police, the Mossos d'Esquadra, was placed under investigation for the torture of a minor in a judicial inquiry in Lleida (Catalonia). Jordi Vilaseca Cantacorps had been arrested in April 2003 in connection with alleged acts of street violence and held incommunicado under "anti-terrorism" legislation. He claimed he was forced to stand motionless for up to eight hours without food or water, and then to kneel without moving for several hours more. Exhausted and dehydrated, he eventually collapsed and was taken to hospital.

☐ In March the Supreme Court confirmed prison sentences of seven and a half years for two men for the abduction and physical abuse of three North African workers, including Hichan Brahini and Garmai Bou Bakelir, in El Ejido in 1997. The municipal council had requested a pardon for the men. The Andalusian Ombudsman opened an inquiry into allegations that an officer of the Local Police was continuing to harass and ill-treat North African immigrants in the town. The number of complaints reportedly increased after the 11 March bombings.

☐ In a disturbing judgment in May the Provincial Court of Girona established that the Moroccan national Driss Zraidi had "undoubtedly" been tortured and racially abused in the police station of Roses (Catalonia) in August 1998. However, the court acquitted 14 officers of the Mossos d'Esquadra because it could not identify the officers involved. It also decided that the torture inflicted was probably "light" torture, consisting of pushing about and vigorous shaking hours after Driss Zraidi had sustained broken ribs. The Catalan Interior Minister reportedly expressed surprise at the judgment and asked the Supreme Court to review it.

Minors in detention

There was an increase in complaints of ill-treatment of minors in detention centres and several judicial proceedings were opened into allegations of violence against minors by supervisors in centres throughout Spain. There were also reports of ill-treatment of minors in police custody. In November the Attorney General prohibited the systematic repatriation of foreign minors. He stated the practice was in contravention of the UN Children's Convention.

☐ In October the parents of Enrique Rincón Alguacil complained that he had been ill-treated in police custody in Madrid after attending a gathering in the Plaza de España. He was allegedly kicked, beaten with a baton, handcuffed and verbally abused. His parents were not informed of his detention, despite their son's requests. A medical report referred to "multiple haematoma" compatible with Enrique Rincón's assertion that he had been assaulted. The parents of Pablo Armando Castro complained that their son had been similarly ill-treated after arrest following the same event. Again, the parents claimed they were not informed at any time of their child's detention, despite the fact that he was held overnight.

Prisons

There were reports of violent deaths and torture and ill-treatment in various prisons, many of which were suffering intense overcrowding. They included Salto del Negro (Gran Canaria) and Tahíche (Lanzarote), where the prosecutor attached to the High Court of the Canary Islands described the problem as "urgent". Judicial investigations were carried out into complaints that prison staff had been involved in acts of brutality against prisoners.

🗀 In May a series of inquiries was held into a riot at Quatre Camins prison in Catalonia on 30 April, in which the deputy director was badly injured and over 70 prisoners were reportedly ill-treated by guards. In July the Justice Ministry of the *Generalitat*, the government of the autonomous region of Catalonia, submitted a report to the public prosecutor, recognizing that up to 26 prisoners had been ill-treated. In July the Justice Ministry dismissed the deputy medical director of Quatre Camins and in September it announced that the director and deputy director of the prison had also been dismissed.

🗀 In September the prosecutor attached to the Provincial Court in Lugo (Galicia) concluded that the chief doctor and two prison officers had assaulted a Moroccan prisoner in February 2002, in the prison of Monterroso. The attack, which was racially motivated, occurred after Magdare Rabay had threatened to injure himself if the doctor did not change his medicine. Two guards reportedly beat him until he lost consciousness, then the doctor beat him again. The prosecutor claimed that Magdare Rabay had also been urinated on, racially abused and called a "terrorist".

Violence against women

Over 60 women were reported killed in incidents of domestic violence. According to the General Council of the Judiciary, 47,000 complaints of violence against women were recorded in the first half of 2004, an increase of 24 per cent over the comparable period in 2003. The figures showed a constant increase in complaints and reflected a lack of effectiveness of public policies in combating violence. Problems associated with cases of violence against women included inadequate medical reports or legal representation. In July the UN Committee on the Elimination of Discrimination against Women examined Spain's fifth periodic report and called on Spain to intensify its efforts to address the issues of domestic violence, discrimination against migrant women and the trafficking of women.

Victims of the Civil War/Franco regime

In his annual report in June the Spanish Ombudsman criticized the authorities' lack of response to individuals and associations attempting to exhume and to identify remains from burial pits containing the bodies of some of the thousands killed during or after the 1936-39 Civil War. In June, AI's Secretary General urged the new government to "recuperate the memory, dignity and remains of the forgotten victims of the Civil War and Franco's regime". In September the Spanish Council of Ministers approved a royal decree setting up an inter-ministerial committee to investigate the "moral and legal rehabilitation" of thousands who were victims of the Civil War and Franco regime. The committee began work in November.

AI country reports/visits

Report
· Europe and Central Asia: Summary of Amnesty International's concerns in the region, January-June 2004: Spain (AI Index: EUR 01/005/2004)

Visit
In June the AI Secretary General led a delegation to Madrid, Barcelona and Vitoria.

SRI LANKA

DEMOCRATIC SOCIALIST REPUBLIC OF SRI LANKA
Head of state: Chandrika Bandaranaike Kumaratunga
Head of government: Mahinda Rajapakse (replaced Ranil Wickremasinghe in April)
Death penalty: abolitionist in practice
International Criminal Court: not signed
UN Women's Convention and its Optional Protocol: ratified

The ceasefire between the government and the Liberation Tigers of Tamil Eelam (LTTE) remained in place, despite a number of violations and a failure to resume peace talks. The human rights situation in the north-east deteriorated following a violent split within the LTTE in April and a dramatic increase in politically motivated killings. Although a large number of child soldiers were released during the internal fighting, the LTTE continued to recruit children, including through abduction. In November the government announced a "reactivation" of the death penalty. Torture in police custody was widely reported and victims seeking redress faced threats and violence. There was little progress towards holding security forces to account for past human rights violations. Religious minorities came under threat, with attacks on Christians and Muslims, as well as the tabling of a bill aimed at curbing religious conversions.

Background

Elections on 2 April brought to power a fragile coalition headed by the President's United People's Freedom Alliance. The LTTE-affiliated Tamil National Alliance (TNA) took the majority of seats in the north-east, where elections were marred by vote rigging, intimidation and violence, including the killing of United National Party and TNA candidates and an Eelam People's Democratic Party (EPDP) activist.

In March the LTTE's eastern commander, known as Colonel Karuna, split from the organization, taking with him a large number of cadres. In April thousands of LTTE troops moved into the east to engage Colonel Karuna and his supporters in battle, resulting in substantial casualties. After four days of fighting Colonel Karuna disbanded the majority of his supporters and went into hiding. However, he continued to speak out against the LTTE and formed his own political party, which in October joined with the Eelam National Democratic Liberation Front. Throughout 2004 the east remained volatile with continued skirmishes between the LTTE and remaining Karuna supporters, growing numbers of political assassinations and widespread child recruitment.

Despite efforts by Norwegian mediators, there was no return to peace talks. Amid an atmosphere of mistrust, the LTTE continued to insist that their proposals for an Interim Self-Governing Authority (ISGA) form the basis of any talks and the coalition government struggled to define its position. On 7 July an LTTE suicide bomber, allegedly sent to kill EPDP MP Douglas Devananda, blew herself up in a Colombo police station killing four policemen.

On 27 November, in his annual "Heroes' Day" speech, LTTE leader Velupillai Prabhakaran stated that the LTTE might return to the "freedom struggle" if peace talks did not resume on the basis of the LTTE's ISGA proposals. On 24 December the LTTE formally rejected the government's latest offer of talks amid growing fears of a return to war.

On 26 December a massive earthquake in the Indian Ocean caused tsunami waves to break on Sri Lanka's coastline, killing more than 30,000 people. Most deaths occurred on the southern and eastern coasts, although there was widespread devastation of infrastructure and over 400,000 people were displaced across the island. Following this disaster, local communities across the country responded quickly with support for the victims, government and LTTE forces began emergency rescue and relief operations, and a large amount of international assistance began to arrive.

Politically motivated killings

There was a dramatic escalation in political killings, especially in the east, following the split in the LTTE. From April onwards an increasing number of civilians, including members of opposition Tamil groups, were assassinated by the LTTE and Colonel Karuna's supporters. Some of these killings took place in government-controlled territory or near Sri Lankan Army (SLA) checkpoints, leading the LTTE to accuse the SLA of providing support to Colonel Karuna's faction. The continued killings and intimidation created an atmosphere of fear among the civilian population in the east as well as putting the ceasefire under strain. A number of people were also killed in Colombo.

▢ On 31 May journalist Aiyathurai Nadesan was shot and killed on his way to work in Batticaloa. It was believed that Colonel Karuna's supporters carried out the killing.

▢ On 8 July the LTTE publicly executed Balasuntaram Sritharan and Thillaiampalam Sundararajan in the eastern village of Illuppaiadaichenai. In a statement released by its Batticaloa-Amparai political wing, the LTTE claimed the two men had been sentenced to death as "traitors".

▢ On 10 August Balanadarajah Iyer, a senior EPDP spokesman, was shot and killed in Wellawatte, Colombo. It was believed that the LTTE carried out the killing.

Child soldiers

The UN Children's Fund (UNICEF) reported the recruitment of 448 children as soldiers in the first half of 2004, while acknowledging that the actual figure was probably far higher.

It was reported that a large number of child soldiers were deployed in the fighting between the LTTE and the Karuna faction in April and that there were some child casualties. Following the fighting, over 1,600 child soldiers from the east, who had fought alongside Colonel Karuna, were disbanded and spontaneously returned to their homes. In May and June it was reported that the LTTE were re-recruiting many of these demobilized children, using tactics of intimidation, abduction and violence. Parents in the east, angry that their children had been used in internecine fighting, attempted to mobilize in an effort to resist re-recruitment. There was also an increase in child recruitment in the north in mid-2004 as the LTTE tried to make up for the large number of cadres it had lost during the split.

▢ In May and June, families in Vaharai, Batticaloa district, who tried to prevent the LTTE from forcibly recruiting their children were beaten with wooden sticks. One woman was knocked unconscious and another was cut on the face.

▢ In May, four boys from Trincomalee were forcibly re-recruited from their homes in the middle of the night. The mother of one of the boys was beaten and injured during the incident.

Torture

There were numerous reports of torture by police, as well as some reports of death in police custody. Some torture victims seeking redress in the courts were reportedly put under pressure to withdraw their cases. Among them was Gerald Perera, a torture victim due to give evidence against seven police officers in the High Court, who was shot on 21 November and subsequently died.

In August the National Police Commission announced that addressing torture by police would be its top priority. It also announced that it would be responsible for the disciplinary control of all police officers, revoking the previous authority of the Inspector General of Police (IGP) in disciplinary matters relating to officers below the rank of inspector. The National Human Rights Commission (NHRC) established a Torture Prevention and Monitoring Unit to investigate allegations and carry out surprise checks on places of detention. However, in September the IGP issued a directive, based on the Attorney General's advice, stating that the NHRC must notify senior police officials before inspecting police barracks and other unauthorized places of detention.

Death penalty

On 20 November the Office of the President announced that "the death penalty will be effective from today for rape, murder and narcotics dealings". This signalled the end of a 27-year moratorium on executions. The reactivation of the death penalty was in response to the murder of a High Court judge and a policeman guarding him. Since the last execution in 1976, all death sentences had been automatically commuted by consecutive presidents.

Prevention of Terrorism Act

It was reported that around 40 prisoners remained in detention under the Prevention of Terrorism Act (PTA) at the end of the year.

In July, in response to a complaint brought under the Optional Protocol to the International Covenant on Civil and Political Rights, the UN Human Rights Committee concluded that the rights of Nallaratnam Singarasa had been violated and that he should be given an appropriate remedy such as "release or retrial and compensation". Nallaratnam Singarasa was detained under the PTA in 1993 and sentenced to 50 years' imprisonment in 1995. Nallaratnam Singarasa claimed that while in detention he was tortured and forced to put his thumbprint to a confession written in Sinhalese, a language he did not understand. This confession formed the main basis for his conviction.

Religious minorities

In July a private members' bill, the Prohibition of Forcible Conversion of Religion Act, was tabled in Parliament. The bill placed restrictions on the circumstances under which a person can be converted. Following objections that the bill was unconstitutional, in August the Supreme Court ruled that some amendments should be made to it. In November another private members' bill was tabled for a constitutional amendment to make Buddhism the national religion. By the end of the year neither of these bills had been passed.

Christian groups reported a few attacks by Buddhist villagers on pastors and churches in the south during the year. In October there was rioting between different Muslim sects in the east, resulting in the demolition of a mosque belonging to a minority Muslim sect and reports of families fleeing their homes. Around the same time tension between Muslims and Tamils led to rioting in Mannar and Akkaraipattu.

AI country reports/ visits

Reports

· Sri Lanka: Put human rights first during the elections (AI Index: ASA 37/001/2004)
· Sri Lanka: Tamil Tigers beating up families to recruit child soldiers (AI Index: ASA 37/002/2004)
· Sri Lanka: Human rights organizations urge visiting Tamil Tiger delegation to end killings and recruitment of child soldiers (AI Index: ASA 37/005/2004)

· Sri Lanka: Free Nallaratnam Singarasa (AI Index: ASA 37/006/2004)
· Sri Lanka: Amnesty International concerned at reactivation of death penalty (AI Index: ASA 37/007/2004)

SUDAN

REPUBLIC OF SUDAN
Head of state and government: Omar Hassan Ahmad al-Bashir
Death penalty: retentionist
International Criminal Court: signed
UN Women's Convention and its Optional Protocol: not signed

In Darfur in western Sudan government forces and allied militias continued to kill thousands and displace tens of thousands of people living in rural areas, especially during the first three months of 2004. Hundreds of those killed were extrajudicially executed by armed forces, military intelligence or militias. A ceasefire signed in April by the government and armed groups based in Darfur – the Sudan Liberation Army (SLA) and the Justice and Equality Movement (JEM) – was violated by all sides. By December about 1.8 million displaced people remained in camps within Darfur or elsewhere in Sudan and more than 200,000 Darfur refugees remained in Chad. The SLA and JEM abducted people from nomad groups, attacked humanitarian convoys and reportedly executed individuals. The final protocols of the North-South peace process were signed on 31 December. During the year the ceasefire between the government and the Sudan People's Liberation Army (SPLA), led by John Garang, continued but was breached by attacks by government-supported militias around Malakal which displaced tens of thousands of people. Hundreds of people were detained without charge for political reasons by national security, intelligence and police forces; at least 100 remained in detention at the end of the year. Torture was widespread, especially in Darfur. At least three detainees died in custody in circumstances where torture appeared to have caused their death. More than 100 death sentences were imposed; executions were believed to have been carried out. Floggings were imposed for numerous offences and usually carried out immediately. Amputations, including cross-amputations, were also imposed but none was known to have been carried out in 2004. Scores of people were sentenced before specialized criminal courts in Darfur after summary and unfair trials. In areas controlled by the SPLA people were sentenced to cruel punishments such as flogging and held in cruel, inhuman or degrading conditions of detention.

Southern Sudan

Peace talks between the SPLA and the government continued intermittently during the year. In January a protocol on wealth-sharing was signed and in May three protocols on power sharing and on the resolution of conflict in the areas of Abyei, South Kordofan and the Nuba Mountains, and the southern Blue Nile Province (the three so-called "marginal areas") were agreed. The power-sharing protocol contained a list of human rights and fundamental freedoms to be respected by both parties.

Despite the ceasefire and continuing peace process, fighting broke out in Bahr al-Ghazal and Upper Nile. In May, hundreds of Shilluk people were killed in Upper Nile and more than 60,000 were reportedly displaced after attacks by government-supported militias. At least 20,000 remained displaced by the end of the year. About 400,000 people displaced in previous years returned to the Bahr al-Ghazal and Equatoria regions. In areas under SPLA control detainees were reportedly sentenced to cruel, inhuman or degrading punishment such as flogging after summary trials or without trial; SPLA commanders reportedly frequently overturned court decisions. Conditions for detainees constituted cruel, inhuman or degrading treatment or punishment. Most prisons were simply large holes in the ground.

Crisis in Darfur

The conflict in Darfur intensified at the start of the year. Attacks were carried out by government forces, sometimes using Antonov bomber planes and helicopter gunships, and by nomad militias known as the Janjawid, armed and supported by the government. Thousands of civilians were killed and tens of thousands made homeless. Others were abducted. Hundreds of villages were destroyed or looted. Thousands of women were raped, sometimes in public, and many were taken as sexual slaves by soldiers or Janjawid militiamen. In April a Humanitarian Ceasefire Agreement was signed by the Sudanese government, the SLA and the JEM in N'Djaména, Chad. Both sides breached the agreement not to target civilians.

By March, with more than one million internally displaced people (IDPs) living in camps while the government continued to restrict access to humanitarian aid, fears of a famine grew. The then UN Humanitarian Coordinator described Darfur as the "greatest humanitarian crisis of our time". In May, following intense international pressure, the government agreed to grant free access to humanitarian organizations. In July, African Union (AU) ceasefire monitors and a protection force were deployed in the main towns. In October the AU Peace and Security Council widened the mandate of the force to include protection of civilians in imminent danger but a planned increase of personnel to more than 3,000 had not been fully implemented by the end of the year.

In July and September UN Resolutions 1556 and 1564 threatened action if the government failed to disarm the Janjawid and protect civilians. However, the Janjawid remained armed and were largely incorporated into Sudanese paramilitary forces such as the Popular Defence Forces. In November Humanitarian and Security Protocols were signed in Abuja, Nigeria, by the government, the SLA and the JEM, committing them to respect international humanitarian law. However, attacks by both sides continued, causing thousands more people to be displaced. Government planes violated the agreement and bombed civilians.

Unlawful killings

Government forces and Janjawid militias carried out hundreds of extrajudicial executions.

🗁 In March, Sudanese military intelligence and army officers and Janjawid militiamen arrested more than 135 Fur people in 10 villages in Wadi Saleh province in West Darfur state. Those arrested were detained in the village of Deleij, blindfolded and taken in groups of about 40 in army trucks to an area behind a hill near Deleij. They were reportedly told to lie on the ground and shot by about 45 members of the military intelligence and the Janjawid.

Violence against women

Armed forces and militia members raped thousands of women and tens of thousands of women suffered other violence and forced displacement in the conflict in Darfur. Women were raped during attacks and frequently abducted into sexual slavery for days or months. Women continued to be raped outside IDP camps.

🗁 An 18-year-old woman described how after an attack on Mukjar in January about 45 women were taken from the village by soldiers and militiamen wearing military uniform and raped. She was raped by six men and given to a soldier who kept her in sexual slavery for one month in Nyala and then took her to Khartoum, where she remained for two months before escaping. The soldier was under investigation at the end of the year.

🗁 In August, armed men in uniform, apparently from militias, reportedly raped three teenage girls gathering wood outside Ardamata IDP camp. The women reported the rape to the police who sent them for a medical examination but subsequently dropped the case.

Refugees and displaced people

The number of displaced people in Darfur more than doubled. By December about 1.8 million people were displaced within Darfur and some 200,000 were refugees in Chad.

Until May, when the government gave access to humanitarian agencies, most IDPs lacked food, water and medical aid and were constantly harassed by Janjawid militias. IDPs continued to report attacks outside camps by the Janjawid and harassment by the security and police forces. Government officials put pressure on IDPs to return to unsafe areas and police forcibly relocated IDPs at night.

🗁 In April, a UN mission described how 1,700 IDPs, whose villages had been burnt, were confined to the town of Kailek in Shattaya district, West Darfur, without access to food or water. The town was encircled by the Janjawid who would take women to rape at night and subject men to forced labour.

◻ At least 40 IDPs from Abu Shouk camp in al-Fasher and Kabkabiya were arrested in July after talking to foreign delegations, including those of US Secretary of State Colin Powell and French Foreign Minister Michel Barnier.

◻ In November, police attacked IDPs in al-Jeer in Nyala, South Darfur state, at least four times in order to empty the camp. On the night of 9-10 November they used tear gas, rubber bullets and bulldozers to drive people out in the presence of international monitors and the media.

Abuses by armed groups
The SLA and JEM were responsible for unlawful killings, attacks on humanitarian convoys and abductions.

◻ In October, 18 passengers from nomad groups were taken off a bus between Niyertiti and Thur in South Darfur state by SLA members. Thirteen of those abducted were believed to have been killed.

Torture
Torture of detainees by the security forces, military intelligence and police was widespread, particularly in Darfur.

◻ Twelve people from Mellit, North Darfur state, arrested by the Positive Security in August were tortured to make them confess to fabricating a video tape showing rapes. Four women, Mariam Mohamed Dinar, Su'ad Ali Khalil, Su'ad al-Nur Abdel Rahman and Fatma Rahma were beaten with a belt, kicked and punched. Mariam Mohamed Dinar had her nails pulled out with pincers. Men arrested at the same time were also reportedly tortured. The charges were dropped and all were released in November.

Deaths in custody
At least three people died in custody. Torture appeared to have caused or hastened their deaths.

◻ Abdel Rahman Mohamed Abdel Hadi died in custody on the day of his arrest, apparently as a result of torture. He was one of nine people arrested in August by military intelligence who were reportedly tortured in the army barracks in Mellit.

◻ Shamseddin Idris, a Nuba student, and Abdel Rahman Suleiman Adam, a student from Darfur – both members of the Popular Congress party (an Islamist opposition to the ruling National Congress Party) arrested in September as part of a crackdown on the party – died immediately after arrest, apparently after being severely beaten. An investigation into the deaths was continuing at the end of the year.

Incommunicado detention
Political detainees, including many prisoners of conscience, continued to be held in prolonged incommunicado detention without trial under Article 31 of the National Security Forces Act.

◻ Six Darfuris arrested in Khartoum in February remained detained without charge and mostly incommunicado at the end of the year. One of them, 50-year-old Fur leader Ma'mun Issa Abdel Gader from Niyertiti, West Darfur, was first detained in Kober prison in Khartoum, later transferred to Dabak prison north of Khartoum, and then to the prison of Wad Medani, south of Khartoum. His family was only allowed to visit him twice.

◻ More than 100 Popular Congress party members were arrested in Khartoum in September, following government allegations of a coup plot. Detainees, including high-profile party members, student activists, people of Darfur origin and relatives of party members, were held incommunicado. Party leader Hassan al-Turabi was transferred from house detention, where he had been held without charge for months, to Kober prison. He had previously been released in October 2003 after two years' detention without trial. By the end of the year some had been released and about 90 were reported to have been charged with involvement in a coup.

Human rights defenders
Human rights defenders continued to be harassed and arrested.

◻ Dr Mudawi Ibrahim Adam, Director of the Sudan Social Development Organization, was arrested at his home in Khartoum in December 2003 after visiting Darfur. He was subsequently charged with offences relating to crimes against the state, some carrying the death penalty. The evidence against him included public AI documents. All charges against him were dropped in August.

◻ Saleh Mahmud Osman, a human rights lawyer from Darfur, was arrested in February in Wad Medani and held without access to the outside world for six weeks. He was released without charge in September after seven months in detention.

Death penalty and other cruel, inhuman and degrading punishments
In Darfur, Specialized Criminal Courts handed down death sentences and corporal punishment after summary trials which failed to meet international fair trial standards. In Khartoum women and men continued to be brought before public order courts and sentenced to flogging for offences such as illegal sexual intercourse, breaching the dress code, selling alcohol or selling tea without a licence.

◻ The sentence of 100 lashes imposed on a 14-year-old pregnant unmarried girl in Nyala convicted of illegal sexual intercourse in 2003 was commuted.

◻ Al-Tayeb Ali Ahmad, an SLA member, was sentenced to death in January for crimes against the state, accused of participating in an attack on al-Fasher airport in 2003. He and two co-defendants, who received prison sentences, were tortured by being beaten with water pipes and sticks before their trial by al-Fasher Specialized Criminal Court and had no legal representation.

◻ Alakor (Madina) Lual Deng was sentenced to death by stoning in Nahud, Kordofan, for adultery. At her trial she had no defence lawyer and was sentenced to death solely on the basis of her own confession. In June the High Court of Justice upheld her appeal and quashed the sentence.

☐ The death sentences on 88 Rizeiqat people, including two children, imposed in July 2002 were quashed in December 2004 and they were released.

Restrictions on freedom of expression

Freedom of the press continued to be restricted. Journalists were detained and summoned for questioning by the authorities and newspapers were censored. The security forces also forced editors to withdraw articles about Darfur.

☐ Zuhair al-Sarraj, a journalist with the newspaper al-Sahafa, was summoned to the offices of the security services several times in November after writing an article complaining of the use of loudspeakers for the calls to prayer during Ramadan. On one occasion he was reportedly severely beaten.

International organizations

In April the Office of the UN High Commissioner for Human Rights sent a fact-finding mission to Chad and Darfur which issued two reports on killings and forced displacement in Darfur and the government's role in these. In July the UN Secretary-General appointed a Special Representative to Sudan. UN human rights monitors were deployed in Darfur in August. The UN High Commissioner for Human Rights, the Special Adviser on the Prevention of Genocide, the Special Representative on Internally Displaced Persons and the UN Special Rapporteurs on extrajudicial, summary or arbitrary executions and on violence against women visited Sudan. Three Security Council resolutions were passed on Sudan. Resolution 1564 established a UN Commission of Inquiry to investigate reports of violations of international human rights and humanitarian law and determine whether acts of genocide had occurred.

The AU Peace and Security Council sent ceasefire monitors and a protection force to Darfur. The AU also brokered a ceasefire and peace protocols between parties to the conflict in Darfur. The African Commission sent a fact-finding mission.

European Union (EU) representatives visited Darfur. The EU maintained an arms embargo and threatened other sanctions on Sudan.

The Arab League sent a fact-finding mission to Darfur in April which drew attention to the deteriorating humanitarian situation.

AI country reports/ visits
Reports
- Sudan/Darfur: "Too many people killed for no reason" (AI Index: AFR 54/008/2004)
- Sudan/Darfur: Incommunicado detention, torture and special courts — Memorandum to the government of Sudan and the Sudanese Commission of Inquiry (AI Index: AFR 54/058/2004)
- Sudan/Darfur: Rape as a weapon of war — Sexual violence and its consequences (AI Index: AFR 54/076/2004)
- Sudan: Intimidation and denial — Attacks on freedom of expression in Darfur (AI Index: AFR 54/101/2004)
- Sudan: Civilians still under threat in Darfur — an agenda for human rights protection (AI Index: AFR 54/131/2004)
- Sudan: Arming the perpetrators of grave abuses in Darfur (AI Index: AFR 54/139/2004)
- Sudan: No one to complain to — no respite for the victims, impunity for the perpetrators (AI Index: AFR 54/138/2004)
- Sudan: What hope for the future? Civilians in urgent need of protection (AI Index: AFR 54/164/2004)

Visits
In May, AI delegates visited Sudanese refugees in Chad. In September and October AI delegates visited Khartoum and Darfur and met government officials.

SWAZILAND

KINGDOM OF SWAZILAND
Head of state: King Mswati III
Head of government: Absalom Themba Dlamini
Death penalty: retentionist
International Criminal Court: not signed
UN Women's Convention: ratified
Optional Protocol to UN Women's Convention: not signed

There was an unresolved crisis in the rule of law which affected the rights of victims of forcible evictions. Food shortages and an increasing rate of HIV infection were also serious concerns. Rape and other forms of sexual abuse of women and girls increased. Reports of torture by members of the police and military persisted and there were several suspicious deaths in police custody. Three people were under sentence of death.

Legal and constitutional developments

By the end of 2004, the two houses of parliament were deadlocked over amendments to the Constitution of the Kingdom of Swaziland Bill. In October the High Court had dismissed an application from non-governmental organizations seeking to suspend parliamentary debate pending full consideration of a legal challenge to the legitimacy of the Constitution drafting process. Civil society organizations were also concerned that the draft Constitution would not protect the human rights of all Swazis. AI campaigned for the draft Constitution to be strengthened.

In September Prime Minister Themba Dlamini publicly withdrew a statement made two years previously by the former Prime Minister that the government would not obey two rulings of the Court of Appeal. The judges of the Court of Appeal, who had resigned in protest in 2002, resumed their duties on 10 November. However, the judges discovered that the government had not implemented one of their rulings, which had upheld the rights of people forcibly evicted in 2000 to return to their homes. Under pressure from the judges, the Minister of Justice and Constitutional Affairs assured the court that the evictees could return. One of the evictees, Madeli Fakudze, attempted to return home, but was again forcibly evicted by police on 14 November, reportedly on the orders of the King. Although Madeli Fakudze was later able to return to his home on terms set down by the King, other evictees remained internally displaced or in exile as refugees. AI condemned the forcible evictions as human rights violations.

The Criminal Procedure and Evidence (Amendment) Act (CPEA Act) came into force in September, restoring the courts' right to hear bail applications in serious cases. Twenty-two unlawfully detained pre-trial suspects, who had been granted bail following a 2002 ruling of the Court of Appeal, had been released by September 2004.

Some provisions of the CPEA Act, however, still infringed the presumption of innocence, the right to liberty and the right to information of arrested suspects. One provision denies the right of redress to those granted bail but unlawfully detained before September 2004.

International human rights obligations

Swaziland ratified the UN Women's Convention; the UN Convention against Torture; the International Covenant on Civil and Political Rights; and the International Covenant on Economic, Social and Cultural Rights. It entered no reservations.

Violence against women and girls

Police officials and non-governmental organizations (NGOs) expressed concern at an increase in rape and sexual abuse of children and young women. In February, the Commissioner of Police stated that in one weekend alone the police received 12 reports of rape, with the victims ranging in age from five to 80. SWAGAA (Swaziland Action Group Against Abuse), an NGO, dealt with 160 cases of rape and sexual abuse between April and September, of which more than half involved girls. Many of the victims, particularly those repeatedly abused, developed sexually transmitted infections, including HIV. Perpetrators included family members and teachers. AI campaigned for improved access to justice and care and treatment for rape survivors.

In July the High Court acquitted a police officer charged with repeatedly raping his seven-year-old daughter. The child had to give evidence and was cross-examined in open court. No expert witnesses were called to explain the impact of sexual abuse on a child. A week after the acquittal, the child was confirmed as HIV-positive.

On 11 September a group of about 20 men stripped and sexually assaulted an 18-year-old student at a bus stop in Manzini. Despite repeated requests by members of the public, police from a nearby police station failed to come to the scene. The victim was eventually rescued and taken to the police station where she made a statement before receiving urgent hospital treatment. Subsequently, three men were arrested and charged. AI called for a full public investigation into why the police failed to intervene to protect the victim.

In February the Commissioner of Police launched a "pilot project" to provide private interview rooms for victims of sexual violence, starting with the regional police headquarters in Manzini. In September the CPEA Act allowed vulnerable young people to give evidence in court through "intermediaries" and from a separate room.

There was limited access within the public health system for survivors of sexual assault to counselling, anti-retroviral drugs or other necessary treatment for sexually transmitted infections. Swaziland has the highest rate of HIV infection globally at over 38 per cent.

Torture and deaths in custody

Torture and ill-treatment by members of the police and military were reported. Several criminal suspects died in police custody in suspicious circumstances.

Mandi Hlophe died in police custody at Manzini police station on 2 April shortly after her arrest. The police reportedly claimed that she had committed suicide. Her family were not given the results of an official postmortem and no inquest was ordered.

On 21 May, 31-year-old Mandlenkhosi Ngubeni died at Matsapha police station within 12 hours of his arrest. There was a public outcry after photographs of his body were published. The Prime Minister ordered a public inquest, which had not concluded by the end of 2004. During the inquest, evidence emerged that the police failed to provide urgent medical treatment. A witness testified he had seen the police torturing Mandlenkhosi Ngubeni with a rubber tube pulled over his face. The results of independent forensic medical analysis were consistent with this allegation.

In April the High Court ruled in a civil damages case that the police acted unlawfully when they arrested, shot and seriously wounded an investigation witness, Thomas Mamba, eight years previously. AI could not obtain confirmation from the police authorities that they had ordered a criminal investigation.

Political trial

In June the trial began in the Mbabane magistrate's court of Roland Rudd, a member of the Swaziland Agricultural and Plantations Workers Union (SAPWU), and three other SAPWU members – Alex Langwenya, Lynn Dingani Mazibuko and Samkeliso Ncongwane. The four men were charged under the Arms and Ammunitions Act after being arrested during a trade union demonstration in August 2003. Roland Rudd was assaulted by police and denied access to medical care. The prosecution withdrew charges against Samkeliso Ncongwane at the opening of the trial, which had not concluded by the end of 2004.

Death penalty

No new death sentences were imposed during 2004. In its November session the Court of Appeal upheld the conviction and death sentence imposed on one prisoner, Richard Mabaso, in 2003. As a result three prisoners were under sentence of death at the end of 2004, all of whom had had their sentences confirmed on appeal.

AI country reports/visits

Reports and statements

- Swaziland: Human rights at risk in a climate of political and legal uncertainty (AI Index: AFR 55/004/2004)
- Stop violence against women — Violence fuels the HIV/AIDS pandemic in Swaziland (AI Index: AFR 55/003/2004)
- Swaziland: Constitution Bill and the rule of law "deal" fail to protect human rights (AI Index: AFR 55/008/2004)
- Swaziland: Judges' stand supports human rights (AI Index: AFR 55/009/2004)

Visit

An AI delegate visited Swaziland to undertake research on human rights aspects of the HIV/AIDS pandemic.

SWEDEN

KINGDOM OF SWEDEN
Head of state: King Carl XVI Gustaf
Head of government: Göran Persson
Death penalty: abolitionist for all crimes
International Criminal Court: ratified
UN Women's Convention and its Optional Protocol: ratified

Discrimination against ethnic minorities and foreign nationals, prison overcrowding, and failures to investigate complaints against the police promptly or independently were among a range of concerns raised by international monitoring bodies. Further revelations were made about the forcible deportation of two asylum-seekers to Egypt in 2001, raising concerns that the Swedish authorities had colluded in their unlawful "rendition" to the custody of the USA before their eventual transfer to Egypt.

International scrutiny

In March, after considering Sweden's 15th and 16th periodic reports under the UN Convention against Racism, the Committee on the Elimination of Racial Discrimination adopted its Concluding Observations. Among the Committee's concerns were the lack of statistical data on the ethnic composition of the

population; reports that few hate crimes led to prosecutions and that relevant legislation was not applied; difficulties faced by a large part of the Roma community in areas such as employment, education and housing; unresolved issues relating to Sami land rights; persistent discrimination against immigrants in relation to social and economic rights; and the possibility of expulsions without a right of appeal under the Special Control of Foreigners Act.

The automatic — instead of exceptional — imposition of restrictive regimes, isolation in particular, on remand detainees, the overcrowding in some prisons and detention facilities, and "unacceptable" outdoor facilities at the Kronobergs remand and detention centre in Stockholm were some of the concerns raised by the Council of Europe's Commissioner for Human Rights in his July report of a visit to Sweden in April. Other concerns were the absence of legislative provisions setting out the maximum time adult asylum-seekers could be detained; the whereabouts of unaccompanied children — feared to have become victim to paedophile and trafficking networks — who had gone missing from the care of the Migration Service; and the insufficient assistance provided to victims of trafficking, including children. Sami land rights issues, and discrimination faced by migrants and Roma in accessing employment, education, housing and the provision of services were also highlighted. The Commissioner's recommendations included the establishment of a separate and independent institution for investigating complaints against the police.

In November the Council of Europe's Committee for the Prevention of Torture and Inhuman or Degrading Treatment or Punishment (CPT) issued a report of its visit to Sweden in January and February 2003. The CPT found that some initial investigations into complaints of police ill-treatment in the county of Västra Götaland had not been prompt, independent or effective, and that detainees in police custody were still not formally guaranteed rights to inform someone of their own choice of their arrest or to have access to a lawyer and a doctor. The CPT urged the government to reconsider the need for a demonstrably independent police complaints agency. With respect to prisons, the CPT recommended that the authorities take further action to mitigate the damaging effects of prolonged periods of isolation, impose restrictions on remand prisoners only in exceptional circumstances, and vigorously pursue strategies to address inter-prisoner violence. The CPT found arrangements for outdoor exercise to be unsatisfactory for remand prisoners subject to restrictions at Gothenburg and Umeå Remand Prisons, and for all inmates at Västberga prison.

Prison conditions

Overcrowding in Kronobergs remand and detention centre led to remand detainees being held in cells not intended to house them, such as isolation cells ordinarily used for intoxicated people, which contained only a plastic mattress and a drain in the floor. Detainees should have been kept in such cells for only brief periods, but sometimes spent up to 10 days in them, according to the chief executive of the prison. Such conditions amounted to cruel and inhuman treatment. Detainees were also held in common areas, depriving all detainees of the use of those facilities, or in storage or laundry rooms.

There were reports that several prisoners with mental disabilities were held in ordinary prisons in contravention of international standards.

Update: policing of 2001 protests in Gothenburg

In December the Court of Appeal confirmed the controversial acquittal in February of the chief police commissioner in charge of the police operation against demonstrators at the Hvitfeldtska school in June 2001, during the European Union summit in Gothenburg. He had been charged with unlawful detention and misconduct in public duty. The Court of Appeal ruled that, even though people held at the school had been detained unlawfully, the chief police commissioner did not act with criminal intent. Following the disturbances at the summit, which led to mass arrests, complaints were lodged against approximately 170 police officers. The complaints resulted in five officers being charged with misconduct, none of whom was subsequently convicted.

Update: 'war on terror' deportations

Two asylum-seekers were handed over by Swedish police to hooded men and placed on an aeroplane leased by the US Defense Department for their transport to Egypt, according to revelations in a Swedish television programme in May. The two men were allegedly hooded and subjected to other forms of ill-treatment before and during their handover and transport. Muhammad Muhammad Suleiman Ibrahim El-Zari and Ahmed Hussein Mustafa Kamil Agiza were forcibly and secretly expelled to Egypt in December 2001, where they later alleged they were tortured, after the Swedish government received "assurances" that they would not be subjected to human rights violations. AI called for an international investigation into all aspects of the case, including alleged collusion between the Swedish and US authorities and failure to protect the two men by Egypt, Sweden and the USA (see Egypt entry). Hanan Attia, the wife of Ahmed Hussein Mustafa Kamil Agiza, and their five children were granted permanent residence in Sweden in June on humanitarian grounds. AI believed that she should have been granted refugee status and protection arising from such a status rather than on humanitarian grounds. During the year, it emerged that the Swedish authorities had withheld information about Hanan Attia from the UN Committee against Torture in an attempt to undermine the credibility of her complaint to the Committee.

Violence against women

Following a survey of Swedish municipalities, AI expressed concern about the ability of local authorities to help survivors of domestic violence. It transpired that for some municipalities it was not a priority, and most of them lacked strategic plans for addressing violence against women.

AI country reports/ visits
Statement
- Sweden: Concerns over the treatment of deported Egyptians (AI Index: EUR 42/001/2004)

SWITZERLAND

SWISS CONFEDERATION
Head of state and government: Joseph Deiss
Death penalty: abolitionist for all crimes
International Criminal Court: ratified
UN Women's Convention: ratified with reservations
Optional Protocol to UN Women's Convention: not signed

There were further allegations of ill-treatment, use of excessive force and racist abuse by police officers. An amendment to the asylum law impeded the effective exercise by many foreign nationals of the right to seek asylum. Government proposals to make further amendments to the law, greatly restricting access to the asylum determination process, risked violating the UN Refugee Convention. Domestic violence against women remained a significant problem.

Racism

In a report published in January, the European Commission against Racism and Intolerance (ECRI) acknowledged that Switzerland had taken a number of steps to combat racism and intolerance but noted the lack of a comprehensive body of anti-discrimination legislation. It was concerned by "the rise in racism and discrimination towards black Africans" displayed "in public opinion, political and media discourse, and also in the behaviour of officials, notably the police". ECRI urged action to counter "a general stigmatisation of black Africans as being involved in the drug trade and in other illegal activities such as prostitution." It noted that the issue of asylum-seekers and refugees was also the subject of negative and hostile debate in public and political spheres, and that there were a number of problems in the field of asylum procedure.

Asylum

Evidence emerged that the individual examination of asylum applications by federal authorities often lacked thoroughness.

Changes to the asylum law which came into force in April included reducing the period within which many asylum-seekers could appeal against the rejection of their initial asylum applications from 30 to five days. The amendment affected those whose initial applications were rejected automatically, without individual examination, on grounds that the authorities categorized their country of origin as safe for return. AI and other organizations working for refugees' human rights expressed concern that the amendment did not allow rejected asylum-seekers sufficient time to access appropriate legal advice and lodge an appeal.

Government proposals for further changes to the asylum law were under parliamentary discussion. In July the Office of the UN High Commissioner for Refugees suggested that some were "focused on restricting access to the asylum procedure and to international protection, and risked running counter to the spirit and the letter of the 1951 Refugee Convention." It was particularly concerned that proposed restrictions on access to normal asylum procedures for people unable to submit valid travel or identity documents within 48 hours could lead to breaches of the UN Refugee Convention. In public statements made during a visit to Switzerland in December, the Council of Europe's Commissioner for Human Rights also expressed concern that changes to asylum procedures were putting the rights of asylum-seekers at risk.

Police racism, ill-treatment and use of excessive force

There were regular reports of ill-treatment, often accompanied by racist abuse. Police accountability mechanisms were unsatisfactory and such abuses were often committed with impunity.

ECRI called for an end to what it identified as "clearly discriminatory police practices" such as carrying out identity checks, taking people into police custody, and carrying out body searches – often on the street, solely on the basis of skin colour. The government rejected the assertion that the police behaved in a racist, discriminatory and violent way towards minorities, in particular black Africans, but acknowledged that mistakes might sometimes occur.

Many detainees, including children, were denied fundamental safeguards against ill-treatment in police custody such as the right to have prompt access to a lawyer and to have relatives informed of their arrest.

More cantonal police forces acquired tasers (dart-firing, high-voltage stun guns). AI continued to raise concerns about the health risks associated with such weapons, as well as their potential for abuse.

Use of force during deportations

In November the government presented, for public consultation, a draft federal law regulating the use of means of restraint by police during deportations and during the transport of detainees ordered by a federal authority. The text largely reflected cross-cantonal guidelines for police on restraint methods to be used during forcible deportation operations, endorsed by the Conference of Directors of the Cantonal Justice and Police Departments in 2002. The Conference had requested legislation to regulate police restraint methods at the federal level. AI welcomed the text insofar as it aimed to make a number of essential safeguards for deportees legally binding, and viewed as particularly positive the banning of any police restraint methods restricting breathing, in view of recent deaths attributable to such methods. However, AI was concerned about certain aspects, in particular a provision allowing the use of electro-shock weapons including tasers. In December the Council of Europe's Commissioner for Human Rights also expressed concern about the use of tasers in the context of forcible deportations.

In December the European Committee for the Prevention of Torture (CPT) published the findings of a visit carried out in October 2003. The principal purpose of the visit was to assess the implementation of measures the CPT had previously recommended concerning procedures and restraint methods applied in the context of forcible deportation operations from Zürich-Kloten Airport. The CPT also reviewed the treatment of foreign nationals detained in the airport transit zone and airport Prison No 2 pending deportation.

The CPT noted "the considerable work" carried out by the authorities to implement its past recommendations. Nevertheless, it said it had gathered a number of allegations, mainly of racist insults, threats and occasional physical ill-treatment during body searches by police officers responsible for checking passports at the border. According to these allegations, such treatment was aimed at persuading foreign nationals to return voluntarily to their country of origin and not to enter Swiss territory or to lodge an asylum request in Switzerland. The CPT said that the most "worrying" allegations concerned physical violence inflicted in retaliation for aborted deportation operations. It formulated a number of recommendations to address such concerns, emphasizing, amongst other things, the need to remind police officers that allegations of ill-treatment would be investigated and, if proven, severely sanctioned; the importance of systematically offering a medical examination, on return to detention, to every foreigner following an aborted deportation operation; and of integration into the general police training programme of information concerning the risk of positional asphyxia during the physical restraint of recalcitrant people. Upon the report's publication, the Swiss authorities stated that they had already taken a number of measures to implement these and other recommendations made by the CPT.

Demonstrations

There were further allegations of police using excessive and unwarranted force in the context of some demonstrations and inappropriately using police equipment designed to temporarily disable or incapacitate people. AI called for weapons firing projectiles such as rubber bullets and "markers" (plastic bullets containing paint and metal), tasers, and disabling chemical irritant gases not to be used in any canton without rigorous independent investigations into their potential for abuse and medical effects. AI also called for strict rules, in line with international standards, regulating the use of such weapons. In addition, AI urged that all officers engaged in direct interventions with the public during policing operations surrounding demonstrations prominently display some form of individual identification – such as a service number.

Updates

⌐ Denise Chervet appealed against a magistrate's decision not to indict the police officer who fired a kinetic impact weapon at her, causing her permanent facial injury, following a demonstration in Geneva in March 2003, and called for him to be charged with causing serious bodily harm. In December a Geneva court endorsed the magistrate's decision but indicated that certain aspects of the shooting incident still needed clarification. A decision by the magistrate as to whether or not to pursue further investigation was awaited at the end of the year. The officer who authorized the use of the weapon was awaiting trial on a charge of causing bodily harm through negligence.

⌐ In May the Geneva government published the report of the extra-parliamentary Commission of Inquiry established to investigate the general handling by Geneva cantonal authorities, including the police, of security and demonstrations surrounding the G8 Summit held in neighbouring France in June 2003. Dozens of people alleged police brutality and excessive and gratuitous use of force by police officers during the G8 demonstrations in and around Geneva, and at least 15 individuals lodged formal criminal complaints against the police. In June it was reported that the Geneva Attorney General had notified eight of them that the investigation into their complaint was being terminated without any further criminal action on the grounds that it was impossible to identify the officers involved.

The commission informed AI that it was not its task to investigate specific cases. Its eventual report made no specific mention of the allegations of police use of excessive force apart from recording that, according to certain testimony, "the principle of proportionality appears not always to have been respected" in the context of a demonstration held on 3 June. It made 52 recommendations to the authorities and other key actors involved in G8 events, including demonstration organizers. The recommendations concerning the police included the proposed creation of specialized police units to deal with such policing operations in future, in view of their complexity and frequency and current police lack of expertise. It also emphasized the principle of proportionality in policing, recommended the acquisition and management of police equipment in a coordinated manner across cantons and called for police officers to wear a service number during public order interventions.

Violence against women

Domestic violence remained prevalent. An amendment to the Swiss Penal Code allowed the authorities to prosecute crimes of domestic violence, including rape, without needing an official complaint from the victim. Legislation aimed at protecting victims of domestic violence and allowing police to ban offenders temporarily from the shared place of residence was introduced or in preparation in several cantons. Further protection measures were needed, including greater efforts to prosecute offenders, to provide an adequate number of refuges for victims, and to address the situation of foreign women whose permission to stay in Switzerland depended directly on continued marriage or cohabitation with their husband during the first three years of residence.

AI country reports/visits
Report
- Europe and Central Asia: Summary of Amnesty International's concerns in the region, January-June 2004: Switzerland (AI Index: EUR 01/005/2004)

SYRIA

SYRIAN ARAB REPUBLIC
Head of state: Bashar al-Assad
Head of government: Muhammad Naji 'Otri
Death penalty: retentionist
International Criminal Court: signed
UN Women's Convention: ratified with reservations
Optional Protocol to UN Women's Convention: not signed

Hundreds of people were arrested for political reasons. Most of them were Kurds detained following violent disturbances in north-eastern Syria in March during which over 30 people were killed. Many of those arrested were held incommunicado at unknown locations. Torture and ill-treatment, including of children, were widely reported. At least nine people reportedly died as a result. Freedom of expression and association remained severely restricted and scores of people were arrested for political reasons, including some solely involved in peaceful activities. Human rights defenders were harassed although in general they could work more openly than in previous years. Two people were reportedly executed. Over 200 political prisoners, including prisoners of conscience, were released.

Background

On 12 March clashes broke out between Arab and Kurdish fans at a football stadium in Qamishli, north-eastern Syria. Security forces responded by firing into the crowd, killing several people. Police attacked Syrian Kurdish mourners the next day, resulting in two days of rioting by Syrian Kurds in several towns in the mainly Kurdish north-east. At least 36 people, mostly Kurds, were reportedly killed and over 100 injured. More than 2,000 people, most of them Kurds, were believed to have been arrested. Most were held incommunicado at unknown locations and there were widespread reports of torture and ill-treatment of detainees, including children. About 200 Kurds remained detained at the end of the year. At least six Kurds were killed while carrying out their military service. No investigations were known to have been initiated into the killings. The predominantly Kurdish areas of north and north-east Syria continued to lag behind the rest of the country in terms of social and economic indicators.

In August Syria acceded to the UN Convention against Torture.

On 2 September the UN Security Council passed Resolution 1559, drafted by the USA and France, calling on foreign forces (that is, Syrian forces) to withdraw from Lebanon and warning against (Syrian) interference in Lebanon's presidential election.

On 26 September in Damascus, 'Izz al-Din al-Sheykh Khalil, a Palestinian, was killed in a car bomb. Israeli security sources reportedly claimed responsibility.

In a cabinet reshuffle on 4 October in which eight ministerial posts changed hands, Ghazi Kan'an, the former head of Syrian intelligence in Lebanon, replaced General 'Ali Hammoud as Interior Minister, and Mahdi Dakhlallah, editor of the ruling party's daily newspaper, al-Ba'ath, replaced Ahmad al-Hassan as Information Minister.

On 19 October the European Union and Syria initialled an Association Agreement, which contains a clause on human rights, committing both sides to work towards free trade.

On 10 December the UN General Assembly voted 161-2 for Israel to abide by international law in the Golan Heights, which it occupied in 1967.

Prisoners of conscience

Prisoners of conscience and possible prisoners of conscience remained in prolonged detention without trial or serving sentences imposed after unfair trials. Others were sentenced during 2004.

🗀 On 1 April, four men were sentenced after grossly unfair secret trials before a Field Military Court (FMC) for "attempting to establish a religious organization, involvement in unlicensed social activities and attending unlicensed religious and intellectual classes". Haythem al-Hamwi and Yahya Sharabajee were sentenced to four years' imprisonment, and Mu'atez Murad and Muhammad Shehada to three years' imprisonment. They had been arrested with about 20 others in May 2003 for their involvement in peaceful activities such as discouraging people from smoking and giving bribes, and participating in a silent demonstration opposing the expected US-led invasion of Iraq, in the town of Darya near Damascus.

🗀 Between June and November dozens of Islamist students and clerics were arrested, mostly in the Hama and Qatana areas. Many of those arrested reportedly had links with the banned Hizb al-Tahrir (Islamic Liberation Party) and were to be tried before FMCs. At least 30 remained in detention at the end of the year.

🗀 Of the "Damascus Spring" detainees – people arrested in 2001 during repression of a pro-reform movement – six remained in solitary confinement at the end of the year. In September information emerged that Habib 'Isa had been beaten severely by guards in May 2002, the same month, it was already known, that Dr 'Aref Dalilah was also beaten. Both men were reportedly in need of medical treatment. Two others, Habib Salih and Kamal al-Labwani, were released on 9 September after completing their sentences.

🗀 'Abd al-'Aziz al-Khayyir remained in Sednaya Prison since his arrest in February 1992. He was sentenced in August 1995 by the Supreme State Security Court (SSSC), whose procedures fall far short of international fair trial standards, to 22 years' imprisonment for membership of the Party for Communist Action.

Releases of political prisoners

More than 200 political prisoners, including prisoners of conscience, were released. Scores were members of the Muslim Brotherhood. Others included members or affiliates of Hizb al-Tahrir or of the pro-Iraqi Ba'th Party. Many had been held beyond the expiry of their sentences. Faris Murad and 'Imad Shiha were released in February and August respectively after being imprisoned in 1975 for membership of the Arab Communist Organization.

Freedom of expression and association

Freedom of expression and association continued to be curtailed.

🗀 On 24 April, 11 university students were arrested by officers of Political Security near Damascus University. Some of the students were among dozens expelled from Aleppo University after peacefully protesting on 25 February against a new law that ended guaranteed employment for engineering graduates. At least seven were reportedly beaten during arrest, and then tortured and ill-treated in custody. They were reportedly beaten and kicked, sometimes while tied to a frame, and subjected to the "flying carpet" torture method whereby the victim is strapped to a piece of wood shaped like the human body and beaten or given electric shocks.

Nine of the 11 were released on 9 May. Muhammad 'Arab and Muhammad al-Dabas remained detained and their trial began on 26 September before the SSSC. Their lawyer told the court that the students retracted "confessions" they had made as a result of beatings and psychological torture.

🗀 The SSSC sentenced four people for "disseminating false information" via the Internet. On 20 June 'Abdel

Rahman al-Shaghouri was sentenced to two and a half years' imprisonment; and on 25 July Haytham Qutaysh received a sentence of four years in prison, his brother Muhammad three years and Yahya al-Aws two years.

☐ On 27 June, seven Kurdish men were convicted by the SSSC of "belonging to a secret organization" and "attempting to sever part of the Syrian territory and annex it to a foreign entity". They were arrested on 25 June 2003 for participating in a peaceful demonstration in front of the UN Children's Fund (UNICEF) building in Damascus calling for the rights of Syrian Kurds to be respected. They said they were tortured and ill-treated in detention, and held in solitary confinement in small cells. One detainee, Muhammad Mustafa, stated before the SSSC that he was being held in a toilet. Muhammad Mustafa, Sherif Ramadhan and Khaled Ahmad 'Ali were sentenced to two years' imprisonment. Four others were sentenced to one year in prison and were ordered to be released as they had already spent a year in detention.

☐ Kurdish student Mas'oud Hamid was sentenced to five years' imprisonment by the SSSC on 10 October after he posted photographs he had taken of the June 2003 UNICEF demonstration on the Internet. He was convicted of being a member of a "secret organization" and "attempting to sever part of the Syrian territory and annex it to a foreign entity".

Torture and deaths in custody

Torture of political and criminal detainees was widely reported, including of children. At least nine people reportedly died as a result; five of them were Kurds and two had been arrested on their return from exile in Iraq.

☐ Four Kurdish schoolchildren – Nijirfan Saleh Mahmoud, Ahmad Shikhmous 'Abdallah, Walat Muhammad Sa'id and Serbest Shikhou – all aged 12 or 13, were reportedly tortured in the minors' section of Qamishli Prison after their arrest by Political Security officers on 6 April. They were reportedly beaten with electric cables, had their heads banged together, were ordered to strip almost naked while counting from one to three and were beaten if they did not complete the stripping in time.

☐ On 1 or 2 August, Ahmad Husayn Hasan (also named as Ahmad Husayn Husayn) died in custody at the Military Intelligence Branch in al-Hasaka, north-eastern Syria, reportedly as a result of torture. He had been detained incommunicado since 13 July. Military Intelligence officers did not allow his family to see the body or have a postmortem conducted.

Violence and discrimination against women

Women's groups called for the lifting of Syria's reservations to the UN Women's Convention, focusing on Article 9 concerning the nationality of children.

The Penal Code continued to fail to afford sufficient protection for women. For example, it declares that a man who spontaneously kills a close female relative committing adultery or in any other extramarital sexual relationship will benefit from a reduced sentence; discriminates against women in cases of adultery; and permits a rapist to escape punishment if he marries the victim. The Personal Code discriminates against women in the areas of marriage, divorce, the family and inheritance.

Women's groups called for shelters and legal and counselling services for women and girls who suffer violence, for better documentation of crimes committed against women, and for labour laws to include provisions to punish sexual harassment in the workplace.

Human rights defenders

Human rights defenders faced harassment but in general could work more openly than in the past. Of three unlicensed human rights organizations that operated during the year, members of the Committees for the Defence of Democratic Liberties and Human Rights (CDDLHR) faced particular persecution. Lawyer Aktham Nu'aysa, President of the CDDLHR, was arrested on 13 April. He was put on trial before the SSSC on charges including "publishing false news to cause public anxiety" and "opposing the objectives of the revolution", which could carry a sentence of up to 15 years' imprisonment. The CDDLHR had published an annual report on human rights violations in Syria and led a campaign for the lifting of the state of emergency, in force since 1963, which gives the security forces sweeping powers and established special security courts whose procedures fall short of international fair trial standards. Aktham Nu'aysa had also expressed concerns about the fate of Lebanese people who had "disappeared" in Syria. He was permitted to travel to Europe where, on 8 October, he received the 2004 Ludovic Trarieux International Human Rights Award, but was denied permission on 7 December to travel to attend a human rights conference in Rabat, Morocco.

☐ CDDLHR members Ahmad Khazim and Hasan Watfa were arrested in mid-March following their participation in a sit-down protest in Damascus on 8 March calling for the lifting of the state of emergency. They were released on 9 May.

Returnees

Dozens of Syrians were reportedly arrested on their return from exile, often after they had obtained permission from the Syrian authorities to return. Many were suspected of personal or family links with the Muslim Brotherhood. Two men died in custody after being arrested on their return from Iraq.

☐ It was reported in August that Mus'ab al-Hariri, aged 18, whose parents moved to Saudi Arabia in 1981, remained detained since his arrest in July 2002 during his first visit to Syria. He faced trial before the SSSC, charged with belonging to the Muslim Brotherhood. In 1998 his brothers Yusef and 'Ubada, then aged 15 and 18, were arrested shortly after entering Syria, and sentenced by FMCs for alleged membership of a secret organization. They were released in 2000 and January 2004. All three brothers were reportedly tortured, including by the *dulab* ("the tyre", whereby the victim is forced into a tyre, which is suspended, and beaten with sticks and cables) and *al-kursi al-almani* ("the German chair", whereby the victim is put into a chair with moving parts which bend the spine backwards).

🗁 Information came to light in October that dual Syrian-Canadian national Arwad Muhammad 'Izzat al-Boushi had received a grossly unfair trial before an FMC in July 2003 after which he was apparently sentenced to 12 years' imprisonment for alleged membership of the Muslim Brotherhood. He was reportedly tortured during the 12 months he was detained awaiting trial. He had left Syria in 1980 and was arrested on 3 July 2002 when he returned to visit his ailing father.

🗁 Syrian-born German national Muhammad Haydar Zammar remained held in prolonged incommunicado detention in solitary confinement at the Palestine Branch (*Far' Falastin*) of Military Intelligence in Damascus since his arrest in November 2001. He was said to be held in appalling conditions in a tiny underground cell. US security forces were reportedly involved in his detention and interrogation in Morocco, where he was initially arrested, and in his secret transfer to Syria. His arrest was reportedly related to his alleged links to al-Qa'ida but he was not charged.

Death penalty

On 5 July the authorities announced that 16 people had been executed in 2002, and 11 in 2003. On 29 August the SSSC sentenced Mahmud al-Nabahan to death for being affiliated to the Muslim Brotherhood, and then commuted the sentence to 12 years in prison. According to Law 49 of July 1980, membership of or affiliation to the Muslim Brotherhood is punishable by death.

On 17 October it was reported that two people were executed in Aleppo, but no further details were made public. On 30 December, two men were sentenced to death by the SSSC, after being convicted of involvement in a bomb attack and gunfight in Damascus in April.

AI country reports/visits
Statements
- Syria: 41 years of the State of Emergency – Amnesty International reiterates its concerns over a catalogue of human rights violations (AI Index: MDE 24/016/2004)
- Syria: Amnesty International calls on Syria to end repressive measures against Kurds and to set up an independent judicial inquiry into the recent clashes (AI Index: MDE 24/029/2004)
- Syria: End persecution of human rights defenders and human rights activists (AI Index: MDE 24/076/2004)

Visits
Amnesty International repeated requests during the year to visit Syria for research and talks with government officials but received no response from the authorities.

TAIWAN

TAIWAN
President: Chen Shui-bian
Head of government: Yu Shyi-kun
Death penalty: retentionist

Human rights reforms made little or no progress during 2004, despite pressure from non-governmental organizations and academics.

Background
President Chen Shui-bian of the Democratic Progressive Party was narrowly re-elected in March. On the day before the elections, he and Vice-President Lu Hsiu-lien were shot at and slightly wounded in an incident which the opposition claimed had been staged. A coalition, led by the former ruling Kuomintang (Nationalist Party), narrowly retained control of the Legislative *Yuan* in December elections.

Death penalty
The death penalty remained in effect for a range of crimes. Three executions were carried out by civilian authorities, continuing a downward trend.

The government made no move to introduce a moratorium on executions. Proposed amendments to the Criminal Code to restrict the scope of the death penalty did not progress in the *Yuan*.

A draft law "to counter terror activities" was proposed which, if passed, would introduce a new group of crimes, including attempted crimes, for which the death penalty could be imposed.

🗁 The 10th retrial of Liu Bing-lang, Su Chien-ho and Chuang Lin-hsun, known as the "Hsichih Trio" – was continuing at the end of the year.

🗁 The Council of Grand Justices granted death row inmate Hsu Tzu-chiang another chance to file an extraordinary appeal to the Supreme Court in July. Hsu Tzu-chiang had been sentenced to death in 2000 for kidnapping and murder. One of the two alleged accomplices provided a signed statement retracting his earlier testimony and stating that Hsu Tzu-chiang had not been involved in the crime.

Legislation
In July, the Legal Aid Foundation was established to implement the new Legal Aid Law and improve access to justice for poorer members of society.

Major human rights reforms announced by President Chen in previous years made slow progress. Laws establishing a Human Rights Commission and incorporating international standards into national law had still not been approved by the end of 2004.

In August, the *Yuan* passed the 3-19 Shooting Truth Investigation Special Commission Act. The Act, passed in response to the shootings of the President and Vice-President in March, established a Commission to conduct an investigation into the incident. There were concerns that the Commission was not subject to any judicial or executive supervision and was authorized to suspend the majority of civil liberties during its investigation. In December, the Council of Grand Justices ruled that parts of the Act were unconstitutional. At the end of the year, the political parties were discussing the implications of this ruling.

Discrimination

Indigenous people were subjected to discrimination in employment in cities. The unemployment rate among indigenous people was 15 per cent – compared to an average of four per cent for the population as a whole – and 48 per cent received less than a third of the average wage.

Women's rights groups continued to press for the establishment of a designated position in the cabinet with responsibility for the protection of women's rights, and for national law to be brought into line with the UN Women's Convention.

Refugees and asylum-seekers

Draft legislation to address the lack of formal asylum procedures, which had been announced in August 2003, made no progress in 2004. People who entered Taiwan illegally, particularly those from China, were often held indefinitely in detention centres.

TAJIKISTAN

REPUBLIC OF TAJIKISTAN
Head of state: Imomali Rakhmonov
Head of government: Akil Akilov
Death penalty: retentionist
International Criminal Court: ratified
UN Women's Convention: ratified
Optional Protocol to UN Women's Convention: signed

At least four men were executed in secret, days before a moratorium on death sentences and executions took effect from 30 April. The location of graves of executed prisoners remained secret, thus subjecting the relatives to continued cruel and inhuman treatment. Reports of torture and ill-treatment by police, and of impunity for such violations, continued.

Background

Many independent journalists alleged harassment and intimidation by the authorities and that the perpetrators enjoyed impunity. The publication of several independent newspapers was suspended, allegedly for political reasons.

The European Union and Tajikistan signed a Partnership and Cooperation Agreement (PCA) in October which included a commitment to cooperate in the protection of human rights. In addition, an Interim Agreement on trade and trade-related matters was signed pending the ratification of the PCA.

Russia opened a military base in Tajikistan in October.

Torture, ill-treatment and impunity

AI continued to receive reports of torture and ill-treatment, including in cases of alleged Islamists. In a large majority of cases there were allegedly no thorough and impartial investigations conducted and the perpetrators enjoyed impunity. The death penalty moratorium was particularly welcome in this respect as torture and ill-treatment, including to extract "confessions", had in many cases played a crucial role in cases resulting in death sentences.

⌐ Vladimir Vasilchikov, Viktor Dudenkov and Elena Dudenkova – Viktor Dudenkov's wife – all members of the Awakening Baptist Church in the town of Nurek, were believed to have been ill-treated by police at the local Department of Internal Affairs between 16 and 23 June. They had been summoned for investigations into the case of Vladimir Vasilchikov's mother, Mariya Vasilchikova, who was last seen in June 2002. While no formal charges were brought, police accused the two men of having killed her. Elena Dudenkova was reportedly insulted, forced to stand up for several hours and denied food and drink. The men, who consistently maintained their innocence, alleged they were pressurized into signing "confessions". Following complaints by both men to the General Procuracy, they were examined by doctors at the Republican Centre of Forensic Medicine in the capital, Dushanbe. On 25 June the doctors concluded that both men were suffering from concussion and other head injuries. Both had to be hospitalized for two weeks. In August the procuracy of Khatlon region closed the investigation into the allegations of ill-treatment as it had found "no sign of a crime" and the General Procuracy confirmed this conclusion in October.

Death penalty

President Imomali Rakhmonov declared a moratorium on death sentences and executions on 30 April. A new law, brought into force in July, set the maximum penalty in the Criminal Code at 25 years' imprisonment. However, in November parliament voted in favour of a draft law increasing the maximum penalty to life imprisonment. This law had not come into force by the end of 2004.

Relatives of those executed before the moratorium still had no right to know the location of the graves. According to domestic law, "[t]he body [of an executed prisoner] shall not be given out for burial, and the burial place shall not be disclosed."

Executions only days before the moratorium was declared brought to at least seven the number of executions carried out despite interventions by the UN Human Rights Committee. By proceeding with the executions Tajikistan violated its obligations as a party to the first Optional Protocol to the International Covenant on Civil and Political Rights (ICCPR).

In August the Human Rights Committee ruled that serious violations of Tajikistan's obligations under the ICCPR had taken place in the cases of Gaybullojon Saidov and Bakhrom Khomidov, in particular that the men's trials were unfair and that their "confessions" had been extracted under torture. Gaybullojon Saidov was executed in April 2001 despite an intervention by the Committee requesting a stay of execution. Bakhrom Khomidov's death sentence was commuted to 25 years' imprisonment by the Supreme Court in September 2004.

◻ At least four men were executed in secret in April. The Human Rights Committee had intervened on behalf of two of them – Rachabmurod Chumayev and Umed Idiyev – urging Tajikistan to stay the executions while the Committee considered allegations that the men's trials had been unfair and that they were tortured. They had been sentenced to death in February 2003 on charges including "terrorism" and murder.

AI country reports/visits
Reports
- Europe and Central Asia: Summary of Amnesty International's concerns in the region, January-June 2004: Tajikistan (AI Index: EUR 01/005/2004)
- Belarus and Uzbekistan: The last executioners – The trend towards abolition in the former Soviet space (AI Index: EUR 04/009/2004)

TANZANIA

UNITED REPUBLIC OF TANZANIA
Head of state: Benjamin Mkapa
Head of government: Frederick Sumaye
Head of Zanzibar government: Amani Abeid Karume
Death penalty: retentionist
International Criminal Court: ratified
UN Women's Convention: ratified
Optional Protocol to UN Women's Convention: not signed

Large numbers of asylum-seekers from Burundi and Rwanda were denied adequate protection of their refugee rights. They were required to stay in refugee camps where conditions were poor, were often threatened with forcible return, and in some cases were forcibly returned. Violence against women was a major human rights concern, including the practice of female genital mutilation. Zanzibar enacted a harsh new law against gay and lesbian people. Prison conditions were severe. Several death sentences were imposed, leaving at least 387 people under sentence of death at the end of 2004. There were no executions.

Zanzibar
Reconciliation (*Muafaka*) talks continued between the ruling Chama Cha Mapinduzi (Party of the Revolution, CCM) and the opposition Civic United Front (CUF). This helped to control political tensions in semi-autonomous Zanzibar. Some electoral reforms were implemented in anticipation of elections due in October 2005. A youth and a CCM militia leader were killed in Pemba island where there were several incidents of pre-election violence in December.

In August, Zanzibar abolished the legal penalty of corporal punishment, still applied on the mainland. Some other issues of legal and judicial reform in Zanzibar were not addressed.

Violence against women
Female genital mutilation continued to be widely practised in several regions, despite a 1998 law criminalizing this harmful traditional practice for girls under 18 and imposing a penalty of up to 15 years' imprisonment. No prosecutions were reported, but there were extensive awareness-raising and campaigning activities by non-governmental organizations.

Killings of elderly women accused of witchcraft were still reported. Local leaders were among 20 people charged with murdering women they said were witches in Iringa district in the south in August.

Freedom of association and expression
Activities of opposition parties, non-governmental organizations and the privately owned media were still restricted in Zanzibar, where the government continued to deny registration to the Zanzibar Association for Human Rights. International and national media groups criticized the 2003 Media Regulation Act for failing to protect media rights sufficiently.

Laws against lesbian and gay people
A law enacted in Zanzibar in August created the new offences of "lesbianism", punishable by up to five years' imprisonment, and of entering into, arranging, celebrating or living in a same-sex marriage or union, punishable by up to seven years in prison. The maximum penalty for a male homosexual act continued to be a five-year prison term.

The Penal Code of the United Republic of Tanzania, applicable on the mainland, continued to provide a maximum penalty of 14 years' imprisonment for a male homosexual act. Sexual acts between women were not criminalized.

There were no known arrests under these laws in 2004 or recent years.

'Terrorism' trial
The trial of a suspect in the 1998 bombing of the US embassy in the capital, Dar es Salaam, in which 11 Tanzanians were killed, concluded in late 2004 with the acquittal of the accused.

Human rights commission

The Commission for Human Rights and Good Governance continued its public inquiry into evictions and police brutality in Serengeti district in 2001.

Death penalty

Several death sentences for murder were reported during the year. In August, 389 people, including two in Zanzibar, were under sentence of death, following presidential commutation of 100 sentences in April 2002. There had been no executions in Tanzania since 1995. Prisoners on death row were held in virtual solitary confinement, with permanent artificial lighting for 24 hours a day, and allowed religious books only. They were reported to be frequently abused and intimidated by guards. Food and medical treatment were poor.

At the end of December, 16 prisoners on death row in Ukonga prison in Dar es Salaam had been on hunger strike for two weeks, started in protest at beatings and harsh conditions.

Refugees

During the year, Tanzanian officials, reportedly in cooperation with Burundian officials, urged the estimated 700,000 Burundian refugees in Tanzania to return home. After fleeing Burundi between 1972 and 2004, about half of them were living in sites for refugees. Officials sometimes threatened refugees with forcible return if they did not go voluntarily. Security concerns in Burundi, conflicts over land ownership, limited access to education, health and housing, and the slow pace of political transition and army reform discouraged many from returning. According to reports, more than 90,000 refugees returned voluntarily during 2004 but some were forced to return, such as 68 Burundians in Ngara region in October.

Rwandese refugees were no longer given refugee status by the Tanzanian government. For those who met the criteria for recognition as refugees, the Office of the UN High Commissioner for Refugees (UNHCR) was able to provide international protection under its mandate. Fewer than 200 UNHCR-recognized Rwandese refugees remained in Tanzania. Some of the hundreds who dispersed across the countryside during the repatriation of Rwandese refugees in 2002 and 2003 returned unofficially to the refugee camps. Without official registration or ration cards, they faced a precarious existence.

AI country reports/ visits
Visits

AI representatives visited Tanzania to conduct research on the treatment of Burundian and Rwandese asylum-seekers and to launch a report about Rwandese refugees in the Great Lakes region (see Rwanda entry).

THAILAND

KINGDOM OF THAILAND
Head of state: King Bhumibol Adulyadej
Head of government: Thaksin Shinawatra
Death penalty: retentionist
International Criminal Court: signed
UN Women's Convention: ratified with reservations
Optional Protocol to UN Women's Convention: ratified

Violence erupted in the four Muslim-majority southern provinces in January, when members of a Muslim armed group attacked an army base. In the course of the year over 500 people were killed in the southern provinces. At least three human rights defenders were killed or "disappeared". The deaths of over 2,000 people in a government-sponsored anti-drugs campaign in 2003 were not properly investigated, reinforcing a climate of impunity among the security forces. The government registered over one million migrant workers in July but many of them were denied basic labour rights. Some 900 people were reported to be under sentence of death. No executions were known to have taken place. Over 5,000 people in Thailand were killed by the tsunami that struck Indian Ocean countries on 26 December. Hundreds of migrant workers from Myanmar were reportedly killed but not included in official casualty figures. Other workers from Myanmar were arrested and harassed by the security forces, and hundreds went into hiding as a result.

Violence in the south

Prime Minister Thaksin Shinawatra extended existing martial law provisions in some areas of Narathiwat, Yala and Pattani provinces in the south of the country after an upsurge in violence which began in January. During the year over 500 people were killed, including civilians, civil servants, members of the security forces and members of armed groups.

On 28 April, 11 police outposts and stations were attacked by Muslim men, mostly armed with knives and a few firearms. Five policemen were killed. The security forces retaliated by opening fire on the attackers, killing over 100 of them.

In October a group of Muslims gathered in front of Tak Bai police station, Narathiwat Province, protesting against the detention of six people for allegedly passing weapons to insurgents. When demonstrators threw rocks and attempted to storm the police station, security forces used tear gas and gunfire in response.

Human rights violations

🗀 In March, Somchai Neelaijaipit, a prominent Muslim lawyer who campaigned for an end to martial law and was representing five Muslim men who had been tortured after their arrest in Narathiwat Province, "disappeared" in Bangkok. Five policemen were arrested in connection with the "disappearance" and released on bail pending court hearings.

🗁 On 28 April, 32 Muslim men were killed by security forces using heavy weapons at Krue Se Mosque, Pattani Province, following an attack on a police station. A government-appointed commission investigated the incident, reportedly finding that the security forces had used force disproportionate to the threat, although their report was not made public. The attacks on 10 other police stations and the security forces' response were not known to have been independently investigated.

🗁 In October at Tak Bai police station at least six demonstrators were killed and some 1,300 arrested and transported to an army base where many were beaten. At least 78 of them died, reportedly as a result of overcrowding during the journey and ill-treatment. The vast majority were released without charge after interrogation, but 58 were charged with unlawful gathering. The government appointed an 11-member commission to conduct an investigation. They reported their findings to the government in December, but the findings were not made public. No one was known to have been brought to justice for the killings.

Abuses by armed opposition groups
Attacks against government officials and installations by unidentified armed groups continued in the south.

🗁 In September, Rapin Ruankaew, a provincial judge, was shot dead by unknown armed men on motorcycles while he was driving to work in Pattani town.

🗁 In November, Ran Tulae, a Buddhist village headman, was killed by an unknown group in Narathiwat Province. A note left near his severed head claimed revenge for the October deaths of demonstrators at Tak Bai police station.

Human rights defenders
At least three human rights defenders were killed or "disappeared" during 2004. In July the Minister of Justice announced that a list of human rights defenders at risk would be compiled and protection provided. However, the government was not known to have initiated independent investigations into abuses against human rights defenders.

🗁 In June environmental activist Charoen Wat-aksorn was killed by unknown assailants after filing a complaint with a Senate committee. He was a small-scale fisherman who had led a campaign against the construction of a coal-fired power plant in Ba Nok district, Prachuab Kiri Khan Province, on the Gulf of Thailand. By the end of 2004 no one was known to have been brought to justice for his killing.

In March the UN Secretary-General's Special Representative on human rights defenders reported the findings of her visit in May 2003. Her report included a recommendation that the government reassess its approach to the rights to peaceful protest and freedom of assembly.

Refugees and migrant workers
Some 142,000 Karen and Karenni refugees from Myanmar remained in camps on the border. Hundreds of other refugees from Myanmar were resettled to third countries.

Small numbers of refugees, most of them members of the Hmong ethnic minority, entered Thailand fleeing armed conflict between Hmong armed groups and the Lao army (see Laos entry). Some 4,500 Hmong refugees living at Wat Thamkrabok, a Buddhist temple in Saraburi Province, were resettled to third countries during 2004.

Over one million migrant workers from Laos, Cambodia and Myanmar were registered by the government in July. Registration allowed them to work legally for one year in some sectors of the economy. However, many of them were denied basic labour rights, most notably a legal minimum wage set by the government.

Impunity
The deaths of over 2,000 people in a 2003 government-sponsored anti-drugs campaign were not properly investigated, reinforcing a climate of impunity among the security forces. No one was known to have been brought to justice for the killings of Muslims in the southern provinces by security forces in April and October 2004.

In September the government told AI that there had been no extrajudicial killings during the 2003 "drugs war". They also said that the use of deadly force by the security forces in the south was strictly legal in all cases.

Prisoner of conscience
Sok Yoeun, a Cambodian prisoner of conscience and refugee held in Thailand since 1999, was released in March and resettled to a third country.

Death penalty
Some 900 people were reported to be under sentence of death, many held continuously in shackles. No executions were known to have taken place during the year.

AI country reports/visits
Report
· Thailand: Memorandum on human rights concerns (AI Index: ASA 39/013/2004)
Visits
AI delegates visited Thailand in April/May, May/June, July, and in November/December.

TIMOR-LESTE

DEMOCRATIC REPUBLIC OF TIMOR-LESTE
Head of state: Jose Alexandre "Xanana" Gusmão
Head of government: Dr Marí Bim Amude Alkatiri
Death penalty: abolitionist for all crimes
International Criminal Court: acceded
UN Women's Convention and its Optional Protocol: acceded

Progress towards the rule of law and the protection and promotion of human rights was undermined by weaknesses in key institutions. These weaknesses led to unlawful arrests and detention, delays in the justice system, infringements of freedom of expression and association, and effective impunity for police accused of human rights violations. Prosecutions of serious crimes committed in 1999 continued amidst uncertainty about the future of the process.

Background

The mandate of the UN Mission of Support in East Timor (UNMISET) was extended in May and again in November for a further and final six months. This reflected the view that, despite steady progress in its institution-building efforts, Timor-Leste had not yet reached the critical threshold of self-sufficiency. Dissatisfaction among former combatants, high unemployment and poverty increased the challenge of building a cohesive and stable democracy. A law establishing the office of Provedor for Human Rights and Justice (Ombudsman), with a mandate to monitor activities of the police, military and other government agencies and to promote and protect human rights, was promulgated but no appointment was made.

Police

The National Police Service of Timor-Leste (PNTL) continued to lack training, professionalism, effective supervision and accountability. Reported violations by the PNTL included frequent use of excessive force, misuse of firearms, arbitrary arrests and over 45 alleged assaults on suspects during arrest or in custody. Suspects were often unlawfully detained beyond the permitted 72 hours, sometimes apparently for punitive reasons.

In a rare case, four officers were convicted in May of ill-treating detainees, but most cases were referred to under-resourced internal procedures and few resulted in effective disciplinary action or prosecution.

Justice system

Courts outside the capital, Dili, were mostly inoperative. Pre-trial detainees were frequently imprisoned beyond the expiry of judicial detention warrants. Delays and limited capacity throughout the legal system obstructed access to justice and perpetuated reliance on "traditional" justice mechanisms, where fair trial standards were not guaranteed.

Violence against women

Widespread sexual and domestic violence constituted a significant proportion of reported crimes but was largely perceived as a matter to be resolved privately or through "traditional" justice mechanisms, where women were at particular risk of discrimination. Although improvements were noted, the relatively few cases brought to court were subject to delays and were sometimes dealt with insensitively.

Freedom of expression and association

Individuals allegedly linked to dissident groups were subject to arrest and detention on uncertain legal grounds. Although the Constitution guarantees freedom of expression, some were charged with disseminating or expressing hostility, hatred or contempt towards the government. Police used excessive force in dispersing demonstrations. In December parliament passed the Law on Freedom of Assembly and Demonstrations, which threatens to inhibit the right to peaceful assembly.

◻ In September, two men were arrested and charged for raising an Indonesian flag.

◻ In July, police used tear gas to disperse a largely peaceful demonstration and arrested 31 people on unclear charges. They were released late the next day.

Past human rights violations

By the end of the year, 74 individuals had been convicted and two acquitted of serious crimes, including crimes against humanity, in connection with the independence ballot in 1999. A total of 391 had been indicted since 2000, of whom 304 were people residing in Indonesia. Indonesia continued to refuse to transfer suspects for trial. Pursuant to a UN Security Council resolution, Serious Crimes Unit investigations concluded in November and Special Panels trials must conclude by May 2005. Trials for 13 defendants remained pending before the Special Panels at the end of the year.

The Indonesia and Timor-Leste governments announced the establishment of a bilateral Truth and Friendship Commission. Although the terms of reference had not been finalized, there were concerns that it might provide impunity for perpetrators of serious crimes committed in Timor-Leste in 1999.

AI country reports/visits
Report
· Indonesia and Timor-Leste: Justice for Timor-Leste — the way forward (AI Index: ASA 21/006/2004)
Visit
An AI delegate visited Timor-Leste in May.

TOGO

TOGOLESE REPUBLIC
Head of state: Gnassingbé Eyadéma
Head of government: Koffi Sama
Death penalty: abolitionist in practice
International Criminal Court: not signed
UN Women's Convention: ratified
Optional Protocol to UN Women's Convention: not signed

There was continuing concern about the safety of military officers held in Lomé civil prison. Harassment of human rights defenders was reported. Widespread torture and ill-treatment continued to be reported. Little progress was made in improving the human rights situation in the country, despite pressure from the European Union (EU) to release prisoners of conscience and adopt new legislation on the press.

Background
In April, the EU began a six-month consultation process with Togo under the Cotonou Agreement. The Agreement provides for the suspension of cooperation with a country if it fails to respect human rights, democratic principles and the rule of law; the EU had suspended cooperation with Togo since 1993.

In April, the Togolese authorities gave 22 undertakings to the EU. They committed to resume "national dialogue with the traditional opposition and civil society"; to prevent and punish extrajudicial killings, torture and other forms of cruel, inhuman or degrading treatment; to release political prisoners; to reform the justice system; to revise the press and communication code; and to ensure that the media, non-governmental organizations and civil society representatives were not harassed, censored or intimidated. While recognizing that "a significant number of measures had been taken by the Togolese authorities", the EU stated in November that "a number of points continue to give rise to concern especially as regards the restoration of democracy". As a consequence the European Council decided that full cooperation with the EU would resume "once free and fair elections have been held".

Freedom of expression
In August, the National Assembly adopted a new code of press and communication. Prison sentences were abolished for several offences including causing offence to the President of the Republic, the President of the National Assembly and other senior establishment figures; and defamation. The new code provides instead for heavy fines of up to 5 million CFA francs (Communauté Financière Africaine francs, approximately US$10,000). Pre-trial detention remained possible for a limited number of offences.

Access was restored to several Internet sites which had previously been censored.

People raising concerns about the human rights situation in Togo were harassed and intimidated, despite the legal reforms and undertakings given to the EU.

◻ In April, Yves Kpeto, a journalist at *Nana FM* radio, was severely beaten by security forces during a demonstration in Lomé.

◻ In October, Dimas Dzikodo, Publishing Director of newly created weekly *Le Forum de la semaine*, received anonymous threats after the publication of an opinion piece denouncing embezzlement by the head of state and his family.

◻ In July during a public radio interview, the President of the National Assembly called the Togolese League of Human Rights (Ligue togolaise des droits de l'homme) "delinquents" after the International Federation for Human Rights (Fédération internationale des ligues des droits de l'homme) released a report on the human rights situation in the country.

Releases
Dozens of prisoners of conscience and people who had been arbitrarily detained were released throughout the year. Other common law prisoners who had spent prolonged periods of time in detention were also released as part of the authorities' efforts to fulfil the undertakings given to the EU.

◻ Prisoners of conscience Marc Palanga and Boboli Panamnéwé, both members of the Union of Forces for Change (Union des forces du changement, UFC), were released in May. The two men had been arrested in February 2003 and sentenced by a court in Kara, northern Togo, in May 2004 to 12 months' imprisonment (with five months suspended) for violence against public authorities. They were arrested solely on account of their peaceful involvement with the UFC.

◻ Marc Atidépé and Kokou Alowou were released in July after spending 11 years in detention without trial. They had been held since 1993 on suspicion of being members of an armed group.

◻ Seven out of a group of nine refugees arrested in Ghana in 1997 and handed over to the Togolese authorities were released in August, after seven years in detention without trial in Kara. The two others had died in detention in previous years.

Arbitrary detention of military officers
Dozens of military officers arrested in May 2003 remained in detention without trial in Lomé civil prison throughout the year. A mission mandated by the EU to verify the implementation of the undertakings given by the Togolese authorities was denied access to this group of detainees while visiting Lomé civil prison. It was unclear whether charges had been brought against them. They were apparently accused of plotting against the state.

Deaths in custody
◻ In January, Komi Kouma Tengué reportedly died after three days in incommunicado detention (*garde à vue*) in the police station in Kévé. The police authorities

claimed he drowned. However, a medical report indicated that he died from a violent blow. His family claimed he died as a result of torture.

🗁 Lieutenant Kpandang and Yao Mensah, two of the military officers detained in Lomé civil prison since May 2003, died in detention. Reports suggested that their deaths may have been linked to harsh prison conditions and inadequate medical treatment.

Torture, ill-treatment and harsh conditions of detention

Torture and ill-treatment remained widespread. Former prisoners reported that they had been tortured by the security forces, especially during pre-trial detention, and held in harsh conditions in Lomé and Kara civil prisons. No action was known to have been taken to hold to account those responsible for torturing and ill-treating detainees and no measures were known to have been taken to improve conditions of detention in Togo.

Arrest of returned asylum-seekers

There were reports that security forces arrested returned asylum-seekers on their arrival in Togo. Some were released after a few days while others remained in unlawful detention for several weeks.

AI country reports/ visits
Report
· Préoccupations d'une coalition d'ONG sur la situation des droits de l'homme au Togo (AI Index: AFR 57/001/2004)

TRINIDAD AND TOBAGO

REPUBLIC OF TRINIDAD AND TOBAGO
Head of state: George Maxwell Richards
Head of government: Patrick Manning
Death penalty: retentionist
International Criminal Court: ratified
UN Women's Convention: ratified
Optional Protocol to UN Women's Convention: not signed

Prison conditions remained poor and in some instances amounted to cruel, inhuman and degrading treatment. Death sentences continued to be imposed. There were continuing reports of torture and ill-treatment by the police.

Abuses by police
Torture and ill-treatment by police continued to be reported. At least 24 people were fatally shot by police.

🗁 In January, Kevin Cato was shot dead by police officers reportedly after he intervened in an altercation between officers and his friends. A police officer was charged with murder.

🗁 In April, Galene Bonadie was shot by police in disputed circumstances. Eyewitnesses alleged that she attempted to intervene as police officers beat a man and was then shot in the head. Police officers stated that she was shot while attempting to take a gun from a police officer. In June the Director of Public Prosecutions ordered an inquest. The inquest opened in December but was adjourned until 2005.

Death penalty
In July, the Judicial Committee of the Privy Council in the UK, the highest court of appeal for Trinidad and Tobago, overturned its own 2004 ruling in the case of Balkissoon Roodal that the mandatory death penalty was in violation of the Constitution.

The mandatory death penalty therefore continued to be the only sentence available for those convicted of murder. However, the court commuted the sentences of all 86 prisoners then under sentence of death to terms of imprisonment on the grounds that they had expected to benefit from the previous ruling.

Death sentences continued to be imposed. At least three people had been sentenced to death by the end of 2004 but no executions had been carried out.

Abuses in detention
Conditions in places of detention continued to cause grave concern and in some cases amounted to cruel, inhuman and degrading treatment. A task force on prison reform announced in 2003 failed to address the vast majority of problems.

In April, after the government granted an AI delegation unrestricted access to all the major prisons of Trinidad, delegates witnessed appalling conditions of detention in Port of Spain Prison and Golden Grove Remand Prison. Both suffered from severe overcrowding and prisoners were forced to defecate and urinate into containers and then place the human waste in buckets outside the cells. Cells of approximately 3m x 3m contained up to 17 prisoners.

Violence in prisons persisted. In October Kern Phillips was stabbed to death by another prisoner. In September, Ignatius Owen died after allegedly being beaten by other inmates. Both men were held at Golden Grove Remand Prison.

Corporal punishment

Laws allowing corporal punishment for crimes including rape remained. No known sentences of flogging were imposed. The government informed AI that corporal punishment had not been imposed on any prisoner since 2002.

AI country reports/ visits
Visit
An AI delegation visited Trinidad in April and met the Minister of National Security and the Acting Commissioner of Prisons.

TUNISIA

REPUBLIC OF TUNISIA
Head of state: Zine El 'Abidine Ben 'Ali
Head of government: Mohamed Ghannouchi
Death penalty: abolitionist in practice
International Criminal Court: not signed
UN Women's Convention: ratified with reservations
Optional Protocol to UN Women's Convention: not signed

Scores of political prisoners, including prisoners of conscience, were released. Dozens of people were sentenced to lengthy prison terms following unfair trials on "terrorism"-related charges. Torture and ill-treatment continued to be reported. Hundreds of political prisoners, including prisoners of conscience, remained in prison. Many had been held for more than a decade. Solitary confinement and denial of medical care in prisons continued to be reported despite recommendations for improvements in conditions in prisons and detention centres made by a government-appointed commission of inquiry in early 2003. Freedom of expression and association continued to be severely restricted.

Background

On 24 October, Zine El 'Abidine Ben 'Ali was elected President for the fourth consecutive time. According to official figures, he received nearly 95 per cent of votes cast. His party, the Democratic Constitutional Rally (Rassemblement constitutionnel démocratique, RCD), won 152 of the 189 seats in the Chamber of Deputies. Amendments to the electoral code introduced in 2003 restricted the use of the media to national public channels, which were dominated by the government, thus severely limiting the electoral campaign of the opposition. There were reports that harassment and intimidation of political opponents and activists as well as known critics of the government intensified in the run-up to the elections. Among those targeted were Hamma Hammami, head of the unauthorized Tunisian Workers' Communist Party (Parti communiste des ouvriers tunisiens, PCOT), who was physically assaulted by men believed to be plain-clothes police officers, and Moncef Marzouki, President of the unauthorized Republican Congress (Congrès pour la République), who was stopped at the airport and interrogated by police.

In January new laws were introduced to establish stricter controls on migrants. Tighter controls of Tunisia's territorial waters and of ships that could be used to carry migrants to Europe illegally were established. Changes to travel documents and measures to deal with criminal networks suspected of involvement in people trafficking were also introduced. Arrests of hundreds of migrants being trafficked to Europe were reported during the year. Scores of migrants also reportedly died during attempts to cross the Mediterranean to Europe.

Releases of political prisoners

At least 79 political prisoners, including prisoners of conscience, were conditionally released in November. Most had been imprisoned for over a decade because they were members or sympathizers of the unauthorized Islamist movement, Ennahda (Renaissance). They were arrested, tortured and imprisoned after grossly unfair trials in the early 1990s. Those released were predominantly prisoners whose sentences would shortly have been completed.

Violence against women

A law on manners and sexual harassment was promulgated in August, amending Article 226 of the Penal Code. The law extends the definition of sexual harassment to words, gestures or actions that undermine a person's dignity and feelings. It increases penalties for sexual harassment at work or in public places to one year in prison and a fine of 3,000 dinar (around US$ 2,430). This penalty is doubled if the victim is a child or a mentally or physically vulnerable individual. Women's rights activists welcomed the law but expressed concern that it linked sexual harassment to safeguarding manners, lacked an adequate definition of harassment and did not contain adequate provisions for investigating allegations.

'War on terror': unfair trials and other violations

At least 15 people were charged under the new "anti-terrorism" law introduced in December 2003. Concerns persisted about the law, which allows for the extension of pre-trial detention for an undefined period and lacks safeguards in relation to people facing extradition to countries where they could face serious human rights violations.

▢ Adil Rahali, aged 27, was deported from Ireland in April after his application for asylum was refused. He was arrested on arrival in Tunisia and taken to the State Security Department of the Ministry of the Interior where he was held in secret detention for several days and reportedly tortured. Adil Rahali, who had worked in Europe for more than a decade, was charged under the 2003 "anti-terrorism" law with belonging to a "terrorist" organization operating abroad. The organization was not named and no details were provided about the exact nature of its activities. His lawyer filed a complaint about the allegation of torture, but no investigation was known to have been initiated by the end of the year. Adil Rahali was scheduled to be tried in February 2005.

Dozens of people were sentenced to lengthy prison terms following unfair trials on "terrorism"-related charges. In the cases highlighted below, the defendants were not charged under the 2003 "anti-terrorism" law because their arrests predated the law's introduction.

▢ In April, seven young men were convicted, following an unfair trial, of membership of a "terrorist" organization, possessing or manufacturing explosives, theft, using banned websites and holding unauthorized meetings. Two others were convicted in absentia. They were among dozens of people arrested in Zarzis, southern Tunisia, in February 2003, most of whom had been released the same month.

The trial failed to respect international fair trial standards. According to defence lawyers, most arrest dates in police reports were falsified, and in one case the place of arrest was falsified. There were no investigations into allegations that the defendants were beaten, suspended from the ceiling and threatened with rape. The convictions rested almost entirely on confessions extracted under duress. The defendants denied all charges brought against them in court.

In July the Tunis Appeal Court reduced the sentences of six of them from 19 years and three months to 13 years' imprisonment. Their appeal was rejected by the Court of Cassation in December. Another defendant, who was a minor at the time of the arrest, had his sentence reduced to 24 months in prison.

▢ In June, 13 students were sentenced, following an unfair trial, to prison terms of between four years and 16 years and three months plus up to 10 years' administrative control; one student was tried in absentia. The students, most of whom were originally from Ariana, were convicted of "terrorism"-related charges. Arrested on 14 and 15 February 2003, all stated in court that their statements had been extracted under torture while held by the State Security Department of the Ministry of the Interior. The prosecution case rested almost exclusively on the

confessions. No investigation was carried out into the allegations of torture. Their appeal was postponed until January 2005.

Freedom of expression

Human rights' and journalists' organizations accused the authorities of stifling press freedom and seeking even tighter government control of the press, contrary to assurances given by the authorities that measures would be introduced to safeguard freedom of expression. Internet access was routinely blocked and e-mails addressed to certain e-mail accounts never reached the intended recipient.

▢ In January the Ministry of the Interior again refused to give authorization for a printed version of the weekly on-line magazine *Kalima*. Under Tunisian law, those seeking to issue a printed publication are required to deposit a declaration and should automatically receive a receipt from the Ministry of the Interior. Printers cannot legally print a publication without this receipt. The authorities gave no reason for withholding the receipt for *Kalima*.

In August the government promulgated a law on data protection which the authorities said was intended to protect personal privacy. However, its apparent effect was to prevent journalists, writers and non-governmental organizations from using personal data for publication without authorization while imposing no restrictions on the personal data that can be held and used by the authorities. The law also established a national commission with ultimate authority over data protection issues. The commission's annual reports are submitted to the President and not made public.

Human rights activists and organizations

The authorities gave no reason for withholding recognition from several human rights organizations that had been asking to be legalized for several years. Among these organizations were the International Association for the Support of Political Prisoners, the Association to Combat Torture in Tunisia, the National Council for Liberties, and the Centre for the Independence of the Judiciary. Members of such non-governmental organizations reported harassment and intimidation by the police.

▢ In June the founders of the Association to Combat Torture in Tunisia were beaten by police as they attempted to register the organization. The authorities had repeatedly refused to register the organization without giving a reason. Three leading members – Radhia Nasraoui, Ali Ben Salem and Ridha Barakati – went to the office of the Governor of Tunis District and insisted on meeting the official in charge. After a six-hour sit-in, the three were assaulted by men believed to be plain-clothes police officers after they were forcibly removed from the office.

Torture and ill-treatment in prison

Overcrowding in prisons and discriminatory treatment of political prisoners continued to be reported. There was continuing concern about lack of medical care, poor hygiene, torture and ill-treatment in prisons.

Dozens of political prisoners continued to be held in prolonged solitary confinement in tiny cells. Some had been held in solitary confinement for more than a decade, in violation of both Tunisian law and international standards. Prisoners often staged prolonged hunger strikes to protest against their conditions of detention.

In June political prisoner Nabil El-Ouaer, held in Borj Er-Roumi prison in Tunis, alleged that he was beaten and placed in a punishment cell and that four criminal prisoners were let into his cell late at night in order to sexually assault and rape him. After the assault, he was transferred to Rabta Hospital in Tunis without explanation. He was transferred between three prisons in a period of one month, apparently in an attempt by the authorities to keep the incident quiet. He was reported to be psychologically distressed as a result of the assault. Despite several requests by his lawyer for an independent criminal inquiry into the assault, no investigation was carried out. In November, he was conditionally released from prison together with scores of other political prisoners. Nabil El-Ouaer had been imprisoned since 1992 following an unfair trial before a military tribunal.

Death in custody

Badreddine Reguii, aged 29, died in Bouchoucha prison in Tunis on 8 February. Police informed the family that he had committed suicide. The family called for a further investigation as the original investigation failed to establish the cause of extensive bruising on his body and a deep wound on his back.

AI country reports/ visits
Statements
- Tunisia: Amnesty International calls for greater respect for human rights as President Ben 'Ali is re-elected (AI Index: MDE 30/007/2004)
- Tunisia: Release of scores of political prisoners is positive step (AI Index: MDE 30/009/2004)

TURKEY

REPUBLIC OF TURKEY
Head of state: Ahmet Necdet Sezer
Head of government: Recep Tayyip Erdoğan
Death penalty: abolitionist for all crimes
International Criminal Court: not signed
UN Women's Convention and its Optional Protocol: ratified

The government introduced further legal and other reforms with the aim of bringing Turkish law into line with international standards. However, implementation of these reforms was patchy and broad restrictions on the exercise of fundamental rights remained in law. Despite positive changes to detention regulations, torture and ill-treatment by security forces continued. The use of excessive force against demonstrators remained a serious concern. Those responsible for such violations were rarely brought to justice. Those who attempted to exercise their right to demonstrate peacefully or express dissent on certain issues continued to face criminal prosecution or other sanctions. State officials failed to take adequate steps to prevent and punish violence against women.

Background

The government continued to introduce constitutional and legal reforms in order to fulfil the criteria required to begin accession negotiations with the European Union. On 17 December, the European Council declared that it intended to start these negotiations with Turkey in October 2005.

In January Turkey signed Protocol No. 13 of the European Convention on Human Rights and in April it signed the Second Optional Protocol of the International Covenant on Civil and Political Rights, aiming at the abolition of the death penalty.

In June, the Kurdistan People's Congress (Kongra Gel), successor to the Kurdistan Workers' Party (PKK), announced that it was ending its unilateral ceasefire. In the second half of the year there were many reports of clashes between members of the armed group and Turkish military and security forces in the south-east of the country.

During the year at least 33 people, 13 of them minors, were killed by landmines or abandoned ordnance. Many more were injured.

Law reform

Many significant changes were introduced in 2004. The State Security Courts were abolished and replaced with Special Felony Courts. International law was given precedence over domestic legislation. All references to the death penalty were removed from the Constitution and the Penal Code. Members of the army were removed from the Higher Education Council (YÖK) and the Higher Board for Radio and Television (RTÜK).

New legislation included a new Press Law, a new Law on Associations, a new Criminal Procedure Law and a new Penal Code. All of these laws contained positive developments and were often less restrictive than their predecessors. For example, the new Penal Code removed many articles which discriminated on grounds of gender and introduced a definition of torture that was closer to that laid down in international law. However, many of these new laws carried over provisions from the old ones that had been used to unnecessarily restrict fundamental rights. In addition, implementation of legislative changes was often uneven and in some cases appeared to be resisted by state officials.

A Law on Compensation of Losses Resulting from Terrorism and the Struggle with Terrorism was also passed which aimed to recompense individuals who had been forcibly displaced in the 1990s during the conflict between government forces and the PKK. Human rights groups expressed concern about the low level of compensation envisaged and suggested that the law was designed to prevent applications to the European Court of Human Rights.

Torture and ill-treatment

Detention regulations that provided better protection for detainees led to an apparent reduction in the use of some torture techniques, such as suspension by the arms and *falaka* (beatings on the soles of the feet). However, the regulations were often not fully implemented. Torture and ill-treatment in police and gendarmerie custody continued to be a serious concern with cases of beatings, electric shock, stripping naked and death threats being reported.

Torture methods which did not leave lasting marks on the detainee's body were also widely reported. Deprivation of food, water and sleep and making detainees stand in uncomfortable positions continued to be reported, despite a circular from the Minister of the Interior prohibiting the use of such techniques. In addition, people were beaten during arrest, while being driven around or after being taken to a deserted place for questioning.

◻ Derya Aksakal was reportedly pulled into a minibus as she was walking along the street in Istanbul on 3 March. She was then blindfolded and questioned about her political activities by three masked men, one of whom she recognized as a police officer. The men reportedly extinguished cigarettes on her body, threatened her with rape and subjected her to a mock execution before releasing her about two hours later.

◻ Aydın Ay was detained on suspicion of theft at Çarşı Police Station in Trabzon on 27 October. He alleged that he was stripped naked, given electric shocks and that his testicles were squeezed in order to make him sign documents without knowing the contents.

A high proportion of complaints of ill-treatment related to excessive use of force by the security forces during demonstrations. Despite a circular from the Minister of the Interior instructing officers not to use disproportionate force, there were continuing reports of protesters being beaten and sprayed with pepper gas even after they had been apprehended.

Impunity

There was a lack of effective mechanisms to monitor the implementation of detention regulations and investigate patterns of abuse by the security forces. The Provincial and Regional Human Rights Boards failed to investigate effectively complaints regarding incidents of torture or ill-treatment and did not demonstrate the necessary impartiality or independence.

Investigations into allegations of torture and ill-treatment by prosecutors were rarely adequate and usually resulted in a decision not to prosecute. The lack of thoroughness of such investigations brought into question their impartiality. Decisions were often based upon medical examinations of detainees which were themselves insufficient and often carried out in the presence of security officials, despite regulations forbidding this. Investigations, and subsequent trials, generally did not examine the chain of command and the accused officers were often not suspended from active duty during such proceedings.

Judicial proceedings against individuals accused of torture and ill-treatment were usually severely prolonged and as a result some prosecutions were halted as the statute of limitations had expired.

◻ On 10 November the Court of Appeal upheld the sentence of a police officer for involvement in the death of trade unionist Süleyman Yeter who died in police custody as a result of torture in March 1999. The trial court had reduced his 10-year sentence to four years and two months' imprisonment for "good conduct", of which he will have to serve only 20 months. Meanwhile, legal proceedings against nine police officers accused of having tortured Süleyman Yeter and 14 other detainees in another incident in 1997 were dropped when the statute of limitations expired on 11 November.

◻ On 2 December, the trial of four police officers for the torture including sexual torture of two high-school students in March 1999 in Iskenderun was postponed for the 30th time, despite the existence of medical reports corroborating the allegations. Meanwhile one of the students, Fatma Deniz Polattaş, remained in prison for membership of the PKK on the basis of statements allegedly extracted under torture.

Those who lodged complaints that the police had used excessive force during arrest or demonstrations were often charged with "resisting a public official by force and violence or threats" or violating Law No. 2911 on Meetings and Demonstrations.

◻ Student demonstrators detained on 12 April in Ankara were reportedly ill-treated by riot police who used excessive force to disperse and detain the protesters. The students were reportedly also ill-treated in the police station and at the courthouse. The judge presiding over the case ignored the complaints of ill-treatment and the students were charged with violating the Law on Meetings and Demonstrations but released pending trial.

Killings in disputed circumstances

Up to 21 civilians were reportedly shot dead by the security forces, many in the south-eastern and eastern provinces. In the majority of cases, the security forces said the victims had failed to heed orders to stop.

☐ Şiyar Perinçek, a suspected member of Kongra Gel, was shot by a plain-clothes police officer after being knocked off a motorcycle in the city of Adana on 28 May. Witnesses claimed that he was unarmed and no warning was issued. He died in hospital two days later. The driver of the motorcycle, Nurettin Başçı, was detained and reportedly tortured. On 4 October, three police officers went on trial for the "ill-treatment" of Nurettin Başçı; one officer was also charged with the "unintentional killing" of Şiyar Perinçek which the indictment alleges occurred after he was shot at by Şiyar Perinçek. The trial was continuing at the end of the year.

☐ Police officers shot dead Mehmet Kaymaz and his 12-year-old son Uğur outside their house in Kızıltepe on 21 November. The authorities claimed that they were armed members of Kongra Gel and that they had shot at police officers who returned fire. Witnesses alleged that it was an extrajudicial execution and that weapons were planted on them after they were killed.

Freedom of expression and human rights defenders

People were prosecuted for the peaceful expression of their opinions, although the Court of Appeal and some lower courts issued landmark judgements upholding the right to freedom of expression. Cases and investigations were opened against individuals because of their peaceful opinions and activities. Such prosecutions constituted a form of judicial harassment; they rarely ended in custodial sentences, but often resulted in heavy fines. Such trials were opened under various articles of the Turkish Penal Code, for example, those which criminalize "insults" to different state bodies or "incitement to enmity and hatred". However, trials were opened under many other laws as well – these included the Anti-Terror Law, the Law on Meetings and Demonstrations, as well as laws on public order and on associations and foundations. Politicians were prosecuted for making election propaganda in languages other than Turkish. Severe fines were handed down under both the old and new press laws to newspapers and journalists.

☐ Journalist Hakan Albayrak was released from prison in Ankara province in November having served six months of a 15-month prison sentence for an article in which he commented on the funeral rites of Mustafa Kemal Atatürk, the founder of the Turkish Republic.

☐ On 30 December a court in Ankara continued to hear the case opened against the writer Fikret Başkaya for having intentionally "insulted or derided the Turkish state" in his book *Against the Current*. He faced a sentence of up to three years' imprisonment if convicted.

Such laws were also used against human rights defenders – including lawyers, doctors, environmentalists and trade unionists who continued to be targeted despite a greater willingness on the part of the government to consult with representatives of civil society. Such harassment varied from province to province. In some cases people were prohibited from organizing petitions, reading press statements or holding demonstrations. The UN Special Representative on Human Rights Defenders visited Turkey in October and expressed her concern at the opening of large numbers of cases and recommended that all cases pending against human rights defenders be reviewed. Individuals who participated in human rights activities were also often subjected to professional sanctions such as dismissal, suspension or transfer to postings away from their home towns.

☐ In June a case was opened seeking the closure of the largest trade union in Turkey, the teachers' trade union Eğitim Sen. The case was based on a statement in the union's statute that it would "defend the rights of individuals to education in their mother tongues" which the prosecuting authorities claimed was unconstitutional. The acquittal of Eğitim Sen in September was overturned by the Court of Appeal in November.

☐ In June, Professors Şebnem Korur Fincancı and Sermet Koç were removed from their positions as heads of the two faculties of Forensic Medicine at hospitals attached to Istanbul University. They had expressed their concerns about the lack of independence of the Forensic Medical Institute to the press. Şebnem Korur Fincancı had previously been removed from her duties at the Institute for writing a report in which she concluded that an individual had died in custody as a result of torture.

Release of prisoners of conscience

On 21 April, Ankara No. 1 State Security Court upheld the 15-year prison sentences imposed on four former Democracy Party (DEP) parliamentarians: Leyla Zana, Hatip Dicle, Orhan Doğan and Selim Sadak. The retrial had been initiated as a result of legislation that allowed for new judicial proceedings to be opened where the European Court of Human Rights had found the original judgement to be in breach of the European Convention on Human Rights. However, in early June the Chief Prosecutor of the Court of Appeal requested that the conviction be overturned, emphasizing that the retrial had also been in breach of international fair trial standards and that they should be retried again but released during these proceedings. On 9 June, the four former parliamentarians were released from Ulucanlar Prison in Ankara. A new retrial began at the Ankara Special Felony Court No. 11 on 21 October.

Violence against women

The human rights of hundreds of thousands of women in Turkey continued to be violated as a result of violence in the family. There were reports of beatings, rape and murder or enforced suicide. State officials failed to take steps to protect women adequately. Investigations into reports of family violence were often inadequate and the perpetrators were rarely brought to justice. Shelters for women at risk of violence were extremely rare.

As a result of concerted lobbying efforts by women's organizations, many provisions which had discriminated on grounds of gender were removed in the new Penal Code. Positive measures introduced included: the abolition of the possibility that someone convicted of rape could have their sentence reduced, postponed or annulled if he agreed to marry the victim; the explicit recognition of marital rape as a crime; and the definition of sustained and systematic violence in the family as torture.

AI country reports/ visits
Reports
- Turkey: From paper to practice – making change real, Memorandum to the Turkish Prime Minister on the occasion of the visit to Turkey of a delegation led by Irene Khan, Amnesty International's Secretary General (AI Index: EUR 44/001/2004)
- Turkey: Restrictive laws, arbitrary application – the pressure on human rights defenders (AI Index: EUR 44/002/2004)
- Turkey: Women confronting family violence (AI Index: EUR 44/013/2004)
- Europe and Central Asia: Summary of Amnesty International's concerns in the region, January-June 2004: Turkey (AI Index: EUR 01/005/2004)

Visits
AI delegates visited Turkey in February, June and December. In February, the Secretary General of AI met senior government figures, including Prime Minister Recep Tayyip Erdoğan.

TURKMENISTAN

TURKMENISTAN
Head of state and government: Saparmurad Niyazov
Death penalty: abolitionist for all crimes
International Criminal Court: not signed
UN Women's Convention: ratified
Optional Protocol to UN Women's Convention: not signed

Human rights abuses were widespread. Small steps to fend off criticism of the country's human rights record failed to adequately address concerns raised by human rights groups and intergovernmental bodies including the Organization for Security and Co-operation in Europe (OSCE), the UN Commission on Human Rights (CHR), and the UN General Assembly. Religious minorities, civil society activists and others exercising their right to freedom of expression faced harassment and imprisonment or were forced into exile. Relatives of dissenters continued to be targeted. Those imprisoned following an alleged assassination attempt on the President in November 2002 continued to be held incommunicado. Conscientious objectors to military service were imprisoned.

Background
President Niyazov and his personality cult continued to dominate all aspects of life in the country. No efforts were made to address impunity or to counter the widespread abuse of human rights.

In October the Khalk Maslakhaty (People's Council), comprising representatives of the legislative, executive and judicial branches of government, reiterated calls for President Niyazov to remain President-for-life. In the absence of independent political parties, parliamentary elections in December were won by the President's party.

Ethnic minorities continued to be at risk of harassment and intimidation including dismissal from employment.

In January the President abolished a requirement for residents to obtain government permission to leave the country. However, the authorities reportedly prevented many dissenters and their relatives from leaving. Freedom of movement inside the country was severely curtailed.

A new mosque, envisaged to become the largest in Central Asia, was inaugurated in the President's home village of Kipchak in October. The walls show inscriptions of verses of the Koran alongside quotations from *Rukhnama,* a "spiritual guidebook" attributed to the President. The mosque was the latest in a series of monumental buildings completed by a French construction firm for the Turkmen authorities.

The authorities forcibly evicted people from their homes for government architectural projects or to implement apparently arbitrary presidential decisions. Reportedly, little notice was given and residents received little or no compensation.

International scrutiny

In April, in its second resolution on Turkmenistan, the CHR reiterated its "grave concern" about the human rights situation. It highlighted "repression of all political opposition activities", the "abuse of the legal system through arbitrary detention, imprisonment and surveillance of persons who try to exercise their freedoms of thought, expression, assembly and association, and harassment of their families", and "restrictions on the exercise of freedoms of ... conscience, religion and belief". It deplored the continued refusal to grant access to those convicted following the November 2002 events. It also urged Turkmenistan to "enable non-governmental organizations ... and other civil society actors to carry out their activities without hindrance".

In its second resolution on Turkmenistan adopted on 20 December, the UN General Assembly expressed "its grave concern at the continuing and serious human rights violations occurring in Turkmenistan" and reiterated the key points raised by the CHR earlier in the year.

None of the UN's human rights experts were allowed to visit Turkmenistan, despite requests by many of them.

In its new strategy on Turkmenistan adopted in July, the European Bank for Reconstruction and Development voiced concern about the "deterioration of the situation with regard to the protection of human rights and the rule of law".

Repression of dissent

Anyone perceived to be critical of the regime and their relatives remained at risk of repression. The relatives of exiled dissidents continued to be targeted in an attempt to stop those in exile from criticizing government policies and speaking out about human rights violations.

The authorities took a number of steps to avoid being classified as a "country of particular concern" under the USA's International Religious Freedom Act, including the registration of the Adventist, Baha'i and Hare Krishna communities and the release of six conscientious objectors from prison. Such a classification can lead to the USA taking steps ranging from diplomatic protest to targeted trade sanctions. However, harassment and intimidation of registered and unregistered religious minorities continued.

The 2003 law criminalizing activities of unregistered non-governmental organizations was annulled in November, but it remained impossible for independent civil society groups to operate. Several civil society activists and a *Radio Liberty* journalist were forced into exile. Several people who had given interviews to *Radio Liberty* and members of their families were harassed, intimidated or arbitrarily detained. International human rights monitors and foreign journalists were in many cases refused access to the country. The authorities routinely harassed civil society activists who attempted to meet representatives of intergovernmental organizations.

▭ In February Gurbandurdy Durdykuliyev was forcibly confined to a psychiatric hospital for exercising his right to freedom of expression. He was a prisoner of conscience. He had sent a letter to President Niyazov and the Balkan region governor in January, urging them to authorize a peaceful demonstration and to refrain from using force against participants. He had earlier criticized President Niyazov's policies in interviews with *Radio Liberty* and had openly spoken about the need for an opposition political party.

▭ In March former Mufti Nasrullah ibn Ibadullah was sentenced to 22 years' imprisonment on treason charges by a court in Ashgabat. He was accused of involvement in the 2002 alleged assassination attempt. In May he was allegedly beaten by Interior Ministry officers in the maximum security prison in Turkmenbashi. There were allegations that the charges were fabricated and that he was targeted for expressing dissent over the extensive use of the President's book *Rukhnama* in mosques and for expressing opposition to proposals in December 2002 to reintroduce the death penalty before the President had made his position clear. It was also alleged that he was targeted because of his Uzbek ethnicity and a government policy to remove members of ethnic minorities from particularly influential posts.

▭ Two female Jehovah's Witnesses – Gulkamar Dzhumayeva and Gulsherin Babakuliyeva – were reportedly detained overnight at a police station in Gagarin district in the town of Turkmenabad in September for practising their religion. Two procuracy officials reportedly sexually harassed Gulsherin Babakuliyeva and one of them reportedly threatened to rape her and hit her several times. A third officer was reportedly present throughout but did not come to her aid.

▭ Rakhim Esenov, aged 78, was detained on 23 February, accused of inciting social, national and religious hatred using the mass media and of smuggling copies of his banned historical novel *Ventsenosny Skitalets* (The Crowned Wanderer) into Turkmenistan. Although he suffered a stroke in detention, interrogation continued shortly afterwards. Following international pressure, he was released on 9 March. However, he was placed under travel restrictions and the charges against him were not dropped. Igor Kaprielov, Rakhim Esenov's son-in-law, was accused of conspiring with him and given a suspended five-year prison sentence for "smuggling" in March.

▭ Mukhametkuli Aymuradov, convicted following an unfair trial on charges of anti-state crimes in 1995, was transferred back to extremely harsh prison conditions in the maximum security prison in Turkmenbashi in May or June where he had previously spent several years. AI was concerned about his health, particularly in light of reports that he was not receiving appropriate medical attention.

Incommunicado imprisonment

Dozens of people imprisoned following unfair trials in connection with the November 2002 events continued to be held incommunicado, without access to families, lawyers, or independent bodies such as the International Committee of the Red Cross. The authorities did not respond to allegations that at least two prisoners died in custody as a result of torture, ill-treatment and harsh prison conditions in 2003. In April the Foreign Ministry informed the Office of the UN High Commissioner for Human Rights that no access would be granted to these prisoners for five years.

Conscientious objectors

To AI's knowledge, seven conscientious objectors – all Jehovah's Witnesses – were released, six of them in June. However, Mansur Masharipov, Vepa Tuvakov and Atamurat Suvkhanov were sentenced to 18 months' imprisonment inMay, June and December respectively for refusing military service on religious grounds. They were prisoners of conscience.

AI country reports/ visits

Reports

- Europe and Central Asia: Summary of Amnesty International's concerns in the region, January-June 2004: Turkmenistan (AI Index: EUR 01/005/2004)
- Belarus and Uzbekistan: The Last Executioners – The trend towards abolition in the former Soviet space (AI Index: EUR 04/009/2004)

UGANDA

REPUBLIC OF UGANDA

Head of state and government: Yoweri Kaguta Museveni
Death penalty: retentionist
International Criminal Court: ratified
UN Women's Convention: ratified
Optional Protocol to UN Women's Convention: not signed

Abuses by the armed opposition Lord's Resistance Army (LRA) increased during the first half of the year. The government asked the International Criminal Court (ICC) to investigate war crimes and crimes against humanity in the context of the war in northern Uganda. Rape of girls was widespread, and other torture persisted. The media continued to be attacked.

Background

Throughout 2004, debate continued over the recommendations of the Constitutional Review Commission (CRC) on moving the country towards a multi-party political system and on lifting the two-term presidential limit ahead of elections due in 2006. The government presented a White Paper containing its counter-proposals to the CRC's recommendations in September.

In November the Constitutional Court held that certain sections of the hotly contested Political Parties and Organizations Act (PPOA) of 2002 were unconstitutional and infringed civil and political rights such as the rights to freedom of association and assembly.

Harassment of politicians continued. In November, four members of parliament from northern Uganda were reportedly beaten by soldiers, allegedly to prevent them holding consultative meetings on the constitutional proposals.

On 9 December, eight suspects from an alleged armed group, the People's Redemption Army (PRA), were charged with plotting to overthrow the government. The previous day, the Constitutional Court had ordered that 25 suspects from the same organization be released on bail immediately. The 25 were charged with treason before the Military General Court Martial.

The war in northern Uganda

The first half of the year saw an upsurge in LRA attacks on civilians in Gulu, Kitgum, Lira and Pader districts. In February the LRA attacked Barlonyo Internally Displaced People Camp in Lira District, killing over 200 people. President Museveni visited the district and apologized for the lack of protection provided by the Uganda People's Defence Force (UPDF).

From July onwards, UPDF military interventions in Sudan and LRA defections led to a downturn in LRA attacks. The government renewed the Amnesty Act for a further three months in August. The Act offered full pardon for those involved in insurgency who abandoned acts of rebellion. In August President Museveni reversed the government's previous position of excluding the LRA leadership from possible pardon by declaring that Joseph Kony, leader of the LRA, had only one chance to seek amnesty.

On 14 November President Museveni ordered a seven-day ceasefire, suspending UPDF operations in a limited area of Acholi region to allow the LRA leadership to meet in an effort to end hostilities. The peace initiative was apparently instigated by Betty Bigombe, former Minister of State in charge of the pacification of northern Uganda.The ceasefire was renewed on several occasions until the end of the year.

Referral to the International Criminal Court

In January the Prosecutor of the ICC announced that he would takes steps to investigate and prosecute war crimes and crimes against humanity committed in the conflict in northern Uganda. This followed a request from the Ugandan government at the end of 2003 for the ICC to investigate crimes committed by the LRA. In July the ICC Prosecutor indicated that he would investigate crimes by both the LRA and government forces. The government pledged its support for the ICC investigations and published the International Criminal Court Bill to implement the ICC Statute in domestic law. The Bill had not been enacted by the end of 2004.

In November, during government efforts to resolve the conflict, officials announced that if leaders of the

LRA were to stop fighting and engage in internal reconciliation mechanisms, the state could withdraw its case from the ICC. However, there is no evidence that once a state party has referred a situation to the ICC that it can "withdraw" the referral.

Violence against women

Reports of rape, including of young girls, were widespread and appeared to be on the increase. In Kabarole, in the west, 54 children were reportedly raped in the first quarter of 2004. In Gulu, the figure rose from 55 in August to 65 in September. Between January and June, 320 child rape cases were reported in the southern area in the districts of Rakai, Kalangala, Masaka and Sembalule, and 682 in Kampala, compared to 437 for the same period in 2003. Nearly half those facing capital charges were accused of raping children.

Support services remained inadequate, and in the absence of appropriate medication, the population, especially children and women, was highly vulnerable to sexually transmitted infections, including HIV/AIDS.

Torture

Reports of torture by law enforcement officers, security agents and the army persisted. Torture continued to be used to extract confessions and as a means of punishment.

In April, a survivor of torture by security agents of the Chieftaincy of Military Intelligence was awarded financial compensation by the Uganda Human Rights Commission. The Commission held the government liable for violating the survivor's rights to liberty and protection from torture and ill-treatment. The government had not settled the award by the end of 2004.

Freedom of expression

Freedom of expression in the media continued to be under serious attack.

In June, six journalists were detained by order of the Chairperson of the Military General Court Martial. They were convicted of contempt of court on the same day. Together with a defence lawyer, they were accused of publishing stories about the trial of a former Army Chief of Staff, which the military court had ordered should be held behind closed doors. The accused were fined and cautioned.

In February, in a landmark judgement, the Supreme Court ruled the offence of "publication of false news" as void and unconstitutional, reaffirming that freedom of expression is a fundamental human right. The Supreme Court ruled that the language in the Penal Code providing for the offence was too imprecise.

Freedom of association and assembly

On several occasions, police impeded the constitutionally guaranteed right to freedom of association by dispersing peaceful demonstrations, gatherings and rallies by opposition parties and groupings.

The Constitutional Court judgement of 17 November nullifying certain sections of the PPOA 2002 removed constraints on political parties' right to hold public rallies in any part of the country. The Court also nullified Section 13(b), which barred a Ugandan citizen who had lived outside the country for more than three years from leading a political party or from being a political office-bearer.

Persecution of sexual minorities

The climate of hostility against lesbians, gays, bisexuals and transgender (LGBT) people persisted and discriminatory legislation against sexual minorities remained in force. Security agents continued to harass members of the LGBT community, causing gay rights activists at one of the main universities to fear for their personal safety.

In October, a radio station was compelled to pay a fine for hosting a live talk show with sexual rights activists. The Broadcasting Council imposed a fine on *FM Radio Simba*, claiming that the programme was "contrary to public morality" and breached existing laws.

Death penalty

Death sentences continued to be imposed. There were at least 525 inmates on death row by December 2004. No civilians have been executed since May 1999, when 28 death row inmates were hanged at Luzira Prison. Three soldiers were executed by firing squad in March 2003. Top prison officers repeatedly called for executions to be carried out by privately employed hangmen, not Prison Department employees, if the government were to maintain the death penalty.

Despite calls for its abolition, the Constitutional Review Commission recommended that the death penalty be retained and should remain mandatory for the crimes of murder, aggravated robbery, kidnapping with intent to murder, and rape of minors below the age of 15. The government responded in September by accepting the recommendations and noting that treason was not listed among the crimes carrying a mandatory death sentence.

AI country reports/visits
Reports/statements
- Uganda: Freedom of the press upheld (AI Index: AFR 59/002/2004)
- Uganda: Government should address attacks on civilians urgently (AI Index: AFR 59/003/2004)
- Uganda: Concerns about the International Criminal Court Bill 2004 (AI Index: AFR59/005/2004)

UKRAINE

UKRAINE
Head of state: Leonid Kuchma
Head of government: Viktor Yanukovych
Death penalty: Abolitionist for all crimes
International Criminal Court: signed
UN Women's Convention and its Optional Protocol: ratified

Allegations of torture and ill-treatment in police detention were widespread. Demonstrations were banned and protesters were detained and harassed. Racist attacks were reported throughout the country. Investigations into the "disappearance" of Georgiy Gongadze made no progress.

Background
The second round of the presidential elections in November was followed by civil unrest and mass protests after the opposition leader, Viktor Yushchenko, refused to accept the official results. The Organization for Security and Co-operation in Europe (OSCE) stated that the elections "did not meet a considerable number of OSCE, Council of Europe and other European standards for democratic elections." In particular, the rights to peaceful assembly and freedom of association were violated and there was an overwhelming bias in favour of the government candidate, Viktor Yanukovych, in the state-controlled media. A third round of the elections on 26 December resulted in an apparent win for Viktor Yushchenko, but the official announcement of the results could only be made after Viktor Yanukovych had completed the appeal process.

Torture and ill-treatment
In December the European Committee for the Prevention of Torture and Inhuman or Degrading Treatment or Punishment published the report of its visit to Ukraine in 2002. This repeated the conclusion of previous reports of visits in 1998 and 2000 that people deprived of their liberty by the Militia run a significant risk of being physically ill-treated at the time of their apprehension or while in custody. Conditions in temporary holding facilities (ITT) run by the Ministry of the Interior were described as intolerable, and overcrowding remained a problem. Access to fresh air was limited and standards of hygiene inadequate. High rates of infection with tuberculosis were reported.

□ Beslan Kutarba and Revaz Kishikashvili were detained by police officers from the Nakhimovsky police station in Sevastopol on the Crimean peninsula, southern Ukraine, in August. They were accused of petty theft and breaking and entering, a crime to which they reportedly confessed. Their lawyers were concerned that their confessions had been extracted under torture. The men received no medical attention and had limited access to families and lawyers. They

remained in the temporary detention centre in Sevastopol at the end of the year; their lawyer reported that their conditions had improved and they were no longer being ill-treated. The local Procurator and the office of the Ministry of the Interior in Sevastopol denied the torture allegations, although no prompt, comprehensive and impartial investigation into them was carried out.

□ Andrey Ovsiannikov, a detainee who contracted tuberculosis (TB) in the temporary holding facility in Sevastopol, finally received treatment in March when he was admitted to hospital as a result of the efforts of his family and the Sevastopol Human Rights Group. He had been arrested in June 2003 on suspicion of drug dealing and was subsequently diagnosed as having TB, but not informed of this and only found out by chance in November 2003 when his health worsened. On 30 June 2004 he was returned to the temporary holding facility, where he remained at the end of the year.

□ On 28 July, 10 young members of a revolutionary communist group who had been arrested in December 2002 were found guilty of involvement in an attempted coup, banditry and attempted murder and sentenced to between six and 14 years' imprisonment. The defendants alleged that they were tortured during the criminal investigation. One member of the group, a 17-year-old woman, was reportedly raped in detention. No investigation was carried out into the allegations. An 11th member of the group died in suspicious circumstances in November 2003.

'Disappearance' of Georgiy Gongadze
Pressure on the Ukrainian government to identify those responsible for the "disappearance" in September 2000 of investigative journalist Georgiy Gongadze increased, but no real progress was made. In March the head of the Parliamentary Investigative Commission working on the case called for President Kuchma's impeachment for "serious, violent crimes". In June the UK-based *Independent* newspaper published leaked documents alleging that high-ranking government officials had blocked the investigation into the "disappearance" and that Georgiy Gongadze had been under surveillance by the Ministry of the Interior before his abduction. In June the Prosecutor General's Office announced that a convicted murderer had confessed to the journalist's killing.

Freedom of expression and association
Opposition supporters were detained in the run-up to the first round of the presidential elections in October; some protesters were ill-treated by police.

□ Members of the youth opposition organization Pora (It is time) were arbitrarily detained and harassed. Aleksander Tsitsenko was detained by masked police on 21 October in Kirovograd as he was collecting leaflets and stickers. He was released without charge on 25 October. Twenty-year-old Andriiy Kulibaba was detained on 20 October in Vinnytsya and sentenced to 10 days in detention for "intentional disobedience to demands of the police". The sentence was later reduced to a fine and he was released on 23 October.

Aleksander Pugach, aged 18, was detained in Vinnytsya on 21 October for refusing to give his name to the police, but was acquitted of that offence. Minutes later, as he stood on the steps of the courthouse, he was detained again for "hooliganism". All charges against all three men were subsequently dropped, but Pora members continued to be targeted prior to the elections.

Refugees

In June the Parliamentary Assembly of the Council of Europe recommended that Ukraine observe the fundamental principles of international law concerning the protection of refugees and asylum-seekers, and show commitment and political will in tackling the problems of migration. Refugee law in Ukraine breaches international standards by imposing a strict time limit of between three and five days after arrival during which asylum-seekers may submit applications.

Violence against women

Trafficking for sexual exploitation remained a serious concern, with Turkey and Russia continuing to be the destination of most of the women and girls trafficked from Ukraine. The government has taken steps to address the problem and prosecutions increased after Article 149 of the Criminal Code — which establishes trafficking as an offence — was introduced in 1998. However, conviction rates remained low. Judges often lacked experience of the issue and witness protection was rarely offered to trafficked women and girls. Although a special department was established within the Ministry of the Interior to deal with trafficking, law enforcement officers often lacked resources and training.

Discrimination

Anti-Semitic and racist attacks were reported in various parts of Ukraine. Members of the Jewish community in Donetsk, for example, reported a dramatic increase in anti-Semitic acts in 2004. Police continued to deny that attacks on Jewish cemeteries and places of worship were racially motivated. In Odessa attacks on foreign nationals, particularly those from Africa, increased; many were attributed to "skinhead" gangs.

AI country reports/ visits
Report
· Europe and Central Asia: Summary of Amnesty International's concerns in the region, January-June 2004: Ukraine (AI Index: EUR 001/005/2004)
Visit
AI delegates visited Ukraine in June.

UNITED ARAB EMIRATES

UNITED ARAB EMIRATES
Head of state: Al-Sheikh Khalifa bin Zayed Al-Nahyan (replaced Al-Sheikh Zayed bin Sultan Al-Nahyan in November)
Head of government: Al-Sheikh Maktoum bin Rashid Al Maktoum
Death penalty: retentionist
International Criminal Court: signed
UN Women's Convention: acceded
Optional Protocol to UN Women's Convention: not signed

Political detainees arrested in the aftermath of the 11 September 2001 attacks in the USA remained held without charge or trial. A UAE national arrested in Abu Dhabi "disappeared". Corporal punishment was imposed in the Emirate of Ras al-Khaimah. One death sentence was passed but no executions were known to have been carried out. Women called for greater rights.

Background

An application by a group of human rights activists to form the UAE's first independent human rights organization was submitted to the Ministry of Labour and Social Affairs in July, but had not been approved by the end of 2004.

In December a Dubai newspaper reported that three such applications had been submitted by three different groups.

Women's rights

In October the UAE acceded without reservation to the UN Women's Convention.

In November Sheikha Lubna al-Qassimi, a member of the Sharjah ruling family, became the UAE's first woman minister when she was appointed Economics and Planning Minister.

In January, the General Women's Union (GWU) debated a draft amended personal status law, proposed by the Ministry for Justice, Islamic Affairs and Awqaf. The GWU demanded extensive changes to ensure greater rights for women and called for greater protection for a first wife in the event of polygamy; improved financial protection for divorced women; and the amendment of a clause authorizing a husband to prevent his wife from working despite a premarital agreement allowing her to work.

Domestic migrant workers continued to be denied the protection of labour legislation. Unconfirmed allegations of ill-treatment included physical abuse — including sexual abuse — and non-payment of wages.

Continued impact of the 'war on terror'

After 11 September 2001, more than 250 people were arrested and detained, including military personnel and judges. The number still detained remained unknown, but they were reportedly held without access to lawyers or family, and their legal status was unclear.

Security provisions continued to be strengthened with the introduction of the Anti-terrorism Act in July. Penalties for involvement with organizations defined as "terrorist" included the death penalty and life imprisonment.

The "war on terror" was also used to restrict freedom of expression, belief and association. Those perceived to have "Islamist" tendencies, including lawyers, judges, teachers and university professors, reportedly faced restrictions on work opportunities and participation in public life. The Anti-terrorism Act provided for up to five years' imprisonment for "propagating, by word, in writing or by any other means" any "terrorist" act or purpose. Organizations such as teachers', lawyers', and journalists' associations faced harassment because some of their board members were perceived to hold "Islamist" views. Some Islamic charities reportedly had their assets confiscated or frozen, and their activities blocked.

Forcible return

On 23 November, Abdelaziz Khalid Osman, a Sudanese political activist and former political prisoner in Sudan, was forcibly returned to Sudan. He was arrested at Abu Dhabi airport upon arrival from Egypt on 23 September, reportedly at the request of the Sudanese authorities. He was arrested when he arrived in Sudan and detained for "crimes against the state", and was subsequently released on 18 December.

'Disappearance'

A 34-year-old employee of the telecommunications company Etisalat, Hassan al-Za'abi, was arrested and "disappeared" after his car was stopped by members of the State Security (Amn al-Dawla) on 1 August in Abu Dhabi. Despite several appeals by his family his fate and whereabouts remained unknown. The reasons for his arrest were not clear but were thought to be politically motivated.

Cruel judicial punishments

In December, two women domestic migrant workers — Indonesian national Wasini bint Sarjan and Indian national Rad Zemah Sinyaj Mohammed — were sentenced to flogging, after becoming pregnant outside marriage, by a Shari'a (Islamic) Court in Ras al-Khaimah. Rad Zemah Sinyaj Mohammed was sentenced to 150 lashes, to be received in two sessions, followed by deportation. Wasini bint Sarjan was sentenced to one year's imprisonment and 100 lashes, followed by deportation.

The sentences were to be carried out once the women had given birth and their children had been weaned.

AI country reports/visits

Report

· The Gulf and the Arabian Peninsula: Human rights fall victim to the "war on terror" (AI Index: MDE 04/002/2004).

Visit

AI visited the UAE in January to conduct research on detainees held in the context of the "war on terror", in July and August to conduct research for the Gulf Stop Violence Against Women project (see Middle East/North Africa Regional Overview 2004), and in November to take part in a police training seminar.

UNITED KINGDOM

UNITED KINGDOM OF GREAT BRITAIN AND NORTHERN IRELAND
Head of state: Queen Elizabeth II
Head of government: Tony Blair
Death penalty: abolitionist for all crimes
International Criminal Court: ratified
UN Women's Convention: ratified with reservations
Optional Protocol to UN Women's Convention: ratified

The UK's highest court ruled that indefinite detention without trial of non-deportable foreign "suspected international terrorists" discriminated against them unjustifiably and was unlawful. Another court held that "evidence" obtained by torture of a third party would be inadmissible only if it had been directly procured by UK agents or if they had connived in its procurement. The authorities sought to circumvent their obligations under international and domestic human rights law in respect of the conduct of UK armed forces in Iraq and Afghanistan. Self-inflicted deaths, self-harm, overcrowding and detention conditions in prisons were of major concern. Public inquiries into cases of alleged collusion by security forces in killings in Northern Ireland were announced. However, the authorities further delayed the establishment of an inquiry into the killing of Patrick Finucane.

Internment in the UK

Eleven foreign nationals continued to be interned under the Anti-terrorism, Crime and Security Act 2001 (ATCSA) — legislation adopted after the 11 September 2001 attacks in the USA. Most had been detained for more than three years in high-security facilities under severely restricted regimes. A 12th person, an Algerian former torture victim, was "released" in April under strict bail conditions amounting to house arrest.

☐ In March the Special Immigration Appeals Commission ruled that the authorities' case for detaining a Libyan man as a "suspected international terrorist" under the ATCSA was "not established", and that some of their assertions had been "clearly misleading", "inaccurate", and "unreasonable". He was the sole person to win an appeal against certification as a "suspected international terrorist" under the ATCSA.

In August the Court of Appeal of England and Wales concluded that the ATCSA permitted (indeed required) the admission of "evidence" procured by torture of a third party, provided that the torture was not committed or connived at by UK officials. Permission to appeal against the ruling was pending at the end of 2004.

In October, 12 senior doctors concluded that all the ATCSA internees they had examined had suffered serious damage to their health. They stated that the indefinite nature of their detention had been a major factor in the deterioration of their mental health and that of their spouses. In November, two internees were transferred to a high-security psychiatric hospital because of the effects of internment on their mental health.

In November, the UN Committee against Torture (CAT) expressed concern about: potentially indefinite detention under the ATCSA; the strict detention regime under which some internees were held at Belmarsh prison; and the interpretation of domestic legislation as preventing the use of evidence obtained through torture only if UK officials were complicit.

In December the Appellate Committee of the House of Lords ruled by a majority of eight to one that indefinite detention without charge or trial of non-deportable foreign "suspected international terrorists" under the ATCSA unjustifiably discriminated against them, and was, therefore, unlawful. AI had intervened in writing in these proceedings.

⊟ In December the application of Mahmoud Abu Rideh, a Palestinian refugee and torture victim, to be released on bail from detention under the ATCSA was adjourned indefinitely. At the end of 2004, he continued to be held in a high-security psychiatric hospital.

Guantánamo Bay

The UK authorities continued to play a duplicitous role in the detention – without any legal basis – of UK residents and nationals in Guantánamo Bay, Cuba, in US custody. UK intelligence officers had taken advantage of the legal limbo and the coercive detention conditions at Guantánamo Bay to conduct interrogations and to extract information to use in proceedings under the ATCSA.

⊟ In March Ruhal Ahmed, Tarek Dergoul, Jamal Udeen, Asif Iqbal and Shafiq Rasul, UK nationals held at Guantánamo Bay since early 2002, were returned to the UK where they were freed without charges.

In June the UK authorities acknowledged for the first time that some detainees interrogated by UK intelligence personnel had complained about their treatment, but refused to provide any further details.

At the end of 2004, four UK nationals and at least five UK residents remained in US custody at Guantánamo Bay. These included Bisher al-Rawi, an Iraqi national

legally resident in the UK, and Jamil Al-Banna, a Jordanian national with refugee status in the UK. The UK authorities may have played some part in their unlawful rendering to US custody, and refused to make representations on their behalf to the US authorities.

UK armed forces in Iraq

There were allegations of unlawful killings, torture, ill-treatment and other violations of international human rights and humanitarian law by UK forces at the time when the UK was recognized as an occupying power in Iraq (see Iraq entry). The UK authorities tried to circumvent domestic and international human rights obligations by asserting that human rights law did not bind UK armed forces in Iraq. AI urged the authorities to establish a civilian-led mechanism to investigate all allegations of serious violations of human rights and humanitarian law by UK armed forces.

In November the CAT expressed concern at the UK's assertion that certain provisions of the UN Convention against Torture could not be applied to actions of the UK in Afghanistan and Iraq. The CAT stated that the Convention applied to all areas under the de facto control of the UK authorities.

⊟ Baha Dawood Salem al-Maliki was among eight Iraqi hotel workers arrested and reportedly beaten in September 2003 by UK soldiers in Basra, Iraq. Three days later Baha al-Maliki's father was handed his son's body, severely bruised and covered in blood. Another detainee, Kefah Taha, was admitted to hospital in a critical condition. In December, a domestic court ruled in a case concerning the deaths of Iraqi civilians in incidents involving UK troops while the UK was an occupying power in Iraq. The court held that – in limited circumstances – both domestic and international human rights law could apply to UK forces during the occupation of Iraq, and that there had not yet been an adequate inquiry into the death of Baha al-Maliki.

Northern Ireland
Collusion and political killings

⊟ In March, in a case with profoundly detrimental implications for human rights and the rule of law, the Law Lords held that the authorities were not obliged under the Human Rights Act 1998 to conduct an "effective and independent" investigation into the 1982 killing of Gervaise McKerr by members of a special "anti-terrorist" unit of the Royal Ulster Constabulary because it had occurred before the Act's entry into force in 2000.

⊟ In February Justice Peter Cory, a retired Canadian Supreme Court judge, publicly confirmed that he had recommended four separate public inquiries into alleged collusion by security forces in the killings of Patrick Finucane, Rosemary Nelson, Robert Hamill and Billy Wright. In April, the authorities finally published Justice Cory's reports, and announced the establishment of public inquiries in three cases, but not that of Patrick Finucane. The three inquiries had not started by the end of 2004.

⊟ In September, Kenneth Barrett, a former Loyalist paramilitary, was convicted of the 1989 murder of

Patrick Finucane. Shortly thereafter, the authorities announced that an inquiry into the Finucane case would be established on the basis of new legislation to take account of "national security". Concern remained over how public the announced inquiry would be and the possible use of "national security" to prevent the full exposure of state collusion in Patrick Finucane's killing.

Abuses by non-state actors

Despite a significant decrease, high levels of paramilitary violence continued, particularly by Loyalist groups. Three killings were attributed to members of Loyalist groups and one to members of Republican groups during 2004. There were on average two shootings and two to three assault victims every week.

The Independent Monitoring Commission reported that members of Loyalist paramilitary organizations were responsible for a series of violent racist attacks in Belfast. According to the Police Service of Northern Ireland the number of racist and homophobic incidents recorded had more than doubled from 226 and 35 respectively in 2002/03, to 453 and 71 in 2003/04. In December, however, the authorities reported that the rate of increase in racist attacks was slowing down.

Prisons

A parliamentary committee found that more people than ever were held in custody and for longer periods. It found that many of them should not have been there, in particular the mentally ill. It expressed concern about overcrowding, unsatisfactory detention conditions and the extreme paucity of prosecutions of police and prison officers involved in custodial deaths. It concluded that the authorities were failing "properly to protect the lives of vulnerable people in the state's care". It found that "someone is either killed, kills themselves or dies in otherwise questionable circumstances every other day" in prison. It expressed deep concern at the number of people dying in custody and at the rate of self-harm incidents, especially among women.

Official statistics showed that there were more than 100 self-inflicted deaths in prisons during 2004. Fourteen or 15 were women. Although women comprised only five to six per cent of the prison population, they accounted for 13 to 15 per cent of self-inflicted deaths.

The Chief Inspector of Prisons for England and Wales issued some highly critical reports following her visits to a number of institutions. Among other things, she raised concerns about risks to inmates' safety, unsatisfactory regimes for women, and poor detention conditions. The Chief Inspector of Prisons for Scotland reported that overcrowding had worsened and that in some facilities sanitary conditions were grossly inadequate.

⬠ In November a public inquiry opened into the killing of Zahid Mubarek by his cellmate, a known racist, at Feltham Young Offenders Institution in March 2000.

Deaths in police custody

⬠ In April a television broadcast showed Christopher Alder choking to death on the floor of Queen's Gardens police station in Hull while handcuffed, in 1998. In December, four of the five police officers involved in his death retired on ill-health grounds. A review of the case by the independent police complaints commission was ongoing at the end of 2004. The Alder family demanded an independent public inquiry.

⬠ In November the verdict of unlawful killing returned by a jury in October 2003 following the inquest into the death of Roger Sylvester in January 1999 was quashed.

Police shootings

⬠ In October an inquest jury returned an unlawful killing verdict following a second inquest into the 1999 fatal police shooting of Harry Stanley. Although the prosecuting authorities were still considering whether to charge the officers involved, in December they were allowed to return to work on "non-operational duties".

⬠ In December an inquest jury returned a lawful killing verdict following an inquest into the fatal police shooting of Derek Bennett in 2001.

Army deaths in disputed circumstances

In November the CAT expressed concern about "reports of incidents of bullying followed by self-harm and suicide in the armed forces, and the need for full public inquiry into these incidents and adequate preventive measures".

⬠ In December, the authorities appointed a human rights lawyer to review four deaths of young soldiers at Deepcut Barracks.

Freedom of expression

⬠ In February the prosecution dropped charges against Katharine Gun, a former government employee accused of leaking an e-mail on US plans to eavesdrop on UN Security Council members in the run-up to the Iraq war. The prosecution stated that there was no reasonable prospect of securing a conviction.

⬠ In December the Court of Appeal of England and Wales upheld the judgement in a case concerning three coachloads of anti-war protesters who were stopped from reaching the Royal Air Force base at Fairford – used by US B52 bombers to fly to Iraq – and forcibly returned to London in March 2003. The court found that detaining Jane Laporte to forcibly return her to London was unlawful and violated her right to liberty under the European Convention on Human Rights. However, the court found that preventing the coaches from reaching Fairford was lawful, and that, as a result, the police had not violated Jane Laporte's right to freedom of peaceful assembly and expression.

Refugees and asylum-seekers

Legislation further restricted the right to appeal against a refusal to grant asylum, replacing the two-tier immigration appeals system with a single tier. The authorities' initial decision-making on asylum claims was frequently inadequate. Restrictions on public funds for immigration and asylum work left many asylum applicants without expert legal advice and representation.

In May the Court of Appeal of England and Wales ruled that legislation allowing the authorities to deny any support to adult asylum-seekers could not be reconciled with the UK's international human rights obligations.

AI country reports/visits
Reports
- United Kingdom: Briefing for the Committee against Torture (AI Index: EUR 45/029/2004)
- UK: Text of Amnesty International submission to House of Lords opposing indefinite detention (AI Index: EUR 45/027/2004)
- Iraq: Killings of civilians in Basra and al-'Amara (AI Index: MDE 14/007/2004)

Visits
AI delegates observed judicial hearings pertaining to internment proceedings under the ATCSA, the prosecution of Katharine Gun, and proceedings in Northern Ireland arising from the killing of Patrick Finucane.

UNITED STATES OF AMERICA

UNITED STATES OF AMERICA
Head of state and government: George W. Bush
Death penalty: retentionist
International Criminal Court: signed
UN Women's Convention: signed
Optional Protocol to UN Women's Convention: not signed

Hundreds of detainees continued to be held without charge or trial at the US naval base in Guantánamo Bay, Cuba. Thousands of people were detained during US military and security operations in Iraq and Afghanistan and routinely denied access to their families and lawyers. Military investigations were initiated or conducted into allegations of torture and ill-treatment of detainees by US personnel in Abu Ghraib prison in Iraq and into reports of deaths in custody and ill-treatment by US forces elsewhere in Iraq, and in Afghanistan and Guantánamo. Evidence came to light that the US administration had sanctioned interrogation techniques that violated the UN Convention against Torture. Pre-trial military commission hearings opened in Guantánamo but

were suspended pending a US court ruling. In the USA, more than 40 people died after being struck by police tasers, raising concern about the safety of such weapons. The death penalty continued to be imposed and carried out.

International Criminal Court
The US government intensified its efforts to curtail the power of the International Criminal Court (ICC). In December, Congress approved a provision in a government spending bill mandating the withholding of certain economic assistance to governments that refuse to grant immunity for US nationals before the ICC.

Guantánamo Bay
By the end of the year, more than 500 detainees of around 35 nationalities continued to be held without charge or trial at the US naval base in Guantánamo Bay on grounds of possible links to al-Qa'ida or the former Taleban government of Afghanistan. While at least 10 more detainees were transferred to the base from Afghanistan during the year, more than 100 others were transferred to their home countries for continued detention or release. At least three child detainees were among those released, but at least two other people who were under 18 at the time of their detention were believed to remain in Guantánamo by the end of the year. Neither the identities nor the precise numbers of detainees held in Guantánamo were provided by the Department of Defense, fuelling concern that individual detainees could be transferred to and from the base without appearing in official statistics.

In a landmark decision, the US Supreme Court ruled in June that the US federal courts had jurisdiction over the Guantánamo detainees. However, the administration tried to keep any review of the detainees' cases as far from a judicial process as possible. The Combatant Status Review Tribunal (CSRT), an administrative review body consisting of panels of three military officers, was established to determine whether the detainees were "enemy combatants". The detainees were not provided with lawyers to assist them in this process and secret evidence could be used against them. Many detainees boycotted the process, which by the end of the year had determined that more than 200 detainees were "enemy combatants" and two were not and could be released. The authorities also announced that all detainees confirmed as "enemy combatants" would have a yearly review of their cases before an Administrative Review Board (ARB) to determine if they should still be held. Again, detainees would not have access to legal counsel or to secret evidence. Both the CSRT and the ARB could draw on evidence extracted under torture or other coercion. In December, the Pentagon announced that it had conducted its first ARB.

The government informed the detainees that they could file habeas corpus petitions in federal court, giving them the address of the District Court in Washington DC. However, it also argued in the same court that the detainees had no basis under constitutional or international law to challenge the lawfulness of their detention. By the end of the year, six months after the Supreme Court ruling, no detainee had had the lawfulness of his detention judicially reviewed.

Detentions in Afghanistan and Iraq

In August, the Independent Panel to Review Department of Defense Detention Operations, appointed by Secretary of Defense Donald Rumsfeld following the publication of photographs of torture and ill-treatment committed by US personnel in Abu Ghraib prison in Iraq (see below), reported that since the invasions of Afghanistan and Iraq, about 50,000 people had been detained during US military and security operations.

US forces operated some 25 detention facilities in Afghanistan and 17 in Iraq (see below). Detainees were routinely denied access to lawyers and families. In Afghanistan, the International Committee of the Red Cross (ICRC) had access only to some detainees in Bagram and Kandahar air bases.

Detentions in undisclosed locations

A number of detainees, reported to be those considered by the US authorities to have high intelligence value, were alleged to remain in secret detention in undisclosed locations. In some cases, their situation amounted to "disappearance". Some individuals were believed to have been held in secret locations for as long as three years. The refusal or failure of the US authorities to clarify the whereabouts or status of the detainees, leaving them outside the protection of the law for a prolonged period, clearly violated the standards of the UN Declaration on the Protection of All Persons from Enforced Disappearance.

Allegations that the US authorities were involved in the secret transfer of detainees between countries, exposing detainees to the risk of torture and ill-treatment, continued.

Military commissions

By the end of the year, 15 detainees were subject to the 2001 Military Order on the Detention, Treatment, and Trial of Certain Non-Citizens in the War Against Terrorism. Detainees named under the Military Order can be detained without charge or trial or tried before a military commission. Military commissions are executive bodies, not independent or impartial courts, with the power to hand down death sentences; there is no right of appeal against their decisions to any court.

Four of the 15 — Yemeni nationals Ali Hamza Ahmed Sulayman al Bahlul and Salim Ahmed Hamdan; Australian national David Hicks; and Ibrahim Ahmed Mahmoud al Qosi of Sudan — were charged with conspiracy to commit war crimes and other offences. The first pre-trial hearings were held for these four detainees in August.

On 8 November, US District Court Judge James Robertson presiding over Salim Hamdan's habeas corpus appeal issued an order stating that Salim Hamdan could not be tried by military commission as charged. Judge Robertson ordered that unless and until a "competent tribunal", as required under Article 5 of the Third Geneva Convention, determined that Salim Hamdan was not entitled to prisoner of war status, he could only be tried by court-martial under the USA's Uniform Code of Military Justice.

Judge Robertson held that even if Salim Hamdan was found not to have prisoner of war status by a "competent tribunal" which satisfied the requirements of the Third Geneva Convention (which the judge said neither presidential nor CSRT determinations would satisfy), his trial before the military commission would be unlawful because of military commission rules permitting the exclusion of the defendant from certain sessions and the withholding of certain classified or "protected" evidence from him. Military commission proceedings were still suspended at the end of the year, with the government having appealed against Judge Robertson's ruling.

Torture and ill-treatment of detainees outside the USA

Photographic evidence of the torture and ill-treatment of detainees in Abu Ghraib prison in Iraq by US soldiers became public in late April, causing widespread national and international concern. President Bush and other officials immediately asserted that the problem was restricted to Abu Ghraib and a few wayward soldiers.

On 22 June, after the leaking of earlier government documents relating to the "war on terror" suggesting that torture and ill-treatment had been envisaged, the administration took the step of declassifying selected documents to "set the record straight". However, the released documents showed that the administration had sanctioned interrogation techniques that violated the UN Convention against Torture and that the President had stated in a central policy memorandum dated 7 February 2002 that, although the USA's values "call for us to treat detainees humanely", there are some "who are not legally entitled to such treatment". The documents discussed, among other things, ways in which US agents could avoid the international prohibition on torture and other cruel, inhuman or degrading treatment, including by arguing that the President could override international and national laws prohibiting such treatment. These and other documents also indicated that President Bush's decision not to apply the Geneva Conventions to detainees captured in Afghanistan followed advice from his legal counsel, Alberto Gonzales, that this would free up US interrogators in the "war on terror" and make future prosecutions of US agents for war crimes less likely. Following the presidential elections in November, President Bush nominated Alberto Gonzales to the post of Attorney General in his new administration.

On 30 December, shortly before Alberto Gonzales' nomination hearings in the Senate, the Justice Department replaced one of its most controversial memorandums on torture, dated August 2002. Although the new memorandum was an improvement on its predecessor, much of the original version lived on in a Pentagon Working Group Report on Detainee Interrogations in the Global War on Terrorism, dated 4 April 2003, which remained operational at the end of the year.

A February report by the ICRC on abuses by Coalition forces in Iraq, which in some cases were judged to be "tantamount to torture", was also leaked as was the report of an investigation by US Army Major General Antonio Taguba. The Taguba report had found "numerous incidents of sadistic, blatant, and wanton criminal abuses" against detainees in Abu Ghraib prison between October and December 2003. It had also found that US agents in Abu Ghraib had hidden a number of detainees from the ICRC, referred to as "ghost detainees". It was later revealed that one of these detainees had died in custody, one of several such deaths that were revealed during the year where torture or ill-treatment was thought to be a contributory factor.

During the year, the authorities initiated various criminal investigations and prosecutions against individual soldiers as well as investigations and reviews into interrogation and detention policies and practices. The investigations found that there had been "approximately 300 recorded cases of alleged abuse in Afghanistan, Guantánamo and Iraq." On 9 September, Major Paul Kern, who oversaw one of the military investigations, told the Senate Armed Services Committee that there may have been as many as 100 cases of "ghost detainees" in US custody in Iraq. Secretary of Defense Rumsfeld admitted to having authorized the Central Intelligence Agency (CIA) to keep at least one detainee off any prison register.

However, there was concern that most of the investigations consisted of the military investigating itself, and did not have the power to carry the investigation into the highest levels of government. The activities of the CIA in Iraq and elsewhere, for example, remained largely shrouded in secrecy. No investigation dealt with the USA's alleged involvement in secret transfers between countries and any torture or ill-treatment that may have ensued. Many documents remained classified. AI called for a full commission of inquiry into all aspects of the USA's "war on terror" and interrogation and detention policies and practices.

During the year, released detainees alleged that they had been tortured or ill-treated while in US custody in Afghanistan and Guantánamo. Evidence also emerged that others, including Federal Bureau of Investigation (FBI) agents and the ICRC, had found that such abuses had been committed against detainees.

Detentions of 'enemy combatants' in the USA

In June the US Supreme Court ruled that Yaser Esam Hamdi, a US citizen held for more than two years in military custody without charge or trial as an "enemy combatant", was entitled to due process and habeas

corpus review of his detention by the US courts. His case was remanded for further proceedings before the lower courts. While the latter were pending, he was released from US custody in October and transferred to Saudi Arabia, under conditions agreed between his lawyers and the US government. These included renouncing his US citizenship and undertaking not to leave Saudi Arabia for five years and never to travel to Afghanistan, Iraq, Israel, Pakistan or Syria.

José Padilla, a US national, and Ali-Saleh Kahlah Al-Marri, a Qatari national, remained detained without charge or trial as "enemy combatants". José Padilla had filed a similar petition to Yaser Hamdi before the US Supreme Court but the Court rejected his petition on the grounds that his appeal had been filed in the wrong jurisdiction. The case was pending a rehearing in South Carolina, where he was detained in a military prison at the end of 2004.

Prisoners of conscience

Conscientious objectors Staff Sergeant Camilo Mejía Castillo and Sergeant Abdullah William Webster were imprisoned; they were prisoners of conscience. Both men remained in prison at the end of the year.

Staff Sergeant Camilo Mejía Castillo was sentenced to one year's imprisonment for desertion after he refused to return to his unit in Iraq on moral grounds relating to his misgivings about the legality of the war and the conduct of US troops towards Iraqi civilians and prisoners. His trial in May went ahead despite a pending decision by the army on his application for conscientious objector status.

In June, Sergeant Abdullah William Webster, who had served in the US army since 1985, was sentenced to 14 months' imprisonment and loss of salary and benefits for refusing to participate in the war in Iraq on the basis of his religious beliefs. He had been ordered to deploy to Iraq despite submitting an application to be reassigned to non-combatant services. His application for conscientious objector status was refused on the ground that his objection was not to war in general but to a particular war.

Refugees, migrants and asylum-seekers

In November, National Public Radio (NPR) reported allegations of abuse of immigration detainees held at three New Jersey jails, including Passaic Jail and Hudson County Correctional Center. They included claims that two prisoners were beaten while handcuffed and that others were bitten by guard dogs. AI had reported on similar abuses in 2003. Most of the alleged victims in the NPR report were deported before investigations could be completed. The Department of Homeland Security said it was reviewing various contract detention facilities but did not confirm which jails were covered in the review.

Ill-treatment and excessive use of force by law enforcement officials

There were reports of ill-treatment and deaths in custody involving "new generation" tasers: powerful dart-firing electroshock weapons deployed or trialled by more than 5,000 US police and correctional agencies. More than 40 people died after being struck by US police tasers, bringing to more than 70 the total number of such deaths reported since 2001. While coroners generally attributed cause of death to factors such as drug intoxication, in at least five cases they found the taser played a role.

Most of the people who died were unarmed men who did not appear to pose a serious threat when they were electroshocked. Many were subjected to multiple shocks and some to additional force such as pepper spray or dangerous restraint holds, including hogtying (placing someone face-down with their hands and feet bound together from behind).

There were reports that tasers were used by officers routinely to shock people who were mentally disturbed or simply refused to obey commands. Children and the elderly were among those shocked. In most such cases, the officers involved were cleared of wrongdoing. In some departments tasers had become the most common force tool used by officers against a wide range of suspects.

AI reiterated its call on the US authorities to suspend use and transfers of tasers and other stun weapons pending a rigorous, independent inquiry into their use and effects.

Death penalty

In 2004, 59 people were executed, bringing to 944 the total number of prisoners put to death since the US Supreme Court lifted a moratorium on executions in 1976. Texas accounted for 23 of the year's executions, and 336 of all the executions in the USA since 1976. Five people were released from death row in 2004 on grounds of innocence, bringing to 117 the total number of such cases since 1973.

Eight people prosecuted in the Texas jurisdiction of Harris County were executed during the year, despite concern around the reliability of forensic evidence processed through the Houston Police Department (HPD) crime laboratory where serious problems had been uncovered in 2003. In October, a judge on the Texas Court of Criminal Appeals said that there should be "a moratorium on all executions in cases where convictions were based on evidence from the HPD crime lab until the reliability of the evidence has been verified". His was the only dissenting voice when the Court denied death row inmate Dominique Green's request for a stay of execution on the basis of concern around the accuracy of the HPD's ballistics work in his case, and the discovery of 280 boxes of mislabelled evidence that could affect thousands of criminal cases. Dominique Green was executed on 26 October.

The USA continued to contravene international law by using the death penalty against child offenders – people who were under 18 at the time of the crime. Around 70 child offenders remained on death row during the year, more than a third of them in Texas.

🗀 In January, the US Supreme Court agreed to hear an appeal from the State of Missouri in the case of Christopher Simmons, who was 17 years old at the time of the crime. The Missouri Supreme Court had overturned his death sentence in 2003 on the grounds that a national consensus had evolved against the execution of child offenders. The scheduled executions of a number of child offenders were stayed pending the US Supreme Court's ruling, which was expected in early 2005.

On 31 March, the International Court of Justice (ICJ) handed down its judgement following a lawsuit brought by Mexico on behalf of its nationals arrested, denied their consular rights, and sentenced to death in the USA. The ICJ found that the USA had violated its international obligations under the Vienna Convention on Consular Relations and that it must provide effective judicial review and reconsideration of the impact of the violations on the cases of the foreign nationals involved. The ICJ noted with "great concern" that an execution date had been set for Osvaldo Torres Aguilera, one of the Mexican nationals named in the lawsuit. Osvaldo Torres' execution was subsequently commuted by the governor of Oklahoma following an appeal for clemency from the President of Mexico and a recommendation for commutation from the state clemency board. On 10 December, the US Supreme Court agreed to hear the appeal of José Medellin, a Mexican national on death row in Texas, to determine what effect US courts should give to the ICJ ruling. The case was due to be considered during 2005.

Prisoners with histories of serious mental illness continued to be sentenced to death and executed.

🗀 Charles Singleton was executed in Arkansas on 6 January. At times on death row, his mental illness had been so acute that he had been forcibly medicated.

🗀 Kelsey Patterson, diagnosed as suffering from paranoid schizophrenia, was executed in Texas on 18 May. The Texas governor rejected a recommendation for clemency from the state Board of Pardons and Paroles in his case.

🗀 On 5 August James Hubbard was executed in Alabama. He was 74 years old – the oldest person to be put to death in the USA since 1977 – and had been on death row for more than a quarter of a century. James Hubbard was reported to suffer from dementia which sometimes led him to forget who he was and why he was on death row.

AI country reports/ visits
Reports
- USA: Dead wrong – the case of Nanon Williams, child offender facing execution on flawed evidence (AI Index: AMR 51/002/2004)
- USA: "Where is the compassion?" – The imminent execution of Scott Panetti, mentally ill offender (AI Index: AMR 51/011/2004)
- USA: Another Texas injustice – the case of Kelsey Patterson, mentally ill man facing execution (AI Index: AMR 51/047/2004)
- USA: Osvaldo Torres, Mexican national denied consular rights, scheduled to die (AI Index: AMR 51/057/2004)
- USA: Undermining security – Violations of human dignity, the rule of law and the National Security

Strategy in "war on terror" detentions (AI Index: AMR 51/061/2004)
- USA: An open letter to President George W. Bush on the question of torture and cruel, inhuman or degrading treatment (AI Index: AMR 51/078/2004)
- USA: Appealing for justice – Supreme Court hears arguments against the detention of Yaser Esam Hamdi and José Padilla (AI Index: AMR 51/065/2004)
- USA: Restoring the rule of law – the right of Guantánamo detainees to judicial review of the lawfulness of their detention (AI Index: AMR 51/093/2004)
- USA: A deepening stain on US justice (AI Index: AMR 51/130/2004)
- USA: Human dignity denied – torture and accountability in the "war on terror" (AI Index: AMR 51/145/2004)
- USA: Guantánamo: Military commissions – Amnesty International observer's notes, No. 3 – Proceedings suspended following order by US federal judge (AI Index: AMR 51/157/2004)
- USA: Excessive and lethal force? Amnesty International's concerns about deaths and ill-treatment involving police use of tasers (AI Index: AMR 51/139/2004)
- USA: Proclamations are not enough, double standards must end – more than words needed this Human Rights Day (AI Index: AMR 51/171/2004)

Visits

AI delegates visited Yemen in April and spoke with relatives of detainees from the Gulf region held in Guantánamo Bay. An AI delegate attended pre-trial military commission hearings in Guantánamo Bay in August and November.

URUGUAY

EASTERN REPUBLIC OF URUGUAY
Head of state and government: Jorge Batlle Ibáñez
Death penalty: abolitionist for all crimes
International Criminal Court: ratified
UN Women's Convention and its Optional Protocol: ratified

Progress in bringing to justice those responsible for past human rights violations was slow. There were reports of torture and ill-treatment. Violence against women was a concern.

Background

The October presidential election was won by Tabaré Ramón Vázquez Rosas from Frente Amplio, a left-wing coalition. He was due to take power in March 2005.

Impunity

Limited action was taken to bring to justice those responsible for past human rights violations. President-elect Tabaré Vázquez promised to implement Article 4 of the 1986 Expiry Law. The article, which obliged the executive to order immediate investigations into any cases of "disappearance" referred to it by the courts, had never been enforced. However, taken as a whole, the Expiry Law sanctioned impunity by exempting from punishment police and military personnel responsible for human rights violations committed before March 1985, in blatant violation of Uruguay's international obligations.

▢ Legal proceedings continued against former Minister of Foreign Affairs Juan Carlos Blanco for the unlawful imprisonment of Elena Quinteros Almeida who "disappeared" in 1976. Juan Carlos Blanco was also summoned to testify, together with former President Juan María Bordaberry, at the investigation into the murders of senator Zelmar Michelini and deputy Héctor Gutiérrez Ruiz in Argentina in 1976.

▢ In September, three military officials appealed against a ruling that they should be extradited to Chile in connection with the kidnap and murder of Chilean national Eugenio Berríos. Eugenio Berríos, a biochemist and former military agent, "disappeared" in 1992. His body was found three years later.

Torture and ill-treatment

There were reports of torture and ill-treatment in prisons, children's detention centres and police stations.

Prison conditions

Conditions in several prisons, including those holding children, fell below internationally accepted standards. There were reports of serious overcrowding and inadequate food, water, lighting and heating.

Violence against women

One woman or girl reportedly died as a result of violence every nine days. Women's organizations were concerned that legislation on domestic violence was not being implemented.

Economic, social and cultural rights

A constitutional amendment was passed making access to clean water a right and declaring that water should not be classed as a commodity.

UZBEKISTAN

REPUBLIC OF UZBEKISTAN
Head of state: Islam Karimov
Head of government: Shavkat Mirzioiev
Death penalty: retentionist
International Criminal Court: signed
UN Women's Convention: ratified
Optional Protocol to UN Women's Convention: not signed

Hundreds of men and women, said to be either devout Muslims or their relatives, were arbitrarily detained following a series of explosions and attacks on police checkpoints in March and April and three suicide bombings in July. Scores of men and dozens of women, all accused of "terrorism"-related offences, were sentenced after unfair trials to long prison terms for their alleged participation in the violence. Evidence reportedly obtained under torture was routinely admitted in court and there was no presumption of innocence. Death sentences and secret executions continued on a large scale, bucking the regional trend towards abolition.

Background

A series of suicide bombings against the US and Israeli embassies as well as the state prosecutor's office killed six people and injured at least nine others in the capital Tashkent on 30 July. These followed a series of explosions and attacks on police checkpoints in Tashkent and the city of Bukhara between 28 March and 1 April, which killed more than 40 people — mostly police officers and alleged attackers. Uzbek authorities blamed the violence on "Islamic extremists", including the banned armed group the Islamic Movement of Uzbekistan (IMU) and the Islamist opposition party Hizb-ut-Tahrir, which they accused of intending to destabilize the country. Hizb-ut-Tahrir denied involvement in the violence. On 9 April the General Prosecutor announced that over 700 people had been questioned in connection with the March-April violence and that 54 suspects had been arrested, of whom 45 had been charged with

"terrorism", including 15 women. He also blamed the bombings on a previously unknown Islamist group, Zhamoat (Society). Seventeen women and 63 men were detained in connection with the July bombings. However, local human rights organizations continued to report sweeping arbitrary detentions across the country of men and women said to be either devout Muslims or their relatives.

The authorities linked the attacks to Uzbekistan's participation in the US-led "war on terror" and claimed that members of Hizb-ut-Tahrir and Zhamoat had been trained in al-Qa'ida camps in Waziristan, Pakistan. A special commission headed by President Karimov oversaw the investigations into the violence.

In June, during the summit of the Shanghai Cooperation Organization (SCO), a regional "anti-terrorist" centre was opened in Tashkent. The centre was to coordinate the fight of SCO member states — China, Kazakstan, Kyrgyzstan, the Russian Federation, Tajikistan and Uzbekistan — against the so-called "three evils of extremism, separatism and terrorism" as part of the "war on terror". During the two-day summit in Tashkent, Uzbek law enforcement forces prevented demonstrators from protesting against human rights violations in Uzbekistan.

Despite Uzbekistan's cooperation in the US-led "war on terror", the US State Department in July decided to stop aid to Uzbekistan. The State Department said that the US Secretary of State was unable to certify that the Uzbek government had made "substantial and continuing progress" in meeting its commitments made to the USA under the joint Declaration on the Strategic Partnership and Cooperation Framework, signed in March 2002. This followed an unprecedented decision in April by the European Bank for Reconstruction and Development (EBRD) to cut aid and investment because of the Uzbek government's failure to meet the EBRD's human rights benchmarks. However, the Uzbek government continued to receive substantial military aid from the US Department of Defense.

On 1 November, in an unprecedented move, thousands of people reportedly took to the streets in the city of Kokand in violent protests against new restrictive trade regulations.

Independent opposition political parties such as Erk and Birlik were unsuccessful in registering ahead of the 26 December parliamentary election. The Organization for Security and Co-operation in Europe criticized the election as falling "significantly short of... international standards for democratic elections."

'Terrorism'-related trials

On 26 July a first group of 15 defendants went on trial before the Supreme Court in Tashkent charged with "anti-state" offences, "terrorism" and membership of illegal religious groups in relation to the March-April violence. Although President Karimov had pledged that the "terrorism trials" would be open and conform to international fair trial standards, the Procurator General published a letter the same day declaring all 15 defendants guilty as charged, thereby denying them presumption of innocence.

Although the defendants in this first trial did not raise torture allegations in court, pleaded guilty and asked for forgiveness, this was not the case in most subsequent trials of those accused of "terrorism". Most of the defendants were not granted adequate access to a lawyer in pre-trial detention and several had been held incommunicado. All were presumed guilty before trial and the majority reportedly were not offered adequate time or resources to mount a defence.

🗁 Nilufar Khaidarova went on trial in Tashkent on 6 September as part of a second group of 15 people, including seven other women, accused of participation in the March-April violence. Along with most of the defendants, she pleaded not guilty to all the charges. She stated in court that during a recess of the trial she had been visited in the investigation-isolation prison (SIZO) in Tashkent by officers of the Ministry of Internal Affairs (MVD) who threatened her with violence if she disclosed that she had been beaten and ill-treated in detention. The court did not investigate any of the allegations of torture and ill-treatment and found all of the defendants guilty. Nilufar Khaidarova was sentenced to six years' imprisonment. In November her sentence was reduced on appeal to four years.

According to reports, Nilufar Khaidarova and her parents had been awakened at 5.30am on 5 April at their home in Tashkent by 20 uniformed police officers, who took them to the Chilanzar district police station still dressed in their nightclothes. The officers searched the premises, causing serious damage, and said they found "Islamic fundamentalist" materials. At the police station Nilufar Khaidarova and her parents were interrogated separately and then taken to the Tashkent City Department of Internal Affairs (GUVD). Nilufar Khaidarova was allegedly beaten by two police officers. Her parents were released without charge the following evening. The GUVD reportedly refused to acknowledge to the parents that Nilufar Khaidarova was in detention or to provide any information on her whereabouts.

In June the Uzbek Ambassador to the UK said that Nilufar Khaidarova had been charged with attempting to overthrow the constitutional order in relation to the March-April violence and that she was being detained at the number 1 SIZO in Tashkent. He said she had been granted regular access to her lawyer and that her mother had visited her several times. She had also reportedly been visited by staff of the International Committee of the Red Cross. According to other sources, however, she had not had regular access to her lawyer, nor had her mother been able to visit her before June.

There was concern that Nilufar Khaidarova was detained because her two brothers and husband, all devout Muslims, were serving long prison sentences for "anti-state" activities and membership of banned religious organizations.

Death penalty

President Karimov stated at a press conference in December that between 50 and 60 people were sentenced to death in 2004. Death sentences were passed within a criminal justice system seriously flawed by widespread corruption and the failure of courts to investigate allegations of torture.

Death row prisoners and their relatives were not informed of the date of execution in advance, and the location of the burial sites of executed prisoners remained secret, constituting cruel and inhuman treatment of relatives.

Comprehensive statistics on the number of death sentences and executions remained a secret, making it impossible to verify government statements that the number of death sentences had decreased.

At least three death sentences highlighted by the international community were commuted to prison terms. At least four prisoners were executed while their cases were under consideration by the UN Human Rights Committee, despite Uzbekistan's commitments under the first Optional Protocol to the International Covenant on Civil and Political Rights. This brought the total number of such cases to at least 14.

Prison conditions on death row continued to fall far short of international standards. There were allegations that death row prisoners were regularly beaten and not allowed outdoor exercise.

The authorities continued to harass and intimidate anti-death penalty activists and their relatives, and to prevent public debate about the death penalty.

🗁 In February, Azizbek Karimov was sentenced to death by the Supreme Court on charges including "terrorism" and setting up or participating in a "religious extremist organization". His family was reportedly not permitted to see him for several months after his arrest. It was also alleged that he was tortured and ill-treated while held in the detention facilities of the Security Service in Tashkent. In June the UN Human Rights Committee urged the Uzbek authorities to stay his execution following allegations that his arrest and sentencing violated key principles of international law. However, Azizbek Karimov was executed in secret in August.

Human rights defender Ruslan Sharipov

Ruslan Sharipov, a 26-year-old correspondent for the Russian news agency *PRIMA* and chairman of the unregistered human rights organization Civic Assistance (Grazhdanskoe sodeystvye), was granted political asylum in the USA in October. He had been convicted in August 2003 on charges of homosexuality and having sex with minors in August 2003 and sentenced to five and a half years in prison.

Ruslan Sharipov had always insisted that the charges against him were fabricated because of his critical reporting and human rights work. He said that the court had ignored forensic medical evidence that exonerated him, and alleged that he was tortured into changing his plea to guilty. He said he was threatened with rape and suffocation, had a gas mask put over his head and the air supply turned off, and was injected with an unknown substance.

In June a district court in Tashkent reviewed Ruslan Sharipov's prison sentence in secret and reduced it to two years' community service in the city of Bukhara. He had been transferred in March from the penal colony in Tavaksay to the more relaxed regime at a so-called colony settlement in Tashkent region. In an open letter published after he arrived in the USA, Ruslan Sharipov explained that he fled Uzbekistan in June with the tacit agreement of the Uzbek authorities during his transfer from Tashkent to Bukhara. He claimed that he was given the choice between leaving the country or being sent back to prison.

AI country reports/ visits
Reports
- Belarus and Uzbekistan: The last executioners – The trend towards abolition in the former Soviet space (AI Index: EUR 04/009/2004)
- Europe and Central Asia: Summary of Amnesty International's concerns in the region, January-June 2004: Uzbekistan (AI Index: EUR 01/005/2004)

VENEZUELA

BOLIVARIAN REPUBLIC OF VENEZUELA
Head of state and government: Hugo Chávez Frías
Death penalty: abolitionist for all crimes
International Criminal Court: ratified
UN Women's Convention: ratified with reservations
Optional Protocol to UN Women's Convention: ratified

Political polarization continued to destabilize Venezuela. There were violent confrontations between supporters of the opposition and the security forces throughout the country. Scores of people were killed and injured. Hundreds more were detained amid allegations of excessive use of force and torture and ill-treatment. There were reports of unlawful killings of criminal suspects. Relatives and those who witnessed abuses were threatened and intimidated. The lack of independence of the judiciary remained a concern. Attempts were made to undermine the legitimacy of the work of human rights defenders.

Background
In August the President won a referendum on whether he should serve out the remaining two years of his six-year term. The opposition made allegations of electoral fraud but international observers and electoral authorities confirmed the legitimacy of the result. After the referendum violent confrontations between government and opposition supporters decreased. However, in November the leading prosecutor

investigating a 2002 coup attempt was killed in a car bomb attack in Caracas, the capital, raising fears of renewed unrest in the country.

After local elections at the end of October, the ruling party controlled the capital and the majority of states.

In May up to 100 alleged Colombian paramilitaries were detained. Judicial proceedings against them on charges of conspiracy to overthrow the government were continuing at the end of the year.

Abuses during demonstrations
At least 14 people died during nationwide anti-government demonstrations in February and March. As many as 200 were wounded and several of those detained were ill-treated or tortured by members of the security forces. Investigations into the abuses were slow and inadequate, reportedly due to the lack of impartiality of the police and judiciary.

⌐ Carlos Eduardo Izcaray stated that he was observing one of the demonstrations in Caracas on 1 March when the situation became increasingly violent. He tried to leave the area but was detained with others by members of the National Guard and repeatedly beaten and threatened with death in an attempt to make him admit to participating in violent acts. He filed a complaint with the Attorney General's Office after he was released without charge.

Police brutality
There were continuing reports of unlawful killings of criminal suspects by members of the police. Relatives and witnesses who reported such abuses were frequently threatened or attacked. No effective protection was granted to them despite calls by the Inter-American Court of Human Rights for the authorities to do so.

⌐ Luis Barrios was killed in September, allegedly by members of the Aragua State police. Two days before his death he was reportedly told by members of the police that hooded men were going to pay him a visit. His brother, Narciso Barrios, was allegedly killed by the police in 2003. Since then the family had been threatened, intimidated and harassed during their quest for justice.

⌐ Mariela Mendoza was shot and wounded by unidentified gunmen outside her home in July in the Baraure de Araure sector of Portuguesa State. She had been a witness to the alleged police killings of her three brothers and prior to the shooting had received death threats.

Equal access to justice
There were continued concerns that the justice system lacked impartiality and independence, particularly in the context of political polarization. The failure of the justice sector to guarantee impartial and effective responses to human rights violations undermined the credibility of the judiciary, the Public Prosecutor's Office and the Human Rights Ombudsman.

There were also concerns that proposed legislative reforms would undermine the rights to freedom of expression and association.

Human rights defenders

President Hugo Chávez suggested at the beginning of the year that the activities of human rights defenders were intended to fuel political turmoil. These allegations exposed human rights defenders to serious dangers, including threats and intimidation.

◻ In May, Liliana Ortega and other members of the human rights organization Committee of the Relatives of the Victims of 27 February (Comité de Familiares de Víctimas del 27 de febrero, COFAVIC) were threatened and intimidated by a leafleting campaign that targeted the organization's headquarters. The leaflets made death threats against Liliana Ortega and contained insulting language.

AI country reports/ visits

Report
- Venezuela: Human rights under threat (AI Index: AMR 53/005/2004)

VIET NAM

SOCIALIST REPUBLIC OF VIET NAM
Head of state: President Tran Duc Luong
Head of government: Phan Van Khai
Death penalty: retentionist
International Criminal Court: not signed
UN Women's Convention: ratified with reservations
Optional Protocol to UN Women's Convention: not signed

The human rights situation worsened in the Central Highlands following demonstrations by members of ethnic minority groups (Montagnards) in April. The ensuing government crackdown resulted in the deaths of at least eight protesters and many injured. This was followed by tight government controls on access and communications with the region. Freedom of expression nationally remained severely limited. Trials of political dissidents continued throughout 2004. Repression of religious denominations not sanctioned by the state continued. A high number of death sentences and executions were reported.

Background

Indicators such as life expectancy, literacy, health and living standards suggested real progress towards the realization of economic, cultural and social rights. However, ethnic minority areas fell behind national trends.

Corruption scandals involving government officials dominated the domestic news. In the first stage of the most significant prisoner amnesties since 1998, more than 8,000 prisoners were given early release. No prisoners of conscience were known to have been released. In October Viet Nam hosted the biennial Asia-Europe (ASEM) meeting. A parallel non-governmental organization People's Forum attended by some Asian and European human rights and development groups also took place under tight control and media restrictions. The Vietnamese authorities prevented one Cambodian group from taking part. Vietnamese participation was restricted to organizations under state control.

A new Criminal Procedure Code came into effect on 1 July. A raft of new Internet regulations were introduced to further control access to information, especially sites run by overseas Vietnamese opposition groups. Viet Nam continued to deny access to independent human rights monitors.

Central Highlands

On 10 and 11 April, thousands of Montagnard people, including women and children, protested against government policies in three provinces of the Central Highlands. Most of the protesters were Christians who had planned five days of peaceful protests about long-standing land ownership and religious freedom issues, and about additional restrictions on freedom of movement, communication and religious practice imposed since the last major protests in 2001. Disproportionate and brutal force was used to break up the demonstrations. At least eight people were unlawfully killed and many hundreds injured in the ensuing crackdown.

The Central Highlands was effectively cut off for several months after April. All communication, including telephone contact, was extremely difficult. Diplomats and journalists were permitted to visit the region only under close supervision.

Arrests and trials continued of those linked to the 2001 unrest, its aftermath, and the April 2004 incidents. Hundreds of Montagnard asylum-seekers continued to attempt to flee to neighbouring Cambodia. At least 142 people have been sentenced to long prison terms since the 2001 unrest, including 31 in 2004. The fate of hundreds of others arrested was not known.

◻ Nine members of the Ede ethnic group – Y Hoang Bkrong, Y K'rec Bya, Y Kuang E Cam, Y Nguyen Kdoh, Y Ruan Bya, Y Tan Nie, Y Tlup Adrong, Yben Nie and Y Som H'mok – were sentenced to between five and 12 years' imprisonment by Dak Lak Provincial People's Court on 11 and 12 August under Article 87 of the Criminal Code. All were accused of "on many occasions, [having] gathered a large group of Ede people to persuade them to oppose the state policy on nationalities".

Detention and trial of government critics

Dissidents critical of government policies who used the Internet to share information continued to be prosecuted. In January a decree was issued classifying as "state secrets" official documents related to trials of people accused of national security offences.

In July Dr Nguyen Dan Que, 62, a former prisoner of conscience and human rights advocate arrested in March 2003, was sentenced to 30 months' imprisonment following a three-hour trial at which he had no legal representation. He was charged with "abusing democratic rights to jeopardize the interests of the State" under Article 258 of the Penal Code. After the trial he was moved to a prison camp in northern Viet Nam, more than two days' journey from his family home. Dr Que had previously spent 18 years in prison, also for his public opposition to government policies. He was in poor health.

Pham Que Duong, 73, a well-respected military historian critical of government policies, was tried in July and sentenced to 19 months' imprisonment under Article 258 of the Penal Code. He had already spent this period in pre-trial detention and was released shortly afterwards.

Suppression of religious freedom

A new religious decree came into effect in November. It was criticized by several religious groups in Viet Nam as codifying existing state control over all aspects of religious life.

Members of unauthorized religious denominations continued to face repression including harassment, forced renunciation of their faith, administrative detention and imprisonment. Members of the Unified Buddhist Church of Vietnam (UBCV) faced particularly harsh treatment and their leadership remained under house arrest. Members of evangelical protestant churches also faced harassment.

Mennonite pastor and human rights activist Nguyen Hong Quang was arrested and sentenced to three years' imprisonment in November. Pastor Quang had been outspoken about the situation of religious freedoms in the Central Highlands for ethnic minority groups, and had defended farmers in land rights cases.

Father Nguyen Van Ly, a Catholic priest and vocal critic of government policies, had his prison sentence reduced for the second time, to five years, in response to international criticism. He had been sentenced to 15 years' imprisonment in 2001 under vaguely worded national security legislation.

Thich Tri Luc, a UBCV monk, was tried in March and sentenced to 20 months' imprisonment on charges of having "distorted the government's policies on national unity and contacted hostile groups to undermine the government's internal security and foreign affairs". He was released in late March having already spent 20 months in pre-trial detention, and gained asylum in Sweden. He had been recognized as a refugee by the UN High Commissioner for Refugees in Cambodia in 2002, but was abducted from Cambodia by Vietnamese agents and held for almost a year incommunicado before his trial. On his release, Thich Tri Luc confirmed both the Vietnamese and Cambodian authorities' role and collusion in his abduction.

Death penalty

At least 88 people — including 12 women — were sentenced to death in 2004; 44 for drug offences and six for fraud, according to official sources. At least 64 people, four of them women, were reported executed. The true figures were believed to be much higher.

In January, the Prime Minister issued a decree making the reporting and dissemination of statistics on the use of the death penalty a "state secret". However, some death penalty and execution cases continued to be reported in the Vietnamese news media.

In October, the Prime Minister asked the police to consider changing the method of execution because nervous members of firing squads with trembling hands frequently missed the target. It was reported that relatives of executed prisoners had to bribe officials for the return of bodies which were otherwise buried in the execution ground.

Despite reports that the authorities were considering the abolition of the death penalty for economic crimes, two executions for fraud were reported. Some executions continued to take place in public, in front of hundreds of onlookers.

Tran Thi My Ha, 31, was executed on 17 November by firing squad at Tan Xuan execution ground in Quang Nam province. She had been sentenced to death in August 2003 after being convicted of running a network trafficking counterfeit money.

Nguyen Thi Ha, 48, was executed at Long Binh execution ground in Ho Chi Minh City on 9 April in front of hundreds of spectators. She had been sentenced to death for smuggling heroin.

AI country reports/ visits
Reports
- Socialist Republic of Viet Nam: Renewed concern for the Montagnard minority (AI Index: ASA 41/005/2004)
- Viet Nam: Early release of cyber-dissident Le Chi Quang (AI Index: ASA 41/007/2004)
- Viet Nam: Death penalty – a dirty secret (AI Index: ASA 41/003/2004)

YEMEN

REPUBLIC OF YEMEN
Head of state: 'Ali 'Abdullah Saleh
Head of government: 'Abdul Qader Bajammal
Death penalty: retentionist
International Criminal Court: signed
UN Women's Convention: ratified with reservations
Optional Protocol to UN Women's Convention: not signed

Hundreds of people were killed, including many who may have been killed unlawfully, during armed clashes between security forces and political opponents in Sa'da Province. Hundreds of people were arrested and most of those detained from previous years remained held without charge or trial. In the rare instances where detainees were brought to trial, the proceedings invariably failed to meet international standards. There were increased punitive measures against journalists and restrictions on press freedom. The government continued to forcibly return people to countries where they were at risk of human rights violations. There were reports of torture or ill-treatment. The punishment of flogging continued to be imposed by courts and carried out. Women's organizations continued to campaign against discrimination and violence against women. At least six people were executed and scores, possibly hundreds, remained under sentence of death.

Background

Governmental and non-governmental human rights conferences and workshops were held in Yemen, raising the profile of human rights. They included the intergovernmental "Sana'a Regional Conference on Human Rights and the Role of the International Criminal Court" and the conference "Human Rights for All", which was organized by AI and HOOD, a local non-governmental organization (see Middle East/North Africa Regional Overview 2004).

However, the human rights situation, already gravely affected by the government's pursuit of the "war on terror" with disregard for the rule of law, was exacerbated by armed clashes in Sa'da Province between security forces and followers of the late Hussain Badr al-Din al-Huthi, a cleric from the Zaidi community.

In August the Ministry of Social Affairs and Labour granted refugees the right to work. Tens of thousands of refugees from countries including Somalia and Ethiopia had been living in Yemen as refugees for years without the right to seek employment.

Killings in Sa'da Province

In June violence erupted in Sa'da Province between security forces and followers of Hussain Badr al-Din al-Huthi. Tensions between the government and Hussain Badr al-Din al-Huthi began with protests by the latter's followers before and during the US-led invasion of Iraq in 2003. After the war, the followers carried on the protests after Friday prayers every week outside mosques, particularly the Grand Mosque in Sana'a, during which they shouted anti-US and Israeli slogans. The protests were invariably followed by arrests and detentions (see below). In June the government called on Hussain Badr al-Din al-Huthi to surrender. When he refused the tension escalated into armed clashes, which lasted until September when government officials announced the death of Hussain Badr al-Din al-Huthi.

Hundreds of people were killed during the clashes. Security forces reportedly used heavy weaponry, including helicopter gunships. Exact details about the killings were not available as the security forces denied journalists access to Sa'da, but in at least one case a helicopter gunship reportedly attacked civilian targets and a number of people were killed. Excessive use of force and extrajudicial killings may have been the main or contributory factors behind the death toll. Reports indicated that children were among the dead. AI called for an investigation into the killing of civilians but no such investigation was known to have been initiated by the end of the year.

Mass arrests and detention without charge or trial

Hundreds of people were arrested during the year and hundreds detained from previous years remained held without charge or trial. They included followers of Hussain Badr al-Din al-Huthi and people arrested in the context of the "war on terror".

Up to 250 followers of Hussain Badr al-Din al-Huthi were reportedly arrested in January alone. Hundreds more were arrested in subsequent months, particularly after the clashes in Sa'da. They included children as young as 11. Many of those detained were said to have not been involved in violent activities.

▢ Adil Shalli was arrested after reportedly circulating a statement opposing the government's military action against followers of Hussain Badr al-Din al-Huthi.

With the exception of a few cases such as that of Judge Muhammad Ali Luqman, who was accused of supporting Hussain Badr al-Din al-Huthi and subsequently tried and sentenced to 10 years' imprisonment, the remaining hundreds of detainees continued to be held without charge or trial. None was allowed access to legal assistance.

No details about those arrested in connection with the "war on terror" were available, but they included at least 17 people who had been returned to Yemen from abroad.

▢ Walid Muhammad Shahir al-Qadasi, a 24-year-old Yemeni national who had been detained in Guantánamo Bay, Cuba, since 2002, was returned to Yemen in April and immediately arrested. Eleven days after his arrival in the Political Security prison, he told AI that his family had not been informed of his arrival in Yemen and that he had been given no access to a lawyer or a judge. It was not known if he remained held at the end of the year.

Over 100 of those held from previous years in connection with the "war on terror" were released, but up to 200 remained in detention without charge or trial. Those freed were reportedly released after agreeing to engage in religious dialogue with Islamic figures and signing a pledge that they had renounced their "extremist" views. However, they remained under restrictions. For example, some were required to report regularly to police, stay near their homes and only contact journalists with the permission of the security forces.

Targeting of journalists

There were increased punitive measures against journalists, including imprisonment, detentions, fines and suspended prison sentences.

Abdulkarim al-Khaiwani, editor-in-chief of *al-Shura*, the weekly publication of the opposition Union of Popular Forces, was sentenced to one year's imprisonment in September by a court in Sana'a. He was accused of supporting Hussain Badr al-Din al-Huthi. *Al-Shura* was also closed down for six months. An appeal hearing was scheduled for December but was delayed.

Saeed Thabet, a Yemeni correspondent for a London-based news agency, was detained in March for a week after reporting that the Yemeni President's son had been shot. The alleged shooting was denied by officials. In April a court imposed a fine and suspended him from working as a journalist for six months.

In late December, four men, including Abdul Wahid Hawash and Abdul Jabbar Saad, respectively editor and journalist for *Al-Ehyaa Al-Araby* newspaper, received suspended prison terms of between four and six months after writing and publishing articles reportedly criticizing Saudi Arabia.

Unfair trials

Three men were sentenced to death and 18 others received prison terms after two lengthy trials which fell short of international standards of fairness. Both trials suffered numerous delays. Defence lawyers were initially prevented from reading relevant documents and could only speak to their clients during court hearings, and not in private. Subsequently, some of the lawyers withdrew from the defence team stating that the accused could not receive a fair trial.

Hizam Saleh Megalli was sentenced to death on 28 August in Sana'a in connection with the bombing of the *Limberg*, a French oil tanker, in October 2002. Fourteen other men, including one tried in absentia, were sentenced to between three and 10 years' imprisonment for the attack on the *Limberg*, a shooting incident involving an aircraft belonging to the US company Hunt Oil, and an assassination attempt. All lodged appeals which were pending at the end of the year.

Jamal Mohammed al-Badawi was sentenced to death on 29 September in Sana'a in connection with the bombing of the *USS Cole* in October 2000. Abd Al Rahim al-Nashiri, who was tried in absentia, was also sentenced to death. He remained in custody in the USA

at the end of the year. Four other men were sentenced to prison terms of between five and 10 years. All lodged appeals which were pending at the end of the year.

Forcible returns

The government continued to forcibly return people to countries where they were at risk of human rights violations. Those returned during the year included 15 Egyptians who had been detained in Yemen since 2001. Among them were Dr Sayyid 'Abd al-Aziz Imam al-Sharif on whose behalf AI had issued an appeal in February 2002 urging the Yemeni government not to return him to Egypt, and Uthman al-Samman and Muhammed 'Abd al-Aziz al-Gamal, who had been sentenced to death by a military court in Egypt in 1994 and 1999 respectively. All were returned in February in exchange for the forcible return to Yemen of Colonel Ahmed Salem Obeid, Former Deputy Minister for Defence in the People's Democratic Republic of Yemen, who had been living in Egypt since fleeing the civil war in Yemen in 1994. After his return he was detained in secret until May when he was released without charge or trial. The fate and whereabouts of the 15 Egyptians were not known to AI and were also said not to be known to their families and friends.

Update: 'Abd al-Salam al-Hiyla

'Abd al-Salam al-Hiyla, a 32-year-old Yemeni businessman and former high-ranking officer in the Yemeni Political Security, travelled to Egypt on a business trip in September 2002 but did not return. His family only learned about his whereabouts in October 2004 when they received information that he was being held in Kabul and then Bagram in Afghanistan. They subsequently received a letter through the International Committee of the Red Cross informing them that he had been transferred to Guantánamo Bay.

Torture

Torture and ill-treatment continued to be reported. Flogging continued to be imposed and carried out in public for a number of offences, including for the consumption of alcohol, for slander and for sexual offences.

Journalist Muhammed al-Qiri was beaten around the face when he was arrested by security forces outside the Grand Mosque on 26 March for photographing arrests. During interrogation he was reportedly blindfolded, told to stand facing a wall with his hands raised over his head, insulted and threatened with further beatings. His head was also reportedly smashed into an iron bar. He was released the following morning on condition that he would not photograph arrests in future. No investigation was known to have been carried out into the allegations.

In June, 14 suspects in the *Limberg* trial (see above) told the court they had been tortured by intelligence officers in pre-trial detention. One of the men reportedly shouted out during the trial proceedings that some of them had received electric shocks. The court ordered an investigation into the allegations. There was no further information by the end of the year.

Discrimination and violence against women

Women's organizations continued to campaign against the many forms of discrimination facing women and violence against women. In January the Justice Minister announced that female judges would be appointed as heads of the juvenile courts. In September the Ministry of Local Administration began a training programme for women to increase their participation in local administration. The National Women's Committee announced that its aim was to ensure that women made up 30 per cent of all elected and unelected bodies including parliament, the *Shura* Council, ministries and the diplomatic corps. The Head of the Committee said that proposals to modify some laws that discriminated against women were awaiting parliamentary approval.

In September women leaders in the three main political parties called for a quota system for women in the next parliamentary elections. In December "Women's Political Empowerment is a necessary step for Political Reform in the Arab World", a conference organized by the Sisters Arab Forum for Human Rights under the patronage of the Minister of Human Rights, was held. Delegates reportedly requested that the election law be amended temporarily to give women a 30 per cent quota of parliamentary seats until at least 2010.

Death penalty

Death sentences continued to be passed and at least six people were executed. Up to hundreds of people may have remained under sentence of death.

▭ In August the death sentence against Fuad 'Ali Mohsen al-Shahari, who had been convicted of murder in 1996, was referred back to the Supreme Court by the President for review. In March the Supreme Court had upheld the sentence. Fuad al-Shahari had reportedly been tortured and ill-treated to force a confession. He was at risk of imminent execution.

▭ Nabil al-Mankali, a Spanish national, remained under sentence of death. The sentence had been ratified by the President in September 2003. He was at risk of imminent execution.

▭ Layla Radman 'A'esh, a Yemeni woman sentenced to death by stoning for adultery in 2000, was released in March.

AI country reports/visits

Report

- The Gulf and Arabian Peninsula: Human rights fall victim to the "war on terror" (AI Index: MDE 04/002/2004)

Visits

Three separate AI delegations visited Yemen in 2004 for research, talks with government officials and to organize the conference "Human Rights for All".

ZAMBIA

REPUBLIC OF ZAMBIA
Head of state and government: Levy Mwanawasa
Death penalty: retentionist
International Criminal Court: ratified
UN Women's Convention: ratified
Optional Protocol to UN Women's Convention: not signed

Journalists and members of opposition or civil society organizations remained at risk of arbitrary detention or harassment, and members of parliament were among opposition leaders detained. Legal reforms to strengthen official responses to violence against women were promised. President Mwanawasa commuted some 60 death sentences but the death penalty was not abolished.

Background

The Constitutional Review Commission largely appointed by President Mwanawasa in 2003 to review the Constitution was the focus of demands for popular consultation on fundamental constitutional reforms. In September, Justice Minister George Kunda threatened treason charges against critics demanding that a new Constitution be adopted by an elected assembly before elections were held in 2006. A petition to the Supreme Court challenging the results of the 2001 presidential elections, which observers regarded as unfair, had still not been heard by the end of 2004. Corruption charges against former President Frederick Chiluba, arrested in 2003 and released on bail to await trial, were drastically scaled down after the prosecution withdrew charges.

Threats to freedom of expression

Journalists, opposition supporters and members of civil society organizations perceived as critical of the government remained at risk of harassment or arrest. Although the courts have usually reversed unconstitutional government orders, they continued to be issued.

▭ On 5 January, Roy Clarke, a British national resident in Zambia for 40 years and columnist for *The Post* newspaper, was given 24 hours to leave the country after he had allegedly insulted President Mwanawasa in an article published the same day. The courts later rescinded the order.

▭ In May the women's organization Women for Change was threatened with deregistration and its Chairperson Emily Sikazwe with removal of her citizenship and deportation to Malawi, apparently because of her human rights work and criticism of the government.

▭ In November the authorities deregistered the Southern Africa Centre for Constructive Resolution of Disputes (SACCORD), a critic of the constitutional review process, claiming its activities were a threat to national security. The courts stayed the deregistration.

In December, 11 members of parliament and 57 other protesters were briefly detained in Lusaka and charged with unlawful assembly after they attempted to demonstrate in support of their demand for a new Constitution before the 2006 elections. Journalists covering the protest were reportedly beaten by police officers.

Some opposition parties were denied permits to hold rallies by the police. Opposition officials were also unable to gain the same level of access to the state-controlled media as the ruling party.

Permission to hold rallies was denied to the Zambia Republican Party in Lusaka in January, and the United Party for National Development in Mumbwa in July. At a rally in Lusaka in August by the opposition Patriotic Front, two people were injured when supporters of the ruling party attacked participants.

Violence against women

The high level of violence against women in Zambia was highlighted in a US Agency for International Development survey published in June, which found that 48 per cent of women respondents said they had been subjected to physical or sexual abuse. One Lusaka hospital alone was reported in June to be treating four new rape cases every day. The police Victim Support Unit lacked capacity, particularly in rural areas where customary law continues to limit women's sexual and reproductive rights.

In June lawyers' organizations criticized the inadequacy of laws on violence against women. In response, President Mwanawasa directed that the law be strengthened. A bill to amend the law had not come before parliament by the end of 2004.

Police abuses

Torture of suspects in police custody continued. In May, a member of the government expressed concern at the high cost of compensation paid to victims of police brutality.

In August, Lusaka police officers reportedly beat Joseph Bwalya with an iron bar after he demanded payment of a debt from a former member of parliament.

Police officers in Munali were alleged to have tied Aliyele Sakala to a grille for three days in March and beat him until he fainted, after he failed to pay a debt. He reportedly suffered long-term paralysis as a result.

Death penalty

In May, President Mwanawasa commuted the death sentences on 15 prisoners convicted in separate cases of murder and armed robbery. In February he commuted the death sentences on 44 soldiers convicted of involvement in a failed coup in 1997, and repeated assurances that there would be no executions during his presidency. In June, one of the 44, Jack Chiti, was released from prison on health grounds.

ZIMBABWE

REPUBLIC OF ZIMBABWE
Head of state and government: Robert Mugabe
Death penalty: retentionist
International Criminal Court: signed
UN Women's Convention: ratified
Optional Protocol to UN Women's Convention: not signed

The government continued its campaign of repression aimed at eliminating political opposition and silencing dissent. Hundreds of people were arrested for holding meetings or participating in peaceful protests. The police, army, supporters of the ruling Zimbabwe African National Union-Patriotic Front (ZANU-PF) and youth militia were implicated in numerous human rights violations, including torture, assault and arbitrary detention. Despite compelling evidence that Zimbabwe would continue to experience food shortages, the government terminated most international food aid programmes. In December parliament passed legislation banning foreign human rights groups from operating in Zimbabwe and imposing restrictions on local human rights organizations, including prohibiting them from receiving foreign funding for human rights work.

Background

After a protracted court case the leader of the opposition Movement for Democratic Change (MDC), Morgan Tsvangirai, was acquitted of treason on 15 October. In November the state filed an application with the Supreme Court for leave to appeal against the acquittal. The matter had not been heard by the end of the year. Morgan Tsvangirai also faced a second charge of treason in connection with mass protests during 2003. This case, repeatedly postponed, was still pending at the end of the year.

In August the MDC, the main opposition party, announced that it was suspending its participation in elections until the government put in place reforms that would enable free and fair elections to take place. At the end of the year it remained unclear whether the MDC would contest parliamentary elections scheduled for March 2005.

On 9 December parliament passed the Electoral Commission Act, ostensibly as part of efforts to bring Zimbabwe into line with the Southern African Development Community (SADC) Principles and Guidelines Governing Democratic Elections. However, human rights and democracy groups criticized some aspects of this legislation, which violate the rights to freedom of association and information.

In February President Mugabe used the Presidential Powers (Temporary Measures) Act to amend the Criminal Procedures and Evidence Act (CPEA). The amendments allowed for pre-trial detention of up to 28 days of people suspected of certain economic crimes or certain offences under the repressive Public Order and Security Act (POSA).

In July the African Union Assembly was due to consider the annual activity report of the African Commission on Human and Peoples' Rights on the human rights situation in Zimbabwe, which contained in an appendix the findings and recommendations of a fact-finding mission to Zimbabwe in 2002. However, the Zimbabwean authorities argued that they had not been given a proper opportunity to respond to the report of the African Commission's fact-finding mission, and consideration of the annual activity report was postponed. By the end of 2004, neither the annual activity report, nor the full report of the 2002 fact-finding mission – which was known to be critical of the human rights situation in Zimbabwe – had been officially published.

In October a senior delegation of the Congress of South African Trade Unions (COSATU) visiting Zimbabwe on a fact-finding mission was summarily deported from the country. The government of Zimbabwe claimed that the visit was of a political nature, apparently because COSATU intended to meet civic and human rights organizations that were critical of the government.

Human rights defenders
Human rights organizations came under renewed attack by the authorities. Following widespread publicity given to the unpublished African Commission report (see above), local human rights organizations were subjected to a campaign of vilification through the state-controlled media. Several non-governmental organizations (NGOs) were accused of "writing" the report or supplying false information to the Commissioners.

On 9 December parliament passed legislation requiring all NGOs to register with a government-appointed NGO Council. The Council was given sweeping powers to interfere with the operations of NGOs, including refusing registration and thereby shutting down NGOs. The legislation singles out organizations that work on "governance", defined as including human rights, banning foreign governance and human rights groups from operating in Zimbabwe and prohibiting national organizations involved in governance and human rights work from receiving foreign funding.

Freedom of association and assembly
The POSA continued to be used selectively to prevent the political opposition and civil society groups from meeting or engaging in peaceful protest. Hundreds of civil society activists and members of the MDC were arrested under POSA. Many of those arrested were subjected to ill-treatment and intimidation while in police custody.

▭ On 28 September, 48 members of the women's organization, Women of Zimbabwe Arise (WOZA), as well as four men working with them, were detained by police, citing POSA, as they neared the end of a 440km sponsored walk from Bulawayo to Harare. They were reportedly intimidated and threatened by police officers. Another woman activist, Siphiwe Maseko, was arbitrarily detained the same day when she attempted to deliver food to those in custody; she was released the following day without charge. The rest of the group was held in custody until 1 October, when a magistrate ruled that they had no case to answer. All were released.

On 29 September, WOZA activists who had not been arrested the previous day finished the walk, gathered at Africa Unity Square in Harare and held a brief prayer service for those in detention. As they began to disperse nine women were arrested by police, who reportedly claimed that the women had contravened Section 19 of POSA by "praying in public". Section 19 of POSA refers to "gatherings conducing to riot, disorder or intolerance". The activists were detained at Harare Central Police Station where three of the women were allegedly assaulted by a plain-clothes officer during interrogation. All were released on bail on 1 October. When they appeared in court on 13 October to answer the charges, no charge sheets were presented and all were released. No further action had been taken by the end of the year.

Repression of independent media
The authorities continued to use the repressive Access to Information and Protection of Privacy Act (AIPPA) to harass, intimidate and silence journalists and newspapers viewed as critical of the government. In November parliament amended the AIPPA, making the practice of journalism without accreditation a criminal offence punishable by up to two years in prison.

▭ On 9 January the High Court ordered the Zimbabwe Republic Police to vacate the offices of Zimbabwe's only independent daily newspaper, the *Daily News*. The police had occupied the newspaper's offices in December 2003, just hours after a court had ordered that the paper – closed down in September 2003 – be allowed to resume publication. The police initially failed to obey the 9 January court order, and the *Daily News* was only able to recommence publication on 21 January. On 22 January the Media Information Commission (MIC) and the Minister for Information and Publicity initiated court proceedings to once again prevent the *Daily News* from publishing. The MIC had consistently refused to register the *Daily News*, despite a court order compelling it to do so.

On 5 February the Supreme Court ruled that the AIPPA was constitutional. The decision was in response to a constitutional challenge by the Independent Journalists Association of Zimbabwe to sections of the AIPPA. This ruling effectively forced the *Daily News* to cease publication as it meant that publishers and journalists faced arrest. The *Daily News* remained unable to publish at the end of the year.

▭ On 10 January, Iden Wetherall, Vincent Kahiya and Dumisani Muleya, editor, news editor and chief reporter respectively of the weekly *Zimbabwe Independent* newspaper, were arrested and charged with criminal defamation in connection with a story printed in the newspaper on 9 January which alleged that President Mugabe had commandeered an Air Zimbabwe plane for personal travel. A fourth journalist, Itai Dzamara, was arrested on 14 January and also charged with criminal defamation. All were released on bail. The case was still pending at the end of the year.

Excessive use of force
The Zimbabwe Republic Police continued to use excessive force when policing public gatherings. Police also used excessive force during forced evictions which took place in the second half of the year.

On 2 September police, war veterans and youth militia attempted to forcibly evict some 10,000 residents from Porta Farm, an informal settlement on the outskirts of Harare. The police were acting in defiance of a court order prohibiting the eviction. The police reportedly fired tear gas directly into the homes of some of the Porta Farm residents. One man, who had been ill with tuberculosis, died shortly after being exposed to the tear gas. At least 10 other people died during the following three weeks. Residents claimed that all those who died, several of whom were reported to have had pre-existing illnesses, had been exposed to the tear gas. Five of the dead were children under the age of one. Hundreds of other residents complained of chest and stomach pains and other ill effects resulting from their exposure to tear gas.

Torture and ill-treatment
State security agents, including members of the Zimbabwe Republic Police and the Central Intelligence Organization (CIO), were implicated in numerous cases of torture, assault and ill-treatment. Victims were primarily members of the political opposition and those perceived as critical of the government. Throughout the year ZANU-PF supporters and youth militia were also implicated in the assault, abduction and intimidation of those believed to be members or supporters of the political opposition. Both state and non-state perpetrators appeared to operate with impunity.

On 14 October, three unidentified men assaulted Philani Zamchiya, President of the Zimbabwe National Students Union (ZINASU), near the union headquarters in Harare. Several police officers then reportedly arrived on the scene and Philani Zamchiya was pushed into a vehicle. He reported that the police officers then assaulted him. He managed to escape by jumping from the moving vehicle and subsequently spent several days in hospital. While Philani Zamchiya was in hospital, men believed to be state security agents reportedly entered his hospital room and demanded information on ZINASU activities, although he was unable to speak as a result of his injuries. No one had been arrested in connection with the assault on Philani Zamchiya by the end of the year.

On 22 April police in Harare brutally assaulted Tinashe Chimedza, a youth activist and former ZINASU president. He had been due to speak at an education forum in Harare. Police detained him at the venue and kicked, punched and beat him with batons. He was hospitalized for several days as a result of his injuries.

Lovemore Madhuku, Chairman of the National Constitutional Assembly (NCA), was severely beaten on 4 February when police officers broke up a peaceful NCA demonstration outside parliament. He was taken from the site of the demonstration to another location in Harare where police punched him and beat him with batons before dumping him on the outskirts of the city centre. Lovemore Madhuku was hospitalized for several days. No one had been arrested in connection with the assault by the end of the year.

Workers and their families on the Charleswood Estate farm of the opposition member of parliament (MP) for Chimanimani, Roy Bennett, were systematically targeted in a series of violent attacks by state agents and ruling party supporters. The farm workers had been repeatedly targeted since 2000 because they worked for an MDC MP. During the year dozens of farm workers were beaten, harassed and intimidated. In one incident children as young as eight were reportedly assaulted by soldiers. At least two women were raped, one allegedly by a police officer. One man was fatally shot (see below). On 9 April state agents, including the police and army, took possession of Roy Bennett's farm in defiance of court orders which prohibited acquisition of the farm by the state, and which directed the state and its functionaries to vacate the farm and cease interference with its operations and staff.

On 8 February a group of some 20 ZANU-PF supporters attacked the home of Amos Makaza, a security officer at Charleswood Estate. When other farm workers came to Amos Makaza's assistance the assailants left, but later returned with members of the Zimbabwe Army. The soldiers opened fire on some of the farm workers. Shemi Chimbarara was shot and died instantly. Another farm worker, John Kaitano, was shot in the leg. A soldier was reported to have been arrested in connection with the shooting of Shemi Chimbarara.

Elections
By-elections held during the year were marked by politically motivated violence and intimidation. Scores of MDC supporters were assaulted and intimidated during a by-election in Zengeza in March. The main perpetrators of this violence were reported to be ZANU-PF supporters. MDC supporters were also the targets of violence before, during and after by-elections in Gutu-North in February and in Lupane in May.

On 28 March, MDC activist Francis Chinozvina was shot dead when a group of ZANU-PF supporters reportedly attacked the house of the MDC candidate for Zengeza, James Makore. Another MDC activist was shot in the leg. Eyewitnesses reportedly implicated a senior ruling party figure in the shooting. However, on 6 April police arrested a different man in connection with the killing.

Administration of justice
On 28 October, in a parliamentary procedure which failed to meet many of the requirements for a fair trial, MDC MP Roy Bennett was sentenced to a 15-month jail term with hard labour for pushing the Minister for Justice, Legal and Parliamentary Affairs to the ground

during a heated exchange in parliament on 18 May. Roy Bennett was denied the right of appeal and placed in Harare Central Prison. On 26 November he was transferred to Mutoko prison in north-east Zimbabwe, which restricted the ability of his family and lawyers to visit him. Initial attempts by lawyers acting for Roy Bennett to bring the matter before the courts were blocked by the Speaker of Parliament. However, on 9 November an urgent application was heard in the High Court of Zimbabwe. The judgement had not been delivered by the end of the year and Roy Bennett remained in prison.

Violations of the right to food

In May the government announced that Zimbabwe had had a "bumper" harvest and no longer needed international food aid. By June most food aid distribution had stopped although some programmes aimed at very vulnerable populations continued. The government's claims about the size of the 2004 harvest were widely discredited, and by the end of the year there was mounting evidence of hunger and food shortages in many areas of Zimbabwe. There were also reports that ZANU-PF party cards were being demanded in some areas before people could access state-controlled grain. The government-controlled Grain Marketing Board (GMB) has an almost total monopoly on the import of and trade in maize, the staple food of most Zimbabweans, and a history of discriminatory allocation of the food it controls.

In November the government agreed to allow the World Food Programme to undertake a one-off distribution of food aid to 1.6 million people during December.

Forced evictions

In the last four months of 2004 the police and army forcibly evicted thousands of people from farms where they had settled between 2000 and 2002. Homes and belongings were destroyed and families left destitute. Human rights lawyers subsequently obtained court orders which allowed people to return to the farms, but some families reported that government officials and state agents continued to harass them and threaten them with removal.

AI country reports/ visits
Report
· Zimbabwe: Power and hunger — violations of the right to food (AI Index: AFR 46/026/2004)
Visits
AI delegates visited Zimbabwe in February and June.

AI REPORT 2005
PART 3

WHAT DOES AI DO?

Amnesty International (AI) mobilizes volunteer activists – people who give freely of their time and energy in solidarity with the victims of human rights abuses. At the latest count there were more than 1.8 million AI members and supporters in over 150 countries and territories in every region of the world.

AI members come from many different backgrounds, with widely different political and religious beliefs, united by a determination to work for a world where everyone enjoys all human rights. AI members may be organized in groups in local communities, schools and colleges. Others participate in networks focused on particular countries and themes or using particular campaigning techniques.

During 2004, AI's members and supporters in countries around the world campaigned to stop the global human rights scandal of violence against women, which devastates the lives of countless women and girls. They sought to build controls over the international arms trade, which fuels conflict, poverty and human rights abuses. They urged their governments to support the International Criminal Court and end impunity for the perpetrators of the worst crimes known to humanity. They tried to protect human rights defenders working on the frontline and to defend the rights of refugees and asylum-seekers in an often hostile environment. Networks of activists focused on the rights of children and of lesbian, gay, bisexual and transgender people. Other networks worked on issues to do with business and economic relations. Some networks mobilize particular sectors: these include students and youth; trade unionists; and health professionals.

One of the year's main campaigns drew attention to the human rights crisis in Darfur, Sudan, where thousands of civilians were killed, tens of thousands made homeless and thousands of women were raped by government-backed militias. AI called for an end to arms transfers that perpetuate the conflict and for those responsible for human rights crimes to be brought to justice. Other major campaigning projects addressed: people-trafficking in Europe; the human rights crisis in Haiti; "disappearances" in Nepal; continuing human rights concerns in Iraq in the wake of the US-led invasion and occupation; and child soldiers across the world. On the 20th anniversary of the gas explosion in Bhopal, India, AI highlighted the facts that the survivors have still not received just compensation or adequate medical help, the plant site has still not been cleaned up and so continues to contaminate the area, and no one has been held responsible for the deaths of over 20,000 people and the debilitating illnesses of thousands of others.

Whatever the particular focus, the activities of AI's members, supporters and staff aim to support the victims of human rights abuses and people working on their behalf and to influence those who have the power to make a difference.

A democratic movement

AI is a democratic, self-governing movement. Major policy decisions are taken by an International Council made up of representatives from all national sections. The Council meets every two years, and has the power to amend the Statute which governs AI's work and methods. (The Statute is available from the International Secretariat or on the AI website, www.amnesty.org.) The Council elects an International Executive Committee of volunteers which carries out its decisions and appoints the movement's Secretary General, who heads up the International Secretariat and is the movement's chief spokesperson.

AI's Secretary General is Irene Khan (Bangladesh), and the members of the International Executive Committee (elected for 2003-5) are Margaret Bedggood (New Zealand), Alvaro Briceño (Venezuela), Ian Gibson (Australia), Paul Hoffman (USA, chair until September 2004), Mariam Lam (Senegal), Claire Paponneau (France), Marian Pink (Austria), Hanna Roberts (Sweden) and Jaap Rosen Jacobson (Netherlands, chair from September 2004).

AI's national sections and local volunteer groups and networks are primarily responsible for funding the movement through donations from members and the public. No funds are sought or accepted from governments for AI's work investigating and campaigning against human rights violations. Information about AI's finances is published annually in the *Amnesty International Review*.

Information about AI is available from national section offices, on the AI website, www.amnesty.org, and from the International Secretariat, Peter Benenson House, 1 Easton Street, London WC1X 0DW, United Kingdom.

AI's guiding principles

AI is independent of any government, political persuasion or religious creed. AI does not support or oppose the views of the victims whose rights it seeks to protect. It is concerned solely with the impartial protection of human rights.

AI forms a global community of human rights defenders whose principles include international solidarity, effective action for the individual victim, the universality and indivisibility of human rights, impartiality and independence, and democracy and mutual respect.

AI's vision is of a world in which every person enjoys all the human rights enshrined in the Universal Declaration of Human Rights and other international human rights standards. Its ambition is to promote ethical globalization to strengthen the forces of justice – the forces that provide hope for the many people worldwide whose rights have been abused.

AI's mission is to undertake research and action focused on preventing and ending grave abuses of the rights to physical and mental integrity, freedom of conscience and expression, and freedom from discrimination, within the context of its work to promote all human rights.

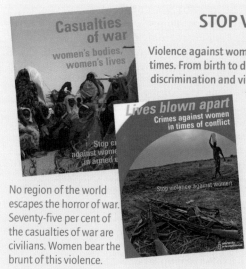

STOP VIOLENCE AGAINST WOMEN

Casualties of war
women's bodies,
women's lives

Lives blown apart
Crimes against women in times of conflict

Violence against women is one of the greatest human rights scandals of our times. From birth to death, in times of peace as well as war, women face discrimination and violence at the hands of the state, the community and the family.

AI's Stop Violence Against Women Campaign, launched in March 2004, shows that violence against women is universal, but it is not inevitable.

No region of the world escapes the horror of war. Seventy-five per cent of the casualties of war are civilians. Women bear the brunt of this violence.

AI's campaign is designed to mobilize both men and women in organizing to counter violence, and to use the power and persuasion of the human rights framework in the efforts to stop violence against women. It calls on everybody – the state, the community and individuals – to acknowledge their responsibility to stop this worldwide human rights scandal.

AI's areas of work

AI's work to build a better world is organized around eight global goals.

Reform and strengthen the justice sector

The central importance of the rule of law for any field of human activity is widely recognized across societies and governing systems. Yet many of the domestic institutions which are meant to uphold the rule of law are seriously flawed, resulting in continuing widespread human rights violations, committed with impunity. Such human rights violations include the imprisonment of prisoners of conscience, unfair political trials, torture and ill-treatment, "disappearances" and unlawful killings. International mechanisms to compensate for domestic failures have evolved rapidly in the last decade, but remain still embryonic and contested.

AI's objectives are to:
- Reform police practice and strengthen the judiciary.
- Address discrimination in the justice sector, particularly with regard to Lesbian, Gay, Bisexual and Transgender people (LGBT) and ethnic and religious minorities.
- Consolidate international criminal justice, specifically by supporting the International Criminal Court and universal jurisdiction.
- Ensure human rights in transitional justice.
- Strengthen national, regional and international mechanisms of state accountability, focusing in particular on UN reform.
- Further develop international standards, for example on "disappearances" and with regard to companies.
- Study the impact of corruption on the administration of justice.

Abolish the death penalty

The momentum for abolition of the death penalty continues, particularly at the inter-governmental level, through the emergence of a World Coalition against the Death Penalty, and the work of national organizations working to abolish the death penalty. However, a sizeable number of countries remain opposed to abolition, and the threats of "terrorism", drugs and organized crime are being used to justify the retention or even in some cases the reinstatement of capital punishment.

AI's objectives are to:
- Promote abolition of the death penalty and moratoriums on its use, in specific countries and internationally, especially by showing the impact of discrimination.
- Monitor death penalty developments globally and respond quickly to events such as action on emblematic cases.
- Produce global statistics, thematic reports and action.
- End the use of the death penalty for child offenders.

Protect the rights of defenders

Human rights defenders are at the frontline of work on human rights. There is increasing recognition of the important role that activists play in promoting human rights. Throughout the world, however, they are deliberately targeted in a variety of ways. Governments use many pretexts to stifle legitimate criticism of their policies, including security and the "war on terror".

AI's objectives are to:
- Engage defenders from all sectors of society, building coalitions, skills and greater visibility for women.
- Highlight the contribution of defenders to the security of society at large and address abuses impacting on their rights, including those arising from security measures.
- Promote the protection and safety of human rights defenders and counter the misuses of the judicial system to persecute them.
- Widen and deepen the use of the UN Declaration on human rights defenders, and support the work of UN and regional protection mechanisms.

Resist human rights abuses in the 'war on terror'

The framework of international law and multilateral action is undergoing the most sustained attack since its establishment. International human rights law and international humanitarian law are being challenged as ineffective in responding to security issues. Governments are eroding human rights standards. Armed groups continue to carry out abuses, and some operate in a loose global alliance. Public opinion is polarized.

AI's objectives are to:

- Address the human rights impact of "counter-terrorism" measures, focusing specifically on detention and trial safeguards, torture, killings and discriminatory laws and practices.
- Address the impact of cooperation agreements among states on human rights protection.
- Engage with the development of treaties on "terrorism".
- Promote international and regional mechanisms for state accountability.
- Report on abuses by armed groups, and explore strategies for raising human rights concerns with these groups.
- Advance progressive interpretations of international human rights and humanitarian law as relevant to the "war on terror".

Uphold the rights of refugees and migrants

The debate relating to the rights of refugees, migrants and the displaced has become increasingly high profile, controversial and politicized. People will continue to move across borders seeking protection from persecution or driven by the prospects of economic opportunities. Demand for cheap and exploitative migrant labour will continue. Xenophobic and racist responses to refugees, asylum-seekers and migrants will continue in both developed and developing countries. Restrictive migration control measures and security measures targeting non-nationals will force people "underground". The vulnerability of non-nationals to a wide variety of human rights abuses will increase.

AI's objectives are to:

- Defend refugees' right not to be returned to countries where they might suffer abuses of their fundamental human rights.
- Defend the right of asylum-seekers to access fair and satisfactory asylum procedures.
- Ensure a human rights approach to solutions to refugee problems.
- Promote the human rights of migrants.
- Monitor and address arbitrary detention practices applied to refugees and migrants.
- Enhance economic, social and cultural rights of refugees and migrants.
- Improve protection of refugee and displaced girls and women vulnerable to sexual exploitation and abuse.

Promote economic, social and cultural rights for marginalized communities

Growing global inequities, and the failure of governments to significantly reduce the number of people living in extreme poverty, are among the defining human rights issues of our times. There is still little acceptance that poverty raises fundamental issues of human rights. However, there is growing activism around economic, social and cultural rights. Mass social movements are beginning to use the language of rights in global campaigns on issues including trade, aid, investment, debt and access to medicines.

CONTROL ARMS CAMPAIGN

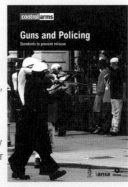

The arms trade is out of control. Worldwide, arms are fuelling conflict, poverty, and human rights abuses. AI, in collaboration with two other non-governmental organizations, Oxfam and IANSA (International Action Network on Small Arms), launched the Control Arms campaign in October 2003.

At the global level, governments should establish an international Arms Trade Treaty that would oblige governments not to transfer arms internationally if they are likely to be used to commit serious violations of human rights and war crimes.

At the community and national level, the campaign is calling for measures to protect people from armed violence. These include strict laws and procedures to control small arms; reducing the quantity of surplus and illegal arms in circulation; and improving the accountability and training of law enforcers and armed forces through work based on respect for international human rights and humanitarian law and standards. Campaigners are calling for more effective civic education about community safety to counter cultures of violence, including the destructive link between arms and conventional notions of masculinity.

Around the world, many police and law enforcement officials misuse their right to use force, with fatal consequences. Most police forces are armed, but many are inadequately trained on how to assess when and where to fire a gun.

The Wire is AI's monthly international newsletter for members, subscribers and sections. Featuring summaries of forthcoming AI reports, accounts of AI actions and a full page of Worldwide Appeals – appeals to the public to support victims of torture, unfair imprisonment and other human rights abuses – **the Wire** informs readers of AI campaigns and developments while urging them to take direct action.

Published in English, French and Arabic, **the Wire** is available on subscription in printed format or free online at web.amnesty.org/wire/

To subscribe, e-mail: ppmsteam@amnesty.org or write to: Marketing & Supply Team (*the Wire* subscriptions), Amnesty International, International Secretariat, Peter Benenson House, 1 Easton Street, London WC1X 0DW, United Kingdom.

AI's objectives are to:
- Promote economic, social and cultural rights as human rights, including by participating in global processes such as those on trade.
- Strengthen legal recognition of economic, social and cultural rights, through national law reform initiatives and development of international standards and mechanisms.
- Address severe abuses of economic, social and cultural rights suffered by marginalized communities
- Address abuses arising from HIV/AIDS.
- Highlight the obligations of economic actors such as companies and expose abuses, for example discrimination in employment.
- Promote human rights principles for privatization and in investment and trade agreements.

Stop violence against women

Violence against women is one of the most widespread and pervasive human rights violations. It is also one of the most hidden. It cuts across cultural, regional, religious and economic boundaries. It is manifested in the context of the family, in the community, in state institutions and in conflict and post-conflict situations. Thanks in particular to the women's movement, there have been significant advances in the promotion of women's rights in international law, including criminal law. However, such advances have made little difference for women on the ground and much remains to be done.

AI's objectives are to:
- Demand that governments criminalize rape and ratify the UN Women's Convention without reservations.
- Challenge impunity for rape and other forms of violence against women, including by armed groups, in conflict and post-conflict situations.
- Ensure that states protect, respect and fulfill women's rights, using the standard of due diligence nationally and internationally to hold states accountable to their obligations.
- Challenge the tolerance of violence against women within society and urge traditional and informal authorities to take effective action to fight it.
- Support women human rights activists.
- Develop policies to address reproductive health rights and other related concerns.

Protect civilians and close the taps that fuel abuses in conflict

In parts of the world conflict appears chronic. Identity issues, poverty and, paradoxically, mineral wealth are among the causes. Sometimes weak states are confronted with economically powerful armed groups; often conflict is prolonged by foreign governments, private companies and diaspora communities. Mass abuses against civilians persist, and despite significant international and national legal developments, impunity still reigns. Effective protection seems to depend too often on the presence of foreign troops.

AI's objectives are to:
- Demand accountability for abuses in armed conflict by states and armed groups.
- Promote an agenda for protecting civilians, including through peacekeeping and peace-building.
- Campaign against the use of child soldiers.
- Demand accountability of external actors complicit in abuses, including second states and economic actors.
- Campaign to restrict the arms trade, including by promoting an arms trade treaty.
- Campaign against indiscriminate weapons, such as cluster weapons.
- Advance the debate on the use of military force.

You can make a difference

AI works to improve human rights through the actions of ordinary people around the world. AI's members and supporters have a record of real achievement. Prisoners of conscience have been released. Death sentences have been commuted. Torturers have been brought to justice. Governments have been persuaded to change their laws and practices.

Sometimes solidarity keeps hope alive. Hope is a precious weapon for prisoners battling to survive, relatives trying to obtain justice or human rights defenders bravely continuing their work despite danger and isolation. However bleak the situation, AI's members and supporters, acting together, can make a difference.

CONTACT AI

AI SECTIONS

Algeria Amnesty International, BP 377, Alger,
RP 16004
e-mail: amnestyalgeria@hotmail.com

Argentina Amnistía Internacional,
Av. Rivadavia 2206 - P4A,
C1032ACO Ciudad de Buenos Aires
e-mail: info@amnesty.org.ar
http://www.amnesty.org.ar

Australia Amnesty International, Locked Bag 23,
Broadway, New South Wales 2007
e-mail: hello@amnesty.org.au
http://www.amnesty.org.au

Austria Amnesty International, Moeringgasse 10,
A-1150 Vienna
e-mail: info@amnesty.at
http://www.amnesty.at

Belgium Amnesty International (Flemish-speaking),
Kerkstraat 156, 2060 Antwerpen
e-mail: directie@aivl.be
http://www.aivl.be
Belgium Amnesty International (francophone),
rue Berckmans 9, 1060 Bruxelles
e-mail: aibf@aibf.be
http://www.aibf.be

Benin Amnesty International, 01 BP 3536,
Cotonou
e-mail: aibenin@leland.bj

Bermuda Amnesty International, PO Box HM 2136,
Hamilton HM JX
e-mail: aibda@ibl.bm

Canada Amnesty International (English-speaking),
312 Laurier Avenue East, Ottawa, Ontario, K1N 1H9
e-mail: info@amnesty.ca
http://www.amnesty.ca
Canada Amnistie Internationale (francophone),
6250 boulevard Monk, Montréal, Québec, H4E 3H7
e-mail: info@amnistie.qc.ca
http://www.amnistie.qc.ca

Chile Amnistía Internacional, Oficina Nacional,
Huelén 188 A, 750-0617 Providencia, Santiago
e-mail: info@amnistia.cl
http://www.amnistia.cl

Côte d'Ivoire Amnesty International, 04 BP 895,
Abidjan 04
e-mail: amnestycotedivoire@aviso.ci

Denmark Amnesty International, Gammeltorv 8, 5,
1457 Copenhagen K.
e-mail: amnesty@amnesty.dk
http://www.amnesty.dk

Faroe Islands Amnesty International, PO Box 1075,
FR-110 Tórshavn
e-mail: amnesty@amnesty.fo
http://www.amnesty.fo

Finland Amnesty International,
Ruoholahdenkatu 24,
D 00180 Helsinki
e-mail: amnesty@amnesty.fi
http://www.amnesty.fi

France Amnesty International, 76 Bd de La Villette,
75940 Paris, Cédex 19
e-mail: info@amnesty.asso.fr
http://www.amnesty.asso.fr

Germany Amnesty International, Heerstrasse 178,
53111 Bonn
e-mail: info@amnesty.de
http://www.amnesty.de

Greece Amnesty International, Sina 30,
106 72 Athens
e-mail: info@amnesty.org.gr
http://www.amnesty.org.gr

Guyana Amnesty International, PO Box 101679,
Georgetown
e-mail: rightsgy@yahoo.com

Hong Kong Amnesty International,
Unit D, 3F, Best-O-Best Commercial Centre,
32-36 Ferry Street, Kowloon
e-mail: admin-hk@amnesty.org
http://www.amnesty.org.hk

Iceland Amnesty International, PO Box 618,
121 Reykjavík
e-mail: amnesty@amnesty.is
http://www.amnesty.is

Ireland Amnesty International,
Sean MacBride House, 48 Fleet Street,
Dublin 2
e-mail: info@amnesty.ie
http://www.amnesty.ie

Israel Amnesty International, PO Box 14179,
Tel Aviv 61141
e-mail: amnesty@netvision.net.il
http://www.amnesty.org.il

Italy Amnesty International,
Via Giovanni Battista De Rossi 10, 00161 Roma
e-mail: info@amnesty.it
http://www.amnesty.it

Japan Amnesty International,
2-7-7F Kanda-Tsukasa-cho, Chiyoda-ku,
Tokyo, 101-0048
e-mail: info@amnesty.or.jp
http://www.amnesty.or.jp

Korea (Republic of) Amnesty International,
Gwangehwamun PO Box 2045, Chongno-gu,
Seoul, 110-620
e-mail: amnesty@amnesty.or.kr
http://www.amnesty.or.kr

Luxembourg Amnesty International,
Boîte Postale 1914, 1019 Luxembourg
e-mail: amnesty@pt.lu
http://www.amnesty.lu

Mauritius Amnesty International, BP 69,
Rose-Hill
e-mail: amnestymtius@intnet.mu

Mexico Amnistía Internacional,
Zacatecas 230, Oficina 605, Colonia Roma Sur,
Delegación Cuahutemoc, CP 06700,
Mexico DF
e-mail: informacion@amnistia.org.mx
http://www.amnistia.org.mx

Morocco Amnesty International,
281 avenue Mohamed V, Apt. 23, Escalier A,
Rabat
e-mail: admin-ma@amnesty.org

Nepal Amnesty International, PO Box 135,
Balaju, Kathmandu
e-mail: amnesty@ccsl.com.np
http://www.amnestynepal.org

Netherlands Amnesty International, PO Box 1968,
1000 BZ Amsterdam
e-mail: amnesty@amnesty.nl
http://www.amnesty.nl

New Zealand Amnesty International, PO Box 5300,
Wellesley Street, Auckland
e-mail: campaign@amnesty.org.nz
http://www.amnesty.org.nz

Norway Amnesty International, PO Box 702,
Sentrum, N-0106 Oslo
e-mail: info@amnesty.no
http://www.amnesty.no

Peru Amnistía Internacional, Enrique Palacios 735-A,
Miraflores, Lima
e-mail: admin-pe@amnesty.org
http://amnistia.org.pe

Philippines Amnesty International,
17-B, Kasing Kasing Street, Corner K-8th, Kamias,
Quezon City
e-mail: amnestypilipinas@meridiantelekoms.net

Poland Amnesty International,
Piêkna 66 a lok.2, 00-672, Warszawa
e-mail: amnesty@amnesty.org.pl
http://www.amnesty.org.pl

Portugal Amnistia Internacional,
Rua Fialho de Almeida 13-1,
PT-1070-128 Lisboa
e-mail: aiportugal@amnistia-internacional.pt
http://www.amnistia-internacional.pt

Puerto Rico Amnistía Internacional,
Calle El Roble 54-Altos, Oficina 11,
Río Piedras, 00925
e-mail: amnistiapr@amnestypr.org

Senegal Amnesty International,
BP 269 Dakar Colobane
e-mail: aisenegal@sentoo.sn

Sierra Leone Amnesty International, PMB 1021,
16 Pademba Road, Freetown
e-mail: aislf@sierratel.sl

Slovenia Amnesty International, Beethovnova 7,
1000 Ljubljana
e-mail: amnesty@amnesty.si
http://www.amnesty.si

Spain Amnistía Internacional, Apdo 50318,
28080 Madrid
e-mail: amnistia.internacional@a-i.es
http://www.es.amnesty.org

Sweden Amnesty International, PO Box 4719,
S-11692 Stockholm
e-mail: info@amnesty.se
http://www.amnesty.se

Switzerland Amnesty International,
PO Box 3001, Bern
e-mail: info@amnesty.ch
http://www.amnesty.ch

Taiwan Amnesty International, No. 89,
7th floor #1, Chung Cheng Two Road,
Kaohsiung
e-mail: aitaiwan@seed.net.tw
http://www.aitaiwan.org.tw

Togo Amnesty International, BP 20013, Lomé
e-mail: aitogo@cafe.tg

Tunisia Amnesty International,
67 rue Oum Kalthoum, 3ème étage, Escalier B,
1000 Tunis
e-mail: admin-tn@amnesty.org

United Kingdom Amnesty International,
The Human Rights Action Centre, 17-25 New Inn Yard,
London EC2A 3EA
e-mail: info@amnesty.org.uk
http://www.amnesty.org.uk

United States of America Amnesty International,
5 Penn Plaza, 14th floor, New York, NY 10001
e-mail: admin-us@aiusa.org
http://www.amnestyusa.org

Uruguay Amnistía Internacional, Colonia 871,
apto. 5, CP 11100, Montevideo
e-mail: amnistia@chasque.apc.org
http://www.amnistiauruguay.org.uy

Venezuela Amnistía Internacional,
Apartado Postal 5110, Carmelitas, Caracas 1010A
e-mail: admin-ve@amnesty.org
http://www.amnistia.int.ve

AI STRUCTURES

Belarus Amnesty International, PO Box 10P,
246050 Gomel
e-mail: amnesty@tut.by

Bolivia Amnistía Internacional, Casilla 10607, La Paz
e-mail: perescar@ceibo.entelnet.bo

Burkina Faso Amnesty International,
303 rue 9.08, 08 BP 11344, Ouagadougou 08
e-mail: aburkina@sections.amnesty.org

Croatia Amnesty International, Martičeva 24,
10000 Zagreb
e-mail: admin@amnesty.hr
http://www.amnesty.hr

Curaçao Amnesty International, PO Box 3676,
Curaçao, Netherlands Antilles
e-mail: eisdencher@interneeds.net

Czech Republic Amnesty International,
Palackého 9, 110 00 Praha 1
e-mail: amnesty@amnesty.cz
http://www.amnesty.cz

Gambia Amnesty International, PO Box 1935, Banjul
e-mail: amnesty@gamtel.gm

Hungary Amnesty International, Rózsa u. 44,
II/4, 1064 Budapest
e-mail: info@amnesty.hu
http://www.amnesty.hu

India Amnesty International, C-161, 4th Floor,
Hemkunt House, Guatam Nagar,
New Delhi 110-049
e-mail: admin-in@amnesty.org
http://www.amnesty.org.in

Malaysia Amnesty International, E6, 3rd Floor,
Bangunan Khas, Jalan 8/1E, 46050 Petaling Jaya,
Selangor
e-mail: amnesty@tm.net.my
http://www.aimalaysia.org

Mali Amnesty International, BP E 3885, Bamako
e-mail: amnesty.mali@afribone.net.ml

Moldova Amnesty International, PO Box 209,
MD-2012 Chişinău
e-mail: amnestyrm@araxinfo.com

Mongolia Amnesty International, PO Box 180,
Ulaanbaatar 21 0648
e-mail: aimncc@magicnet.mn
http://www.amnesty.mn

Pakistan Amnesty International, B-12,
Shelezon Centre, Gulsan-E-Iqbal, Block 15,
University Road, Karachi - 75300
e-mail: amnesty@cyber.net.pk

Paraguay Amnistía Internacional,
Tte. Zotti No. 352 e/Hassler y Boggiani,
Asunción
e-mail: ai-info@py.amnesty.org

Slovakia Amnesty International, Benediktiho 5,
811 05 Bratislava
e-mail: amnesty@amnesty.sk
http://www.amnesty.sk

South Africa Amnesty International,
PO Box 29083, Sunnyside 0132, Pretoria,
Gauteng
e-mail: info@amnesty.org.za
http://www.amnesty.org.za

Thailand Amnesty International,
641/8 Vara Place, Ladprao Soi 5, Ladprao Road,
Chatuchak, Bangkok 10900
e-mail: info@amnesty.or.th
http://www.amnesty.or.th

Turkey Amnesty International,
Muradiye Bayiri Sok, Acarman ap. 50/1,
Tesvikiye 80200, Istanbul
e-mail: amnesty@superonline.com
http://www.amnesty-turkiye.org

Ukraine Amnesty International, PO Box 60,
Kiev-15, 01015
e-mail: office@amnesty.org.ua

Zambia Amnesty International, PO Box 40991,
Mufulira
e-mail: azambia@sections.amnesty.org

Zimbabwe Amnesty International, Office 25 E,
Bible House, 99 Mbuya Nehanda Street, Harare
e-mail: amnesty@mweb.co-zw

AI GROUPS

There are also AI groups in:
Angola, Aruba, Azerbaijan, Bahamas, Bahrain, Barbados, Bosnia and Herzegovina, Botswana, Cameroon, Chad, Dominican Republic, Egypt, Estonia, Grenada, Jamaica, Jordan, Kuwait, Kyrgyzstan, Lebanon, Liberia, Lithuania, Malta, Mozambique, Palestinian Authority, Romania, Russian Federation, Serbia and Montenegro, Trinidad and Tobago, Uganda, Yemen

AI OFFICES

International Secretariat (IS)
Amnesty International, Peter Benenson House, 1 Easton Street, London WC1X 0DW, United Kingdom
e-mail: amnestyis@amnesty.org
http://www.amnesty.org

ARABAI (Arabic translation unit)
c/o International Secretariat, Peter Benenson House, 1 Easton Street, London WC1X 0DW, United Kingdom
e-mail: arabai@amnesty.org
http://www.amnesty-arabic.org

Éditions Francophones d'Amnesty International (EFAI)
17 rue du Pont-aux-Choux, 75003 Paris, France
e-mail: ai-efai@amnesty.org
http://www.efai.org

Editorial de Amnistía Internacional (EDAI)
Calle Valderribas 13, 28007 Madrid, Spain
e-mail: mlleo@amnesty.org
http://www.edai.org

European Union (EU) Office
Amnesty International, Rue d'Arlon 37-41, B-1000 Brussels, Belgium
e-mail: amnesty-eu@aieu.be
http://www.amnesty-eu.org

IS Beirut – Middle East and North Africa Regional Office
Amnesty International, PO Box 13-5696, Chouran Beirut 1102 - 2060, Lebanon
e-mail: mena@amnesty.org

IS Dakar – Development Field Office
Amnesty International, Sicap Liberté II, Villa 1608, BP 47582, Dakar Liberté, Dakar, Senegal
e-mail: Kolaniya@amnesty.org

IS Geneva – UN Representative Office
Amnesty International, 22 rue du Cendrier, 4ème étage, CH-1201 Geneva, Switzerland
e-mail: gvunpost@amnesty.org

IS Hong Kong – Asia Pacific Regional Office
Amnesty International, 16/F Siu on Centre, 188 Lockhart Rd, Wanchai, Hong Kong
e-mail: admin-ap@amnesty.org

IS Kampala – Africa Regional Office
Amnesty International, Plot 20A, Kawalya Kaggwa Close, Kololo, Uganda
e-mail: admin-kp@amnesty.org

IS Moscow – Russia Resource Centre
Amnesty International, PO Box 212, Moscow 121019, Russian Federation
e-mail: russiaresourcecentre@amnesty.org

IS New York – UN Representative Office
Amnesty International, 777 UN Plaza, 6th Floor, New York, NY 10017, USA

IS Paris – Research Office
Amnesty International, 76 Bd de la Villette, 75940 Paris, Cédex 19, France
e-mail: pro@amnesty.org

IS San José – Americas Regional Office
Amnistía Internacional, 75 metros al norte de la Iglesia de Fatima, Los Yoses, San Pedro, San José, Costa Rica
e-mail: admin-cr@amnesty.org

Selected international human rights treaties
(AT 31 DECEMBER 2004)

States which have ratified or acceded to a convention are party to the treaty and are bound to observe its provisions. States which have signed but not yet ratified have expressed their intention to become a party at some future date; meanwhile they are obliged to refrain from acts which would defeat the object and purpose of the treaty.

Legend:
- ● became a state party in 2004
- ○ state is a party
- ◐ signed in 2004
- D signed but not yet ratified
- 10 Countries making a declaration under Article 10 of the Optional Protocol to CEDAW do not recognize the competence of the Committee on the Elimination of Discrimination against Women to undertake confidential inquiries into allegations of grave or systematic violations of the Convention

	International Covenant on Civil and Political Rights (ICCPR)	(first) Optional Protocol to the ICCPR	Second Optional Protocol to the ICCPR, aiming at the abolition of the death penalty	International Covenant on Economic, Social and Cultural Rights	Convention on the Elimination of All Forms of Discrimination against Women (CEDAW)	Optional Protocol to CEDAW	Convention on the Rights of the Child (CRC)	Optional Protocol to the CRC on the involvement of children in armed conflict	International Convention on the Elimination of All Forms of Racial Discrimination
Afghanistan	○			○	○		○	○	○
Albania	○			○	○	○	○		○
Algeria	○	○		○	○		○		○
Andorra	D	D	D		○	○	○	○	D
Angola	○			○	○		○		
Antigua and Barbuda					○		○		○
Argentina	○	○		○	○	D	○	○	○
Armenia	○	○		○	○		○	D	○
Australia	○	○	○	○	○		○	D	○
Austria	○	○	○	○	○	○	○	○	○
Azerbaijan	○	○	○	○	○	○	○	○	○
Bahamas					○		○		
Bahrain					○		○	●	○
Bangladesh	○			○	○	○10	○	○	○
Barbados	○	○		○	○		○		○
Belarus	○	○		○	○	●	○		○
Belgium	○	○	○	○	○	●	○	○	○
Belize	○			D	○	○10	○	○	○
Benin	○	○		○	○	D	○	D	○
Bhutan					○		○		D
Bolivia	○	○		○	○	○	○	●	○
Bosnia and Herzegovina	○	○	○	○	○	○	○	○	○
Botswana	○				○		○	●	○
Brazil	○			○	○	○	○	●	○
Brunei Darussalam							○		
Bulgaria	○	○	○	○	○	D	○	○	○
Burkina Faso	○	○		○	○	D	○	D	○
Burundi	○			○	○	D	○	D	○
Cambodia	○	◐		○	○	D	○	●	○
Cameroon	○			○	○		○	D	○
Canada	○	○		○	○	○	○	○	○
Cape Verde	○	○	○	○	○		○		○
Central African Republic	○	○		○	○		○		○
Chad	○	○		○	○		○	○	○

	International Covenant on Civil and Political Rights (ICCPR)	(first) Optional Protocol to the ICCPR	Second Optional Protocol to the ICCPR, aiming at the abolition of the death penalty	International Covenant on Economic, Social and Cultural Rights	Convention on the Elimination of All Forms of Discrimination against Women (CEDAW)	Optional Protocol to CEDAW	Convention on the Rights of the Child (CRC)	Optional Protocol to the CRC on the involvement of children in armed conflict	International Convention on the Elimination of All Forms of Racial Discrimination
Chile	○	○	D	○	○	D	○	○	○
China	D			○	○		○	D	○
Colombia	○	○	○	○	○	D	○	D	○
Comoros					○		○		●
Congo (Democratic Republic of the)	○	○		○	○		○	○	○
Congo (Republic of the)	○	○		○	○		○		○
Cook Islands							○		
Costa Rica	○	○	○	○	○	○	○	○	○
Côte d'Ivoire	○	○		○	○		○		○
Croatia	○	○	○	○	○	○	○	○	○
Cuba					○	D	○	D	○
Cyprus	○	○	○	○	○	○	○		○
Czech Republic	○	○	●	○	○	○	○	○	○
Denmark	○	○	○	○	○	○	○	○	○
Djibouti	○	○		○	○		○		○
Dominica	○			○	○		○	○	
Dominican Republic	○	○		○	○		○	D	○
Ecuador	○	○	○	○	○	○	○	●	○
Egypt	○			○	○		○		○
El Salvador	○	○		○	○	D	○	○	○
Equatorial Guinea	○	○		○	○		○		○
Eritrea	○			○	○		○		○
Estonia	○	○	●	○	○		○	D	○
Ethiopia	○			○	○		○		○
Fiji					○		○		○
Finland	○	○	○	○	○	○	○	○	○
France	○	○		○	○	○	○	○	○
Gabon	○			○	○	●	○	D	○
Gambia	○	○		○	○		○	D	○
Georgia	○	○	○	○	○	○	○		○
Germany	○	○	○	○	○	○	○	●	○
Ghana	○	○		○	○	D	○	D	○
Greece	○	○	○	○	○	○	○	○	○
Grenada	○			○	○		○		D
Guatemala	○	○		○	○	○	○	○	○
Guinea	○	○		○	○		○		○
Guinea-Bissau	D	D	D	○	○	D	○	D	D
Guyana	○	○		○	○		○		○
Haiti	○				○		○	D	○
Holy See							○	○	○
Honduras	○	D	D	○	○		○	○	○
Hungary	○	○	○	○	○	○	○	D	○
Iceland	○	○	○	○	○	○	○	○	●
India	○			○	○		○	▶	○
Indonesia					○	D	○	D	○
Iran (Islamic Republic of)	○			○			○		○
Iraq	○			○	○		○		○

● became a state party in 2004

○ state is a party

▶ signed in 2004

D signed but not yet ratified

10 Countries making a declaration under Article 10 of the Optional Protocol to CEDAW do not recognize the competence of the Committee on the Elimination of Discrimination against Women to undertake confidential inquiries into allegations of grave or systematic violations of the Convention

	International Covenant on Civil and Political Rights (ICCPR)	(first) Optional Protocol to the ICCPR	Second Optional Protocol to the ICCPR, aiming at the abolition of the death penalty	International Covenant on Economic, Social and Cultural Rights	Convention on the Elimination of All Forms of Discrimination against Women (CEDAW)	Optional Protocol to CEDAW	Convention on the Rights of the Child (CRC)	Optional Protocol to the CRC on the involvement of children in armed conflict	International Convention on the Elimination of All Forms of Racial Discrimination
Ireland	○	○	○	○	○	○	○	○	○
Israel	○			○	○		○	▷	○
Italy	○	○	○	○	○	○	○	○	○
Jamaica	○			○	○		○	○	○
Japan	○			○	○		○	●	○
Jordan	○			○	○		○	▷	○
Kazakstan	▷			▷	○	○	○	○	○
Kenya	○			○	○		○	○	○
Kiribati					●		○		
Korea (Democratic People's Republic of)	○			○	○		○		
Korea (Republic of)	○	○		○	○		○	●	○
Kuwait	○			○	○		○	●	○
Kyrgyzstan	○	○		○	○	○	○	○	○
Lao People's Democratic Republic	▷			▷	○		○		○
Latvia	○	○		○	○		○	▷	○
Lebanon	○			○	○		○	▷	○
Lesotho	○	○		○	○	●	○		○
Liberia	●	▶		●	○	▶	○	▶	○
Libyan Arab Jamahiriya	○	○		○	○	●	○	●	○
Liechtenstein	○	○	○	○	○	○	○	▷	○
Lithuania	○	○		○	○		●	○	○
Luxembourg	○	○	○	○	○	○	○	●	○
Macedonia (former Yugoslav Republic of)	○	○		○	○	○	○	●	○
Madagascar	○	○		○	○	▷	○	●	○
Malawi	○	○		○	○	▷	○	▷	○
Malaysia					○		○		
Maldives					○		○	●	○
Mali	○	○		○	○	○	○	○	○
Malta	○	○	○	○	○		○	○	○
Marshall Islands							○		
Mauritania	●			●			○		○
Mauritius	○	○		○	○	▷	○	▷	○
Mexico	○	○		○	○	○	○	○	○
Micronesia (Federated States of)					●		○	▷	
Moldova	○			○	○		○	●	○
Monaco	○		○	○			○	○	○
Mongolia	○	○		○	○	○	○	●	○
Morocco	○			○	○		○	○	○
Mozambique	○		○		○		○	●	○
Myanmar					○		○		
Namibia	○	○		○	○	○	○	○	○
Nauru	▷	▷					○	▷	▷
Nepal	○	○	○	○	○	▷	○	▷	○
Netherlands	○	○	○	○	○	○	○	▷	○
New Zealand	○	○	○	○	○	○	○	○	○
Nicaragua	○	○	▷	○	○		○		○
Niger	○	○		○	○	●	○		○

● became a state party in 2004

○ state is a party

▶ signed in 2004

▷ signed but not yet ratified

10 Countries making a declaration under Article 10 of the Optional Protocol to CEDAW do not recognize the competence of the Committee on the Elimination of Discrimination against Women to undertake confidential inquiries into allegations of grave or systematic violations of the Convention

SELECTED INTERNATIONAL HUMAN RIGHTS TREATIES

	International Covenant on Civil and Political Rights (ICCPR)	(first) Optional Protocol to the ICCPR	Second Optional Protocol to the ICCPR, aiming at the abolition of the death penalty	International Covenant on Economic, Social and Cultural Rights	Convention on the Elimination of All Forms of Discrimination against Women (CEDAW)	Optional Protocol to CEDAW	Convention on the Rights of the Child (CRC)	Optional Protocol to the CRC on the involvement of children in armed conflict	International Convention on the Elimination of All Forms of Racial Discrimination
Nigeria	○			○	○	●	○	D	○
Niue							○		
Norway	○	○	○	○	○	○	○	○	○
Oman							○	●	○
Pakistan				▶	○		○	D	○
Palau							○		
Panama	○	○	○	○	○	○	○	○	○
Papua New Guinea					○		○		○
Paraguay	○	○	○	○	○	○	○	○	○
Peru	○	○		○	○	○	○	○	○
Philippines	○	○		○	○	○	○	○	○
Poland	○	○	D	○	○	○	○	D	○
Portugal	○	○	○	○	○	○	○	○	○
Qatar							○	○	○
Romania	○	○	○	○	○	○	○	○	○
Russian Federation	○	○		○	○	●	○	D	○
Rwanda	○			○	○		○	○	○
Saint Kitts and Nevis					○		○		
Saint Lucia					○		○		
Saint Vincent and the Grenadines	○	○		○	○		○		○
Samoa					○		○		
San Marino	○	○	●	○	○		○	D	○
Sao Tome and Principe	D	D	D	D	○	D	○		D
Saudi Arabia					○		○		○
Senegal	○	○		○	○	○	○	●	○
Serbia and Montenegro	○	○	○	○	○	○	○	○	○
Seychelles	○	○	○	○	○	D	○	D	○
Sierra Leone	○	○		○	○	D	○	○	○
Singapore					○		○	D	
Slovakia	○	○	○	○	○	○	○	D	○
Slovenia	○	○	○	○	○	●	○	●	○
Solomon Islands				○	○	○	○		○
Somalia	○	○		○			D		○
South Africa	○	○	○	D			○	D	○
Spain	○	○	○	○	○	○	○	○	○
Sri Lanka	○	○		○	○	○	○	○	○
Sudan	○			○			○	D	○
Suriname	○	○		○			○	D	○
Swaziland	●			●	●		○		
Sweden	○	○		○	○	○	○	○	○
Switzerland	○		○	○	○	○	○	○	○
Syrian Arab Republic	○			○	○		○		○
Tajikistan	○	○		○	○	D	○		○
Tanzania	○			○	○		○	●	○
Thailand	○			○	○	○	○		○
Timor-Leste	○		○	○	○	○	○	●	○
Togo	○	○		○	○		○	D	○

Legend

● became a state party in 2004

○ state is a party

▶ signed in 2004

D signed but not yet ratified

10 Countries making a declaration under Article 10 of the Optional Protocol to CEDAW do not recognize the competence of the Committee on the Elimination of Discrimination against Women to undertake confidential inquiries into allegations of grave or systematic violations of the Convention

	International Covenant on Civil and Political Rights (ICCPR)	(first) Optional Protocol to the ICCPR	Second Optional Protocol to the ICCPR, aiming at the abolition of the death penalty	International Covenant on Economic, Social and Cultural Rights	Convention on the Elimination of All Forms of Discrimination against Women (CEDAW)	Optional Protocol to CEDAW	Convention on the Rights of the Child (CRC)	Optional Protocol to the CRC on the involvement of children in armed conflict	International Convention on the Elimination of All Forms of Racial Discrimination
Tonga							○		○
Trinidad and Tobago	○			○	○		○		○
Tunisia	○			○	○		○	○	○
Turkey	○	▶	▶	○	○	○	○	●	○
Turkmenistan	○	○	○	○	○		○		○
Tuvalu					○		○		
Uganda	○	○		○	○		○	○	○
Ukraine	○	○		○	○	○	○	D	○
United Arab Emirates					●		○		○
United Kingdom	○		○	○	○	●	○	○	○
United States of America	○			D	D		D	○	○
Uruguay	○	○	○	○	○	○	○	○	○
Uzbekistan	○	○		○	○		○		○
Vanuatu					○		○		
Venezuela	○	○		○	○	○	○	○	○
Viet Nam	○			○	○		○	○	○
Yemen	○			○	○		○		○
Zambia	○	○		○	○		○		○
Zimbabwe	○			○	○		○		○

● became a state party in 2004

○ state is a party

▶ signed in 2004

D signed but not yet ratified

10 Countries making a declaration under Article 10 of the Optional Protocol to CEDAW do not recognize the competence of the Committee on the Elimination of Discrimination against Women to undertake confidential inquiries into allegations of grave or systematic violations of the Convention

Selected international human rights treaties
(AT 31 DECEMBER 2004)

States which have ratified or acceded to a convention are party to the treaty and are bound to observe its provisions. States which have signed but not yet ratified have expressed their intention to become a party at some future date; meanwhile they are obliged to refrain from acts which would defeat the object and purpose of the treaty.

	Convention against Torture and Other Cruel, Inhuman or Degrading Treatment or Punishment	Optional Protocol to the Convention against Torture**	Convention relating to the Status of Refugees (1951)	Protocol relating to the Status of Refugees (1967)	International Convention on the Protection of the Rights of All Migrant Workers and Members of Their Families (1990)	Rome Statute of the International Criminal Court
Afghanistan	○²⁸					○
Albania	○	○	○	○		○
Algeria	○²²		○	○		D
Andorra	D					○
Angola			○	○		D
Antigua and Barbuda	○		○	○		○
Argentina	○²²	●	○	○	D	○
Armenia	○		○	○		D
Australia	○²²		○	○		○
Austria	○²²	D	○	○		○
Azerbaijan	○²²		○	○	○	
Bahamas			○	○		D
Bahrain	○					D
Bangladesh	○				D	D
Barbados						○
Belarus	○		○	○		
Belgium	○²²		○	○		○
Belize	○		○	○	○	○
Benin	○		○	○		○
Bhutan						
Bolivia	○		○	○	○	○
Bosnia and Herzegovina	○²²		○	○	○	○
Botswana	○		○	○		○
Brazil	○	D	○	○		○
Brunei Darussalam						
Bulgaria	○²²		○	○		○
Burkina Faso	○		○	○	○	●
Burundi	○²²		○	○		●
Cambodia	○		○	○	▶	○
Cameroon	○²²		○	○		D
Canada	○²²		○	○		○
Cape Verde	○			○	○	D
Central African Republic			○	○		○
Chad	○		○	○		D
Chile	○²²		○	○	D	D

● became a state party in 2004

○ state is a party

▶ signed in 2004

D signed but not yet ratified

22 Countries making a declaration under Article 22 recognize the competence of the Committee against Torture to consider individual complaints

28 Countries making a reservation under Article 28 do not recognize the competence of the Committee against Torture to undertake confidential inquiries into allegations of systematic torture if warranted

* Countries making a declaration under Article 124 decline to recognize the jurisdiction of the International Criminal Court over war crimes for seven years after ratification

** The Optional Protocol to the Convention against Torture will enter into force after 20 ratifications

	Convention against Torture and Other Cruel, Inhuman or Degrading Treatment or Punishment	Optional Protocol to the Convention against Torture**	Convention relating to the Status of Refugees (1951)	Protocol relating to the Status of Refugees (1967)	International Convention on the Protection of the Rights of All Migrant Workers and Members of Their Families (1990)	Rome Statute of the International Criminal Court
China	○28		○	○		○*
Colombia	○		○	○	○	○*
Comoros	D				D	D
Congo (Democratic Republic of the)	○		○	○		○
Congo (Republic of the)	○		○	○		●
Cook Islands						
Costa Rica	○22	D	○	○		○
Côte d'Ivoire	○		○	○		D
Croatia	○22	D	○	○		○
Cuba	○28					
Cyprus	○22	◗	○	○		○
Czech Republic	○22	◗	○	○		D
Denmark	○22	●	○	○		○
Djibouti	○		○	○		○
Dominica			○	○		○
Dominican Republic	D		○	○		D
Ecuador	○22		○	○	○	○
Egypt	○		○	○	○	D
El Salvador	○		○	○	○	
Equatorial Guinea	○28		○	○		
Eritrea						D
Estonia	○	◗	○	○		○
Ethiopia	○		○	○		
Fiji			○	○		○
Finland	○22	D	○	○		○
France	○22		○	○		○*
Gabon	○	◗	○	○	◗	○
Gambia	D		○	○		○
Georgia	○		○	○		○
Germany	○22		○	○		○
Ghana	○22		○	○	○	○
Greece	○22		○	○		○
Grenada						
Guatemala	○22	D	○	○	○	
Guinea	○		○	○	○	○
Guinea-Bissau	D		○	○	D	D
Guyana	○					●
Haiti			○	○		D
Holy See	○		○	○		
Honduras	○	◗	○	○		○
Hungary	○22		○	○		○
Iceland	○22	D	○	○		○
India	D					
Indonesia	○28				◗	
Iran (Islamic Republic of)			○	○		D
Iraq						
Ireland	○22		○	○		○
Israel	○28		○	○		D

● became a state party in 2004

○ state is a party

◗ signed in 2004

D signed but not yet ratified

22 Countries making a declaration under Article 22 recognize the competence of the Committee against Torture to consider individual complaints

28 Countries making a reservation under Article 28 do not recognize the competence of the Committee against Torture to undertake confidential inquiries into allegations of systematic torture if warranted

* Countries making a declaration under Article 124 decline to recognize the jurisdiction of the International Criminal Court over war crimes for seven years after ratification

** The Optional Protocol to the Convention against Torture will enter into force after 20 ratifications

	Convention against Torture and Other Cruel, Inhuman or Degrading Treatment or Punishment	Optional Protocol to the Convention against Torture**	Convention relating to the Status of Refugees (1951)	Protocol relating to the Status of Refugees (1967)	International Convention on the Protection of the Rights of All Migrant Workers and Members of Their Families (1990)	Rome Statute of the International Criminal Court
Italy	○22	D	○	○		○
Jamaica			○	○		D
Japan	○		○	○		
Jordan	○					○
Kazakstan	○		○	○		
Kenya	○		○	○		D
Kiribati						
Korea (Democratic People's Republic of)						
Korea (Republic of)	○		○	○		○
Kuwait	○28					D
Kyrgyzstan	○		○	○	○	D
Lao People's Democratic Republic						
Latvia	○		○	○		○
Lebanon	○					
Lesotho	○		○	○	▶	○
Liberia	●	●	○	○	▶	●
Libyan Arab Jamahiriya	○				●	
Liechtenstein	○22		○	○		○
Lithuania	○		○	○		○
Luxembourg	○22		○	○		○
Macedonia (former Yugoslav Republic of)	○		○	○		○
Madagascar	D	D	○			D
Malawi	○		○	○		○
Malaysia						
Maldives	●					
Mali	○	▶	○	○	○	○
Malta	○22	○	○	○		○
Marshall Islands						○
Mauritania	●28		○	○		
Mauritius	○					○
Mexico	○22	D	○	○	○	D
Micronesia (Federated States of)						
Moldova	○		○	○		D
Monaco	○22		○			D
Mongolia	○					○
Morocco	○28		○	○	○	D
Mozambique	○		○	○		D
Myanmar						
Namibia	○		○	○		○
Nauru	D					○
Nepal	○					
Netherlands	○22		○	○		○
New Zealand	○22	D	○	○		○
Nicaragua	D		○	○		
Niger	○		○	○		○
Nigeria	○		○	○		○
Niue						
Norway	○22	D	○	○		○

● became a state party in 2004

○ state is a party

▶ signed in 2004

D signed but not yet ratified

22 Countries making a declaration under Article 22 recognize the competence of the Committee against Torture to consider individual complaints

28 Countries making a reservation under Article 28 do not recognize the competence of the Committee against Torture to undertake confidential inquiries into allegations of systematic torture if warranted

* Countries making a declaration under Article 124 decline to recognize the jurisdiction of the International Criminal Court over war crimes for seven years after ratification

** The Optional Protocol to the Convention against Torture will enter into force after 20 ratifications

	Convention against Torture and Other Cruel, Inhuman or Degrading Treatment or Punishment	Optional Protocol to the Convention against Torture**	Convention relating to the Status of Refugees (1951)	Protocol relating to the Status of Refugees (1967)	International Convention on the Protection of the Rights of All Migrant Workers and Members of Their Families (1990)	Rome Statute of the International Criminal Court
Oman						D
Pakistan						
Palau						
Panama	○		○	○		○
Papua New Guinea			○	○		
Paraguay	○22	▶	○	○	D	○
Peru	○22		○	○	▶	○
Philippines	○		○	○	○	D
Poland	○22 28	▶	○	○		○
Portugal	○22		○	○		○
Qatar	○					
Romania	○	D	○	○		○
Russian Federation	○22		○	○		D
Rwanda			○	○		
Saint Kitts and Nevis			○			
Saint Lucia						D
Saint Vincent and the Grenadines	○		○	○		○
Samoa			○	○		○
San Marino	D					○
Sao Tome and Principe	D		○	○	D	D
Saudi Arabia	○28					
Senegal	○22	D	○	○	○	○
Serbia and Montenegro	○22	D	○	○	▶	○
Seychelles	○22		○	○	○	D
Sierra Leone	○	D	○	○	D	○
Singapore						
Slovakia	○22		○	○		○
Slovenia	○22		○	○		○
Solomon Islands			○	○		D
Somalia	○		○	○		
South Africa	○22		○	○		○
Spain	○22		○	○		○
Sri Lanka	○				○	
Sudan	D		○	○		D
Suriname			○	○		
Swaziland	●		○	○		
Sweden	○22	D	○	○		○
Switzerland	○22	▶	○	○		○
Syrian Arab Republic	●28					D
Tajikistan	○		○	○	○	○
Tanzania			○	○		○
Thailand						D
Timor-Leste	○		○	○	●	○
Togo	○22		○	○	D	
Tonga						
Trinidad and Tobago			○	○		○
Tunisia	○22		○	○		
Turkey	○22		○	○	●	

● became a state party in 2004

○ state is a party

▶ signed in 2004

D signed but not yet ratified

22 Countries making a declaration under Article 22 recognize the competence of the Committee against Torture to consider individual complaints

28 Countries making a reservation under Article 28 do not recognize the competence of the Committee against Torture to undertake confidential inquiries into allegations of systematic torture if warranted

* Countries making a declaration under Article 124 decline to recognize the jurisdiction of the International Criminal Court over war crimes for seven years after ratification

** The Optional Protocol to the Convention against Torture will enter into force after 20 ratifications

	Convention against Torture and Other Cruel, Inhuman or Degrading Treatment or Punishment	Optional Protocol to the Convention against Torture**	Convention relating to the Status of Refugees (1951)	Protocol relating to the Status of Refugees (1967)	International Convention on the Protection of the Rights of All Migrant Workers and Members of Their Families (1990)	Rome Statute of the International Criminal Court
Turkmenistan	○		○	○		
Tuvalu			○	○		
Uganda	○		○	○	○	○
Ukraine	○²²		○	○		ⅅ
United Arab Emirates						ⅅ
United Kingdom	○	○	○	○		○
United States of America	○			○		ⅅ
Uruguay	○²²	❱	○	○	○	○
Uzbekistan	○					ⅅ
Vanuatu						
Venezuela	○²²			○		○
Viet Nam						
Yemen	○		○	○		ⅅ
Zambia	○		○	○		○
Zimbabwe			○	○		ⅅ

● became a state party in 2004

○ state is a party

❱ signed in 2004

ⅅ signed but not yet ratified

22 Countries making a declaration under Article 22 recognize the competence of the Committee against Torture to consider individual complaints

28 Countries making a reservation under Article 28 do not recognize the competence of the Committee against Torture to undertake confidential inquiries into allegations of systematic torture if warranted

∗ Countries making a declaration under Article 124 decline to recognize the jurisdiction of the International Criminal Court over war crimes for seven years after ratification

∗∗ The Optional Protocol to the Convention against Torture will enter into force after 20 ratifications

Selected regional human rights treaties
(AT 31 DECEMBER 2004)

African Union (formerly the Organization of African Unity)

States which have ratified or acceded to a convention are party to the treaty and are bound to observe its provisions. States which have signed but not yet ratified have expressed their intention to become a party at some future date; meanwhile they are obliged to refrain from acts which would defeat the object and purpose of the treaty.

This chart lists countries which were members of the African Union at the end of 2004.

Legend:
- ● became a state party in 2004
- ○ state is a party
- ◗ signed in 2004
- D signed but not yet ratified

	African Charter on Human and Peoples' Rights (1981)	Protocol to the African Charter on the Establishment of an African Court on Human and Peoples' Rights	African Charter on the Rights and Welfare of the Child	Convention Governing the Specific Aspects of Refugee Problems in Africa
Algeria	○	○	○	○
Angola	○		○	○
Benin	○	D	○	○
Botswana	○	D	○	○
Burkina Faso	○	○	○	○
Burundi	○	○	●	○
Cameroon	○		○	○
Cape Verde	○		○	○
Central African Republic	○	D	D	○
Chad	○	◗	○	○
Comoros	○	○	●	●
Congo (Democratic Republic of the)	○	D		○
Congo (Republic of the)	○	D	D	○
Côte d'Ivoire	○	○	◗	○
Djibouti	○		D	
Egypt	○	D	○	○
Equatorial Guinea	○	D	○	○
Eritrea	○		○	
Ethiopia	○	D	○	○
Gabon	○	●	D	○
Gambia	○	○	○	○
Ghana	○	D	D	○
Guinea	○	D	○	○
Guinea-Bissau	○	D		○
Kenya	○	D	○	○
Lesotho	○	○	○	○
Liberia	○	D	D	○
Libya	○	○	○	○
Madagascar	○	D	D	D
Malawi	○	D	○	○
Mali	○	○	○	○
Mauritania	○	D		○
Mauritius	○	○	○	D
Mozambique	○	●	○	○
Namibia	○	D	●	
Niger	○	●	○	○
Nigeria	○	●	○	○
Rwanda	○	○	○	○
Sahrawi Arab Democratic Republic	○		D	
Sao Tome and Principe	○			

African Union (formerly the Organization of African Unity)

	African Charter on Human and Peoples' Rights (1981)	Protocol to the African Charter on the Establishment of an African Court on Human and Peoples' Rights	African Charter on the Rights and Welfare of the Child	Convention Governing the Specific Aspects of Refugee Problems in Africa
Senegal	○	○	○	○
Seychelles	○	D	○	○
Sierra Leone	○	D	○	○
Somalia	○		D	D
South Africa	○	○	○	○
Sudan	○	D		○
Swaziland	○	◗	D	○
Tanzania	○	D	○	○
Togo	○	○	○	○
Tunisia	○	D	D	○
Uganda	○	○	○	○
Zambia	○	D	D	○
Zimbabwe	○	D	○	○

● became a state party in 2004

○ state is a party

◗ signed in 2004

D signed but not yet ratified

Organization of American States (OAS)

States which have ratified or acceded to a convention are party to the treaty and are bound to observe its provisions. States which have signed but not yet ratified have expressed their intention to become a party at some future date; meanwhile they are obliged to refrain from acts which would defeat the object and purpose of the treaty.

This chart lists countries which were members of the OAS at the end of 2004.

Legend:
- ● became a state party in 2004
- ○ state is a party
- ◗ signed in 2004
- Ɗ signed but not yet ratified
- 62 Countries making a Declaration under Article 62 recognize as binding the jurisdiction of the Inter-American Court of Human Rights (on all matters relating to the interpretation or application of the American Convention)

	American Convention on Human Rights (1969)	Protocol to the American Convention on Human Rights to Abolish the Death Penalty	Additional Protocol to the American Convention on Human Rights in the area of Economic, Social and Cultural Rights	Inter-American Convention to Prevent and Punish Torture (1985)	Inter-American Convention on Forced Disappearance of Persons (1994)	Inter-American Convention on the prevention, punishment and eradication of violence against women
Antigua and Barbuda						○
Argentina	○[62]			○	○	○
Bahamas						○
Barbados	○[62]					○
Belize						○
Bolivia	○[62]		Ɗ	Ɗ	○	○
Brazil	○[62]	○	○	○	Ɗ	○
Canada						
Chile	○[62]	Ɗ	Ɗ	○	Ɗ	○
Colombia	○[62]		○	○	Ɗ	○
Costa Rica	○[62]	○	○	○	○	○
Cuba*						
Dominica	○					○
Dominican Republic	○[62]		Ɗ	○		○
Ecuador	○[62]	○	○	○	Ɗ	○
El Salvador	○[62]			○	○	○
Grenada	○					○
Guatemala	○[62]			○	○	○
Guyana						○
Haiti	○[62]		Ɗ	Ɗ		○
Honduras	○[62]			Ɗ	Ɗ	○
Jamaica	○					
Mexico	○[62]			○	○	○
Nicaragua	○[62]	○	Ɗ	Ɗ	Ɗ	○
Panama	○[62]	○	○	○	○	○
Paraguay	○[62]	○	○	○	○	○
Peru	○[62]		○	○	○	○
Saint Kitts and Nevis						○
Saint Lucia						○
Saint Vincent and the Grenadines						○
Suriname	○[62]			○	○	○
Trinidad and Tobago						○
United States of America	Ɗ					
Uruguay	○[62]	○	○	○	○	○
Venezuela	○[62]	○	Ɗ	○	○	○

* In 1962, by resolution of the VIII Meeting of Consultation of Ministers of Foreign Affairs, the current Government of Cuba was excluded from participation in the OAS.

Council of Europe

States which have ratified or acceded to a convention are party to the treaty and are bound to observe its provisions. States which have signed but not yet ratified have expressed their intention to become a party at some future date; meanwhile they are obliged to refrain from acts which would defeat the object and purpose of the treaty.

This chart lists countries which were members of the Council of Europe at the end of 2004.

Legend:

- ● became a state party in 2004
- ○ state is a party
- ◗ signed in 2004
- D signed but not yet ratified

* Protocol No. 6 to the European Convention for the Protection of Human Rights and Fundamental Freedoms concerning the abolition of the death penalty in times of peace (1983).

** Protocol No. 12 to the European Convention for the Protection of Human Rights and Fundamental Freedoms concerning the general prohibition of discrimination (2000). The Protocol will enter into force after 10 ratifications.

*** Protocol No. 13 to the European Convention for the Protection of Human Rights and Fundamental Freedoms concerning the abolition of the death penalty in all circumstances.

	European Convention for the Protection of Human Rights and Fundamental Freedoms (1950)	Protocol No. 6*	Protocol No. 12**	Protocol No. 13***	Framework Convention on the Protection of National Minorities
Albania	○	○	●	D	○
Andorra	○	○		○	
Armenia	○	○	●		○
Austria	○	○	D	●	○
Azerbaijan	○	○	D		○
Belgium	○	○	D	○	D
Bosnia and Herzegovina	○	○	○	○	○
Bulgaria	○	○		○	○
Croatia	○	○	○	○	○
Cyprus	○	○	○	○	○
Czech Republic	○	○	D	●	○
Denmark	○	○		○	○
Estonia	○	○	D	●	○
Finland	○	○	●	●	○
France	○	○		D	
Georgia	○	○	○	○	D
Germany	○	○	D	●	○
Greece	○	○	D	D	D
Hungary	○	○	D	○	○
Iceland	○	○	D	●	D
Ireland	○	○	D	○	○
Italy	○	○	D	D	○
Latvia	○	○	D	D	D
Liechtenstein	○	○	D	○	○
Lithuania	○	○		●	○
Luxembourg	○	○	D	D	D
Macedonia	○	○	●	●	○
Malta	○	○		○	○
Moldova	○	○	D	D	○
Monaco	◗	◗		◗	
Netherlands	○	○	●	D	D
Norway	○	○	D	D	○
Poland	○	○		D	○
Portugal	○	○	D	○	○
Romania	○	○	D	○	○
Russian Federation	○	D	D		○
San Marino	○	○	○	○	○
Serbia and Montenegro	●	●	●	●	○
Slovakia	○	○	D	D	○
Slovenia	○	○	D	○	○
Spain	○	○		D	○
Sweden	○	○		○	○
Switzerland	○	○		○	○
Turkey	○	○	D	◗	
Ukraine	○	○	D	○	○
United Kingdom	○	○		○	○

WHETHER IN A HIGH-PROFILE CONFLICT OR A FORGOTTEN CORNER OF THE GLOBE, AMNESTY INTERNATIONAL CAMPAIGNS FOR JUSTICE AND FREEDOM FOR ALL AND SEEKS TO GALVANIZE PUBLIC SUPPORT TO BUILD A BETTER WORLD.

WHAT CAN YOU DO?

■ Join Amnesty International and become part of a worldwide movement campaigning for an end to human rights violations. Help us make a difference.

■ Make a donation to support Amnesty International's work.

In a dangerous and divided world, it is more important than ever that the global human rights movement remains strong, relevant and vibrant.

Together we can make our voices heard.

I WANT TO HELP

■ I am interested in receiving further information on becoming a member of Amnesty International

name

address

country

email

■ I wish to make a donation to Amnesty International

amount

Please debit my   Visa ■   Mastercard ■

number

expiry date

signature

Please return this form to the Amnesty International office in your country. (See pages 291-294 for further details of Amnesty International offices worldwide.) If there is not an Amnesty International office in your country, please return this form to Amnesty International's International Secretariat in London:

Peter Benenson House, 1 Easton Street, London WC1X 0DW, United Kingdom (donations will be taken in UK£, US$ or €)

www.amnesty.org

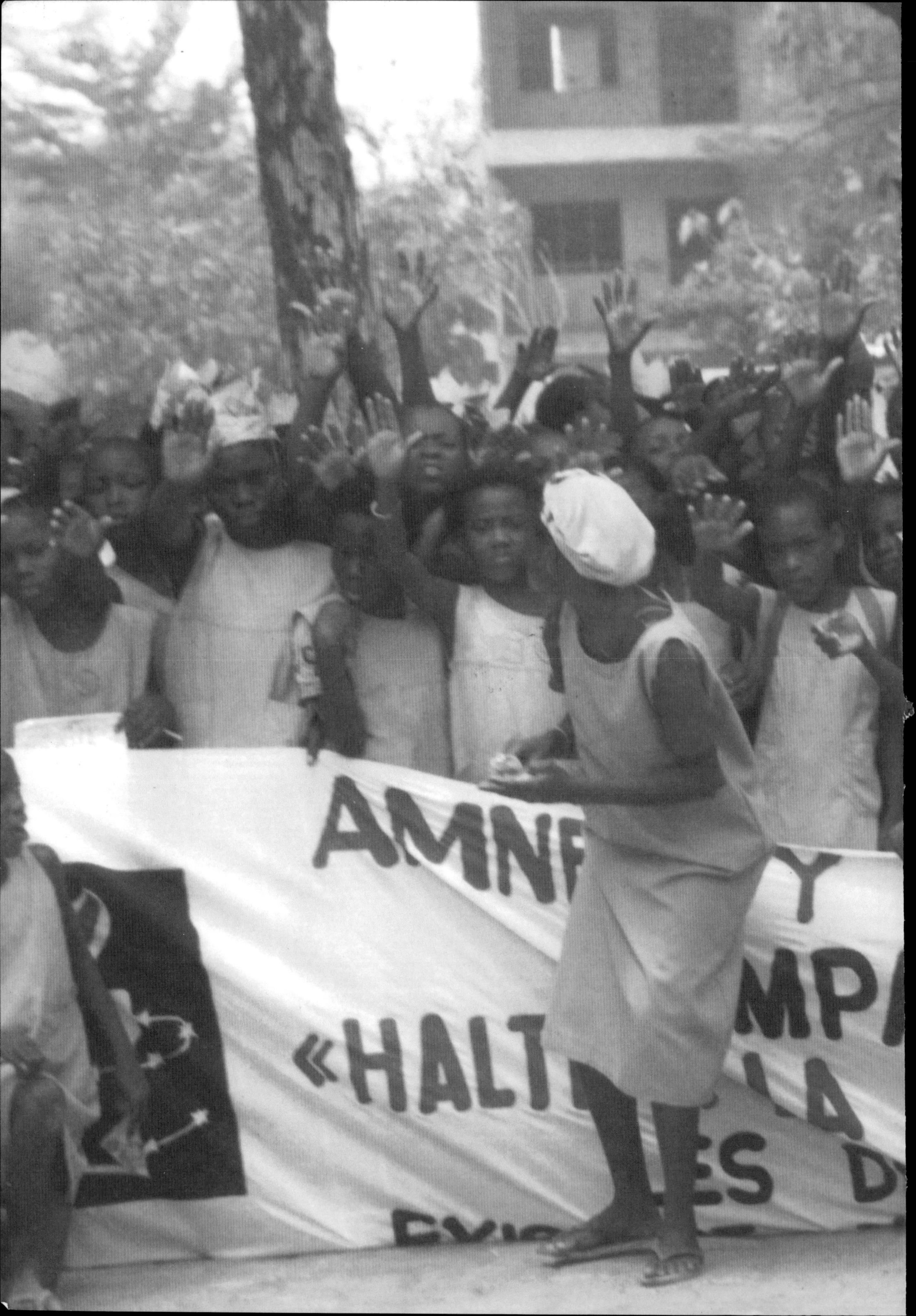
AMN
Y
MPA
«HALT
ES D